Torts: Doctrine and Process

Donald H. Beskind
Doriane Lambelet Coleman

About This Book

There are many torts textbooks on the market, including several excellent editions from which we have been privileged to learn and teach. Each serves its authors' particular pedagogical objectives as well as their sense of the needs of the students who will use it. This textbook was designed with three principal objectives in mind:

First, we want to offer a complete first-year course that is appropriately rigorous — that best meets the highest intellectual and analytical capabilities of our own students and of students at similar institutions. Thus, the cases and materials we have included are designed primarily for extraction learning: they are framed so that their doctrinal context is clear, but as with law practice, the rule and other relevant information are generally derived from careful reading and analysis of a set of materials. Throughout, we have also sought to use cases and materials whose factual contexts exemplify the complex circumstances our graduates are likely to encounter in sophisticated, modern practice settings.

Second, we want the course to prepare students to litigate difficult torts issues in the most contemporary settings. To this end, our approach is primarily doctrinal, and where other approaches — normative, economic, philosophical, and theoretical — are included, students are encouraged to think about their utility and merits as they implicate and fit within the law's existing doctrinal structure. The doctrine is presented consistent with the reality that tort law has evolved from its judge-made "common law" roots to be a true hybrid of common law and legislatively promulgated statutory rules.

Third, and also to this pragmatic end, the materials feature the relationship between the "black letter" or substantive law of torts, the rules of civil procedure, and the decisions and judgments required of practicing lawyers. Our goal is for students to see torts where they exist in the practice of law: at the juncture of the rules that govern the litigation process and the choices lawyers make using the facts and law to build arguments within those rules. The problems we have included throughout are derived from our own past exam questions and specifically test students' understanding of the doctrine and this juncture.

It was ultimately the search for materials that combined these three objectives—a combination we did not find in existing texts — that led us to develop this book. Our commitment has always been to provide the strongest possible educational foundation for our students, grounded in our own experience as academics and practitioners. We look forward to working with you.

Donald Beskind and Doriane Coleman
Duke Law School

DEDICATION AND GRATITUDE

To Professor Joseph (Joe) A. Page, for introducing me to Torts in law school and for helping to launch my academic career thereafter. Among many other things, I owe my understanding of proximate cause and the baseball cases to you. Your keen intelligence, seriousness of purpose, and playfulness live on in my classroom. And to Professor George C. Christie, for teaching me, through his own exceptional book and personal mentorship, how best to think about and teach doctrine, and also how to use Torts to teach legal method and process. Generations of students have benefitted directly from your pedagogical thoughtfulness; generations more will continue to benefit because you gave us these gifts, which we will pass along in turn. dlc

I join in the dedication to George Christie and add my dedication to all those whose life's work is or was keeping tort law connected to the scales of justice. dhb

We are grateful to the Duke Press and to Marlyn Dail at Duke Law School for working with us every year to produce an up-to-date edition worthy of all of our aspirations. You are both terrific partners in this collaboration. Thank you for working with us.

ACKNOWLEDGMENTS

We are grateful for the generosity of the following individuals and institutions that have permitted us to include their copyrighted material either free of charge or for a nominal fee so that we could, in turn, pass the savings along to students who purchase these course materials:

George C. Christie, James B. Duke Professor Emeritus of Law, Duke Law School

Johanna M. Shepherd, Professor of Law, Emory Law School

The American Law Institute

CONVENTIONS

We use certain conventions throughout the book that are important to note at the outset.

The most important is that we omit string citations in original materials that are unnecessary for our immediate purposes. These omissions are not otherwise noted. We also omit text that is unnecessary for our purposes, but in this instance, we mark omissions with ellipses. Should you be interested in reading omitted material, you can find it in the full text of the original.

We use two different footnoting conventions. Footnotes in replicated material are numbered as they are in the original. Thus, if a case has ten footnotes numbered 1 through 10 and we include three of those in our excerpt — for example, the first, third, and tenth footnotes will be numbered "1," "3," and "10." We use symbols instead of numbers for our own editorial footnotes.

Finally, we have not altered the citation forms used in original materials. This means, for example, that you will see courts' own — and thus often different — citation forms throughout the text.

Table of Contents

Table of Cases

INTRODUCTION

Welcome to law school! We look forward to working with you this year. The material in this introductory chapter is designed to ensure that you are properly prepared for your courses in general; although it uses examples from Torts, it is not otherwise specific to this class. We hope that by being most transparent about our assumptions and expectations at the outset, you will have the opportunity to do your best work and also to enjoy a most engaging, intellectual and professional experience.

I. PREPARING FOR CLASS

Preparing for and "being prepared" for law school classes may be different from what you had to do to be successful in the past. At the risk of being too basic, this is because there are always different possible degrees of preparedness: You can be entirely unprepared because you didn't read the assignment. You can be partially prepared because you only read a portion of the assignment, although you did that carefully. You can be generally prepared because you skimmed and maybe "book briefed"[*] the entire assignment. Or you can be fully prepared because you read and briefed the entire assignment carefully. Like your future employers, your professors, especially your 1L professors, will expect you to be fully prepared every day, and they will consider you "unprepared" if your preparation falls short of this standard. Even in your 2 and 3L years, you will find that students who are consistently prepared in this sense are better able to engage the material. This translates, inevitably, into better lawyering skills, better grades, and a better reputation.[**]

You want to be thought of by your fellow students, law school professors, and eventual employers as a person with an impeccable professional approach to your work. Preparedness is central to this approach, as is timeliness, courtesy toward peers and superiors, and the ability to work collaboratively in team settings, among other things. Notice that these attributes are separate from your substantive legal knowledge and analytical skills. You can get the equivalent of an "A" on every one of your exams, but if it's clear to your professors that you weren't professional in your approach to class on a daily basis, they won't be there to write your letters of recommendation; by definition, the latter are designed to speak to more than just your grades since these are clear from your transcript. The same goes for your eventual work in the legal profession: although very bright lawyers are obviously an asset, the nature of the work is such that weak professional attributes will make difficult the case for hiring or promotion.

---

[*] Editors' note: Book briefing is explained below. Essentially, it means making margin notes in your casebook.

[**] Editors' note: Being prepared is important whether or not you are called on. Even if you are not called on, you are expected to engage — respond, analyze, critique — silently. You won't be able to do this if you don't prepare.

To be prepared for class on a daily basis, you must carefully read the assigned material and brief the assigned cases. The first year of law school is notoriously difficult, not because the substance of the material is particularly complex or obscure, but because a lot of reading is assigned and a high level of preparation is expected. For many of you, these demands will be different from what you are accustomed to. You must embrace these demands. If you do, you will be rewarded with an appropriately sophisticated sense of and ability to work with the law. The 1L year is literally the foundation for all that you will do beginning in your 2L year and throughout your legal careers. Your goal this year should be to develop the strongest possible base from which to work in the future. The following provides the template for careful case briefing, which is the best way to ensure (big picture) that you do the groundwork necessary to establish this essential base, and (little picture) that you are appropriately prepared on a daily basis.

II. BRIEFING CASES

Why Lawyers and Law Students Brief Cases

Throughout your lives as law students and lawyers, you will be "briefing" cases. That is, you will be reading them to discover their various formally identifiable parts, and in most cases you will be reducing them — making them brief — so that they are easier to work with. Over time, you will acquire your own style of briefing cases, but even then, there are formal parameters that you will follow. This is necessary (and so even if you're a free spirit you'll toe the line) because law professors and other lawyers talk in a jargon that comprises in part the elements of a case brief, and you'll need to communicate with them.

You should brief carefully for all of your classes this year because:

1. You want to be prepared for class in case you are called on and, even if you're not, so that you can engage the material along with your classmates.

2. It is essential that you learn the law, which is frequently derived from rules as applied in cases.

3. Repeated briefing over time is necessary to the development of your ability to effectively and efficiently read, analyze, and synthesize cases. Relatedly, repeated briefing is also important to the development of your legal reasoning skills.

Note that only the second of these is directly relevant to exam taking; there is a lot more going on in law school and in your growth as lawyers than that.

Commercial materials are available that contain "canned" or already-prepared briefs; briefs for many cases are also available online. It is our strong recommendation that you resist relying on such materials. While they may be helpful either when you have not had adequate time to prepare or when you are not sure you understand a case, relying on them consistently and in lieu of your own preparation is problematic in two ways:

First, relying on the work of others will retard the development of your own ability to read, analyze, and synthesize cases. Because this is a big piece of what lawyers do in practice, the development of these skills is not optional. And it is certainly not something you want to tackle for the first time when you are out of law school, when there are no more canned or prepared briefs available.

Second, although published materials will generally be correct in the sense that they will accurately represent the facts, issue, and rule of a case, they will not necessarily provide you with the detail or depth necessary to a particular professor's approach or class discussion. In this sense, they may function as effectively as skimming a case, but they may not be adequate otherwise.

Relying on others' briefs either much or all of the time is one of the four most frequent patterns we see with students who do not do as well on their exams as they would have expected or liked.

Companies that advise pre-law and first-year law students sometimes also recommend that students "book brief" — make margin notes — in lieu of preparing full case briefs. Whether this is an adequate strategy depends largely on the individual student/lawyer, her ability accurately and comprehensively to retain information that is not captured in the margin notes, and the eventual uses of the case material. In other words, book briefing works for some people sometimes, but not for everyone or for all purposes. It is our recommendation that you not book brief, at least not until you are adept at the skill of full case briefing and you have a good sense of what it is that your professors want from you. If you book brief before then, you are likely to be less-than-fully prepared.

How to Brief a Case

The standard or formal elements of a brief, indeed of all legal analysis, are often helpfully broken down into the acronym "IRAC." IRAC stands for Issue, Rule, Application, Conclusion. Specifically, IRAC requires that the lawyer derive the issue or issues to be resolved, find or develop the law or legal rule that is or should be used to address the issue(s), apply the rule to the facts, and reach a conclusion as to how the issue(s) is/are to be resolved and what happens next in the case. We are not being dramatic when we tell you that what we have just written comprises much of what you will be doing in every course throughout law school and otherwise throughout your legal careers: almost every case you analyze or "brief," and every memorandum, brief, or opinion you write, will follow a version of this paradigm.

As a threshold matter, IRAC assumes that the facts or factual background of a case have already been presented. For purposes of case briefing, however, it is essential always to have ready a good statement of the *relevant* facts. And so if you wish, you may refer to the briefing paradigm as FIRAC instead.

(F)IRAC breaks down this way:

(F) The facts of the case, also called "factual background" or "underlying facts."

These are the underlying events that give rise to the lawsuit. The case facts are to be distinguished from the Procedural History (PH) of the case, that is, the facts that describe the course of the litigation once it has been initiated. In some courses, you may be asked by your professors to provide the procedural history of a case.

Note that proper legal analysis requires that you cull from the facts presented only those that are relevant to the issue(s) presented. For example, if the raw facts tell you that the suit is for damages arising out of a car accident, and that A, who is 20, and B, who is 16, were both passengers in the car, it is likely that their ages will be irrelevant to the analysis of whether their suits against the negligent driver will be successful. That is, their ages have nothing to do with the negligence of the driver. On the other hand, their ages might be relevant if the issue were whether their consents to medical treatment, signed as they were brought into the hospital, were valid as a defense to a battery claim brought against the physician who treated them. This is because the validity of consent may turn, in part, on the age of the person consenting.

(I) The legal issue that is implicated by those facts, also called "question presented."

Lawyers, and certainly your professors, will sometimes break this component down and distinguish between the "procedural issue" and the "substantive issue" in the case. In a nutshell, the procedural issue is the question that arises relating to the stage of the trial or appellate process at which a substantive issue was disposed of; e.g., if the trial court dismissed the plaintiff's case and she appeals the dismissal, an issue might be whether the judge correctly dismissed the case before all the witnesses had been deposed. The substantive issue or question presented relates to what the applicable law is or how it should be construed; e.g., if the case that was dismissed involved a claim for battery, the issue might be whether the plaintiff's evidence amounted to a battery or the applicable law required additional facts plaintiff could not show.

Note that a single appeals court opinion may involve more than one issue. When you brief cases for class, you should focus on the issue most pertinent to the subject at hand. If it is not obvious, the chapter title and subheading under which the case appears should be helpful to you in identifying the issue. For example, if the case you are briefing is in the book to illustrate the rules that apply to offensive battery claims, and the case involves multiple issues including the issue whether the plaintiff has a viable claim for offensive battery, your brief should focus on that issue. Nevertheless, there is value to reading and making notes about peripheral issues; this is one of the ways lawyers learn about the law more generally, including about how different issues intersect with one another.

(R) The rule of law that is or should be used to address the issue, also called "law" or "applicable law."

The applicable law is the law that the court uses to resolve the case. Applicable law generally falls into one of three categories:

Mostly, the courts resolve issues using their interpretation of existing law. Existing law for this purpose includes constitutional (state or federal), statutory (state or federal), and judicially pronounced or common law. The law as it has been articulated in prior cases is often called "precedent" or "applicable precedent."

Sometimes, the issue before the court is whether the existing law ought to be changed. Because lower courts have no power to change existing law, this issue is only properly before the state's highest court, and even then, only if that law itself was judge-made rather than statutory.

On other occasions, there is no existing law on point. If a lower court is confronted with this situation, it will make new law — usually by borrowing the standard in another jurisdiction. Such lawmaking is subject to review by higher courts.

Developing the ability to identify and describe the applicable law and its source is part of what your legal training will be about. Correspondingly, where the law is not entirely clear, or where it might be subject to modification, your legal training also will involve developing the ability to argue convincingly that the court should adopt your position (rather than your opponent's) on what the existing law means or what the newly declared law should be. All of this involves understanding the value of precedent in the law, as well as the ability to synthesize cases and analogize among related areas of law. (You will work most directly on these skills in your legal writing class, and your other professors will assume you are in fact developing them in that context. Thus, as you do your work both in and out of legal writing class, train yourself to think about how these skills apply, not only to your own writing, but also to the structure and articulation of judges' opinions, and to the way advocates and judges in all subject matters engage their analyses.)

(A) The court's application of the facts to the rule or law. This is also called the court's analysis.

It is in this part of the case that the court considers the parties' different arguments about how the law applies to the facts, and also the part in which the court resolves those arguments. This part also may contain the court's rationale, or explanation for the ultimate holding and result.

While courts frequently work methodically through the parties' arguments, sometimes the analysis that appears in the opinions you read will be incomplete or conclusory. When that happens, beyond describing whatever analysis the court provided, your task is to construct and briefly set out in your brief the best arguments for both the result reached and the result urged by the party that lost. Having done that, take care not to confuse the analysis that you've imagined — which will be important to you both in and out of class — with what the court actually wrote.

Note that this is usually the place in a case brief or other legal document (such as a memorandum or advocacy brief) where the lawyer is able to be the most creative; it is the place where facts are brought to bear — proof or evidence is proffered — in support of an argument that the law requires a particular outcome.

(C) The court's conclusion, also called the holding of the case.

This is your precise statement of the new rule that emerges as a result of the court's analysis. Think of the holding as what this court might want a later court to say was the precedent this case established. As with the issue, the conclusion or holding also may be broken down into both a procedural and a substantive holding. There is quite a science to developing the substantive holding in particular; you will spend a lot of time working on this skill, also most directly in your legal writing class. In this regard, note carefully that the conclusion or holding is to be distinguished from the result in the case, which is simply the "yes" or "no" answer to the issue, or more simply the answer to the question, who won in the end.

Final Notes on Briefing

When you work with your other professors, the IRAC formula may be presented a bit differently than we have here. But since we all speak the same language in the end, you should be able to reconcile the different formulas without much difficulty. Note also that while some of your professors will focus class discussion on critical analysis of cases including all the elements of case briefs, others will assume you have engaged this analysis on your own and will use that assumed analysis as a springboard for additional discussion — for example, of the policy implications of the law or its theoretical sources — while yet others will engage a hybrid approach. The professor's approach depends upon his or her pedagogical objectives for the class.

Finally, although critiques of/policy arguments about the law or its application to a particular set of facts may form part of a court's discussion (in the R/Rule and/or A/Application portions of its opinion) the IRAC template does not provide a place for you to do the same. A brief is a summary of the court's opinion, not yours. Nevertheless, intellectual engagement in class materials means more than just briefing. And so as you proceed, be sure to develop your own approach to thinking about and chronicling your (and your professors' and classmates') critiques and policy arguments. You even may wish to include these in a "notes" or "comments" section that you include at the end of your brief, but, again, take care not to conflate your analysis with the court's.

III. INTRODUCTION TO CIVIL LITIGATION

A. The Plaintiff's and Defendant's Cases

Civil litigation begins with a lawsuit being filed. After paying a filing fee, the plaintiff who brings the suit files a complaint and obtains a summons requiring the defendant, the person sued, to respond to the complaint. The summons and the complaint must be "served" on the defendant by the plaintiff. Until the defendant receives the complaint, he ordinarily has no obligation to respond to it. Once served, however, the defendant must respond. His options include a "motion to dismiss" for deficiencies in the claim, an "answer" denying liability and an affirmative defense that, in effect says that even if the defendant is responsible, the law provides an excuse from liability. The defendant also may file any claims he has against the plaintiff or anyone else arising out of the same transaction.

The plaintiff's claim can be based in torts, contracts, property, constitutional law, etc. Regardless of the area of the law at issue, however, all claims raised require the plaintiff to allege facts establishing a set of elements fixed by the relevant law. Thus, for example, as we will see shortly, tort law requires the plaintiff who files a battery claim to establish four elements: (1) the defendant committed *a voluntary act*, (2) with *intent* to cause harmful or offensive bodily contact, (3) which *caused* the plaintiff (4) a relevant *injury*.

Merely alleging facts establishing each element is not enough to get a plaintiff to trial on her complaint. If challenged, after filing the complaint but before trial, she will have to establish that she has evidence on each element that, if not rebutted, would require the case be decided in her favor. This quantum of evidence as to each of the elements is, in the aggregate, called a "prima facie" case. That term comes from the Latin for "at first sight."

Although what follows simplifies things substantially, for present purposes it suffices to know that once the plaintiff has set out a prima facie case, the case can proceed to a trial at which defendant's litigation options are: (1) to rebut one or more of these elements — for example, if the claim at issue is battery, to deny that she committed a voluntary act, and/or (2) to proffer an affirmative defense — for example, to argue that any battery was legally permissible because of consent or self-defense.

As you will see below, the plaintiff can succeed only if she is able to make out and persuade the trier of fact that she is correct as to each and every element of her claim, and the defendant is unable to make out and persuade the trier of fact that he is correct as to any affirmative defense he raised. If the defendant succeeds in persuading the trier of fact either that one or more elements of the plaintiff's case was not proved, or that every element of an affirmative defense has been proved, the plaintiff will lose.

One helpful metaphor is to think of a claim as a box, and to think of its elements as empty compartments within the box. (Imagine a parts box you'd buy at Home Depot with the number of compartments required by your project.) For example, the intentional tort of battery is a box within which (according to the law) there must be four compartments labeled (in shorthand) (1) act, (2) intent, (3) causation, and (4) injury. This means that when the plaintiff files a battery claim, he must allege *both* that all of these four compartments exist within the box *and* that he has facts to put into each. For example, he must allege that the defendant committed a voluntary act and he must describe (at least summarily) facts that will prove this allegation, and then he must do the same for intent, causation, and injury. If the judge sees that there are less than four compartments in the box, she will dismiss the complaint. If the complaint survives this initial check, it will proceed through the litigation process described immediately below, but as it does, the plaintiff will be required to do more than continue to allege the existence of facts to fill each of the compartments: he will have to produce evidence backing up that allegation. For example, he will have to produce a witness who will testify that the defendant voluntarily threw the punch that injured him, etc. If, at any point in the litigation, it becomes clear that there are not sufficient facts for each compartment, the claim will be dismissed.[***]

*** Editors' note: This box metaphor is applicable to any claim or defense where a party has the burden of proof. The compartments are always based on the elements required by law.

B. The Civil Trial and Appellate Process

The Federal Rules of Civil Procedure, about which you will learn in detail when you take the procedure course, establish the process through which litigants in civil cases proceed. Each state has adopted a similar set of rules. Because the cases you read in law school text or casebooks always arise at the intersection of substance and procedure — that is, at a particular point in the process and based on a particular legal rule or set of rules — and because the procedural posture of a case often influences what a court is permitted to do with its substance, it is essential that you are familiar at the outset with the basic outlines of the litigation process. Here it is, in summary and sequential list form.

As you read through this list, note that we have italicized those stages of the process that involve either dispositive motions or other stages involving decisions of law that you will see reviewed most often in law school casebooks. For our purposes, dispositive motions are requests to the court made by one or the other party to dispose (one way or the other) of an entire claim on the basis that it is either (1) unequivocally flawed, or (2) unequivocally good. A claim will be unequivocally flawed if — as described in Part II(A) above — one or more elements of the claim are not alleged or the facts are not there to support each of them.

THE PRETRIAL PROCESS

1. Plaintiff's Complaint
2. *Defendant's Answer or Motion to Dismiss Plaintiff's Complaint*
3. Plaintiff's Response to Motion to Dismiss
4. Defendant's Reply to Plaintiff's Response to Motion to Dismiss
5. Discovery (e.g., Interrogatories, Depositions, Requests for Production of Documents and Things, etc.)
6. *Plaintiff's and/or Defendant's Motion for Summary Judgment*
7. Response of opposing party

THE TRIAL PROCESS

8. Opening Statements
9. Plaintiff's Case in Chief
    A. Plaintiff calls witnesses — direct examination by plaintiff, cross-examination by defense, redirect by plaintiff
    B. Plaintiff offers exhibits
    C. Plaintiff rests

10. *Defendant's Motion for Judgment as a Matter of Law (a/k/a for a Directed Verdict)*

11. Plaintiff's response

12. Defendant's Case in Chief

    A. Defendant calls witnesses — direct examination by defendant, cross-examination by plaintiff, redirect by defense
    B. Defendant offers exhibits
    C. Defendant rests

13. *Plaintiff's and/or Defendant's Motion for Judgment as a Matter of Law (a/k/a for a Directed Verdict)*

14. Response of opposing party

15. Closing Arguments

16. Jury Instructions (if tried to a jury)

17. Jury Deliberations (if tried to a jury)

18. Verdict

19. *Renewed Motion(s) for Judgment as a Matter of Law (if previously made) or Motion for a New Trial (a/k/a Motion for Judgment Non Obstante Veredicto (JNOV))*

20. Response of opposing party

21. Final Decision of Trial Court

THE APPELLATE PROCESS

22. Appeals from that final decision to the intermediate appellate court on issues of law or clearly erroneous factual findings (including brief of appellant, response of respondent, reply of appellant, oral arguments, and decision of court).

23. Appeals to the Supreme Court on issues of law or clearly erroneous factual findings (including brief of Appellant, response of Respondent, reply of Appellant, oral arguments, and decision of court).

    Depending on the jurisdiction, appeals to the Supreme Court may be "as of right," meaning that the appellant (the party who lost below and who seeks reversal of that adverse decision) has a right to be heard by the high court, or they may be "discretionary," meaning that the high court has the power to determine whether it wishes to hear the dispute or not. In the latter situation, appellant files a petition for certiorari or, colloquially, a "cert petition," explaining why the court should take the case. In some places, this is known as a petition for discretionary review. Respondent (the party who won below and who would like that decision to stand) is permitted to file an opposition brief explaining why the court should not take the case.

C. Standards and Burdens of Proof

The law assigns different standards of proof to different kinds of cases based on a formula that considers the significance of the parties' respective interests, including as compared with each other, and on an evaluation of the risks of error that it is willing to bear in the circumstances. There is a substantial body of constitutional law on this point, but for present purposes, it suffices to appreciate the following:

Preponderance of the evidence. If the law considers a deprivation to be important, but not very important, and it is willing to bear the risk of more significant error given the interests on the other side, it requires that the potential depriver prove her case by a "preponderance of the evidence." This standard requires the depriver to show that each element is "more likely than not" true, or that the metaphorical scales that would weigh the evidence are "tipped past equipoise" in their favor. Equipoise is the equally balanced scale. The preponderance standard is also called "the greater weight of the evidence." This is the standard used in civil (including tort) litigation, which generally deprives the defendant "only" of money; money is considered to be relatively unimportant — in contrast with the deprivation of liberty or of one's child, for example — and the risk of relatively significant error bearable, considering the plaintiff's and society's interest in the existence of a system that provides effective compensation for injuries.

Clear and convincing evidence. If the law considers a deprivation to be very important, but not of utmost importance, and if it is willing to bear some but not a big risk of error to protect a competing interest, it will demand proof of fault by "clear and convincing evidence." Aspects of proceedings to terminate parental rights on the basis of permanent abuse, neglect, or abandonment are conducted according to this standard, on the view that the permanent loss of one's child is a very important deprivation, but one that must be balanced against the child's interest in a settled parental relationship and the state's *parens patriae* interest in protecting child welfare. Increasingly, this standard is being made relevant to tort cases by legislatures enacting it to, for example, reduce the number of punitive damage verdicts, make it more difficult to sue emergency room health care providers, or otherwise protect potential defendants.

Beyond a reasonable doubt. If the law considers a potential deprivation to be of utmost gravity and importance, and (at least formally) it is only willing to bear a miniscule risk of error, it will demand that the eventual depriver prove fault "beyond a reasonable doubt." This is the standard that attaches to criminal prosecutions, because they typically risk one of the ultimate deprivations, i.e., a deprivation of personal liberty, including the freedom of mobility. (Death falls into the same category, of course.) This is the basis for the well-known mantra that, "It is better to let a guilty man go free than to risk improperly imprisoning an innocent one." This burden of proof is not relevant to tort cases though jurors who watch too much television are often confused.

The law is loathe formally to assign numerical values to burdens of proof, but it is sometimes said that "beyond a reasonable doubt" means 98 or 99% sure; "clear and convincing evidence" might be valued (depending on the court) at between 65 and 90% sure; and "by a preponderance of the evidence" or "greater weight" both mean more than 50% sure.

It is generally said that the plaintiff bears the ultimate burden of proof in a civil case, including a torts case. However, this is merely a generalization. In fact, there are several different burdens in a case and some of them can shift depending on the stage of the litigation.

Specifically, there are three different, sequential burdens of proof in a civil case:

The burden of pleading. This requires the plaintiff to file a complaint that pleads (states or alleges) the facts required to prove each and every element of the claim. The plaintiff will survive a dispositive motion, as described in the immediately preceding section, if she alleges in good faith sufficient facts to support each element. The defendant also has this burden if she files an affirmative defense or her own claim against the plaintiff or others.

The burden of production. This requires the plaintiff to produce evidence to prove or support every essential factual allegation made in the complaint. For example, if the complaint alleges that the defendant's negligence was in running a red light, the plaintiff must prove this — e.g., with an eyewitness or the defendant's admission that she was speeding. Plaintiff will survive a dispositive motion on the issue if he is able to produce this evidence. Once the plaintiff makes out a prima facie case, the burden of production shifts to the defendant to rebut the case. The defendant also has a burden of production if she has an affirmative defense or her own claims.

The burden of persuasion. This requires the party who brought the claim or affirmative defense to satisfy the trier of fact that the fact is true. This burden never shifts; it always remains on the party who brought the claim or asserted the defense.

* * *

Chapter One will introduce you to Torts as a subject. From that chapter, you will get a sense of its origins, its objectives, and also of common threshold issues that may affect the viability of claims regardless of their category. As you move forward from this chapter to the next, and so on, be sure to take prior knowledge and lessons forward. This will help you integrate material from the beginning so that by mid-semester and later, you have the best sense possible of how methodology and doctrine fit together.

CHAPTER ONE
OVERVIEW OF TORT LAW

> Tort. A private or civil wrong or injury . . . for which the court will provide a remedy in the form of an action for damages. A violation of a duty imposed by general law . . . A legal wrong committed upon the person or property independent of contract.
>
> *Black's Law Dictionary*, 6th ed.

The traditional 1L curriculum in U.S. law schools includes Torts, Contracts, Criminal Law, Constitutional Law, Property, and Civil Procedure. Although some law schools have a slightly different slate or have introduced an additional subject from the upper level curriculum, this core has been a constant focus of the first year for over a century. Mainly this is because practicing lawyers will do work in one or more of these areas and because they are the foundation for the more specialized courses that build from their basic principles. While you will study each of them separately as a formal matter, you should quickly notice — including in this course – that there is quite some overlap, that they are not actually siloed in practice.

I. PRACTICAL AND THEORETICAL RATIONALES

The traditional justifications for tort law — its "first principles" — are preventing self-help, deterring (regulating) harmful behavior, and compensating victims for injuries inflicted by others. Although all three continue to support modern tort law, the compensation and deterrence rationales are most salient in the present era.

The compensation rationale is paramount. Those who are injured as a result of the wrongdoing of others have four possible sources of financial relief: their own resources including insurance, if any; charitable donations, if any; government benefits, if any; and tort damages. Not everyone has money in the bank, insurance, access to charity, or government benefits, but everyone has access to the courts to enforce applicable tort law. This means that for many in the society, tort law is the only recourse when they suffer personal injuries or property damage. This situation is in contrast with many other Western democracies where there is universal health care and mandatory insurance coverage for other forms of harm.

The deterrence rationale also remains central to the doctrine. It assumes that the possibility of tort liability (including the possibility of lost compensation due to contributory fault) causes people to take more care than they might otherwise contemplate, which results in fewer or less serious accidents. In this respect, and at least in theory, tort law acts as *ex ante* behavior regulation for individuals and corporations that would be subject to tort damages: one can take risks outside of the range of what is considered reasonable by others, but the costs of doing so must be factored into the decision to proceed. Although the assumption that people know the law is questionable in many areas, it is likely to be relatively strong in this context because it is largely based in community norms.

Consistent with these rationales, tort law supports three kinds of damages: compensatory damages—literally, damages to compensate the plaintiff for actual losses suffered; nominal damages, also called dignitary damages—designed to compensate the plaintiff symbolically for intentional torts that do not cause measurable economic loss; and punitive damages—also called exemplary damages—awarded in some contexts where the defendant's behavior has been particularly egregious. Consistent with the most important modern rationale for tort law, compensatory damages are the most common.

Depending upon one's theoretical leanings, the rules that govern tort law, including rules on damages, should do more than simply compensate or deter or punish in individual cases. For example, proponents of distributive justice might argue with proponents of an economic approach to the law about the law's broader, societal implications. Although elements of these perspectives will be evident at various points in this course, our focus is primarily doctrinal, not theoretical. That is, our pedagogical objective is to teach you the substantive law of torts; how this law intersects with procedure in the context of litigation; and the legal method more generally.

II. THE EVOLUTION OF UNITED STATES TORT LAW

United States tort law has its origins in British tort law; indeed, our law continues to refer to British law in certain areas, and the British will sometimes also refer to ours. At its origins, British tort law was mostly judge-made. Judge-made law is also called "common law." Common law is to be distinguished from statutory law, which is promulgated by legislative bodies. When the Colonies declared their independence from England in 1776, so that the tort system would continue uninterrupted, the colonial legislatures passed "statutes of incorporation" which literally incorporated the relevant common law of England into their new legal systems. Since then, state courts and legislatures across the United States have worked with and evolved this law.

For present purposes, the two most significant evolutions are (1) the move from being a body of law that was almost exclusively judge-made and thus almost exclusively located in case law, to a body of law that is a true hybrid of judicially and legislatively made law; and (2) the move from a focus on strict liability to a preference for liability based on mental (rather than causal) fault.

A. The Increasing Role of Legislatures

When politicians and commentators talk about "activist judges" who overstep their bounds by "making rather than interpreting law," they are ignoring (either conveniently or naively) the fact that much of U.S. law is and has always been intentionally judge-made. Tort law is a prime but certainly not the only example. Historically, legislatures only infrequently stepped in to make tort law; and even when they did — for example, when they passed the statutes of incorporation in 1776 — their incursion was only momentary or periodic. In the present period, however, legislatures are increasingly stepping in to abrogate the common law and to establish new legal rules. Many of these changes, particularly in the area of medical malpractice law, are the result of the "tort reform" movement. For example, as part of these efforts, state legislatures have enacted special statutes of limitations, caps on damages, and liability rules that are designed specifically to override longstanding judge-made law. As a result, modern lawyers and law students can no longer assume that the law they read in cases is dispositive, particularly if it reflects older precedent; they must look both to existing common law and any related legislative measures.

B. From Strict Liability to Liability Based on Mental Fault

If you think about the range of mental states that can animate a person's conduct, from the most purposefully injurious or morally blameworthy to the most careful and well-meaning, you can draw a mental "fault continuum" that ranges from the most to the least mentally culpable. In tort law, the most mentally culpable acts are called intentional torts and the least are called strict liability torts. In between is negligence, which is defined as careless or unreasonable behavior:

* ____ *

Strict Liability Negligence Intentional Torts

"At common law" — which roughly equates to the law in England before 1776 and the law in the Colonies and then the States for a while thereafter — all torts were strict liability offenses called "trespasses": if the defendant's act was volitional and it caused personal injury or property damage to the plaintiff, the plaintiff could recover regardless of the defendant's mental state; the key facts involved the defendant's act, causation, and harm. This meant that the bulk of tort liability at the time was causation-based and concentrated exclusively on the strict liability side of the fault continuum. Over time, the law came to prefer liability based on mental fault rather than causality. The result is that in the modern era, the bulk of tort liability is concentrated in the negligence and, to a lesser extent, the intentional torts portions of the fault continuum. Strict liability still exists, but it is restricted to a short list of claims, including claims for injuries caused by some animals, by some dangerous activities, and by some products. This preference for fault-based liability is based in the view that legal responsibility is, in most cases, only fairly or justly assigned to those who are mentally culpable.

C. The Tort System's Ability to Deal with Large, Systemic Problems

The tort system is not especially good at dealing with large cases and systemic problems. Cases involving numerous parties, defendants that are critical to the community's economy or infrastructure and thus may be seen as "too big to fail", issues including medical causation that are recurring across cases and jurisdictions, and different sensitivities such as trauma and time, are only awkwardly dealt with using standard tort doctrine and conventional litigation strategies. Because of this, alternative compensation systems have been developed and may be adopted by the parties and courts depending on the facts. The 9-11, BP Oil, and Jeffrey Epstein funds are illustrative of such alternative compensation systems, as are the multi-district (MDL) and aggregate litigation schemes that emerged to deal with the opioid, silicone gel breast implant, and asbestos cases. We will discuss these alternatives as related issues arise in our materials.

III. THRESHOLD ISSUES AFFECTING THE VIABILITY OF CLAIMS

A. The Contingency Fee and Collectability

It is the rare plaintiff who, after having been injured, can afford to pay a lawyer an hourly rate to handle a case. Recognizing this, the common law has long allowed lawyers in tort cases to work on a contingent fee basis. Under a contingent fee, the plaintiff's lawyer is only paid if the plaintiff wins and then the fee is a percentage of the recovery. That fee can vary from less than 10% in large class action cases to as much as 40% in complicated medical malpractice or products liability cases. Since the plaintiff's lawyer is not paid unless the plaintiff prevails, the likelihood of proving liability is an important consideration to the lawyer in deciding whether to take the plaintiff's case.

Another critical decision is damages — not just how badly the plaintiff was hurt physically or economically, but whether compensation for those losses is collectible. The most common source of payment for tort damages is liability insurance coverage. The next most common source is direct payment from the defendant. Even if liability is strong and damages are significant, in the absence of adequate insurance or assets on the part of the defendant, a jury verdict will likely be uncollectible. And, even if the defendant has some assets, the judgment obtained at trial may be discharged in bankruptcy, leaving the plaintiff with a hollow victory and the plaintiff's lawyer unpaid.

A topical example of a line of cases that are likely to fall short as a threshold matter because of collectability issues are those that have or will involve claims of medical malpractice in the first several months of the Covid epidemic. As we will see when we turn our attentions to negligence, doctors who have agreed or are required to take on particular patients generally have a duty to treat them reasonably and prudently, i.e., according to an established medical standard of care; and they will be liable for damages that result and are recoverable. But because Covid is a novel disease that was not well understood in those initial months, it will be difficult for a plaintiff to establish that there was a standard of care in place to which the defendant's conduct can be compared. Moreover, because patients who suffered important consequences including death generally came into care with significant pre-existing conditions, it will be difficult to prove that malpractice rather than the pre-existing conditions caused those consequences. Finally, legislatures are considering bills that would limit if not eliminate Covid-related liability in certain circumstances, including in medical emergencies; where they become law, such limitations would make it difficult-to-impossible to recover damages that can be established in the normal course.

B. Vicarious Liability

When it appears that a defendant may lack sufficient assets, the possibility that a third party might be vicariously liable for the defendant's torts can make a case viable. Vicarious liability attaches in cases where, as a matter of policy, the courts have determined that it is fair and just to impose this obligation on others. The claim against the third party is not that they committed a tort, but rather simply that they are responsible legally for the torts of another.

The categories of vicariously liable defendants are fixed. The most important is the employer-employee relationship. Employers are vicariously liable for the torts their employees commit in the scope or in the course of their employment. Vicarious liability in this setting is also known as *respondeat superior* liability — meaning the superior responds for the torts of the employee. There are exceptions to this rule, the most important of which is that employers are generally not liable for their employees' intentional torts, unless the employment involves committing such torts, for example being a bouncer at a bar, or involves a position of trust, for example being a daycare provider or taxi driver.

The most litigated issues in the employer-employee context are whether the tortious actor is an employee or an independent contractor and, if the actor is an employee, whether the tort was committed in the scope or course of the employment.

The law of agency is complex, but for present purposes, it suffices to know that employees can generally be distinguished from independent contractors by whether their work is closely managed or directed and by whether they use their own materials and supplies; if they are closely managed and do not use their own materials and supplies, they are more likely to be classified as an employee than as an independent contractor.

Of course, employers are not responsible for torts committed when their employees are not at work or working and so defining when they are is often essential. For example, consider what the arguments might be for and against vicarious liability in circumstances where a management-level employee was held responsible for significant burn damage to a motel where he was staying on company business; the fire was started after the employee fell asleep in his bed going over the company's accounts and smoking a cigarette. See Edgewater Motels, Inc. v. Gatzke, 277 N.W.2d 11 (Minn. 1979). Most cases are easier. For example, there likely would be vicarious liability in circumstances where a UPS driver in a UPS truck negligently caused an accident in an intersection on her normal route during her scheduled workday; but there likely would not be vicarious liability in circumstances where the same driver took the truck off her scheduled route without permission to visit her girlfriend during her lunch break.

Outside of the employment context, individuals involved in joint enterprises may be vicariously liable for the torts of others in the enterprise. Joint enterprises can be complicated, but again for now it is sufficient to know that they involve agreements among the parties to the enterprise to work together toward a common goal — for example, establishing and running a law firm, or developing a residential complex, or even simply going on a trip across country together — where each pays an equal share and has an equal say in how the enterprise is conducted.

Finally, some statutes provide for vicarious liability in circumstances where the common law does not. For example, after the school shootings at Columbine High School in 1999, many state legislatures enacted laws abrogating the common law rule that parents are not vicariously liable for the torts of their children. (We will see this common law rule in operation in the next chapter.) The resulting statutes provide that parents can be required to pay for the damage done by their children in certain circumstances; the amount they are subject to paying is generally capped, for example at $5,000.00. The law firm Matthiesen, Wickert & Lehrer in Hartford,

Wisconsin, has developed a very useful summary of the fifty states' parental responsibility laws. It is available online at https://www.mwl-law.com/wp-content/uploads/2018/02/parental-responsibility-laws-chart.pdf.

Persons who are vicariously liable for the torts of others may be able to recover their losses if they are entitled by agreement or otherwise to be "indemnified" by the tortfeasor. For example, "indemnification" provisions are common in employment and publications contracts. These provisions memorialize the parties' understanding that they will hold each other harmless for liability incurred as a result of tortious conduct. And some states have enacted statutes that require manufacturers to indemnify innocent retailers and corporations to indemnify directors and officers in certain circumstances.

C. Statutory and Common Law Immunities

Some claims cannot proceed — if they are filed, they will be dismissed — because the defendant is said to be "immune" from suit. Dismissal in this context is without regard to the merits of the claim otherwise. Thus, even if the plaintiff could make out all of the elements of the prima facie case, the suit would still be dismissed on the basis that, as a threshold matter, the defendant cannot be sued in the context at issue.

The immunities that are of most concern to litigants in modern civil cases are statutes of limitations, workers' compensation statutes, sovereign immunity, and family immunities.

1. Statutes of Limitations

Statutes of limitations are laws enacted by legislatures that limit the amount of time an injured party has within which to file suit against a defendant. The particular limitation period depends on the tort (or other claim) at issue; and it is often different depending on the jurisdiction. Whatever the case, if an injured party fails to file her claim before the end of the limitations period, it will fail from the outset, again regardless of the merits of the underlying claim. Missing the statute of limitations is the most common cause of malpractice claims against tort lawyers. Careful research to establish the limitations period and then multiple reminders as the deadline approaches are essential to protect the client's interests and to avoid this malpractice problem.

However long it lasts, the period begins when the claim arises — for example, in the case of a battery claim, when the defendant touches the plaintiff in a harmful or offensive manner — and it usually ends at the conclusion of the limitations period — for example, depending on the jurisdiction, within two years. This provision from the Illinois Code is typical:

> Actions for damages for an injury to the person, or for false imprisonment, or malicious prosecution, or for a statutory penalty, or for abduction, or for seduction, or for criminal conversation . . . shall be commenced within 2 years next after the cause of action accrued. . . .

75 ILCS 5/13-202 (Personal injury—Penalty). *See also* Hertel v. Sullivan, 261 Ill.App.3d 156 (1994) (applying this statutory provision, discussing the difference between when a statute begins to run in fact and in law, and the relevance of "discovery" and "repose" in this context).

2. Workers Compensation Statutes

At common law a worker could not sue his employer for on-the-job injuries. The theory was that workers were servants who could not sue their masters who had given them a job. As an alternative to allowing those suits, states enacted workers compensation statutes. These are state laws that typically provide that workers who are injured on the job are to be compensated *exclusively* out of a fund established for this purpose; the fund is sustained by a tax on employers. This means that a claim filed in court that is subject to the "exclusive remedy provision" of a workers compensation statute will be dismissed, again regardless of the merits of the underlying claim. The funds are helpful to workers because they are compensated quickly relative to the litigation process, and because they need not prove fault on the part of their employer; they "merely" need to establish that their injuries were work-related. The downside for employees is that the compensation provided is generally fixed and less than they might get if they were able to sue successfully in court. Correspondingly, the funds are helpful to employers who are able thereby to avoid tort litigation; this means that in most cases they do not risk potentially large tort damages awards and they are able better to predict and plan for the costs of accidents. A typical exception to this rule (which is based in the exclusive remedy provision of workers compensation statutes) is claims for intentional torts. Thus, the issue whether the plaintiff has alleged and may be able to prove an intentional tort is the subject of much tort-related litigation.

3. Sovereign (Governmental) Immunity

In general, there are three categories of government defendants: federal, state, and local. At common law, the doctrine of sovereign immunity — based in the old notion that "the king can do no wrong" — provided that the federal and state governments were absolutely immune from suit. Local governments, including counties, townships, cities, and villages, were not usually considered sovereigns; many were and still are corporate entities. Nevertheless, depending on the jurisdiction, local government entities may enjoy significant statutorily-based "governmental" immunity.

a. Federal Government Immunity

The following excerpt from a Report for Congress prepared by the Congressional Research Service provides an excellent summary of the scope of federal sovereign immunity:

> The Federal Tort Claims Act (FTCA), 28 U.S.C. §§ 1346(b), 2671–2680, is the statute by which the United States authorizes tort suits to be brought against itself. As a result of the common law doctrine of sovereign immunity, "the United States cannot be sued without its consent." "Congress alone has the power to waive or qualify that

> immunity." In 1946, by enacting the FTCA, Congress waived sovereign immunity for some tort suits. With exceptions, it made the United States liable:
>
>> for injury or loss of property, or personal injury or death caused by the negligent or wrongful act or omission of any employee of the government while acting within the scope of his office or employment, under circumstances where the United States, if a private person, would be liable to the claimant in accordance with the law of the place where the act or omission occurred.
>
> 28 U.S.C. § 1346(b).
>
> Thus, the FTCA makes the United States liable for the torts of its employees to the extent that private employers are liable under state law for the torts of their employees.* The fact that state law would make a state or municipal entity — as opposed to a *private* person — liable under like circumstances is not sufficient to make the United States liable under the FTCA.
>
> The FTCA, however, contains exceptions under which the United States may not be held liable even though a private employer could be held liable under state law. [The three most important exceptions are] . . . : the *Feres* doctrine, which prohibits suits by military personnel for injuries sustained incident to service; the discretionary function exception; and the intentional tort exception. Among the other exceptions, the United States may not be held liable in accordance with state law imposing strict liability; it may not be held liable for interest prior to judgment or for punitive damages (28 U.S.C. § 2674); for the act or omission of an employee exercising due care in the execution of an invalid statute or regulation (28 U.S.C. § 2680); for claims "arising out of the loss, miscarriage, or negligent transmission of letters or postal matter"; for claims arising in respect of the assessment or collection of any tax or customs duty; for claims caused by the fiscal operations of the Treasury or by the regulation of the monetary system; for claims arising out of combatant activities; or for claims arising in a foreign country.

Henry Cohen and Vivien S. Chu, Federal Tort Claims Act, Congressional Research Service, April 27, 2009, at 1–2, available at https://apps.dtic.mil/sti/pdfs/ADA499631.pdf.

The Discretionary Function Exception

As Cohen and Chu explain, "the discretionary function exception is the most significant exception to government liability that is explicitly provided for in the FTCA . . . [because it] immunizes the United States from claims 'based upon the exercise or performance or the failure

* Editors' note: Among the notable differences between state law claims and claims under the FTCA is that FTCA actions do not begin with the filing of a complaint in court. Instead, the process begins when a plaintiff serves Form 95 on the federal agency at issue. The statute of limitations for filing Form 95 is two years from the date of injury. Form 95 sets out the basic facts of the claim and the amount demanded, along with other information the agency needs to process the claim. The agency then has six months to determine whether it wishes to pay the claim. If the agency does not respond within that time period or the plaintiff declines a settlement, the plaintiff may then file a traditional complaint in federal court.

to exercise or perform a discretionary function.'" *Id.* at 2, citing 28 U.S.C. § 2680(a). The reason this exception is so significant — to the point where the waiver of sovereign immunity that is the FTCA may not have waived much in the end — is that the United States Supreme Court has interpreted "discretion" quite broadly. Thus, it encompasses:

> the discretion of the executive or administrator to act according to one's judgment of the best course. . . . It . . . includes more than the initiation of programs and activities. It also includes determinations made by executives or administrators in establishing plans, specifications or schedules of operations. Where there is room for policy judgment and decision there is discretion. It necessarily follows that acts of subordinates in carrying out the operations of government in accordance with official directions cannot be actionable.

Dalehite v. United States, 346 U.S. 15, 34, 35–36 (1953). Most importantly, the Court has made clear that the "choice or judgment" that provides immunity is not determined by the title or status of the government employee who would exercise it:

> A discretionary act is one that involves choice or judgment; there is nothing in that description that refers exclusively to policy-making or planning functions. Day-to-day management of banking affairs, like the management of other businesses, regularly require[s] judgment as to which of a range of permissible courses is the wisest.

United States v. Gaubert, 499 U.S. 315, 325 (1991).

Discretionary acts are to be distinguished from non-discretionary acts (also called "ministerial" acts) by looking to:

> whether the action is a matter of choice for the acting employee . . . . [C]onduct cannot be discretionary unless it involves an element of judgment or choice. . . . Thus, the discretionary function exception will not apply when a federal statute, regulation, or policy specifically prescribes a course of action for an employee to follow. In this event, the employee has no rightful option but to adhere to the directive. . . . The [discretionary function] exception . . . protects only governmental actions and decisions based on considerations of public policy.

Berkovitz v. United States, 486 U.S. 531, 536–37 (1988).

The Feres Doctrine

The Feres Doctrine is based in the United States Supreme Court's decision in Feres v. United States, 340 U.S. 135 (1950). The issue in the consolidated cases was "whether the Tort Claims Act extends its remedy to one sustaining 'incident to the service' what under other circumstances would be an actionable wrong." *Id.* at 138. The holding of the Court was that the federal government's sovereign immunity was not waived as to injuries sustained by service members "on active duty and not on furlough." *Id.*

The doctrine and its exception are rationalized on three grounds:

First, a contrary decision allowing a member of the armed services to sue the federal government under the FTCA would subject this otherwise "distinctively federal" relationship to the vagaries of different states' laws. *Id.* at 143 ("The relationship between the Government and members of its armed forces is 'distinctively federal in character,' . . . 'To whatever extent state law may apply to govern the relations between soldiers or others in the armed forces and persons outside them or nonfederal governmental agencies, the scope, nature, legal incidents and consequence of the relation between persons in service and the Government are fundamentally derived from federal courses and governed by federal authority.'").

Second, "the Veterans' Benefits Act establishes as a substitute for tort liability, a statutory 'no fault' compensation scheme which provides generous pensions to injured servicemen, without regard to any negligence attributable to the Government." United States v. Johnson, 481 U.S. 681, 684 (1987) (quotations and citations omitted).

Third, there is the matter of "'[t]he peculiar and special relationship of the soldier to his superiors, the effects of the maintenance of such suits on discipline, and the extreme results that might obtain if suits under the Tort Claims Act were allowed for negligent orders given or negligent acts committed in the course of military duty. . . .'" *Id.*

Using one or more of these rationales, the courts typically interpret the Feres Doctrine's "incident to service" rule broadly. *See, e.g.*, Irvin v. U.S., 845 F.2d 126 (6th Cir. 1988) (applying doctrine to preclude a medical malpractice claim seeking recovery for death of a newborn against a military obstetrician for allegedly poor prenatal care of an active duty servicewoman).** Responding to decisions like *Irvin*, the 2020 National Defense Authorization Act permits members of the military to pursue an administrative claim for medical malpractice if the treatment did not occur in an active conflict zone. The government's immunity from suit in federal court stands, however: if the claim is denied or the compensation offered by the administrative process is deemed insufficient by the claimant, they have no further recourse under the FTCA.

The Intentional Torts Exception

The FTCA expressly retains the government's traditional sovereign immunity for "[a]ny claim arising out of assault, battery, false imprisonment, false arrest, malicious prosecution, abuse of process, libel, slander, misrepresentation, deceit, or interference with contract rights." 28 U.S.C § 2680(h). However, "with regard to acts or omissions of investigative or law enforcement officers of the United States Government, the provisions of this chapter [waiving immunity] . . . shall apply to any claim arising . . . out of assault, battery, false imprisonment, false arrest, abuse of process, or malicious prosecution." *Id.* Section 2680(h) defines "investigative or law enforcement officer" as "any officer of the United States who is empowered by law to execute searches, to seize evidence, or to make arrests for violations of Federal law." *Id.*

The scope of the law enforcement waiver to the intentional torts exception was recently clarified in Millbrook v. United States, in which the Supreme Court allowed a suit brought against the United States by a federal prisoner who alleged he was sexually assaulted by federal correctional officers. 133 S.Ct. 1441 (2013). Writing for an unanimous Court, Justice Clarence

** Editors' note: If the plaintiff in *Irvin* had been the wife of the active duty serviceman, she would not have been subject to the Feres doctrine and thus would have been able to sue under the FTCA.

Thomas expressly rejected efforts by the United States and some lower courts to use the statute's definition of "investigative or law enforcement officer" to narrow the scope of the waiver only to circumstances where officers commit intentional torts in the context of "searches, seizures of evidence, arrests, and closely related exercises of investigative or law-enforcement authority." *Id.* at 1445–46 (holding that "the waiver effected by the law enforcement proviso extends to the acts or omissions of law enforcement officers that arise within the scope of their employment, regardless of whether the officers are engaged in investigative or law enforcement activity, or are executing a search, seizing evidence or making an arrest.") "By its terms," wrote Justice Thomas, this [definitional] provision focuses on the *status* of persons whose conduct may be actionable, not the types of activities that may give rise to a tort claim against the United States." *Id.* at 1445.

b. State Government Immunity

State governments have also waived part of their sovereign immunity; many have modeled their waivers on the FTCA. Because of this, both the states' amenability to suit and the remaining areas of immunity are often the same as those described in the FTCA.

c. Local Government Immunity

As we have already noted, although local government entities may have some statutory immunity, they will typically be liable for the torts of their employees up to the limit of their liability insurance policies. For example, in North Carolina,

> [t]he General Assembly has authorized cities and counties to waive the defense of governmental immunity by purchasing liability insurance (G.S. 153-435; 160A-485). Local governments may be inclined to waive this defense for several reasons. First, as just illustrated, for many activities it is difficult to be certain in advance that governmental immunity will protect the local government from liability. Second, by purchasing liability insurance, a local government provides a remedy for citizens who otherwise could not be compensated for injuries caused by the negligence of the local government's employees in performing governmental activities. Third, the defense of governmental immunity is limited to tort claims. It does not extend to claims for violations of constitutional rights or federal or state statutes.
>
> . . .
>
> If the local governing body purchases insurance, a person who sues the local government may not recover more than the policy amount for his or her injuries. This is true even if the person's damages far exceed the policy limits. For example, if the policy is limited to $25,000 per occurrence, even if the plaintiff's injuries are $57,000, the plaintiff may only recover to the extent of the policy limits. Indeed, the waiver statute specifically provides that if a jury returns a verdict in excess of the insurance limits, the judge must reduce the award to the maximum limits of the policy before entering the judgment on the court docket. In other words, governmental immunity is waived only to the extent of insurance coverage. Similarly when a local government's

insurance policy involves a deductible, the local government retains governmental immunity for damages that fall within the amount of the deductible.

Anita R. Brown-Graham, County and Municipal Government in North Carolina, Article 12: Civil Liability of the Local Government and Its Officials and Employees, UNC-Chapel Hill School of Government at 8-9 (2007). *See also* Handbook for Minnesota Cities, Chapter 18: Liability, Publication of the League of Minnesota Cities (2013) (detailing terms of state's and cities' waiver of sovereign immunity, their liability limits, and insurance provisions).

d. Immunities Applicable to Government Employees

All of the sovereign immunity rules described to this point apply when a plaintiff seeks to name a government or governmental entity as defendant. If one wishes to sue a state or local government employee, either in lieu of or in addition to suing their employer, different immunities may apply. The most important of these for our purposes are the following:

Federal employees cannot be sued at all if their employer (an arm of the federal government) is liable under the FTCA; in other words, that remedy is exclusive and it is only against the United States. See, e.g., Alan Feuer and Benjamin Weiser, Biden Justice Department Seeks to Defend Trump in Suit Over Rape Denial, The New York Times, June 8, 2021 (the United States arguing in briefs that "when Mr. Trump had denied raping Ms. Carroll, through the White House press office or in statements to reporters in the Oval Office and on the White House lawn, he was acting within the scope of his office").

Otherwise, state and federal legislators have "legislative immunity," judges have "judicial immunity," and prosecutors have "prosecutorial immunity"; these immunities preclude liability for lawful acts done in an official capacity. Other state and local government officials may have more limited or "qualified" immunity, depending upon the circumstances. For example, most local governments provide immunity to employees of their child protective services departments (CPS or DSS). This immunity typically bars suit against such employees for injuries to children that may be caused in part by child placement or supervision decisions made by CPS or DSS.

Qualified immunity in particular has been in the news a lot lately, as it often applies in cases involving the use of force by police. The goal of the doctrine is to balance, on one hand, the interests of government officers in being able to do their jobs without fear of lawsuits and personal financial liability and, on the other hand, the interests of civilians in deterring unlawful official conduct and obtaining redress for resulting injuries. The "qualification" or limit on the officer's immunity is the Constitution: If official action violates a "clearly established" constitutional right, it is not subject to the immunity and the officer may be liable. If it does not, the immunity will protect them from suit. Over the years, the courts developed the doctrine such that officers were protected from suit unless their actions were directly on the point of and contrary to a well-established constitutional right that average, non-legally trained persons would know and understand. This has allowed for quite egregious results and abundant criticism of the doctrine's evolution. As we write in 2021, we appear to be in a period of at least slight correction by the Supreme Court, although the lower federal courts are still producing results and opinions that test its limits. Compare Taylor v. Riojas, 592 U.S. ___

(2020), 2020 WL 6385693 (2020), with Ramirez v. Guadarrama, No. 20-10055 (5th Cir. June 25, 2021). For an example of recent commentary on this juncture see Evidence ProfBlogger, Fifth Circuit Grants Qualified Immunity To Officers Who Tased Man Soaked in Gasoline, Knowing it Would Light Him on Fire, June 27, 2021.

4. Family Immunities

At common law, spouses could not sue one another on the theory that, once married, the two became one and thus could not be adversaries. This doctrine has been substantially eroded so that today, it is at least possible for spouses to sue one another for intentional torts. Spousal rape is the classic transitional scenario in this regard.

Similarly, for a long time it was not possible for children to sue their parents. Several theories supported this rule including that the harmony of the family would be disturbed by adversarial litigation; that parents' necessary, superior status within the family would be disrupted; and that any damages the child might recover likely would constitute more than his or her share of the family's resources and thus take resources away from another (presumably innocent) family member. This rule has also been substantially eroded. Children are now able to sue their parents for some intentional torts—like spousal rape, child sex abuse was a common transitional scenario. However, a majority of jurisdictions continue to preclude suit on the basis of mere negligence, either on the ground that parents retain traditional immunity in this area, i.e., immunity has only been rejected for some intentional torts, or on the ground that while the courts no longer recognize parent-child immunities, there is still "no duty" reasonably to supervise a child. We will discuss this special "no duty" negligence rule in Chapter Four.

There are exceptions to this rule that children cannot bring negligence suits against their parents. For example, many jurisdictions permit children's negligence claims against their parents where these are based in car accidents involving an insured parent-driver; in such cases, the family's harmony and finances are said not to be in jeopardy because the parent is only a nominal defendant. Some states also permit children to sue their parents in negligence when the alleged injury occurs while the child is "at work" with their parent.

Because children do not often sue their parents, these rules are mostly applicable in circumstances where a defendant who is alleged to have injured a child seeks to include the child's parent as a co-defendant, on the theory that the parent was either solely or also responsible; the impleading of the parent will be permissible only if the child herself could have sued her parent in the circumstances. *See, e.g.,* Brunner v. Hutchinson Division, Lear-Siegler, Inc., 770 F.Supp. 517 (D. S.D. 1991) (setting out the history of the parent-child immunity rule, the exceptions that have been carved out over time, and this typical factual context).

* * *

This chapter has introduced you to the traditional rationales for tort law — compensation, deterrence, and the prevention of self-help. It has provided a sense of the law's most significant modern transformations—the move from a strict liability or causation-based approach to liability to a fault-based approach, and the move from rules that were predominately judge-made to a hybrid system involving both judge-made and legislatively enacted rules. Finally, the chapter has laid the foundation for you to begin to understand the basis for evaluating the viability of claims as a threshold matter, including with respect to collectability, vicarious liability, statutes of limitations, worker's compensation, and immunities. All of these issues are relevant throughout the course; take time to notice them when they arise and then to consider how the lessons set out in this chapter might be helpful to resolving the disputes at issue.

CHAPTER TWO
INTENTIONAL TORTS

I. THE PRIMA FACIE CASE

A. The Basic or "Skeleton" Prima Facie Case

The basic or "skeleton" prima facie case for the intentional torts is: (1) act, (2) intent, (3) causation, and (4) injury. The intent and injury elements of this skeleton are fleshed out differently in each of the specific intentional torts; as we will see below, these differences are what distinguish the torts from each other. First, however, it is important for you to learn the very precise legal meaning of each of the basic terms.

1. The Act Requirement

The first required element of the intentional torts prima facie case is an "act." According to The Restatement (Second) of Torts, § 2, "[t]he word 'act' . . . denote[s] an external manifestation of the actor's will and does not include any of its results, even the most direct, immediate, and intended." The following explanation is also from the Restatement:

Comment:

a. Necessity of volition. There cannot be an act without volition. Therefore, a contraction of a person's muscles which is purely a reaction to some outside force, such as a knee jerk or the blinking of the eyelids in defense against an approaching missile, or the convulsive movements of an epileptic, are not acts of that person. So too, movements of the body during sleep when the will is in abeyance are not acts. Since some outward manifestation of the defendant's will is necessary to the existence of an act which can subject him to liability, it is not enough that a third person has utilized a part of the defendant's body as an instrument to carry out his own intention to cause harm to the plaintiff. In such case, as in the case of the knee jerk, the actor is the third person who has used the defendant's body as an instrument to accomplish some purpose of his own, or who has struck the defendant's leg so as to have caused the knee jerk.

b. Freedom of actor's will. If the actor's will is in fact manifested by some muscular contraction, including those which are necessary to the speaking of words, it is not necessary that his will operate freely and without pressure from outside circumstances. Indeed, the fact that the pressure is irresistible in the sense that it is one which reasonable men cannot be expected to resist, does not prevent its manifestation from being an act, although it may make the act excusable. A muscular reaction is always an act unless it is a purely reflexive reaction in which the mind and will have no share. Thus, if A, finding himself about to fall, stretches his hand out to seize some object, whether a fellow human being or a mere inanimate object, to save himself from falling, the stretching out of his hand and the grasping of the object is an act in the sense in which that word has heretofore been used, since the defendant's mind has grasped the situation and has dictated a muscular contraction which his rapidly formed judgment leads him to believe to be helpful to prevent his fall. While the decision is formed instantaneously, nonetheless the movement of the hand is a response to the will exerted by a mind which has already determined upon a distinct course of action. The exigency in which the defendant is placed, the necessity for a rapid decision, the fact that the decision corresponds to a universal tendency of mankind, may be enough to relieve the defendant from liability, but it is not enough to prevent his grasping of the object from being his own act.

c. Act and its consequences. The word "act" includes only the external manifestation of the actor's will. It does not include any of the effects of such manifestation, no matter how direct, immediate, and intended. Thus, if the actor, having pointed a pistol at another, pulls the trigger, the act is the pulling of the trigger and not the impingement of the bullet upon the other's person. So too, if the actor intentionally strikes another, the act is only the movement of the actor's hand and not the contact with the other's body immediately established.

A Note on the Restatements of Torts

As we have already seen, tort law today is found primarily in cases, but increasingly also in statutes. These are the authoritative sources of the law. Non-authoritative but still persuasive descriptions or statements of particular legal rules may also be found in treatises written by legal academics—for example, Prosser on Torts and Dobbs on Torts—and in the Restatement of Torts, which is produced by the American Law Institute (ALI).

The ALI is an organization of well-respected lawyers and legal academics which publishes the Restatements in various subject matter areas. Courts often refer to the Restatements' descriptions of the law, either because these descriptions reflect or have been adopted as the law in the jurisdiction, or as an example of what the law might be. As you consider Restatement provisions throughout this course and elsewhere, it is important to keep in mind that, although they are often an accurate rendition of the "black letter law" — i.e., the majority rule across the jurisdictions — they are also sometimes aspirational. As Professor Joseph King has explained, "[f]rom the beginning, there have been tensions resulting from differing views of the restatements' proper role. Perhaps the most prominent has been the 'tension . . . between stating what the law is and what [the law] ought to be.'" Joseph H. King, The Torts Restatement's Inchoate Definition of Intent for Battery, and Reflections on the Province of Restatements, 38 Pepperdine L. Rev. 623, 654–660 (2011).

According to Professor King's recent history of the ALI,

> [a] number of influential players in the formative years of the Institute, including its first two directors, have been described as supporting the view that the restatement's purpose was to state what that law is. But other commentators believed that the founders contemplated that the restatements would undertake a broader mission, which would include recommending changes in the law. [For example,] Professor Hull presents a detailed argument that the vision of the Institute's first director, William Draper Lewis, was that of "a group of 'progressive-pragmatic' legal academics, who wished to reform law and promote the influence of law professors in the wider world of legal practice."

In any event, as Professor King and others have noted, "[t]he dispute as to the mission of the [Institute] has not been resolved and, no doubt, will continue well into the future." Id. For present purposes, you can assume that the Restatement provisions you read accurately reflect the black letter law unless it is otherwise noted. Don't forget, though, that the law in any particular jurisdiction may be different, i.e., the jurisdiction may not follow the majority rule.

2. The Intent Requirement

The second required element of the prima facie case for the intentional torts is "intent." This element can be made out in one of two ways. First, intent can be made out by showing that the defendant acted with the "purpose" or the "desire" to cause the consequences of his act. This is sometimes called "true intent." Second, intent can be made out by showing that the defendant knew with "certainty" or "substantial certainty" – the latter defined as "near certainty" not less – that the consequences would follow from his act.* The Comment accompanying Section 8A of the Second Restatement provides this additional detail:

> *a.* "Intent," as it is used throughout the Restatement of Torts, has reference to the consequences of an act rather than the act itself. When an actor fires a gun in the midst of the Mojave Desert, he intends to pull the trigger; but when the bullet hits a person who is present in the desert without the actor's knowledge, he does not intend that result. "Intent" is limited, wherever it is used, to the consequences of the act. All consequences which the actor desires to bring about are intended, as the word is used in this Restatement.
>
> *b.* Intent is not, however, limited to consequences which are desired. If the actor knows that the consequences are certain, or substantially certain, to result from his act, and still goes ahead, he is treated by the law as if he had in fact desired to produce the result. As the probability that the consequences will follow decreases, and becomes less than substantial certainty, the actor's conduct loses the character of intent, and becomes mere recklessness . . . . As the probability decreases further, and amounts only to a risk that the result will follow, it becomes ordinary negligence . . . All three have their important place in the law of torts, but the liability attached to them will differ.
>
> Illustrations:
>
> 1. A throws a bomb into B's office for the purpose of killing B. A knows that C, B's stenographer, is in the office. A has no desire to injure C, but knows that his act is

* Editors' note: The Second and Third Restatements use the terms "substantial certainty" and "substantially certain" instead of "near certainty" or "nearly certain." The authors of the Third Restatement agree, however, that "near certainty" better reflects what the courts require to make out intent, and that the term "substantial certainty" can be misleading in that it tends to suggest that a finding of recklessness — i.e., less than "near certainty" — is sufficient. For our class purposes, we strongly recommend that you consider the intent requirement to be satisfied only by a showing that the defendant had the purpose or desire to cause the consequences of his act or that he was nearly certain these consequences would follow. For a discussion of this issue see item 5 of http://lawprofessors.typepad.com/tortsprof/2014/05/simons-and-pryor-respond-to-wrights-comments-on-the-restatement-of-intentional-torts.html.

> [nearly] certain to do so. C is injured by the explosion. A is subject to liability to C for an intentional tort.
>
> 2. On a curve in a narrow highway A, without any desire to injure B, or belief that he is [nearly] certain to do so, recklessly drives his automobile in an attempt to pass B's car. As a result of this recklessness, A crashes into B's car, injuring B. A is subject to liability to B for his reckless conduct, but is not liable to B for any intentional tort.

In contrast with intent, and according to most courts, an

> actor's conduct is in reckless disregard of the safety of another if he does an act or intentionally fails to do an act which it is his duty to the other to do, knowing or having reason to know of facts which would lead a reasonable [person] to realize not only that his conduct creates an unreasonable risk of physical harm to another, but also such risk is substantially greater than that which is necessary to make his conduct negligent.

Restatement (Second) of Torts § 500. The Restatement situates the place of recklessness (and related concepts) on the fault continuum:

> Terms conveying the idea of wrongdoing that is aggravated — even though falling short of the wrongdoing involved in intentional torts— are common in the discourse of torts. Sometimes, the term used is "gross negligence." Taken at face value, this term simply means negligence that is especially bad. Given this literal interpretation, gross negligence carries a meaning that is less than recklessness. The term "willful or wanton misconduct" is also frequently employed. "Willful misconduct" sometimes refers to conduct involving an intent to cause harm; but "wanton misconduct" is commonly understood to mean recklessness. Frequently, courts refer to conduct that displays a "reckless disregard for risk" or a "reckless indifference to risk." When a person's conduct creates a known risk that can be reduced by relatively modest precautions, to state that the person displays a reckless disregard for risk is equivalent to stating that the person's conduct is reckless.

Restatement (Third) Torts: Physical And Emotional Harm, Section 2, Comment (a). Recklessness is also sometimes described as indifference.

Consistent with this continuum, courts generally consider recklessness to be a "higher" or "aggravated" form of negligence, so that the prima facie case for recklessness is the same as that for negligence but with the addition of the necessary aggravating facts. See Hutchinson v. Tudubaev, 2010 WL 4514367 (Sup. Ct. Conn. 2010) ("There is no reason why a plaintiff, relying on the same set of facts in a negligence count cannot set forth in a separate count a cause of action arising out of those same facts alleging recklessness . . . reckless conduct is an aggravated form of negligence . . . included in that definition is a claimed departure from ordinary care which forms the basis of a negligence claim. . . . If we have a negligence count which sets forth facts that support a negligence claim, a motion to strike will not lie against a recklessness count which incorporates those facts, if they also support a reckless conduct theory of liability."); Hatch v. V.P. Fair Foundation, Inc., 990 S.W.3d 126, 139 (Mo. App. 1999) ("Recklessness is an aggravated form of negligence which differs in quality, rather than in degree, from ordinary lack of care. It is applied to conduct which is negligent, rather than intentional, but which is so far from a proper state of mind that it is treated in many respects as if it were so intended."); Royal Indemnity Company v. Love, 630 N.Y.S.2d (652, 654) (Sup. Ct. N.Y. 1995) ("A person acts recklessly if he or she is aware of and consciously disregards a substantial and unjustifiable risk.").

Notes and Questions

1. Draw the fault continuum, this time including the intermediate forms of negligence described above.

2. The issue whether an act is intentional — according to the "near certainty" standard — or merely reckless is mostly addressed in the context of claims that an employee is entitled to bypass the exclusive remedy provided in a workers compensation statute and instead to seek a remedy in tort. Workers' compensation statutes provide statutory levels of compensation to workers injured on the job (which ensures that some compensation is available relatively quickly) and preclude negligence lawsuits (which gives employers the incentive necessary to invest in the workers compensation fund). These same statutes often include an exception for intentional torts. For this purpose, "intent" is usually defined as provided by the Restatement; however, some jurisdictions require workers to prove "true intent" (a purpose or desire to injure) before they can bypass the workers compensation system.

3. It is often difficult to discern a defendant's intent. (In most cases, the defendant is unlikely to offer up evidence as plain as a declaration, "My goal was to cause the plaintiff physical pain and harm.") Nevertheless, the inquiry is designed to be subjective; it seeks to establish what the defendant actually intended. What kind of information is the fact finder permitted to consider in doing this work? Here is how one court instructed the jury:

> Intentional conduct is purposeful conduct rather than conduct that is accidental or inadvertent. Now intent is a mental process. A . . . person may take the stand and testify as to what his or her intention was and you may believe the testimony or not according to whether or not you find that it warrants belief. But intention often can only be proven by the actions and statements of the person whose act is being examined.
>
> No one can be expected to come into court and testify that he looked into another person's mind and saw there a certain intention. It is often impossible and never necessary to prove intent by direct evidence. Intent may be proven by circumstantial evidence, as I have explained that term to you.
>
> Therefore, one way in which the . . . jury can determine what a person's intention was at any given time, aside from that person's own testimony, is first by determining what that person's conduct was, including any statement he made and what the . . . circumstances were surrounding that conduct, and then from that conduct and those circumstances, inferring what his intention was.

> In other words, a person's intention may be inferred from his conduct. You may infer from the fact that the person engaged in conduct that he intended to engage in that conduct. This inference is not a necessary one. That is, you are not required to infer intent from the person's conduct, but it is an inference that you may draw if you find it reasonable and a logical inference. I remind you that the burden of proving intent by a preponderance of evidence is on the plaintiff.

Suarez v. Dickmont Plastics Corp., 698 A.2d 838, 844 n. 7 (Conn. 1997).

Problem One: Intent v. Recklessness

It is often difficult to distinguish intentional conduct from merely reckless conduct. The following hypothetical exemplifies this difficulty. Did Ichiro have the intent necessary for battery? For recklessness? What would make you more comfortable saying it is one rather than the other?

Ichiro plays professional baseball. He is playing at another team's stadium and has been commenting all game long to his teammates about the huge and obnoxious crowd. They constantly boo him and his teammates. Ichiro's team loses. He is in the outfield when the game ends. There's no booing as he walks towards the dugout and the crowd starts to file out. As he walks past the pitcher's mound, he sees a baseball lying on the ground. He picks it up and throws it into the stands with a high arc saying loudly, "There goes another one." Anita is leaving the stadium with her back to the field. The ball hits Anita on the head causing surface wounds, intracranial bleeding, and a concussion.

3. The Causation Requirement

To make out a prima facie case, regardless of the tort or the mental state requirement, a plaintiff must show that the defendant's act was an actual (factual) cause of the injuries at issue; this is called the actual cause requirement. The plaintiff must also show that the defendant's act was a legal or "proximate" cause of the injuries; this requirement involves an inquiry into the fairness of holding the defendant liable for the plaintiff's damages. We will focus closely on these two parts of the causation requirement in our study of negligence.

4. The Injury Requirement

Finally, the plaintiff must show that the defendant's act caused the requisite "injury." According to The Restatement (Second) § 7(1), "[t]he word "injury" is used . . . to denote the invasion of any legally protected interest of another." In contrast, "[t]he word "harm" is used . . . to denote the existence of loss or detriment in fact of any kind to a person resulting from any cause." Id. at (2). And "[t]he words "physical harm" are used . . . to denote the physical impairment of the human body, or of land or chattels." Id. at (3). The accompanying Comment amplifies as follows:

a. "Injury" and "harm" contrasted. The word "injury" is used throughout the Restatement of this Subject to denote the fact that there has been an invasion of a legally protected interest which, if it were the legal consequence of a tortious act, would entitle the person suffering the invasion to maintain an action of tort. It differs from the word "harm" in this: "harm" implies the existence of loss or detriment in fact, which may not necessarily be the invasion of a legally protected interest. The most usual form of injury is the infliction of some harm; but there may be an injury although no harm is done. Thus, any intrusion upon land in the possession of another is an injury, and, if not privileged, gives rise to a cause of action even though the intrusion is beneficial, or so transitory that it constitutes no interference with or detriment to the land or its beneficial enjoyment. So too, the mere apprehension of an intentional and immediate bodily contact, whether harmful or merely offensive, is as much an "injury" as a blow which breaks an arm. It is desirable to have a word to denote the type of result which, if the act which causes it is tortious, is sufficient to sustain an action even though there is no harm for which compensatory damages can be given. The meaning of the word "injury," as here defined, differs from the sense in which the word "injury" is often used, to indicate that the invasion of the interest in question has been caused by conduct of such a character as to make it tortious.

b. "Harm" implies a loss or detriment to a person, and not a mere change or alteration in some physical person, object or thing. Physical changes or alterations may be either beneficial, detrimental, or of no consequence to a person. In so far as physical changes have a detrimental effect on a person, that person suffers harm. Acts or conditions which affect the personal tastes, likes, or dislikes of a person may be either beneficial to him, or detrimental, or of no consequence, the same as acts which affect physical things. In so far as these acts or conditions are detrimental to him, he suffers harm. Thus harm, as defined in this Section, is the detriment or loss to a person which occurs by virtue of, or as a result of, some alteration or change in his person, or in physical things, and also the detriment resulting to him from acts or conditions which impair his physical, emotional, or aesthetic well-being, his pecuniary advantage, his intangible rights, his reputation, or his other legally recognized interests. Frequently, where "harm" is used in this Restatement, it is qualified by some limiting adjective, such as bodily harm, physical harm, pecuniary harm, and the like. In each such case the intent is to limit the rule stated to the particular kind of harm specified. Where no such limiting adjective appears, the word is to be understood in the general sense here defined.

. . .

e. Physical harm. The words "physical harm" are used to denote physical impairment of the human body, or of tangible property, which is to say land or chattels. Where the harm is impairment of the body, it is called "bodily harm."

B. The Specific or "Fleshed Out" Prima Facie Cases

As we have already noted, the specific intentional torts — battery and assault, for example — are based in the skeleton prima facie case but are distinguished from one another by the way in which the intent and injury elements are fleshed out. The following sections cover the specific prima facie cases for the intentional torts of battery, assault, intentional infliction of emotional distress, fraud, and false imprisonment. We will see two more, trespass and conversion, in the affirmative defenses part of the chapter.

1. Battery, Assault, and Intentional Infliction of Emotional Distress

HALL v. McBRYDE
919 P.2d 910 (Colo. App. 1996)

Opinion by Judge Hume.

Plaintiff, Eric Hall, appeals from a judgment entered in favor of defendant, Marcus McBryde (Marcus), on a claim of battery, and in favor of Marcus' parents, defendants, James McBryde and Kathleen McBryde, on claims of negligent maintenance of a weapon and negligent supervision. We affirm in part, reverse in part, and remand with directions.

On January 14, 1993, Marcus was at his parents' home with another youth after school. Although, at that time, Marcus was, pursuant to his parents' wishes, actually living in a different neighborhood with a relative and attending a different high school in the hope of avoiding gang-related problems, he had sought and received permission from his father to come to the McBryde house that day to retrieve some clothing. Prior to that date, Marcus had discovered a loaded gun hidden under the mattress of his parents' bed. James McBryde had purchased the gun sometime earlier.

Soon after midday, Marcus noticed some other youths in a car approaching the McBryde house, and he retrieved the gun from its hiding place. After one of the other youths began shooting towards the McBryde house, Marcus fired four shots toward the car containing the other youths.

During the exchange of gunfire one bullet struck plaintiff, who lived next to the McBryde residence, causing an injury to his abdomen that required extensive medical treatment. Although plaintiff testified that it was Marcus who shot him, the trial court made no finding as to whether plaintiff was struck by a bullet fired by Marcus.

Neither James McBryde nor Kathleen McBryde was home at the time of the shooting. In a deposition, the transcript of which was introduced at trial, James McBryde testified that he had no recollection of telling Marcus that he had purchased the gun and that he believed he was the only one in the house who was aware of it. Marcus testified in a deposition, also introduced at trial, that his father had never told him about the gun and that he discovered it on his own.

Although none of the defendants appeared for trial, the trial court received testimony from plaintiff and reviewed prior deposition testimony in the case. Thereafter, the trial court entered its "Verdict of the Court and Entry of Judgment" in which it found in favor of defendants on all three of plaintiff's claims.

I.

Plaintiff first contends that the trial court erred in entering judgment for James and Kathleen McBryde on plaintiff's claim of negligent maintenance of a weapon. We disagree. . . . we find no error as to the trial court's judgment in favor of James and Kathleen McBryde on the claim of their negligent maintenance of a weapon.

II.

Plaintiff next contends that the trial court erred in entering judgment for James and Kathleen McBryde on the claim of negligent supervision. Again, we disagree.

A parent is not liable for the torts committed by his or her child merely because of the parent-child relationship. However, when a child has a known propensity to commit a potentially harmful act, the parent has a duty to use reasonable care to prevent the child from causing such harm if the parent knows or should know of the propensity and has the ability and opportunity to control the child. Horton v. Reaves, 186 Colo. 149, 526 P.2d 304 (1974); Mitchell v. Allstate Insurance Co., supra.

Here, the trial court found no evidence that Marcus had been a member of a gang, that he had ever been arrested prior to the shooting incident, or that he otherwise had any history of violent or improper behavior. The trial court also determined that allowing Marcus to return to the McBryde home unsupervised during the afternoon of the shooting to pick up clothing "was not a breach of [the parents'] duty of supervision that any reasonable person would recognize." Once again, because more than one inference or conclusion may be drawn from the facts and because the trial court's determination is supported by evidence in the record, it will not be disturbed. See Mitchell v. Allstate Insurance Co., supra.

III.

Finally, plaintiff contends that the trial court erred in entering judgment for Marcus on the claim of battery. We agree.

An actor is subject to liability to another for battery if he or she acts intending to cause a harmful or offensive contact with the person of the other or a third person, or an imminent apprehension of such a contact, and a harmful or offensive contact with the person of the other directly or indirectly results.

Here, the trial court found that there was no evidence indicating that Marcus intended to shoot at plaintiff. Furthermore, based upon statements by Marcus that he was not purposely trying to hit the other youths but, instead, was shooting at their car, the trial court also determined that plaintiff had failed to prove Marcus intended to make contact with any person other than plaintiff. Based upon this second finding, and relying on CJI-Civ.3d 20:5 and CJI-Civ.3d 20:8 (1989), the trial court concluded that the doctrine of transferred intent could not apply to create liability for battery upon plaintiff. We conclude that, in reaching its determination that no battery occurred, the trial court did not properly analyze the intent required for battery or the transferability of such intent.

As set forth above, the intent element for battery is satisfied if the actor either intends to cause a harmful or offensive contact or if the actor intends to cause an imminent apprehension of such contact. Moreover, with respect to the level of intent necessary for a battery and the transferability of such intent, Restatement (Second) of Torts § 16 (1965) provides as follows:

> (1) If an act is done with the intention of inflicting upon another an offensive but not a harmful bodily contact, or of putting another in apprehension of either a harmful or offensive bodily contact, and such act causes a bodily contact to the other, the actor is liable to the other for a battery although the act was not done with the intention of bringing about the resulting bodily harm.
>
> (2) If an act is done with the intention of affecting a third person in the manner stated in Subsection (1), but causes a harmful bodily contact to another, the actor is liable to such other as fully as though he intended so to affect him.

See also Restatement (Second) of Torts § 20 (1965); Alteiri v. Colasso, 168 Conn. 329, 362 A.2d 798 (1975) (when one intends an assault, then, if bodily injury results to someone other than the person whom the actor intended to put in apprehension of harm, it is a battery actionable by the injured person); Brown v. Martinez, 68 N.M. 271, 361 P.2d 152 (1961).

Here, the trial court considered only whether Marcus intended to inflict a contact upon the other youths. It did not consider whether Marcus intended to put the other youths in apprehension of a harmful or offensive bodily contact.

However, we conclude, as a matter of law, that by aiming and firing a loaded weapon at the automobile for the stated purpose of protecting his house, Marcus did intend to put the youths who occupied the vehicle in apprehension of a harmful or offensive bodily contact. Hence, pursuant to the rule set forth in Restatement (Second) of Torts § 16(2) (1965), Marcus' intent to place other persons in apprehension of a harmful or offensive contact was sufficient to satisfy the intent requirement for battery against plaintiff.

Accordingly, we conclude that the cause must be remanded for additional findings as to whether the bullet that struck plaintiff was fired by Marcus. If the trial court finds that the bullet was fired by Marcus, it shall find in favor of plaintiff on the battery claim and enter judgment for damages as proven by plaintiff on that claim.

The judgment is affirmed as to plaintiff's negligence and negligent supervision claims against defendants James McBryde and Kathleen McBryde. As to the plaintiff's battery claim against defendant Marcus McBryde, the judgment is reversed, and the cause is remanded for further proceedings consistent with this opinion.

Notes and Questions

1. Because he was under 18, the law considered Marcus McBryde a "child" for purposes of the plaintiff's claims against his parents, who, because of his age, continued to have various parental rights and responsibilities. The court also properly treated Marcus as an adult for purposes of the plaintiff's battery claim, because adolescents are considered to be capable of

forming intent to cause harm or offense. Thus, leaving aside the parental supervision claims, you should consider this case to be representative of the analysis a court would engage when dealing with an adult defendant in a battery case.

2. *McBryde* is an example of a "harmful battery" case, because the plaintiff suffered bodily harm as a result (allegedly) of the defendant's actions. We will see shortly that harmful batteries are distinguished from "offensive batteries" in which the direct harm caused by the defendant is dignitary. Of course, a battery can be both harmful and offensive; depending on the facts, for example, sexual batteries can meet both requirements.

3. *McBryde* describes the basic requirements for the torts of battery and assault. Can you develop their list forms — flesh out their four-part skeleton prima facie cases — from the narrative description in the opinion?

4. Make sure you understand the transferred intent rule. Based on its application in *McBryde*, how would you describe it? There were two transfers at issue in *McBryde*. What were they?

HORTON v. REAVES
526 P.2D 304 (Colo. 1974)

En Banc

On March 4, 1970, Mrs. Reaves placed her five-week-old daughter upon a bed, encompassed by pillows and blankets to prevent the baby from falling off the bed. Mrs. Reaves then left the child unattended for two and one-half hours while she visited a next-door neighbor, Mrs. Horton. As Mrs. Reaves was returning to her home, Johnny and Keith Horton, four and three year-old children of Mrs. Horton, were seen jumping from the porch of the Reaves home and running across the yard to their home. Johnny said something to his mother which indicated that the Reaves baby might need attention. In response to the severe questioning of his mother, Johnny admitted that he had dropped the Reaves baby. Mrs. Horton immediately called to Mrs. Reaves to check on her child. Mrs. Reaves found the infant on the bedroom floor with a crushed skull.

Through her legal guardian, the infant plaintiff brought this personal injury action against Johnny and Keith Horton, Mrs. Horton, and Mrs. Reaves. The complaint alleged: That Johnny and Keith Horton entered the Reaves home without authority and assaulted and battered the child; that Mrs. Horton negligently supervised or failed to supervise her children, thereby allowing the assault and battery to occur; that Mrs. Reaves negligently failed to care for her child by leaving it unattended; that the action of Mrs. Reaves also constituted wanton or reckless disregard for the infant's well-being.

Prior to trial, the district court dismissed the simple negligence claim against Mrs. Reaves on grounds of parental immunity. At the close of the plaintiff's case, the court dismissed the claim against Mrs. Horton and the remaining claim against Mrs. Reaves by reason of insufficiency of evidence. The trial proceeded to conclusion against the two remaining defendants, Johnny and Keith Horton. Judgment was entered upon a jury verdict in favor of these defendants.

The Court of Appeals affirmed the district court in all respects except that it reversed and remanded the claim against Johnny and Keith Horton for a new trial on the basis of an improper jury instruction. We granted two petitions for certiorari to the Court of Appeals decision, Reaves v. Horton, Colo.App., 518 P.2d 1380 (1973). One petition for certiorari was by the infant against Mrs. Reaves and Mrs. Horton; and the other was by the boys, complaining as to the reversal. We have consolidated the writs. We affirm as to the first writ and reverse as to that of the boys.

LIABILITY OF DELORES HORTON

I.

The plaintiff first argues that the Court of Appeals erred in affirming the district court's ruling that there was insufficient evidence to submit the issue of Mrs. Horton's negligence to the jury.

As pointed out by the Court of Appeals, under the great weight of authority a parent is not liable for the torts of a child merely because of the parent-child relationship. Rather, a parent is liable for the tortious acts of the child only if the parent's negligence in supervising the child is the proximate cause of the injury. In cases involving a battery committed by a child, the parent's liability is predicated upon three factors: (1) that the child had a propensity to commit the particular abuse which caused the injury; (2) that the parent knew of the child's propensity; and (3) that the parent failed to restrain the child from committing the particular type of wrongful conduct causing injury.

In this case there was no competent evidence establishing Mrs. Horton's liability. The only testimony concerning any previous assault-like behavior on the part of Johnny or Keith was supplied by Mrs. Reaves. She testified that on one occasion Johnny and Keith had pushed another Horton child off a bed. Mrs. Reaves' testimony states that Mrs. Horton reprimanded her children for this behavior. This latter testimony indicates that Mrs. Horton exercised due care in watching over Johnny and Keith. In fact, we have been unable to find any evidence in the record tending to show that Mrs. Horton was negligent in not preventing Johnny and Keith from engaging in the particular type of behavior of which the plaintiff has complained. Under these circumstances, the Court of Appeals was correct in concluding that the issue of Mrs. Horton's negligence should not have been submitted to the jury.

. . .

LIABILITY OF JOHNNY AND KEITH HORTON

III.

The Court of Appeals ruled that the trial court failed to properly instruct the jury concerning the intent requirement of an infant charged with an intentional tort.

The jury was instructed that in order to find Keith and Johnny Horton liable, it had to find: (1) that the defendants were 'capable of intending the harmful contact of another;' and (2) that the defendants 'acted with the intent of making a harmful contact with the plaintiff's person.' The question of the nature of the intent required of infants charged with intentional torts is a matter of first impression in this state. . . .

It is recognized that, often as a matter of policy, other jurisdictions hold infants liable for their intentional torts, so as to avoid inflicting financial loss upon an innocent victim. It is our view, however, that the requisite intent required must include some awareness of the natural consequences of intentional acts. Though the extent of the resulting harm need not be intended, nor even foreseen, the infant must appreciate the offensiveness or wrongfulness of his act before liability inures.

The instructions given by the trial court are consistent with our pattern jury instructions.

> 'In order for plaintiff, (name), to recover from defendant, (name), on his claim of battery, you must find that both of the following have been established:
>
> '1. The defendant acted with the intent of making a (harmful) (or) (offensive) contact with the plaintiff's person (or with the person of another).
>
> '2. The defendant's act resulted in a (harmful) (or) (offensive) contact with the person of the plaintiff. . . .' Colorado Jury Instructions 20:5.

See Restatement (Second) of Torts § 13 (1965).

There is sufficient authority to support the Court of Appeals ruling on this issue. However, we believe that the law of this state should require, in the commission by the infant of the intentional act, an intent to make a harmful contact. As already indicated the infant need not intend the consequences which actually follow, but it must appreciate the fact that the contact may be harmful.

LIABILITY OF MRS. REAVES
IV.

The plaintiff argues that the trial court erred in dismissing the claims asserted against Mrs. Reaves. We agree with the trial court and the Court of Appeals' analysis and conclusion that, under the doctrine of parental immunity, liability of a parent can be predicated only upon willful and wanton misconduct. Therefore, the simple negligence claim against Mrs. Reaves was properly dismissed. We also agree with the trial court and the Court of Appeals that there was insufficient evidence of willful and wanton misconduct on the part of Mrs. Reaves to submit the question to the jury.

The ruling of the Court of Appeals is affirmed, except the portion thereof relating to the instructions on the liability of Johnny and Keith Horton, as to which it is reversed, and the cause is returned to the Court of Appeals with directions that it issue an affirming remittitur to the district court.

PRINGLE, Chief Justice (concurring in part and dissenting in part):

I concur in Sections, I, II and III of the majority opinion. I must, however, respectfully dissent to Section IV of the opinion of the Court. In my view when a mother leaves a five-week-old child alone on a bed in an unlocked house for two and one-half hours while she engages in conversation with a neighbor and injury results to her child as a result of her negligence, there is at least a jury question as to whether her conduct was willful and wanton under the circumstances.

KELLEY, Justice (specially concurring):

In reference to the liability of Johnny Horton and Keith Horton for an intentional tort, I would hold that infants below some specific age cannot, as a matter of law, be held liable.

We have held here that in the commission by the infant of an intentional tort the law requires a harmful contact. The infant need not intend the consequences which actually result from the harmful contact, but he must appreciate the fact that the contact may be harmful.

In Benallo v. Bare, 162 Colo. 22, 427 P.2d 323 (1967), we adopted a rule that a child six years of age or younger is incapable of being contributorily negligent as a matter of law. If this is a reasonable presumption, then it seems to me that, at least, in the case of infants three and four years of age, we should hold, as a matter of law, that they are incapable of appreciating that their intentionally tortious contacts may be harmful.

Notes and Questions

1. What are the rules that apply to the issues whether and when children are liable for their intentional torts and for battery in particular? Are they the same as those that govern the liability of adults for these same torts?

2. Justice Kelley writes a short concurring opinion suggesting that children under the age of five ought to be considered incapable of forming tortious intent as a matter of law. If this were the case, what would be the procedural effect on the claim against Johnny and Keith Horton? How might this rule be rationalized?

3. Justice Kelley also notes that the law typically finds that children under the age of seven are incapable of negligence as a matter of law. As we will see in the negligence materials, this rule has since changed so that children are now considered capable of negligence as young as (approximately) five years old. In any event, the minimum age for negligence remains higher than the minimum age for intentional torts. What might be the basis for holding children liable for their intentional torts earlier than for their negligent conduct?

4. What are the rules that apply to resolving the issue whether a parent is responsible for harm caused by (and the torts of) her children? Why was Mrs. Horton not responsible for her sons' actions?

5. What rules apply to resolving the issue whether a parent is responsible for harm suffered by her child? Why was Mrs. Reaves not responsible even in part for the injury to her daughter?

6. The common law in the United States on the issue of parental responsibility for children's torts is unusual comparatively speaking. In most if not all other countries, parents are vicariously liable for damage done by their children. What particular political or policy views might account for the American position? Recall from our discussion of parental immunity in

Chapter One that many states have enacted statutes at least partially abrogating this position. Look carefully at the extent of these abrogations and then characterize the legislatures' commitment to providing plaintiffs with a compensatory remedy when children commit intentional torts.

7. Following the states' development of common law parental immunity rules beginning in the late 1800s, the United States Supreme Court established constitutional doctrine which provides for "family privacy" and "parental autonomy" — in political discussions, the same doctrine is often referred to as "parents' rights." In general terms, this doctrine provides that

> parents are entitled to raise their children as they see fit, including to make most decisions for them until they reach the age of majority. This doctrine of parental autonomy resides principally in the Fourteenth Amendment, and is rationalized on the grounds of the following syllogism: Children lack the "maturity, experience, and capacity for judgment" necessary to make good decisions for themselves. Thus, someone needs to make decisions for them. Parents are best suited for this purpose (as opposed to the state or another third party) because they are most likely to make decisions in their children's best interests. Based on this rights and responsibilities framework—the Supreme Court typically speaks of "the right, coupled with the high duty" — the law formally presumes that whatever the parent's decision, it is the child's best interests. Among the many routine day-to-day decisions parents make, this doctrine protects their right to decide such fundamental questions as where their children go to school, with whom they associate, what treatment they receive in the event they become ill or injured, and in general the values according to which they are raised.
>
> As between parents and third parties, including the state and other individuals, the presumption that parents act in their children's best interests is rebuttable only when there is evidence that a parent is causing or risking harm to a child. State child protection laws traditionally have defined the sorts of harm that will place a parent's decisions or conduct outside the scope of parental authority. Among other things, these laws proscribe abuse . . . and neglect. Federal constitutional law generally embraces these boundaries on the ground that states have a compelling interest in protecting children from harm and risk that is intentionally inflicted by their parents.

Doriane Lambelet Coleman, *The Legal Ethics of Pediatric Research*, 57 Duke L.J. 517, 546-46 (2007).

State courts deciding cases under state law typically abstain from invoking federal law—they want their rule of decision to be their own—and thus this constitutional doctrine is generally not mentioned in opinions in torts cases decided by state court judges. Nevertheless, because the federal Constitution is the supreme law of the land, the doctrine is the proverbial elephant in the room. This excerpt from the New York Court of Appeals in Holodook v. Spencer, 43 A.D.2d 129, 135 (1974), explaining the corresponding tort law doctrine of negligent supervision of a child, is illustrative:

> In most areas of tort law, the reasonable man standard well serves the law's general aim of structuring human activity in accordance with the community's understanding and expectations of proper conduct. In the family relation between parent and child,

however, we do not believe that application of this standardized norm is the wisest course. The result . . . would be to circumscribe the wide range of discretion a parent ought to have in permitting his child to undertake responsibility and gain independence. As Mr. Justice Greenblott [explained below]:

> The duty to supervise a child in his daily activities has as its objective the fostering of physical, emotional and intellectual development, and is one whose enforcement can depend only on love. Each child is different, as is each parent; as to the former, some are to be pampered while some thrive on independence; as to the latter, some trust in their children to use care, others are very cautious. Considering the different economic, educational, cultural, ethnic and religious backgrounds which must prevail, there are so many combinations and permutations of parent-child relationships that may result that the search for a standard would necessarily be in vain — and properly so. Supervision is uniquely a matter for the exercise of judgment. For this reason parents have always had the right to determine how much independence, supervision and control a child should have, and to best judge the character and extent of development of their child.

The mutual obligations of the parent-child relation derive their strength and vitality from such forces as natural instinct, love and morality, and not from the essentially negative compulsions of the law's directives and sanctions. Courts and Legislatures have recognized this, and consequently have intruded only minimally upon the family relation. This is so, and properly, because the law's external coercive incentives are inappropriate to assuring performance of the subtle and shifting obligations of family.

Do these doctrines explain why the majority on the Colorado Supreme Court disagreed with Justice Pringle about Mrs. Reaves's responsibility for the harm caused to her daughter?

POLMATIER v. RUSS
537 A.2d 468 (Conn. 1988)

GLASS, Associate Justice.

The principal issue on this appeal is whether an insane person is liable for an intentional tort. The plaintiff, Dorothy Polmatier, executrix of the estate of her deceased husband, Arthur R. Polmatier, brought this action against the defendant, Norman Russ, seeking to recover damages for wrongful death. The state trial referee, exercising the power of the Superior Court, rendered judgment for the plaintiff. The defendant has appealed from that judgment. We find no error.

The trial court's memorandum of decision and the record reveal the following undisputed facts. On the afternoon of November 20, 1976, the defendant and his two month old daughter visited the home of Arthur Polmatier, his father-in-law. Polmatier lived in East Windsor with his wife, Dorothy, the plaintiff, and their eleven year old son, Robert. During the early evening Robert noticed a disturbance in the living room where he saw the defendant astride Polmatier on a couch beating him on the head with a beer bottle. Robert heard Polmatier exclaim, "Norm, you're killing me!" and ran to get help. Thereafter, the defendant went into Polmatier's bedroom where he took a box of 30-30 caliber ammunition from the bottom drawer of a dresser and went to his brother-in-law's bedroom where he took a 30-30 caliber Winchester rifle from the closet. He then returned to the living room and shot Polmatier twice, causing his death.

About five hours later, the defendant was found sitting on a stump in a wooded area approximately one half mile from the Polmatier home. The defendant was naked and his daughter was in his arms wrapped in his clothes, and was crying. Blood was found on his clothes, and he had with him the Winchester rifle, later determined to be the murder weapon.

The defendant was taken to a local hospital and was later transferred to Norwich Hospital. While in custody he was confined in Norwich Hospital or the Whiting Forensic Institute. The defendant was charged with the crime of murder pursuant to General Statutes § 53a–54a(a), but was found not guilty by reason of insanity pursuant to General Statutes § 53a-13. Dr. Walter Borden, a psychiatrist, testified at both the criminal and this civil proceeding regarding the defendant's sanity. In the present civil case Borden testified that, at the time of the homicide, the defendant was suffering from a severe case of paranoid schizophrenia that involved delusions of persecution, grandeur, influence and reference, and also involved auditory hallucinations. He concluded that the defendant was legally insane and could not form a rational choice but that he could make a schizophrenic or crazy choice. He was not in a fugue state. The trial court found that at the time of the homicide the defendant was insane.

The substitute complaint for the wrongful death of Polmatier alleged in the first count that the death resulted from an assault, beating and shooting by the defendant, and included a second count for exemplary damages and a third count based on negligence. The defendant filed a substitute answer denying all material allegations of the plaintiff's substitute complaint and asserted three special defenses: (1) as to all counts, the defendant was non compos mentis at the time of the alleged assault and, therefore, not capable of forming the intent necessary for tort liability; (2) the third count was barred by General Statutes § 52-584, the statute of limitations; and (3) as to all counts, the plaintiff or the plaintiff's decedent was comparatively or contributorily negligent. . . .

After a trial to the court, the court found for the plaintiff on the first count and awarded compensatory damages. On appeal the defendant claims that the trial court erred in failing to apply the following two-pronged analysis to his claim: first, whether the defendant intended the act which produced the injury; and second, whether he intended the resulting injury. We find no error.

I.

Connecticut has never directly addressed the issue of whether an insane person is civilly liable for an intentional tort. The majority of jurisdictions that have considered this issue have held insane persons liable for their intentional torts. See 4 Restatement (Second), Torts § 895J. This rule is reflected in the Restatement (Second) of Torts § 283B, which provides: "Unless the actor is a child, his insanity or other mental deficiency does not relieve the actor from liability for conduct which does not conform to the standard of a reasonable man under like circumstances." The majority rule has been applied to cases involving intentional homicide. Commentators trace the majority rule back to the dictum of a seventeenth century English case. The majority rule is not, however, without criticism. For example, Professor Bohlen has stated:

> [W]here a liability, like that for the impairment of the physical condition of another's body or property, is imposed upon persons capable of fault only if they have been guilty of fault, immaturity of age or mental deficiency, which destroys the capacity for fault, should preclude the possibility of liability. . . . But so long as it is accepted as a general principle that liability for injuries to certain interests are to be imposed only upon those guilty of fault in causing them, it should be applied consistently and no liability should be imposed upon those for any reason incapable of fault.

F. Bohlen, "Liability in Tort of Infants and Insane Persons," 23 Mich.L.Rev. 9, 31–32 (1924–25). For a similar view, see R. Ague, "The Liability of Insane Persons in Tort Actions," 60 Dick.L.Rev. 211(1956). Nonetheless, we are persuaded by the proponents of the majority rule, especially when the cases in which it has been applied are examined.

A leading case is *Seals v. Snow,* 123 Kan. 88, 254 P. 348 (1927). In *Seals,* the widow of Arthur Seals brought a civil action against Martin Snow to recover damages for the death of her husband. Several interrogatories were submitted to the jury, including: "Was Martin Snow insane when he shot Arthur Seals? A. Yes. If you answer the last question in the affirmative, was Martin Snow at the time he shot Arthur Seals able to distinguish right from wrong? A. No." *Id.,* at 89, 254 P. 348. The jury returned a verdict for the plaintiff. In upholding the ensuing judgment, the Kansas Supreme Court stated: "The defendant challenges the doctrine generally sustained by the courts that an insane person is liable to make compensation for his torts. It is conceded that the great weight of authority is that an insane person is civilly liable for his torts. This liability has been based on a number of grounds, one that where one of two innocent persons must suffer a loss, it should be borne by the one who occasioned it. Another, that public policy requires the enforcement of such liability in order that relatives of the insane person shall be led to restrain him and that tort-feasors shall not simulate or pretend insanity to defend their wrongful acts causing damage to others, and that if he was not liable there would be no redress for injuries, and we might have the anomaly of an insane person having abundant wealth depriving another of his rights without compensation." *Id.,* 90, 254 P. 348.

Like *Seals,* another homicide case applying the majority rule is *McIntyre v. Sholty,* 121 Ill. 660, 13 N.E. 239 (1887), where recovery was allowed against an insane person's estate for the wrongful killing of the plaintiff's wife. The court reasoned: "There is, to be sure, an appearance of hardship in compelling one to respond for that which he is unable to avoid for want of the control of reason. But the question of liability in these cases is one of public policy. If an insane person is not held liable for his torts, those interested in his estate, as relatives or otherwise, might not have a sufficient motive to so take care of him as to deprive him of opportunities for inflicting injuries upon others. There is more injustice in denying to the injured party the recovery of damages for the wrong suffered by him, than there is in calling upon the relatives or friends of the lunatic to pay the expense of his confinement, if he has an estate ample enough for that purpose. The liability of lunatics for their torts tends to secure a more efficient custody and guardianship of their persons. Again, if parties can escape the consequences of their injurious acts upon the plea of lunacy, there will be a strong temptation to simulate insanity with a view of masking the malice and revenge of an evil heart." *Id.,* at 664–65, 13 N.E. 239.

Our adoption of the majority rule holding insane persons civilly liable, in appropriate circumstances, for their intentional torts finds support in other Connecticut case law. We have elsewhere recognized the vitality of the common law principle that "'where one of two innocent persons must suffer loss from an act done, it is just that it should fall on the one who caused the loss rather than upon the other who had no agency in producing it and could not by any means have avoided it.'" *Verrilli v. Damilowski,* 140 Conn. 358, 360, 100 A.2d 462 (1953), citing *Granniss v. Weber,* 107 Conn. 622, 625, 141 A. 877 (1928); *Grissell v. Housatonic R. Co.,* 54 Conn. 447, 461, 9 A. 137 (1887).

II.

We now turn to the defendant's claim that the trial court should have applied a two-pronged analysis to his claim. The first prong is whether the defendant intended the act that produced the injury. The defendant argues that for an act to be done with the requisite intent, the act must be an external manifestation of the actor's will. The defendant specifically relies on the Restatement (Second) of Torts § 14, comment b, for the definition of what constitutes an "act," where it is stated that "a muscular movement which is purely reflexive or the convulsive movements of an epileptic are not acts in the sense in which that word is used in the Restatement. So too, movements of the body during sleep or while the will is otherwise in abeyance are not acts. An external manifestation of the will is necessary to constitute an act, and an act is necessary to make one liable [for a battery]. . . ." The defendant argues that if his "activities were the external manifestations of irrational and uncontrollable thought disorders these activities cannot be acts for purposes of establishing liability for assault and battery." We disagree.

We note that we have not been referred to any evidence indicating that the defendant's acts were reflexive, convulsive or epileptic. Furthermore, under the Restatement (Second) of Torts § 2, "act" is used "to denote an external manifestation of the actor's will and does not include any of its results, even the most direct, immediate, and intended." Comment b to this section provides in pertinent part: "A muscular reaction is always an act unless it is a purely reflexive reaction in which the mind and will have no share." Although the trial court found that the defendant could not form a rational choice, it did find that he could make a schizophrenic or crazy choice. Moreover, a rational choice is not required since "[a]n insane person may have an intent to invade the interests of another, even though his reasons and motives for forming that intention may be entirely irrational." 4 Restatement (Second), Torts § 895J, comment c. The following example is given in the Restatement to illustrate the application of comment c: "A, who is insane believes that he is Napoleon Bonaparte, and that B, his nurse, who confines him in his room, is an agent of the Duke of Wellington, who is endeavoring to prevent his arrival on the field of Waterloo in time to win the battle. Seeking to escape, he breaks off the leg of a chair, attacks B with it and fractures her skull. A is subject to liability to B for battery."

We recognize that the defendant made conflicting statements about the incident when discussing the homicide. At the hospital on the evening of the homicide the defendant told a police officer that his father-in-law was a heavy drinker and that he used the beer bottle for that reason. He stated he wanted to make his father-in-law suffer for his bad habits and so that he would realize the wrong that he had done. He also told the police officer that he was a supreme being and had the power to rule the destiny of the world and could make his bed fly out of the window. When interviewed by Dr. Borden, the defendant stated that he believed that his father-in-law was a spy for the red Chinese and that he believed his father-in-law was not only going to kill him, but going to harm his infant child so that he killed his father-in-law in self-defense. The explanations given by the defendant for committing the homicide are similar to the illustration of irrational reasons and motives given in comment c to § 895J of the Restatement, set out above.

Under these circumstances we are persuaded that the defendant's behavior at the time of the beating and shooting of Polmatier constituted an "act" within the meaning of comment b, § 2, of the Restatement. Following the majority rule in this case, we conclude that the trial court implicitly determined that the defendant committed an "act" in beating and shooting Polmatier. Accordingly, the trial court did not err as to the first prong of the defendant's claim.

III.

The second prong of the defendant's claim is that the trial court erred in failing to determine whether the defendant intended the resulting injury to the decedent. The defendant argues in his brief that "[t]he trial court must satisfy the second prong of its intentional tort analysis with a finding that the defendant acted 'for the *purpose* of causing' [1 Restatement, Torts § 13, comment d] or with a '*desire* to cause' [1 Restatement (Second), Torts § 8A] the resulting injury." (Emphasis added.) This argument is more persuasive in its application to proof of the elements of crimes than in its relation to civil liability.

In the criminal law the "act" and the "intent" of the actor are joined to determine the culpability of the offender. For example, the allegations of the essential elements of murder are as follows: "A person is guilty of murder when, with intent to cause the death of another person, he causes the death of such person." General Statutes § 53a–54a (a). The defendant claims that "[i]ntent need not involve ill will or malice, but must include a design, purpose and intent to do wrong and inflict the injury." Under the Restatement, "intent" is used "to denote that the actor desires to cause consequences of his act, or that he believes that the consequences are substantially certain to result from it." 1 Restatement (Second), Torts § 8A. Comment b to § 8A of the Restatement provides in pertinent part: "All consequences which the actor desires to bring about are intended, as the word is used in this Restatement. Intent is not, however, limited to consequences which are desired. If the actor knows that the consequences are certain, or substantially certain, to result from his act, and still goes ahead, he is treated by the law as if he had in fact desired to produce the result." We have stated that "[i]t is not essential that the precise injury which was done be the one intended." *Alteiri v. Colasso,* 168 Conn. 329, 334, 362 A.2d 798 (1975).

As discussed above, the defendant gave the police and Borden several reasons why he killed Polmatier. Under Comment c to § 895J of the Restatement, it is not necessary for a defendant's reasons and motives for forming his intention to be rational in order for him to have the intent to invade the interests of another. Considering his statements to the police and to Borden that he intended to punish Polmatier and to kill him, we are persuaded that the defendant intended to beat and shoot him. . . . There is no error.

WHITE v. MUNIZ
999 P.2d 814 (Colo. 2000)

Justice Kourlis delivered the Opinion of the Court.

Petitioner, Barbara White, as personal representative of the estate of Helen Everly, appeals the decision of the court of appeals in *Muniz v. White,* 979 P.2d 23, 25 (Colo.App.1998), which determined that a mentally incapacitated adult should be held liable for her intentional tort even if she was unable to appreciate the wrongfulness of her actions.[1] We disagree with the court of appeals. Rather, we conclude that under the facts present in this case, in order to recover on a theory of intentional tort, the plaintiff, Sherry Lynn Muniz, was required to prove that Everly intended to commit an act and that Everly intended the act to result in a harmful or offensive contact. Accordingly, we reverse the court of appeals, and remand for reinstatement of the jury verdict in favor of the defendant.

I.

In October of 1993, Barbara White placed her eighty-three year-old grandmother, Helen Everly, in an assisted living facility, the Beatrice Hover Personal Care Center.[2] Within a few days of admission, Everly started exhibiting erratic behavior. She became agitated easily, and occasionally acted aggressively toward others.

On November 21, 1993, the caregiver in charge of Everly's wing asked Sherry Lynn Muniz, a shift supervisor at Hover, to change Everly's adult diaper. The caregiver informed Muniz that Everly was not cooperating in that effort. This did not surprise Muniz because she knew that Everly sometimes acted obstinately. Indeed, initially Everly refused to allow Muniz to change her diaper, but eventually Muniz thought that Everly relented. However, as Muniz reached toward the diaper, Everly struck Muniz on the jaw and ordered her out of the room.

The next day, Dr. Haven Howell, M.D. examined Everly at Longmont United Hospital. Dr. Howell deduced that "she [had] a progressive dementia with characteristic gradual loss of function, loss of higher cortical function including immediate and short term memory, impulse control and judgement." She diagnosed Everly with "[p]rimary degenerative dementia of the Alzheimer type, senile onset, with depression."

In November of 1994, Muniz filed suit alleging assault and battery[3] against Everly, and negligence against Barbara and Timothy White. The case proceeded to a jury trial on March 17, 1997.[5] While arguing outside the presence of the jury for specific jury instructions, the

---

[1] We granted certiorari to determine: "Whether the element of 'intent' in an intentional tort requires that the defendant appreciate the offensiveness of her conduct, and whether the court of appeals erred by refusing to apply this court's rule in *Horton v. Reaves,* 186 Colo. 149, 526 P.2d 304 (1974), to a mentally incapacitated adult." Because we received this issue in the context of an assault and battery, we answer this question in regard to those intentional torts only.

[2] Everly died on March 18, 1996.

[3] For simplicity, we address the issues in this case in terms of the battery claim only. The same principles would apply in the assault context.

[5] Prior to trial, the trial court dismissed the negligence claim brought by Muniz against the Whites.

parties took differing positions on the mental state required to commit the alleged intentional torts. Muniz requested the following instruction: "A person who has been found incompetent may intend to do an act even if he or she lacked control of reason and acted unreasonably." White tendered a different instruction:

> A person intends to make a contact with another person if he or she does an act for the purpose of bringing about such a contact, whether or not he or she also intends that the contact be harmful or offensive. The intent must include some awareness of the natural consequences of intentional acts, and the person must appreciate the consequences of intentional acts, and the person must appreciate the offensiveness or wrongfulness of her acts.

The trial court settled on a slightly modified version of White's instruction. It read:

> A person intends to make a contact with another person if she does an act for the purpose of bringing about such a contact, whether or not she also intends that the contact be harmful or offensive.

The fact that a person may suffer from Dementia, Alzheimer type, does not prevent a finding that she acted intentionally. You may find that she acted intentionally if she intended to do what she did, even though her reasons and motives were entirely irrational. *However, she must have appreciated the offensiveness of her conduct.*

(Emphasis added.) In selecting the instruction on intent, the trial court determined that Everly's state was comparable to that of a child.

Muniz's counsel objected to the last sentence of the instruction, claiming that it misstated the law. He argued that the instruction improperly broadened the holding in *Horton v. Reaves,* 186 Colo. 149, 526 P.2d 304 (1974), where the supreme court held that an infant must appreciate the offensiveness or wrongfulness of her conduct to be liable for an intentional tort. The jury rendered verdicts in favor of Everly and White.

The court of appeals reversed the decision of the trial court and remanded the case for a new trial. The court of appeals reasoned that most states continue to hold mentally deficient plaintiffs liable for their intentional acts regardless of their ability to understand the offensiveness of their actions. "[W]here one of two innocent persons must suffer a loss, it should be borne by the one who occasioned it." *Muniz v. White,* 979 P.2d 23, 25 (Colo.App.1998). The court of appeals reasoned that insanity may not be asserted as a defense to an intentional tort, and thus, concluded that the trial court erred in "instructing the jury that Everly must have appreciated the offensiveness of her conduct." *Id.* at 26.

II.

The question we here address is whether an intentional tort requires some proof that the tortfeasor not only intended to contact another person, but also intended that the contact be harmful or offensive to the other person.

A.

State courts and legal commentators generally agree that an intentional tort requires some proof that the tortfeasor intended harm or offense. *See* W. Page Keeton et al., *Prosser and Keeton on the Law of Torts* § 8 (5th ed.1984); Dan B. Dobbs, *The Law of Torts* § 30 (2000). According to the Restatement (Second) of Torts,

> (1) An actor is subject to liability to another for battery if
>
> > (a) he acts *intending to cause a harmful or offensive contact* with the person of the other or a third person, or an imminent apprehension of such a contact, and
> >
> > (b) an offensive [or harmful] contact with the person of the other directly or indirectly results.
>
> (2) An act which is not done with the intention stated in Subsection (1, a) does not make the actor liable to the other for a mere offensive contact with the other's person although the act involves an unreasonable risk of inflicting it and, therefore, would be negligent or reckless if the risk threatened bodily harm.

Restatement (Second) of Torts § 18 (1965)(emphasis added); *see also Hall v. McBryde,* 919 P.2d 910, 913–14 (Colo.App.1996); Restatement, *supra,* § 13.

Historically, the intentional tort of battery required a subjective desire on the part of the tortfeasor to inflict a harmful or offensive contact on another. *See* Restatement, *supra,* § 8A; Keeton, *supra,* § 8; 6 Am.Jur.2d *Assault and Battery* § 8 (1999). Thus, it was not enough that a person intentionally contacted another *resulting* in a harmful or offensive contact. *See* Restatement, *supra,* § 18 cmt. e;[6] Keeton § 8. Instead, the actor had to understand that his contact would be harmful or offensive. *See* Keeton, *supra,* § 8; Dobbs, *supra,* § 29. The actor need not have intended, however, the harm that actually resulted from his action. *See* Restatement, *supra,* § 16(1). Thus, if a slight punch to the victim resulted in traumatic injuries, the actor would be liable for all the damages resulting from the battery even if he only intended to knock the wind out of the victim. *See id.*

Juries may find it difficult to determine the mental state of an actor, but they may rely on circumstantial evidence in reaching their conclusion. No person can pinpoint the thoughts in the mind of another, but a jury can examine the facts to conclude what another must have been thinking. *See* Keeton, *supra,* § 8. For example, a person of reasonable intelligence knows with substantial certainty that a stone thrown into a crowd will strike someone and result in an offensive or harmful contact to that person. *See id.* Hence, if an actor of average intelligence

---

[6] According to the Restatement:

> [I]t is necessary that an act be done for the purpose of bringing about a harmful or offensive contact . . . to another or to a third person or with knowledge that such a result will, to a substantial certainty, be produced by his act. . . .

Restatement, *supra,* § 18 cmt. e.

performs such an act, the jury can determine that the actor had the requisite intent to cause a harmful or offensive contact, even though the actor denies having such thoughts. *See id.*

B.

More recently, some courts around the nation have abandoned this dual intent requirement in an intentional tort setting, that being an intent to contact and an intent that the contact be harmful or offensive, and have required only that the tortfeasor intend a contact with another that *results* in a harmful or offensive touching. *See Brzoska v. Olson,* 668 A.2d 1355, 1360 (Del.1995) (stating that battery is an intentional, unpermitted contact on another which is harmful or offensive; and that the intent necessary for battery is the intent to contact the person); *White v. University of Idaho,* 118 Idaho 400, 797 P.2d 108, 111 (1990) (determining that battery requires an intent to cause an unpermitted contact, not an intent to make a harmful or offensive contact). Under this view, a victim need only prove that a voluntary movement by the tortfeasor resulted in a contact which a reasonable person would find offensive or to which the victim did not consent. *See University of Idaho,* 118 Idaho 400, 797 P.2d at 111. These courts would find intent in contact to the back of a friend that results in a severe, unexpected injury even though the actor did not intend the contact to be harmful or offensive. *See id.* 118 Idaho 400, 797 P.2d at 109. The actor thus could be held liable for battery because a reasonable person would find an injury offensive or harmful, irrespective of the intent of the actor to harm or offend.

Courts occasionally have intertwined these two distinct understandings of the requisite intent. *See Brzoska,* 668 A.2d at 1360 (approving the Restatement view of the intent element of a battery, but summarizing the rule as "the intentional, unpermitted contact upon the person of another which *is* harmful or offensive") (emphasis added); Keeton, *supra,* § 8 (noting that applying the element of intent frequently confuses authorities). In most instances when the defendant is a mentally alert adult, this commingling of definitions prejudices neither the plaintiff nor the defendant. However, when evaluating the culpability of particular classes of defendants, such as the very young and the mentally disabled, the intent required by a jurisdiction becomes critical.

In *Horton v. Reaves,* 186 Colo. 149, 526 P.2d 304 (1974), we examined the jury instructions used to determine if a four-year-old boy and a three-year-old boy intentionally battered an infant when they dropped a baby who suffered skull injuries as a result. We held that although a child need not intend the resulting harm, the child must understand that the contact may be harmful in order to be held liable. *See Horton,* 186 Colo. at 155–56, 526 P.2d at 307–08. Our conclusion comported with the Restatement's definition of intent; it did not state a new special rule for children, but applied the general rule to the context of an intentional tort of battery committed by a child. Because a child made the contact, the jury had to examine the objective evidence to determine if the child actors intended their actions to be offensive or harmful. This result complied with both the Colorado jury instruction at the time, and the definition of battery in the Restatement. *See id.*

C.

In this case, we have the opportunity to examine intent in the context of an injury inflicted by a mentally deficient, Alzheimer's patient. White seeks an extension of *Horton* to the mentally ill,[7] and Muniz argues that a mere voluntary movement by Everly can constitute the requisite intent. We find that the law of Colorado requires the jury to conclude that the defendant both intended the contact and intended it to be harmful or offensive.

III.

Because Colorado law requires a dual intent, we apply here the Restatement's definition of the term. As a result, we reject the arguments of Muniz and find that the trial court delivered an adequate instruction to the jury.[8]

Operating in accordance with this instruction, the jury had to find that Everly appreciated the offensiveness of her conduct in order to be liable for the intentional tort of battery. It necessarily had to consider her mental capabilities in making such a finding, including her age, infirmity, education, skill, or any other characteristic as to which the jury had evidence. We presume that the jury "looked into the mind of Everly," and reasoned that Everly did not possess the necessary intent to commit an assault or a battery. *See Hall v. Walter,* 969 P.2d 224, 238 (Colo.1998) (stating that the court presumes the jury followed instructions in reaching its verdict).

A jury can, of course, find a mentally deficient person liable for an intentional tort, but in order to do so, the jury must find that the actor intended offensive or harmful consequences. As a result, insanity is not a defense to an intentional tort according to the ordinary use of that term, but is a characteristic, like infancy, that may make it more difficult to prove the intent element of battery. Our decision today does not create a special rule for the elderly, but applies Colorado's intent requirement in the context of a woman suffering the effects of Alzheimer's.

Contrary to Muniz's arguments, policy reasons do not compel a different result. Injured parties consistently have argued that even if the tortfeasor intended no harm or offense, "where one of two innocent persons must suffer a loss, it should be borne by the one who occasioned it." Keeton, *supra,* § 135. Our decision may appear to erode that principle. Yet, our decision does not bar future injured persons from seeking compensation. Victims may still bring intentional

---

[7] Authorities often classify the insane with infants in analyzing tort liability. *See* Keeton, *supra,* § 135. White argues that Alzheimer's patients residing in elder care facilities owe no duty of care to their caretakers because the patients reside there due to their infirmities. She contends that the caregiver assumes some risk of injury when he accepts employment serving such patients who have no capacity to control their conduct. Several jurisdictions have approved of this so-called "fireman's rule" approach. *See Mujica v. Turner,* 582 So.2d 24 (Fla. Dist. Ct. App. 1991); *Anicet v. Gant,* 580 So.2d 273, (Fla.Dist.Ct.App.1991); *Gould v. American Family Mut. Ins. Co.,* 198 Wis.2d 450, 543 N.W.2d 282 (1996). We conclude that an examination of this approach falls beyond the scope of the issue on certiorari. Further, since this case was not tried to the jury on a negligence claim, the duty of care owed by the patient to the caregiver for negligence purposes was not an issue.

[8] The actual instruction used by the court in this case is not consistent with our holding today; however, the error worked in favor of the plaintiff. Since the jury found for the defendant even in the face of the error, the error has no bearing on our decision. The error relates to Instruction 11 and to the first paragraph of Instruction 13, in which there is a suggestion that the conduct need only result in harmful or offensive contact, even without the actor's intent to harm or offend. As we hold today, the actor's intent to harm or offend is an element of the claim. The last paragraph of Instruction 13 cures the error to some extent because the court instructed the jury that the defendant "must have appreciated the offensiveness of her conduct."

tort actions against mentally disabled adults, but to prevail, they must prove all the elements of the alleged tort. Furthermore, because the mentally disabled are held to the reasonable person standard in negligence actions, victims may find relief more easily under a negligence cause of action. *See Johnson v. Lambotte,* 147 Colo. 203, 206, 363 P.2d 165, 166 (1961).

IV.

With regard to the intent element of the intentional torts of assault and battery, we hold that regardless of the characteristics of the alleged tortfeasor, a plaintiff must prove that the actor desired to cause offensive or harmful consequences by his act. The plaintiff need not prove, however, that the actor intended the harm that actually results. Accordingly, we reverse the decision of the court of appeals, and remand the case to that court for reinstatement of the jury verdict in favor of White and consideration of any remaining issues.

Notes and Questions

1. What is the "single intent" rule as described in *White*? What is the "dual intent" rule?

2. Assume that *Polmatier* states the majority rule. Was the Colorado appellate court in *White* correct in finding that, as characterized by the State's Supreme Court, "most states continue to hold mentally deficient defendants liable for their intentional acts regardless of their ability to understand the offensiveness of their actions"?

3. Was the jury instruction given by the trial judge in *White* consistent with the rule in *Polmatier*? If so, what are the facts that distinguish the two cases that explain the different results?

4. Notice that *White* signals an important development in this area of the law; that is, as neuroscientists grow our understanding of how the brain functions, litigants and courts will have to work harder to fit their facts within the traditional mind-body or will-reflex dichotomy described in *Polmatier*. For commentary on this issue, see, e.g., Dov Fox and Alex Stein, Dualism and Doctrine, 90 Ind. L. J. 975 (2015).

5. *White* suggests that a few jurisdictions require only "single intent." In fact, there is an important debate among torts scholars about how many jurisdictions follow the "single intent" rule and separately about whether "single intent" or "dual intent" is the best policy in any event. It is unlikely that the accounting debate will be settled anytime soon, simply because the relevant case law is often ambiguous on the point. The policy debate is thriving in the meantime. It centers on which approach (single or dual intent) is truer to the historical rationales for battery law — the protection of bodily integrity and decisional autonomy. It has also re-focused attention on the question whether, consistent with the fault continuum set out in Chapter 1, intentional torts in the modern era require a degree of mental fault higher than recklessness. As of this writing, the authors of the Tentative Draft No. 1 of the Restatement of the Law Third, Torts: Intentional Torts to Persons (April 8, 2015), have indicated that they are likely to adopt the "single intent" rule in the final version, and more generally to revise (or clarify, depending on how one reads the cases) the prima facie case for battery as follows:

§ 101. Battery by Harmful Contact

An actor is subject to liability to another for battery if:

(a) the actor intends to cause a contact with the person of the other . . . ;

(b) the actor's affirmative conduct causes such a contact;

(c) the contact (i) causes bodily harm to the other or (ii) is offensive . . . ; and

(d) the other does not effectively consent to the otherwise tortious conduct ....

Note that in addition to its preference for single intent, this formulation makes consent—which is usually an affirmative defense—part of the plaintiff's prima facie case and burden. We will discuss this last move further as we proceed through the consent materials below.

Problem Two: Single v. Dual Intent

Consider the different implications of the "single intent" and "dual intent" rules in the context of the following fact pattern. If you were the plaintiff's lawyer in a dual-intent jurisdiction, what would your options be?

Defendant is raised from birth until the age of twenty-two in an isolated, patriarchal cult community. He has had no exposure of any kind to the outside world, or to any of its behavioral norms. A central tenet of the cult is that women exist to serve men in all respects, including sexually. The women in the cult are, as far as Defendant can tell, happy to fulfill this role; there is no evidence suggesting that he is wrong in this assumption. If a man wants a woman to feed him or to have sex with him, whoever she is, cult etiquette requires simply that he order her to comply. She does not resist in any objectively ascertainable way. Boys in the cult are entitled to exercise their privileges in these respects beginning at the age of thirteen. Girls in the cult are expected to comply also beginning at the age of thirteen. Defendant has been exercising his rights for nine years.

One day the authorities raid the cult's compound in search of a man wanted for tax evasion. The leader of the cult orders the members to disperse temporarily. Defendant thus leaves the compound for the first time in his life. He ends up in an ordinary American town approximately thirty miles away, hungry and emotionally disoriented. He grabs the Plaintiff, a junior at the local college and the first woman he encounters, and orders her to feed and bed him. Having no idea who he is she resists. He (in his view) asserts his rights. She (in her view) is raped. Throughout, his disorientation blinds him to her unusual reaction. Previously known among her friends as "Happy-Go-Lucky," she suffers long-term, debilitating physical and emotional injuries as a result.

WISHNATSKY v. HUEY
584 N.W.2d 859 (N.D. App. 1998)

Martin Wishnatsky appealed a summary judgment dismissing his battery action against David W. Huey, and an order denying his motion for an altered judgment. We conclude, as a matter of law, that no battery occurred, and we affirm the judgment and the order.

On January 10, 1996, Huey, an assistant attorney general, was engaged in a conversation with attorney Peter B. Crary in Crary's office. Without knocking or announcing his entry, Wishnatsky, who performs paralegal work for Crary, attempted to enter the office. Huey pushed the door closed, thereby pushing Wishnatsky back into the hall. Wishnatsky reentered the office and Huey left.

Wishnatsky brought an action against Huey, seeking damages for battery. Huey moved for summary judgment of dismissal. The trial court granted Huey's motion and a judgment of dismissal was entered. Wishnatsky moved to alter the judgment. The trial court denied Wishnatsky's motion.

Wishnatsky also sought a disorderly conduct restraining order under N.D.C.C. Ch. 12.1-31.2 against Huey, based on the January 10, 1996, incident, and another on January 25, 1996. In affirming a judgment dismissing Wishnatsky's petition, our Supreme Court concluded "Huey's conduct did not rise to the level of intrusive behavior which would warrant a reasonable person to conclude Huey committed the offense of disorderly conduct."

Wishnatsky appealed, contending the evidence he submitted in response to Huey's motion for summary judgment satisfies the elements of a battery claim and the trial court erred in granting Huey's motion. Wishnatsky also contends Huey is not entitled to prosecutorial or statutory immunity.

Summary judgment is a procedural device for the prompt and expeditious disposition of a controversy without trial if either party is entitled to judgment as a matter of law, if no dispute exists as to either the material facts or the inferences to be drawn from undisputed facts, or if resolving factual disputes would not alter the result. "In considering a motion for summary judgment, a court must view the evidence in the light most favorable to the party opposing the motion, who must be given the benefit of all favorable inferences which reasonably can be drawn from the evidence." *Mougey Farms v. Kaspari,* 1998 ND 118, ¶ 12, 579 N.W.2d 583. "Disputes of fact become questions of law if reasonable persons can draw only one conclusion from the evidence." *Id.* In reviewing a summary judgment, an appellate court views the evidence in the light most favorable to the non-moving party to determine if the trial court properly granted summary judgment as a matter of law. On a defendant's motion for summary judgment, the question for the court is "whether a fair-minded jury could return a verdict for the plaintiff on the evidence presented. The mere existence of a scintilla of evidence in support of the plaintiff's position will be insufficient; there must be evidence on which the jury could reasonably find for the plaintiff." *Anderson v. Liberty Lobby, Inc.,* 477 U.S. 242, 252, 106 S.Ct. 2505, 91 L.Ed.2d 202 (1986).

"In its original conception [battery] meant the infliction of physical injury." VIII Sir William Holdsworth, *A History of English Law* 422 (2d Impression 1973). By the Eigteenth Century, the requirement of an actual physical injury had been eliminated:

> At Nisi Prius, upon evidence in trespass for assault and battery, Holt, C.J. declared,
>
> 1. That the least touching of another in anger is a battery.
>
> 2. If two or more meet in a narrow passage, and without any violence or design of harm, the one touches the other gently, it is no battery. 3. If any of them use violence against the other, to force his way in a rude inordinate manner, it is a battery; or any struggle about the passage, to that degree as may do hurt, is a battery.

Blackstone explained:

> The least touching of another's person willfully, or in anger, is a battery; for the law cannot draw the line between different degrees of violence, and therefore totally prohibits the first and lowest stage of it: every man's person being sacred, and no other having a right to meddle with it, in any the slightest manner.

3 William Blackstone, *Commentaries* *120. On the other hand, "in a crowded world, a certain amount of personal contact is inevitable, and must be accepted." W. Page Keeton et al., *Prosser and Keeton on the Law of Torts* § 9, at 42 (5th ed.1984).

The American Law Institute has balanced the interest in unwanted contacts and the inevitable contacts in a crowded world in *Restatement (Second) of Torts* §§ 18, 19 (1965):

> 18. Battery: Offensive Contact
>
> (1) An actor is subject to liability to another for battery if
>
>> (a) he acts intending to cause a harmful or offensive contact with the person of the other or a third person, or an imminent apprehension of such a contact, and
>>
>> (b) an offensive contact with the person of the other directly or indirectly results.
>>
>> . . .
>
> 19. What Constitutes Offensive Contact
>
> A bodily contact is offensive if it offends a reasonable sense of personal dignity.

Comment *c* to § 18 notes that the contact need not be "directly caused by some act of the actor" and also notes that "the essence of the plaintiff's grievance consists in the offense to the dignity involved in the unpermitted and intentional invasion of the inviolability of his person and not in any physical harm done to his body." Comment *a* to § 19 explains what kind of conduct offends a reasonable sense of personal dignity:

> In order that a contact be offensive to a reasonable sense of personal dignity, it must be one which would offend the ordinary person and as such one not unduly sensitive as to his personal dignity. It must, therefore, be a contact which is unwarranted by the social usages prevalent at the time and place at which it is inflicted.

Huey moved for summary judgment of dismissal, because, among other things, "as a matter of law, a battery did not occur on January 10, 1996." Huey supported the motion with his affidavit stating in part:

> 8. That Attorney Crary and I had settled into a serious discussion about the case and had established a good rapport when the door to his office suddenly swung open without a knock. An unidentified individual carrying some papers then strode in unannounced. I had not been told that anyone would be entering Attorney Crary's office during the private meeting. . . . I subsequently learned that the individual's name is Martin Wishnatsky.

Wishnatsky responded to Huey's motion for summary judgment with an affidavit of Crary and with his own affidavit stating in part:

> 1. I am a born-again Christian and cultivate holiness in my life. [A]s a result I am very sensitive to evil spirits and am greatly disturbed by the demonic. However, in Christ there is victory.
>
> 2. On January 9, 1996, Mr. David Huey of the North Dakota Attorney General's office, visited the ministry where I was working at 16 Broadway in Fargo, North Dakota with an ex parte court order.
>
> 3. The following morning I entered the office of Peter Crary, an attorney for whom I do paralegal work, to give him certain papers that had been requested. Mr. Crary was speaking with Mr. David Huey at the time. As I began to enter the office Mr Huey threw his body weight against the door and forced me out into the hall. I had not said a word to him. At the same time, he snarled: "You get out of here." This was very shocking and frightening to me. In all the time I have been working as an aide to Mr. Crary, I have never been physically assaulted or spoken to in a harsh and brutal manner. My blood pressure began to rise, my heart beat accelerated and I felt waves of fear in the pit of my stomach. My hands began to shake and my body to tremble. Composing myself, I reentered the office, whereupon Mr. Huey began a half-demented tirade against me and stormed out into the hall. I looked at Mr. Crary in wonder.

We certainly agree with the Supreme Court's determination that when Wishnatsky attempted to enter the room in which Huey was conversing with Crary, "Huey apparently reacted in a rude and abrupt manner in attempting to exclude Wishnatsky from that conversation." *Wishnatsky v. Huey,* 1997 ND 35, ¶ 15, 560 N.W.2d 878. As a matter of law, however, Huey's "rude and abrupt" conduct did not rise to the level of battery.

The evidence presented to the trial court demonstrates Wishnatsky is "unduly sensitive as to his personal dignity." *Restatement (Second) of Torts* § 19 cmt. a (1965). Without knocking or otherwise announcing his intentions, Wishnatsky opened the door to the office in which Huey and Crary were having a private conversation and attempted to enter. Huey closed the door opened by Wishnatsky, thereby stopping Wishnatsky's forward progress and pushing him back into the hall. The bodily contact was momentary, indirect, and incidental. Viewing the evidence in the light most favorable to Wishnatsky, and giving him the benefit of all favorable inferences which can reasonably be drawn from the evidence, we conclude Huey's conduct in response to Wishnatsky's intrusion into his private conversation with Crary, while "rude and abrupt," would not "be offensive to a reasonable sense of personal dignity." In short, an "ordinary person . . . not unduly sensitive as to his personal dignity" intruding upon a private conversation in Wishnatsky's manner would not have been offended by Huey's response to the intrusion. We conclude that Huey's conduct did not constitute an offensive-contact-battery, as a matter of law, and the trial court did not err in granting Huey's motion for summary judgment dismissing Wishnatsky's action.

Because we have concluded there was no battery as a matter of law, we need not address the immunity issues Wishnatsky has raised. We need not consider questions, the answers to which are unnecessary to the determination of the case. *See, e.g., Kaler v. Kraemer,* 1998 ND 56, 10, 574 N.W.2d 588; *Hospital Servs., Inc. v. Brooks,* 229 N.W.2d 69, 71 (N.D.1975).

Affirmed.

Notes and Questions

1. Do you agree with the *Wishnatsky* court's conclusion that the defendant did not commit an offensive battery? In other words, are you persuaded by the court's articulation of the defendant's argument? Using the facts provided in the opinion, how would you state the plaintiff's best argument that (contrary to the result in the case) Huey's act did constitute an offensive battery?

2. Martin Wishnatsky appeared pro se, as his own attorney, in both the North Dakota Court of Appeals and Supreme Court. Some years later he attended and graduated from Liberty Law School in Lynchburg, Virginia. Had he consulted you as his lawyer, what advice could you have given him about his case that might have helped him better present it?

3. Mr. Wishnatsky had a fascinating personal and professional history in politics, religion, and law.In 1996, when he worked as a paralegal for Peter Crary, both were involved with a Christian ministry doing anti-abortion work. As the case implies, the ministry had a complicated relationship with the Attorney General, who was at the time seeking the ministry's involuntary dissolution; this effort culminated in the North Dakota's Supreme Court decision in State ex rel. v. Heitkamp, 616 N.W.2d 826 (N.D. 2000), in which Wishnatsky successfully intervened, id., "to preserve his religious rights in the ministry." Telephone Interview with Justin Howell, June 9, 2014 (notes on file with authors). With respect to the shoving incident at issue in Wishnatsky v. Huey, Wishnatsky explains that, "I was always in and out of Pete's office. For me to open the door and stick my head in and say something was completely customary." Id. Does this additional information change your sense of the facts and thus of the merits of Wishnatsky's offensive battery claim? A graduate of Andover (1966) and Harvard twice (A.B. magna cum laude in 1966, Ph.D. in 1975), Wishnatsky ultimately got his law degree in 2012. He worked for Roy Moore when Moore was the Chief Justice of the Alabama

Supreme Court, and, it turns out, for a while after Moore left the bench. See Abigail Abrams, Roy Moore's 'Jewish Attorney' is a Practicing Christian, Time, Jan. 5, 2018.

COHEN v. SMITH
648 N.E.2d 329 (Ill. App. 1995)

Justice CHAPMAN delivered the opinion of the court:

Patricia Cohen was admitted to St. Joseph Memorial Hospital ("Hospital") to deliver her baby. After an examination, Cohen was informed that it would be necessary for her to have a cesarean section. Cohen and her husband allegedly informed her physician, who in turn advised the Hospital staff, that the couple's religious beliefs prohibited Cohen from being seen unclothed by a male. Cohen's doctor assured her husband that their religious convictions would be respected.

During Cohen's cesarean section, Roger Smith, a male nurse on staff at the Hospital, allegedly observed and touched Cohen's naked body. Cohen and her husband filed suit against Nurse Smith and the Hospital. The trial court allowed defendants' motions to dismiss. We reverse.

In reviewing a motion to dismiss for failure to state a cause of action, the court must view all well-pleaded facts in the light most favorable to the plaintiff. A trial court may dismiss a cause of action for failing to state a cause of action, based solely on the pleadings, only if it is clearly apparent that no set of alleged facts can be proven which will entitle a plaintiff to recovery. Therefore, we will consider only the facts alleged . . . in the[] complaints.

This case was originally filed as two separate cases, one against Nurse Smith and the other against the Hospital. The cases were consolidated on appeal. There are strong similarities between the complaints filed, and the arguments made, in each case. Plaintiffs' complaints against both Nurse Smith and the Hospital [include a claim for battery].

. . .

The Restatement (Second) of Torts provides that an actor commits a battery if:

> (a) he acts intending to cause a harmful or offensive contact with the person of the other or a third person, or an imminent apprehension of such a contact, and
>
> (b) a harmful contact with the person of the other directly or indirectly results." Restatement (Second) of Torts, § 13 (1965).

Liability for battery emphasizes the plaintiff's lack of consent to the touching. "Offensive contact" is said to occur when the contact "offends a reasonable sense of personal dignity." Restatement (Second) of Torts § 19 (1965).

Historically, battery was first and foremost a systematic substitution for private retribution. Protecting personal integrity has always been viewed as an important basis for battery. "Consequently, the defendant is liable not only for contacts which do actual physical harm, but also for those relatively trivial ones which are merely offensive and insulting." (Prosser, § 9, at 41.) This application of battery to remedy offensive and insulting conduct is deeply ingrained in our legal history. As early as 1784, a Pennsylvania defendant was prosecuted for striking the cane of a French ambassador. The court furthered the distinction between harmful offensive batteries and nonharmful offensive batteries:

> As to the assault, this is, perhaps, one of that kind, in which the insult is more to be considered than the actual damage; for, though no great bodily pain is suffered by a blow on the palm of the hand, or the skirt of the coat, yet these are clearly within the definition of assault and battery, and among gentlemen too often induce duelling and terminate in murder.

Causing actual physical harm is not an element of battery. "A plaintiff is entitled to demand that the defendant refrain from the offensive touching, although the contact results in no visible injury." Prosser, § 9, at 41.

With these definitions in mind, we examine plaintiffs' allegations against Nurse Smith. In count 1, plaintiffs charge defendant with a battery:

> 1. That defendant, Roger Smith, on or about December 9, 1990, was acting in his capacity as an agent and employee of St. Joseph Memorial Hospital, Inc., which is located in Jackson County, Illinois;
>
> 2. That on or about December 9, 1990, the plaintiff, Patricia K. Cohen, was a patient admitted to St. Joseph Memorial Hospital, Inc. for the purpose of delivery of a baby, and after her admittance it was determined that the baby should be delivered by cesarean section;
>
> 3. That based upon information sufficient to form a belief, plaintiff alleges that Roger Smith was made aware that Patricia K. Cohen had strongly held and deeply ingrained moral and religious views which prohibited her from being seen or observed in an unclothed condition by a member of the opposite sex;
>
> 4. That Roger Smith is male and was a member of the operating team which was to perform a cesarean section upon Patricia K. Cohen;
>
> 5. That Patricia K. Cohen was informed, by and through her husband, Joe Cohen, by the physician who was to perform the cesarean section that Roger Smith's presence in the operating room was necessary for the procedure but the cesarean section could be performed without him seeing Patricia K. Cohen in an unclothed condition;
>
> 6. The physician who was to perform the cesarean section instructed Roger Smith that the operation was to be performed without any male seeing Patricia K. Cohen in an unclothed condition;
>
> 7. Relying about the assurances provided her by her physician, that no male would observe her in an unclothed condition, Patricia K. Cohen consented to have the cesarean section performed at St. Joseph Memorial Hospital, Inc.;

> 8. That Roger Smith did act so as to place himself in such a position so as to view and touch Patricia K. Cohen's naked, unclothed, body, and did in fact observe and touch her naked and unclothed body;
>
> 9. That based upon information sufficient to form a belief, plaintiff alleges that Roger Smith did intentionally touch and observe Patricia K. Cohen's naked and unclothed body although informed of Patricia K. Cohen's moral and religious beliefs regarding members of the opposite sex observing her in an unclothed condition;
>
> 10. That Roger Smith's actions were taken while Patricia K. Cohen was incapacitated, was on the surgical table, and was under the control of Roger Smith.

It is apparent from these quotations, which must be taken as true for purposes of the motion to dismiss, that the plaintiffs in the instant case are not alleging that the cesarean section performed on Cohen violated any medical standard or was performed incorrectly or that any attendant procedure was improper because of any deviation from any appropriate medical standard. The plaintiffs' claim is in no way based upon medical malpractice. Cohen alleges instead that Roger Smith knowingly violated her privacy interests and religious standards and beliefs by touching her without her consent.

The only reason there is some hesitancy over the issue of whether a battery occurred in this case is because the contact took place in a hospital between a medical professional and a patient. If Patricia Cohen had been struck in the nose by Nurse Smith on a public street, everyone would agree that a battery occurred, and under those limited facts, there would be no defense to the battery. In contrast, medical professionals are allowed to touch patients during the course of medical treatment because patients consent, either explicitly or implicitly, to the touching. The violation of a plaintiff's right to bodily and personal integrity by an unconsented-to touching is the essence of a claim for battery.

. . .

The plaintiffs' complaint against Nurse Smith alleges that Smith touched Cohen's naked body after being informed of her moral and religious beliefs against such touching by a male. Similarly, the plaintiffs' complaint against the Hospital alleges that the doctor performing the surgery told Nurse Smith that the operation was to be performed without any male seeing Cohen naked. According to the complaint, despite being informed of Cohen's religious beliefs, Nurse Smith, an agent and employee of the Hospital, intentionally saw and touched Cohen's naked body.

The allegation that both Nurse Smith and the Hospital were informed in advance of plaintiffs' religious beliefs is important in this case, because the religious convictions of plaintiffs might not be those of most people who enter the hospital to give birth. As a matter of fact, plaintiffs' counsel candidly conceded that there would be no cause of action for battery if Patricia Cohen had been placed in Nurse Smith's and the Hospital's care in an emergency situation in which Patricia had been unable to inform the Hospital or its agents of her beliefs. Plaintiffs' attorney acknowledged that his clients' moral and religious views are not widely held in the community and, because of this, plaintiffs could state a claim against defendants only if the plaintiffs plead that the defendants had knowledge of those beliefs. But, he contends, the defendants' knowledge of the plaintiffs' religious beliefs was pleaded in their complaint. Specifically, plaintiffs contend that defendants' knowledge is clearly illustrated by an allegation in the plaintiffs' amended complaint that Nurse Smith requested the presence of the Murphysboro City Police at the Hospital to prevent Mr. Cohen from objecting to Nurse Smith's presence in the operating room while Mrs. Cohen was naked, and to physically restrain Mr. Cohen if necessary.

The fact that the plaintiffs hold deeply ingrained religious beliefs which are not shared by the majority of society does not mean that those beliefs deserve less protection than more mainstream religious beliefs. The plaintiffs were not trying to force their religion on other people; they were only insisting that their beliefs be respected by the Hospital and the Hospital staff.

As we have stated previously, Patricia Cohen was not trying to, and was not entitled to, impose her religious beliefs on others. When she informed the Hospital of her moral and religious beliefs against being viewed and touched by males, the Hospital was free to refuse to accede to those demands. But, according to her complaint, when Cohen made her wishes known to the Hospital, it, at least implicitly, agreed to provide her with treatment within the restrictions placed by her beliefs.

Although most people in modern society have come to accept the necessity of being seen unclothed and being touched by members of the opposite sex during medical treatment, the plaintiffs had not accepted these procedures and, according to their complaint, had informed defendants of their convictions. This case is similar to cases involving Jehovah's Witnesses who were unwilling to accept blood transfusions because of religious convictions. (*In re Estate of Brooks* (1965), 32 Ill.2d 361, 205 N.E.2d 435.) Although most people do not share the Jehovah's Witnesses' beliefs about blood transfusions, our society, and our courts, accept their right to have that belief. Similarly, the courts have consistently recognized individuals' rights to refuse medical treatment even if such a refusal would result in an increased likelihood of the individual's death. *Cruzan v. Director, Missouri Department of Health* (1990), 497 U.S. 261, 110 S.Ct. 2841, 111 L.Ed.2d 224.

A person's right to refuse or accept medical care is not one to be interfered with lightly. As Justice Cardozo stated, "Every human being of adult years and sound mind has a right to determine what shall be done with his own body; and a surgeon who performs an operation without his patient's consent commits an assault, for which he is liable in damages." *Schloendorff v. Society of New York Hospital* (1914), 211 N.Y. 125, 105 N.E. 92.

Knowing interference with the right of determination is battery. Our examination of the record reveals that facts charging that interference are pleaded in plaintiffs' complaint against Nurse Smith and against the Hospital. For purposes of a motion on the pleadings, a court must accept these facts as true. Accepting as true the plaintiffs' allegations that they informed defendants of their religious beliefs and that defendants persisted in treating Patricia Cohen as they would have treated a patient without those beliefs, we conclude that the trial court erred in dismissing the battery . . . count[].

Reversed and remanded.

Notes and Questions

1. *Wishnatsky* and *Cohen* were decided by courts in different jurisdictions, which could have different approaches to the relevance of minority religious sensibilities in the establishment of offensive batteries. On the other hand, maybe their positions are aligned. Can the two cases be reconciled? How would you state the prima facie case for offensive batteries that emerges from this reconciliation or synthesis?

2. The jury generally decides whether a bodily contact is offensive to a reasonable sense of personal dignity. (As we will see in our discussion of negligence, the issue of reasonableness is mostly for the jury.) This means that reasonableness is established according to community customs and norms—time and place matter for this purpose. Occasionally, however, a judge will take the reasonableness issue away from the jury and decide it himself or herself, as a matter of law. When might this happen?

3. *Cohen* suggests that a plaintiff can make out an offensive battery claim either by showing that the defendant acted with the intent to cause a contact they knew would be offensive to a reasonable sense of personal dignity, or by showing that the defendant acted knowing that the plaintiff had an unusual sense of personal dignity. This alternative approach exists in a number of jurisdictions.

4. In describing the rationale for the rule that patients are entitled to reject even sound medical judgment, the *Cohen* court quotes from then-New York State Justice Benjamin Cardozo's opinion in Schloendorff v. Society of New York Hospital. (Cardozo later became a Justice on the United States Supreme Court.) This case and Cardozo's quoted language in particular are widely recognized as the foundation for the law in this area. The principle that adults are generally free to withhold consent even in medical situations in which their lives are at risk has implications beyond tort law. For example, a person who withholds consent for religious reasons is protected in their decision by the First Amendment's right to free exercise; someone who withholds consent for purely secular reasons may be protected by the Fourteenth Amendment's right to decisional autonomy (due process/privacy). This means that if a state changed its tort law to deny competent adults the right to withhold medical consent in life-threatening situations — for example, as a pro-life tort reform measure — the federal Constitution would continue to provide that privilege. The standard exception to the right to withhold medical consent also arises out of these constitutional privileges. That is, our constitutional rights are enforceable only so long as the government does not have a suitable — rational, important, or compelling, depending on the issue — reason for violating them. Many jurisdictions have determined that financial responsibility for minor children is a sufficient reason for forcing life-saving medical treatment on competent adults.

5. *Cohen* alludes to a different rule that applies in cases of emergency, when neither the patient nor a proxy decision maker is available to consent to necessary medical treatment. Can you tell from the case what that rule is? In an emergency, the patient is said not to be "available" when they are unconscious or else incapable of making an intelligent and voluntary choice about treatment. A proxy decision maker is someone close to the patient who is legally authorized to provide consent. Such a decision maker is unavailable in an emergency if they cannot be reached in time to ensure that the patient's best medical interests are met.

6. Cases where medical professionals proceed to treat the patient without any consent are typically considered batteries. Cases where consent is obtained but it is insufficiently informed are typically considered negligent medical malpractice. We will deal with the latter categories of cases in our treatment of medical negligence.

7. Note that the plaintiffs sued both the hospital and Nurse Smith. Be sure you can distinguish the different factual bases for the claims against each. If you were counsel for the plaintiffs and Nurse Smith was found liable, what would be your strategy for collecting those damages? As you consider this question, revisit the discussion on Vicarious Liability in Chapter One's coverage of Threshold Issues Affecting the Viability of Claims.

DICKENS v. PURYEAR
276 S.E.2d 325 (N.C. 1981)

EXUM, Justice.

Plaintiff's complaint is cast as a claim for intentional infliction of mental distress. It was filed more than one year but less than three years after the incidents complained of occurred. Defendants moved for summary judgment before answer was due or filed. Much of the factual showing at the hearing on summary judgment related to assaults and batteries committed against plaintiff by defendants. Defendants' motions for summary judgment were allowed on the ground that plaintiff's claim was for assault and battery; therefore it was barred by the one-year statute of limitations applicable to assault and battery.

Thus this appeal raises two questions. First, whether defendants, by filing motions for summary judgment before answer was due or filed, properly raised the affirmative defense of the statute of limitations. Second, whether plaintiff's claim is barred by the one-year statute of limitations applicable to assault and battery. We hold that defendants properly raised the limitations defense but that on its merits plaintiff's claim is not altogether barred by the one-year statute because plaintiff's factual showing indicates plaintiff may be able to prove a claim for intentional infliction of mental distress a claim which is governed by the three-year statute of limitations. . . .

The facts brought out at the hearing on summary judgment may be briefly summarized: For a time preceding the incidents in question plaintiff Dickens, a thirty-one year old man, shared sex, alcohol and marijuana with defendants' daughter, a seventeen year old high school student. On 2 April 1975 defendants, husband and wife, lured plaintiff into rural Johnston County, North Carolina. Upon plaintiff's arrival defendant Earl Puryear, after identifying himself, called out to defendant Ann Puryear who emerged from beside a nearby building and, crying, stated that she "didn't want to see that SOB." Ann Puryear then left the scene. Thereafter Earl Puryear pointed a pistol between plaintiff's eyes and shouted "Ya'll come on out." Four men wearing ski masks and armed with nightsticks then approached from behind plaintiff and beat him into semi-consciousness. They handcuffed plaintiff to a piece of farm machinery and resumed striking him with nightsticks. Defendant Earl Puryear, while brandishing a knife and cutting plaintiff's hair, threatened plaintiff with castration. During four or five interruptions of the beatings defendant Earl Puryear and the others, within plaintiff's hearing, discussed and took votes on whether plaintiff should be killed or castrated. Finally, after some two hours and the conclusion of a final conference, the beatings ceased. Defendant Earl Puryear told plaintiff to go home, pull his telephone off the wall, pack his clothes, and leave the state of North Carolina; otherwise he would be killed. Plaintiff was then set free.[1]

Plaintiff filed his complaint on 31 March 1978. It alleges that defendants on the occasion just described intentionally inflicted mental distress upon him. He further alleges that as a result of defendants' acts plaintiff has suffered "severe and permanent mental and emotional distress, and physical injury to his nerves and nervous system." He alleges that he is unable to sleep, afraid to go out in the dark, afraid to meet strangers, afraid he may be killed, suffering from chronic diarrhea and a gum disorder, unable effectively to perform his job, and that he has lost $1000 per month income.

On 7 September and 15 November 1978 defendants filed . . . motions for summary judgment. The motions made no reference to the statute of limitations nor did they contest plaintiff's factual allegations. Judge Braswell, after considering arguments of counsel, plaintiff's complaint, plaintiff's deposition and evidence in the criminal case arising out of this occurrence, concluded that plaintiff's claim was barred by G.S. 1-54(3), the one-year statute of limitations applicable to assault and battery. On 29 March 1979 he granted summary judgment in favor of both defendants.

. . .

II.

We turn now to the merits of defendants' motions for summary judgment. Defendants contend, and the Court of Appeals agreed, that this is an action grounded in assault and battery. Although plaintiff pleads the tort of intentional infliction of mental distress, the Court of Appeals concluded that the complaint's factual allegations and the factual showing at the hearing on summary judgment support only a claim for assault and battery. The claim was, therefore, barred by the one-year period of limitations applicable to assault and battery. Plaintiff, on the other hand, argues that the factual showing on the motion supports a claim for intentional infliction of mental distress a claim which is governed by the three-year period of limitations.[8] At least, plaintiff argues, his factual showing is such that it cannot be said as a matter of law that he will be unable to prove such a claim at trial. We agree with plaintiff's position.

---

[1] This same occurrence gave rise to a criminal conviction of defendant Earl Puryear for conspiracy to commit simple assault. See State v. Puryear, 30 N.C.App. 719, 228 S.E.2d 536, appeal dismissed, 291 N.C. 325, 230 S.E.2d 678 (1976).

[8] Although defendants argue that even the tort of intentional infliction of mental distress is governed by the one-year statute of limitations, we are satisfied that it is not. The one-year statute, G.S. 1-54(3), applies to "libel, slander, assault, battery, or false imprisonment." As we go to some length in the opinion to demonstrate, the tort of intentional infliction of mental distress is none of these things. Thus the rule of statutory construction embodied in the maxim, expressio unius est exclusio alterius, meaning the expression of one thing is the exclusion of another, applies. No statute of limitations addresses the tort of intentional infliction of mental distress by name. It must, therefore, be governed by the more general three-year statute of limitations, G.S. 1-52(5), which applies to "any other injury to the person or rights of another, not arising on contract and not hereafter enumerated." Even if we had substantial doubt about which statute of limitations applies, and we do not, the rule would be that the longer statute is to be selected.

To resolve the question whether defendants are entitled to summary judgment on the ground of the statute of limitations we must examine both the law applicable to the entry of summary judgment and the law applicable to the torts of assault and battery and intentional infliction of mental distress. We think it better to begin with a discussion of applicable tort law.

A

North Carolina follows common law principles governing assault and battery. An assault is an offer to show violence to another without striking him, and a battery is the carrying of the threat into effect by the infliction of a blow. The interest protected by the action for battery is freedom from intentional and unpermitted contact with one's person; the interest protected by the action for assault is freedom from apprehension of a harmful or offensive contact with one's person. The apprehension created must be one of an immediate harmful or offensive contact, as distinguished from contact in the future. As noted in State v. Ingram, 237 N.C. 197, 201, 74 S.E.2d 532, 535 (1953), in order to constitute an assault there must be:

> (A)n overt act or an attempt, or the unequivocal appearance of an attempt, with force and violence, to do some immediate physical injury to the person of another . . . The display of force or menace of violence must be such to cause the reasonable apprehension of immediate bodily harm.

A mere threat, unaccompanied by an offer or attempt to show violence, is not an assault. The damages recoverable for assault and battery include those for plaintiff's mental disturbance as well as for plaintiff's physical injury.

Common law principles of assault and battery as enunciated in North Carolina law are also found in the Restatement (Second) of Torts (1965) (hereinafter "the Restatement"). As noted in § 29(1) of the Restatement, "(t)o make the actor liable for an assault he must put the other in apprehension of an imminent contact." (Emphasis supplied.) The comment to § 29(1) states: "The apprehension created must be one of imminent contact, as distinguished from any contact in the future. 'Imminent' does not mean immediate, in the sense of instantaneous contact. . . . It means rather that there will be no significant delay." Similarly, § 31 of the Restatement provides that "(w)ords do not make the actor liable for assault unless together with other acts or circumstances they put the other in reasonable apprehension of an imminent harmful or offensive contact with his person." (Emphasis supplied.) The comment to § 31 provides, in pertinent part:

> a. Ordinarily mere words, unaccompanied by some act apparently intended to carry the threat into execution, do not put the other in apprehension of an imminent bodily contact, and so cannot make the actor liable for an assault under the rule stated in § 21 (the section which defines an assault). For this reason it is commonly said in the decisions that mere words do not constitute an assault, or that some overt act is required. This is true even though the mental discomfort caused by a threat of serious future harm on the part of one who has the apparent intention and ability to carry out his threat may be far more emotionally disturbing than many of the attempts to inflict minor bodily contacts which are actionable as assaults. Any remedy for words which are abusive or insulting, or which create emotional distress by threats for the future, is to be found under §§ 46 and 47 (those sections dealing with the interest in freedom from emotional distress).

Illustration:

> 1. A, known to be a resolute and desperate character, threatens to waylay B on his way home on a lonely road on a dark night. A is not liable to B for an assault under the rule stated in § 21. A may, however, be liable to B for the infliction of severe emotional distress by extreme and outrageous conduct, under the rule stated in § 46.

. . .

The tort of intentional infliction of mental distress is recognized in North Carolina. Stanback v. Stanback, 297 N.C. 181, 254 S.E.2d 611 (1979). "(L)iability arises under this tort when a defendant's 'conduct exceeds all bounds usually tolerated by decent society' and the conduct 'causes mental distress of a very serious kind.'" In Stanback plaintiff alleged that defendant breached a separation agreement between the parties. She further alleged, according to our opinion in Stanback, "that defendant's conduct in breaching the contract was 'willful, malicious, calculated, deliberate and purposeful' . . . (and) that 'she has suffered great mental anguish and anxiety . . .' as a result of defendant's conduct in breaching the agreement . . . (and) that defendant acted recklessly and irresponsibly and 'with full knowledge of the consequences which would result. . . .' " We held in Stanback that these allegations were "sufficient to state a claim for what has become essentially the tort of intentional infliction of serious emotional distress. Plaintiff has alleged that defendant intentionally inflicted mental distress."

The tort alluded to in Stanback is defined in the Restatement § 46 as follows:

> One who by extreme and outrageous conduct intentionally or recklessly causes severe emotional distress to another is subject to liability for such emotional distress, and if bodily harm to the other results from it, for such bodily harm.

The holding in Stanback was in accord with the Restatement definition of the tort of intentional infliction of mental distress. We now reaffirm this holding.

There is, however, troublesome dictum in Stanback that plaintiff, to recover for this tort, "must show some physical injury resulting from the emotional disturbance caused by defendant's alleged conduct" and that the harm she suffered was a "foreseeable result." Plaintiff in Stanback did not allege that she had suffered any physical injury as a result of defendant's conduct. We noted in Stanback, however, that "physical injury" had been given a broad interpretation in some of our earlier cases, e. g., Kimberly v. Howland, 143 N.C. 398, 403-04, 55 S.E. 778, 780 (1906), where the Court said,

> The nerves are as much a part of the physical system as the limbs, and in some persons are very delicately adjusted, and when 'out of tune' cause excruciating agony. We think the general principles of the law of torts support a right of action for physical injuries resulting from negligence, whether wilful or otherwise, none the less strongly because the physical injury consists of a wrecked nervous system instead of lacerated limbs.

We held in Stanback that plaintiff's "allegation that she suffered great mental anguish and anxiety is sufficient to permit her to go to trial upon the question of whether the great mental anguish and anxiety (which she alleges) has caused physical injury." We held, further, that plaintiff's allegation that "defendant acted with full knowledge of the consequences of his actions . . . sufficiently indicated that the harm she suffered was a foreseeable result of his conduct."

After revisiting Stanback in light of the earlier authorities upon which it is based and considering an instructive analysis of our cases in the area by Professor and former Dean of the University of North Carolina Law School, Robert G. Byrd, we are satisfied that the dictum in Stanback was not necessary to the holding and in some respects actually conflicts with the holding. We now disapprove it.

If "physical injury" means something more than emotional distress or damage to the nervous system, it is simply not an element of the tort of intentional infliction of mental distress. As noted, plaintiff in Stanback never alleged that she had suffered any physical injury, yet we held that she had stated a claim for intentional infliction of mental distress. In Wilson v. Wilkins, 181 Ark. 137, 25 S.W.2d 428 (1930), defendants came to the home of the plaintiff at night and accused him of stealing hogs. They told him that if he did not leave their community within 10 days they "would put a rope around his neck." Defendants' threats caused the plaintiff to remove his family from the area. Plaintiff testified that he was afraid they would kill him if he did not leave and that he suffered great mental agony and humiliation because he had been accused of something of which he was not guilty. In sustaining a jury verdict in favor of plaintiff, the Arkansas Supreme Court rejected defendants' contention that plaintiff was required to show some physical injury before he could recover. The Court said:

> The (defendants) rely upon the rule . . . that in actions for negligence there can be no mental suffering where there has been no physical injury.
>
> The rule is well settled in this state, but it has no application to willful and wanton wrongs and those committed with the intention of causing mental distress and injured feelings. Mental suffering forms the proper element of damages in actions for willful and wanton wrongs and those committed with the intention of causing mental distress.

Similarly, the question of foreseeability does not arise in the tort of intentional infliction of mental distress. This tort imports an act which is done with the intention of causing emotional distress or with reckless indifference to the likelihood that emotional distress may result. A defendant is liable for this tort when he "desires to inflict severe emotional distress . . . (or) knows that such distress is certain, or substantially certain, to result from his conduct . . . (or) where he acts recklessly . . . in deliberate disregard of a high degree of probability that the emotional distress will follow" and the mental distress does in fact result. Restatement § 46, Comment i, p. 77. "The authorities seem to agree that if the tort is wilful and not merely negligent, the wrong-doer is liable for such physical injuries as may proximately result, whether he could have foreseen them or not." Kimberly v. Howland, supra, 143 N.C. at 402, 55 S.E. at 780.

We are now satisfied that the dictum in Stanback arose from our effort to conform the opinion to language in some of our earlier cases the holdings of which led ultimately to our recognition in Stanback of the tort of intentional infliction of mental distress.

The earliest of these cases is Kirby v. Jules Chain Stores Corp., 210 N.C. 808, 188 S.E. 625 (1936). This case involved a bill collector who used highhanded collection tactics against plaintiff debtor. In an effort to collect the debt defendant said to plaintiff, "By G , you are like all the rest of the damn deadbeats. You wouldn't pay when you could. . . . If you are so damn low you won't pay, I guess when I get the sheriff and bring him down here you will pay then." Plaintiff, who was pregnant, became emotionally distraught and her evidence tended to show that her distress caused her child to be prematurely stillborn. This Court sustained a verdict and judgment for the plaintiff. The Court recognized that earlier cases permitting recovery under such circumstances required that there be a forcible trespass. Without deciding whether a forcible trespass existed in the case before it the Court concluded that "(t)he gravamen of plaintiff's cause of action is trespass to the person. (Citation omitted.) This may result from an injury either willfully or negligently inflicted." The Court said further:

> It is no doubt correct to say that fright alone is not actionable, but it is faulty pathology to assume that nervous disorders of serious proportions may not flow from fear or fright. Fear long continued wears away one's reserve.
>
> As a general rule, damages for mere fright are not recoverable; but they may be recovered where there is some physical injury attending the cause of the fright, or, in the absence of physical injury, where the fright is of such character as to produce some physical or mental impairment directly and naturally resulting from the wrongful act".

. . .

Kirby, rightly or wrongly, has been read to require some physical injury in addition to emotional distress.

Statements that "fright" alone is not actionable and that the harm suffered must be a foreseeable result of defendant's conduct appear in other cases relied on in Stanback, all of which, in turn, rely on Kirby. These are: Crews v. Finance Co., 271 N.C. 684, 157 S.E.2d 381 (1967) (highhanded debt collection efforts; held, plaintiff could recover for resulting nervousness, acute angina, and high blood pressure); Slaughter v. Slaughter, 264 N.C. 732, 142 S.E.2d 683 (1965) (defendant, son of plaintiff, exploded firecrackers outside his home where plaintiff was a guest with the purpose of frightening his children who were in the room with plaintiff; held, plaintiff could recover for a fractured left hip suffered when she fell as a result of becoming emotionally upset at the noise); Langford v. Shu, 258 N.C. 135, 128 S.E.2d 210 (1962) (plaintiff, defendant's next door neighbor, frightened by defendant's practical joke, a "mongoose box," stumbled while fleeing the box, fell and tore a cartilage in her knee; held, plaintiff could recover for damages to her knee); Martin v. Spencer, 221 N.C. 28, 18 S.E.2d 703 (1942) (defendant directed verbal abuse at plaintiff and engaged in altercation with plaintiff's brother in a dispute over a boundary; held, plaintiff could recover for a miscarriage which, according to her evidence, resulted from "fright occasioned by the conduct of the defendant."); Sparks v. Products Corp., 212 N.C. 211, 193 S.E. 31 (1937) (held, plaintiff could recover for "shock and injury to her nerves, resulting in loss of weight, nervousness, periodical confinement in bed, and other ailments" caused by defendant's blasting operation which hurled a rock through the roof of plaintiff's home).

Although these earlier cases, except for Sparks v. Products Corp., did permit recovery under circumstances similar to those to which the modern tort of intentional infliction of mental distress is directed, the cases did not actually come to grips with the tort as it is now recognized by Prosser and the Restatement and as we recognized it in Stanback. These earlier cases were concerned with a broader concept of liability than the relatively narrow one now known as intentional infliction of mental distress. They were concerned with permitting recovery for injury, physical and mental, intentionally or negligently inflicted. The opinion in Kirby consistently refers to injuries which result from either wilful or negligent conduct. Crews, which relied on Kirby, dealt with intentional actions of a bill collector. The opinion, however, relied on § 436 of the Restatement. This section deals with negligent infliction of mental distress which results in physical harm. . . . To the extent, then, that these earlier cases required some "physical injury" apart from mere mental or emotional distress and, in addition, talked in terms of foreseeability, they did so in the context of negligently inflicted injuries and not in the context of the tort, as it is now recognized, of intentional infliction of mental distress. This Court in Williamson v. Bennett, 251 N.C. 498, 112 S.E.2d 48 (1960) denied recovery for a serious nervous disorder unaccompanied by physical injury, allegedly caused by defendant's negligent operation of an automobile. Denial, however, was on the ground that the connection between the relatively minor accident and plaintiff's condition was too tenuous and too "highly extraordinary" to permit recovery. The Court noted, however, id. at 503, 112 S.E.2d at 51:

> This cause involves mental distress and invasion of emotional tranquility. It concerns itself with fear and resultant neurasthenia allegedly caused by ordinary negligence. In so far as possible we shall avoid consideration of those situations wherein fright, mental suffering and nervous disorder result from intentional, wilful, wanton or malicious conduct.

Stanback, then, should not be read as grafting "physical injury" and "foreseeability" requirements on the tort of intentional infliction of mental distress. Neither should it be read as grafting the requirements of this tort on other theories of recovery for mental and emotional distress dealt with in our earlier cases. We leave those theories where they lay before Stanback.

Stanback, in effect, was the first formal recognition by this Court of the relatively recent tort of intentional infliction of mental distress. This tort, under the authorities already cited, consists of: (1) extreme and outrageous conduct, (2) which is intended to cause and does cause (3) severe emotional distress to another. The tort may also exist where defendant's actions indicate a reckless indifference to the likelihood that they will cause severe emotional distress. Recovery may be had for the emotional distress so caused and for any other bodily harm which proximately results from the distress itself.

B

We now turn to some principles governing the entry of summary judgment. The movant must clearly demonstrate the lack of any triable issue of fact and entitlement to judgment as a matter of law. The record is considered in the light most favorable to the party opposing the motion. "(A)ll inferences of fact from the proofs proffered at the hearing must be drawn against the movant and in favor of the party opposing the motion."

In ruling on summary judgment, a court does not resolve questions of fact but determines whether there is a genuine issue of material fact. An issue is material "if the facts alleged are such as to constitute a legal defense or are of such nature as to effect the result of the action, or if the resolution of the issue is so essential that the party against whom it is resolved may not prevail." Thus a defending party is entitled to summary judgment if he can show that claimant cannot prove the existence of an essential element of his claim, or cannot surmount an affirmative defense which would bar the claim.

Summary judgment is, furthermore, a device by which a defending party may force the claimant to produce a forecast of claimant's evidence demonstrating that claimant will, at trial, be able to make out at least a prima facie case or that he will be able to surmount an affirmative defense. Under such circumstances claimant need not present all the evidence available in his favor but only that necessary to rebut the defendant's showing that an essential element of his claim is non-existent or that he cannot surmount an affirmative defense.

C

The question, then, is whether in light of the principles applicable to motions for summary judgment and those applicable to the torts of assault and battery and intentional infliction of mental distress, the evidentiary showing on defendants' motions for summary judgment demonstrates as a matter of law the non-existence of a claim for intentional infliction of mental distress. Stated another way, the question is whether the evidentiary showing demonstrates as a matter of law that plaintiff's only claim, if any, is for assault and battery. If plaintiff, as a matter of law, has no claim for intentional infliction of mental distress but has a claim, if at all, only for assault and battery, then plaintiff cannot surmount the affirmative defense of the one-year statute of limitations and defendants are entitled to summary judgment on the ground of the statute.

Although plaintiff labels his claim one for intentional infliction of mental distress, we agree with the Court of Appeals that "(t)he nature of the action is not determined by what either party calls it. . . ." The nature of the action is determined "by the issues arising on the pleading and by the relief sought," id., and by the facts which, at trial, are proved or which, on motion for summary judgment, are forecast by the evidentiary showing.

Here much of the factual showing at the hearing related to assaults and batteries committed by defendants against plaintiff. The physical beatings and the cutting of plaintiff's hair constituted batteries. The threats of castration and death, being threats which created apprehension of immediate harmful or offensive contact, were assaults. Plaintiff's recovery for injuries, mental or physical, caused by these actions would be barred by the one-year statute of limitations.

The evidentiary showing on the summary judgment motion does, however, indicate that defendant Earl Puryear threatened plaintiff with death in the future unless plaintiff went home, pulled his telephone off the wall, packed his clothes, and left the state. The Court of Appeals characterized this threat as being "an immediate threat of harmful and offensive contact. It was a present threat of harm to plaintiff. . . ." The Court of Appeals thus concluded that this threat was also an assault barred by the one-year statute of limitations.

We disagree with the Court of Appeals' characterization of this threat. The threat was not one of imminent, or immediate, harm. It was a threat for the future apparently intended to and which allegedly did inflict serious mental distress; therefore it is actionable, if at all, as an intentional infliction of mental distress.

The threat, of course, cannot be considered separately from the entire episode of which it was only a part. The assaults and batteries, construing the record in the light most favorable to the plaintiff, were apparently designed to give added impetus to the ultimate conditional threat of future harm. Although plaintiff's recovery for injury, mental or physical, directly caused by the assaults and batteries is barred by the statute of limitations, these assaults and batteries may be considered in determining the outrageous character of the ultimate threat and the extent of plaintiff's mental or emotional distress caused by it.[11]

Having concluded, therefore, that the factual showing on the motions for summary judgment was sufficient to indicate that plaintiff may be able to prove at trial a claim for intentional infliction of mental distress, we hold that summary judgment for defendants based upon the one-year statute of limitations was error and we remand the matter for further proceedings against defendant Earl Puryear not inconsistent with this opinion. . . .

Notes and Questions

1. Now that you have read and briefed a case focusing on assault specifically, you should be able to state the full, detailed prima facie case for battery and assault. Remember that because a failed battery can be an assault and a failed assault can be a battery, there is, in effect, a single prima facie case for both torts.

2. Note from all of the cases in this section that, although the *Restatement* states the intent required for assault as (in relevant part) "intent to cause . . . imminent apprehension of harmful or offensive bodily contact," what the cases actually require is intent to cause apprehension of imminent harmful or offensive bodily contact.

3. Imagine that the two individuals —Christian Cooper and Amy Cooper —in the following news story both brought assault claims against each other. What is the best argument each could develop in support of their claim and what problems can you identify? Sarah Maslin Nir, White Woman is Fired After Calling Police on Black Man in Central Park, The New York Times, May 26, 2020; see alsoAndrea Salcedo, White woman who called 911 on Black birder loses suit over termination, Washington Post, September 22, 2022. If you are interested in the intersection of race and sex in the intentional torts context, see "In 'Reasonable' Fear of Deadly Force?" which we have included in the Appendix at the back of the book. It assumes you know self-defense doctrine and so we recommend that you wait to try to resolve the issues it raises until after we have finished that material. It comes up shortly.

4. Notice that the state's statute of limitations was a threshold issue that affected the viability of the plaintiff's claim regardless of whether he could make out the prima facie case for intentional infliction of emotional distress (IIED). Ultimately, the *Dickens* court concludes that

[11] We note in this regard plaintiff's statement in his deposition that "(i) t is not entirely (the future threat) which caused me all of my emotional upset and disturbance that I have complained about. It was the ordeal from beginning to end." If plaintiff is able to prove a claim for intentional infliction of mental distress it will then be the difficult, but necessary, task of the trier of fact to ascertain the damages flowing from the conditional threat of future harm. Although the assaults and batteries serve to color and give impetus to the future threat and its impact on plaintiff's emotional condition, plaintiff may not recover damages flowing directly from the assaults and batteries themselves.

this claim is not barred by the statute of limitations but it does not address the merits. Imagine that you were the plaintiff's lawyer on remand. How would you develop the IIED claim? If you were the defendants' lawyer, would you file a second motion for summary judgment, this time on the merits?

5. *Dickens* discusses the differences between intentional and negligent infliction of emotional distress (NIED). We will revisit these when we cover NIED in Chapter Three.

6. Notice that unlike the other intentional torts we have studied, IIED's intent element can be made out in most jurisdictions by a showing of "mere" recklessness. Thus, even a defendant who is genuinely unaware that his or her outrageous behavior could result in severe emotional distress can be liable for IIED so long as that objective standard is met. See, e.g., *Blakely v. Shortal's Estate*, 236 Iowa 787 (plaintiff's IIED claim — based in facts showing that plaintiff suffered serious emotional distress after discovering that her recently divorced neighbor, defendant, had committed suicide in her kitchen — should have been submitted to the jury). The lower standard of fault required for IIED may be explained by the focus on outrageous conduct: the rules governing IIED assign "liability only for conduct exceeding all bounds which could be tolerated by a society, of a nature especially calculated to cause mental damage of a very serious kind." William L. Prosser, Intentional Infliction of Mental Suffering: A New Tort, 37 Mich. L. Rev. 888, 889 (1938–39) (emphasis added).

7. Federal law, including federal constitutional law, trumps state law when the two are in conflict. This rule is based in the Constitution's Supremacy Clause (Article VI) and related preemption doctrine. Thus, when an IIED claim is based in speech or religious beliefs protected by the First Amendment, it may be preempted. Specifically, the First Amendment's Free Speech Clause is implicated whenever emotional distress is alleged to result from speech; where that speech touches on matters of public concern, federal law is an especially strong barrier to tort liability. In *Snyder v. Phelps*, 131 S.Ct. 1207 (2011), for example, the father of a deceased American soldier sued members of the Westboro Baptist Church for picketing at his son's funeral. The members' signs included messages like "Thank God for Dead Soldiers," and "God Hates You," among others. *Id.* at 1213. The United States Supreme Court acknowledged that Westboro's conveyance of its views in conjunction with the funeral made the expression of those views particularly harmful. *Id.* at 1217. Nonetheless, it held that the First Amendment protected the Westboro members' "picketing peacefully on matters of public concern at a public place adjacent to a public street." *Id.* at 1218. *See also Collin v. Smith*, 578 F.2d 1197 (7th Cir. 1978), cert denied, 439 U.S. 916 (1978) (despite possibility of serious psychological harm to residents, including a large number of concentration camp survivors, city cannot prevent an American Nazi group from marching in a predominantly Jewish community). Speech-based IIED claims are particularly vulnerable on First Amendment grounds when the plaintiff is a public figure; to survive constitutional challenge, such claims require a showing that the publication at issue contains a false statement of fact made with knowledge that the statement was false or with reckless disregard as to whether or not it was true. *Hustler v. Falwell*, 485 U.S. 46, 56 (1988). *Id.* The First Amendment's Free Exercise Clause is implicated when emotional distress is alleged to result from behavior based in or mandated by a religious belief. For example, in *Paul v. Watchtower Bible and Tract Society of New York, Inc.*, 819 F.2d 875 (9th Cir. 1987), the court held that defendants could not be liable in tort for distress caused by the practice of "shunning," because such liability would directly burden a traditional religious practice of Jehovah's Witnesses. *Id.* at 880–881.

8. The intersection of presidents, presidential politics, and IIED has an interesting history. In a case brought by Paula Jones against President William Jefferson (Bill) Clinton, the United States Supreme Court decided that sitting presidents are not immune from tort claims, including IIED claims, brought by private citizens based on conduct that had taken place prior to their inauguration. Clinton v. Jones, 520 U.S. 681 (1997). It was in a deposition on remand in that case that Clinton perjured himself when he was asked if he had ever had sexual relations with Monica Lewinsky; this act of perjury ultimately led to his impeachment by the House of Representatives in 1998. See, e.g., David A. Graham and Cullen Murphy, The Clinton Impeachment As Told By The People Who Lived It, The Atlantic, Dec. 2018. All of Jones's claims, including her IIED claim, were eventually dismissed — either on motions to dismiss or for summary judgment — for failure to make out a prima facie case. The opinion of the United States District Court dismissing Jones's IIED claim is a textbook application of the IRAC formula and of black letter law. The substance of the law itself can be critiqued, of course. Jones v. Clinton, 990 F.Supp 657 (E.D. Ark. 1998) (IIED claim discussed in Part 3 of the opinion). A series of tweets by President Donald J. Trump in May 2020 attacking MSNBC host Joe Scarborough led to speculation that the Jones precedents could be the basis for yet another IIED claim against a sitting president. See, e.g., Peter H. Schuck, Trumps 'Horrifying Lies' About Lori Klausutis May Cross a Legal Line, The New York Times, May 28, 2020 (applying immunity and IIED doctrine). Distinguish the Clinton and Trump facts and consider whether a Klausutis v. Trump claim would fare better than did the Jones v. Clinton claim.

2. Fraud aka Intentional or Fraudulent Misrepresentation

ROBLIN v. SHANTZ
311 P.2d 459 (Or. 1957)

Rossman, Justice.

This is an appeal by Charles Dana Roblin, contestant, from a decree of the Circuit Court for Marion County which dismissed proceedings he had instituted to contest the will of his father, Charles Ernest Roblin, and which ordered that the will be admitted to probate.

Charles Ernest and Ollie M. Roblin, both now deceased, were the parents of the appellant, Charles Dana Roblin, and of a daughter, Ruth Emily Shantz, proponent and respondent. For convenience we will refer to the elder Charles Roblin as Mr. Roblin and to the younger as Charles.

The family resided for many years in Salem. When Ruth Married Carl Shantz they took their residence in Milwaukie, Oregon. Charles became a peripatetic, but during summer months returned to Salem for extended visits in the family home. In 1950 Mr. Roblin left the family home and made his abode in a Salem hotel. Ruth testified that he left in aggravation over his wife's conduct in sending money to Charles and paying his bills. In 1951 Mr. Roblin suffered a stroke and shortly repaired to a nursing home in Salem.

In the fall of 1951, Ruth, at her father's instance, arranged for him to undergo an eye operation in Portland. In that period he resided with Ruth and her husband for seven months. After he had recovered from the operation he returned to the nursing home where Ruth visited him every two weeks. Mrs. Roblin also called upon him from time to time, being driven to the nursing home in the Roblins' car by Charles. The latter, however, did not enter the home. Upon an earlier occasion when he attempted to visit his father, the latter ordered him out of the room in no unmistakable language.

Mrs. Roblin executed a will on July 3, 1953, and died five days later. Her will bequeathed all of her property equally to both children. Its terms were operative on property appraised at $1,581. But Charles received, in addition to his half of that sum, property worth $12,301.06 which was not part of the estate proper. This greater amount represented accounts and chattels the title to which was in Charles and the mother jointly, and to which he survived.

On either the evening of July 8 or the morning of July 9, 1953, Ruth visited her father in the nursing home and informed him, perhaps in response to his inquiry, that her mother had left everything to Charles except a diamond ring. Immediately Mr. Roblin ordered Ruth to obtain for him a lawyer. Ruth suggested a Mr. Steelhammer who was her husband's cousin. The suggestion was acceptable to her father, he having known Mr. Steelhammer through their mutual membership in the Salem Elks Lodge. On the morning of July 9 Mr. Steelhammer went to the nursing home and conversed in privacy with Mr. Roblin, who directed him to prepare a will, leaving Charles one dollar only and the remainder to Ruth. The father also requested Mr. Steelhammer to prepare a petition for a conservatorship of the father's property with Ruth as conservator. That afternoon, Ruth, upon Mr. Steelhammer's request, drove him to the nursing home. When they arrived, the attorney alone met with the testator, who then executed his will, with Steelhammer and the operator of the home as witnesses. The will nominated Ruth as executrix and left to her everything except one dollar which was bequeathed to Charles. The petition for conservatorship was filed on July 20. Mr. Roblin died September 6, 1953, aged 83.

* * *

The principal thrust of contestant's attack upon the will is that, according to him, Ruth's statement to her father that she received nothing from her mother but a ring while her brother took all, was knowingly false and fraudulent and that its effect was, as intended, to cause Mr. Roblin to give his entire estate to Ruth. Contestant submits that, though his father may have executed his will voluntarily, the execution resulted from a misunderstanding of fact intentionally created by a false statement made to him.

Courts set aside wills whose provisions reflect the testator's belief in false data arising from fraudulent misrepresentation made to him by a beneficiary.

> 'Fraud which causes testator to execute a will consists of statements which are false, which are known to be false by the party who makes them, which are material, which are made with the intention of deceiving testator, which deceive testator, and which cause testator to act in reliance upon such statements.'

Page on Wills, 3d Ed. 347, § 176. Absent any one of the elements of that definition of fraud, no ground for contest is established.

The statement which we are considering, and the consequences of its utterance, must be measured against the elements of fraud which vitiates a solemnly executed will.

The statement must be false and known to be such by the maker. In fact, Ruth's mother did not leave everything, except a ring, to her brother. Ruth was to receive half of $1,581; the other half of which went to Charles along with the $12,301.06 in jointly held property to which Charles survived. After the expenses of administration and taxes were paid by that estate, Ruth received $61.90. Charles received from his mother $12,367.96. The disparity is so great that Ruth may be excused for having been piqued, as is Charles now.

We must distinguish between a belief in the literal truth and falsity of a statement and that type of belief in falsity that underlies the fraudulent misrepresentation. Ruth testified at trial that 'The only thing one could say, or I did say, was that Mother had left everything to Charlie.' In this context a belief in the falsity of an utterance must be defined with regard to the nature of man and his reactions to an unexpected disappointment. The testimony just quoted demonstrates that at the time of utterance, and indeed at the time of trial, after reflection, Ruth doubted not that the hyperbole fairly described the division of her mother's estate.

The speaker must intend to deceive, and succeed. We are unwilling to decide that even a conscious exaggeration necessarily imports an intent to deceive. Even people of high character often exaggerate in order to express their belief with clarity and force. The purpose in instances of that kind is not to deceive, but better to communicate the belief. We are convinced that the statement made by Ruth is an example of that process. The speaker may in perfect good faith omit what he considers to be a non-material qualification upon his broad statement, thinking that a recital of all the details merely obfuscates the main point.

The misrepresentation must cause the testator to act upon it. In other words, the will must be the fruit of the fraud. In the Roblin family, little family unity or mutuality of attitude toward life bound father and son together. We know that the father emphatically expressed a desire that Charles stay away from the nursing home so that the two would not meet. Evidently, the wanderlust of the son was a canker to the parent. The learned trial judge would have been justified in a conclusion that the statement made by Ruth did not cause her father to rely upon it in the execution of his will, but rather that the statement merely provided an occasion for the taking of a step which the disappointed parent may have independently taken even if the statement had never been uttered.

The testimony of Ruth and of Charles conflicts in that she states, and he denies, that all her information about the division of their mother's estate came from him. If one believes her account, which the judge below may have done, her statement to her father cannot be objectionable. In that event, she merely relayed information which Charles gave her.

Both parties testified on direct and on cross-examination at some length about the amount of money each had received from Mr. and Mrs. Boblin inter vivos. We deem this evidence irrelevant. The statement of Ruth which is objected to refers only to the disposition of her mother's property upon her death. It does not relate to the inter vivos gifts to the children, of which Ruth received the greater share. Consequently the truth or falsity of the statement stands independent of the history of inter vivos donations.

Agreeing, as we do, with the disposition of this matter by the judge below, we affirm his decree.

Notes and Questions

1. As the heading to this section indicates, the intentional tort of fraud is also known as fraudulent misrepresentation, intentional misrepresentation, or just misrepresentation. As explained in Dan B. Dobbs, Paul T. Hayden, and Ellen M. Bublick, The Law of Torts, 2nd ed. (2011), at Chapter 52 sections 662, 663, and 664:

> Both the torts of intentional misrepresentation and negligent misrepresentation are derived from the old tort of *Deceit*, which covered pure economic harm caused by misrepresentations of fact made directly or indirectly to, and justifiably relied upon by the plaintiff. The misrepresentation normally must induce the plaintiff to enter into a transaction, or sometimes to avoid a transaction, as where it induces the plaintiff to retain shares of stock rather than sell them. The traditional tort of deceit required an intentional misrepresentation as well as certain other elements, but in a limited number of cases, the defendant is now under a duty of care so that negligent misrepresentation is sometimes actionable. Misrepresentations include those made in advertisements and other widely published material if they are likely to induce an economic transaction. They also include misrepresentations presented as friendly counsel by a fiduciary, although more commonly misrepresentations are made by an adversarial bargainer such as a seller. False communications, including misleading nondisclosures, are often referred to as fraud or deceit when the falsity is intentional.
>
> . . .
>
> The terms fraud, deceit, and misrepresentation are used as the name of the economic tort. However, these terms can also be used, not as a name for a cause of action but as a description of facts such as an actual event or the communication unrelated to economic transactions. In that descriptive sense, many misrepresentations are important in establishing legal liability for some tort, but not the tort of misrepresentation or fraud.
>
> . . .
>
> "The requirement of pecuniary damages might best be understood as a reference to the economic character of the tort claim for damages.

The Dobbs treatise is often an invaluable resource for law students and lawyers working to understand a doctrine or line of cases in additional depth.

2. The elements of this tort are also often described differently in different jurisdictions and treatises. For example, the relevant Restatement Second provision §525 "Liability for Fraudulent Misrepresentation" reads: "One who fraudulently makes a misrepresentation of fact, opinion, intention or law for the purpose of inducing another to act or to refrain from action in reliance upon it, is subject to liability to the other in deceit for pecuniary loss caused to him by his justifiable reliance upon the misrepresentation." Does the Restatement's version differ in substance from Oregon's? Can you standardize both according to the usual four-part intentional torts prima facie case, i.e., (1) act, (2) intent, (3) causation, (4) injury?

3. In fraud cases, intent to make a misrepresentation of fact can be proved when the false representation was made (a) knowingly, (b) with belief but not knowledge of its truth, or (c) recklessly. The first category typically includes intentionally misleading ambiguities. The second category includes situations in which a defendant asserts she knows something to be true when in fact she only believes it to be so. The third category includes cases where "the person is aware of, but consciously disregards, a substantial and unjustifiable risk of such a nature that its disregard constitutes a gross deviation from the standard of care that an ordinary person would exercise under all the circumstances." Davis v. McGuigan, 325 S.W.3d 149 (Tenn. 2010). If you need to revisit recklessness, see supra Part I(A)(2) (Intent).

4. As noted in Part I(A)(2) of this Chapter, the intent element of an intentional tort normally cannot be made out using recklessness; recklessness is typically considered to be a negligence-based tort and thus to be on the negligence side of the line between intent and negligence on the fault continuum. Why might fraud, like intentional infliction of emotional distress, be an exception to this rule?

5. Intent in this context is otherwise the same as it is in others, that is, it can be made out by showing that the defendant's purpose was to cause reliance or that they were nearly certain reliance would result.

6. The reasonableness of the plaintiff's reliance on another's representations sometimes depends on whether the person making the representations is a "fiduciary." A fiduciary is a person in a relationship with another, whose position requires them to be trustworthy and honest, and to act in good faith toward the other. For example, an attorney in an attorney-client relationship is the client's fiduciary; and the two are said to be in a fiduciary relationship. Others commonly deemed to be fiduciaries include guardians, trustees, administrators of estates, real estate agents, bankers, and stockbrokers.

7. Fraud can occur in the myriad settings where a relied-upon false statement can cause a financial loss. These settings include real estate and other sales transactions, securities offerings, contract formation, and the provision of professional services. In some cases, for example securities fraud, state or federal statutes may provide an additional or exclusive cause of action and remedy.

8. The *Roblin* case illustrates the claim's application in the context of a challenge to a last will and testament. This challenge arose in probate — a special court or court's jurisdiction that involves the processing of decedents' estates and guardianships. The word "probate" and many of the other terms of art in the case are from the area of the law known as Trusts and Estates. This law governs the treatment of many property transfers before and after death.

Problem Three: "Hydroxychloroquine Cures Covid"

Rather than presenting this problem in the usual narrative form, we present it as a complaint to give you a sense of what facts and claims look like in a pleading. Every jurisdiction has different requirements for pleadings. This one is based on North Carolina's rules and practices.

Your task is to analyze the complaint and the underlying case based on what you have learned about threshold issues affecting the viability of claims and the prima facie case for fraud.

Specifically, as it is written, do you have any concerns about the viability of the fraud claim based on those threshold issues or the plaintiff's ability to make out an element or elements of the prima facie case? We have not yet covered affirmative defenses, but simply using your intuition and experience, are there arguments the defendant might raise that could weaken the chances for a plaintiff's verdict?

STATE OF NORTH CAROLINA COUNTY OF DURHAM	IN THE GENERAL COURT OF JUSTICE SUPERIOR COURT DIVISION 22 CVS 1345
ELI CUMMINGS, Plaintiff, v. FLUSH LIMBURGER, III, Defendant.	**COMPLAINT** **(JURY TRIAL DEMANDED)**

Plaintiff, Eli Cummings, complaining of the Defendant alleges:

Parties and Jurisdiction

1. At all times relevant to this complaint, Eli Cummings was a citizen and resident of the City of Durham and County of Durham, North Carolina. He was married and had two children, ages 6 and 8.

2. At all times relevant to this complaint, Flush Limburger III ["Defendant Limburger" or "Defendant"], was a citizen and resident of the State of Florida.

3. This court has jurisdiction over Defendant Limburger under the North Carolina Long Arm Statute, G.S. § 1-75.4 (1)(a) because Defendant on his radio show broadcast in the City and County of Durham and State of North Carolina solicited a purchase made by Eli Cummings.

Facts

4. When Covid-19 came to North Carolina Eli Cummings and his family never contracted it, but he was greatly concerned that if he did and had to miss work, he would lose wages because he had used most of his sick leave for the year 2020 due to a knee he injured while out running in January 2020.

5. Defendant Limburger had a syndicated radio show carried by a station in Raleigh, North Carolina whose broadcast signal covered Durham, North Carolina.

6. Eli Cummings listened to Defendant's show and heard him extoll the virtues of various products available from companies who were advertisers on the show. Many products were over-the-counter drugs and supplements.

7. As the Covid-19 pandemic worsened, Eli Cummings had increased concerns about what would happen to his family if he got sick.

8. On or about April 11, 2020, when listening to Defendant Limburger, Eli Cummings heard him advertise for a company that could, without a prescription, ship consumers hydroxychloroquine.

9. Defendant Limburger said that hydroxychloroquine taken daily would greatly reduce or eliminate the chances of getting Covid-19.

10. Defendant Limburger said the company had a one-time, limited supply and there would not be more.

11. Defendant Limburger said the drug was so safe that people all over the world took it to prevent malaria and treat lupus without harmful side effects.

12. Defendant did not share with his radio audience that he did not take it himself because he was aware that a small percentage of those who did take it had potentially fatal heart arrythmias.

13. On or about April 15, 2020, Eli Cumming learned that a person he had been around had the virus and became panic-stricken about getting Covid. To hear the about hydroxychloroquine again, he made a point of listening to Defendant's radio broadcast that day.

14. While listening to Defendant, he heard the same things he heard every time he heard Defendant talk about hydroxychloroquine. In response he ordered a year's supply.

15. The hydroxychloroquine Eli Cummings ordered arrived in one or two days and Eli Cummings took it daily as Defendant has suggested.

16. After two weeks of taking hydroxychloroquine, Elijah suffered a near fatal bout of heart failure. He was in the intensive care unit for several days and his heart was permanently damaged. Though he survived and has now spent three years in intensive rehabilitation, he will be unable to work to support his family for the rest of his life.

17. Before taking hydroxychloroquine, Eli Cummings had no heart problems.

18. The heart failure Eli Cummings suffered was not due to an arrhythmia but rather to massive destruction of his red blood cells, a process called hemolysis. Testing revealed that he had glucose 6 phosphate dehydrogenase deficiency [G6PDD].

19. G6PDD is a genetic disorder that occurs almost exclusively in males. In the US it mostly affects men of African descent like Eli Cummings, about 10% of whom have it. In those who do, red blood cells carrying oxygen from the lungs to the body's tissues break down

prematurely when exposed to a variety of chemical compounds ranging from those in certain foods (fava beans, for example) to the components of many drugs (including common ones such as sulfa-containing antibiotics).

20. Quinine-based antimalarials such as hydroxychloroquine (and chloroquine) cause hemolysis in people with G6PDD.

First Cause of Action — Fraud

21. Plaintiff incorporates in this First Cause of Action for Fraud the previous paragraphs.

22. The Defendant falsely represented material facts including, but not limited to, the safety of hydroxychloroquine when taken to prevent contracting Covid-19.

23. The Defendant concealed material facts including, but not limited to, the heart health risks of taking hydroxychloroquine to prevent contracting Covid-19.

24. Each false representation and concealment by Defendant was reasonably calculated to deceive.

25. Each false representation and concealment by Defendant was made intending to deceive.

26. Eli Cummings was deceived by Defendant's false representations and concealments.

27. As a direct and proximate result of defendant's deceptions and concealments, Eli Cumming suffered heart failure, permanent disability, loss of income, pain and suffering, emotional distress and other injuries and losses.

Plaintiff demands a jury trial on all issues of fact.

WHEREFORE, Plaintiff, Eli Cummings. prays that he have of the Defendant, Flush Limburger, III, the following relief:

1. Compensatory damages as determined by the jury but in no event less than $25,000.00,
2. Punitive damages as determined by the jury;
3. Costs and interest as permitted by law; and
4. Such other and further relief as is just and proper.

This 2nd day of May, 2022.

Coleman & Beskind, P.A.

By: /s/ Donald H. Beskind
Donald H. Beskind
Bar No. 8138
210 Science Drive
Durham, NC 27708
(919) 613-7085

Problem Four: "In Pristine Condition"

Priya has a thing for 1962 Chevrolet Corvettes. As you can see, it's a gorgeous car. She's obsessed because she prefers classic cars and because, in high school, this was the car that she and her friends all said they would want when they grew up. For them, at that time and in that place, it was a symbol of having made it in life. That one could afford not only to buy but also to maintain such an iconic and sensitive vehicle this many years later would signal all of that and more. As Barry Kluczyk explains in the January 2020 issue of Muscle Machines,

> [d]espite their bowtie DNA, classic Corvettes are most assuredly not like other Chevys. Their unique architecture and advanced technologies separate them from their Chevelle and Camaro cousins in wonderful and confounding ways — often simultaneously.
>
> That's the dichotomy of buying and living with a vintage 'Vette: For all the familiarities of small-block and big-block engines and Muncie gearboxes, the fiberglass body structure and features such as hidden headlamps and independent rear suspension bring with them a whole new level of consideration, and demand unique skills for proper care and feeding.
>
> "Buying your first vintage Corvette brings with it a singular and special ownership experience," says Werner Meier, a 50-year Corvette professional who is a nationally respected judge, [and] collector, . . . "To get the most out of it, you've got to know exactly what you're getting into, as well as be prepared for maintenance and repair idiosyncrasies unlike other American vehicles — and even with the challenges, it will probably still hook you for the rest of your life."
>
> As a member of an active, dedicated Facebook group, Priya knew that she wasn't the only one in her high school class who was hooked and for whom this particular dream never died. Now, the '62 Corvette isn't only about having made it in the sense of having a good job that pays well enough to buy one, but also about having gotten to the place where such extraordinary luxuries are commonplace, and life can still be pure, unadulterated fun.

And so, when Priya saw an ad for this red one, above, she made the call. Deena answered. Deena explained that it had been her father's car; he had just died and she was the administrator of his estate; he had kept it in a climate-controlled garage basically since he purchased it new in 1962; and it was still in pristine condition inside and out — not only had he mostly driven a more basic car for his everyday transportation needs, but he had also treated it with kid gloves throughout the time he owned it. Deena offered to let Priya drive it and have it checked out by a specialist before she made a decision about purchasing.

Priya took Deena up on her offer to go for a test drive. Everything about the Corvette was exhilarating, from its appearance to the feel of the seats and steering wheel to the way it hugged the road. When Priya got back to Deena's, she told Deena that she would make an appointment to have the car checked out by experts, explaining that if all was as expected, she would make an offer. Priya then scheduled the appointment for the evaluation and appraisal.

Two days before the appointment, Deena notified Priya that Werner Meier — the well-known collector mentioned in the magazine article excerpt above — had just called with an offer to purchase the car sight unseen. Meier had apparently known Deena's father and the car. Deena told Priya that, in these circumstances, she would be selling to Meier unless Priya agreed to buy it that day at her asking price, i.e., at $79k. Priya, who had been unable to think of much else since she had driven the Corvette, decided to go for it. She posted her news on Facebook, of course!

That night, Priya paid Deena for the car. As she drove it out of Deena's driveway, she was struck by a drunk driver in a Lamborghini who wasn't watching the road. The Corvette was totaled in the crash. The driver was a wealthy man. In an effort to avoid the more complicated — for him — ramifications of the accident, he wrote Priya a check for the $79k she had paid Deena.

In the aftermath of the accident, Priya learned that the Corvette had not been worth $79k. Specifically, she learned that while this was a competitive price for a '62 Corvette that was actually in the pristine shape Deena had advertised, hers hadn't been in that kind of shape. Rather, its cosmetically perfect exterior had covered a "birdcage" that was rusted through and through. As Kluczyk explains in the same January 2020 issue of Muscle Machines,

> [t]he big irony with vintage Corvettes is the assumption that, because of their fiberglass bodies, rust isn't an issue, when it's actually the most important factor to consider. The two areas of concern are the frame and the "birdcage" structure that serves as the underlying framework to which the body is attached.
>
> Pervasive corrosion in the birdcage is the bigger problem," he says. "You want to run, not walk, away from a car with it, because the labor hours and consequential costs involved with tackling it are so high that you might as well throw away the car. For most people, and for all but a handful of the most valuable Corvette models, addressing birdcage rust makes no practical sense."

It turns out, Deena's father didn't keep the car in a climate-controlled garage until later in his life. He took care of it when he could, but mostly kept it looking good on the outside; and especially in the early years, he drove it a lot, including on salted roads in the winters. (Road salt is used to melt snow and ice which makes roads safer to drive on, but it's also a corrosive that causes rust.) Deena hadn't paid much attention to how her father used and maintained the car when she was growing up; she was focused mostly on the latter years, when her father really pampered the car. She later explained that this is where her mind was when she was selling it after her father's death.

Priya is angry about how the whole deal went down. The idea that Deena would get to keep the entire $79k makes her crazy. Although she's not a lawyer, the first thing that pops into her head is "fraud." Is her instinct correct? Put differently, how might this prima facie case be made out and what are its strengths and weaknesses? Are any of the weaknesses significant enough to cause a judge to grant a defendant's dispositive motion?

3. False Imprisonment

EILERS v. COY
582 F.Supp. 1093 (D. Minn. 1984)

MacLAUGHLIN, District Judge.

The plaintiff in this case, William Eilers, has moved the Court to enter a directed verdict against the defendants on his claims that the defendants falsely imprisoned him and violated his civil rights during a deprogramming attempt in 1982. Both sides have submitted briefs on the question and the Court has heard oral argument.

After careful consideration the Court has decided as follows:

1. Plaintiff's motion for a directed verdict on the issue of false imprisonment is granted and the Court holds, as a matter of law, that plaintiff William Eilers was falsely imprisoned without legal justification.

2. Plaintiff's motion for a directed verdict with respect to 42 U.S.C. § 1985(3) is granted as to certain elements of the plaintiff's claim that a conspiracy on the part of the defendants deprived him of certain of his federal constitutional rights.

FACTS

The evidence in this case has established the following facts. The plaintiff William Eilers and his pregnant wife Sandy were abducted from outside a clinic in Winona, Minnesota in the early afternoon of Monday, August 16, 1982, by their parents and relatives and by the defendant deprogrammers who had been hired by the parents of the plaintiff and his wife. The plaintiff was 24 years old at the time and his wife Sandy was 22. The couple was living on a farm near Galesville, Wisconsin and had traveled to Minnesota for Sandy's pre-natal examination.

At the time of the abduction, Bill and Sandy Eilers were members of the religious group Disciples of the Lord Jesus Christ. There is ample evidence that this group is an authoritarian religious fellowship directed with an iron hand by Brother Rama Behera. There is also evidence that Bill Eilers' personality, and to some extent his appearance, changed substantially after he became a member of the group. These changes were clearly of great concern to members of the plaintiff's family. However, other than as they may have affected the intent of the parents of Bill and Sandy Eilers in the actions they took in seizing Bill and Sandy, the beliefs and practices of the Disciples of the Lord Jesus Christ should not be, and are not, on trial in this case.

While leaving the Winona Clinic on August 16, 1982 the plaintiff, who was on crutches at the time due to an earlier fall, was grabbed from behind by two or more security men, forced into a waiting van, and driven to the Tau Center in Winona, Minnesota. Forcibly resisting, he was carried by four men to a room on the top floor of the dormitory-style building. The windows of this room were boarded over with plywood, as were the windows in his bathroom and in the hallway of the floor. The telephone in the hallway had been dismantled.

The plaintiff was held at the Tau Center for five and one-half days and subjected to the defendants' attempts to deprogram him. Shortly after his arrival at the Tau Center, and after a violent struggle with his captors, the plaintiff was handcuffed to a bed. He remained handcuffed to the bed for at least the first two days of his confinement. During this initial period, he was allowed out of the room only to use the bathroom, and was heavily guarded during those times. On one occasion, the plaintiff dashed down the hall in an attempt to escape, but was forcibly restrained and taken back to the room. After several days of resistance, the plaintiff changed tactics and apparently pretended to consent to his confinement.

The defendants and the plaintiff's relatives had agreed in advance of the abduction that the plaintiff would be kept at the Tau Center for one week, regardless of whether the plaintiff consented to their actions. At no time during the week was the plaintiff free to leave the Tau Center, nor at any time were reasonable means of escape available to him. Three of the eight people hired by the parents were designated "security men." These individuals, described by witnesses as at least six feet tall and weighing over 200 pounds, guarded the exits on the floor at all times.

On the evening of Saturday, August 21, 1982, as the plaintiff was leaving the Tau Center to be transported to Iowa City, Iowa for further deprogramming, he took advantage of his first opportunity to escape and jumped from the car in which he was riding. Local residents, attracted by the plaintiff's calls for help, assisted the plaintiff in making his escape and the police were summoned.[2]

The evidence has also shown that within three weeks before the abduction occurred, the plaintiff's relatives had contacted authorities in Trempealeau County, Wisconsin in an attempt to have the plaintiff civilly committed. Family members have testified that they believed the plaintiff was suicidal because of a letter he had written to his grandmother before joining the Disciples of the Lord Jesus Christ in which he wrote that demons were attacking his mind and telling him to kill himself rather than go to the Lord. Defendants' Exhibit A at 13–14. Joyce Peterson, a psychiatric social worker, interviewed the plaintiff in person on July 26, 1982. After interviewing the plaintiff and consulting with the Trempealeau County Attorney, Peterson informed the plaintiff's relatives that no legal grounds existed in Wisconsin for confining the plaintiff because he showed no signs of being a danger to himself or to others. The defendants in this case were aware of that information at the time they abducted and held the plaintiff.

DISCUSSION

In considering the plaintiff's motion for a directed verdict, the Court is required to view the evidence in the light most favorable to the defendants and to resolve all conflicts in the evidence in the defendants' favor. *Dace v. ACF Industries, Inc.,* 722 F.2d 374, 375 (8th Cir.1983). A directed verdict motion should be granted only when reasonable jurors could not differ as to the conclusions to be drawn from the evidence. *Id.*

[2] The plaintiff's wife Sandy stayed with the deprogrammers and has not returned to the group Disciples of the Lord Jesus Christ of which the plaintiff is still a member. She has since divorced the plaintiff and has sole custody of the couple's infant son.

The plaintiff has alleged two main causes of action against the defendants: false imprisonment and conspiracy to deprive the plaintiff of his constitutional rights in violation of 42 U.S.C. § 1985(3). These claims will be discussed separately.

A. False Imprisonment

The plaintiff's first claim is that the defendants' conduct in confining him at the Tau Center constituted false imprisonment for which the defendants had no legal justification. False imprisonment consists of three elements:

1) words or acts intended to confine a person;

2) actual confinement; and

3) awareness by the person that he or she is confined.

Blaz v. Molin Concrete Products Co., 309 Minn. 382, 385, 244 N.W.2d 277, 279 (1976); Restatement (Second) of Torts § 35 (1965).

The evidence in this case has overwhelmingly established each of the elements of false imprisonment. By their own admission, the defendants intended to confine the plaintiff for at least one week. While the defendants maintain that their purpose was to help the plaintiff, it is not a defense to false imprisonment that the defendants may have acted with good motives. Malice toward the person confined is not an element of false imprisonment. *Strong v. City of Milwaukee,* 38 Wis.2d 564, 567, 157 N.W.2d 619, 621 (1968); *Witte v. Haben,* 131 Minn. 71, 74, 154 N.W. 662, 663 (1915); W. Prosser, *Law of Torts* 48 (4th ed. 1971).

There is also no question that the plaintiff was actually confined. Relying on the Minnesota Supreme Court's decision in *Peterson v. Sorlien,* 299 N.W.2d 123, 129 (Minn.1980), *cert. denied,* 450 U.S. 1031, 101 S.Ct. 1742, 68 L.Ed.2d 227 (1981), the defendants contend that there was no actual confinement because there is evidence that the plaintiff consented to the defendants' actions, at least by the fourth day of his confinement. The plaintiff, in contrast, has testified that he merely pretended to consent in order to gain an opportunity to escape. The plaintiff's apparent consent is not a defense to false imprisonment. Many people would feign consent under similar circumstances, whether out of fear of their captors or as a means of making an escape. But in this case, unlike the *Peterson* case relied on by the defendants, it is undisputed that the plaintiff was at no time free to leave the Tau Center during the week in question, nor were any reasonable means of escape available to him. Under these circumstances, the Court finds, in agreement with many other authorities, that the plaintiff's apparent consent is not a defense to false imprisonment. 32 Am.Jur.2d False Imprisonment § 15 (1982); Restatement (Second) of Torts § 36 (1965). The Court therefore holds, as a matter of law, that the plaintiff has proven the necessary elements of false imprisonment.

The next question is, given that the defendants falsely imprisoned the plaintiff, were their actions legally justified so as to preclude liability for false imprisonment? As justification for their actions, the defendants rely on the defense of necessity. They claim that the confinement and attempted deprogramming of the plaintiff was necessary to prevent him from committing suicide or from otherwise harming himself or others. *See State v. Hembd,* 305 Minn. 120, 130, 232 N.W.2d 872, 878 (1975).

The defense of necessity has three elements. The first element is that the defendants must have acted under the reasonable belief that there was a danger of imminent physical injury to the plaintiff or to others.

It is not clear that such a danger existed on August 16, 1982. The alleged threats of suicide made by the plaintiff were contained in a letter dated June 14, 1982, and that letter recounted impressions the plaintiff had had some time earlier. Moreover, Joyce Peterson, the psychiatric social worker who personally interviewed the plaintiff on July 26, 1982, concluded in her report, and reported to the plaintiff's relatives, that the plaintiff was not dangerous to himself or to others. Nevertheless, viewing the evidence in the light most favorable to the defendants, the Court will assume for purposes of this motion that the plaintiff was in imminent danger of causing physical injury to himself or to others.

The second and third elements of the necessity defense are intertwined. The second element is that the right to confine a person in order to prevent harm to that person lasts only as long as is necessary to get the person to the proper lawful authorities. The third element is that the actor must use the least restrictive means of preventing the apprehended harm.

In this case, the defendants' conduct wholly fails to satisfy either of these elements of the necessity defense. Once having gained control of the plaintiff, the defendants had several legal options available to them. They could have:

1) turned the plaintiff over to the police;

2) sought to initiate civil commitment proceedings against the plaintiff;

3) sought professional psychiatric or psychological help for the plaintiff with the possibility of emergency hospitalization if necessary.

At no time did the defendants attempt, or even consider attempting, any of these lawful alternatives during the five and one-half days they held the plaintiff, the first five of which were business days. Instead, they took the plaintiff to a secluded location with boarded-up windows, held him incommunicado, and proceeded to inflict their own crude methods of "therapy" upon him — methods which even the defendants' own expert witness has condemned. Well aware that the police were searching for the plaintiff, the defendants deliberately concealed the plaintiff's location from the police.

It must be emphasized that the Minnesota Legislature has prescribed specific procedures that must be followed before a person can be deprived of his or her liberty on the basis of mental illness. Those procedures include examination of the proposed patient by qualified professionals, and a judicial determination that the proposed patient is dangerous and in need of treatment. Manifold procedural protections, including the right to counsel, are afforded the proposed patient at all stages of this civil commitment proceeding. Obviously, none of these protections were afforded the plaintiff in this case.

Minnesota law also provides that, in situations where there is not time to obtain a court order, a person may be admitted or held for emergency care and treatment in a hospital, without a court order, upon a written statement by a licensed physician or psychologist that the person is mentally ill and is in imminent danger of causing injury to himself or to others. The defendants in this case — unlicensed and untrained individuals — made no effort to obtain any such statement from a licensed physician or psychologist.

The defendants' failure to even attempt to use the lawful alternatives available to them is fatal to their assertion of the necessity defense. Where the Legislature has prescribed specific procedures that must be followed before a person can be deprived of his or her liberty on the ground of mental illness, not even parents or their agents acting under the best of motives are entitled to disregard those procedures entirely.

The Court has assumed for the purposes of this motion that the defendants were justified in initially restraining the plaintiff based upon their belief that he was in imminent danger of harming himself or others. But even under those circumstances, the defense of necessity eventually dissipates as a matter of law. No specific time limit can be set, because the period during which an actor is acting out of necessity will vary depending on the circumstances of each case. In this particular case, however, where the defendants held the plaintiff, a 24-year-old adult, for five and one-half days with no attempt to resort to lawful alternatives available to them, the Court could not sustain a jury verdict in the defendants' favor on the issue of false imprisonment. Accordingly, the Court rules as a matter of law that the plaintiff was falsely imprisoned without justification. The issue of what amount of damages, if any, the plaintiff suffered from this false imprisonment is a question for the jury.

B. Section 1985(3)

The next claim upon which the plaintiff has moved for a directed verdict is that the defendants conspired to and did deprive him of his federal constitutional rights in violation of 42 U.S.C. § 1985(3). The Court will direct a verdict as to some, but not all, of the elements of this claim.

A cause of action under section 1985(3) consists of the following elements:

1) a conspiracy;

2) for the purpose of depriving any person or class of persons of the equal protection of the laws or of equal privileges and immunities under the laws;

3) an act or acts in furtherance of the conspiracy; and

4) an injury to the person or property of a citizen or a deprivation of the rights and privileges of any citizen.

Three of these elements are clearly present in this case. By their own admission, the defendants planned and conspired to abduct the plaintiff and to hold him against his will. They committed several acts in furtherance of this conspiracy including seizing the plaintiff at the Winona Clinic, transporting him to the Tau Center, and holding him there against his will for five and one-half days. These actions were in clear violation of the plaintiff's constitutional rights, including his right not to be deprived of liberty without due process of law, and his right to freedom of interstate travel.[8] The Court holds as a matter of law that the plaintiff has established the first, third, and fourth elements of his section 1985(3) cause of action.

The remaining element is that the conspiracy be for the purpose of depriving the plaintiff of the equal protection of the laws. The United States Supreme Court has interpreted this element as requiring that the defendants' conduct be motivated by class-based, invidiously discriminatory animus. In other words, in order for the plaintiff to recover under section 1985(3), the defendants must have taken action against him because of his membership in a group or class that is protected by that statute. The Court has previously ruled in this case that the religious group Disciples of the Lord Jesus Christ is a group protected by the statute. The remaining question is whether the defendants took action against the plaintiff because of an animus toward that group or, as the defendants contend, because of a concern for the welfare of the plaintiff. The Court finds that the defendants' motivation is an issue upon which reasonable jurors could differ. The Court therefore denies the plaintiff's motion for a directed verdict on this element of the plaintiff's section 1985(3) cause of action.

C. Conclusion

This will not be a popular decision. While the Court has substantial sympathy for the feelings and reactions of the parents of Bill and Sandy Eilers, this Court is sworn to uphold the law and the Constitution of the United States. If the basic rights of an American citizen are not recognized in a federal court by a federal judge, where will they be recognized?

Based on the foregoing, IT IS ORDERED that the plaintiff's motion for a directed verdict is granted as to his claim for false imprisonment (Count IV of the Second Amended Complaint), and as to certain elements of his 42 U.S.C. § 1985(3) claim (Count I of the Second Amended Complaint) described herein. The plaintiff's motion is in all other respects denied.

Notes and Questions

1. The action for false imprisonment "protects the personal interest in freedom from restraint of movement." *Broughton v. State*, 37 N.Y.2d 451, 457 (1975). As a result, the tort is made out when a defendant "confines one intentionally without lawful privilege and against his consent within a limited area *for any appreciable time, however short*." *Feliciano v. Kreiger*, 362 N.E.2d 646 (Ohio 1977) (quoting 1 Harper & James, The Law of Torts (1956) 226, § 3.7) (emphasis added).

2. A defendant may be liable for actions that indirectly result in confinement. Thus, for example, a company that rents a vehicle to a plaintiff then reports the vehicle as stolen to the police, knowing the truth to be otherwise, may be liable to the plaintiff if he or she is

---

[8] The Court does not decide whether the defendants' actions deprived the plaintiff of his first amendment right to freedom of religion as that question is intimately tied up with the question of the defendants' motivation. As discussed below, the defendants' motivation is a question for the jury. In any event, absent state action or state involvement, a deprivation of first amendment rights is not actionable under section 1985(3). *United Bhd. of Carpenters and Joiners, Local 610 v. Scott,* 463 U.S. 825, 103 S.Ct. 3352, 3357, 77 L.Ed.2d 1049 (1983).

subsequently detained by the police as a result. *See Braumon v. U-Haul, Inc.*, 945 S.W.2d 676, 680–81 (Mo. Ct. App. 1997).

3. Although consent and privilege are possible defenses for all intentional torts, they are so ubiquitous in this context that many states require the plaintiff to show a lack of consent or the absence of a lawful privilege as additional elements of the claim.

4. The defendant's subjective belief in the lawfulness of the confinement is irrelevant. Rather, whether confinement is lawful depends on the status of the defendant at the time of the confinement. If the defendant is a merchant who suspected the plaintiff of shoplifting, or a law enforcement officer who suspected the plaintiff of having committed a crime, the lawfulness of the confinement turns on its reasonableness. *See e.g., Niskanen v. Giant Eagle, Inc.*, 912 N.E.2d 595, 601 (Ohio 2009) ("a merchant with probable cause to suspect shoplifting may detain the suspect in a reasonable manner and for a reasonable length of time."); *Serpico v. Menard, Inc.*, 927 F.Supp. 276, 281 (N.D.Ill. 1996) ("defendant had to have reasonable grounds to believe that plaintiff committed retail theft and could only detain plaintiff a reasonable amount of time to make that determination"); *Bennett v. Ohio Dept. of Rehab. & Corr.*, 60 Ohio St.3d 107 (1991) (false imprisonment will lie where an inmate was imprisoned beyond the expiration of his sentence); *Coblyn v. Kennedy's, Inc.* 359 Mass. 319, 323 (1971) ("there were no reasonable grounds for believing that the plaintiff was committing larceny and, therefore, he should not have been detained. . ."); *Sturgeon v. Holtan*, 486 S.W.2d 209, 211 (Mo. 1972) (pleadings were sufficient to state a claim for false imprisonment where police officer restrained plaintiff on a sidewalk and took him to the station without filing any charges).

5. As footnote 8 of the court's opinion in *Eilers* suggests, claims for violations of a plaintiff's constitutional rights are only viable if the defendant is a state actor or was acting on behalf of the state in some respect. Could the plaintiff in *Eilers* meet this threshold requirement?

II. THE AFFIRMATIVE DEFENSES

Once the plaintiff has made out his or her prima facie case, the defendant has one of two non-exclusive options: she can rebut one or more of its elements, and/or she can mount an affirmative defense. For example, a defendant responding to a battery claim can argue that there was no battery, but that, even if there was the plaintiff consented to it. The plaintiff bears the burden of proof on the prima facie case; rebuttals by the defendant go to weakening that case and making it less likely that the burden will be met. On the affirmative defense of consent the burden of proof is on the defendant; rebuttals by the plaintiff similarly weaken that case. The following material covers the principal affirmative defenses applicable to intentional torts claims: consent, self-defense, and necessity.

A. Consent

HELLRIEGEL v. THOLL
417 P.2d 362 (Wash. 1966)

Donworth, Judge.

This is an appeal by a plaintiff from the dismissal of his complaint at the end of the plaintiff's evidence. Wolf-Jurgen Hellriegel, plaintiff's teen-age son, was seriously injured when three of his friends tried to throw him into Lake Washington during an afternoon spent in water-skiing, sunbathing, and engaging in horseplay. The defendants in the suit are these three teen-age friends of plaintiff's son. Plaintiff sued in his own behalf for recovery of the cost of the medical care for his son, and sued in his son's behalf for the loss of income and for the temporary total disability and the alleged permanent partial disability, as well as for general damages for the alleged negligence and recklessness by which his son was harmed. Before trial, the complaint was amended by changing the grounds of the liability from negligence and recklessness to that of battery.

The only issue on this appeal is the issue decided by the trial court in the granting of the nonsuit — did the plaintiff present sufficient evidence to take the question of liability of any of the three defendants to the jury?

We need not review in detail all the evidence in the case. The rule which the trial court must apply in passing on a motion for a nonsuit is stated in *Parrish v. Ash*, 32 Wash.2d 637, 648, 203 P.2d 330, 337 (1949). It reads:

> A challenge to the sufficiency of the evidence, motion for nonsuit, a motion for a directed verdict, or a motion for judgment notwithstanding the verdict admits the truth of the opposing party's evidence and all inferences that reasonably can be drawn therefrom and requires that the evidence be interpreted most strongly against the moving party and in the light most favorable to the party against whom the motion is made.

There has been considerable reliance by respondents (both in the trial motion and on appeal) on the testimony of several witnesses other than appellant's son. We believe that, except to the extent that appellant's son admitted that such testimony was accurate, he is not bound by it for the purposes of the motion for nonsuit. Appellant's son testified extensively under direct and cross-examination concerning the circumstances leading up to and culminating in his injury. We need only consider his own testimony in order to determine the issue presented on this appeal, because he testified at length .... What the other witnesses stated, in so far as their testimony was not corroborated by appellant's son, need not be considered in passing on the motion for nonsuit. *Parrish v. Ash*, supra.

Certain background against which to consider the sufficiency of appellant's evidence should be stated. On the afternoon of July 26, 1963, appellant's son, Wolf-Jurgen Hellriegel (called Dicka by his friends), a 15- or 16-year-old high school student, joined a group of friends and fellow students at the Mount Baker Beach, on Lake Washington, for an afternoon of water-skiing.

Although there may have been other teenagers coming and going and for a time sunbathing and mingling with them, the group consisted primarily of the 6 witnesses whose testimony was presented to the trial court and is considered by this court on appeal. They were appellant's son, Miss Nina Trippy, Miss Darci Johnson, and the 3 minor respondents John Tholl, Gregory Haverfield, and Michael Dorris. Although these witnesses recall the general setting and the incident with varying details and with varying degrees of clarity about what happened, there appears to be no dispute that, in general, the circumstances leading up to the injury of minor appellant Hellriegel occurred approximately as young Hellriegel himself described it.

[Editors' note: The following is exerpted from Hellriegel's direct examination.]

> I had just come home from the YMCA after two hours of the workout, and, well, I felt like water skiing; my brother did too. And we decided we would go. And my brother phoned Dick Bila and picked up Darci and Nina. We brought them down to our house, which is on the lake, and we were laying on our beach waiting for Dick Bila to come by, when Mike Dorris came by. [A]bout the same time Dick Bila arrived with his boat, and we rode in the boats over to the Mount Baker Beach and we started water skiing, taking turns, and taking turns driving the boat and skiing and watching the skier.
>
> After skiing it was, oh, I'd say, 3:00 o'clock, 3:30. We went up onto the beach, and, well, we sat around quite close. And somebody started throwing a pillow-I don't know who it was-it was Nina's pillow. And we threw it around, and after a while it got so far out of reach-we were kind of lazy at the time-and we just-I don't think we bothered about it and started throwing grass, and I guess after we tired of throwing grass we got around-talk got around to throwing people into the lake. And after a while of talking like this — I don't know — somebody must have said they could throw me in, or something to this effect, and I stated, 'Oh, you couldn't throw me in even if you tried.' And with that the three boys, Mike, Greg and John, jumped up and, well, tried to throw me into the water. I struggled for a while and I ended up in a sitting position parallel to the lake, facing, my head facing north, and Mike was behind me. Again, I was in a sitting position and John and Greg had my legs up in the air.
>
> I was trying to get them off, and I had my hands reaching toward my legs when Mike, trying to reach my hands, must have slipped or lost his balance, and he fell on the back of my head and pushed it forward. I heard two cracks like somebody snapping his knuckles, and right after that I lost all control, I couldn't move my legs, and it was kind of a numb sensation all over.
>
> I yelled out, I knew what had happened. I yelled out, 'Please, let me down, I am paralyzed.'

[Editors' note: The following is our summary of the main points from Hellreigel's cross-examination. The complete Q and A is in the unexerpted version of the case online.]

- The pillow throwing lasted two or three minutes and no one was angry at anybody. It was all in the spirit of fun.

- Somebody said they could throw Hellreigel in the lake and he said they wouldn't be able to do it. And then they basically "jumped" him.

- Greg and John were towards Hellreigel's feet and he was looking towards his feet, with his head more or less ducked as he was trying to free their hands from his legs.

- He was in a sort of sitting position, squirming around.

- During the struggle, Mike apparently lost his balance and slipped and fell against Hellreigel's head. That's when Hellreigel heard a snap and felt it.

- Right after the snap, Hellreigel yelled to the boys to let him down.

- At the time this happened, Hellreigel was strong and husky.

Appellant has assigned error solely to the trial court's determination that there was not sufficient evidence of a battery to establish a prima facie case of liability against respondents. Appellant acknowledges that the basis for the trial court's ruling is shown in the colloquy between counsel and the court just prior to the granting of respondents' motion. The record shows that the trial court ruled that respondents were not liable because:

> (1) The actions of respondents in trying to throw appellant's son into the lake were not such as to constitute an offensive touching of his person.
>
> (2) The actions of respondents were consented to by appellant's son by his participation in the 'horseplay' and his statement to the effect that all three of the boys could not throw him into the lake.

If the trial court is correct on either point, its judgment must be affirmed.

We shall first discuss the issue of consent before considering the issue of offensive touching.

It is agreed by all parties to the suit that consent is a defense to battery, except for some exceptions (not presently applicable) when consent cannot be given. The points on which the parties differ is whether the words and actions of Dicka amounted to consent to engage in the horseplay, and whether this consent was broad enough to encompass the events which caused his injury.

First, with regard to the significance of Dicka's words and actions, we agree with the trial court that his words were an invitation to respondents to try to throw him into the water if they thought they could. His statement to them (quoted above) constituted a consent that the boys could try to throw him into the lake (as distinguished from a consent to being thrown into the lake) and he thereby assumed the risk that he might be accidentally injured during the horseplay that necessarily would result from their attempt to throw him into the lake and his resistance to such attempt. Even if what he said was in response to someone's statement to the effect 'Let's throw Dicka into the lake,' his words were an invitation to try, as distinguished from a warning to the other boys not to try to throw him in because he did not want to be thrown in and would resist.

The setting in which these words were spoken is the key to their meaning. The boys had been throwing a pillow around, apparently at each other, rather like a ball. They also threw grass when the pillow was thrown out of reach. They were all good friends. No one was angry, nor had anyone tried to withdraw from the horseplay. It was in good-natured fun.

If there had been the slightest indication that Dicka had not wanted to participate in this horseplay but had engaged in it only to the extent necessary to protect himself, then appellant's position might be plausible. However, we have Dicka's own statement that he had joined in the pillow throwing and the grass throwing. Dicka also stated that he and the boy who fell on him, Mike Dorris, were used to wrestling together prior to this accident. Dicka was very athletic and this activity was regarded by all of the boys as 'fun.' Under the circumstances shown by the evidence, it would be a strained and unreasonable interpretation of Dicka's statement to the boys to construe it as a warning not to try to throw him into the lake, because he did not want to be thrown in, even in fun, and that he would resist such an attempt.

Appellant's counsel argues in his brief that, even if Dicka gave any consent, it was consent to being thrown into the lake, and not a consent to have his neck broken, i.e., that the scope of the consent did not include this battery. Of course, Dicka did not consent to having his neck broken. As we pointed out above, Dicka did not even consent to being thrown into the lake-he consented only to having his three friends try to throw him into the lake, while he resisted their attempt. In other words, he consented to rough and tumble horseplay.

Appellant's counsel argues in connection with this issue that Restatement, Torts § 53, and Comment a clearly show that the particular invasion was not consented to by Dicka. That section reads:

> To constitute a consent, the assent must be to the invasion itself and not merely to the act which causes it.

The two comments that follow this section state . . .

> A. If the act to which assent is given is such that a reasonable man would recognize that a particular invasion is substantially certain to result from it, an assent to the act is tantamount to an assent to the invasion, and, therefore, is as effective as a consent thereto.
>
> B. If two persons engage in a boxing match, neither of them assents to receiving any particular blow, since each hopes to avoid his adversary's blows by dodging, sidestepping or blocking. However, he does sufficiently express a willingness that the other shall try to hit him, and the expression of such willingness is a sufficient assent to those blows which he is unable to avoid, since while he may avoid some blows, he is substantially certain to receive others.

Appellant argues (1) that the invasion to which this section refers in the present case is the breaking of Dicka's neck, and (2) that the breaking of his neck was not substantially certain to result from being thrown into the lake, and that, therefore, he did not consent to this invasion. We do not agree with appellant's understanding of what the term 'invasion' means as used in § 53 of the restatement. Comment b of that section shows that the 'invasion' refers to the intentional acts, such as blows received in a boxing match, and not the injuries which may result from accidents such as accidental slipping, as in the case at bar.

The invasion consented to in this instance, as we stated earlier, was rough and tumble horseplay. The question which § 53 of the restatement does not answer is, who takes the risk of injury which may accidentally result from such rough and tumble play? It seems to us that rough and tumble play is like an informal boxing match, which is described in Comment b above. The boxer accepts the risk of serious injuries from the blows received. Persons who engage in roughhouse horseplay also accept the risk of accidental injuries which result from participation therein.

It should be clear from the foregoing discussion that, when we apply the test (stated earlier in this opinion) of taking all of appellant's favorable evidence as true, and drawing all the favorable inferences therefrom, the only conclusion that can reasonably be drawn is that Dicka consented to the rough and tumble play. Therefore, there is no jury question on the issue of consent.

The second question is whether there was evidence of any intentional act which could be called 'offensive contact' committed by respondents beyond the limits of that consent? The record is completely barren of any such evidence. The contact (when Mike Dorris slipped and fell onto Dicka) which actually broke Dicka's neck was accidental. All other contact was a part of the rough and tumble play.

Therefore, we must affirm the trial court.

Appellant has argued that the trial court erred in holding that there was no evidence of offensive contact in this case. We have read the colloquy between court and counsel on this issue. As we understand the record, the trial court was simply saying that, if the contact was within the consent, it could not be 'offensive.' Nothing would be gained by our discussing the separate legal analysis of the concept of 'offensive contact' as that term is defined by Restatement, Torts §19, and as that term is used in Restatement, Torts §13. It is sufficient to say (so that our opinion will not be misunderstood) that, in the absence of consent, the other facts in this case might present a jury question on the issue of 'offensive contact.' Since consent was admitted in Dicka's testimony, we are not called upon to decide that question.

For the reasons given above, we agree with the trial court that appellant's evidence was not sufficient to require the case to be submitted to the jury. Therefore, we affirm the trial court's judgment of dismissal.

Notes and Questions

1. Wolf-Jurgen Hellriegel (Dicka) apparently recovered from his injuries. He is a licensed lawyer in Washington state.

2. Depending on the jurisdiction, consent is either part of the plaintiff's prima facie case or an affirmative defense. As we saw in the notes following White v. Muniz, the authors of the Third Restatement have suggested that the burden may be on the plaintiff seeking to recover in battery to prove that she did not consent to the touching at issue; the effect of this rule choice is to add this as a fifth element to the plaintiff's prima facie case. Or, the burden may be on the defendant to prove that the touching was done with the plaintiff's consent. How is this distinction meaningful both conceptually and practically? We present consent as an affirmative defense here because this is the rule in most jurisdictions, and also because the issue is usually joined by the defendant regardless.

3. Otherwise, the rules defining lawful consent are the basically same across the jurisdictions. What do you learn about these rules from the *Hellriegel* case? Would the result in the case have been different if, after the boys had begun wrestling but before the plaintiff was injured, the plaintiff had yelled out in a serious tone, "Put me down! I don't want to play anymore!"? What additional rules can you derive from your analysis of this question?

4. In addition to "express" and "implied" consent, the law also distinguishes between "actual" and "apparent" consent, and provides that apparent consent is legally effective consent. Why might the law provide that apparent consent trumps actual consent in cases where the two diverge? What does this rule require of plaintiffs? Of defendants? As you think through these questions, consider this discussion from Gerber v. Veltri, 203 F. Supp. 3d 846, 852–53 (N.D. Ohio 2016), aff'd, 702 F. App'x 423 (6th Cir. 2017). One of the issues in *Gerber* was whether the jurisdiction follows the single or the dual intent rule for battery:

> The *Restatement (Third)* . . . includes an illustration that closely mirrors [the defendant's] explanation.
>
> Illustration 11 describes the following scenario: "Ellen taps Roberta on the shoulder in a movie theater, asking Roberta to turn off her cell phone. The tap aggravates a preexisting shoulder injury, causing Roberta bodily harm. Ellen is not subject to liability to Roberta for battery." *Restatement (Third)* § 101 cmt. f. The *Restatement* further explains:
>
> In this case, Ellen satisfies single intent (because she intends to contact Roberta), but does not satisfy dual intent (because she does not intend to cause harm or offense).
>
> Nevertheless, the choice of rule [single versus dual intent] is immaterial, because apparent consent precludes liability [either way]: it is reasonable for Ellen to believe that Roberta does not object to the ordinary, minor physical contact of a tap on the shoulder to get her attention. The doctrine of apparent consent significantly limits an actor's potential liability for battery. It applies, of course, even in cases where the plaintiff does not actually consent to the contact intended by the actor.

5. For consent to be effective, it "must be given (a) by one who has the capacity to consent or by a person empowered to consent for him, and (b) to the particular conduct, or to substantially the same conduct." Restatement (Second) of Torts § 892A (1979). States across the country have enacted statutes providing that certain categories of individuals—for example, underage

children, individuals with relevant intellectual disabilities, and employees with respect to violations of workplace safety regulations — lack the capacity to consent as a matter of law. See also Robins v. Harris, 740 N.E.2d 914 (Ind. App. 2000) (holding that female inmates who engaged in sexual contact with prison guard were legally incapable of consenting to such contact because of the dependent custodial relationship; on the facts, the inmates approached the guard and offered the contact in exchange for other favors). In the absence of such law, the issue whether the plaintiff had the capacity to consent for the trier of fact to establish.

6. Related to the effectiveness of the consent is the requirement that any consent given be both knowing and voluntary. Litigation about whether the plaintiff consented knowingly generally turns on the argument that the consent was "procured by fraud or concealment." Hogan v. Tavzel, 660 So.2d 350, 352, n. 3 (Fla. App. 1995) (sexual battery claim is viable where husband and wife had consensual sex but husband concealed the fact that he had a sexually transmitted disease). Litigation about whether the plaintiff consented voluntarily generally turns on the argument that the consent was procured under undue pressure or duress. Here, with some exceptions, judges are quite strict, finding sufficient evidence of duress when physical violence but not economic harm is threatened. See, e.g., Lucas v. Redig, Not Officially Published, Available at 2004 WL 1700517 (Cal. App. 2004) (over objections from the dissent, court rejects as insufficient evidence of duress testimony from plaintiff that he agreed to sex acts with this supervisor because he was afraid of losing his job if he refused); Reavis v. Slominski, 551 N.W.2d 528 (Neb. 1996) (same).

7. Review your notes on Cohen v. St. Joseph Memorial Hospital, Inc. In addition to the issue of offensiveness in battery, the case also features the consent issue as it arises in the medical context.

B. Self-Defense

LANE v. HOLLOWAY
1 Q.B. 379 (1968)

. . .

APPEAL from Dorchester County Court.

LORD DENNING M.R.

On July 21, 1966, the peace of the ancient borough of Dorchester was disturbed. Mr. Lane, the plaintiff, was a retired gardener aged 64. He was living in a quiet court just off High East Street. Backing onto that court there was a café which was run by a young man, Mr. Holloway, the defendant, aged 23. The people in the court did not like the sound of a juke-box from the café. They also objected because the customers relieved themselves at night in the courtyard. To meet their objection Mr. Holloway began to build some lavatories. But relations were strained. On July 21, 1966, at about 11 o'clock at night Mr. Lane, the 64-year-old, came back from the public-house. He stopped outside his door and started talking to his neighbour, Mrs. Brake. Mr. Holloway was in bed drinking a cup of coffee. His wife, hearing Mr. Lane and Mrs. Brake talking, called out to them: "You bloody lot." Mr. Lane replied: "Shut up, you monkey-faced tart." Mr. Holloway sprang up and said: "What did you say to my wife?" He said it twice. Mr. Lane said: "I want to see you on your own," implying a challenge to fight. Whereupon Mr. Holloway came out in his pyjamas and dressing-gown. He walked up the courtyard to the place where Mr. Lane was standing at his door. He moved up close to Mr. Lane in a manner which made Mr. Lane think that he might himself be struck by Mr. Holloway. Whereupon Mr. Lane threw a punch at Mr. Holloway's shoulder. Then Mr. Holloway drew his right hand out of his pocket and punched Mr. Lane in the eye, a very severe blow. Mr. Holloway said: "You hit me first." Mr. Lane said: "If I had two good pins you would not have done this. I shall make a case of it." Mr. Lane was taken to hospital. It was indeed a very severe wound. It needed 19 stitches. He had also to have an operation. He was in hospital for a month. It made worse his chronic glaucoma. The surgeon of the Dorset General Hospital said that in his view the injury was caused by a hard object, not a soft one. He had never seen injuries of this kind caused by a fist. It was suggested that Mr. Holloway must have used a weapon or a hard instrument. But the judge found that that was not so: it was caused by a fist. Nevertheless it caused this very severe injury.

. . .

The first question is: Was there an assault by Mr. Holloway for which damages are recoverable in a civil court? I am quite clearly of opinion that there was. It has been argued before us that no action lies because this was an unlawful fight: that both of them were concerned in illegality; and therefore there can be no cause of action in respect of it. Ex turpi causa oritur non actio. To that I entirely demur. Even if the fight started by being unlawful, I think that one of them can sue the other for damages for a subsequent injury if it was inflicted by a weapon or savage blow out of all proportion to the occasion. I agree that in an ordinary fight with fists there is no cause of action to either of them for any injury suffered. The reason is that each of the participants in a fight voluntarily takes upon himself the risk of incidental injuries to himself. Volenti non fit injuria. But he does not take on himself the risk of a savage blow out of all proportion to the occasion. The man who strikes a blow of such severity is liable in damages unless he can prove accident or self-defence.

In this case the judge found that "with a young man of 23 and a man of 64, whom he knows to be somewhat infirm, the young man cannot plead a challenge seriously: nor is he entitled to go and strike him because of an insult hurled at his wife."

I quite agree. Mr. Holloway in anger went much too far. He gave a blow out of proportion to the occasion for which he must answer in damages.

Thus far I entirely agree with the judge. Then the question arises as to the amount of damages. The judge said that "to a substantial extent the plaintiff brought the injury on himself: first, by insulting the defendant's wife; secondly, by challenging the defendant to fight; and, thirdly, by striking the first blow. These matters in my judgment must operate to reduce the damages extensively."

He gave a sum of £75, saying it would have been very much higher but for reasons stated.

Now there is an appeal. It is said that the judge ought not to have reduced the damages. The judge had cases before him, both in this country and New Zealand and Canada, where it was held that provocation could be used to reduce the damages. But most of these cases were considered by the High Court of Australia in 1962 in Fontin v. Katapodis. The plaintiff struck the defendant with a weapon, a wooden T-square. It broke on his shoulder. There was not much trouble from that. But then the defendant picked up a sharp piece of glass with which he was working and threw it at the plaintiff, causing him severe injury. The judge reduced the damages from £2,850 to £2,000 by reason of the provocation. But the High Court of Australia, including the Chief Justice, Sir Owen Dixon, held that provocation could be used to wipe out the element of exemplary or aggravated damages but could not be used to reduce the actual figure of pecuniary compensation. So they increased the damages to the full £2,850.

I think that the Australian High Court should be our guide. The defendant has done a civil wrong and should pay compensation for the physical damage done by it. Provocation by the plaintiff can properly be used to take away any element of aggravation. But not to reduce the real damages. I ought to say in fairness to the judge that he did not have the benefit of the case in the High Court of Australia. We have had the benefit of it.

On the evidence this young man went much too far in striking a blow out of all proportion to the occasion. It must have been a savage blow to produce these consequences. I think the damages ought to be increased from £75 to £300 and I would allow the appeal accordingly.

SALMON L.J.

Mr. O'Brien has addressed a most interesting argument to us to the effect that his client ought to have succeeded in the court below on the ground of ex turpi causa non oritur actio or volenti non fit injuria. These are recondite topics about which there is much learning. Mr. O'Brien has given us the advantage of his very thorough researches.

In considering these matters, however, I think it is very necessary to keep one's feet firmly on the ground and focus on the facts of this particular case. The salient facts, as I see them, are these:

The defendant owns a café at the corner of a quiet court in Dorchester. The plaintiff lives in this court. The plaintiff and his neighbours are not very pleased about the activities of the defendant's customers either inside or outside the café and they have expressed their displeasure to the defendant. The defendant has done all he could to meet their points but still much noise comes from the café and there is a good deal of bad blood between the defendant on the one hand and his neighbours, including the plaintiff, on the other. The plaintiff is a rather cantankerous old man of 64 years of age and slightly infirm. The defendant is a healthy young man of 23 years of age. On the night in question an interchange of pleasantries was apparently started by the defendant's wife shouting out of the window to the plaintiff, who was enjoying the air with his neighbour, Mrs. Brake: "You bloody lot," to which he replied with scant courtesy: "Shut up, you monkey-faced tart." This was just vulgar abuse on the one side and the other. The defendant was very angry and got out of bed and said: "What did you call my wife?" and the old gentleman, no doubt encouraged and fortified by the beer which he had been drinking that evening, said: "I'll take you on at any time" or words to that effect. The judge, as my Lord has pointed out, has said what must be obvious to any sensible man: nobody of 23 in those circumstances could seriously believe he was being challenged to a fight by this troublesome old man 40 years older than he was, rather infirm and full of beer. What occurred is clear. The defendant was extremely annoyed, and that perhaps is not surprising. What I think is surprising is that he got out of bed, put on his dressing-gown and went down to the plaintiff; and it seems fairly obvious that he went down to beat him up and teach him a lesson. He walked up very close to the plaintiff, as the judge has found, in a menacing way, giving the plaintiff the impression that he was no doubt about to be struck; the plaintiff then punched this man 40 years younger than himself on the shoulder, whereupon the defendant smashed his fist into the plaintiff's face. The ophthalmic surgeon, who apparently had spent some 21 years at Basingstoke and East Grinstead (very famous centres of plastic surgery) with vast experience of injuries of this kind, said that he, at any rate, had never seen any such injuries produced by a fist alone; there must have been some hard object to produce these injuries which he said could be described as major wounds. I am bound to say, having seen the photographs, that I am not at all surprised at the view expressed by the ophthalmic surgeon. However, in cross-examination he said in effect: "I suppose anything is possible and I cannot say it is impossible that those injuries could have been caused by a fist." The judge rejected the suggestion that the defendant might have been wearing a knuckle-duster or had some pennies between his fingers and came to the conclusion that he did no more than hit the plaintiff with his fist, and that is a finding which we, of course, entirely accept: it is binding on us. According to the evidence of the surgeon, this man was kept in hospital for a month. He was moved from the local hospital to the Royal Eye Infirmary. He had to have two operations for the removal of blood clots and the correction of a skin flap and no fewer than 19 stitches were inserted around his eye. Since the injuries were inflicted with the fist alone, the conclusion is inescapable that it must have been a savage blow, that the plaintiff must have smashed his fist with great force into the eye of this man 40 years older than he was, after coming up to him in a threatening manner and having received no more than a slight punch on the shoulder.

To say in circumstances such as those that ex turpi causa non oritur actio is a defence seems to me to be quite absurd. Academically of course one can see the argument, but one must look at it, I think, from a practical point of view. To say that this old gentleman was engaged jointly with the defendant in a criminal venture is a step which, like the judge, I feel wholly unable to take.

The defence of volenti non fit injuria seems to me to be equally difficult. It is inconceivable that the old man, full of beer as he was, was voluntarily taking the risk of having an injury of this kind inflicted upon him. I think the judge was quite right in rejecting the defence of volenti non fit injuria.

As to the damages, but for one matter which the judge (wrongly, I think) took into consideration, it is obvious that £75 is a ludicrously inadequate sum to award for injuries such as those I have described. The judge, however, thought that the old man had behaved very badly, and indeed no one could question that view. He had been very impolite, he had also been rather impolitic in saying: "I'll take you on at any time"; he had been extremely rude to the defendant's wife; and, for good measure, when he went into the witness-box he was not very particular about what he said, as he thought it might increase the amount of money he would receive; the judge said that the plaintiff gave some dishonest evidence on damages and indeed that he did not believe anything the plaintiff said unless it was corroborated. I entirely reject the contention that because a plaintiff who has suffered a civil wrong has behaved badly, this is a matter which the court may take into account when awarding him compensatory damages for physical injuries which he has sustained as the result of the wrong which has been unlawfully inflicted upon him.

I would unhesitatingly come to that view without any authority at all. I cannot see how logically or on any principle of law the fact that the plaintiff has behaved rather badly and is a cantankerous old man can be even material when considering what is the proper compensation for the physical injury which he has suffered.

. . .

In my judgment the sum of £75 is far too little and I do not dissent from my Lord's proposal that the damages should be increased to £300. My only doubt is as to whether that sum is sufficient. I would allow the appeal accordingly.

Notes and Questions

1. Opinions in British cases are written differently from those in the United States. For example, they typically include the opinions of all of the judges who heard the case, and the judges often discuss the lawyers in the case by name.

2. The defendant in *Lane* argued that he should be absolved of responsibility for the plaintiff's injuries for three separate reasons: the fight was illegal, he acted in self-defense, and the plaintiff provoked him. What are the rules that apply to each of these arguments?

3. Do you agree with the rule that verbal provocation by the plaintiff cannot (ever) be used by the defendant to reduce the amount of compensatory damages owed? In this regard, the Law Lords refer several times to the arguments made by (losing) defense counsel, Mr. O'Brien. As to the provocation rule in particular, Mr. O'Brien argued that:

> One should not take a figure for damages regardless of the surrounding facts, because those surrounding facts colour the value of the physical injury. It is conceded that damages for loss of earnings would not be affected in this way. In the case of physical injury, one is dealing with corporeal integrity. In assessing damages for the loss of a leg, the court is entitled to assess the damage on the basis of the value of that leg to the plaintiff. Here the plaintiff shouted abuse at the defendant in such a way as to invite assault and behaved so badly that he could not be heard to say that his corporeal integrity was of substantial value to him.

BROWN v. MARTIN
53 So.3d 643 (La. App. 2010)

This is a tort suit arising out of an off-duty deputy, who was working a private detail for a parking lot owner, shooting and injuring an armed parking lot patron. The narrow issue presented is whether the trial court correctly concluded that the deputy, Taraunce Charles Martin, acted in self-defense and thus that the deputy's private employer, Central Parking System of Louisiana, Inc., could not be vicariously liable to the injured patron, Kyle Aaron Brown. Finding no error in the trial court's conclusion, we affirm the granting of Central Parking's motion for summary judgment and dismissing Mr. Brown's suit against it.

FACTUAL AND PROCEDURAL BACKGROUND

On the night of January 26, 2008, Kyle Brown and two female friends went out partying in the New Orleans French Quarter. At about 4:00 a.m. on January 27, 2008, the trio returned to Mr. Brown's car, which was parked in Central Parking's lot located on Conti Street. When they reached the Conti Street lot, Mr. Brown became embroiled in a dispute with the occupants of a red truck. The driver of the red truck began to drive in circles around the trio, and the occupants in the truck began taunting and shouting at Mr. Brown. The trio continued walking towards Mr. Brown's car. When they reached the car, Mr. Brown armed himself with a handgun, which he removed from under the driver's seat. Despite the cold January weather, Mr. Brown took off his shirt. The two females got into the car, and Mr. Brown proceeded towards the red truck.

Meanwhile, the cashier and some customers in the parking lot alerted Deputy Martin that a man (later identified as Mr. Brown) was running around the lot with a gun and screaming and shouting at people. Deputy Martin, who was on foot, requested his partner, Walter Wilson, who was stationed in his vehicle, provide him with backup assistance. At that time, both Deputy Martin and Deputy Wilson were working a private detail for Central Parking. Deputy Martin then went to investigate the disturbance.

When Deputy Martin approached Mr. Brown in the parking lot, Mr. Brown was having words with the occupants of the red truck. Deputy Martin neither detained nor questioned the occupants of the red truck. Nor did he inform Mr. Brown that he was a law enforcement officer. Deputy Martin unsuccessfully attempted to calm down Mr. Brown, who was agitated. Deputy Martin instructed Mr. Brown, who appeared to be intoxicated, to get into his car and to leave the parking lot. In order to attempt to get Mr. Brown to leave, Deputy Martin told him "Go home. You been drinking. Go chill out and go home." Deputy Martin also warned him that he was going to have to arrest him. Mr. Brown then drew his weapon, pointed it at the ground, and shouted several racial expletives. Deputy Martin then drew his gun and commanded several times, each time more forcefully, that Mr. Brown drop the gun. Mr. Brown ignored the commands. Instead, Mr. Brown pointed the gun at Deputy Martin and threatened to kill him, stating, "Well, f . . . it, I'll kill you." In response to the threat, Deputy Martin fired several shots at Mr. Brown. It is undisputed that Deputy Martin fired nine shots and that Mr. Brown was hit between five and seven times. Although both Deputy Martin and his partner, Deputy Wilson, believed that Mr. Brown had fired a shot, it is undisputed that Mr. Brown did not fire any shots.

Mr. Brown was criminally charged with and convicted of aggravated battery of a peace officer with a firearm, a violation of La. R.S. 14:37.2. This court affirmed the conviction. *State v. Brown,* 09-0863 (La.App. 4 Cir. 12/2/09), 26 So.3d 845.

On January 29, 2009, Mr. Brown commenced this tort suit against Mr. Martin and both his alleged private employer, Central Parking, and his public employer, the Orleans Parish Criminal Sheriff, Marlin N. Gusman. Mr. Brown alleged that Deputy Martin was Central Parking's employee at the time of the shooting and that Central Parking thus was vicariously responsible for his actions.

After answering the suit and generally denying the allegations of the petition, Central Parking filed a motion for summary judgment. In support of its motion for summary judgment, Central Parking introduced the entire transcript Mr. Brown's January 27, 2009, criminal trial. The

State's three witnesses at the criminal trial were Deputy Martin; Deputy Wilson, who was Deputy Martin's partner; and Derika Gibson, an off-duty deputy who witnessed the shooting from a vehicle parked near the parking lot entrance. The defense's two witnesses were Alexandra Biggs, one of the females who accompanied Mr. Brown to the French Quarter; and Sergeant Randy Mannix, who served in the army with Mr. Brown and trained him in gun safety. The facts of this case, as presented at the criminal trial, are outlined in detail in this court's opinion in *Brown, supra.* Summarizing, the pertinent facts are as follows:

> The deputies' [Deputy Martin's and Deputy Wilson's] testimony reflects that customers reported to the cashier that the defendant [Mr. Brown] was belligerent, hostile, and appeared to have been drinking, and he was running around the parking lot with a gun. Deputy Martin approached the defendant [Mr. Brown], and the defendant [Mr. Brown] pulled a gun from his waistband. Deputy Martin took cover behind a parked vehicle and Deputy Wilson provided backup. The testimony of the deputies as well as that of an observing, off-duty deputy [Deputy Gibson] reflects that the defendant [Mr. Brown] pointed the gun at Deputy Martin.
>
> Deputy Martin testified that after making repeated attempts to calm him, the defendant [Mr. Brown] continued to resist his efforts. The defendant [Mr. Brown] grew increasingly belligerent, yelling expletives and racial slurs. Deputy Martin ordered the defendant [Mr. Brown] to drop his weapon and he refused. Deputy Martin then fired shots at the defendant [Mr. Brown]. The 911 supervisor authenticated the tape of the 911 call received in connection with the incident, in which a code 108, "officer needs assistance," request was made.

In opposing the summary judgment, Mr. Brown submitted excerpts from the criminal transcript and his own affidavit. In his affidavit, which is dated January 6, 2010, Mr. Brown attested that:

> 1. When Deputy Martin approached me I did not know he was a peace Deputy or law enforcement officer.
>
> 2. I armed myself only to protect my life and the lives of my companions as we were being threatened by the occupants of a red truck.
>
> 3. I would have been relieved to know that Deputy Martin was providing security as he did nothing in my presence to get rid of the threat presented by the occupants of the red truck and the truck itself.
>
> 4. I was shot five or six times and critically wounded as a result of those nine shots fired by Deputy Martin. (see exhibit "B", an excerpt of my initial hospitalization and diagnosis.)
>
> 5. I had never formed the intent to fire my weapon at anyone before I was shot.
>
> 6. I never threatened Deputy Martin as I had nothing going on with him.
>
> 7. I merely reacted to a loud voice behind me which caused me to turn my body while armed.

The trial court granted Central Parking's motion for summary judgment, denied Mr. Brown's motion for new trial, and certified its judgment as final. This appeal followed.

DISCUSSION

Appellate courts review the grant of a summary judgment motion *de novo* using the same standard applied by the trial court in deciding the motion for summary judgment. In determining whether summary judgment is appropriate the two issues a court must resolve are whether there is any genuine issue of material fact, and whether the mover is entitled to judgment as a matter of law. Summary judgment shall be granted if the pleadings, depositions, answers to interrogatories, and admissions on file, together with the affidavits, if any, show that there is no genuine issue as to material fact and that the mover is entitled to judgment as a matter of law.

A genuine issue is one as to which reasonable persons could disagree; if reasonable persons could reach only one conclusion, there is no need for trial on that issue and summary judgment is appropriate. *Hines v. Garrett,* 04-0806, p. 1 (La.6/25/04), 876 So.2d 764, 765. A fact is material if it potentially insures or precludes recovery, affects a litigant's ultimate success, or determines the outcome of the legal dispute. *Id.* (citing *Smith v. Our Lady of the Lake Hosp., Inc.,* 93-2512, p. 27 (La.7/5/94), 639 So.2d 730, 751). Simply stated, a "material" fact is "one that would matter on the trial on the merits." *Smith, supra.*

The party seeking the summary judgment has the initial burden of affirmatively showing the absence of a genuine issue of material fact. After the mover has met its initial burden of proof, the burden shifts to the non-moving party to produce factual support sufficient to establish that he will be able to satisfy his evidentiary burden at trial. If the non-moving party fails to meet this burden, there is no genuine issue of material fact, and the mover is entitled to summary judgment.

"Favored in Louisiana, the summary judgment procedure 'is designed to secure the just, speedy, and inexpensive determination of every action' and shall be construed to accomplish these ends." *King v. Parish National Bank,* 04-0337, p. 7 La.10/19/04), 885 So.2d 540, 545 (quoting La. C.C.P. art. 966(A)(2)). Despite the legislative mandate that summary judgments are now favored, factual inferences reasonably drawn from the evidence must be construed in favor of the party opposing the motion, and all doubt must be resolved in the opponent's favor.

Central Parking's motion for summary judgment was based on the affirmative defense of self-defense — that it could not be liable because its employee, Deputy Martin, was acting in self-defense when "he fired at the pistol [w]ielding plaintiff after the plaintiff threatened to kill the uniformed deputy." As the party pleading an affirmative defense Central Parking had the burden of proof.

Because the applicable substantive law determines materiality, whether a particular fact in dispute is material can be seen only in light of the substantive law applicable to the case. The law on self-defense involving deadly force is that generally "a person cannot use 'deadly force' (force likely to cause death or great bodily harm) unless he reasonably believes he is threatened with serious bodily harm." Frank L. Maraist and Thomas C. Galligan, Jr., *Louisiana Tort Law,* § 2.09[2] (2nd ed. 2009) (*Maraist & Galligan*) (citing *Mathews v. Stewart,* 293 So.2d 209

(La.App. 3rd Cir.1974)).[7] The factors the jurisprudence considers in deciding whether the circumstances justified the use of deadly force include: (i) the character and reputation of the attacker, (ii) the attacker's belligerence, (iii) the difference in size and strength between the parties, (iv) the attacker's overt acts or threats of bodily harm, and (v) the possibility of a peaceful retreat. "Many of these are the same factors applicable in any self-defense case." *Maraist & Galligan, supra.*[8]

Applying these factors to the facts of this case, we find the record reflects that the attacker, Mr. Brown, was belligerent — hostile and ready to start a fight. Indeed, Deputy Martin testified that he attempted to calm Mr. Brown down and instructed Mr. Brown to go home and cool off. The record further reflects that Mr. Brown engaged in an overt act — aimed a gun at Deputy Martin — and threatened bodily harm — threatened to kill. An analysis of these facts thus supports a finding that Deputy Martin was justified in using deadly force.

. . . [T]he issue of the applicability of the affirmative defense of self-defense is a fact-intense, totality of the circumstances determination. As such, this determination is generally inappropriate for summary judgment. However, where reasonable minds cannot differ, the question of self-defense with a dangerous weapon is a question of law that may be resolved by summary judgment.

. . .

Mr. Brown acknowledges that his conviction for aggravated assault of a peace officer with a firearm can be used to establish that Deputy Martin was placed in a reasonable apprehension of receiving a battery. However, he contends that does not mean Deputy Martin's subsequent actions of shooting him six to seven times were reasonable. He further contends that the outcome of the criminal case is not dispositive of this civil case. Mr. Brown argues that "[t]he undisputed facts in this case are that the Plaintiff was shot at nine times and was struck, six to seven times while the Plaintiff never fired his gun." He points out that in his petition he alleged that the shots Deputy Martin fired at him were disproportionate to the degree of force necessary because after being shot, he fell down and then was repeatedly shot after he was already on the ground. The particular paragraph of the petition reads:

---

[7] We note that in 2006, the Legislature provided by statute, that "any person who uses reasonable and apparently necessary or deadly force to prevent a forcible offense against the person or his property, in accordance with La. R.S. 14:19 or 20 (criminal provisions governing self defense and justifiable homicide), is immune from civil action for the use of such force." *Maraist & Galligan, supra.*

[8] As Mr. Brown points out, the use of force by law enforcement officers is governed by the reasonable force standard under La. C.Cr.P. art. 220 (which governs use of force for a lawful arrest) and *Kyle v. City of New Orleans,* 353 So.2d 969 (La.1977). To determine whether an officer acted reasonably under the circumstances the jurisprudence considers the so-called *Kyle* factors; to wit: (1) the known character of the arrestee; (2) the risks and dangers faced by the officer; (3) the nature of the offense involved; (4) the chance of the arrestee's escape if the particular means are not employed; (5) the existence of alternative methods of arrest; (6) the physical size, strength, and weaponry of the officer as compared to the arrestee; and (7) the exigency of the moment. *See also Mathieu v. Imperial Toy Corp.,* 94-0952 (La.11/30/94), 646 So.2d 318 (finding *Kyle* factors apply in judging an officer's reasonableness in approaching a suspect). Many of these factors are the same factors used in analyzing self-defense with deadly force.

> Taraunce Charles Martin observed the Petitioner pull the handgun out of his pocket and immediately drew his firearm and pointed it at the Petitioner. When Petitioner turned in the direction of Taraunce Charles Martin, Taraunce Charles Martin fired at the Petitioner, knocking him to the ground. Taraunce Charles Martin then looked down at the Petitioner and fired at least five more shots at the Petitioner, hitting him four more times and critically wounding him.

Mr. Brown's primary contention is that summary judgment was improper because a genuine issue of material fact exists regarding whether Deputy Martin used excessive force. In support of this contention, Mr. Brown cites the testimony of the State's three witnesses at the criminal trial. First, he cites Deputy Martin's testimony that he remembered firing once, looking down, thinking that he heard return fire, and firing four more rounds. Second, he cites Ms. (Deputy) Gibson's testimony that within a couple of shots Mr. Brown was down. Third, he cites Deputy Wilson's testimony that he did not shoot his gun because once Mr. Brown was hit there was no need for him to fire. Based on this evidence, Mr. Brown contends that there is a genuine issue of material fact.

Central Parking counters that the State's three witnesses all testified that Deputy Martin stopped shooting as soon as Mr. Brown went down. Although Ms. (Deputy) Gibson testified that Mr. Brown was down "[w]ithin a couple of shots," she further testified that she did not see Deputy Martin stand over Mr. Brown and shoot. Deputy Wilson testified that "[o]nce he [Mr. Brown] fell, that was the end of the shooting." Deputy Martin testified that that he shot Mr. Brown until he went down. Deputy Martin further testified that he thought he shot Mr. Brown about five times and denied shooting him again after he hit the ground.

The opponent to a properly supported motion for summary judgment may not rest on the mere allegations or denials of his or her pleadings, but must respond by affidavits or as otherwise provided by law setting forth specific facts showing that there exists a genuine issue of material fact for trial. If he does not so respond, summary judgment, if appropriate, shall be rendered against him. Such is the case here. The record is devoid of any evidence supporting Mr. Brown's contention that Deputy Martin used unreasonable force. Although Mr. Brown submitted his own affidavit in opposition to the motion for summary judgment, his affidavit does not state that Deputy Martin continued to shoot once Mr. Brown was on the ground.

Mr. Brown contends, in his brief, that "[d]iscovery as to the trajectory of the bullets and the angle of entry can certainly be sought through the use of medical experts and since none of the bullets exited the Plaintiff's body, it is reasonable to assume that the Plaintiff was lying on a hard surface, such as the ground, that prevented the six to seven bullets from exiting the Plaintiff's body." Mr. Brown's speculation regarding the potential outcome of discovery, which was never requested in the trial court, is insufficient to establish a genuine issue of material fact. "While parties should be given a fair opportunity to present their claim, there is no absolute right to delay action on a motion for summary judgment until discovery is completed." *Jeanmarie,* 09-1059 at pp. 8–9, 34 So.3d at 951. In this case, as Central Parking points out, Mr. Brown neither conducted any discovery nor represented that any discovery was needed before the trial court decided the motion for summary judgment. The record thus supports the trial court's decision granting Central Parking's motion for summary judgment.

. . .

For the foregoing reasons, the judgment of the trial court is affirmed.

Notes and Questions

1. What does the *Brown* case add to your understanding of the self-defense doctrine?

2. Which of these arguments did the plaintiff in *Brown* make? (1) The defendant was not privileged to use force to defend himself against the plaintiff's actions. (2) The defendant was not privileged to use deadly force to defend himself. (3) The defendant was not privileged to continue to use deadly force after the plaintiff was on the ground.

3. Imagine a set of facts where the use of a gun would not constitute deadly force.

4. In the case, Deputy Martin was off duty from his job with the New Orleans Police Department. Consider the threshold issues that may have been at issue had he been on duty. In particular, return to Chapter One and review the vicarious liability and governmental immunity questions that might have arisen in that different context.

5. Racial slurs sometimes trigger violent reactions. Because of the "words alone" rule, traditional torts doctrine does not excuse such reactions on the grounds that they were provoked by the speaker. As we saw in *Lane*, their only effect may be to cause a factfinder to reduce any punitive (exemplary) damages that might otherwise have been awarded. Does this rule make sense? What are the policy arguments for and against an amendment that would permit a defendant to use physical and verbal provocations equivalently? Provocation or "the heat of passion" rule is generally discussed further in criminal law.

C. Property-Related Defenses

Analogous to the right to bodily autonomy protected by battery, lawful owners and occupiers of land have traditionally had the right to determine, at least in the first instance, who enters their property under what conditions. The ancient idea of trespass represents a violation of that right and its associated terms. At common law, merely stepping onto the land of another — even when the entrant didn't know they were on another's land and no actual damage was caused — satisfied the requirements for what was then the strict liability tort of trespass. Today, these facts are mostly still sufficient. For example, to make out a trespass claim in California, the plaintiff must establish the following by a preponderance of the evidence:

> (1) the plaintiff's ownership or control of the property; (2) the defendant's intentional, reckless, or negligent entry onto the property; (3) lack of permission for the entry or

acts in excess of permission; (4) harm; and (5) the defendant's conduct was a substantial factor in causing the harm.

Hanson v. Piecuch, Not Reported in P.3d, 2016 WL5373072 (Cal. App. 2016).

Notice that the first and third requirements are atypical for an intentional tort's prima facie case. Ordinarily, the plaintiff's affirmative case does not require proof of (1) standing and (3) lack of a privilege. Defenses to intentional trespass, such as lack of the right to bring the case (standing) or privileges defeating the claim (various forms of permission, e.g.invitations, leases, and easements), and necessity — both private and public, are first pled by the defendant and then responded to by the plaintiff.

When the property intentially affected is moveable property, what the law calls "chattels," conversion is usually the applicable tort. Conversion is civil theft whose prima facie case requires a plantiff to establish that the defendant intentionally exercised "substantial dominion" over plaintiff's property, interfering seriously with plaintiff's rights. Dobbs, V. 1, Sec. 61, p. 168]. In conversion the harm can be denying plaintiff access to the property, destroying the property, or refusing to return loaned property after a proper demand.

The first case in this section, Katko v. Briney, describes the common law limits of a property holder's rights to use physical force in defense of trespass and conversion. The next four cases, Rossi v. Delduca, Vincent v. Lake Erie Transportation Company, Surocco v. Geary, Wegner v. Milwaukee Mutual Insurance Company, describe the defense of necessity in both its private and public forms.

KATKO v. BRINEY
183 N.W.2d 657 (Iowa 1971)

MOORE, Chief Justice.

The primary issue presented here is whether an owner may protect personal property in an unoccupied boarded-up farm house against trespassers and thieves by a spring gun capable of inflicting death or serious injury.

We are not here concerned with a man's right to protect his home and members of his family. Defendants' home was several miles from the scene of the incident to which we refer infra.

Plaintiff's action is for damages resulting from serious injury caused by a shot from a 20-gauge spring shotgun set by defendants in a bedroom of an old farm house which had been uninhabited for several years. Plaintiff and his companion, Marvin McDonough, had broken and entered the house to find and steal old bottles and dated fruit jars which they considered antiques.

At defendants' request plaintiff's action was tried to a jury consisting of residents of the community where defendants' property was located. The jury returned a verdict for plaintiff and against defendants for $20,000 actual and $10,000 punitive damages.

After careful consideration of defendants' motions for judgment notwithstanding the verdict and for new trial, the experienced and capable trial judge overruled them and entered judgment on the verdict. Thus we have this appeal by defendants.

. . .

II.

Most of the facts are not disputed. In 1957 defendant Bertha L. Briney inherited her parents' farm land in Mahaska and Monroe Counties. Included was an 80-acre tract in southwest Mahaska County where her grandparents and parents had lived. No one occupied the house thereafter. Her husband, Edward, attempted to care for the land. He kept no farm machinery thereon. The outbuildings became dilapidated.

For about 10 years, 1957 to 1967, there occurred a series of trespassing and housebreaking events with loss of some household items, the breaking of windows and 'messing up of the property in general'. The latest occurred June 8, 1967, prior to the event on July 16, 1967 herein involved.

Defendants through the years boarded up the windows and doors in an attempt to stop the intrusions. They had posted 'no trespass' signs on the land several years before 1967. The nearest one was 35 feet from the house. On June 11, 1967 defendants set 'a shotgun trap' in the north bedroom. After Mr. Briney cleaned and oiled his 20-gauge shotgun, the power of which he was well aware, defendants took it to the old house where they secured it to an iron bed with the barrel pointed at the bedroom door. It was rigged with wire from the doorknob to the gun's trigger so it would fire when the door was opened. Briney first pointed the gun so an intruder would be hit in the stomach but at Mrs. Briney's suggestion it was lowered to hit the legs. He admitted he did so 'because I was mad and tired of being tormented' but 'he did not intend to injure anyone.' He gave no explanation of why he used a loaded shell and set it to hit a person already in the house. Tin was nailed over the bedroom window. The spring gun could not be seen from the outside. No warning of its presence was posted.

Plaintiff lived with his wife and worked regularly as a gasoline station attendant in Eddyville, seven miles from the old house. He had observed it for several years while hunting in the area and considered it as being abandoned. He knew it had long been uninhabited. In 1967 the area around the house was covered with high weeds. Prior to July 16, 1967 plaintiff and McDonough had been to the premises and found several old bottles and fruit jars which they took and added to their collection of antiques. On the latter date about 9:30 p.m. they made a second trip to the Briney property. They entered the old house by removing a board from a porch window which was without glass. While McDonough was looking around the kitchen area plaintiff went to another part of the house. As he started to open the north bedroom door the shotgun went off striking him in the right leg above the ankle bone. Much of his leg, including part of the tibia, was blown away. Only by McDonough's assistance was plaintiff able to get out of the house and after crawling some distance was put in his vehicle and rushed to a doctor and then to a hospital. He remained in the hospital 40 days.

Plaintiff's doctor testified he seriously considered amputation but eventually the healing process was successful. Some weeks after his release from the hospital plaintiff returned to work on crutches. He was required to keep the injured leg in a cast for approximately a year and wear a special brace for another year. He continued to suffer pain during this period.

There was undenied medical testimony plaintiff had a permanent deformity, a loss of tissue, and a shortening of the leg.

The record discloses plaintiff to trial time had incurred $710 medical expense, $2056.85 for hospital service, $61.80 for orthopedic service and $750 as loss of earnings. In addition thereto the trial court submitted to the jury the question of damages for pain and suffering and for future disability.

III.

Plaintiff testified he knew he had no right to break and enter the house with intent to steal bottles and fruit jars therefrom. He further testified he had entered a plea of guilty to larceny in the nighttime of property of less than $20 value from a private building. He stated he had been fined $50 and costs and paroled during good behavior from a 60-day jail sentence. Other than minor traffic charges this was plaintiff's first brush with the law. On this civil case appeal it is not our prerogative to review the disposition made of the criminal charge against him.

IV.

The main thrust of defendants' defense in the trial court and on this appeal is that 'the law permits use of a spring gun in a dwelling or warehouse for the purpose of preventing the unlawful entry of a burglar or thief. They repeated this contention in their exceptions to the trial court's instructions 2, 5 and 6. They took no exception to the trial court's statement of the issues or to other instructions.

In the statement of issues the trial court stated plaintiff and his companion committed a felony when they broke and entered defendants' house. In instruction 2 the court referred to the early case history of the use of spring guns and stated under the law their use was prohibited except to prevent the commission of felonies of violence and where human life is in danger. The instruction included a statement breaking and entering is not a felony of violence.

Instruction 5 stated:

> You are hereby instructed that one may use reasonable force in the protection of his property, but such right is subject to the qualification that one may not use such means of force as will take human life or inflict great bodily injury. Such is the rule even though the injured party is a trespasser and is in violation of the law himself.

Instruction 6 stated:

> An owner of premises is prohibited from willfully or intentionally injuring a trespasser by means of force that either takes life or inflicts great bodily injury; and therefore a person owning a premise is prohibited from setting out 'spring guns' and like dangerous devices which will likely take life or inflict great bodily injury, for the purpose of harming trespassers. The fact that the trespasser may be acting in violation of the law does not change the rule. The only time when such conduct of setting a

> 'spring gun' or a like dangerous device is justified would be when the trespasser was committing a felony of violence or a felony punishable by death, or where the trespasser was endangering human life by his act.

Instruction 7, to which defendants made no objection or exception, stated:

> To entitle the plaintiff to recover for compensatory damages, the burden of proof is upon him to establish by a preponderance of the evidence each and all of the following propositions:
>
> 1. That defendants erected a shotgun trap in a vacant house on land owned by defendant, Bertha L. Briney, on or about June 11, 1967, which fact was known only by them, to protect household goods from trespassers and thieves.
>
> 2. That the force used by defendants was in excess of that force reasonably necessary and which persons are entitled to use in the protection of their property.
>
> 3. That plaintiff was injured and damaged and the amount thereof.
>
> 4. That plaintiff's injuries and damages resulted directly from the discharge of the shotgun trap which was set and used by defendants.

The overwhelming weight of authority, both textbook and case law, supports the trial court's statement of the applicable principles of law.

Prosser on Torts, Third Edition, pages 116–118, states:

> * * * the law has always placed a higher value upon human safety than upon mere rights in property, it is the accepted rule that there is no privilege to use any force calculated to cause death or serious bodily injury to repel the threat to land or chattels, unless there is also such a threat to the defendant's personal safety as to justify a self-defense. * * * spring guns and other mankilling devices are not justifiable against a mere trespasser, or even a petty thief. They are privileged only against those upon whom the landowner, if he were present in person would be free to inflict injury of the same kind.

Restatement of Torts, section 85, page 180, states:

> The value of human life and limb, not only to the individual concerned but also to society, so outweighs the interest of a possessor of land in excluding from it those whom he is not willing to admit thereto that a possessor of land has, as is stated in § 79, no privilege to use force intended or likely to cause death or serious harm against another whom the possessor sees about to enter his premises or meddle with his chattel, unless the intrusion threatens death or serious bodily harm to the occupiers or users of the premises. * * * A possessor of land cannot do indirectly and by a mechanical device that which, were he present, he could not do immediately and in person. Therefore, he cannot gain a privilege to install, for the purpose of protecting his land from intrusions harmless to the lives and limbs of the occupiers or users of

> it, a mechanical device whose only purpose is to inflict death or serious harm upon such as may intrude, by giving notice of his intention to inflict, by mechanical means and indirectly, harm which he could not, even after request, inflict directly were he present.

In Volume 2, Harper and James, The Law of Torts, section 27.3, pages 1440, 1441, this is found:

> The possessor of land may not arrange his premises intentionally so as to cause death or serious bodily harm to a trespasser. The possessor may of course take some steps to repel a trespass. If he is present he may use force to do so, buy only that amount which is reasonably necessary to effect the repulse. Moreover if the trespass threatens harm to property only — even a theft of property — the possessor would not be privileged to use deadly force, he may not arrange his premises so that such force will be inflicted by mechanical means. If he does, he will be liable even to a thief who is injured by such device.

. . .

In Hooker v. Miller, 37 Iowa 613, we held defendant vineyard owner liable for damages resulting from a spring gun shot although plaintiff was a trespasser and there to steal grapes. At pages 614, 615, this statement is made: 'This court has held that a mere trespass against property other than a dwelling is not a sufficient justification to authorize the use of a deadly weapon by the owner in its defense; and that if death results in such a case it will be murder, though the killing be actually necessary to prevent the trespass. The State v. Vance, 17 Iowa 138.' At page 617 this court said: '(T)respassers and other inconsiderable violators of the law are not to be visited by barbarous punishments or prevented by inhuman inflictions of bodily injuries.')

The facts in Allison v. Fiscus, 156 Ohio 120, 110 N.E.2d 237, 44 A.L.R.2d 369, decided in 1951, are very similar to the case at bar. There plaintiff's right to damages was recognized for injuries received when he feloniously broke a door latch and started to enter defendant's warehouse with intent to steal. As he entered a trap of two sticks of dynamite buried under the doorway by defendant owner was set off and plaintiff seriously injured. The court held the question whether a particular trap was justified as a use of reasonable and necessary force against a trespasser engaged in the commission of a felony should have been submitted to the jury. The Ohio Supreme Court recognized plaintiff's right to recover punitive or exemplary damages in addition to compensatory damages.

In Starkey v. Dameron, 96 Colo. 459, 45 P.2d 172, plaintiff was allowed to recover compensatory and punitive damages for injuries received from a spring gun which defendant filling station operator had concealed in an automatic gasoline pump as protection against thieves.

. . .

In addition to civil liability many jurisdictions hold a land owner criminally liable for serious injuries or homicide caused by spring guns or other set devices. See State v. Childers, 133 Ohio 508, 14 N.E.2d 767 (melon thief shot by spring gun); Pierce v. Commonwealth, 135 Va. 635,

115 S.E. 686 (policeman killed by spring gun when he opened unlocked front door of defendant's shoe repair shop); State v. Marfaudille, 48 Wash. 117, 92 P. 939 (murder conviction for death from spring gun set in a trunk); State v. Beckham, 306 Mo. 566, 267 S.W. 817 (boy killed by spring gun attached to window of defendant's chili stand); State v. Green, 118 S.C. 279, 110 S.E. 145, 19 A.L.R. 1431 (intruder shot by spring gun when he broke and entered vacant house. Manslaughter conviction of owner-affirmed); State v. Barr, 11 Wash. 481, 39 P. 1080 (murder conviction affirmed for death of an intruder into a boarded up cabin in which owner had set a spring gun).

In Wisconsin, Oregon and England the use of spring guns and similar devices is specifically made unlawful by statute. 44 A.L.R., section 3, pages 386, 388.

The legal principles stated by the trial court in instructions 2, 5 and 6 are well established and supported by the authorities cited and quoted supra. There is no merit in defendants' objections and exceptions thereto. Defendants' various motions based on the same reasons stated in exceptions to instructions were properly overruled.

. . . Affirmed.

Notes and Questions

1. One Justice dissented on the ground that the trial court erred in failing to require the plaintiff to prove that the defendants intended to injure him. How do we know he was right? Why did the majority treat this error as (in effect) harmless?

2. The same Justice also disagreed with the majority's holding that setting a spring gun to protect just property (and not also life or limb) should in all instances result in liability for harm done to a trespasser. Here are the relevant portions of his dissent in this respect:

> Since our decision in Hooker v. Miller, supra, we have recognized in this state the doctrine that the owner of a premise is liable in damages to a mere trespasser coming upon his property for any injury occasioned by the unsafe condition of the property which the owner has intentionally permitted to exist, such as installed spring guns, unless adequate warning is given thereof. In Hooker, which involved stealing grapes from a vineyard, we held a property owner had no right to resist such a trespass by means which may kill or inflict great bodily injury to the trespasser. But it does appear therein that we recognized some distinction between a mere trespass against property and a trespass involving a serious crime or involving a dwelling. Except when the trespass involves a serious crime, a crime posing a threat to human life, it may be argued that the law in this jurisdiction should limit the right of one to protect his property, that he does not have a privilege to resist a mere trespass by using a spring gun or other device which poses a threat to life.
>
> However, left unsettled by this and other court pronouncements is the means which may be used to repel, prevent, or apprehend a trespasser engaged in a more serious criminal offense. True, there is a line of cases which seem to apply the same rule to all criminal trespasses except those involving arson, rape, assault, or other acts of

> violence against persons residing on the property invaded. There are others which at least infer that any serious law violation by the trespasser might permit the reasonable use of dangerous instrumentalities to repel the intruder and prevent loss or damage to one's valuable property.
>
> . . .
>
> Although I am aware of the often-repeated statement that personal rights are more important than property rights, where the owner has stored his valuables representing his life's accumulations, his livelihood business, his tools and implements, and his treasured antiques as appears in the case at bar, and where the evidence is sufficient to sustain a finding that the installation was intended only as a warning to ward off thieves and criminals, I can see no compelling reason why the use of such a device alone would create liability as a matter of law.

3. According to Wikipedia citing Gary A. Munneke and the Chicago Tribune:

> Four years after the case was decided, Briney was asked if he would change anything about the situation. Briney replied: "There's one thing I'd do different, though, I'd have aimed that gun a few feet higher."

4. Nearly 50 years after the case, Randy Maniloff, an attorney in Philadelphia who writes the informative and amusing newletter and website www.CoverageOpinions.info, interviewed 93-year-old Garold Heslinga, Marvin Katko's attorney. https://www.law.com/2017/01/30/meet-the-lawyer-93-who-tried-the-torts-spring-gun-case/. Maniloff's article covers the case's post-trial history and characterizes law students' reactions to it over the years.

ROSSI v. DELDUCA
181 N.E.2d 591 (Mass. 1962)

Spalding, Justice.

Although the declaration contains thirteen counts against several defendants, we are now concerned with only the first and seventh. The plaintiff in the first count (hereinafter called the plaintiff) is Patricia Rossi, a minor, who seeks by her next friend to recover for injuries inflicted upon her by two dogs owned by the defendant, Ernest V. DelDuca. In the seventh count John Rossi, Patricia's father, seeks to recover for medical expenses incurred by him on behalf of his daughter. Both counts were submitted to the jury who returned verdicts for the plaintiffs. The case comes here on the defendant's exception to the denial of his motion for a directed verdict on each count.

There was evidence of the following: The plaintiff lived with her parents on Oak Street, Methuen. Oak Street runs north and south. In order to reach the Rossi house coming from the south it is necessary to pass Cambridge Street which joins Oak Street from the east. On the east side of Oak Street starting at the junction of Cambridge and Oak streets and proceeding northward there are three houses occupied by the defendant and members of his family. The first house (No. 105) is owned and occupied by Arthur DelDuca, a brother of the defendant.

To the north of, and next to, Arthur's house is a house (No. 119) owned and occupied by Samuel DelDuca, also a brother of the defendant. Next to and north of Samuel's house is the defendant's house (No. 121). At 70 Cambridge Street (on the north side of the street) is a garage owned by the defendant's wife, which the defendant uses in his contracting business. There is a small shed near the back of the garage, slightly to the west, which is also used in the business. Cambridge Street is a dead-end street to the east of the garage, and there are no streets running off Oak Street north of Cambridge Street. In connection with his business, the defendant owned and maintained bulldozers, graders, and equipment which he kept outdoors on a field owned by his father, Vincenzo, located east of 105, 119, and 121 Oak Street, and north of the garage at 70 Cambridge Street. 'Going north of the east side of Oak Street starting at Cambridge Street there were no fences between the houses. The field on the east side of Oak Street was to the north of 70 Cambridge Street and east of * * * [the defendant's] land at 121 Oak Street. The land was all open in there.' On this field, the defendant, with the permission of his father, had erected a pen to house two great Dane dogs which he owned. The defendant's brother Arthur was the owner of a purplish-gray German Weimaraner dog.

In September, 1955, Ida Celia and the plaintiff, both aged eight, were students in the third grade of the Ashford school. In the afternoon of September 26, school having closed, they started walking up Oak Street toward their homes. As they reached the corner of Cambridge Street, they saw the German Weimaraner ahead of them on Oak Street. The dog started to come toward them, and, as the plaintiff testified, 'We got frightened so we * * * ran down Cambridge Street * * * [and the dog was] [f]ollowing us.' Realizing that Cambridge Street was a dead-end street, the girls left Cambridge Street on the north side, passing around the garage at 70 Cambridge Street and the shed. The dog continued to follow them. After they passed the shed, they ran along a path in the field belonging to the defendant's father. The plaintiff then saw, for the first time, a black great Dane. '[T]he dog was on its hind legs and it was going to jump on her. It did jump on her. She doesn't remember after that, and then she remembers two black dogs on her. She didn't feel anything but they were biting her neck. She shouted for help.' The plaintiff's father observed the defendant's great Dane dogs in the field. They 'were worrying some object' which he learned was his daughter Patricia who was 'crouched down on her knees * * * with her hands on her face.' He picked her up and took her to the hospital.

The defendant testified that on September 26, 1955, he owned two 'black Dane dogs.' The dogs were 'trained to stay in the field to the rear of this defendant's home where his equipment was kept. * * * He had a lot of equipment and was concerned about it.' The defendant's arrangement with his father regarding this land was that the 'defendant could use all of that property for parking his equipment and doing anything he wanted with it in connection with his business. * * * He had full control of the field.'

1.

It is clear both from the pleadings and the evidence that the plaintiff seeks to recover under G.L. c. 140, § 155, which, as amended by St.1934, c. 320, § 18 reads: 'If any dog shall do any damage to either the body or property of any person, the owner or keeper, or if the owner or keeper be a minor, the parent or guardian of such minor, shall be liable for such damage, unless such damage shall have been occasioned to the body or property of a person who, at the time such damage was sustained, was committing a trespass or other tort, or was teasing, tormenting or abusing such dog.' Under this statute, unlike the common law, 'the owner or keeper of a dog is liable * * * for injury resulting from an act of the dog without proof * * * that its owner or keeper was negligent or otherwise at fault, or knew, or had reason to know, that the dog had any extraordinary, dangerous propensity, and even without proof that the dog in fact had any such propensity.' Leone v. Falco, 292 Mass. 299, 300, 198 N.E. 273, 274. It is to be noted that the strict liability imposed by the statute is of no avail to a plaintiff if at the time of his injury he 'was committing a trespass or other tort, or was teasing, tormenting or abusing such dog.' And it is incumbent upon a plaintiff to plead and prove that he has done none of these things.

The defendant contends that the plaintiff is barred from recovery because on her own testimony — and there is no evidence more favorable to her — she was committing a trespass at the time the defendant's dogs attacked her. We assume that, although the field where the plaintiff was attacked was owned by the defendant's father, the defendant had possessive rights in the property sufficient to render the principle enunciated in Sarna v. American Bosch Magneto Corp., 290 Mass. 340, 195 N.E. 328, inapplicable. We are of opinion, nevertheless, that the jury could have found that the plaintiff was not a trespasser, as that word is used in the statute. A finding was warranted that the plaintiff, an eight year old girl, was frightened by the German Weimaraner dog which was between her and the only means of access to her house; that she turned and ran down a side street; and that because this was a dead-end street she went north across the field in the rear of the defendant's house in order to get home, the Weimaraner following her all the while. This evidence brings the case, we think, within the principle that one is privileged to enter land in the possession of another if it is, or reasonably appears to be, necessary to prevent serious harm to the actor or his property. Restatement 2d: Torts, Tent. draft no. 2, 1958, § 197. This privilege not only relieves the intruder from liability for technical trespass . . . but it also destroys the possessor's immunity from liability in resisting the intrusion. Ploof v. Putnam, 81 Vt. 471, 71 A. 188, 20 L.R.A.,N.S., 152. See Bohlen, Incomplete Privilege to Inflict Intentional Invasions of Interests of Property & Personality, 39 Harv. L. Rev. 307. 'The important difference between the status of one who is a trespasser on land and one who is on the land pursuant to an incomplete privilege is that the latter is entitled to be on the land and therefore the possessor of the land is under a duty to permit him to come and remain there and hence is not privileged to resist.' Restatement 2d: Torts, Tent. draft no. 2, 1958, § 197, comment k. We assume that the statute evidences a legislative recognition of the right of a possessor of land to keep a dog for protection against trespassers. Nevertheless, we do not believe that the Legislature intended to bar recovery in a case like the present.

2.

In support of his motion for a directed verdict on count seven, the defendant contends that it is not possible to recover consequential damages under G.L. c. 140, § 155. He argues that the phrase 'damage to either the body or property of any person' must be interpreted to mean damage which is the direct result of an injury, and cannot include consequential damage which was sustained by the plaintiff John Rossi. A full answer to this contention is found in M'Carthy v. Guild, 12 Metc. 291 (construing a predecessor of the present statute, which, while different in some particulars, is essentially similar on the point in issue). There, in permitting recovery for consequential damage by the parent of a child bitten by a dog, it was said: 'The object of the statute is to protect from injury by dogs. * * * But it is quite apparent that a remedy, confined to the case of an injury to the person, and to be enforced only by an action in the name of such person, would fall short of giving complete redress for injuries by dogs. * * * [The statute] provides an adequate remedy for the entire damages that may result from any such injur[ies]. The parent * * * will recover his appropriate damages, and the minor * * * will, in his own name, recover for the personal suffering.' Pp. 292–293. Compare Wilson v. Grace, 273 Mass. 146, 154–155, 173 N.E. 524; Zarba v. Lane, 322 Mass. 132, 135, 76 N.E.2d 318.

Exceptions overruled.

VINCENT v. LAKE ERIE TRANSPORTATION CO.
124 N.W. 221 (Minn. 1910)

O'Brien, J.

The steamship Reynolds, owned by the defendant, was for the purpose of discharging her cargo on November 27, 1905, moored to plaintiff's dock in Duluth. While the unloading of the boat was taking place a storm from the northeast developed, which at about 10 o'clock p. m., when the unloading was completed, had so grown in violence that the wind was then moving at 50 miles per hour and continued to increase during the night. There is some evidence that one, and perhaps two, boats were able to enter the harbor that night, but it is plain that navigation was practically suspended from the hour mentioned until the morning of the 29th, when the storm abated, and during that time no master would have been justified in attempting to navigate his vessel, if he could avoid doing so. After the discharge of the cargo the Reynolds signaled for a tug to tow her from the dock, but none could be obtained because of the severity of the storm. If the lines holding the ship to the dock had been cast off, she would doubtless have drifted away; but, instead, the lines were kept fast, and as soon as one parted or chafed it was replaced, sometimes with a larger one. The vessel lay upon the outside of the dock, her bow to the east, the wind and waves striking her starboard quarter with such force that she was constantly being lifted and thrown against the dock, resulting in its damage, as found by the jury, to the amount of $500.

We are satisfied that the character of the storm was such that it would have been highly imprudent for the master of the Reynolds to have attempted to leave the dock or to have permitted his vessel to drift away from it. One witness testified upon the trial that the vessel could have been warped into a slip, and that, if the attempt to bring the ship into the slip had failed, the worst that could have happened would be that the vessel would have been blown ashore upon a soft and muddy bank. The witness was not present in Duluth at the time of the storm, and, while he may have been right in his conclusions, those in charge of the dock and the vessel at the time of the storm were not required to use the highest human intelligence, nor were they required to resort to every possible experiment which could be suggested for the preservation of their property. Nothing more was demanded of them than ordinary prudence and care, and the record in this case fully sustains the contention of the appellant that, in holding the vessel fast to the dock, those in charge of her exercised good judgment and prudent seamanship.

It is claimed by the respondent that it was negligence to moor the boat at an exposed part of the wharf, and to continue in that position after it became apparent that the storm was to be more than usually severe. We do not agree with this position. The part of the wharf where the vessel was moored appears to have been commonly used for that purpose. It was situated within the harbor at Duluth, and must, we think, be considered a proper and safe place, and would undoubtedly have been such during what would be considered a very severe storm. The storm which made it unsafe was one which surpassed in violence any which might have reasonably been anticipated.

The appellant contends by ample assignments of error that, because its conduct during the storm was rendered necessary by prudence and good seamanship under conditions over which it had no control, it cannot be held liable for any injury resulting to the property of others, and claims that the jury should have been so instructed. An analysis of the charge given by the trial court is not necessary, as in our opinion the only question for the jury was the amount of damages which the plaintiffs were entitled to recover, and no complaint is made upon that score.

The situation was one in which the ordinary rules regulating property rights were suspended by forces beyond human control, and if, without the direct intervention of some act by the one sought to be held liable, the property of another was injured, such injury must be attributed to the act of God, and not to the wrongful act of the person sought to be charged. If during the storm the Reynolds had entered the harbor, and while there had become disabled and been thrown against the plaintiffs' dock, the plaintiffs could not have recovered. Again, if which attempting to hold fast to the dock the lines had parted, without any negligence, and the vessel carried against some other boat or dock in the harbor, there would be no liability upon her owner. But here those in charge of the vessel deliberately and by their direct efforts held her in such a position that the damage to the dock resulted, and, having thus preserved the ship at the expense of the dock, it seems to us that her owners are responsible to the dock owners to the extent of the injury inflicted.

In Depue v. Flatau, 100 Minn. 299, 111 N. W. 1, 8 L. R. A. (N. S.) 485, this court held that where the plaintiff, while lawfully in the defendants' house, became so ill that he was incapable of traveling with safety, the defendants were responsible to him in damages for compelling him to leave the premises. If, however, the owner of the premises had furnished the traveler with proper accommodations and medical attendance, would he have been able to defeat an action brought against him for their reasonable worth?

In Ploof v. Putnam, 71 Atl. 188, 20 L. R. A. (N. S.) 152, the Supreme Court of Vermont held that where, under stress of weather, a vessel was without permission moored to a private dock at an island in Lake Champlain owned by the defendant, the plaintiff was not guilty of trespass, and that the defendant was responsible in damages because his representative upon the island unmoored the vessel, permitting it to drift upon the shore, with resultant injuries to it. If, in that case, the vessel had been permitted to remain, and the dock had suffered an injury, we believe the shipowner would have been held liable for the injury done.

Theologians hold that a starving man may, without moral guilt, take what is necessary to sustain life; but it could hardly be said that the obligation would not be upon such person to pay the value of the property so taken when he became able to do so. And so public necessity, in times of war or peace, may require the taking of private property for public purposes; but under our system of jurisprudence compensation must be made.

Let us imagine in this case that for the better mooring of the vessel those in charge of her had appropriated a valuable cable lying upon the dock. No matter how justifiable such appropriation might have been, it would not be claimed that, because of the overwhelming necessity of the situation, the owner of the cable could not recover its value.

This is not a case where life or property was menaced by any object or thing belonging to the plaintiff, the destruction of which became necessary to prevent the threatened disaster. Nor is it a case where, because of the act of God, or unavoidable accident, the infliction of the injury was beyond the control of the defendant, but is one where the defendant prudently and advisedly availed itself of the plaintiffs' property for the purpose of preserving its own more valuable property, and the plaintiffs are entitled to compensation for the injury done.

Order affirmed. Lewis, J.

I dissent. It was assumed on the trial before the lower court that appellant's liability depended on whether the master of the ship might, in the exercise of reasonable care, have sought a place of safety before the storm made it impossible to leave the dock. The majority opinion assumes that the evidence is conclusive that appellant moored its boat at respondent's dock pursuant to contract, and that the vessel was lawfully in position at the time the additional cables were fastened to the dock, and the reasoning of the opinion is that, because appellant made use of the stronger cables to hold the boat in position, it became liable under the rule that it had voluntarily made use of the property of another for the purpose of saving its own. In my judgment, if the boat was lawfully in position at the time the storm broke, and the master could not, in the exercise of due care, have left that position without subjecting his vessel to the hazards of the storm, then the damage to the dock, caused by the pounding of the boat, was the result of an inevitable accident. If the master was in the exercise of due care, he was not at fault. The reasoning of the opinion admits that if the ropes, or cables, first attached to the dock had not parted, or if, in the first instance, the master had used the stronger cables, there would be no liability. If the master could not, in the exercise of reasonable care, have anticipated the severity of the storm and sought a place of safety before it became impossible, why should he be required to anticipate the severity of the storm, and, in the first instance, use the stronger cables?

I am of the opinion that one who constructs a dock to the navigable line of waters, and enters into contractual relations with the owner of a vessel to moor at the same, takes the risk of damage to his dock by a boat caught there by a storm, which event could not have been avoided in the exercise of due care, and further, that the legal status of the parties in such a case is not changed by renewal of cables to keep the boat from being cast adrift at the mercy of the tempest.

Notes and Questions

1. *Rossi* is, of course, a private necessity case. Just to be clear, what distinguishes a public necessity from a private necessity?

2. Why was the plaintiff in *Rossi* not considered a trespasser and thus responsible for her own injuries? Was this decision reached by looking to the common law or to the statute that governs the responsibility of dog owners? Notice that this case is illustrative of the hybrid statutory-common law nature of modern tort law. And notice how the two are used by the court to resolve the issue presented.

3. Keep track of the rules that apply to the liability of dog owners for dog bites. What general rules can you derive from the *Katko* and *Rossi* cases that would apply to dog bite cases

generally? We will revisit the subject toward the end of the course in the context of our discussion of strict liability.

4. The *Vincent* case sets out what has become the Restatement position on the doctrine of private necessity. This position has generated important scholarly controversy. *See, e.g.*, George C. Christie, The Defense of Necessity Considered from the Legal and Moral Points of View, 48 Duke L.J. 975 (1999). First, its holding is not required by the common law, i.e., precedent does not clearly require payment when damage is done. Second, requiring payment in circumstances where a trespass to land or chattels is justified by the need to save life and limb is, at least for some, morally and legally questionable. On the latter point, is it so clear (as the court suggests it is) that the law ought to require a man to pay compensation for bread taken in circumstances of need? Or for one life taken in circumstances where this is necessary to save the lives of more than one person? The latter question is derived from cases or hypotheticals where, for example, one man is thrown off of a lifeboat so that it does not sink and result in the death of others on the boat. How would the rule in *Vincent* resolve the claims of the decedent's estate on these facts? Does this resolution absolve the defendants from moral responsibility for their conduct?

5. Among other things, the law and economics movement seeks to encourage development of legal rules that incentivize socially useful behavior. Is this goal different from tort law's generally held mission? If the goal is socially useful behavior instead of or in addition to compensation, is the rule in *Vincent* a good or a bad one? Does it depend on the facts? For example, if instead of sacrificing less valuable property to save more valuable property — an efficient choice by some accounts — the sacrifice was of one person to save a number of individuals, as in the lifeboat hypothetical above. Would this also be socially useful?

SUROCCO v. GEARY
3 Cal. 69, 1853 WL 639 (Cal. 1853)

Dwinelle and Holt, for appellant.

The question of law is, whether a person or public officer has a right to pull down a building, acting in good faith for the purpose of preventing the spreading of a public conflagration, without being personally liable therefor in damages.

The law of Mexico prevailed at the time of the conflagration, when the damage is alleged to have been done, in December, 1849. 1 Peters, 511, 542. By that law the individual who in *good faith* destroyed a building, to prevent the spread of a public conflagration, was expressly held not liable in damages. 7 Partides, Title 15, Law 10.

Such destruction is not done solely on one's own account, but for that of the whole city; for it might happen that if not thus arrested, the fire might spread over the whole town, or a great part of it; and acting with a good intention, he is not answerable in damages. Ib. pp. 39, 440. If a private individual could do this, *a fortiori,* could the chief magistrate of the city do it.

The same rule prevails at common law, and is a principle of public law everywhere.

And property so destroyed is not "taken for public use," nor does the principle of compensation apply. Constitution California, Art. 1, Sec. 8.

The act is not that of the sovereign exercising the right of eminent domain, but an act of private necessity, done for private advantage, like that which authorizes the appropriation of a plank by one, which will not sustain two in the water. Although the act of destruction is for the public benefit, in one sense, it is so only as a matter of police, and those whose property is saved by it, reap the benefit, and ought to contribute, if any one is to be held accountable, on the principle of general average.

The mode of compensation in certain cases, and who is to make it, is provided for by the application of general principles. The party benefited may be sued for compensation . . . and if several, for contribution.

As to the necessity for the act complained of, that must be taken to be necessary, which is judged to be so by the judgment of discreet men, who have knowledge of all the circumstances. We are not bound to await the event in judging of the necessity of a protective measure, as in throwing goods overboard to lighten the vessel; the gale may cease, but the master is not liable for the loss. "Doing the act with good intentions," taken from the Spanish law, is a phrase illustrative of the principle of justification. In this case the fire actually reached the site of the building after its destruction.

We ask that the judgment be reversed, and that an absolute judgment be entered for the appellant. The case is governed by the Practice Act of 1850, under which this court have authority to render such judgment as substantial justice may require, sects. 162, 271, 275, 279; and this appeal was taken before that act was repealed, Min. Sup. Ct., vol. 2, p. 5, and is saved by the repealing Act of 1851, sect. 648.

No brief on file for respondent.

MURRAY, Chief Justice, delivered the opinion of the Court — HEYDENFELDT, Justice, concurred.

This was an action, commenced in the court below, to recover damages for blowing up and destroying the plaintiffs' house and property, during the fire of the 24th of December, 1849.

Geary, at that time Alcalde of San Francisco, justified, on the ground that he had the authority, by virtue of his office, to destroy said building, and also that it had been blown up by him to stop the progress of the conflagration then raging.

It was in proof, that the fire passed over and burned beyond the building of the plaintiffs', and that at the time said building was destroyed, they were engaged in removing their property, and could, had they not been prevented, have succeeded in removing more, if not all of their goods.

The cause was tried by the court sitting as a jury, and a verdict rendered for the plaintiffs, from which the defendant prosecutes this appeal under the Practice Act of 1850.

The only question for our consideration is, whether the person who tears down or destroys the house of another, in good faith, and under apparent necessity, during the time of a conflagration, for the purpose of saving the buildings adjacent, and stopping its progress, can be held personally liable in an action by the owner of the property destroyed.

This point has been so well settled in the courts of New York and New Jersey, that a reference to those authorities is all that is necessary to determine the present case.

The right to destroy property, to prevent the spread of a conflagration, has been traced to the highest law of necessity, and the natural rights of man, independent of society or civil government. "It is referred by moralists and jurists to the same great principle which justifies the exclusive appropriation of a plank in a shipwreck, though the life of another be sacrificed; with the throwing overboard goods in a tempest, for the safety of a vessel; with the trespassing upon the lands of another, to escape death by an enemy. It rests upon the maxim, *Necessitas inducit privilegium quod jura privata.*"

The common law adopts the principles of the natural law, and places the justification of an act otherwise tortious precisely on the same ground of necessity. (See American Print Works *v.* Lawrence, 1 Zab. 258, 264, and the cases there cited.)

This principle has been familiarly recognized by the books from the time of the saltpetre case, and the instances of tearing down houses to prevent a conflagration, or to raise bulwarks for the defence of a city, are made use of as illustrations, rather than as abstract cases, in which its exercise is permitted. At such times, the individual rights of property give way to the higher laws of impending necessity.

A house on fire, or those in its immediate vicinity, which serve to communicate the flames, becomes a nuisance, which it is lawful to abate, and the private rights of the individual yield to the considerations of general convenience, and the interests of society. Were it otherwise, one stubborn person might involve a whole city in ruin, by refusing to allow the destruction of a building which would cut off the flames and check the progress of the fire, and that, too, when it was perfectly evident that his building must be consumed.

The respondent has invoked the aid of the constitutional provision which prohibits the taking of private property for public use, without just compensation being made therefor. This is not "a taking of private property for public use," within the meaning of the Constitution.

The right of taking individual property for public purposes belongs to the State, by virtue of her right of eminent domain, and is said to be justified on the ground of state necessity; but this is not a taking or a destruction for a public purpose, but a destruction for the benefit of the individual or the city, but not properly of the State.

The counsel for the respondent has asked, who is to judge of the necessity of the destruction of property?

This must, in some instances, be a difficult matter to determine. The necessity of blowing up a house may not exist, or be as apparent to the owner, whose judgment is clouded by interest, and the hope of saving his property, as to others. In all such cases the conduct of the individual must be regulated by his own judgment as to the exigencies of the case. If a building should be torn down without apparent or actual necessity, the parties concerned would undoubtedly be liable in an action of trespass. But in every case the necessity must be clearly shown. It is true, many cases of hardship may grow out of this rule, and property may often in such cases be destroyed, without necessity, by irresponsible persons, but this difficulty would not be obviated by making the parties responsible in every case, whether the necessity existed or not.

The legislature of the State possess the power to regulate this subject by providing the manner in which buildings may be destroyed, and the mode in which compensation shall be made; and it is to be hoped that something will be done to obviate the difficulty, and prevent the happening of such events as those supposed by the respondent's counsel.

In the absence of any legislation on the subject, we are compelled to fall back upon the rules of the common law.

The evidence in this case clearly establishes the fact, that the blowing up of the house was necessary, as it would have been consumed had it been left standing. The plaintiffs cannot recover for the value of the goods which they might have saved; they were as much subject to the necessities of the occasion as the house in which they were situate; and if in such cases a party was held liable, it would too frequently happen, that the delay caused by the removal of the goods would render the destruction of the house useless.

The court below clearly erred as to the law applicable to the facts of this case. The testimony will not warrant a verdict against the defendant.

Judgment reversed.

Notes and Questions

1. *Surocco* is often cited as a seminal "public necessity" case. Yet the court itself rejected this characterization. Why?

2. Generalize from the facts of the case to develop a statement that explains what a "necessity" is that would justify a trespass, and also what attributes would be sufficient to make the necessity a "public" one.

3. Who is entitled to claim the defense of "public necessity"?

4. *Surocco* held that public necessity justifies a trespass so that the defendant is not responsible in tort for the plaintiff's damages. Was it also comfortable with this result? What are the arguments for and against this holding? What are the possible solutions for the plaintiff?

WEGNER v. MILWAUKEE MUTUAL INSURANCE COMPANY
479 N.W.2d 38 (Minn. 1991)

Tomljanovich, Justice.

The Minneapolis police department severely damaged a house owned by Harriet G. Wegner while attempting to apprehend an armed suspect. Wegner sought compensation from the City of Minneapolis on trespass and constitutional "taking" theories. The district court granted the City's motion for summary judgment on the "taking" issue. The court of appeals affirmed, reasoning that although there was a "taking" within the meaning of the Minnesota Constitution, the "taking" was noncompensable under the doctrine of public necessity. We reverse.

The salient facts are not in dispute. Around 6:30 p.m. on August 27, 1986, Minneapolis police were staking out an address in Northeast Minneapolis in the hope of apprehending two suspected felons who were believed to be coming to that address to sell stolen narcotics. The suspects arrived at the address with the stolen narcotics. Before arrests could be made, however, the suspects spotted the police and fled in their car at a high rate of speed with the police in pursuit. Eventually, the suspects abandoned their vehicle, separated and fled on foot. The police exchanged gunfire with one suspect as he fled. This suspect later entered the house of Harriet G. Wegner (Wegner) and hid in the front closet. Wegner's granddaughter, who was living at the house, and her fiancé then fled the premises and notified the police.

The police immediately surrounded the house and shortly thereafter called an "Operation 100" around 7:00 p.m. The term "Operation 100" refers to the calling of the Minneapolis Police Department's Emergency Response Unit (ERU) to the scene. The ERU, commonly thought of as a "SWAT" team, consists of personnel specially trained to deal with barricaded suspects, hostage-taking, or similar high-risk situations. Throughout the standoff, the police used a bullhorn and telephone in an attempt to communicate with the suspect. The police, receiving no response, continued efforts to establish contact with the suspect until around 10:00 p.m. At that time the police decided, according to ERU procedure, to take the next step in a barricaded suspect situation, which was to deliver chemical munitions. The police fired at least 25 rounds of chemical munitions or "tear gas" into the house in an attempt to expel the suspect. The police delivered the tear gas to every level of the house, breaking virtually every window in the process. In addition to the tear gas, the police cast three concussion or "flash-bang" grenades into the house to confuse the suspect. The police then entered the home and apprehended the suspect crawling out of a basement window.

The tear gas and flash-bang grenades caused extensive damage to the Wegner house. For example: a pink film from the tear gas covered the walls and furniture; some walls were dented from the impact of the tear gas canisters; one tear gas canister went through one of the upstairs walls. Wegner alleges damages of $71,000. The City denied Wegner's request for reimbursement, so she turned to her insurance carrier, Milwaukee Mutual Insurance Company (Milwaukee Mutual) for coverage. Milwaukee Mutual paid Wegner $26,595.88 for structural damage, $1,410.06 for emergency board and glass repair and denied coverage for the rest of the claim. Milwaukee Mutual is subrogated to the claims of Wegner against the City to the extent of its payments under the policy.

Wegner commenced an action against both the City of Minneapolis and Milwaukee Mutual to recover the remaining damages. In conjunction with a trespass claim against the City, Wegner asserted that the police department's actions constituted a compensable taking under Minn. Const. art. I, § 13. Milwaukee Mutual cross-claimed against the City for its subrogation interest and any additional amounts the insurer may be found liable for in the future.

Milwaukee Mutual and the City both brought motions for summary judgment on all claims. The district court granted partial summary judgment in favor of the City on the "taking" issue, holding that "Eminent domain is not intended as a limitation on [the] police power." Both Wegner and Milwaukee Mutual appealed the trial court's determination.

The court of appeals affirmed the trial court, reasoning that although there was a "taking" within the meaning of Minn. Const. art. I, § 13, the "taking" was noncompensable under the doctrine of public necessity. *Wegner v. Milwaukee Mut. Ins. Co.,* 464 N.W.2d 543 (Minn.App.1990).

I.

Article I, section 13, of the Minnesota Constitution provides: "Private property shall not be taken, destroyed or damaged for public use without just compensation, first paid or secured." This provision "imposes a condition on the exercise of the state's inherent supremacy over private property rights." *Johnson v. City of Plymouth,* 263 N.W.2d 603, 605 (Minn.1978). This type of constitutional inhibition "was designed to bar Government from forcing some people alone to bear public burdens which, in all fairness and justice, should be borne by the public as a whole." *Armstrong v. United States,* 364 U.S. 40, 49, 80 S.Ct. 1563, 1569, 4 L.Ed.2d 1554 (1960).

The purpose of the damage clause is to ensure that private landowners are compensated, not only for physical invasion of their property, but also damages caused by the state where no physical invasion has occurred. A more significant restriction on recovery under this provision is the requirement that the taking or damaging must be for a public use. What constitutes a public use under this provision is a judicial question which this court historically construes broadly.

The City contends there was no taking for a public use because the actions of the police constituted a legitimate exercise of the police power. The police power in its nature is indefinable. However, simply labeling the actions of the police as an exercise of the police power "cannot justify the disregard of the constitutional inhibitions." *Petition of Dreosch,* 233 Minn. 274, 282, 47 N.W.2d 106, 111 (1951).[2]

---

[2] One commentator explained:

> [The police power] is used by the court to identify those state and local governmental restrictions and prohibitions which are valid and which may be invoked without payment of compensation. In its best known and most traditional uses, the police power is employed to protect the health, safety, and morals of the community in the form of such things as fire regulations, garbage disposal control, and restrictions upon prostitution and liquor. But it has never been thought that government authority under the police power was limited to those narrow uses.

The City argues that Wegner and Milwaukee Mutual are confusing the concept of police power and eminent domain. We agree that this is not an eminent domain action and should not be analyzed as such. This action is based on the plain meaning of the language of Minn. Const. art I, § 13, which requires compensation when property is damaged for a public use. Consequently, the issue in this case is not the reasonableness of the use of chemical munitions to extricate the barricaded suspect but rather whether the exercise of the city's admittedly legitimate police power resulted in a "taking".

In resolving this case of first impression, the well-reasoned decision of *Steele v. City of Houston,* 603 S.W.2d 786 (Tex.1980) provides guidance. In *Steele,* the Texas Supreme Court addressed a constitutional taking claim involving facts strikingly similar to the present case. There, a group of escaped prisoners had taken refuge in a house apparently selected at random. After discovering the prisoners in the house, the Houston police discharged incendiary material into the house for the purpose of causing the house to catch fire. The police allegedly let the house burn, even after the fire department arrived, in order to ensure all the prisoners had been forced out. The court, interpreting the taking provision of the Texas Constitution, which is virtually identical to the Minnesota taking provision, stated, "this court has moved beyond the earlier notion that the government's duty to pay for taking property rights is excused by labeling the taking as an exercise of police powers." *Id.* at 789. In discussing the city's governmental immunity argument, the court stated:

> The Constitution itself is the authorization for compensation for the destruction of property and is a waiver of governmental immunity for the taking, damaging or destruction of property for public use.

The court further stated:

> The City argues that the destruction of the property as a means to apprehend escapees is a classic instance of police power exercised for the safety of the public. We do not hold that the police officers wrongfully ordered the destruction of the dwelling; we hold that the innocent third parties are entitled by the Constitution to compensation for their property.

Id. at 791, 793. The court reversed the grant of summary judgment and remanded the case to the trial court so the plaintiffs could prove that the house was intentionally set on fire and that the destruction of the house and its contents was for a public use.

It is unnecessary to remand this case for a determination of whether the police intentionally damaged the Wegner house for a public use. It is undisputed the police intentionally fired tear gas and concussion grenades into the Wegner house. Similarly, it is clear that the damage inflicted by the police in the course of capturing a dangerous suspect was for a public use within the meaning of the constitution.

The court of appeals cited the *Steele* decision for the simple proposition that the apprehension of criminal suspects has been held to be a public use but did not address the rest of the case despite the factual similarities to the case at bar. Instead, the court of appeals placed heavy

---

Sax, *Takings and the Police Power,* 74 Yale L.J. 36, n. 6 (1966).

reliance on the Georgia Intermediate Court of Appeals case of *McCoy v. Sanders,* 113 Ga.App. 565, 148 S.E.2d 902 (1966). The *McCoy* court held the draining of a pond by the police while searching for a murder victim's body was a proper exercise of the police power not requiring compensation under the Georgia Constitution. *Id.,* 113 Ga.App. at 566, 148 S.E.2d at 903. As in *Steele,* the Georgia Constitution also mirrors the Minnesota Constitution. The Georgia courts, however, interpret the damage provision of their constitution as limited to those situations where there is physical interference with the property "in connection with an improvement for public use." *Id.,* 113 Ga.App. at 569, 148 S.E.2d at 905. This court never has held that the takings provision of Minn. Const. art. I, § 13 is to be applied in such a limited way. We believe the *Steele* decision is more directly on point and provides a much better analysis than *McCoy.*

We hold that where an innocent third party's property is damaged by the police in the course of apprehending a suspect, that property is damaged within the meaning of the constitution.

II.

We briefly address the application of the doctrine of public necessity to these facts. The Restatement (Second) of Torts § 196 describes the doctrine as follows:

> One is privileged to enter land in the possession of another if it is, or if the actor reasonably believes it to be, necessary for the purpose of averting an imminent public disaster.[6]

See McDonald v. City of Red Wing, 13 Minn. 38 (Gil. 25) (1868) (city excused from paying compensation under the doctrine of "public safety" where city officers destroyed building to prevent the spread of fire). Prosser, apparently somewhat troubled by the potential harsh outcomes of this doctrine, states:

> It would seem that the moral obligation upon the group affected to make compensation in such a case should be recognized by the law, but recovery usually has been denied.

Prosser and Keeton, *The Law of Torts,* § 24 (5th ed. 1984); *see also Restatement (Second) of Torts* § 196 comment h. Here, the police were attempting to apprehend a dangerous felon who had fired shots at pursuing officers. The capture of this individual most certainly was beneficial

---

[6] Prosser explains:

> Where the danger affects the entire community, or so many people that the public interest is involved, that interest serves as a complete justification to the defendant who acts to avert the peril to all. Thus, one who dynamites a house to stop the spread of a conflagration that threatens a town, or shoots a mad dog in the street, or burns clothing infected with smallpox germs, or in time of war, destroys property which should not be allowed to fall into the hands of the enemy, is not liable to the owner, so long as the emergency is great enough, and he has acted reasonably under the circumstances. This notion does not require the "champion of the public" to pay for the general salvation out of his own pocket. The number of persons who must be endangered in order to create a public necessity has not been determined by the courts.

Prosser and Keeton, *The Law of Torts,* § 24 (5th ed.1984).

to the whole community. In such circumstances, an individual in Wegner's position should not be forced to bear the entire cost of a benefit conferred on the community as a whole.

Although the court of appeals found there to be a "taking" under Minn. Const. art. I, § 13, the court ruled the "taking" was noncompensable based on the doctrine of public necessity.

We do not agree. Once a "taking" is found, compensation is required by operation of law. Thus, if the doctrine of public necessity were to apply to a given fact situation, no taking could be found under Minn. Const. art. I, § 13.

We are not inclined to allow the city to defend its actions on the grounds of public necessity under the facts of this case. *But see Steele,* 603 S.W.2d at 792. We believe the better rule, in situations where an innocent third party's property is taken, damaged or destroyed by the police in the course of apprehending a suspect, is for the municipality to compensate the innocent party for the resulting damages. The policy considerations in this case center around the basic notions of fairness and justice. At its most basic level, the issue is whether it is fair to allocate the entire risk of loss to an innocent homeowner for the good of the public. We do not believe the imposition of such a burden on the innocent citizens of this state would square with the underlying principles of our system of justice. Therefore, the City must reimburse Wegner for the losses sustained.

As a final note, we hold that the individual police officers, who were acting in the public interest, cannot be held personally liable. Instead, the citizens of the City should all bear the cost of the benefit conferred.

The judgments of the courts below are reversed and the cause remanded for trial on the issue of damages.

Affirmed in part, reversed in part and remanded.

Notes and Questions

1. *Wegner* is a contemporary public necessity case. How has the State of Minnesota resolved the concerns raised by the *Surocco* court?

2. The difference between a "taking" for which the Constitution requires "just compensation" and a "trespass" excused by "public necessity" is not always clear. As the United States Supreme Court has noted, "each case must be judged on its own facts." *United States v. Caltex*, 344 U.S. 149, 156 (1952). For our (torts class) purposes, it suffices to note that the closer case facts are to those in *Surocco*, where there was an imminent threat to public safety requiring decisive, destructive action by the state or someone acting on behalf of the state to protect the public welfare, the more likely they are to be characterized as a trespass and not a taking. *See, e.g., id.* (the Court characterizes the demolition by the retreating United States military of private oil companies' facilities to ensure they could not be used by the advancing enemy as a trespass justified by public necessity and thus rejects the companies' claim that this action was a taking requiring just compensation). On the other hand, examples of cases where the Court has agreed with the plaintiff that there was a "taking" include *United States v. Commodities*

Trading Corporation, 339 U.S. 950 (1950) (the Court agreed that the requisitioning by the War Department of 760,000 pounds of black pepper from the defendant for use in the war effort was a "taking" and the only issue was the price the Department needed to pay to satisfy the just compensation requirement), and *United States v. Miller*, 317 U.S. 369 (1943) (the United States exercises its eminent domain authority to condemn private property for the relocation of a railroad line). Does the court in *Wegner* decide that the defendants' actions were a trespass or a taking? Using the United States Supreme Court decisions set out in this note, how would you argue that it was a taking? That it was not?

AN OVERVIEW OF NEGLIGENCE

Chapters Three to Six focus on negligence, which may be generally defined as carelessness that causes a physical injury or property damage. As a category, negligence is to be contrasted with intentional torts, which require a more culpable mental state — either the purpose to or near certainty that an act will cause harm, and with strict liability torts — which are causation- rather than fault-based. See Chapter 1(B) (discussing the fault continuum). Although it is the newest of the three categories of tort law, having emerged only in the late 18th century to early 19th century, most tort claims today are based in negligence.

The negligence prima facie case has four elements: (1) duty, (2) breach of duty, (3) causation, and (4) injury or damage. In narrative form, this means that for a plaintiff to make out a case in negligence, it must be established that the defendant owed them a duty of care that was breached, and that this breach caused the plaintiff's physical injuries or property damage. You will see that some opinions set out a three-part prima facie case which combines the causation and injury elements, and some set out a five-part prima facie case which breaks out causation into its two principal sub-parts. However, the four-part breakdown is most common. The chapters that follow track these four required elements.

Chapter 3 focuses on the first element of the prima facie case — duty. Duty is generally described as "an obligation, to which the law will give recognition and effect, to conform to a particular standard of conduct toward another." W. Page Keeton, et al., *Prosser and Keeton on The Law of Torts* § 53 (5th ed.1984). As such, it is a question of law for the court to decide in the first instance, based on a consideration of the policy implications inherent in the imposition of the obligation across the category of cases represented by the claim.

The first part of Chapter 3 addresses duty as it exists in the most common circumstances; that is, those in which a plaintiff's physical injuries or property damage are alleged to be the result of affirmative conduct by the defendant. In these circumstances, when the defendant acts, they are said to owe a duty to the plaintiff whenever it is reasonably foreseeable that their actions risk injury. We will see that in the run-of-the-mill case, this duty is treated as established, and mostly as a result the issue is not litigated; instead, the parties turn straight to breach. For example, duty will likely never be litigated (or summary judgment on the issue will be proper) where the allegation and uncontroverted evidence are that the defendant drove his car through a red light into an intersection and crashed into the plaintiff whose car was proceeding legally: if there is any "obligation[] to which the law will give recognition and effect, to conform to a particular standard of conduct toward another[,]" it is this one and others sufficiently like it that they are believed to deserve the same default treatment.

The second part of Chapter 3 addresses particular circumstances in which this default — or automatically established — duty does not exist. These particular circumstances involve those in which, at common law, the defendant either had no duty at all or else had a specifically delineated obligation. These circumstances include the law's traditional "no duty to rescue" rule, special premises liability rules, and the rules governing claims for "stand-alone" negligent infliction of emotional distress and economic loss. (Stand-alone claims assume the plaintiff has not suffered a precedent or concurrent physical injury or property damage.) As in all duty contexts, these special rules were carved out for policy reasons, and to the extent their terms are amended over time these amendments also reflect the courts' policy considerations.

Chapter 4 focuses on the law governing the second element of the prima facie case for negligence — breach of the duty of care. A breach of duty is established by evidence that the defendant acted "unreasonably." (This requirement and legal term of art usually translates well to our lay understandings of "carelessness" and even of "negligence.") Conversely, satisfying the duty is established by evidence that the defendant acted "reasonably." In either case, reasonableness is the "standard of care" (another term of art) required by negligence law. The special standards of care (definitions of "reasonableness") for children, the physically handicapped, and experts including professionals are developed in this chapter, as well as the tools and methods lawyers use to prove and disprove breach.

Chapter 5 focuses on negligence law's third required element — causation. Most basically, a breach of due care must in fact cause a plaintiff's personal injuries or property damage before these can be compensable. For liability finally to attach, however, the breach must also be found to be their proximate cause. Proximate cause is also sometimes called "legal cause." It is designed to be a final check on the policy merits of the plaintiff's claim; it is the point in the prima facie case where the fact finder (usually the jury) can undo an injustice that it believes would result from a finding of liability. In this respect it is both similar to and different from duty analysis: like duty analysis, it is an inquiry that is ultimately steeped in policy; unlike duty analysis, it is fact-based by definition, both in terms of its decision maker and of its focus on the particular defendant's specific breach. You will see that because of these similarities and differences, courts that have occasion to discuss duty often also discuss proximate cause. Noticing these discussions and then taking the time to understand how the two analyses relate will help you to develop a most sophisticated understanding of the negligence prima facie case.

Chapter 6 addresses the fourth and final element of the negligence prima facie case — injury. It also focuses on the damages that flow from different kinds of injuries. Unlike claims for intentional torts which can be based in a mere dignitary harm, successful claims in negligence require an allegation and proof that the plaintiff has suffered an injury for which at least compensatory damages are warranted. Although punitive damages are rarely awarded in the negligence context, they may be possible if the plaintiff can prove that the defendant acted knowing that the conduct was unreasonable or reckless.

CHAPTER THREE
DUTY

The first element of the prima facie case for negligence is duty. Consistent with the doctrine, this chapter is divided into two parts: The first focuses on the duty rule that applies in the typical negligence case, which involves a defendant whose affirmative actions are alleged to have risked harm. The second focuses on the traditional policy exceptions to this general rule. These exceptions include the "no duty to rescue" rule, the "no duty" rules that apply in cases in which plaintiffs allege only emotional distress or economic loss, and the special duties that apply in premises liability cases.

I. THE GENERAL OR "DEFAULT" DUTY RULE

The general rule is that duty exists as a matter of law in circumstances where the defendant "acts" — as that term was defined in Chapter Two — in a way that poses a risk of harm to others. A very simple example is a case arising out of a car accident in an intersection allegedly caused by the defendant who was texting while driving. The parties in such cases rarely litigate duty, because there will rarely be the legal basis to argue that it does not exist; hence our use of the term "default" duty. This default reflects a policy decision — made at some earlier point in time by a court considering the matter — that when individuals act in a way that risks harm, they assume a legal obligation to others. The duty is this legal obligation.

A. The Different Judicial Approaches to the Default Duty

What parties do sometimes litigate in this area are big questions about the *scope* of the default duty. For example, they might litigate the issues whether every person is owed a duty who is in fact injured as a result of the defendant's actions, or whether the duty is owed regardless of the nature of the risks the defendant posed. (Note that because these are big questions, and because they are questions of law, their answers are generally established in most jurisdictions and only infrequently come up for review by the appellate courts.) The three opinions that follow — *Palsgraf*, *Barker*, and *Strauss* — reflect historical and modern approaches to the *scope* of the default duty. As you read the opinions, be sure to note the ways in which the judges approach the scope issue differently, and how these differences affect individual case outcomes and the law's expressive function — the message the law sends to individuals in the society about their obligations to themselves and to others.

PALSGRAF v. LONG ISLAND RAILROAD
162 N.E. 99 (N.Y. 1928)

CARDOZO, C. J.

Plaintiff was standing on a platform of defendant's railroad after buying a ticket to go to Rockaway Beach. A train stopped at the station, bound for another place. Two men ran forward to catch it. One of the men reached the platform of the car without mishap, though the train was already moving. The other man, carrying a package, jumped aboard the car, but seemed unsteady as if about to fall. A guard on the car, who had held the door open, reached forward to help him in, and another guard on the platform pushed him from behind. In this act, the package was dislodged, and fell upon the rails. It was a package of small size, about fifteen inches long, and was covered by a newspaper. In fact it contained fireworks, but there was nothing in its appearance to give notice of its contents. The fireworks when they fell exploded. The shock of the explosion threw down some scales at the other end of the platform many feet away. The scales struck the plaintiff, causing injuries for which she sues.

The conduct of the defendant's guard, if a wrong in its relation to the holder of the package, was not a wrong in its relation to the plaintiff, standing far away. Relatively to her it was not negligence at all. Nothing in the situation gave notice that the falling package had in it the potency of peril to persons thus removed. Negligence is not actionable unless it involves the invasion of a legally protected interest, the violation of a right. 'Proof of negligence in the air, so to speak, will not do.' Pollock, Torts (11th Ed.) p. 455. . . . The plaintiff, as she stood upon the platform of the station, might claim to be protected against intentional invasion of her bodily security. Such invasion is not charged. She might claim to be protected against unintentional invasion by conduct involving in the thought of reasonable men an unreasonable hazard that such invasion would ensue. These, from the point of view of the law, were the bounds of her immunity, with perhaps some rare exceptions, survivals for the most part of ancient forms of liability, where conduct is held to be at the peril of the actor. If no hazard was apparent to the eye of ordinary vigilance, an act innocent and harmless, at least to outward seeming, with reference to her, did not take to itself the quality of a tort because it happened to be a wrong, though apparently not one involving the risk of bodily insecurity, with reference to some one else. 'In every instance, before negligence can be predicated of a given act, back of the act must be sought and found a duty to the individual complaining, the observance of which would have averted or avoided the injury.' McSherry, C. J., in West Virginia Central & P. R. Co. v. State, 96 Md. 652, 666, 54 A. 669, 671 (61 L. R. A. 574). 'The ideas of negligence and duty are strictly correlative.' Bowen, L. J., in Thomas v. Quartermaine, 18 Q. B. D. 685, 694. The plaintiff sues in her own right for a wrong personal to her, and not as the vicarious beneficiary of a breach of duty to another.

A different conclusion will involve us, and swiftly too, in a maze of contradictions. A guard stumbles over a package which has been left upon a platform. It seems to be a bundle of newspapers. It turns out to be a can of dynamite. To the eye of ordinary vigilance, the bundle is abandoned waste, which may be kicked or trod on with impunity. Is a passenger at the other end of the platform protected by the law against the unsuspected hazard concealed beneath the waste? If not, is the result to be any different, so far as the distant passenger is concerned, when the guard stumbles over a valise which a truckman or a porter has left upon the walk? The passenger far away, if the victim of a wrong at all, has a cause of action, not derivative, but original and primary. His claim to be protected against invasion of his bodily security is neither greater nor less because the act resulting in the invasion is a wrong to another far removed. In this case, the rights that are said to have been violated, are not even of the same order. The man was not injured in his person nor even put in danger. The purpose of the act, as well as its effect, was to make his person safe. I[f] there was a wrong to him at all, which may very well be doubted it was a wrong to a property interest only, the safety of his package. Out of this wrong to property, which threatened injury to nothing else, there has passed, we are told, to the plaintiff by derivation or succession a right of action for the invasion of an interest of another order, the right to bodily security. The diversity of interests emphasizes the futility of the effort to build the plaintiff's right upon the basis of a wrong to some one else. The gain is one of emphasis, for a like result would follow if the interests were the same. Even then, the orbit of the danger as disclosed to the eye of reasonable vigilance would be the orbit of the duty. One who jostles one's neighbor in a crowd does not invade the rights of others standing at the outer fringe when the unintended contact casts a bomb upon the ground. The wrongdoer as to them is the man who carries the bomb, not the one who explodes it without suspicion of the danger. Life will have to be made over, and human nature transformed, before prevision so extravagant can be accepted as the norm of conduct, the customary standard to which behavior must conform.

The argument for the plaintiff is built upon the shifting meanings of such words as 'wrong' and 'wrongful,' and shares their instability. What the plaintiff must show is 'a wrong' to herself; i.e., a violation of her own right, and not merely a wrong to some one else, nor conduct 'wrongful' because unsocial, but not 'a wrong' to any one. We are told that one who drives at reckless speed through a crowded city street is guilty of a negligent act and therefore of a wrongful one, irrespective of the consequences. Negligent the act is, and wrongful in the sense that it is unsocial, but wrongful and unsocial in relation to other travelers, only because the eye of vigilance perceives the risk of damage. If the same act were to be committed on a speedway or a race course, it would lose its wrongful quality. The risk reasonably to be perceived defines the duty to be obeyed, and risk imports relation; it is risk to another or to others within the range of apprehension. This does not mean, of course, that one who launches a destructive force is always relieved of liability, if the force, though known to be destructive, pursues an unexpected path. 'It was not necessary that the defendant should have had notice of the particular method in which an accident would occur, if the possibility of an accident was clear to the ordinarily prudent eye.' Some acts, such as shooting are so imminently dangerous to any one who may come within reach of the missile however unexpectedly, as to impose a duty of prevision not far from that of an insurer. Even to-day, and much oftener in earlier stages of the law, one acts sometimes at one's peril. Under this head, it may be, fall certain cases of what is known as transferred intent, an act willfully dangerous to A resulting by misadventure in injury to B. These cases aside, wrong is defined in terms of the natural or probable, at least when unintentional. The range of reasonable apprehension is at times a question for the court, and at times, if varying inferences are possible, a question for the jury. Here, by concession, there was nothing in the situation to suggest to the most cautious mind that the parcel wrapped in newspaper would spread wreckage through the station. If the guard had thrown it down knowingly and willfully, he would not have threatened the plaintiff's safety, so far as appearances could warn him. His conduct would not have involved, even then, an unreasonable probability of invasion of her bodily security. Liability can be no greater where the act is inadvertent.

Negligence, like risk, is thus a term of relation. Negligence in the abstract, apart from things related, is surely not a tort, if indeed it is understandable at all. Negligence is not a tort unless it results in the commission of a wrong, and the commission of a wrong imports the violation of a right, in this case, we are told, the right to be protected against interference with one's bodily security. But bodily security is protected, not against all forms of interference or aggression, but only against some. One who seeks redress at law does not make out a cause of action by showing without more that there has been damage to his person. If the harm was not willful, he must show that the act as to him had possibilities of danger so many and apparent as to entitle him to be protected against the doing of it though the harm was unintended. Affront to personality is still the keynote of the wrong. Confirmation of this view will be found in the history and development of the action on the case. Negligence as a basis of civil liability was unknown to mediaeval law. For damage to the person, the sole remedy was trespass, and trespass did not lie in the absence of aggression, and that direct and personal. Liability for other damage, as where a servant without orders from the master does or omits something to the damage of another, is a plant of later growth. When it emerged out of the legal soil, it was thought of as a variant of trespass, an offshoot of the parent stock. This appears in the form of action, which was known as trespass on the case. The victim does not sue derivatively, or by right of subrogation, to vindicate an interest invaded in the person of another. Thus to view his cause of action is to ignore the fundamental difference between tort and crime. He sues for breach of a duty owing to himself.

The law of causation, remote or proximate, is thus foreign to the case before us. The question of liability is always anterior to the question of the measure of the consequences that go with liability. If there is no tort to be redressed, there is no occasion to consider what damage might be recovered if there were a finding of a tort. We may assume, without deciding, that negligence, not at large or in the abstract, but in relation to the plaintiff, would entail liability for any and all consequences, however novel or extraordinary. There is room for argument that a distinction is to be drawn according to the diversity of interests invaded by the act, as where conduct negligent in that it threatens an insignificant invasion of an interest in property results in an unforeseeable invasion of an interest of another order, as, e. g., one of bodily security. Perhaps other distinctions may be necessary. We do not go into the question now. The consequences to be followed must first be rooted in a wrong.

The judgment of the Appellate Division and that of the Trial Term should be reversed, and the complaint dismissed, with costs in all courts.

ANDREWS, J. (dissenting).

Assisting a passenger to board a train, the defendant's servant negligently knocked a package from his arms. It fell between the platform and the cars. Of its contents the servant knew and could know nothing. A violent explosion followed. The concussion broke some scales standing a considerable distance away. In falling, they injured the plaintiff, an intending passenger.

Upon these facts, may she recover the damages she has suffered in an action brought against the master? The result we shall reach depends upon our theory as to the nature of negligence. Is it a relative concept — the breach of some duty owing to a particular person or to particular persons? Or, where there is an act which unreasonably threatens the safety of others, is the doer liable for all its proximate consequences, even where they result in injury to one who would generally be thought to be outside the radius of danger? This is not a mere dispute as to words. We might not believe that to the average mind the dropping of the bundle would seem to involve the probability of harm to the plaintiff standing many feet away whatever might be the case as to the owner or to one so near as to be likely to be struck by its fall. If, however, we adopt the second hypothesis, we have to inquire only as to the relation between cause and effect. We deal in terms of proximate cause, not of negligence.

Negligence may be defined roughly as an act or omission which unreasonably does or may affect the rights of others, or which unreasonably fails to protect one's self from the dangers resulting from such acts. Here I confine myself to the first branch of the definition. Nor do I comment on the word 'unreasonable.' For present purposes it sufficiently describes that average of conduct that society requires of its members.

There must be both the act or the omission, and the right. It is the act itself, not the intent of the actor, that is important. In criminal law both the intent and the result are to be considered. Intent again is material in tort actions, where punitive damages are sought, dependent on actual malice — not one merely reckless conduct. But here neither insanity nor infancy lessens responsibility.

As has been said, except in cases of contributory negligence, there must be rights which are or may be affected. Often though injury has occurred, no rights of him who suffers have been touched. A licensee or trespasser upon my land has no claim to affirmative care on my part that the land be made safe. Where a railroad is required to fence its tracks against cattle, no man's rights are injured should he wander upon the road because such fence is absent. An unborn child may not demand immunity from personal harm.

But we are told that 'there is no negligence unless there is in the particular case a legal duty to take care, and this duty must be one which is owed to the plaintiff himself and not merely to others.' Salmond Torts (6th ed.) 24. This I think too narrow a conception. Where there is the unreasonable act, and some right that may be affected there is negligence whether damage does or does not result. That is immaterial. Should we drive down Broadway at a reckless speed, we are negligent whether we strike an approaching car or miss it by an inch. The act itself is wrongful. It is a wrong not only to those who happen to be within the radius of danger, but to all who might have been there — a wrong to the public at large. Such is the language of the street. Such the language of the courts when speaking of contributory negligence. Such again and again their language in speaking of the duty of some defendant and discussing proximate cause in cases where such a discussion is wholly irrelevant on any other theory. As was said by Mr. Justice Holmes many years ago:

> 'The measure of the defendant's duty in determining whether a wrong has been committed is one thing, the measure of liability when a wrong has been committed is another.' Spade v. Lynn & B. R. Co., 172 Mass. 488, 491, 52 N. E. 747, 748 (43 L. R. A. 832, 70 Am. St. Rep. 298).

Due care is a duty imposed on each one of us to protect society from unnecessary danger, not to protect A, B, or C alone.

It may well be that there is no such thing as negligence in the abstract. 'Proof of negligence in the air, so to speak, will not do.' In an empty world negligence would not exist. It does involve a relationship between man and his fellows, but not merely a relationship between man and those whom he might reasonably expect his act would injure; rather, a relationship between him and those whom he does in fact injure. If his act has a tendency to harm some one, it harms him a mile away as surely as it does those on the scene. We now permit children to recover for the negligent killing of the father. It was never prevented on the theory that no duty was owing to them. A husband may be compensated for the loss of his wife's services. To say that the wrongdoer was negligent as to the husband as well as to the wife is merely an attempt to fit facts to theory. An insurance company paying a fire loss recovers its payment of the negligent incendiary. We speak of subrogation — of suing in the right of the insured. Behind the cloud of words is the fact they hide, that the act, wrongful as to the insured, has also injured the company. Even if it be true that the fault of father, wife, or insured will prevent recovery, it is because we consider the original negligence, not the proximate cause of the injury. Pollock, Torts (12th ed.) 463.

In the well-known Polemis Case, [1921] 3 K. B. 560, Scrutton, L. J., said that the dropping of a plank was negligent, for it might injure 'workman or cargo or ship.' Because of either possibility, the owner of the vessel was to be made good for his loss. The act being wrongful, the doer was liable for its proximate results. Criticized and explained as this statement may have been, I think it states the law as it should be and as it is.

The proposition is this: Every one owes to the world at large the duty of refraining from those acts that may unreasonably threaten the safety of others. Such an act occurs. Not only is he wronged to whom harm, might reasonably be expected to result, but he also who is in fact injured, even if he be outside what would generally be thought the danger zone. There needs be duty due the one complaining, but this is not a duty to a particular individual because as to him harm might be expected. Harm to some one being the natural result of the act, not only that one alone, but all those in fact injured may complain. We have never, I think, held otherwise. Indeed in the Di Caprio Case we said that a breach of a general ordinance defining the degree of care to be exercised in one's calling is evidence of negligence as to every one. We did not limit this statement to those who might be expected to be exposed to danger. Unreasonable risk being taken, its consequences are not confined to those who might probably be hurt.

If this be so, we do not have a plaintiff suing by 'derivation or succession.' Her action is original and primary. Her claim is for a breach of duty to herself — not that she is subrogated to any right of action of the owner of the parcel or of a passenger standing at the scene of the explosion.

The right to recover damages rests on additional considerations. The plaintiff's rights must be injured, and this injury must be caused by the negligence. . . .

The judgment appealed from should be affirmed, with costs.

POUND, LEHMAN, and KELLOGG, JJ., concur with CARDOZO, C. J. ANDREWS, J., dissents in opinion in which CRANE and O'BRIEN, JJ., concur.

Notes and Questions

1. *Palsgraf* is one of the most famous cases in American jurisprudence. It is certainly a traditional highlight of the first year in law school. This is at least in part because of Justice Cardozo's majority opinion. Commenting on his writing style, Christopher Hawthorne wrote:

There is an accuracy that defeats itself by the over-emphasis of details. This was Cardozo's own pronouncement on judicial opinion-writing, and he took his own advice very seriously. Cardozo's writing is regarded as some of the most elliptical in American law.

Cardozo's famously indirect style had a purpose, however. Judge Richard Posner describes Cardozo as a "shy pragmatist" who used a "'professionally' smooth, legal insider's style" to disguise a pragmatic ideology. Cardozo's style gave him a unique advantage, since it allowed him to promulgate innovative or even controversial theories of law, while appearing to take incremental, formalist steps. This "insider's style," delivered with utter confidence, made Cardozo's opinions unassailable, at least until the reader unpacked the rhetoric.

Similarly, Cardozo's talent for aphorism prompted the citing judge to adopt a metonymic approach to Cardozo's opinions, using a single phrase — "danger invites rescue," for instance — to stand for a whole opinion.

Finally, Cardozo extended his skillful use of rhetoric, not just into his statements of law, but also into his statements of facts. This use of the statement of facts as a persuasive device is not unique to Cardozo, but he was a particularly accomplished practitioner.

Nowhere is this more apparent than in Cardozo's brief and abstract statement of facts in *Palsgraf v. Long Island Railroad Co.*:

> Plaintiff was standing on a platform of defendant's railroad after buying a ticket to go to Rockaway Beach. A train stopped at the station, bound for another place. Two men ran forward to catch it. One of the men reached the platform of the car without mishap, though the train was already moving. The other man, carrying a package, jumped aboard the car, but seemed unsteady as if about to fall. A guard on the car, who had held the door open, reached forward to help him in, and another guard on the platform pushed him from behind. In this act, the package was dislodged, and fell upon the rails. It was a package of small size, about fifteen inches long, and was covered by newspaper. In fact it contained fireworks, but there was nothing in its appearance to give notice of its contents. The fireworks when they fell exploded. The shock of the explosion threw down some scales at the other end of the platform many feet away. The scales struck the plaintiff, causing injuries for which she sues.

Here, Cardozo is in no danger of overemphasizing details. We could read *Palsgraf* a hundred times and never know the following facts: that the explosion was so severe that it ripped a huge hole in the platform and could be heard several blocks away; that the scales were as tall as Helen Palsgraf and that the glass in the scales shattered and fell on her; that the crowd on the platform panicked and that the ensuing stampede, not the explosion, may have knocked over the scales; and that the "injury" for which Mrs. Palsgraf sued was a severe stutter which developed several days after the accident. Cardozo also refused to discuss the probable distance between Mrs. Palsgraf and the explosion — more than ten feet but probably less than thirty feet. Leave out

> the actual location of the train platform — East New York — and the reader may feel transported into a strange, featureless world, full of uncertain terror. The statement of facts creates an anxiety in the reader which demands the reassurance of authority — a reassurance which Cardozo was happy to provide in the remainder of the opinion.
>
> . . . Cardozo's phrases, "the eye of ordinary vigilance," and "negligence in the air," are talismans of tort law. Posner describes this style as "gnomic." Certainly, Cardozo speaks in *Palsgraf* with an Olympian authority which suggests that his opinion is the last word on the subject: "Life will have to be made over, and human nature transformed, before prevision so extravagant can be accepted as the norm of conduct," he extravagantly intones, rejecting a more expansive definition of duty and foreseeability.
>
> Posner suggests that this is the reason Cardozo left his statement of facts so abstract and general. An opinion with a more specific set of facts could have been limited to fact patterns "in which the type of injury that occurs is unforeseeable." Instead, Cardozo wanted to write a short primer on negligence. Specific facts would have gotten in the way. The abstraction of facts, the aphoristic phrasing, the tremendous rhetorical confidence with which Cardozo makes his argument — all this has the effect of blurring law, fact, policy, and philosophy until the entire opinion seems like a statement of truth.

Christopher Hawthorne, *Deific Decree: The Short, Happy Life of a Pseudo-Doctrine*, 33 LOY. L.A. L. REV. 1755 (2000).

2. How does Justice Cardozo characterize the duty in negligence? What is his methodology for establishing duty? Contrast this characterization and methodology with Justice Andrews's approach to duty. What different policy objectives are embedded in their respective formulations?

3. In his dissent, Justice Andrews uses "the well-known *Polemis* Case" to support his position that to establish duty, the plaintiff need not show that his or her particular harm was foreseeable ex ante. In re An Arbitration Between Polemis and Furness, Withy & Co., Ltd., 3 K. B. 560 (1921) ("the dropping of a plank was negligent, for it might injure 'workman or cargo or ship'"). The plaintiffs in *Polemis* were successful in their claim for the total loss of their ship which was caused by a fire which itself resulted from the defendants' negligence in allowing their workmen to drop a plank from an upper to a lower deck. When the plank hit the lower deck, it caused a spark that ignited petrol fumes which had accumulated there. The case is mostly known for its proximate cause analysis, but in *Palsgraf*, Justice Andrews used it for the threshold proposition that these same facts were also sufficient to establish duty and breach.

4. *Palsgraf* is the first but not the last case you will read in which courts and judges discuss and distinguish issues of duty and proximate cause. You will not have a complete understanding of the relationship between the two until you have covered both, but in the meantime, it is important that you notice the phenomenon and that you work to see when text is shifting from a discussion and analysis of duty to a discussion and analysis of proximate cause. Justices Cardozo and Andrews made that shift clear in the way they structured and wrote their opinions in *Palsgraf*. The next case is not as clear in this respect, but if you read carefully and with an eye to these issues, you will be able to distinguish them and thus to identify the

rule of the case — the default duty in negligence. What is the difference between that rule and the rule that the judge says applies to proximate cause analysis?

BARKER v. CITY OF PHILADELPHIA
134 F. Supp. 231 (E.D. Pa. 1955)

LORD, District Judge.

This action was instituted by Dolores Barker, administratrix of the estate of Robert P. Ebbecke, deceased, to recover damages under the Wrongful Death, 12 P.S. §§ 1601 et seq., and Survival Statutes of Pennsylvania, 20 P.S. ch. 3 Appendix, § 771, for the death of Robert P. Ebbecke, a minor, on August 18, 1952. Plaintiff alleged the minor's death resulted from the negligent operation of one of the City of Philadelphia's trash trucks.

The case was tried before a jury and resulted in verdicts in favor of the estate and the parents of the deceased minor. Defendant has filed the present motion to set aside the verdicts and for judgment n. o. v.

The question is: Should a prudent or reasonably cautious man have foreseen that the alleged negligent act of defendant would result in the injury sustained?

The accident occurred in a densely populated section of the City of Philadelphia.

The City maintained a garage for its trash trucks approximately one and one-half blocks from the scene of the accident. The street on which the garage is situated is the same street on which the misfortune occurred. The trucks used this street regularly in traveling to and from the garage. As a result of such use, the drivers of the trucks were thoroughly familiar with the fact that this was a neighborhood of children.

On the east side of the block where the accident occurred is a vacant lot which attracts children from time to time. On the west side of the same block is a City playground where at the time of the accident, "quite a gang of" children were playing.

On the afternoon of the accident, the driver of the City's truck was proceeding down this street to the garage. As he approached the scene where the accident occurred, he came upon another City truck double-parked in the street and headed in the same direction. The driver of the double-parked vehicle motioned that it was all right to proceed around him. Thereupon, the driver of the City truck which was in motion turned out into the extreme left-hand side of the street, in attempting to pass the City vehicle which was parked. While doing so, the driver noticed a huge piece of brown wrapping paper approximately six feet in diameter and two or three feet in height. This paper was lying partially in the gutter and partially on the curb on the east side of the street. The driver stated he did not desire to run over the paper because it might contain broken bottles and thus injure the tires of the truck. He attempted to avoid it by judging the distance between the paper and the City trash truck that was double-parked. After endeavoring to pass between these two objects, he then proceeded on to the garage.

What, in fact, actually happened was that the driver misjudged the truck's position with respect to the paper and ran over it, crushing to death the boy who was under the paper with a playmate.

At the conclusion of the trial, the Court charged the jury in substance as follows:

> In the argument of counsel much has been said as to the foreseeability of the danger on the part of the truck driver. The law as to this is that one cannot be held legally liable for injury to the personal property of another unless by the exercise of that degree of care and caution which a prudent or reasonably cautious man, acting under similar circumstances, would exert could he have foreseen, not the extent of the injury or damage, or manner in which it occurred, but could have foreseen that some injury or damage to the person or property of another would reasonably be expected to ensue as the result of his action or conduct.
>
> In this case the question for you to determine as a fact is whether the truck driver acted as a reasonably prudent and cautious man would act in driving his truck under the facts and the evidence as they have been testified to in this case. If he did you should find for the defendant. If he did not your verdict should be for the plaintiff. Could he have foreseen that the injury would reasonably be expected as a result of his conduct? If he could, you should find for the plaintiff. If he could not, your verdict should be for the defendant.

To determine if there was negligence, it is necessary to ascertain first if a prudent or reasonably cautious man should have foreseen that his act would cause injury.

Negligence has long been defined generally as the omission to do something which a reasonable man, guided upon those considerations which ordinarily regulate the conduct of human affairs would do, or doing something which a prudent and reasonable man would not do. Blyth v. Birmingham Water Works, 11 Exchequer 781 (1856).

The American Law Institute in its definition of negligence has said "negligence is * * * conduct * * * which falls below the standard established by law for the protection of others against unreasonable risk of harm" and further in Section 283, that this standard of conduct "is that of a reasonable man under like circumstances." Restatement, Torts §§ 282, 283.

Thus, negligence is a matter of risk — that is to say, of recognizable danger of injury. In most instances, it is caused by an act of heedlessness or carelessness, where the negligent party is unaware of the results which may follow from his act. But it may also exist where he has considered the possible consequences carefully and has exercised his own best judgment as in the present case.

The Restatement of Torts in Section 435, ill. 1, and the Supreme Court of Pennsylvania have adopted the view that a defendant who is negligent must take existing circumstances as he finds them, and may be liable for consequences brought about by his acts, even though they were not reasonably to have been anticipated. Or, as it is sometimes expressed, what he could foresee is important in determining whether he was negligent in the first instance, but not at all decisive in determining the extent of the consequences for which, once negligent, he will be liable.

Applying the law to the facts of the instant case it is readily ascertainable that the driver of the City's truck should have known that some form of injury might ensue if he were to pass over this huge piece of paper. Taking the facts most favorable to the plaintiff, it is a justifiable conclusion to draw that the appearance of the paper, as shown by the fact it was two to three feet in height, would put an ordinarily prudent man on notice that injury might result if he ran over it, and that he should exercise additional precautions to avoid doing so. This is evident by the fact that the driver acknowledged that he was *aware* that something might be under the wrapping paper. Additionally, I believe that this awareness coupled with the fact that the driver was one who consistently handled trash, bundles of paper and similar discarded objects, put him on notice that the nature and position of this object was not of the kind ordinarily encountered in his travels. A person who is employed specifically to collect trash, and does so for a period of time, acquires that additional and somewhat special, knowledge as to the type of ordinary trash set out by inhabitants to be collected.

The evidence shows that the deceased and another little boy were playing "opening envelopes" under this huge piece of paper and that the boys were not sitting absolutely still. The natural tendency of children is to move about causing some movement of the paper.

In Shipley v. City of Pittsburgh, *supra*, the court held that an instruction to the jury that the defendant was not liable if the accident was not "'such accident as should have been reasonably anticipated'", constituted reversible error. However, in some of the earlier cases there is language which is in conflict with the rule there stated. Cf. Wood v. Pennsylvania R. Co., 1896, 177 Pa. 306, 35 A. 699, 35 L.R.A. 199. It is to be noted that in cases following the Wood decision, courts have improperly assumed the defendant's negligence *qua* the plaintiff and considered the "cause" question in language which would have been more appropriately directed to the negligence issue.

In cases in which other elements of a cause of action for negligence were present, the Pennsylvania courts have repeatedly followed the rule of the Shipley case. As early as City of Pittsburgh v. Grier, 1853, 22 Pa. 54, the defendant contended that the "destruction of the boat was a consequence which the agents could not have foreseen as likely to occur."

However, the Court said, "But it is not the law, that men are responsible for their negligence only to the extent of the injuries which they knew would result from it."

It has been held: "If the city was negligent, it was liable for the consequences of its neglect, though those consequences were not, and could not by any ordinary prudence have been, anticipated." Corbin v. City of Philadelphia, 1900, 195 Pa. 461, 45 A. 1070, 1071, 49 L.R.A. 715; Restatement, Torts, § 435.

Accordingly, under Pennsylvania law a defendant who has failed to exercise reasonable care under the circumstances cannot escape liability for damage upon the ground that he could not have foreseen the particular results of his negligent act. Therefore, in the instant case, it is no defense for the City to say that the driver, who carelessly drove over a piece of paper which for reasons of safety he intended to avoid, did not foresee that a child was under the paper. To allow such a defense would exculpate negligent persons from liability for all but deliberate or wantonly malicious acts.

However, assuming the law requires the driver to have foreseen the possibility of injury, the jury, from the facts in evidence, together with all reasonable inferences in favor of plaintiff, might well have found that the driver should have foreseen the possibility that a child was underneath this object.

Moreover, the driver saw this piece of paper and noticed that it was high enough for a little child to be underneath. He then ran over the very piece of paper which he had concluded was unsafe to crush.

The jury resolved as a fact that two little children were underneath the paper, also, that one of the children had been *sitting up* underneath the paper in the street. The jury also could have resolved that the two children had not been lying motionless under the paper, but were playing there. As a matter of fact, the surviving child testified that he had been sitting under the paper with decedent "opening envelopes." The jury may then have concluded that the motion caused by children playing underneath the paper was easily observable by a prudent driver.

The evidence in the case amply supports the jury's verdict that the driver of the truck under these particular circumstances was careless and that his careless act resulted in the decedent's death.

This Court is of the opinion that there was negligence when the driver attempted to avoid the paper and failed to do so, and, as a matter of law, the verdicts of the jury should not be disturbed.

Accordingly, defendant's motion to set aside the verdicts and for judgment n. o. v. is dismissed.

Notes and Questions

1. Notice that this case raises threshold issues that might affect the viability of the negligence claim regardless of how good it is otherwise. That is, even before duty there are the questions whom to sue, whether they have relevant immunities, and whether damages are recoverable. In this case, the plaintiff chose to sue the City of Philadelphia. Return to Chapter One – Threshold Issues and figure out why that made sense. Using the same materials, do you understand why it made sense not to sue Robert Ebbecke's parents?

2. How does Judge Lord in *Barker* describe the rule for establishing duty? How is it similar to and different from Justice Cardozo's approach? From Justice Andrews's approach? What implications does Judge Lord's approach have for litigation? What kind of behavior does it seek to characterize as unreasonable and thus to regulate ex ante?

3. Understanding the rule announced in *Barker*, as the plaintiff would you object to anything the judge said in the instructions quoted in the opinion?

4. The duty rule in most jurisdictions is consistent with *Barker*'s. Would Justice Cardozo criticize it for being ex post analysis?

5. How would Justice Cardozo evaluate the facts in *Barker*? Using Cardozo's methodology, develop the argument that the City of Philadelphia had a duty to the plaintiff; and then develop the argument that it did not.

6. You have just read two cases in which, because duty is a question of law for the court, judges decided whether the defendant had a duty towards the plaintiff. You also saw that foreseeability is embedded in both cases as a factor in the decision whether a duty exists. But foreseeability turns on the facts extant at the time the actor acts or fails to act, and ordinarily, fact questions are for the jury to decide. When facts about foreseeability are contested, does it make sense for the law still to leave it to judges to decide whether a duty exists?

In 2005 the American Law Institute adopted the Restatement of the Law of Torts 3d, Liability for Physical and Emotional Harm. Section 7 proposed a solution to this doctrinal quandary:

1. An actor ordinarily has a duty to exercise reasonable care when the actor's conduct creates a risk of physical harm.

2. In exceptional cases, when an articulated countervailing principle or policy warrants denying or limiting liability in a particular class of cases, a court may decide that the defendant has no duty or that the ordinary duty of reasonable care requires modification.

While § 7 still entrusts decisions about the existence of a duty to the court, it purports to remove foreseeability from that analysis and to focus instead on aspects of the case that do not involve contested facts. Can you identify these, and was the ALI right that they focus judges more clearly on their domain of "law" not "fact"?

In the years since the adoption of § 7, only a handful of jurisdictions have embraced it. For a good example of a court's analysis in doing so, see A.W. Lancaster County School District 0001, 784 N.W.2d 907 (Neb. 2010).

B. Case-By-Case Exceptions to the Default Duty

Occasionally, a particular set of facts suggests that the court ought to make an exception to the default duty. As you read the following illustrative case, pay careful attention to how the defendant (Consolidated Edison) constructs its argument for an exception: What is the rule it uses to do this work? What are the facts it uses to support its argument? Also pay careful attention to how the plaintiff (Julius Strauss) responds; specifically, does he attack the rule, the argument, or the evidentiary support for the argument?

STRAUSS v. BELLE REALTY COMPANY
482 N.E.2d 34 (NY 1985)

KAYE, Justice.

On July 13, 1977, a failure of defendant Consolidated Edison's power system left most of New York City in darkness. In this action for damages allegedly resulting from the power failure, we are asked to determine whether Con Edison owed a duty of care to a tenant who suffered personal injuries in a common area of an apartment building, where his landlord — but not he — had a contractual relationship with the utility. We conclude that in the case of a blackout of a metropolis of several million residents and visitors, each in some manner necessarily affected by a 25-hour power failure, liability for injuries in a building's common areas should, as a matter of public policy, be limited by the contractual relationship.

This court has twice before confronted legal questions concerning the 1977 blackout.

Plaintiff, Julius Strauss, then 77 years old, resided in an apartment building in Queens. Con Edison provided electricity to his apartment pursuant to agreement with him, and to the common areas of the building under a separate agreement with his landlord, defendant Belle Realty Company. As water to the apartment was supplied by electric pump, plaintiff had no running water for the duration of the blackout. Consequently, on the second day of the power failure, he set out for the basement to obtain water, but fell on the darkened, defective basement stairs, sustaining injuries. In this action against Belle Realty and Con Edison, plaintiff alleged negligence against the landlord, in failing to maintain the stairs or warn of their dangerous condition, and negligence against the utility in the performance of its duty to provide electricity.

Plaintiff moved for partial summary judgment against Con Edison (1) to estop it from contesting the charge of gross negligence in connection with the blackout, and (2) to establish that Con Edison owed a duty of care to plaintiff. He argued that Con Edison was prohibited from denying it was grossly negligent by virtue of the affirmed jury verdict in *Food Pageant v. Consolidated Edison Co.,* 54 N.Y.2d 167, 445 N.Y.S.2d 60, 429 N.E.2d 738, *supra,* and that it owed plaintiff a duty even though he was "not a customer of Consolidated Edison in a place where the accident occurred." Con Edison cross-moved for summary judgment dismissing the complaint, maintaining it had no duty to a noncustomer.

The court granted the motion insofar as it sought collateral estoppel regarding gross negligence, and denied Con Edison's cross motion to dismiss the complaint, finding a question of fact as to whether it owed plaintiff a duty of care. The Appellate Division reversed and dismissed the complaint against Con Edison. Citing *Moch Co. v. Rensselaer Water Co.,* 247 N.Y. 160, 159 N.E. 896, the plurality concluded that "Con Ed did not owe a duty to plaintiff in any compensable legal sense" (98 A.D.2d 424, 428, 469 N.Y.S.2d 948). Justice Gibbons dissented, finding extension of the duty tolerable here because "[t]he tenants of the building in question constitute a defined, limited and known group of people" (*id.,* at p. 437, 469 N.Y.S.2d 948). On public policy grounds, we now affirm the Appellate Division order dismissing the complaint against Con Edison.

A defendant may be held liable for negligence only when it breaches a duty owed to the plaintiff[.] The essential question here is whether Con Edison owed a duty to plaintiff, whose injuries from a fall on a darkened staircase may have conceivably been foreseeable, but with whom there was no contractual relationship for lighting in the building's common areas.

Duty in negligence cases is defined neither by foreseeability of injury nor by privity of contract. As this court has long recognized, an obligation rooted in contract may engender a duty owed to those not in privity, for "[t]here is nothing anomalous in a rule which imposes upon A, who has contracted with B, a duty to C and D and others according as he knows or does not know that the subject-matter of the contract is intended for their use" (*MacPherson v. Buick Motor*

Co., 217 N.Y. 382, 393, 111 N.E. 1050). In *Fish v. Waverly Elec. Light & Power Co.,* for example, an electric company which had contracted with the plaintiff's employer to install ceiling lights had a duty to the plaintiff to exercise reasonable care. . . .

But while the absence of privity does not foreclose recognition of a duty, it is still the responsibility of courts, in fixing the orbit of duty, "to limit the legal consequences of wrongs to a controllable degree" and to protect against crushing exposure to liability. "In fixing the bounds of that duty, not only logic and science, but policy play an important role" 9 N.E.2d 406. *also, Becker v. Schwartz,* 46 N.Y.2d 401, 408, 413 N.Y.S.2d 895, 386 N.E.2d 807). The courts' definition of an orbit of duty based on public policy may at times result in the exclusion of some who might otherwise have recovered for losses or injuries if traditional tort principles had been applied.

Considerations of privity are not entirely irrelevant in implementing policy. Indeed, in determining the liability of utilities for consequential damages for failure to provide service — a liability which could obviously be "enormous," and has been described as " *sui generis,* " rather than strictly governed by tort or contract law principles (*see,* Prosser and Keeton, Torts § 92, at 663 [5th ed.]) — courts have declined to extend the duty of care to noncustomers. For example, in *Moch Co. v. Rensselaer Water Co.,* 247 N.Y. 160, 159 N.E. 896, *supra,* a water works company contracted with the City of Rensselaer to satisfy its water requirements. Plaintiff's warehouse burned and plaintiff brought an action against the water company in part based on its alleged negligence in failing to supply sufficient water pressure to the city's hydrants. The court denied recovery, concluding that the proposed enlargement of the zone of duty would unduly extend liability. Similarly, in *Beck v. FMC Corp.,* 42 N.Y.2d 1027, 398 N.Y.S.2d 1011, 369 N.E.2d 10, *affg.* 53 A.D.2d 118, 385 N.Y.S.2d 956), an explosion interrupted a utility's electrical service, which in turn resulted in the loss of a day's pay for hourly workers at a nearby automobile plant. In an action brought by the workers, the court denied recovery on the basis of controlling the unwarranted extension of liability.

Moch involved ordinary negligence, while Con Edison was guilty of gross negligence, but the cases cannot be distinguished on that basis. In reserving the question of what remedy would lie in the case of "reckless and wanton indifference to consequences measured and foreseen" (247 N.Y. at p. 169, 159 N.E. 896), the court in *Moch* contemplated a level of misconduct greater than the gross negligence involved here. The court in *Food Pageant,* in upholding the jury's verdict against Con Edison, noted as instances of Con Edison's misconduct its employee's failure to follow instructions to reduce voltage by "shedding load" after lightning had hit the electrical system, and its staffing decisions (54 N.Y.2d at pp. 173–174, 445 N.Y.S.2d 60, 429 N.E.2d 738, *supra*). Though found by the jury to constitute gross negligence, this behavior was not so consciously culpable as to fall into the category of conduct contemplated as "reckless and wanton" by the court in *Moch.*

In the view of the Appellate Division dissenter, *Moch* does not control because the injuries here were foreseeable and plaintiff was a member of a specific, limited, circumscribed class with a close relationship with Con Edison. The situation was thought to be akin to *White v. Guarente,* 43 N.Y.2d 356, 401 N.Y.S.2d 474, 372 N.E.2d 315, where an accounting firm was retained by a limited partnership to perform an audit and prepare its tax returns. As the court noted there, the parties to the agreement contemplated that individual limited partners would rely on the tax returns and audit. Refusing to dismiss a negligence action brought by a limited partner against the accounting firm, the court said, "the services of the accountant were not extended to a faceless or unresolved class of persons, but rather to a known group possessed of vested rights, marked by a definable limit and made up of certain components" (*id.*, at p. 361, 401 N.Y.S.2d 474, 372 N.E.2d 315; *see also, Glanzer v. Shepard,* 233 N.Y. 236, 135 N.E. 275; *supra; Fish v. Waverly Elec. Light & Power Co.,* 189 N.Y. 336, 82 N.E. 150, *supra*).

Central to these decisions was an ability to extend the defendant's duty to cover specifically foreseeable parties but at the same time to contain liability to manageable levels. In *White,* for instance, liability stemmed from a single isolated transaction where the parties to the agreement contemplated the protection of identified individuals. Here, insofar as revealed by the record, the arrangement between Con Edison and Belle Realty was no different from those existing between Con Edison and the millions of other customers it serves. Thus, Con Edison's duty to provide electricity to Belle Realty should not be treated separately from its broader statutory obligation to furnish power to all other applicants for such service in New York City and Westchester County (Transportation Corporations Law § 12; Public Service Law § 31[1]). When plaintiff's relationship with Con Edison is viewed from this perspective, it is no answer to say that a duty is owed because, as a tenant in an apartment building, plaintiff belongs to a narrowly defined class.

Additionally, we deal here with a system-wide power failure occasioned by what has already been determined to be the utility's gross negligence. If liability could be found here, then in logic and fairness the same result must follow in many similar situations. For example, a tenant's guests and invitees, as well as persons making deliveries or repairing equipment in the building, are equally persons who must use the common areas, and for whom they are maintained. Customers of a store and occupants of an office building stand in much the same position with respect to Con Edison as tenants of an apartment building. In all cases the numbers are to a certain extent limited and defined, and while identities may change, so do those of apartment dwellers. While limiting recovery to customers in this instance can hardly be said to confer immunity from negligence on Con Edison (*see, Koch v. Consolidated Edison Co.,* 62 N.Y.2d 548, 479 N.Y.S.2d 163, 468 N.E.2d 1, *supra*), permitting recovery to those in plaintiff's circumstances would, in our view, violate the court's responsibility to define an orbit of duty that places controllable limits on liability.

Finally, we reject the suggestion of the dissent that there should be a fact-finding hearing to establish the alleged catastrophic probabilities flowing from the 1977 blackout and prospective blackouts, before any limitation is placed on Con Edison's duty to respond to the public for personal injuries. In exercising the court's traditional responsibility to fix the scope of duty, for application beyond a single incident, we need not blind ourselves to the obvious impact of a city-wide deprivation of electric power, or to the impossibility of fixing a rational boundary once beyond the contractual relationship, or to the societal consequences of rampant liability.

In sum, Con Edison is not answerable to the tenant of an apartment building injured in a common area as a result of Con Edison's negligent failure to provide electric service as required by its agreement with the building owner. Accordingly, the order of the Appellate Division should be affirmed, with costs.

MEYER, Justice (dissenting).

My disagreement with the majority results not from its consideration of public policy as a factor in determining the scope of Con Ed's duty, but from the fact that in reaching its public policy conclusion it has considered only one side of the equation and based its conclusion on nothing more than assumption. I, therefore, respectfully dissent.

As Professors Prosser and Keeton have emphasized (Prosser and Keeton, Torts, at 357–358 [5th ed.]), "The statement that there is or is not a duty begs the essential question — whether the plaintiff's interests are entitled to legal protection against the defendant's conduct * * * It is a shorthand statement of a conclusion, rather than an aid to analysis in itself * * * But it should be recognized that 'duty' is not sacrosanct in itself, but is only an expression of the sum total of those considerations of policy which lead the law to say that the plaintiff is entitled to protection." We accepted the concept without reservation in *De Angelis v. Lutheran Med. Center,* 58 N.Y.2d 1053, 1055, 462 N.Y.S.2d 626, 449 N.E.2d 406, stating as to the role played by policy that, "A line must be drawn between the competing policy considerations of providing a remedy to everyone who is injured and of extending exposure to tort liability almost without limit."

Although *De Angelis* did not define the "competing policy considerations" to be reviewed in deciding where the line is to be drawn, it made clear that "absent legislative intervention, the fixing of the 'orbit' of duty, as here, in the end is the responsibility of the courts". Thus, the suggestion in the plurality opinion at the Appellate Division (98 A.D.2d at p. 429, 469 N.Y.S.2d 948) that the liability issue now considered is "best addressed to the Legislature" is no more correct in the present situation than it was when in *Codling v. Paglia,* 32 N.Y.2d 330, 345 N.Y.S.2d 461, 298 N.E.2d 622 we imposed upon manufacturers the economic burden of strict products liability to bystanders as well as to those in privity.

There is, of course, legislative intervention in the regulation of gas and electric companies (Transportation Corporations Law art. 2; Public Service Law art. 4). But the only "legislative" limitation upon the liability of such companies consists of Public Service Commission acceptance and approval of Con Ed's rate schedule, which incorporates the rule, previously enunciated by this court (*Weld v. Postal Telegraph-Cable Co.,* 199 N.Y. 88, 92 N.E. 415, *on second appeal* 210 N.Y. 59, 103 N.E. 957), that liability "be limited to damages arising from the utility's willful misconduct or gross negligence" (*Food Pageant v. Consolidated Edison Co.,* 54 N.Y.2d 167, 172, 445 N.Y.S.2d 60, 429 N.E.2d 738). But, as *Food Pageant* and *Koch v. Consolidated Edison Co.,* 62 N.Y.2d 548, 479 N.Y.S.2d 163, 468 N.E.2d 1, *cert. denied* 469 U.S. 1210, 105 S.Ct. 1177, 84 L.Ed.2d 326) establish, what caused the injuries for which compensation is sought in this action was Con Ed's gross negligence.

What policy considerations are involved in determining whether Con Ed's gross negligence liability should be extended to "bystanders" and where, if at all, a line should be drawn between the varying bystander situations is, then, the issue to be decided. *Codling v. Paglia* looked at the total exclusion of the bystander from opportunity to detect a product defect, the system of mass production and distribution, the ability of the manufacturer to pass on, in part if not in whole, the economic burden of postdistribution liability, and the added incentive toward safety that could be expected to result. To that extent at least it departed from the rationale of *Moch Co. v. Rensselaer Water Co.,* 247 N.Y. 160, 168, 159 N.E. 896 that performance of a contract to supply water to a municipality did not impose "another duty, apart from contract, to an indefinite number of potential beneficiaries."

Ultramares Corp. v. Touche, 255 N.Y. 170, 174 N.E. 441, *Tobin v. Grossman,* 24 N.Y.2d 609, 301 N.Y.S.2d 554, 249 N.E.2d 419 and *Pulka v. Edelman,* 40 N.Y.2d 781, 390 N.Y.S.2d 393,

358 N.E.2d 1019 on which the majority rely, spoke, it is true, to the necessity of avoiding crushing liability, but articulated no factors by which the crushing nature of the potential liability was to be determined. They can, perhaps, be distinguished from *Codling* on the ground that the service businesses they involved (accounting, medicine and parking) do not have the potential of *Codling's* mass distribution system to pass on or absorb the resulting economic burden, but the same cannot be said for the present defendant though it too is involved in furnishing a service.

Criteria more extensive than the unsupported prediction of disaster for determining liability are not wanting, however. Thus, in *Tarasoff v. Regents of Univ.*, 17 Cal.3d 425, 434, 131 Cal.Rptr. 14, 22, 551 P.2d 334, 342), the Supreme Court of California listed the major factors to be balanced in determining duty as "the foreseeability of harm to the plaintiff, the degree of certainty that the plaintiff suffered injury, the closeness of the connection between the defendant's conduct and the injury suffered, the moral blame attached to the defendant's conduct, the policy of preventing future harm, the extent of the burden to the defendant and consequences to the community of imposing a duty to exercise care with resulting liability for breach, and the availability, cost and prevalence of insurance for the risk involved." Prosser and Keeton (*op. cit., supra* at 359), on the basis of the *Tarasoff* case and *Vu v. Singer Co.*, 538 F.Supp. 26, *aff'd*, 9th Cir., 706 F.2d 1027, *cert. denied* 464 U.S. 938, 104 S.Ct. 350, 78 L.Ed.2d 315, list similar factors, which are discussed at greater length in section 4 of their treatise. As to the loss distribution factor, they note (*op. cit.,* at 24–25) that, "The defendants in tort cases are to a large extent public utilities, industrial corporations, commercial enterprises, automobile owners, and others who by means of rates, prices, taxes or insurance are best able to distribute to the public at large the risks and losses which are inevitable in a complex civilization. Rather than leave the loss on the shoulders of the individual plaintiff, who may be ruined by it, the courts have tended to find reasons to shift it to the defendants", except where there are "limitations upon the power of a defendant to shift the loss to the public * * * [as] where the liability may extend to an unlimited number of unknown persons, and is incapable of being estimated or insured against in advance."

The majority's blind acceptance of the notion that Consolidated Edison will be crushed if held liable to the present plaintiff and others like him ignores the possibility that through application to the Public Service Commission Con Ed can seek such reduction of the return on stockholders' equity . . . or increase in its rates, or both, as may be necessary to pay the judgments obtained against it. It ignores as well the burden imposed upon the persons physically injured by Con Ed's gross negligence or, as to those forced to seek welfare assistance because their savings have been wiped out by the injury, the State. Doing so in the name of public policy seems particularly perverse, for what it says, in essence, is the more persons injured through a tort-feasor's gross negligence, the less the responsibility for injuries incurred.

I agree that there are situations encompassed by our tort system that require such a result, perverse though it may be, but before granting public utilities absolution beyond that which they already enjoy through the limitation of their liability to acts of gross negligence, I would put the burden upon the utility to establish the necessity for doing so. I am not suggesting that the issue is to be determined by a jury for, as already noted, I do not question that "duty" is a question of law to be determined by the courts. But the law is not without illustrations of preliminary issues involving facts to be determined by a Judge (*e.g.,* competency and privilege of witnesses, Richardson, Evidence § 117 [Prince 10th ed]; Morgan, Evidence § 53 [3d ed.];

suppression of evidence, CPL 710.60; Richardson, *op cit.* § 550). Nor am I necessarily suggesting that a retrospective determination of how crushing the liability from the 1977 blackout may be, as distinct from a more generalized prospective determination, should govern, although I would not balk at the former if the latter proved impossible of demonstration. All that I am suggesting is that it is Con Ed which claims that its duty does not encompass plaintiff, not because Con Ed was not grossly negligent, but because the effect of that negligence if Con Ed is held liable for it would be to cripple Con Ed as well as the victims of the negligence. There simply is no basis other than the majority's say so for its assumptions (majority opn., at p. 405, 492 N.Y.S.2d at p. 559, 482 N.E.2d at p. 38) that the impact of a city-wide deprivation of electric power upon the utility is entitled to greater consideration than the impact upon those injured; that a rational boundary cannot be fixed that will include some (apartment tenants injured in common areas, for example), if not all of the injured; that the consequence of imposing some bystander liability will be more adverse to societal interests than will follow from blindly limiting liability for tort to those with whom the tort-feasor has a contractual relationship. Before we grant Con Ed's motion to dismiss, therefore, we should require that a rational basis for such assumptions be established.

Con Ed may well be able to do so, but before its motion is granted at the expense of an unknown number of victims who have suffered injuries the extent and effects of which are also unknown, it should be required to establish that the catastrophic probabilities are great enough to warrant the limitation of duty it seeks. . . .

I would, therefore, deny the summary judgment motions of both sides and remit to Supreme Court for determination of the preliminary fact issues involved.

WACHTLER, C.J., and SIMONS, ALEXANDER and TITONE, JJ., concur with KAYE, J.

MEYER, J., dissents and votes to reverse in a separate opinion in which JASEN, J., concurs.

Order affirmed, with costs.

Notes and Questions

1. Why did the majority in *Strauss* reject the default duty rule? Generalize from the facts of this case and state a broader rule about when courts might reject the default. Does the broader rule risk swallowing the default duty; that is, are litigants in the run-of-the-mill case likely to use *Strauss* and its incarnation across the jurisdictions to try to litigate the duty issue in cases where defendants affirmatively act to risk harm to plaintiffs?

2. What was the dissent's principal concern with what the majority did? Was this concern legitimate? Why do you think the majority rejected it?

3. Notice the legislature's reform of the traditional common law duty rule that applies in the utilities setting and how the court works with the hybrid statutory-common law rule.

4. In cases like this one, where the defendant is deemed "too big to fail" by the legislature and/or the courts, they are given a "bye" that allows them to avoid mere negligence claims and only to answer for those where, on the facts, the plaintiff can establish both privity and higher

degrees of fault, i.e., gross negligence, recklessness, and intent. This might be the right policy choice depending on the facts and interests at issue, but it might also be seen as a failure of tort law to meet its fundamental compensation and deterrence goals. Alternative approaches such as insurance and compensation funds may better allocate responsibility and loss in these cases.

5. Notice the relationship between the law of contracts and the law of torts as it is described in *Strauss*. Does the court apply contract law rather than tort law to resolve the related issue, or does it import a contracts-law concept into tort law? What is it about this contracts rule that makes it so easily deployed in this setting?

6. In pandemic conditions involving a highly infectious disease like Covid, policymakers are tasked with balancing competing interests including public and individual health concerns, the effects of restrictions on the economy, and regional and individual preferences — including preferences related to autonomy. Can you see how a version of this interests balancing analysis would be undertaken at the duty stage of a related negligence case? For example, consider the facts and policy considerations you'd expect to see in an analysis of the issue whether shopkeepers and restaurant owners have a duty to require Covid-related precautions of their staff and customers, for example, the wearing of masks and social distancing? As you make the transition from this first "default" duty section of the materials to the next, second "traditional exceptions" section, consider which doctrine best houses that analysis.

II. TRADITIONAL POLICY EXCEPTIONS TO THE DEFAULT DUTY

In Part I of this chapter, we introduced the general or default duty, which applies in cases in which the defendant acted in a way that risked harm. In this second part, we examine the traditional categorical (as opposed to case-by-case) exceptions to the application of the default duty. In general, these exceptions are in play when the case involves a claim that the defendant failed to act to rescue, aid, or warn the plaintiff; a claim that the plaintiff suffered only emotional harm or economic loss; or a claim that something on the defendant's premises (for example a swimming pool or a hidden defect on the land) caused the harm or loss. Just as the default duty is based in a policy choice, so too are the exceptions. That is, for various policy reasons, society and the law are or were believed to be better off in these situations with a "no duty" or "special duty" rule. At the same time, because policy preferences sometimes vary with the circumstances or change over time, as we will see, there are both traditional and modern exceptions to the exceptions — cases where the traditional exception has never been or is no longer valid, so that the default rule is restored. An example of the former is that although there is generally no duty to rescue, there has always been an exception where the defendant and plaintiff are in a legally recognized special relationship. An example of the latter is that although there is generally no duty to trespassers, there is now a duty in some circumstances to children who trespass.

Without belaboring the point, the material in this part of the chapter is steeped in policy analysis, both in support of a "no duty" or "special duty" rule, and in support of exceptions to those rules that would provide for a duty where one normally does not exist. In the cases that follow, you will see that the particular form of analysis the courts engage is relatively standard across the traditional exceptions and also across jurisdictions. This iteration, from the Maryland Court of Appeals decision in Patton v. United States of America Rugby Football, 851 A.2d 566 (Md. 2003), is typical:

> In determining the existence of a duty, we consider, among other things, the foreseeability of harm to the plaintiff, the degree of certainty that the plaintiff suffered the injury, the closeness of the connection between the defendant's conduct and the injury suffered, the moral blame attached to the defendant's conduct, the policy of preventing future harm, the extent of the burden to the defendant and consequences to the community of imposing a duty to exercise care with resulting liability for breach, and the availability, cost and prevalence of insurance for the risk involved.

Id. at 571. As you read through the cases in this chapter, including the *Patton* case, be sure to notice when and how judges use this multi-factor policy analysis.

A. Plaintiff Alleges That Defendant Failed to Act to Rescue, Warn, or Aid

1. The Traditional "No Duty" Rule

THEOBALD v. DOLCIMASCOLA
690 A.2d 1100 (N.J. App. 1997)

The opinion of the court was delivered by DREIER, P.J.A.D.

Plaintiffs, Colleen Theobald as Administrator Ad Prosequendum for the heirs of Sean Theobald and as administrator of his estate, and Colleen Theobald and Harold Theobald (the parents of the late Sean Theobald), individually, appeal from summary judgments dismissing their complaint against the three remaining defendants, Michael Dolcimascola, Robert Bruck, and Amy Flanagan. Settlements or unappealed summary judgments have removed the remaining defendants from this case.

On January 20, 1991, plaintiffs' decedent, Sean Theobald, was in the second floor bedroom of his house with five of his friends. His father was downstairs watching television. The friends had gathered at 6:00 p.m. for a birthday party for one of the friends, Robert Bruck. The other teenagers present were Charles Henn, Michael Dolcimascola, Amy Flanagan and Katherine Gresser. At some time during the evening, the decedent produced an unloaded revolver and ammunition, both of which were examined by all of the teenagers. The discussion turned toward another friend of theirs who had died playing Russian Roulette, and the decedent indicated that he also would try the "game." According to the predominant version of the varying testimony, Sean put a bullet into the gun, pointed it at his head and pulled the trigger several times. He then put the gun down, checked the cylinder, and tried again three or four more times. The gun then went off, killing him. Other versions had the gun going off on the first occasion he tried, or the gun firing by accident without his putting the barrel to his head. There was, however, ample testimony that there were several attempts made while the five other teenagers merely sat around and watched. The trial judge determined that if none of the teenagers actively participated, they had no duty to stop the decedent, and therefore summary judgment was entered.

. . .

The first question before us is whether any of the defendants, if they were mere observers to this tragic event, can be held civilly liable to plaintiffs. We are at a loss for a viable theory. Had this been a joint endeavor in which all were participating in the "game" of Russian Roulette, there is some authority that each of the participants in the enterprise might be held responsible, although the only cases we have been able to retrieve involve the criminal responsibility of participants. *See e.g., Commonwealth v. Atencio,* 345 *Mass.* 627, 189 *N.E.*2d 223, 224–26 (1963) (where the participants were found guilty of manslaughter). There is no reason to suppose that if the participants could be found criminally responsible, they could not also be held civilly liable. A line, however, has been drawn by the courts between being an active participant and merely being one who had instructed a decedent how to "play" Russian Roulette. In the latter case, a defendant was determined to be free of any potential criminal liability. *Lewis v. State*, 474 *So.*2d 766, 771 (Ala.Crim.App.1985). Another court, *in dictum*, stated that inducing an individual to engage in Russian Roulette creates a sufficiently foreseeable harm to engender potential civil liability. *Great Central Ins. Co. v. Tobias*, No. 86 AP-820, 1987 WL 9624, AT *5 (Ohio.Ct.App.1987).

The most comprehensive New Jersey statement of the existence of a duty to another was expressed in *Wytupeck v. City of Camden*, 25 *N.J.* 450, 136 *A.*2d 887 (1957). Although the case involved the question of liability for the use of a dangerous instrumentality on defendant's land, the case explored when a duty to act arises in inter-personal relationships:

> "Duty" is not an abstract conception; and the standard of conduct is not an absolute. Duty arises out of a relation between the particular parties that in right[,] reason and essential justice enjoins the protection of the one by the other against what the law by common consent deems an unreasonable risk of harm, such as is reasonably foreseeable. In the field of negligence, duty signifies conformance "to the legal standard of reasonable conduct in the light of the apparent risk;" the essential question is whether "the plaintiff's interests are entitled to legal protection against the defendant's conduct." *Prosser on Torts* (2d ed., section 36). Duty is largely grounded in the natural responsibilities of social living and human relations, such as have the recognition of reasonable men; and fulfillment is had by a correlative standard of conduct.

. . .

If defendants had either been participants or had induced decedent to play Russian Roulette, or even if there had been some other factor by which we could find a common enterprise, then defendants may have had a duty to act to protect Sean from the consequences of his foolhardy actions. Such a duty would nevertheless invoke the usual principles of comparative negligence. The problem with such potential liability, however, is the significant factor of a decedent's own negligence which, when measured against any participant's breach of a duty of care, would probably preclude recovery in most cases.

What we are left with in the case before us, positing that there was no proof of encouragement or participation, is a claim which is grounded in a common law duty to rescue. As has been explained in texts and reiterated in case law, there is no such duty, except if the law imposes it based upon some special relationship between the parties. *See* W. Page Keeton, et al., *Prosser and Keaton on Torts*, § 56, at 375 (5th ed. 1984) ("[T]he law has persistently refused to impose on a stranger the moral obligation of common humanity to go to the aid of another human being who is in danger, even if the other is in danger of losing his life."); J.D. Lee and Barry A. Lindahl, *Modern Tort Law*, § 3.07, at 36 (1994 and Supp.1996) ("With regard to rescues, it has been stated that the general rule is that there is no liability for one who stands idly by and fails to rescue a stranger. . . ."); *Restatement (Second) of Torts*, § 314 (1965) ("The fact that the actor realizes or should realize that action on his part is necessary for another's aid or protection does not of itself impose upon him a duty to take such action."). The Restatement's Illustration 1 is instructive. It posits the actor, A, viewing a blind man, B, stepping into the street in the path of an approaching automobile, where a word or touch by A would prevent the anticipated harm. The Restatement concludes that "A is under no duty to prevent B from stepping into the street, and is not liable to B."

Recent New Jersey decisions have focused upon the exceptions to this general rule and involve situations where a duty to act exists as a result of the relationship between the parties, namely, police-arrestee (*Del Tufo v. Township of Old Bridge*, 147 *N.J.* 90, 685 *A.*2d 1267 (1996); *Hake v. Manchester Township*, 98 *N.J.* 302, 486 *A.*2d 836 (1985)) and physician-patient (*Olah v. Slobodian*, 119 *N.J.* 119, 574 *A.*2d 411 (1990)). These cases also address the liability of a ship's captain for failing to attempt to rescue a drowning seaman.

All of these cases are distinguishable from the situation before us, assuming the five observers were mere bystanders upon whom the law places no duty to have protected the decedent. While we may deplore their inaction, we, as did the trial judge, find no legal authority to impose liability. We note the ease with which defendants could have reached out and taken away the revolver when Sean put it down between his two series of attempted firings, or the simple act of one of the five walking to the door and summoning Sean's father, or even remonstrating with Sean concerning his actions. But such acts would have been no more or less than the simple preventatives given in the Restatement Illustration of a word or touch necessary to save a blind pedestrian. Where there is no duty, there is no liability.

. . .

In sum, we determine that there was no common law duty owed by defendants to the decedent if defendants were mere observers of his shooting.

Notes and Questions

1. Central to the outcome of the *Theobald* case was the absence of any evidence of affirmative conduct by Sean's friends that could be said to have contributed to his death. What set of facts would have yielded a different result?

2. The issue whether the "no duty to rescue" rule applies or not is resolved as a threshold matter by the distinction between affirmative conduct and omissions – or what the courts traditionally called "misfeasance" and "nonfeasance." As Section 37 of the Third Restatement affirms, "[a]n actor whose conduct has not created a risk of physical or emotional harm to another has no duty of care to the other unless a court determines that one of the [exceptions] . . . is applicable." It is not always easy to sort risk-creating acts from risk-creating omissions or misfeasance from nonfeasance. For example, imagine that a car accident results in part from the defendant's failure to apply the brakes in a timely way. Is the ensuing negligence case governed by the default duty rule because the defendant engaged in a risk-creating activity by driving his car;

or is it governed by the "no duty" rule because his failure to apply the brakes is properly characterized as an "omission" and thus as a failure to aid?

3. *Theobald* sets out some exceptions to the "no duty" rule — for example, where there is a "special relationship" between the parties. We see these exceptions in section A.2.d. below.

GALANTI v. UNITED STATES
709 F.2d 706 (11th Cir. 1983)

LEWIS R. MORGAN, Senior Circuit Judge:

Vivian W. Galanti, plaintiff-appellant, brought this action against the government in the District Court for the Northern District of Georgia under the Federal Tort Claims Act (FTCA), 28 U.S.C. § 1346(b), claiming that her husband, Isaac N. Galanti, died as a result of negligence committed by an agent of the Federal Bureau of Investigation (FBI). The district court concluded that no actionable negligence exists under the pertinent facts and granted the government's motion to dismiss for failure to state a claim. We affirm the district court's order for the following reasons.

The facts giving rise to appellant's claim are undisputed. In October of 1978, Isaac N. Galanti and Roger Dean Underhill were shot to death on a secluded tract of undeveloped property in Fulton County, Georgia. Galanti was interested in purchasing the property from Underhill, and the two men were inspecting it at the time of their deaths. Unknown to Galanti, Underhill was a key witness in the government's investigation into the criminal activity of Michael G. Thevis. Thevis, a convicted felon, had escaped from federal custody six months earlier and was still a fugitive at the time of the murders. He was apprehended a month later and eventually convicted in federal court of violating Underhill's civil rights by having him murdered, along with the innocent bystander Galanti, in order to prevent Underhill's testimony in the government's case.*

For several months before his death, Underhill traveled a great deal and kept a low profile, although he frequently contacted FBI Agent Paul V. King, Jr. King was in charge of the Thevis investigation and knew that Thevis had made earlier attempts to kill Underhill. King considered Underhill to be in extreme danger at all times. For this reason, the government arranged for Underhill to enter a witness protection program in which Underhill would be given a permanent, new identity with government assistance, but Underhill refused to enter the program until he sold the undeveloped property in Fulton County. He ignored advice to retain a real estate agent and insisted on personally handling the sale of his property. In the week preceding his death, Underhill repeatedly visited the property even though King advised him of the needless danger involved. On the night before the murders, Underhill called and informed King that he would be showing the property the next day to Galanti who had answered a newspaper advertisement. King made no attempt to contact and warn Galanti of the potential danger, nor did he arrange for surveillance of the property. This is the conduct which formed the basis of appellant's suit in the district court. She claimed that King's failure

* Editors' note: Thevis has a fascinating personal history set out in *U.S. v. Thevis*, 665 F.2d 616 (5th Cir. 1982).

to warn or protect Nicholas Galanti against a specific, foreseeable danger was a negligent act and the proximate cause of her husband's death.

This action was necessarily filed in federal court under the provisions of the FTCA since appellant seeks to hold the government liable for the negligence of its employee, but both parties agree that Georgia law controls the negligence issue. In Georgia there are four essential elements of a negligence action:

(1) A legal duty to conform to a standard of conduct raised by the law for the protection of others against unreasonable risks of harm;

(2) A breach of this standard;

(3) A legally attributable causal connection between the conduct and the resulting injury; and,

(4) Some loss or damage flowing to the plaintiff's legally protected interest as a result of the alleged breach of the legal duty.

It is the first element with which we are concerned in this appeal. The court below concluded that under no circumstances could appellant establish a legal duty owed by King to Nicholas Galanti, and accordingly granted the government's motion to dismiss for failure to state a claim. Appellant vigorously challenges this conclusion and relies on a large number of state and federal cases, some very recent, in order to support her argument. After a careful review of the various claims and the relevant law, we find that the district court's order must be affirmed.

The general rule in Georgia is that one has no duty to warn or protect another person from a foreseeable risk of harm simply because of one's knowledge of the danger. In other words, the mere foreseeability of injury to another person does not of itself create a duty to act. This rule is not applicable in three distinct factual situations, however, and appellant contends that each of the three exceptions is present here. First, the duty to protect or warn against danger will arise if the defendant has in any way taken an affirmative step to create the danger. . . . In the present case, FBI Agent King did nothing to create the foreseeable danger. He was merely aware of the risk to Galanti and for whatever reason chose not to act. Georgia law does not hold him legally responsible for knowledge alone.

A second exception to the general rule concerns the defendant's failure to properly exercise his ability to control the foreseeably dangerous instrument. . . . This is not the situation we are faced with here. Appellant has not alleged, and the relevant facts do not support the theory, that FBI Agent King or his associates had the ability and failed to control Michael Thevis. Thevis was a wanted fugitive beyond King's control during the relevant time period, and thus King had no duty to warn or protect Galanti merely because of the danger posed by Thevis' known criminal intent.

Finally, law enforcement officials may have the legal duty to warn or protect against danger if they have voluntarily assumed or incurred that duty to a specific individual. . . . However, this duty, if at all applicable here, would extend only to Roger Dean Underhill, and he repeatedly ignored warnings and refused protection. Appellant cannot cite to any Georgia statute or case which charges law enforcement officials with the duty to warn or protect members of the general public simply upon learning of a possible danger.

We recognize that the result in this case may appear harsh because Galanti's death very likely would have been avoided if King had chosen to act rather than to remain silent. Nonetheless, Georgia law did not impose any legal duty on King to act on behalf of Galanti, and therefore appellant's complaint did not establish a viable claim. For this reason, the order of the district court is AFFIRMED.

Notes and Questions

1. If it could be proved that (1) the FBI knew Thevis was in the area, (2) Thevis was likely to show up at the site and try to kill Underhill, and (3) Galanti would be on the site with Underhill, how would you argue for and against the FBI's having a duty to Galanti?

2. In *Galanti*, the court indicates that the suit was brought under the FTCA. Go back to our description of this statute in Chapter 1, identify the specific provision(s) likely used in the case, and make sure you can describe the relationship between that statute and the underlying negligence case.

3. A Duke Law alumna, Amelia Ashton (now Thorn), explained the traditional rationales for the "no duty to rescue" rule in her law review note, *Rescuing The Hero: The Ramifications Of Expanding The Duty To Rescue On Society And The Law*, 59 DUKE L.J. 69 (2009):

> Despite the potential for disturbing outcomes, the no-duty rule was essentially justified by three arguments. First, a legal requirement to rescue would invade autonomy, which is closely related to two other propositions: the consent-of-the-governed rationale and the harm principle. Second, creating a duty would run counter to natural law principles. Finally, religious sensibility was expected to fill any potential gap left by legally requiring so little action.
>
> Of these, the autonomy discussion has been most prevalent. The distinctly American sensibility of autonomy — noted as early as the country's inception by Alexis de Tocqueville — is strongly credited with the formulation of and adherence to this rule, which upholds the freedom to decide whether or not to rescue at the expense of injury to a victim. And despite notorious descriptions of pitiless bystanders who simply look on as victims perish, there is some sense that discomfort with imposing a duty to rescue reflects a genuine and warranted concern about liberty. Viewing the requirement of action as an infringement assumes that one values what is being infringed upon: control over one's own decisions is fundamental from the autonomist's perspective. For some, these are high stakes, and requiring action is seen as an offense to liberty so grave that it equates to "[making] man a slave."
>
> The autonomy argument is linked to the consent-of-the-governed rationale, which holds that citizens legitimize their government by consenting to it because it reflects their autonomous choices. A lack of freedom of choice in the law, then, is an affront both to individual liberty and individuals who would sustain a legitimate government.

> The importance of individual liberty is also linked to the harm principle — the notion that a legal wrong is constituted only when a harm is inflicted. The common law's commitment to punishing misfeasance (essentially, a bad act) but ignoring nonfeasance (essentially, a non act) further supported a system that refrained from prosecuting the absence of rescue. This development grew naturally from a "highly individualistic philosophy of the older common law [which] had no great difficulty in working out restraints upon the commission of affirmative acts of harm, but shrank from converting the courts into an agency for forcing men to help one another." The distinction between omissions and acts is more formally justified by noting that the former results in no change to the victims' situations — at most a missed opportunity to benefit them — whereas the latter inflicts positive harm. The rules of causation, linked to the requirement of an act, only compounded this dilemma.
>
> In addition to the forces of social identity and legal structure that supported an autonomist perspective, the no-duty rule paralleled the psychological underpinnings of early common law, which recognized that the desire to rescue — because of its risks — ran counter to the "natural law" principle of self-preservation. The instinct for survival was so fundamental and ingrained that it could not realistically be expected to subside in times of potentially life-threatening acts of rescue.
>
> Finally, it was also assumed that the strength of moral aspirations and social norms would compensate for the lack of a formal legal duty. Specifically, the existence and understanding of the divide on the legal and moral continuum under common law doctrine was justified by the promise of religion, a moral sphere expected to pick up where the common law's harsh disregard for the would-be rescuee left off. Because religions generally promote altruism and self-sacrifice, they would encourage rescue behavior even without the creation of a legal duty.

Id. at 78–79.

4. Are you personally persuaded that, as a matter of policy, there should normally be no duty to rescue? What are the rationales that are most supportive of this "no duty" rule? What are the flaws in those rationales? Given these competing rationales, analyze the merits of this proposed statutory provision: "An actor whose conduct has not created a risk of physical or emotional harm to another but who sees another in immediate risk of death or grave bodily injury, and who can take reasonable actions act to aid, warn, or rescue the other person at no risk to himself, has an affirmative duty to take reasonable action."

5. Neither of the two principal cases in this section analyzes the question whether there should be a duty to rescue according to the standard multi-factor analysis set out in the introduction to this chapter. This is because the "no duty" rule is so well-established that the analysis according to these factors is not necessary. Assume for the purposes of this question that this is actually a novel issue for the highest appellate court in your jurisdiction. How would it fare according to the standard analysis?

2. Exceptions to the "No Duty" Rule

The common law rule that there is normally no duty to take affirmative action to rescue, aid, or warn is subject to four traditional exceptions: prior conduct, promissory estoppel, special relationships, and volunteer rescue. Because duty is always a policy question, like the traditional "no duty to rescue" rule, these exceptions are also policy-based. As you are reading the cases, consider what these policy bases might be.

a. Volunteer Rescue

HAWKINS v. HOUSER
371 S.E.2d 297 (N.C. App. 1988)

Phillips, J.

These two wrongful death actions were dismissed by an order of summary judgment following a hearing at which the court considered affidavits, depositions, and other materials which indicate the following: In January, 1985 on defendants' 220-acre tract of Lincoln County farm and woodland were situated their dwelling house, a mobile home park containing 25 trailer sites in one area and 30 in another, and about a quarter of a mile from the park an unenclosed, unposted farm pond about 150 feet wide, which residents of the trailer park often visited and fished in. On 28 January 1985 the pond was frozen over and some boys from the trailer park skated on the ice. On 29 January 1985 decedents Pless and Hawkins, both residents of the trailer park, drowned in the pond after Pless, age 12, even though warned by Hawkins not to do so and warned earlier by defendants not to go into the pond, rode his bicycle onto the ice and fell through near the center of the pond and Hawkins, age 26, also on a bicycle, tried to rescue him. Though both fell into the icy water and neither could swim they were able to stay afloat for about 40 minutes by holding onto Hawkins' bicycle which did not sink, as Pless's did. Their calls for help were heard by other park residents, who had defendants telephone the rescue squad in Lincolnton. Two or more unimproved dirt roads on defendants' property led to the pond, one of which leading off from State Road #1280 had been blocked by defendants with felled trees to reduce vehicular traffic near the pond. In telephoning the rescue squad, defendant Sue Houser, with her husband's concurrence, told the crew to use the road off State Road #1280 in getting to the pond. But the rescue crew was unable to get to the pond on that road though they tried to get around the felled tree for about 15 minutes, and when they got to the pond by another unblocked route the victims had just expired.

Plaintiffs' information concerning the misdirected rescue attempt was obtained during discovery after the action was filed and in their complaints they alleged only that defendants were negligent in maintaining the pond, in failing to enclose it, in failing to put warnings around it, and that it was an attractive nuisance to neighborhood children. The defendants denied any negligence and alleged that the decedents were contributorily negligent.

Since our jurisprudence favors the trial of cases on their merits when there are any merits to litigate, it is proper to dismiss an action by summary judgment under the provisions of Rule 56(a), N.C. Rules of Civil Procedure, only when it clearly appears from the materials considered by the trial judge that no genuine issue of material fact exists between the parties with respect to the controversy being litigated. The controversy in litigation here is whether defendants were negligent in causing the drownings of the decedents and whether the decedents were contributorily negligent in causing their own deaths. With respect to these issues the materials considered by the court lead to and require the following conclusions as a matter of law:

First, the order cannot be upheld on the ground that decedents were contributorily negligent as a matter of law, and defendants do not argue otherwise. Because the materials show that an issue of fact does exist as to the decedents' contributory negligence, since decedent Pless was only 12 years old, and the decedent Hawkins was undertaking to save his life under circumstances that do not appear to be rash, even in retrospect.

Second, the materials do show, however, that no genuine issue of fact exists as to the alleged negligence of the defendants in maintaining the unenclosed, unposted pond on their property. Sifted down the evidentiary forecasts on this issue indicate only that defendants maintained the pond in the farm and rural setting described and our law is that maintaining an unfenced, unposted body of water upon one's rural land by itself is not negligence. According to the materials the victims were capable of appreciating the danger of the ice giving way, the decedent Pless was on the pond as a trespasser, defendants did nothing to either conceal or enhance the danger, and the attractive nuisance doctrine does not apply because the decedent Pless was not a child of tender years but an intelligent 12 year old capable of recognizing the danger in riding a bicycle over an ice-covered body of water. Thus, the claims that defendants were negligent in maintaining the pond were properly dismissed, and to that extent the orders are affirmed; but the dismissals of the actions are not affirmed for the reasons stated below.

Third, the materials show that an issue of fact does exist as to defendants' negligence in misdirecting the rescue squad to where the victims were in imminent peril of drowning or dying by hypothermia in the icy water. Defendants, though volunteers in telephoning for aid, had the positive duty to use ordinary care in performing that task, the known and obvious purpose of which, under the circumstances, was to inform the rescue squad where the endangered persons were and an expeditious way to get there. Evidence that in making the call defendants suggested that the rescuers travel to the pond by a time-wasting barricaded road when an unimpeded road was available is evidence that defendants did not use ordinary care. Defendants' only argument on this point is not that the evidentiary forecast does not raise the question of fact, but that negligence by misdirecting the crew was not alleged in the complaint. This deficiency is not automatically fatal to plaintiffs' actions, as it would have been under our former procedure, because under our modern notice pleading system amendments to the pleadings are liberally permitted when the evidence and circumstances warrant, even at trial, and the circumstances in this case appear to warrant such an amendment. In *Hardison v. Williams,* 21 N.C.App. 670, 205 S.E.2d 551 (1974), a summary judgment dismissing the action was reversed because the record indicated an issue of fact existed as to an act of negligence that had not been alleged in the complaint and that grounds existed for allowing an amendment to allege that act. Substantially the same situation exists here. Since the trial is yet to be scheduled and the information as to the unalleged act of negligence was apparently elicited from defendants after the complaint was filed defendants should have no difficulty in preparing to defend this issue. Though the deaths occurred more than two years ago the amendment, if allowed, would not be a "new action" barred by the statute of limitations, as defendants contend. Since the negligence that would be alleged arose out of the drownings in their pond and the complaint notified defendants of these occurrences the amendment would relate back to the filing of the complaint. As stated in *Estrada,* "[t]o hold otherwise would negate the very policies embodied in Rule 15." *Ibid* at 636, 321 S.E.2d at 246.

Thus, we reverse the orders dismissing the actions and remand the matters to the Superior Court for a determination as to whether plaintiffs may amend their complaints to allege that defendants were negligent in misdirecting the rescue squad to the pond in which the decedents were marooned.

Affirmed in part; reversed in part; and remanded.

WELLS and PARKER, JJ., concur.

Notes and Questions

1. *Hawkins* states the traditional common law rule with respect to what constitutes volunteering to rescue and the duty that arises as a result. Like all of the other exceptions in this section, this rule imposes a duty to aid where normally there would not be one. And again like all of the other exceptions, it is based in policy. What policy justifies the traditional volunteer rescuer rule? On the other hand, what disincentives might result from this rule?

2. Section 44 of the Third Restatement provides that "[a]n actor who discontinues aid or protection is subject to a duty of reasonable care to refrain from putting the other in a worse position than existed before the actor took charge of the other and, if the other reasonably appears to be in imminent peril of serious physical harm at the time of termination, to exercise reasonable care with regard to the peril before terminating the rescue." Could the *Hawkins* plaintiffs prove that the defendant put them in a worse position than existed before they misdirected the rescue squad?

3. Good Samaritan laws may, depending on their terms, abrogate the traditional common law rule. Good Samaritan laws take their name from the biblical Parable of the Good Samaritan which tells the story of the aid given by one traveler to another who had been beaten and robbed, despite their different religious and ethnic backgrounds. Luke 10:25-37. The aim of these enactments is to encourage those who would otherwise have no duty to aid to assist those in urgent need. As you will see, different states have taken different approaches to their Good Samaritan statutes.

Vermont's Duty to Aid the Endangered Act is most comprehensive, creating a duty to provide aid; immunizing those who comply from liability in mere negligence; and punishing willful violators with a fine, albeit a quite modest one:

> (a) A person who knows that another is exposed to grave physical harm shall, to the extent that the same can be rendered without danger or peril to himself or without interference with important duties owed to others, give reasonable assistance to the exposed person unless that assistance or care is being provided by others.
>
> (b) A person who provides reasonable assistance in compliance with subsection (a) of this section shall not be liable in civil damages unless his acts constitute gross negligence or unless he will receive or expects to receive remuneration. Nothing contained in this subsection shall alter existing law with respect to tort liability of a practitioner of the healing arts for acts committed in the ordinary course of his practice.

> (c) A person who willfully violates subsection (a) of this section shall be fined not more than $100.00. (1967, No. 309 (Adj. Sess.), §§ 2–4, eff. March 22, 1968.)

12 VT. STAT. ANN. tit. 519 (2013). No Vermont case has held that the statute is enforceable by a civil suit for damages against a bystander who fails to respond to the duty it creates. How does the statute alter the common law rule of liability? Which does more to incentivize rescue, the statute or the common law rule?

Since the first Good Samaritan statute was enacted in 1959, every state has adopted a provision affording some protection to those who render aid. *See* 64 ALR 4th 294 (1989). However, Vermont's particular formulation, first establishing a statutory duty to rescue supported by a sanction for its violation and then immunizing volunteers from mere negligence liability, has not been followed in other jurisdictions. More typically, other states' Good Samaritan statutes merely do the latter — immunize volunteer rescuers from mere negligence liability. They otherwise leave the common law rule intact. Tennessee's statute is illustrative in this respect:

> . . .
>
> (b) Any person, including those licensed to practice medicine and surgery and including any person licensed or certified to render service ancillary thereto, or any member of a volunteer first aid, rescue or emergency squad that provides emergency public first aid and rescue services, shall not be liable to victims or persons receiving emergency care for any civil damages as a result of any act or omission by such person in rendering the emergency care or as a result of any act or failure to act to provide or arrange for further medical treatment or care for the injured person, except such damages as may result from the gross negligence of the person rendering such emergency care, who in good faith . . . [listing of kinds of aid omitted].

TENN. CODE ANN. § 63-6-218 (2010). Notice that this statute applies to "[a]ny person" who would choose to render aid, including ordinary passersby and emergency and medical personnel. Other states' immunizing statutes focus exclusively on emergency and medical personnel, providing (only) them with immunity from liability in mere negligence. In those states, volunteer rescuers who are not emergency and medical personnel are presumably still subject to the common law rule.

A related statutory treatment in this period is to immunize medical professionals from mere negligence liability *whenever* they are rendering aid in an "emergency" — even if they are being paid to do this work and even though (as we will see in the next chapter) emergencies already contextualize the care that is deemed reasonable in the circumstances. This is in contrast with earlier Good Samaritan statutes like Vermont's above, which only immunized medical professionals from negligence liability when they were volunteering their services. In this new setting, the term "emergency" is often construed broadly. For example, the scene of an emergency was deemed to include an injured person's home where he was taken after being injured on an ATV in the woods a considerable distance away. Mueller v. McMillian Warner Ins. Co., 290 Wis.2d 571, 714 N.W.2d 183 (2006). And a pediatrician who was seeing patients in the hospital who was summoned "stat" to provide emergency resuscitation to a newborn baby who had been deprived of oxygen during the birthing process was deemed to be acting in an "emergency," notwithstanding that stat services are routine in hospitals. Burciaga v St.

John's Hospital, 187 Cal App 3d 710, 232 Cal Rptr 75 (2d Dist., 1986). It was significant to the *Burciaga* court that the baby had not been the doctor's patient before the stat call.

4. In the following op-ed, law professors Frank Rudy Cooper, Suzette Malveaux, and Catherine E. Smith argue that there should be a state law-based civil duty "to intervene when fellow officers use excessive force" that is enforceable by injured parties. The authors use existing police department policies and the history of the Reconstruction era federal civil rights laws to explain that *requiring* bystander officers to be Good Samaritans would not be "a novel idea." Read the op-ed to develop a general sense of the federal causes of action; and then use the framework set out *in Patton v. United States of America Rugby Football* — multi-factor duty analysis — to develop the arguments for and against adoption of this special duty. As a reminder, we include that framework in the introduction to this part of the chapter, i.e., II. Traditional Policy Exceptions to the Default Duty. It is also discussed in Justice Meyers dissent in *Strauss v. Belle Realty Company*.

> Police departments across the nation are implementing policies that would require officers to intervene when fellow officers use excessive force. Minneapolis has such a policy, yet it was not enough to spur Derek Chauvin's colleagues to intercede to save George Floyd's life.
>
> Our years of studying constitutional civil rights have taught us that police policies and even criminal statutes are not enough to overcome the "blue wall of silence" among officers. What's needed are state laws that create an affirmative duty for bystander cops to intervene to prevent use of excessive force or other civil rights deprivations, and that allow civil suits against cops who don't.
>
> Victims of police misconduct should not have to rely on inadequate department policies or prosecutorial whims for protection or redress. Criminal charges in cases of police violence are extremely rare. Tellingly, it took a week for Chauvin to be charged with second-degree murder and his fellow officers with accomplice liability as protests against racially motivated police violence erupted around the globe.
>
> By contrast, empowering individuals to bring civil lawsuits against bystander cops who fail to intervene — with the threat of monetary damages — would force officers to act. This might sound like a novel idea, but U.S. history teaches otherwise.
>
> In the late 1800s, despite the Reconstruction amendments to the U.S. Constitution, the Ku Klux Klan and its sympathizers terrorized formerly enslaved blacks and their white allies. Throughout the South, many police would orchestrate and participate in Klan violence. Others would tacitly agree to stand down. Congress passed the Civil Rights Act of 1871, also known as the Ku Klux Klan Act, in an effort to dismantle racist systems and institutions.
>
> This comprehensive legislation empowered individuals to act as private attorneys general to enforce the Constitution in several ways. Section 1983 enabled individuals to seek damages for constitutional violations, Section 1985 prohibited conspiracies against civil rights, and Section 1986 required police and other state officials to intervene in such conspiracies whenever possible.

Consistent with its early hostility toward the Reconstruction agenda, the Supreme Court severely restricted these sections. After lying dormant for about 100 years, they were resurrected in the late 20th century. Section 1986 is still rarely used, but its underlying principle, the duty to intervene, could help address present-day police violence — even if law enforcement is fundamentally restructured in the future.

Requiring officers to intervene makes sense for several reasons. When violence is perpetrated by law enforcement, bystander police officers are often the only people who can safely intervene. Civilians cannot be expected to stop an officer from assaulting a victim: They would risk arrest for obstructing justice and possibly face bodily harm themselves.

Police officers' unwillingness to report misconduct by other officers and their tendency to retaliate against those who do are common dynamics of police culture. If officers were required to intercede and supported in doing so, pressure would be reduced on those who currently hesitate to act. Anti-retaliation provisions, such as those in Colorado's broad new police accountability bill, which also mandates a duty to intervene, would further protect officers who take a stand.

In 1871, Congress knew that law enforcement inaction enabled lynchings, rapes and murders, playing an important role in the continued subjugation of black Americans. Police inaction today perpetuates racial hierarchies by allowing harms ranging from everyday harassment to brutal murders. Police silence results in burdens that are borne largely by the poor, racial minorities and other marginalized communities.

Although the 1871 act targeted the Klan and its sympathizers, reliance on this legislative model does not imply that all police officers are bad actors. Duty-to-intervene laws address the need for systemic change. They would tear down the blue wall of silence, altering police culture.

In medicine, the lowest-ranked members of a surgical team are expected to object if a surgeon is about to operate on the wrong limb or if they see other instances of malpractice. Mandating that police officers intercede would generate greater trust in them, protect civil rights and, ultimately, save lives.

None of Chauvin's fellow officers stopped him from kneeling on the neck of an unarmed and handcuffed man for nearly nine minutes. None of them acted on Floyd's repeated pleas for his life, nor after he lost consciousness. Many law enforcement agencies tell the public, "If you see something, say something." No less should be expected from those who have pledged to protect and serve.

Frank Rudy Cooper, Suzette Malveaux, and Catherine E. Smith, *We must tear down the 'blue wall of silence.' Here's how civil law suits could help.* THE WASHINGTON POST, June 17, 2020.

b. Promissory Estoppel

LIGHT v. NIPSCO INDUSTRIES, INC.
747 N.E.2d 73 (Ind. App. 2001)

Garrard, J.

The Lights commenced this action against Northern Indiana Public Service Company (NIPSCO), asserting that NIPSCO's failure to properly inspect the hookup of natural gas to Lights' residence was a proximate cause of injury to Mr. Light. In due course the trial court granted summary judgment to NIPSCO and this appeal followed.

The materials designated to the court by the parties presented evidence of the following facts. In 1988, Mr. Light was interested in converting the heating system in his home in Howe, Indiana to natural gas. He contacted Hank Platts, the manager of NIPSCO's office in LaGrange to discuss conversion. Mr. Platts referred Mr. Light to others in the office who furnished information on the advantages of using natural gas. Light expressed interest in the safety of natural gas and inquired if NIPSCO had a list of recommended installers or of installers that it had "Black Balled." He assertedly was told that they did not but that "if the work isn't right, we make them correct it before turning on the gas." Subsequently, Light contacted Kim Hummel and when NIPSCO assured him that Hummel could do the work, Light contracted with him to provide and install a furnace, water heater and air conditioner and asked NIPSCO to install the natural gas supply lines.

Light was not present to observe when Hummel installed the appliances, nor was he present when the gas was turned on. When Light returned home he discovered that they had hot water so he presumed everything was all right. Light does not know who turned on the gas but assumed it was NIPSCO because, earlier, when the line was run on the property and the meter was installed, he was told that it was shut off and that "when the installation is complete, he'll have to call us to come out, and we'll turn on the gas, and we'll inspect it and turn on the gas." There is no evidence that Light called NIPSCO to send personnel to inspect Hummel's work or to turn on the gas, and there is no evidence that Hummel did so.

Nine years later, Mr. Light discovered through another contractor that his water heater was not properly vented. He contacted NIPSCO and discovered that this was permitting carbon monoxide to escape into the home. The gas was shut off until a new water heater with the correct flue was installed.

The Lights contend that their carbon monoxide exposure in the home caused health problems Mr. Light had been experiencing.[2]

On appeal, the Lights acknowledge that NIPSCO owed them neither a general duty to inspect the hookup, nor a contract obligation to do so. They contend instead that NIPSCO voluntarily assumed the duty and is therefore liable for its breach. NIPSCO recognizes longstanding Indiana law enforcing voluntarily assumed duties, but argues that a duty may only be

---

[2] No issues are presented concerning Mr. Light's medical condition and its possible nexus with carbon monoxide exposure.

voluntarily assumed by a performance of the undertaking itself. Relying on contract law, it asserts that a mere promise to inspect is unenforceable in the absence of consideration to support it.

From the evidence that the gas was turned on and the representation that NIPSCO would have to be called to accomplish this it is inferable that NIPSCO in fact turned on the gas to the appliances in the dwelling. This evidence, however, does not support the further inference that NIPSCO actually inspected or attempted to inspect the installation of the appliances. Accordingly, the issue presented in this appeal is whether the mere assurance or promise that NIPSCO would inspect the connections and "make them do it right" is sufficient in the absence of any evidence that NIPSCO in fact attempted any such inspection to impose a tort duty of reasonable care.

Indiana tort law has long recognized that where one assumes to act he may thereby become subject to the duty to act with reasonable care towards those who may foreseeably be injured if he does not do so. Commencing with *Baker v. Midland-Ross Corp.,* 508 N.E.2d 32 (Ind.Ct.App.1987), our decisions have equated Indiana law with the provisions of RESTATEMENT (SECOND) OF TORTS, § 324A (1977). . . . Two years later, in *Harper v. Guarantee Auto Stores,* 533 N.E.2d 1258, 1262 (Ind.Ct.App.1989), . . . [t]he court . . . applied the provision but added the requirement that the evidence establish that the defendant should have recognized the careful execution of its undertaking was necessary for the protection of the injured party. The court equated this with the traditional requirement of foreseeability. More recent decisions simply have asserted that Indiana law parallels § 324A.

§ 324A provides:

> One who undertakes, gratuitously or for consideration, to render services to another which he should recognize as necessary for the protection of a third person or his things, is subject to liability to the third person for physical harm resulting from his failure to exercise reasonable care to protect his undertaking, if
>
> (a) his failure to exercise reasonable care increases the risk of such harm, or
>
> (b) he has undertaken to perform a duty owed by the other to the third person, or
>
> (c) the harm is suffered because of reliance of the other or the third person upon the undertaking.

While the Restatement provides the caveat that it expresses no opinion whether a gratuitous promise, without in any way entering upon performance, is sufficient to impose liability, Indiana decisions state that a promise is sufficient when coupled with reliance by the injured promisee. Thus, in *Ember v. B.F.D. Inc.,* 490 N.E.2d 764, 770 (Ind.Ct.App.1986), the court stated, "As [defendant] correctly argues, liability for nonfeasance, in connection with a gratuitous duty, is confined to situations when the beneficiaries detrimentally relied on performance, or when the actor increased the risk of harm." (citations omitted.).[4]

---

[4] As the court explained "nonfeasance" equates with a failure to act despite a gratuitous promise to do so, while "misfeasance" equates with instances where the action was taken or attempted.

Citing *Ember,* in *Johnson v. Owens,* 639 N.E.2d 1016, 1019 (Ind.Ct.App.1994) the court again stated that duty might arise when one assumes a duty to act "through affirmative conduct or agreement" and held that the total failure to act, nonfeasance, would nevertheless be actionable where the beneficiary relied on performance or the defendant increased the risk of harm.

We conclude, therefore, that while a gratuitous promise without more will not impose a duty upon which tort liability may be predicated, when that promise is accompanied by reliance on the part of the promisee, and the reliance was reasonable under the circumstances, a legal duty may be found.

Both the existence and the extent of such a duty are ordinarily questions for the trier of fact.

It follows that the evidence designated to the trial court was not sufficient to determine as a matter of law that NIPSCO had not voluntarily assumed a duty to the Lights based upon its representations, or promises, and Lights' reliance thereon. Accordingly, since genuine issues have not been foreclosed as to any of the other elements of Lights' claim, summary judgment was inappropriate.

The judgment is reversed and the case is remanded for such further proceedings as may be necessary.

Reversed and remanded.

BAKER, J., concurs.

MATHIAS, Judge, dissenting

Without question, a promise should-and usually does-stand for something. However, our legal system has wisely placed limitations on the formal enforceability of *gratuitous* promises. Because I think those limitations should apply here, I must respectfully dissent.

The majority holds that NIPSCO's gratuitous promise may be actionable as a matter of tort law. Specifically, the majority relies on Restatement (Second) of Torts § 324A, which was adopted by this court in *Harper v. Guarantee Auto Stores,* 533 N.E.2d 1258, 1262 (Ind.Ct.App.1989). . . .

The "caveat" immediately following . . . section [324A] declines to express an opinion as to whether making "a gratuitous promise, without in any way entering upon performance, is a sufficient undertaking to result in liability under the rule stated in this Section." Nevertheless, and in the absence of any evidence that NIPSCO actually inspected the work at issue, the majority adopts such a rule: "a promise is sufficient when coupled with reliance by the injured promisee."

. . .

Our lives are filled with many relationships that never do and never should take on legal significance. A friend is no less a friend because the law does not define what friendship is.

Similarly, we often undertake tasks on behalf of others with the explicit or implicit understanding that the beneficiary can make no claim beyond disappointment when things do not turn out as originally promised or represented. When a relative or friend volunteers to "look at" a malfunctioning motor vehicle or a home one is planning to purchase, I do not believe the common law should impose liability when such inspection either never takes place or turns out to be deficient. The majority's position . . . is that liability might well attach. The important limiting concept is one of whether reliance was reasonable, a concept not fully developed by the majority or by the Restatement discussions.

As a matter of contract law, it is well settled that "[n]ot every promise creates a legal obligation which the law will enforce. A promise must be predicated upon adequate consideration before it can command performance." Under the facts and circumstances before us, I believe that the payments NIPSCO would eventually receive from the Lights for the natural gas to fuel the appliances installed by the third-party contractor could serve as adequate consideration to enforce NIPSCO's promise to inspect under traditional contract theory.

Instead, the majority has embarked down a tort path that will likely have far-reaching and undesirable consequences. For this reason, I must respectfully dissent.

Notes and Questions

1. *Light* and the line of cases it represents is an example of the sometimes-porous boundary between tort law and contract law. This porousness reflects the subjects' common origin and the fact that the common law itself is not nearly as segregated by topic as is the 1L curriculum. Specifically in this case, contract law's doctrine of promissory estoppel — which, in some instances, allows for the creation of a contract without consideration so long as the plaintiff can prove a promise and detrimental reliance on the promise — is used by tort law to establish a duty to aid where one does not otherwise exist. Where else in the course have we already seen the intersection of torts and contracts?

2. The dissent in *Light* laments that a gratuitous promise, without more, can have legal (as opposed to moral) consequences. This view finds its way into other jurisdictions' versions of the promissory estoppel rule that require the plaintiff also to show that any reliance on the promise was reasonable, and that hold that reliance is unreasonable unless the plaintiff can show that the defendant had at least begun to act on or "undertake" to effect the promise. Which version of the rule incentivizes the most socially useful conduct?

c. Prior Conduct that Puts Plaintiff in a Position of Peril

PONDER v. NATIONAL CONVOY & TRUCKING CO.
173 S.E. 336 (N.C. 1934)

Appeal from Superior Court, Madison County; McElroy, Judge.

Action by Love Ponder against the National Convoy & Trucking Company and another. Judgment for plaintiff, and defendants appeal.
Affirmed.

This is an action to recover damages for injuries to the person and to the property of the plaintiff, caused, as alleged in the complaint, by the negligence of the defendants in the operation of a truck and trailer owned by the defendant the National Convoy & Trucking Company, and operated by the defendant Floyd S. Williams, its employee.

The evidence at the trial tended to show that on November 3, 1932, a truck owned and driven by the plaintiff collided with a trailer attached to a truck owned by the defendant the National Convoy & Trucking Company, and operated by the defendant Floyd S. Williams, its employee, within the corporate limits of the town of Marshall, N. C., on State Highway No. 20, with the result that plaintiff's truck was badly injured, and that plaintiff suffered painful and permanent injuries to his person.

At the time of the collision, the trailer attached to the truck extended across and completely obstructed the highway. The truck and trailer were about 61 feet in length; the highway through the town of Marshall, and at the place of the collision, was 18 or 20 feet wide. The defendant Floyd S. Williams had undertaken to turn the truck and trailer around on the highway, by driving the truck into a side road, which was not paved, leaving the trailer extending across and completely obstructing the highway. The wheels of the truck stuck in the soft ground of the side road, and for this reason the defendant was unable to move the truck or the trailer. He was in this situation for 10 or 15 minutes before the collision, and during that time made no effort to warn drivers of approaching automobiles or trucks of their peril, although he could see that a curve in the highway would prevent such drivers from seeing the trailer until they were so close to it that they might not be able to stop and thus avoid a collision. All his efforts were devoted to moving the truck and trailer. There were several persons present, attracted by his situation; but defendant did not request any one of them to warn drivers of approaching automobiles or trucks of their peril, by flags or otherwise.

While defendant's trailer thus obstructed the highway, the plaintiff, driving his truck, which was heavily loaded, approached on the highway, coming downgrade. Because of a curve in the highway, the plaintiff did not see, and could not see, the trailer, until he was within 25 or 30 feet of the obstruction. After he saw that the trailer was across the highway, completely obstructing it, the plaintiff was unable to stop his truck, because of the steep grade and his heavy load. Despite his efforts to avoid a collision, he was unable to do so. Plaintiff suffered painful and permanent injuries to his person as the result of the collision. His truck was badly injured.

Issues involving defendants' negligence, plaintiff's contributory negligence, and the amount of damages sustained by the plaintiff, as a result of his injuries, were submitted to the jury and answered in favor of the plaintiff.

From judgment that plaintiff recover of the defendants the sum of $10,150, the amount of the damages assessed by the jury, and the costs of the action, the defendants appealed to the Supreme Court.

CONNOR, Justice.

In the ninth paragraph of his complaint, the plaintiff alleges that the collision between his truck and the truck owned by the defendant the National Convoy & Trucking Company, and operated at the time of the collision by the defendant Floyd S. Williams, its employee, was caused by the negligence of the defendants, in that:

> "(a) Defendants knowingly, wilfully, carelessly, recklessly and negligently attempted to turn an automobile truck more than 61 feet long, on a narrow road, on a curve completely blocking said road to other vehicles using the same;
>
> (b) Defendants wilfully, recklessly, and negligently, without due care for the safety of others, using said road blocked the same without giving warning by flagman or other danger signals, to drivers of vehicles coming down a steep grade and around a curve above the point so blocked by defendants;
>
> (c) By driving and operating upon the highways of the State a truck with a trailer attached dangerous to the traveling public without having thereon some signal of danger to show others using said highways of their danger; said trailer being of a length in excess of that allowed by law."

Conceding that there was no evidence at the trial of this action, tending to show negligence on the part of the defendants as specified in sections (a) and (c) of paragraph 9 of the complaint, we are of the opinion that there was evidence tending to show negligence as specified in section (b) of said paragraph. For this reason, there was no error in the refusal by the trial court of defendants' motion for judgment as of nonsuit, at the close of all the evidence. The defendant Floyd S. Williams, after he found himself unable to move the truck and the trailer, because the wheels of the truck had stuck in the soft ground off the pavement, owed the duty to plaintiff and others approaching the obstruction in the highway, on automobiles or trucks, to exercise reasonable care to warn them of their peril. A failure to perform this duty was negligence. There was evidence tending to show that such negligence was the proximate cause of the collision, resulting in injury to the plaintiff.

The exceptions to the charge of the court to the jury are without merit. The instructions with respect to negligence on the part of the defendants, and contributory negligence on the part of the plaintiff, were in accord with well-settled principles of law. There was no error in the trial. The judgment is affirmed.

No error.

Notes and Questions

1. What was the defendant's negligence? Was it (a) turning in the wrong place, (b) pulling a trailer that wasn't suitable for the particular roadway, or (c) something else? If you think (c) is correct, can you specify the "something else"?

2. How would you use *Ponder* if you were counsel for the plaintiff in the following case: A bartender served the initially sober defendant his last drink of the night, a Long Island Iced Tea containing six ounces of liquor. As the defendant was drinking the Iced Tea, the bartender realized that the defendant was getting very drunk. Because the defendant was a regular patron, the bartender also knew that he intended to drive. When the defendant walked away for a few minutes leaving his car keys on the bar, the bartender remarked to other patrons that the defendant was very drunk. The defendant returned, finished his drink, and without permission, drank some of another patron's drink. The defendant then left the bar, drove off, and within a mile lost control of his car, crossed the centerline of the highway, and hit an oncoming car head-on killing the driver and badly injuring the passenger.

d. Special Relationships

PATTON v. UNITED STATES OF AMERICA RUGBY FOOTBALL
851 A.2D 566 (Md. 2003)

HARRELL, J.

On 17 June 2000, Robert Carson Patton, II, and his father, Donald Lee Patton, while at an amateur rugby tournament in Annapolis, were struck by lightning. Robert, a player in the tournament, was seriously injured, but survived. Donald, a spectator watching his son play, died. Robert and various other members of the Patton family filed suit in the Circuit Court for Anne Arundel County alleging negligence against the rugby tournament organizers, referee, and related organizations with regard to the episode.

Defendants filed Motions to Dismiss arguing they owed no legal duty to Robert and Donald Patton. A hearing was held and, on 10 July 2003, the Circuit Court dismissed the action. The Patton family appealed. This Court, on its own initiative and before the appeal could be decided in the Court of Special Appeals, issued a writ of certiorari to determine whether any of the defendants, under the circumstances alleged in the complaint, owed a legal duty to Robert and Donald Patton. *Patton v. USA Rugby*, 379 Md. 224, 841 A.2d 339 (2004).

I.

A. The Lightning Strike

Based on Appellants' amended complaint, we assume the truth of the following factual allegations:

Sometime during the early morning of 17 June 2000, Robert and Donald Patton arrived at playing fields adjacent to the Annapolis Middle School in Anne Arundel County, Maryland. Robert was to play rugby for the Norfolk Blues Rugby Club. Donald intended to support his son as a spectator. Robert and Donald, along with other participants and spectators, placed their equipment and belongings under a row of trees adjacent to the playing fields.

The rugby tournament was coordinated by Steven Quigg and was sanctioned by the United States of America Rugby Football Union, Ltd., d/b/a USA Rugby [USA Rugby], and Mid-Atlantic Rugby Football Union, Inc. [MARFU]. Rugby matches involving over two dozen teams began at approximately 9:00 a.m. and were planned to continue throughout the day. It was a warm, muggy day. The weather forecast for Annapolis was for possible thunderstorms. At some point prior to the start of the twenty minute match between the Norfolk Blues and the Washington Rugby Football Club ("the match"), a thunderstorm passed through the area surrounding the Annapolis Middle School. At the start of the match, rain commenced; lightning could be seen and thunder could be heard proximate to the lightning flashes. By this time, the National Weather Service had issued a thunderstorm "warning" for the Annapolis area.

Kevin Eager, a member of the Potomac Society of Rugby Football Referees, Inc., was the volunteer referee for the afternoon match in which Robert Patton was a participant. Under the direction of Eager, the match continued as the rain increased in intensity, the weather conditions deteriorated, and the lighting flashed directly overhead. Other matches at the tournament ended. Robert Patton continued to play the match through the rain and lightning and his father continued to observe as a spectator until the match was stopped just prior to its normal conclusion.

Upon the termination of the match, Robert and Donald fled the playing fields to the area under the trees where they left their possessions. As they began to make their exit from under the trees to seek the safety of their car, each was struck by lightning. Donald died. Robert Patton sustained personal injuries and was hospitalized, but recovered.

B. Circuit Court Proceedings

Appellants here and Plaintiffs below are Judith Edwards Patton (wife of Donald Patton), acting in both an individual capacity and as personal representative of the estate of Donald Patton; Sophia P. Patton and Robert C. Patton (the parents of Donald Patton); Robert Carson Patton, II; and Meredith Patton (Donald's daughter). They sued the USA Rugby, MARFU, the Potomac Rugby Union, Inc. ("PRU"), the Potomac Society of Rugby Football Referees, Inc. ("Referees' Society"), Kevin Eager, and Steven Quigg. . . . [Plaintiffs' complaint in the Circuit Court, as amended, alleged that the defendants failed to use proper policy and procedures to protect players and spectators from lightning strikes. Defendants' motions to dismiss asserted, among other things, that they owed no tort duty to either Robert or Donald Patton as a matter of law, and that they had statutory immunity from injuries arising from recreational uses of the premises, i.e. playing rugby on the middle school field. The Circuit Court granted the motion to dismiss and issued a Memorandum Opinion.]

. . .

This appeal follows . . . from a dismissal of the amended complaint based solely on the ground that there was no legal duty owed to Robert or Donald Patton. Appellants present the following question for our consideration:

Did the trial court err, when it found that Appellees had no duty to protect Appellants from lightning injuries and granted Appellees' motions to dismiss for failure to state a claim upon which relief can be granted?

. . .

III.

A.

For a plaintiff to state a prima facie claim in negligence, he or she must prove the existence of four elements by alleging facts demonstrating "(1) that the defendant was under a duty to protect the plaintiff from injury, (2) that the defendant breached that duty, (3) that the plaintiff suffered actual injury or loss, and (4) that the loss or injury proximately resulted from the defendant's breach of the duty." *Remsburg v. Montgomery*, 376 Md. 568, 582, 831 A.2d 18, 26 (2003) (quoting *Muthukumarana v. Montgomery Co.*, 370 Md. 447, 486, 805 A.2d 372, 395 (2002), and cases cited therein). Generally, whether there is adequate proof of the required elements to succeed in a negligence action is a question of fact to be determined by the fact-finder. The existence of a legal duty, however, is a question of law to be decided by the court.

. . .

When assessing whether a tort duty may exist, we often have recourse to the definition in W. Page Keeton, et al., *Prosser and Keeton on The Law of Torts* § 53 (5th ed.1984), which characterizes "duty" as "an obligation, to which the law will give recognition and effect, to conform to a particular standard of conduct toward another." *Id.* In determining the existence of a duty, we consider, among other things:

> the foreseeability of harm to the plaintiff, the degree of certainty that the plaintiff suffered the injury, the closeness of the connection between the defendant's conduct and the injury suffered, the moral blame attached to the defendant's conduct, the policy of preventing future harm, the extent of the burden to the defendant and consequences to the community of imposing a duty to exercise care with resulting liability for breach, and the availability, cost and prevalence of insurance for the risk involved.

. . .

. . . In determining whether a duty exists, "it is important to consider the policy reasons supporting a cause of action in negligence. The purpose is to discourage or encourage specific types of behavior by one party to the benefit of another party." *Valentine*, 353 Md. at 550, 727 A.2d at 950. "While foreseeability is often considered among the most important of these factors, its existence alone does not suffice to establish a duty under Maryland law." *Remsburg*, 376 Md. at 583, 831 A.2d at 26. As we clarified in *Ashburn*:

> [t]he fact that a result may be foreseeable does not itself impose a duty in negligence terms. This principle is apparent in the acceptance by most jurisdictions and by this Court of the general rule that there is no duty to control a third person's conduct so as

> to prevent personal harm to another, unless a "special relationship" exists either between the actor and the third person or between the actor and the person injured.

Ashburn, 306 Md. at 628, 510 A.2d at 1083 (citations omitted). In addition, "a tort duty does not always coexist with a moral duty." *Jacques*, 307 Md. at 534, 515 A.2d at 759 (citing W. Page Keeton, et al., *Prosser and Keeton on The Law of Torts* § 56 (5th ed.1984)). We have held that such a "special duty" to protect another may be established "(1) by statute or rule; (2) by contractual or other private relationship; or (3) indirectly or impliedly by virtue of the relationship between the tortfeasor and a third party." *Bobo*, 346 Md. at 715, 697 A.2d at 1376 (internal citations omitted).

B.

Appellants allege that a "special relationship" existed between Appellees (USA Rugby, MARFU, PRU, the Referees' Society, and Steven Quigg) and Robert and Donald Patton sufficient to recognize the existence of a duty to protect the latter, the breach of which gave rise to an action for negligence. Appellants argue that:

> A participant in a sporting event, by the very nature of the sport, trusts that his personal welfare will be protected by those controlling the event. Stated another way, it is reasonably foreseeable that both the player, and the player's father, will continue to participate in the match, as long as the match is not stopped by the governing bodies in charge. It also is reasonably foreseeable that, when matches are played in thunderstorms, there is a substantial risk of injury from lightning. And finally, it is reasonably foreseeable that a father will not abandon his son, when he sees those who have assumed responsibility for his son's welfare placing his son in a perilous condition. . . .

Appellants essentially contend that the tournament organizers had a duty to protect Robert and Donald, and to extricate them, from the dangers of playing in and viewing, respectively, a sanctioned rugby match during a thunderstorm.

Appellees counter that "there is no 'special relationship' between Mr. Patton, Sr., Mr. Patton and the [A]ppellees which would require the [A]ppellees to protect and warn these individuals of the dangers associated with lightning." Appellees argue that they "had no ability to control the activities of players or spectators at any time," and "there is no evidence in the record that Mr. Patton, Sr. and Mr. Patton were dependent upon or relied upon the [A]ppellees in any way, shape or form." We said in *Remsburg* that "the creation of a 'special duty' by virtue of a 'special relationship' between the parties can be established by either (1) the inherent nature of the relationship between the parties; or (2) by one party undertaking to protect or assist the other party, and thus often inducing reliance upon the conduct of the acting party." *Remsburg*, 376 Md. at 589–90, 831 A.2d at 30. We conclude that Appellants here did not establish by either of these methods a triable issue as to the existence of a "special relationship." *Id.*

In *Remsburg*, among other issues, we focused on whether a "special relationship" was created because of an implied or indirect relationship between the parties. *Id.* We held that the leader of a hunting party was under no special duty to protect a property owner who was shot by a member of the leader's hunting party. We found insufficient the relationship of dependence between the leader of the hunting party and the injured property owner. This meant there was no duty on the part of the leader to protect the property owner from being accidentally shot by a hunting party member. 376 Md. at 593, 831 A.2d at 33. In holding that the inherent nature of the relationship between the parties did not give rise to a "special relationship" and, hence, a tort duty, we again approved the traditional "special relationships" that consistently have been associated with the "special relationship" doctrine. 376 Md. at 593–94, 831 A.2d at 32–33. We adopted previously as Maryland common law § 314A of the Restatement, entitled "Special Relations Giving Rise to a Duty to Aid or Protect," which provides that:

> (1) [a] common carrier is under a duty to its passengers to take reasonable action
>
> (a) to protect them against unreasonable risk of physical harm. . . .
>
> (2) An innkeeper is under a similar duty to his guests.
>
> (3) A possessor of land who holds it open to the public is under a similar duty to members of the public who enter in response to his invitation.
>
> (4) One who is required by law to take or who voluntarily takes the custody of another under circumstance such as to deprive the other of his normal opportunities for protection is under a similar duty to the other.

Restatement (Second) of Torts § 314A (1965); *see Southland Corp. v. Griffith,* 332 Md. 704, 719, 633 A.2d 84, 91 (1993). Although the foregoing list is not exhaustive, our caselaw where we have found a duty arises consistently requires an element of dependence that is lacking in the present case. *See, e.g., Todd v. MTA*, 373 Md. 149, 165, 816 A.2d 930, 939 (2003) (finding that an employee of a common carrier has a legal duty to take affirmative action for the aid or protection of a passenger under attack by another passenger); *Southland*, 332 Md. at 720, 633 A.2d at 91 (finding that a convenience store, through its employee and by virtue of a special relationship between the business and its customers, owed a legal duty to a customer being assaulted in store parking lot to call the police for assistance when requested to do so).

As stated in *Remsburg*, "while we have permitted some flexibility in defining this limited exception, such as including the employer-to-employee relationship and also that of business owner-to-patron, we have been careful not to expand this class of 'special relationships' in such a manner as to impose broad liability for every group outing." *Remsburg*, 376 Md. at 594, 831 A.2d at 33.

. . . We [have] reasoned that for a "special relationship" to exist . . . it must be shown that the [defendant] affirmatively acted to protect the decedent or a specific group of individuals like the decedent, thereby inducing specific reliance by an individual on the [defendant's] conduct. 370 Md. at 496, 805 A.2d at 401.

The element of dependence and ceding of self-control by the injured party . . . is absent in the present case.[5] There is no credible evidence that the two adults, Robert and Donald Patton, entrusted themselves to the control and protection of Appellees. Accordingly, we follow our admonition in *Remsburg* to avoid expanding the "special relationship" exception in such a manner as to impose broad liability for every group activity. *Remsburg*, 376 Md. at 594, 831

[5] There may be a degree of dependency and ceding of control that could trigger a "special relationship" in, for example, a Little League game where children playing in the game are reliant on the adults supervising them.

A.2d at 33. Our decision here, in line with *Remsburg* . . ., is consistent with our view of narrowly construing the "special relationship" exception.

Of the relevant cases from our sister states, we find *Dykema v. Gus Macker Enters., Inc.*, 196 Mich.App. 6, 492 N.W.2d 472 (1992) to be particularly persuasive in the present case. In *Dykema*, the Michigan Court of Appeals held that the sponsors of an outdoor basketball tournament had no duty to warn a tournament spectator of an approaching thunderstorm that ultimately caused his injury. *Dykema*, 492 N.W.2d at 474–75. A thunderstorm struck the area of the tournament. The plaintiff, while running for shelter, was struck by a falling tree limb and paralyzed. *Dykema*, 492 N.W.2d at 473.

Like Maryland, Michigan recognizes the general rule that there is no tort duty to aid or protect another in the absence of a generally recognized " special relationship." *Dykema*, 492 N.W.2d at 474. The Michigan court stated that:

> The rationale behind imposing a legal duty to act in these special relationships is based on the element of control. In a special relationship, one person entrusts himself to the control and protection of another, with a consequent loss of control to protect himself. The duty to protect is imposed upon the person in control because he is in the best position to provide a place of safety. Thus, the determination whether a duty-imposing special relationship exists in a particular case involves the determination whether the plaintiff entrusted himself to the control and protection of the defendant, with a consequent loss of control to protect himself.

Id. (citations omitted). Like the situation of the plaintiff and tournament sponsors in *Dykema*, Appellants here cannot be said to have entrusted themselves to the control and protection of the rugby tournament organizers. *Id.* ("Plaintiff was free to leave the tournament at anytime, and his movements were not restricted by Defendant."). We do not agree that, as Appellants argue, "the participants in the tournament, in effect, cede control over their activities to those who are putting on the event." Robert and Donald Patton were free to leave the voluntary, amateur tournament at any time and their ability to do so was not restricted in any meaningful way by the tournament organizers. An adult amateur sporting event is a voluntary affair, and the participants are capable of leaving the playing field on their own volition if they feel their lives or health are in jeopardy. The changing weather conditions in the present case presumably were observable to all competent adults. Robert and Donald Patton could have sought shelter at any time they deemed it appropriate to do so.

There is a line of cases, not dependent on analysis of whether a special relationship existed, that rely on the ability of competent adults to perceive the approach of thunderstorms and to appreciate the natural risks of lightning associated with thunderstorms to justify finding no breach of an ordinary duty of care owed to a plaintiff, whether that duty is recognized by common law, undertaken by the conduct of a defendant, or implied from the conduct of a defendant. For example, in *Hames*, the Supreme Court of Tennessee held that the State's failure to provide lightning proof shelters and lightning warning devices at a State-owned golf course was not actionable in negligence. *Hames*, 808 S.W.2d at 45. Like Robert and Donald Patton, the golfer in *Hames* began to play his sport of choice on an overcast day. On the day that the golfer was struck by lightning, no signs were posted informing patrons what to do in the event of a thunderstorm and no effort was made to clear the golf course by course employees. *Hames*, 808 S.W.2d at 42. Approximately 25 minutes after the golfer began to play golf, a thunderstorm moved through the area. He was struck and killed by lightning while seeking cover on a small hill underneath some trees.

The plaintiff in *Hames* argued that the U.S. Golf Association's Rules and Regulations created a golf course standard of care that required posting of lightning warnings and precautions. *Hames*, 808 S.W.2d at 43. The plaintiff's argument in *Hames* is analogous to Appellants' argument in the present case, i.e., the National Collegiate Athletic Association guidelines constitute a lightning safety standard of care for outdoor sporting events.

As well as finding no proximate cause, the Tennessee Court found that the "risks and dangers associated with playing golf in a lightning storm are rather obvious to most adults." *Hames*, 808 S.W.2d at 45. The Court noted that it would have taken the decedent golfer two minutes to reach the relative safety of the clubhouse, but instead he remained on the golf course. *Id.* The Court concluded that "it is reasonable to infer that a reasonably prudent adult can recognize the approach of a severe thunderstorm and know that it is time to pack up the clubs and leave before the storm begins to wreak havoc." *Id.* Accordingly, even though the State, as owner-operator of the golf course, owed Hames a general duty "to exercise reasonable care under all the attendant circumstances to make the premises safe . . . the defendant's conduct did not fall below the applicable standard of care." *Hames*, 808 S.W.2d at 44–46.

In *Caldwell v. Let the Good Times Roll Festival*, 717 So.2d 1263, 1274 (La.Ct.App.1998), the Louisiana Court of Appeals held that the City of Shreveport and two co-sponsors of an outdoor festival had neither a general nor specific duty to warn spectators of an approaching severe thunderstorm that caused injuries due to its high winds. The court in *Caldwell* observed that:

> Most animals, especially we who are in the higher order, do not have to be told or warned about the vagaries of the weather, that wind and clouds may produce a rainstorm; that a rainstorm and wind and rain may suddenly escalate to become more severe and dangerous to lives and property. A thundershower may suddenly become a thunderstorm with destructive wind and lightning. A thunderstorm in progress may escalate to produce either or both tornadoes and hail, or even a rare and unexpected micro burst . . . all of which are extremely destructive to persons and property.

Caldwell, 717 So.2d at 1271. . . .

Judgment of the Circuit Court for Anne Arundel County affirmed. Costs to be paid by appellants.

Chief Judge BELL joins in the judgment only.

Notes and Questions

1. Do you agree with the USA Rugby court's conclusion that "Robert and Donald Patton were free to leave the voluntary, amateur tournament at any time and their ability to do so was not restricted in any meaningful way by the tournament organizers"? What could have been the costs to Robert had he walked off the field when he decided (contrary to the views of the officials) that the conditions had become too treacherous to continue? What other information would you like to have before determining whether those costs would have been worth bearing?

2. Do you agree that adult and child athletes are differently dependent on officials and referees? What factors other than chronological age control dependence?

3. Early on in the opinion the court noted that it was not deciding the matter on the basis of the waiver Robert had signed as a condition to membership in USA Rugby. It is typical for organizers of recreational activities, whether these be for profit or not, to require participants to sign waivers exculpating the organizers from liability for risks inherent in the activity and for negligence. We will see this in more detail in our chapter on defenses to negligence.

4. By now you should be comfortable spotting and working through the threshold issues described in Chapter One, particularly those involving collectability and immunities. Do you see those that likely affected the choices the plaintiffs made in USA Rugby, about whom to sue and how to develop their claims?

5. As the ALI explains,

> [t]he term "special relationship" has no independent significance. It merely signifies that courts recognize an affirmative duty arising out of the relationship where otherwise no duty would exist . . . . Whether a relationship is deemed special is a conclusion based on reasons of principle or policy.
>
> . . . No algorithm exists to provide clear guidance about which policies in which proportions justify the imposition of an affirmative duty based on a relationship. The special relationships established by this Section are justified in part because the reasons for the no-duty rule . . . are obviated by the existence of the relationship. A relationship identifies a specific person to be protected and thus provides a more limited and justified incursion on autonomy, especially when the relationship is entered into voluntarily. In addition, some relationships necessarily compromise a person's ability to self-protect, while leaving the actor in a superior position to protect that person. Many of the relationships also benefit the actor. . . .

Restatement (Third) of Torts § 40, Comment (2013).

6. The list of recognized "special relationships" has evolved since the publication of the Restatement Second. This evolution has been the result of courts across the country finding additional relationships of dependence and reliance, the two main criteria underlying the establishment of a special relationship. They also usually involved an analysis of the policy implications of adding a particular new relationship to this list, which was governed by the multi-factor duty analysis introduced in the beginning of this chapter. Section 40 of the Third Restatement provides an up-to-date statement of the majority rule:

> (a) An actor in a special relationship with another owes the other a duty of reasonable care with regard to risks that arise within the scope of the relationship.
>
> (b) Special relationships giving rise to the duty provided in Subsection (a) include:
>
> (1) a common carrier with its passengers,
>
> (2) an innkeeper with its guests,
>
> (3) a business or other possessor of land that holds its premises open to the

public with those who are lawfully on the premises,

(4) an employer with its employees who, while at work, are:

(a) in imminent danger; or

(b) injured or ill and thereby rendered helpless,

(5) a school with its students,

(6) a landlord with its tenants, and

(7) a custodian with those in its custody, if:

(a) the custodian is required by law to take custody or voluntarily takes custody of the other; and

(b) the custodian has a superior ability to protect the other.

7. In the Comment that accompanies this section, the ALI explains that "the list of special relationships provided in this Section is not exclusive. Courts may, as they have since the Second Restatement, identify additional relationships that justify exceptions to the no-duty rule. . . ." It goes on to suggest that

> [o]ne likely candidate for an addition to recognized special relationships is the one among family members. This relationship, particularly among those residing in the same household, provides as strong a case for recognition as a number of the other special relationships recognized in this Section. To date, there has been little precedent addressing the family relationship as a basis for an affirmative duty, although family immunities have long been removed as an impediment to this development. Family exclusions in liability insurance may have stunted doctrinal development in this area. However, bases do exist for affirmative duties that overlap with a duty imposed by an intra-family special relationship. . . . [For example, s]tatutes imposing duties on parents to provide for their children are [a] potential source for an affirmative tort duty. . . .

The suggestion by the ALI that courts consider adding husband-wife and/or parent-child to the list of accepted special relationships is not new; it was first made in the comments associated with Section 314(a) of the Restatement Second. Although these particular relationships may seem intuitively "special" and thus especially deserving of special relationships status, the reason the courts are loathe to include them is that doing so would effectively involve the state in the regulation of relationships within the intact family. As we have already seen, aside from domestic violence (including both spousal and child abuse) and child neglect, the law has stayed away from such interference for both political and constitutional reasons; and state courts routinely rationalize their "hands off" approach to the family on alternative grounds. *See, e.g.*, Bicknell v. Dakota GM, Inc., Not Reported in F.Supp.2d, 2009 WL 799613 *8 (D. Minn. 2009) ("A spousal relationship, however, is not a *per se* 'special relationship' for the purpose of creating a legal duty. . . . the purpose of the special duty exception is to protect an individual who is 'particularly vulnerable and dependent on the defendant, who in turn holds considerable power over the plaintiff's welfare.' (citation omitted) Here, plaintiff and Mr. Bicknell's relationship is not a 'special relationship that creates a legal duty: a party is not dependent on his or her spouse for protection by virtue of any inherent vulnerability.'")

8. As the *Patton* case demonstrates, the special relationship exception to the no duty rule exists or may be the basis for a viable argument in many different factual circumstances. However, there are three frequently recurring fact patterns that are particularly worthy of note: fact patterns involving special relationships that impose a duty on business owners to protect against the criminal acts of third parties; fact patterns involving special relationships that impose a duty on the defendant to protect a third-party plaintiff; and special relationships that impose a duty on governments to protect particular citizens.

Although there is generally no duty to rescue, "a business or other possessor of land that holds its premises open to the public" has traditionally been in a special relationship "with those who are lawfully on the premises" that imposes a duty to aid. Restatement (Second) of Torts § 314A (1965). Notwithstanding this well-established special relationship, courts have been reluctant to impose the obligation in circumstances involving the criminal acts of third parties. In other words, the special relationships exception to the exception to the default duty that there is no duty to aid itself has an exception where the aid is needed as a result of third-party criminal conduct. (We recognize that this last point is torturous – pun intended – but you need to figure it out.) Consider the policy rationales that might motivate this reluctance. They result in the imposition of additional requirements on plaintiffs who seek to recover for a defendant's failure to aid in such circumstances. Depending on the jurisdiction, plaintiffs are generally required to prove that the particular kind of criminal activity at issue was foreseeable to a reasonable person in the defendants' shoes, taking into account prior similar acts, the location of the business, and the time period at issue. They may also be asked to prove that, on balance, the burden of imposing the obligation reasonably to protect patrons against the criminal conduct is less than the value of the business to the community, i.e., that imposing the burden wouldn't cause a valuable enterprise either to leave the community or not to locate there in the first place. See, e.g., Trammell Crow Central Texas v. Gutierrez, 267 S.W.3d 9 (Tex. 2008) (rejecting the imposition of a duty on the owners and operators of a mall complex to protect moviegoers from assailants who shot and killed them because there was insufficient evidence of prior, similarly violent incidents on the premises and noting that the burden to the mall owners of additional prophylactic measures might also factor into the duty analysis). Note that the latter is consistent with the standard methodology in circumstances where duty is a policy question either on specific facts or in across a category of cases.

Health care professionals, including doctors and therapists, are generally considered to be in a special relationship with their patients that derives from their contractual relationship. The question whether that special relationship imposes obligations on the health care professionals to rescue third parties from the foreseeable acts of their patients is a recurring one. Whereas the common law limited this tort obligation consistent with contract privity rules, modern doctrine is slightly more inclusive. Depending on the jurisdiction, reasonably or readily identified or identifiable victims may be owed a duty to warn or protect against patients whose violent or dangerous propensities are foreseeable to their providers. See, e.g., Shea v. Caritas Carney Hospital, Inc., 947 N.E.2d 99 (Mass. App. 2011) (rejecting executrix's duty to warn claim because the defendants, mental health care professionals who treated the patient, "did not have a reasonable basis to believe there was a clear and present danger" that their patient "would attempt to kill or inflict serious bodily injury" on the decedent who was otherwise not a "reasonably identified victim"). This modern rule derives from the California Supreme Court's decision in Tarasoff v. Regents of the Univ. of Cal., 17 Cal.3d 425, 131 Cal.Rptr. 14, 551 P.2d 334 (1976). In *Tarasoff*, "the landmark case on the subject of a mental health professional's duty to warn potential victims[,] . . . .

> a student at the University of California at Berkeley told a school psychologist that he was planning to kill an undergraduate student, with whom he was obsessed, upon her return from a summer trip to Brazil. The student did not name his intended victim, but she was easily identifiable as Tatianna Tarasoff. After the psychologist alerted campus police to the threat and recommended that his patient be committed, the patient was briefly taken into custody, but he was eventually released. Neither the psychologist nor the police took any action to warn Tarasoff, who was killed by the patient a few weeks later. Tarasoff's parents brought a negligence complaint against the university and the psychologist. The Supreme Court of California held that "once a therapist does in fact determine, or under applicable professional standards reasonably should have determined, that a patient poses a serious danger of violence to others, he bears a duty to exercise reasonable care to protect the foreseeable victim of that danger."

Shea v. Caritas Carney Hospital, Inc., supra at note 8. As applied, the *Tarasoff* court held that the therapist acted reasonably to discharge the duty by notifying the campus police of the threat. Nevertheless, the decision was widely condemned by the mental health care community which was concerned that it would require them to violate their therapist-patient confidentiality rules and would result in the imposition of liability whenever a potentially violent patient caused harm. As a result, like Massachusetts, most if not all states have adopted statutory or common law rules limiting and specifying the terms of the duty to warn or protect. *Tarasoff* is otherwise very prominent in the jurisprudence and so you may find it useful at some point to read it in its entirety. Among other things, the case contains an extensive discussion of mental health policy, state sovereign immunity, and waivers of that immunity which may be especially instructional.

Assuming they survive immunity challenges as a threshold matter, claims against the government charging negligence in the decision to parole recidivists or in allowing the escape of violent prisoners also fall into this third-party exception to the traditional no duty to rescue, aid, or warn rule. Compare Thompson v. County of Alameda, 614 P.2d 728 (Cal. 1980) (applying the special relationships test and multi-factor duty analysis to the claim that the county ought to have warned a dangerous parolee's mother, the police, or the neighborhood that he was being paroled and that he had threatened to kill a young child in the neighborhood if he was released into his mother's custody, and rejecting the imposition of the duty on the grounds that the victim was not "readily identifiable"), with Johnson v. State of California, 447 P.2d 352 (Cal. 1968) (engaging the same analysis and concluding that the state did have a duty to warn the foster mother of a child the state knew to be violent before placing the child in her care).

Again assuming they survive immunity challenges as a threshold matter, claims brought by individuals against municipalities for failure to dispatch any or at least effective police or fire rescue personnel may still be barred by the "public duty" doctrine. This doctrine provides that absent a special relationship, the duty to provide government services is owed "to the public at large" and not to any individual specifically. In other words, "the mere existence of rescue services does not, standing alone, impose upon the governmental entity a duty to use them for the benefit of a particular individual." Mullin v. Municipal City of South Bend, 639 N.E.2d 278 (Ind. 1994). As the District of Columbia Court of Appeals detailed in Powell v. District of Columbia,

> [a] number of public policy considerations underlie the public duty doctrine. Courts concerned with separation of powers maintain that the public duty doctrine is necessary to avoid "judicial scrutiny of every act of the other branches of government which has some effect upon the public." Other courts, focusing on fiscal concerns, fear either "a potential drain on the public coffers," or that the encouragement of increased litigation will deprive the municipality of funds for correcting the governmental error that gave rise to the complaint. Other courts have viewed the issue from the government employee's perspective, maintaining that without the public duty doctrine such employees would be subject to an unreasonable litigation risk that could not be "passed on to their 'clients'." In addition to reserving questions about the appropriate allocation of limited resources to the executive and legislature, and concern about the "severe depletion of these resources," the court has emphasized the need for public employees to have broad discretion in responding to demands given limited resources and "the inescapable choices of allocation that must be made." Without such a limitation on liability, the [government] would be potentially liable for "every oversight, omission, or blunder made by a police, [ambulance or building inspection] official."

602 A.2d 1123, 1128 (D.C. 1992). A special relationship in this context may be established where there is evidence of

> (1) an explicit assurance by the municipality, through promises or actions, that it would act on behalf of the injured party;
>
> (2) knowledge on the part of the municipality that inaction could lead to harm; and
>
> (3) justifiable and detrimental reliance

on the government's assurance. Mullin v. Municipal City of South Bend, supra. Depending on the jurisdiction, this reliance must be "by the injured party" specifically, or else by someone acting on their behalf. Id. Be sure you understand and are able to articulate the difference between governmental immunity and the public duty doctrine. In essence, they are both firewalls that insulate the government from liability in tort law.

B. Plaintiff Alleges That Defendant Caused Only Emotional Distress

"Stand-alone" emotional distress claims allege that the defendant owed plaintiff the duty to refrain from negligently inflicting emotional distress (NIED). They are to be distinguished from claims for non-economic damages — including damages for emotional suffering — which flow from physical injuries.

The prima facie case for NIED is (1) a duty to use reasonable care not to inflict emotional distress, (2) a breach of that duty, (3) which causes, (4) emotional distress. As you will see in the cases that follow, the law has traditionally been reluctant to recognize a stand-alone emotional distress claim — hence there was a "no duty" rule at common law. Although the courts have warmed to the claim over time, it remains constrained in many if not most jurisdictions.

JOHNSON v. ROGERS
763 P.2d 771 (Utah 1988)

DURHAM, Justice:

Plaintiffs sought compensatory damages for the wrongful death of their child, as well as for emotional distress to both plaintiffs and physical injury to plaintiff Ray Johnson. The trial court denied defendants' motion on the issue of damages for Ray Johnson's emotional distress. Plaintiffs filed this interlocutory appeal, and defendants cross-appealed. We affirm the trial court's ruling as to the damages for emotional distress.

Facts

At approximately 10:00 p.m. on April 16, 1982, plaintiff Ray Johnson and his eight-year-old son David were waiting for a "walk" signal before crossing a street in downtown Salt Lake City. A truck crossed the intersection and jumped the curb, killing David and injuring Ray. The truck was owned by NAC [the Newspaper Agency Corporation] and operated by Donald Rogers. It is admitted that Rogers was driving under the influence of alcohol and that he negligently caused the injuries.

. . .

IV. Negligent Infliction of Emotional Distress

. . . [B]efore us on appeal is the question of whether a cause of action for negligently inflicted emotional distress exists in Utah and, if so, under what circumstances it exists. . . . "[I]t is well established in Utah that a cause of action for emotional distress may not be based upon mere negligence." The two cases relied on for that principle are *Samms v. Eccles* and *Jeppsen v. Jensen,* 47 Utah 536, 155 P. 429 (1916).

. . .

In view of the age of *Samms v. Eccles* (decided twenty-seven years ago) and *Jeppsen v. Jensen* (decided seventy-two years ago), a reexamination of their premises is timely. This is particularly so in view of the extensive development of the law in this area in the intervening period and the abandonment by other jurisdictions of the precedents which were persuasive to this Court in its earlier opinions. Therefore, we . . . address the question anew: Should a cause of action exist in this jurisdiction for the negligent infliction of emotional distress, and should the cause of action extend to bystanders whose emotional injuries result from the infliction of injury to or death of third persons? We note that all parties have framed the issue in this fashion. It is unclear from the record whether Rogers' conduct is claimed to be sufficiently "wanton" to qualify under the intentional infliction of emotional distress standard.

Virtually all jurisdictions in the United States now recognize a broad protected interest in mental tranquility, first acknowledged in Utah in *Jeppsen.* The negligent infliction of emotional distress as a separate tort (distinct from the "willful and wanton" infliction of emotional distress or the negligent infliction of physical injuries with concomitant emotional injuries) has evolved rapidly only since the 1960s. . . . A common fact pattern for the cause of action is that existing in this case: a bystander observes negligent injury to a victim, which causes the bystander to suffer emotional distress. The courts have developed several rules affecting recovery for the emotional distress. Currently, no jurisdiction precludes recovery under any circumstances. Recovery is based upon satisfaction of one of three standards: the impact rule, the zone-of-danger rule, or a foreseeability standard.

The impact rule requires that a plaintiff sustain some physical impact or injury which itself causes emotional distress. It was the original and most limited approach to emotional distress claims and was responsive to courts' early concerns about speculative damages and floods of litigation over trivial claims. Although this rule was at one time a majority position, it has fallen into disfavor in recent years for a number of reasons. Suspicion regarding the authenticity of claims of mental distress has decreased with medical advances in the field of psychiatry and psychology. The concern over case load impact has come to be seen as inadequate reason to deny legitimate claims, and those courts that have abandoned the impact rule have not in fact seen drastic increases in this type of litigation. Finally, the results of the impact rule were often arbitrary, capricious, and unfair: the existence of a physical impact or injury frequently bore no rational relationship to the existence and severity of emotional injuries. Sometimes even the slightest of physical impacts (e.g., from smoke, dust, small jolts) was a sufficient predicate for recovery for emotional injuries, whereas the absence of such trivial impact could preclude recovery for the same injuries. . . . Because of its irrationality, the majority of courts abandoned the impact rule.

The zone-of-danger rule, relied on by the trial judge in this case, was adopted by many courts as a less restrictive substitute for the impact rule. It is set forth in section 313 of the Restatement (Second) of Torts:

> (1) If the actor unintentionally causes emotional distress to another, he is subject to liability to the other for resulting illness or bodily harm if the actor
>
> > (a) should have realized that his conduct involved an unreasonable risk of causing the distress, otherwise than by knowledge of the harm or peril of a third person, and
> >
> > (b) from facts known to him, should have realized that the distress, if it were caused, might result in illness or bodily harm.
>
> (2) The rule stated in Subsection (1) has no application to illness or bodily harm of another which is caused by emotional distress arising solely from harm or peril to a third person, *unless the negligence of the actor has otherwise created an unreasonable risk of bodily harm to the other.* (Emphasis added.)

The zone-of-danger rule offers many of the same benefits, although more expansive in its application, as did the impact rule. It is an objective standard and serves to identify in consistent fashion those who are eligible to recover. Unfortunately, it also suffers from many of the disadvantages of the impact rule: it is a rigid and inequitable limitation on recovery for injuries which are otherwise indistinguishable from each other. The parent standing next to the child hit by a car has a cause of action; the parent standing twenty feet away does not.

California was the first jurisdiction in the United States to extend liability beyond the zone of danger. *Dillon v. Legg,* 68 Cal.2d 728, 441 P.2d 912, 69 Cal.Rptr. 72 (1968). In *Dillon,* Justice

Tobriner of the California Supreme Court wrote:

> [T]he complaint here presents the claim of the emotionally traumatized mother, who admittedly was *not* within the zone of danger, as contrasted with that of the sister, who *may have been* within it. The case thus illustrates the fallacy of the rule that would deny recovery in the one situation and grant it in the other. In the first place, we can hardly justify relief to the sister for trauma which she suffered upon apprehension of the child's death and yet deny it to the mother merely because of a happenstance that the sister was some few yards closer to the accident. The instant case exposes the hopeless artificiality of the zone-of-danger rule. In the second place, to rest upon the zone-of-danger rule when we have rejected the impact rule becomes even less defensible. We have, indeed, held that impact is not necessary for recovery. The zone-of-danger concept must, then, inevitably collapse because the only reason for the requirement of presence in that zone lies in the fact that one within it will fear the danger of *impact.*

The court went on to observe that it had in the past "rejected the argument that we must deny recovery upon a legitimate claim because other fraudulent ones may be urged," and that "the alleged inability to fix definitions on the different facts of future cases does not justify the denial of recovery on the specific facts of the instant case; . . . proper guidelines can indicate the extent of liability for such future cases." Focusing on the foreseeability of risk, the court enunciated what has come to be known as the "*Dillon* rule," consisting of three factors which when evaluated determine the degree of foreseeability of the plaintiff's injury: (1) whether the plaintiff was located near the scene of the accident; (2) whether the emotional trauma to the plaintiff was caused by actually witnessing the accident; and (3) whether the plaintiff and the victim were closely related. In light of these factors, the court can determine whether the injury was reasonably foreseeable.

Hawaii has broadened the *Dillon* foreseeability standard, using a "pure" foreseeability analysis in bystander cases. Where serious emotional distress to a plaintiff-bystander is the reasonably foreseeable consequence of the defendant's act, the defendant's conduct is the proximate cause of the plaintiff's mental injury and general tort principles are applied to impose liability. *Leong v. Takasaki,* 55 Haw. 398, 520 P.2d 758 (1974); *Rodrigues v. State,* 52 Haw. 156, 472 P.2d 509, *reh'g denied,* 52 Haw. 283, 472 P.2d 509 (1970). In the absence of any limiting rules, however, the circumstances permitting liability extend far beyond ordinary expectations, creating grave theoretical and policy problems.

The distinction between "direct victim" and "bystander" liability and its effect on the standard of recovery used by the courts must also be examined in order for the summary of currently accepted approaches to liability to be complete. Courts have characterized the direct or primary victim as the person to whom a duty was owed and who was directly injured by the breach of that duty. The bystander or secondary victim is anyone who was not directly injured by the defendant, but who suffered mental distress as a result of his or her association with the direct victim's injury. Thus, in fact situations involving car/pedestrian accidents, the person who is physically injured by the defendant may bring an action for emotional trauma as a direct victim, while a bystander to the accident may recover based only on theories of secondary liability.

The direct victim/bystander distinction is important because in some jurisdictions it controls the standard which a plaintiff must meet in order to recover. In California, the *Dillon* standard no longer applies in direct victim cases. Instead, the court has adopted a broader foreseeability test and has abandoned the requirement that the emotional injury be physically manifested. *Molien v. Kaiser Foundation Hosp.,* 27 Cal.3d 916, 616 P.2d 813, 167 Cal.Rptr. 831 (1980). States that have adopted a zone-of-danger rule have, in effect, limited recovery to cases involving direct victims, disallowing recovery to bystanders. Plaintiffs who are allowed to recover because they were present within the zone of danger are direct victims because the defendant breached the duty of care owed them. Other witnesses falling outside of the zone are denied recovery due to the lack of direct injury and breach of a duty. The distinction between direct victims and bystanders must be taken into account in fashioning and applying any standard of recovery for negligent infliction of emotional distress.

A final comment must be added to the discussion of direct victim and bystander liability. As a method by which a defendant's liability can be limited in bystander cases, many jurisdictions require that any claimed emotional injury be manifested physically. This requirement persists in most jurisdictions as a sign of courts' concern that emotional injury claims made by plaintiffs who have not been directly injured are difficult to validate in the absence of physical symptoms and that deletion of this requirement would result in a flood of ill-founded bystander claims. However, some courts have recently dismissed these concerns as unwarranted and now allow recovery in the absence of any physical symptoms. *See, e.g., Rodrigues v. State,* 52 Haw. 156, 472 P.2d 509, *reh'g denied,* 52 Haw. 283, 472 P.2d 509 (1970); *Paugh v. Hanks,* 6 Ohio St.3d 72, 451 N.E.2d 759 (1983) (physical injury is evidence of the *degree* of mental injury).

Our research has not disclosed, nor have the parties identified, any jurisdiction in the United States which bars all recovery for the negligent infliction of emotional distress. The policy considerations in favor of realistic limits on negligence liability have given rise in turn to the impact rule, the zone-of-danger rule, and the *Dillon* rule, but not to a refusal to recognize the cause of action under any circumstances. Although the search for coherent, consistent application of liability principles in this area is difficult, that difficulty is an inappropriate predicate for denial of redress to a whole class of legitimate and serious claims.

It is further to be observed that the argument against allowing such an action because groundless charges may be made is not a good reason for denying recovery. If the right to recover for injury resulting from wrongful conduct could be defeated whenever such dangers exist, many of the grievances the law deals with would be eliminated. That some claims may be spurious should not compel justice to shut their [sic] eyes to serious wrongs and let them go without being brought to account. It is the function of courts and juries to determine whether claims are valid or false. This responsibility should not be shunned merely because the task may be difficult to perform.

We therefore sustain the trial judge in his determination that a cause of action for negligent infliction of emotional distress may be maintained and undertake to establish general guidelines for the availability of recovery. A discussion of the rule of law to be applied must be general because the facts of this case would satisfy any of the three major tests applied in other jurisdictions. The plaintiff here suffered an impact during the accident, receiving physical injuries to his foot. Furthermore, he was in the immediate zone of danger created by Rogers' acts. Finally, all three of the *Dillon* criteria are present: he was located immediately at the scene of the accident, he saw and heard all of the events associated with the violence to the victim, and the victim was his child.

I believe that the analytic approach of the *Dillon* rule is fundamentally sound in its focus on foreseeability as a necessary element of duty in negligence cases, and I would treat it as a legitimate starting point in the treatment of bystander causes of action for negligent infliction of emotional distress. I am aware, however, that the rule as formulated in *Dillon* has not served as an adequate guarantee of certainty in application even by the California courts.

I therefore emphasize that it is impossible to articulate a mechanistic test, as opposed to identifying an analytic approach, in a case which challenges no traditional limitations. In effect, I would hold that one may recover for the negligent infliction of emotional distress when one was in the zone of danger created by the negligence and suffered a physical impact. I nevertheless express the view that the less arbitrary, more traditional tort analysis embodied in the *Dillon* rule is appropriate. It is true that *Dillon* is more flexible than the impact and zone-of-danger rules, but it is not entirely free from the criticism that it too has become hardened and mechanical in practice because the courts attempting to apply [it] have no general policies to guide them in the difficult cases.

. . .

Although I believe that expanding Utah's tort principles to allow recovery for negligent infliction of emotional distress is prudent, I also recognize that philosophical concerns about the proper limits of tort liability exist. While liability standards have been greatly expanded in the past few decades, the pendulum has recently begun to swing back, with courts and commentators now reexamining the effectiveness and cost of the current system. At least one scholar believes that the focus should be on standards that prevent accidents rather than on compensation, a goal that is better served by traditional insurance than by the courts. It is possible that a major redesign of current tort law will become necessary and desirable. In the meantime, I am satisfied that the limits on recovery for negligent infliction of emotional distress contained in the *Dillon* rule strike an appropriate balance between the need for flexibility and the need for predictability.

Affirmed in part and reversed in part. Remanded for trial.

[Concurring opinion by Justice Zimmerman is omitted]

Notes and Questions

1. Recall our earlier work on intentional infliction of emotional distress (IIED). Both torts reflect a strong judicial reluctance to permit an unfettered claim for "mere" emotional harm. Is this reluctance justified? How?

2. The prima facie case for IIED includes two requirements designed to assure that only important cases of emotional distress can be the basis for compensation: the "outrageous act" requirement and the "serious" emotional distress (injury) requirement. Use the *Johnson* case to develop the prima facie case for negligent infliction of emotional distress (NIED). What requirements do the jurisdictions include in this case to assure that liability for negligently inflicted emotional harm is also properly fettered?

3. As you develop your answer to this last question, note that, unlike IIED whose prima facie case is essentially the same across the jurisdictions, NIED appears in several different formulations depending on the jurisdiction. This means that you will need first to catalog the different jurisdictional approaches to the NIED prima facie case, and then to identify their aspects. For purposes of our course, it is sufficient that you have done this cataloging. You do not need to fix on a particular version as the majority rule.

4. Be sure that you understand the factual and legal differences between "direct victim" case and "bystander" cases. What are the policy arguments in favor of expanding and restricting the legal standard (and thus access to damages) in the former? And in the latter?

HARNICHER v. UNIVERSITY OF UTAH MEDICAL CENTER
962 P.2d 67 (Utah 1998)

HOWE, Chief Justice:

Plaintiffs David and Stephanie Harnicher, parents of triplets born after in vitro fertilization using donor sperm, brought this action for medical malpractice alleging negligent infliction of emotional distress against defendant University of Utah Medical Center for using sperm from a donor other than the one that the couple had allegedly selected. The trial court found no evidence of physical injury or illness to support an action for negligent infliction of emotional distress and granted summary judgment in favor of the Medical Center. The Harnichers appeal.

FACTS

David and Stephanie Harnicher sought treatment for infertility at the University of Utah Medical Center Fertility Clinic. Artificial insemination using David's sperm yielded no results. The Harnichers then contacted Dr. Ronald L. Urry of the Fertility Clinic regarding the possibility of in vitro fertilization. Dr. Urry suggested a procedure known as "micromanipulation" wherein holes are drilled in the mother's harvested ova to facilitate fertilization. The ova are then placed in a petri dish with harvested sperm and the fertilized ova are subsequently implanted in the uterine wall, enabling the mother to bear her own child. Dr. Urry recommended using a mixture of the husband's sperm and donor sperm.

The Harnichers agreed. The micromanipulation method increased the chances that Stephanie would bear David's biological child. Additionally, the "mixed sperm" procedure potentially allowed the couple to believe and represent that any child born would be David's because if the donor closely matched David in physical characteristics and blood type, the parents would never be sure which sperm actually fertilized the ovum. Therefore the Harnichers evaluated the donor information provided by the Medical Center on that basis. The Medical Center maintains that the couple narrowed the selection to four donors and signed consent forms acknowledging that their doctor would make the final selection. The Harnichers assert, however, that they specifically and exclusively selected donor # 183. Stephanie testified that when clinic employee Doug Carroll informed her that only frozen sperm, which has a lower success rate than fresh, was available from donor # 183 and asked her if she still wanted to do the donor backup, she replied, "Only if you can get 183. . . . I'll take my lower chances. Let's just go with 183."

The procedure was performed, and Stephanie gave birth to triplets, two girls and one boy. Shortly after their birth, one of the babies became ill, requiring blood tests. Two of the children's blood type revealed that they could not possibly have been the children of either David or donor # 183. A DNA test on one of the children established that the father was actually donor # 83, another donor on the Harnichers' list.

Donor # 183, like David, had curly dark hair and brown eyes. Donor # 83 had straight auburn hair and green eyes. One of the triplets has red hair. The Harnichers maintain that the Medical Center's mistaken use of the wrong donor thwarted their intention of believing and representing that David is the children's biological father. They brought this action against the Medical Center alleging that they have "suffered severe anxiety, depression, grief, and other mental and emotional suffering and distress which has adversely affected their relationship with the children and with each other." However, both David and Stephanie testified in their depositions that they had not experienced any bodily harm as a result of the mistake.

After the Medical Center moved for summary judgment, the Harnichers consulted a psychologist, Jeff Kocherhans, Ph.D., who administered various psychological tests and concluded that David suffered from a variety of symptoms of depression and anxiety, including sleep disturbance, fatigue, impaired concentration, and diminished work productivity. Kocherhans diagnosed Stephanie with "major Depressive Disorder, recurrent, severe, Panic Disorder and Generalized Anxiety Disorder," manifested by low mood, fatigue, crying spells, decreased appetite and weight loss, difficulty concentrating, pounding heart, shaking, cold flashes, shortness of breath, choking sensation, teeth grinding, muscle tension, and fingernail biting. Prior to seeking treatment at the Medical Center, Stephanie had counseled with a psychologist for some of the same symptoms and had also received stress medication from a medical doctor. Kocherhans' diagnoses appeared in an affidavit which the Harnichers filed more than a month after the Medical Center moved for summary judgment.

The trial court concluded that "there has been no physical harm or injury sustained by the plaintiffs that would enable them to maintain an action for negligent infliction of emotional distress" and that the plaintiffs' alleged physical symptoms "are transitory, temporary, and not the kind of physical manifestations of a mental illness that provide the basis for a claim of negligent infliction of emotional distress." The Harnichers contend that their disappointment in the results of the donor mixup has resulted in mental illness accompanied by physical symptoms. They ask this court to hold that a diagnosed mental illness in and of itself is sufficient to support a cause of action for negligent infliction of emotional distress.

ANALYSIS

In order to properly grant summary judgment, the court must view the facts in the light most favorable to the non-moving party and find that there are no disputed issues of material fact and that the moving party is entitled to judgment as a matter of law. We review the trial court's conclusions of law for correctness, granting them no deference.

I. BACKGROUND

In *Johnson v. Rogers,* 763 P.2d 771 (Utah 1988), we first recognized negligent infliction of emotional distress as a cause of action in Utah. In that case, a father and his eight-year-old son were waiting to cross the street at an intersection when a truck jumped the curb and struck them, killing the child and injuring the father. Justice Durham, in the lead opinion, reviewed the history and theoretical foundations of the action for negligent infliction of emotional distress and determined that such an action exists in Utah. *Id.* at 782. A majority of the court recognized the need to establish a clear standard. *Id.* at 785 (Zimmerman, J., concurring in part). The majority selected language mirroring the rule proffered in section 313 of the Restatement (Second) of Torts. This standard provides:

> (1) If the actor unintentionally causes emotional distress to another, he is subject to liability to the other for resulting illness or bodily harm if the actor
>
> > (a) should have realized that his conduct involved an unreasonable risk of causing the distress, otherwise than by knowledge of the harm or peril of a third person, and
> >
> > (b) from facts known to him, should have realized that the distress, if it were caused, might result in illness or bodily harm.
>
> (2) The rule stated in Subsection (1) has no application to illness or bodily harm of another which is caused by emotional distress arising solely from harm or peril to a third person, unless the negligence of the actor has otherwise created an unreasonable risk of bodily harm to the other.

Id. at 780 (emphasis omitted) (quoting Restatement (Second) of Torts § 313 (1965)). Subsection (2) constitutes the zone of danger test. "Simply stated, the zone of danger rule 'allows one who is himself or herself threatened with bodily harm in consequence of the defendant's negligence to recover for emotional distress resulting from viewing the death or serious physical injury of a member of his or her immediate family.' " *Clohessy v. Bachelor,* 237 Conn. 31, 675 A.2d 852, 857 (1996) (quoting *Bovsun v. Sanperi,* 61 N.Y.2d 219, 473 N.Y.S.2d 357, 461 N.E.2d 843 (1984)).

Because the instant case does not involve injury to a third party, we address only the application of subsection (1). We addressed similar circumstances in *Hansen v. Mountain Fuel Supply Co.,* 858 P.2d 970 (Utah 1993). In that case, construction workers who had unknowingly inhaled asbestos sought to recover damages for negligent infliction of emotional distress due to fear of cancer. We observed that "[i]n *Johnson,* we were primarily concerned with application of the rule outlined in [section 313] subsection (2). In the instant case, plaintiffs are not seeking recovery for trauma inflicted on them because of harm or peril to one nearby; plaintiffs allege that they themselves inhaled asbestos." *Id.* at 974. We applied the section 313(1) requirement for "illness or bodily harm" and found that the plaintiffs had neither offered evidence of symptoms so severe as to constitute mental illness, nor shown that they had suffered physical symptoms as a result of their distress. *Id.* at 975. We emphasized that "the emotional distress suffered must be severe; it must be such that 'a reasonable [person,] normally constituted, would be unable to adequately cope with the mental stress engendered by the circumstances of the case.'" *Id.* (quoting *Rodrigues v. State,* 52 Haw. 156, 472 P.2d 509, 520 (1970)). Consequently, we held that "[p]laintiffs' mere unsubstantiated opinions that they have suffered severe anxiety as a result of their exposure do not create a triable issue of fact that would withstand summary judgment." *Id.* Justice Zimmerman, joined by the majority, explicitly declined to postulate whether "mental illness, in the absence of physical manifestation, is sufficient to support a claim." *Id.* at 982 (Zimmerman, J., concurring in part and concurring in the result).

The comments to section 313 restrict the scope of a claim for negligent infliction of emotional distress. Comment "a" declares that the "rule stated in this Section does not give protection to mental and emotional tranquillity in itself." Restatement (Second) of Torts § 313 cmt. a (1965). Comment "c" articulates a form of "reasonable person" test by noting that in contrast to the section 312 rule for intentional creation of emotional distress, "one who unintentionally but negligently subjects another to such emotional distress does not take the risk of any exceptional physical sensitiveness to emotion which the other may have unless the circumstances known to the actor should apprise him of it." Restatement (Second) of Torts § 313 cmt. c (1965). These comments recognize the fact that "[w]e cannot permit every claim for negligent infliction of emotional distress to go to a jury under such varying standards as each trial judge may choose." *Johnson,* 763 P.2d at 785 (Zimmerman, J., concurring in part).

II. BODILY HARM

In opposing the Medical Center's motion for summary judgment, the Harnichers' filed the affidavit of Jeff Kocherans, wherein he listed various conditions allegedly suffered by the Harnichers as a result of their emotional distress. He averred that David Harnicher suffered from sleep disturbance, fatigue, impaired concentration, and diminished work productivity. He further stated that Stephanie suffered from low mood, fatigue, crying spells, decreased appetite and weight loss, difficulty concentrating, pounding heart, shaking, cold flashes, shortness of breath, choking sensation, teeth grinding, muscle tension, and fingernail biting.

In contrast to this affidavit, the Harnichers' both denied having suffered any bodily harm as a result of the alleged donor sperm mix-up in their sworn depositions, which were taken well before Kocherans' affidavit was filed. When David was asked, "[i]s there any other kind of damage [other than mental and emotional stress] that you claim you have suffered," he replied, "[n]o, I can't think we've claimed anything other than that at the moment." Moreover, in response to a question asking Stephanie to describe what bodily harm she claimed she had experienced as a result of the donor sperm mix-up, she responded, "[a]s a result of the mix-up, I have not claimed any bodily harm."

Because of the variance between the Harnichers' sworn deposition and Kocherans' subsequent affidavit, we do not comment on whether the symptoms listed in Kocherans' affidavit qualify as "bodily harm" under section 313(1) of the Restatement (Second) of Torts. The general rule is that in a summary judgment proceeding, "when a party takes a clear position in a deposition, that is not modified on cross-examination, he may not thereafter raise an issue of fact by his own affidavit which contradicts his deposition, unless he can provide an explanation of the discrepancy." *Webster v. Sill,* 675 P.2d 1170, 1172-73 (Utah 1983).

As stated above, the Harnichers did not consult Kocherans until after the Medical Center moved for summary judgment, presumably for the purpose of obtaining an affidavit to oppose summary judgment. The only explanations that they offer for the discrepancy between their deposition testimony and Kocherans' affidavit is that they are "not the type of people who would easily seek medical treatment" and that the questions asked at their depositions were not sufficiently specific to allow them to properly respond. We reject each of these explanations.

First, the Harnichers' reluctance to seek medical treatment fails to explain why they denied any physical harm at the deposition but asserted such harm during their consultation with Kocherans, which occurred after the Medical Center had filed its motion for summary judgment. These types of harm are not of the type that would require diagnosis or discovery by a medical doctor or psychologist. In fact, unless Kocherans observed the Harnichers while they ate, worked, and slept, the Harnichers must have described these conditions to him. Thus it is difficult to understand how the Harnichers were able to describe these conditions so accurately to Kocherans when they were not able to do so during their sworn depositions.

Second, although the deposition questions at issue might not have been as direct and clear as they might have been, the Harnichers' counsel should have understood these questions and clarified his clients' responses thereto on crossexamination, if necessary. As discussed above, in *Mountain Fuel,* we required bodily harm for a cause of action. 858 P.2d at 975. Harnichers' counsel therefore should have known that the Medical Center's questions were directed at evidence of bodily harm. The Harnichers' alleged confusion regarding these questions is not a reasonable explanation for the discrepancy between their deposition testimony and Kocherans' affidavit.

For the reasons stated above, we conclude that the trial court did not err in finding that the Harnichers had not suffered any bodily harm or physical injury that would support an action for negligent infliction of emotional distress.

III. MENTAL ILLNESS

The Harnichers contend that their disappointment in their children has caused them severe emotional distress to the point of mental illness. They ask us to hold that "diagnosed mental illness," standing alone, is sufficient to support a claim for negligent infliction of emotional distress. As in *Hansen v. Mountain Fuel,* it is unnecessary for us to decide that question here. We recognize that severe emotional distress can cause mental illness and that genuine mental illness constitutes real harm. Nonetheless, practicality demands that the standard of proof in such cases be more than merely subjective. *See Molien v. Kaiser Found. Hosps.,* 27 Cal.3d 916, 167 Cal.Rptr. 831, 616 P.2d 813, 818 (1980). As previously stated, in *Mountain Fuel* we emphasized that the "emotional distress suffered must be severe; it must be such that 'a reasonable [person,] normally constituted, would be unable to adequately cope with the mental stress engendered by the circumstances of the case.'" 858 P.2d at 975. Such a threshold test is particularly necessary because the existence of and cause of a mental illness often is not obvious in a manner comparable to a physical injury or illness.

As a result of their fertility treatment, the Harnichers became the parents of three normal, healthy children whom the couple suggest do not look as much like David as different children might have and whose blood type could not be descended from his. This result thwarted the couple's intention to believe and represent that the triplets are David's biological children. Exposure to the truth about one's own situation cannot be considered an injury and has never been a tort. Therefore, destruction of a fiction cannot be grounds for either malpractice or negligent infliction of emotional distress.

The Harnichers' assertion that David did not want children unless they were biologically his own is belied by the couple's knowing consent to the use of donor sperm. Stephanie testified that she could say "with probability," without ever having seen either donor, that the children of donor # 183 would have been better looking than her triplets and that in her mind, she was damaged by that fact. During her deposition, she was asked and testified as follows:

> Q. Do you claim that you have been damaged any by the difference in personality or traits and characteristics inherited by your children versus what you think they would have inherited from 183?
>
> A. Definitely.
>
> Q. How have you been damaged?
>
> A. Feeling-wise, it hurts. I mean, it just — it saddens me.

Realistically, however, it is impossible to know whether the children of donor # 183 would have been superior in any way to the triplets or, indeed, whether the same number of babies or none at all would have resulted from the use of the less effective frozen sperm. The supposition that the road not taken would have led to a better result is a common human fallacy; it cannot support an action for negligent infliction of emotional distress. The Harnichers do not allege that the triplets are unhealthy, deformed, or deficient in any way. Nor do they claim any racial or ethnic mismatch between the triplets and their parents. In fact, the couple has presented no evidence at all that the physiological characteristics of three normal healthy children, which could not have been reliably predicted in any event, present circumstances with which " 'a reasonable [person,] normally constituted, would be unable to adequately cope.' " *Mountain Fuel,* 858 P.2d at 975.

CONCLUSION

As noted above, the section 313(1) rule does not give protection to mental and emotional tranquility per se. Consequently, much of the " 'emotional distress' which we endure . . . is not compensable." *Thing v. La Chusa,* 48 Cal.3d 644, 257 Cal.Rptr. 865, 771 P.2d 814, 829 (1989) (denying recovery for negligent infliction of emotional distress where mother of injured child arrived at the scene after accident had already occurred). The Harnichers have failed to raise a triable issue of fact that they have suffered bodily harm. Furthermore, they have not shown that the Medical Center's alleged negligence is of the type that is likely to cause severe and unmanageable mental distress in a reasonable person normally constituted. *See Mountain Fuel,* 858 P.2d at 975. Therefore, we hold that the Harnichers have failed to "state a claim for negligent infliction of emotional distress, as this claim is defined in Utah." *Boucher,* 850 P.2d at 1182.

Affirmed.

ZIMMERMAN, J., concurs in Chief Justice HOWE's opinion.

RUSSON, J., concurs in the result.

DURHAM, Associate Chief Justice, dissenting:

On review of summary judgment, this court is obligated to view the facts in the light most favorable to the non-moving party and to find that there are no disputed issues of material fact.

Clover v. Snowbird Ski Resort, 808 P.2d 1037 (Utah 1991). This the majority has failed to do.

This court has, as the majority notes, adopted the standard set forth in section 313 of the Restatement of Torts (Second) for recovery for negligent infliction of emotional distress: liability exists for "illness or bodily harm" resulting from negligent acts. I believe first, that the majority opinion has conflated the "illness" factor with the "bodily harm" part of the standard, and second, it has inappropriately resolved disputed issues of material fact regarding the severity of the symptoms actually alleged to have been caused by the defendant's negligence.

The totality of facts in this limited record, in my view, reflect a rather different history than do those highlighted in the majority opinion. The plaintiffs sought treatment from the University of Utah Medical Center Fertility Clinic after a significant period of unsuccessful efforts to conceive a child, including at least two full cycles of unsuccessful artificial insemination. They had been informed before this contact that the likely cause of their infertility was Mr. Harnicher's low sperm count and decreased sperm mobility, which significantly decreased the possibility of conception by natural methods.

During their initial consultation with the medical staff at the University, they discussed alternative treatments including artificial insemination using Mr. Harnicher's sperm and in vitro fertilization using either Mr. Harnicher's sperm or donor sperm. Two artificial insemination attempts at the University were unsuccessful, and Mrs. Harnicher's gynecologist Dr. Hatasaka recommended they consult with Dr. Urry regarding in vitro fertilization. Mrs. Harnicher's deposition reflects her high degree of concern — from the very first interview with Dr. Urry — for identifying the treatment process that would most closely approximate natural conception of their biological child. The following excerpts from her deposition demonstrate this concern:

> Answer [by Mrs. Harnicher]: Dr. Urry said that for us to be able to have our biological child, that we had to do in vitro; and to have our biological child-the chances of in vitro working, period, were 20 to 30 percent a cycle; and that he gave us a 14 percent chance of having our biological child from that in vitro cycle, from each cycle.
>
> And he drew on the chalkboard how he would do it, how he would put David's sperm in one petri dish and David's sperm mixed with a donor in a second petri dish; and that he would micromanipulate the eggs in the one dish with David's-only sperm, and that if he was able to get embryos from that, he would use them first and then he would go to the donor mix next if we didn't get success with David's only.
>
> And I was very apprehensive about the donor. I wanted David's biological child. And that's why I did in vitro . . . .
>
> . . .
>
> I expressed my apprehension to Urry. And I started asking him about how he selects donors, about their personality, what would be their motive to be a donor, whether it was philanthropic or financial — you know, I wanted to know that — and if he had any donors on his list that looked like David.
>
> . . . I cried a lot at that meeting. I can remember that. I was very shook.

> Question: And what was the cause or source of your stress and crying?
>
> Answer: About the possibility of not being able to have David's biological child and having to use a donor . . . .
>
> He said that they did an extensive interview, screening of the donors, and that he screened-that he might only pick one in some large number of available donors based on their appearance and their personality and their intelligence and other inheritable traits . . . .
>
> And I was inquiring more and more about, you know, the type of people and the personality and whether he had anybody that looked like David.

After the first meeting with Dr. Urry described above, he gave plaintiffs his list of donors to review. Mrs. Harnicher described the following exchange with Dr. Urry and another employee of the hospital:

> And he went through-I don't know-three to six different guys. And he gave me descriptions on their personalities. And then he narrowed it down to [donor number] 183. And then he told me that-well, in that same conversation, that if you're not-since you're not going to tell the kids, then you've also got to match the blood type. . . .
>
> I said, Gosh, I didn't even-I didn't even think about the blood type.

Thus, Dr. Urry recommended donor 183 because of matching blood type and the fact that the procedure he contemplated using would leave the actual biological parentage of any offspring entirely unknown as between Mr. Harnicher and the closely matched donor.

After further inquiries about donor 183, which met with reassuring responses about his general resemblance to her husband in physical appearance, Mrs. Harnicher settled on donor 183.

> Answer: [A hospital employee] wanted to know if I had narrowed down my donor choices. And I said, I only have one choice. And I said, 183. And he said 183 was on the frozen [sperm] list only . . . .
>
> . . .
>
> And [he] said, Well, frozen doesn't work as well as fresh, and I can't get a fresh sample from 183, that this guy was on vacation, 183.
>
> And he said, *Do you still want to do donor backup? And I said, Only if you can get 183. . . .*
>
> . . .
>
> *He called up again to confirm my donor just to be cautious because I didn't put down backups to 183.* I just put down one. And he said: I just want to verify that this is what you want to do. Do you want to do a donor mix? And I said, Yes if you can get 183.

> He said, Well, I can only get it frozen. Again, I said: I know. I know. I know. Let's just go with frozen. (Emphasis added.)

Mrs. Harnicher's deposition also details numerous attempts on her part to elicit specific physical details about donor 183, which seem to reflect her extreme concern about the resemblance issue.

> Answer: . . . and then we got to 183. And I asked her about 183. And she said he was very good-looking, really nice, pretty eyes, and that-she said he was tall and thin and he was the most handsome of all the donors, always has a smile. So I asked her what his teeth looked like, because David has straight teeth and I wanted to know.
>
> And then I asked her about his — if he had broad shoulders like David. I remembered that because she got a little annoyed with me because I was being too specific and she didn't want me to find out who the donors were, I assume. So she said: I can't tell you that about his shoulders. He has a nice build. And she said, Out of all of them, he looks most like David. And so then that was it.

Counsel for the defendant suggested — and the majority appears to have accepted the suggestion — that the plaintiffs are disappointed that their children are not "better looking." It is clear from a review of Mrs. Harnicher's deposition testimony that the primary issue for her was always the degree to which her children would look like Mr. Harnicher, their father, not their general "good looks." The majority opinion dismisses the Harnichers' desire to believe and represent that any children born as a result of the treatment they received were David Harnicher's biological offspring as a "fiction," which it cannot be tortious to destroy. But Mrs. Harnicher's testimony asserts that she would not have undergone donor sperm in vitro fertilization without the assurance that she, her husband, and any children they had would never need to know whether a biological bond existed. Had it not been for the University's negligence in mixing sperm from the wrong donor with David's, the "fiction" would never have been labeled a fiction; it would simply have been an "alternative reality" for the Harnicher family. In fact, in a sense, it was this alternative that the Harnichers negotiated for in their contract with the University, and that the University destroyed through its negligent act.

Moreover, the Medical Center actively encouraged the Harnichers to undergo in vitro fertilization and adopt this "fiction" despite the fact that the Harnichers expressed reservations about raising a child who was not biologically their own, and despite current scientific literature which weighs heavily against encouraging such a "fiction." *See, e.g.,* Barbara Eck Menning, *Donor Insemination: the Psychosocial Issues,* 18 Contemp. OB/GYN 155, 162 (1981) (stating that it is "medically reprehensible" to alleviate the "genetic loss" by using semen mixing and telling patients that they will never know "which sperm got there first"); Robert D. Nachtigall et al., *Stigma, Disclosure, and Family Functioning Among Parents of Children Conceived Through Donor Insemination,* Fertility and Sterility, July–Dec., 1997, at 83 (encouraging disclosure of conception through donor insemination). The notion that there can be no loss or harm associated with the destruction of the very circumstance the University counseled the Harnichers to seek and promised to provide is unrealistic in human terms.

The most cursory review of the history of civilization demonstrates that the biological component of parentage has never been trivial in human affairs. *See, e.g.,* Dr. Th. H. Van De Velde, *Fertility and Sterility in Marriage: Their Voluntary Promotion and Limitation* 79-84

(F.W. Stella Browne trans., 1929); C. Lee Buxton & Anna L. Southam, *Human Infertility* 203-16 (1958); Charles A. Joël, *Fertility Disturbances in Men and Women* 317-27 (1971); *Fertility and Sterility* 359-69 (R.F. Harrison et al. eds., 1983). The trial court and the majority appear convinced that the loss of an unassailable assurance that one's children carry one's genes is of negligible value. Such a conviction is belied by the extraordinary lengths to which thousands of people in this era will go to pursue biological parenthood. *See generally Infertility: Diagnosis and Management* 17–19, 23 (James Aiman ed., 1984).

Some women will choose not to have children if they cannot honestly believe (whether the belief is accurate or not) that those children are biologically linked to their husbands; in fact, that was the objective of the in vitro procedure recommended to the Harnichers, as well as Dr. Urry's advice that donor 183 be selected for the donor mix because of his matching blood type and physical resemblance. Mrs. Harnicher testified that she was one of those women who only wanted children if there was a biological link to her husband, and I cannot concede that her choice is illegitimate because I, or any other judge, might view it as misguided. The majority reflects its failure to understand this point when it observes that "the Harnichers' assertion that David did not want children unless they were biologically his own is belied by the couple's knowing consent to the use of donor sperm." This misstates the Harnichers' claim-they have only asserted that they did not want children unless it would be highly unlikely that they would ever know that their child was not biologically David's, thus permitting the assumption of biological continuity. The use of donor sperm from a closely matched donor, when mixed with David's, would not interfere with their objective; that is precisely why the University staff recommended the procedure, and the reason the Harnichers consented to it.

In addition to the flaws in the majority opinion's characterization of the Harnichers' claims, there are analytic problems with its application of the Restatement standard to the facts. Section 313, which this court has adopted, specifies liability for negligent infliction of emotional distress for "illness or bodily harm." I take the position first, that mental illness of an incapacitating severity — standing alone and unassociated with so-called "physical" symptoms or findings — qualifies as "illness" within the meaning of that section, and second, that even if the standard is read to mean "illness with some bodily harm" (which is in fact how the majority opinion seems to read it), there is evidence in the record to get past summary judgment on the Harnichers' damages.

As to the first question-whether mental illness standing alone qualifies as "illness" within the meaning of the Restatement — I find it anomalous that this court would be willing to deny the possibility in this era of awareness about the severe impact of mental disability on the texture and quality of human life. Any number of conditions associated with mental illness can be incapacitating without any overt "bodily" manifestations, as, for example, clinical depression, anxiety disorders and panic response, obsessive-compulsive disorders, and eating disorders, to name a few. "Suffering," as is increasingly understood by medicine, is not a phenomenon in which the physical and the mental sources and causes of pain may be readily differentiated. *See generally* Eric J. Cassell, *The Nature of Suffering and The Goals of Medicine* (1991) (arguing that suffering — the quintessential feature of sickness — cannot be analyzed or relieved). Likewise, it is not the case that we refuse in our tort system to attempt quantification and compensation for suffering that has a mental or emotional component. Indeed we undertake such a calculus regularly in wrongful death and personal injury contexts.

Aside from these considerations, however, there is an affidavit in this record filed by a clinical psychologist, with over ten years of experience in "assessment and treatment of mental disorders," who performed rather extensive testing on the Harnichers. He opines as follows in that affidavit:

> a. David Harnicher is a 45 year old male of estimated above-average intelligence who is currently experiencing symptoms of depression and anxiety which is [*sic*] corroborated by testing.
>
> b. David's depressive symptoms include persistent depressed mood, loss of interest in and enjoyment of usual activities, sleep disturbance, fatigue, feelings of inadequacy and diminished confidence, pessimism regarding the future, irritability, social withdrawal, impaired concentration, decreased motivation, diminished work productivity and thoughts of death.
>
> c. David's anxiety symptoms include persistent apprehension and excessive worry, constantly feeling "keyed up," fatigue, concentration difficulties, irritability, muscle tension, sleep disturbance and abdominal discomfort associated with stressful situations.
>
> . . .
>
> e. The disclosure that his wife's children were not biologically his was especially disappointing and stressful to him because he has not wanted children unless they were his. He had hoped and expected that he would at least be able to believe that the children might be his. This has caused difficulties in his marriage to Stephanie Harnicher.
>
> f. Stephanie Harnicher is a 38 year old female of above average intelligence who suffers from major Depressive Disorder, recurrent, severe, Panic Disorder, and Generalized anxiety disorder which are corroborated by testing.
>
> g. Stephanie's depressive symptoms include the following: Persistent low mood, fatigue, difficulty concentrating, feelings of worthlessness, feelings of hopelessness, decreased appetite with 10 lbs. of weight loss, decreased sexual interest, irritability, periods of crying and having to push herself to do things.
>
> h. Stephanie's panic attacks are characterized by her heart pounding and racing, severe shaking, cold flashes, shortness of breath, inability to speak, a choking sensation, chest and arm pain, dizziness, and fear of losing control or "going crazy."
>
> i. Stephanie further shows more general anxiety symptoms including excessive worry and apprehension, irritability, shaking, grinding her teeth, muscle tension, concentration difficulty, fears about leaving the house and fingernail biting.
>
> j. These symptoms have progressed over time beginning with the disclosure that the donor sperm was mixed up and the children were definitely not Davids [*sic*]. The trauma suffered by Stephanie . . . has gotten progressively worse as she has had to

deal with the issues surrounding the disclosure that the children's biological father was neither David, nor the donor chosen by the Harnichers.

Dr. Kocherhans' affidavit concludes with the opinion that "[t]he fact that [the Harnichers] did not seek treatment sooner is not an indication that they were not experiencing genuine suffering" and that "both David and Stephanie are in need of treatment for the above stated disorders."

In light of the foregoing assertions of fact, none of which are controverted in any fashion by the defendants, Stephanie Harnicher's deposition testimony that she does not claim "bodily harm" as the result of the negligent use of the wrong donor sperm, and David's statement that "I can't think we've claimed anything other than [emotional or mental stress or anguish]" are not dispositive on the question of the existence of mental illness with physical manifestations. Just as one suffering from cancer, from a progressive neurological disease, or even from viral and bacterial infections may not be aware of the disease process and may not attribute symptoms to the correct cause, so a person suffering from mental illness may not be aware of or able to articulate that fact. Indeed, one of the characteristics of the most common form of mental illness-clinical depression-is the lack of insight on the part of the sufferer that an illness process is implicated. Thus I think that even if the Harnichers had explicitly denied suffering from mental illness in their depositions, which they did not, they would still be entitled to offer expert testimony to the contrary, as they have done through the Kocherhans affidavit. An issue of fact sufficient to avoid summary judgment is thus created. Someone with undiagnosed early-stage multiple sclerosis or emphysema might well deny being sick-but not knowing you are ill doesn't mean you aren't.

The Restatement standard under which this court is operating does not require "bodily harm" in addition to "illness," but rather as an alternative. In any event, even if physical symptoms were necessary to establish "illness," as the majority seems to conclude, many of the symptoms described in the Kocherans affidavit readily satisfy such a requirement: e.g., sleep disturbance, fatigue, muscle tension, abdominal discomfort, weight loss, severe shaking, cold flashes, shortness of breath, chest and arm pain, dizziness. Clearly, there are factual questions in this case about causation and the severity of the illness that the Harnichers claim. Those are jury questions. In fact, they are typical jury questions.

The majority appears to be reluctant to view the Harnichers' response to their asserted loss as a damaging one, in view of the fact that they do indeed have three healthy and loved children despite the University's negligence in performing this procedure. The alleged facts, however, clearly meet the traditional standard for negligence: 1) the existence of a duty on the part of the University to use the donor sperm selected by the Harnichers that would have permitted them to believe the children to be their full biological children; 2) a breach of that duty through the University's mistake in using sperm from the wrong donor; 3) injury consisting of the Harnichers' loss of the opportunity to believe their children to be their full biological offspring; and 4) damages in the form of mental illness requiring treatment, accompanied by physical symptoms. I grant that the facts are only alleged at this point, including those relating to the causation question, but Dr. Kocherans' affidavit asserts facts respecting causation and damages sufficient to exceed the summary judgment threshold.

Most troubling to me, and unnecessary to the result of the majority opinion, is its general tone of disdain for and belittlement of the nature of the suffering claimed by the Harnichers. An extensive body of literature analyzing the experience of infertility, and the complexity of the psychoemotional issues raised by in vitro fertilization, and the use of donor sperm, undercuts the majority's apparent assumption that the result of having children-any children by any means-obviates any possible loss associated with not having the children one planned (and in this case contracted) for. *See, e.g.,* Arthur L. Greil, *Infertility and Psychological Distress: A Critical Review of the Literature,* 45 Soc. Sci. Med. 1679, 1679-1704 (1997); Robert D. Nachtigall, *supra* at 83-89; Barbara Eck Menning, *The Psychology of Infertility, in Infertility: Diagnosis and Management* 17 (James Aiman ed., 1984). In *The Psychology of Infertility,* Barbara Eck Menning observes:

> Many women feel that it is "selfish" to achieve a pregnancy without the genetic contribution of the husband. This loss of genetic continuity is an important factor for the husband to discuss and to accept. No matter how well the donor is matched to the husband, this loss is real and has to be grieved over. . . .
>
> Both husband and wife may have exaggerated fears as the time of delivery approaches. One fear frequently verbalized is that somehow a mistake in selection of donor may have been made and the resulting baby will have a totally incongruous racial or physical appearance. This fear is the subject of dreams, fantasies, and general anxiety. There may also be more subtle fears regarding the baby's health, intelligence, and attractiveness. To preserve anonymity, very little information is shared about the donor. A great deal of faith must be placed in the hands of the doctor or clinic doing the screening and selecting of donors. *This is a sacred trust that no facility offering donor insemination should take lightly.*

Menning, *supra* at 24.

In conclusion, I believe that a compensable loss and eligible damages have been asserted by plaintiffs and that they are entitled to have their cause of action tried by a jury. I would reverse.

STEWART, J., concurs in the dissenting opinion of Associate Chief Justice DURHAM.

Notes and Questions

1. *Harnicher* was brought as a torts case. Could it have been brought as a contracts case instead? Very generally, a breach of contract case requires the plaintiff to show that there was a valid contract; that its terms were breached by the defendant; and that this breach caused the plaintiff legally recognized harm. What is it about the Harnichers' facts that suggest this would be a difficult case to make?

2. According to the *Harnicher* majority, this is not a proper torts case either. How do the Justices in the majority arrive at this result? Justice Durham disagrees with their analysis; what does she do differently? Do the Justices use the facts differently? The law? Both? How might one decide who is right?

3. If this is neither a proper contracts nor a proper torts case, what is the legal recourse for what the lab did? Should the law provide a remedy? As you think about this last question, consider whether this might be a circumstance in which the legislature would be better suited than the

courts to address the subject which we might frame more generally as regulating the field or providers of alternative reproductive technologies. Is there an argument that the legislature's particular institutional competence and authority makes it the better forum for such regulation? As it turns out, legislatures are also loath to regulate in this area, which, in addition to errors relating to the loss, destruction, and mixing up of gametes and embryos includes questions about how to characterize both when they are the subject of "ownership" disputes and damages. What might explain the reluctance?

4. Why did the majority reject the plaintiffs' offer of proof of physical manifestations of their emotional distress? Should recovery for NIED depend on plaintiffs' ability to provide such proof? In other words, are physical manifestations a good or the best tool to sort meritorious from unmeritorious claims for NIED?

5. The majority suggested that its result might have been different had the laboratory made a different kind of error, for example, had the laboratory mistakenly used gametes from a man of a different race or ethnicity. How would you describe the legally relevant difference between a mistake about the donor's blood and phenotype and a mistake about his race or ethnicity? Laboratories do make all of these mistakes, as it turns out. See, e.g., Maggie O'Farrell, IVF mother: 'I love him to bits. But he's probably not mine," The Guardian, October 29, 2009, available at http://www.theguardian.com/lifeandstyle/2009/oct/30/ivf-errors-baby-mix-up (summarizing the publicly available instances of such errors); Jennifer Musial, 'Two Babies, Two Races, One Womb, Politics and Culture, August 10, 2010.

6. Justice Durham emphasizes that her opinion with respect to the existence of a duty (and implicitly of breach) does not ultimately resolve the case since causation likely remains an important question. Why is or should this be an obvious point?

7. For a fascinating look at the extensive problems with the University of Utah's fertility program, which included sperm being provided and surreptitiously substituted by Thomas Lippert, an ex-convict employee, see http://www.sltrib.com/sltrib/news/57445054-78/lippert-urry-font-university.html.csp.

C. Plaintiff Alleges that Defendant Caused Only Economic Harm

As in the case of stand-alone emotional harm, courts have long rejected claims for stand-alone economic harm. The policy reasons, largely based in a preference for contracts in this context, are different but notice that the methodology for creating exceptions is constant.

AIKENS v. DEBOW
541 S.E.2D 576 (W. Va. 2000)

SCOTT, Justice.

This case arises upon certified question from the Circuit Court of Berkeley County and presents the issue of entitlement to recovery in tort of economic loss not accompanied by bodily injury or property damage, a matter not previously resolved with precision by this Court.

I. Factual and Procedural Background

Plaintiff Richard Aikens operates a motel and restaurant known as the Martinsburg Econo-Lodge ("Econo-Lodge"), which is located on Route 901 and can be accessed by exiting from Interstate 81 at the Spring Mills Road exit. While the Route 901 overpass bridge permits the shortest, most-convenient means of accessing the Econo-Lodge for south-bound travelers traveling on I-81, the establishment can still be accessed through alternate routing. On September 18, 1996, Defendant Robert Debow, a truck driver and employee of Defendant Craig Paving, Inc., was driving a flatbed truck north on I-81 carrying a trackhoe. Because the trackhoe was too high to pass safely under the Route 901 overpass, an accident resulted which caused substantial damage to the bridge. It was closed for nineteen days to make the necessary repairs.

Plaintiff instituted the underlying cause of action on May 28, 1997, seeking recovery for the decreased revenues he experienced due to closure of the Route 901 overpass. Asserting that his reduced revenues were proximately caused by the accident, Plaintiff seeks recovery of $9,000 in lost income.

Arguing that as a matter of law Plaintiff could not recover for his economic losses in the absence of direct bodily injury or property damage, Defendants moved for summary judgment. The circuit court denied Defendants' motion for summary judgment, ruling that "there are factual issues in this case pertaining to causation and foreseeability which remain appropriate for jury determination." The circuit court further held that, "under West Virginia law, the Plaintiff may not be barred from recovering for economic injuries alleged to have been suffered as a result of the Defendants' negligence."

Following the circuit court's denial of Defendants' motion for summary judgment, the parties requested and the circuit court agreed to certification of the following issue:

> Whether a claimant who has sustained no physical damage to his person or property may maintain an action against another for negligent injury to another's property which results consequentially in purely economic loss to the claimant.

. . .

Recognizing that this Court, in addressing certified questions, has "retained the right to address them with some flexibility[,]" we reframe the question presented in the case sub judice to more thoroughly encompass the full breadth of the question to be answered. *Miller v. Lambert*, 195 W.Va. 63, 69, 464 S.E.2d 582, 588 (1995). The question, as reformulated, is consequently as follows:

> May a claimant who has sustained purely economic loss as a result of an interruption in commerce caused by negligent injury to the property of a third person recover damages absent either privity of contract or some other special relationship with the alleged tortfeasor?

We answer this question in the negative.

. . .

III. The Existence of a Duty

The resolution of any question of tort liability must be premised upon fundamental concepts of the duty owed by the tortfeasor.

> In order to establish a *prima facie* case of negligence in West Virginia, it must be shown that the defendant has been guilty of some act or omission in violation of a duty owed to the plaintiff. No action for negligence will lie without a duty broken.

Syl. Pt. 1, Parsley v. General Motors Acceptance Corp., 167 W.Va. 866, 280 S.E.2d 703 (1981). . . . Importantly, the determination of whether a defendant in a particular case owes a duty to the plaintiff is not a factual question for the jury; rather, "[t]he determination of whether a plaintiff is owed a duty of care by the defendant must be rendered as a matter of law by the court." Only the related questions of negligence, due care, proximate cause, and concurrent negligence which present jury issues, as we explained in syllabus point five of *Hatten v. Mason Realty Co.*, 148 W.Va. 380, 135 S.E.2d 236 (1964): "Questions of negligence, due care, proximate cause and concurrent negligence present issues of fact for jury determination when the evidence pertaining to such issues is conflicting or where the facts, even though undisputed, are such that reasonable men may draw different conclusions from them." *Id.* at 381, 135 S.E.2d at 238, syl. pt. 5.

. . .

We recognized in *Robertson v. LeMaster*, 171 W.Va. 607, 301 S.E.2d 563 (1983), that while foreseeability of risk is a primary consideration in determining the scope of a duty an actor owes to another, "[b]eyond the question of foreseeability, the existence of duty also involves policy considerations underlying the core issue of the scope of the legal system's protection[.]" *Id.* at 612, 301 S.E.2d at 568. "Such considerations include the likelihood of injury, the magnitude of the burden of guarding against it, and the consequences of placing that burden on the defendant." *Id.*

. . .

IV. Restrictions on Limitless Expansion of Duty

The appropriate application of these fundamental tort principles has served as a source of great controversy. Justice Benjamin Cardozo, in *Ultramares Corp. v. Touche*, 255 N.Y. 170, 174 N.E. 441 (1931), expressed the danger of expanding the concept of duty in tort to include economic interests and consequent exposure of defendants "to a liability in an indeterminate amount for an indeterminate time to an indeterminate class. The hazards of a business conducted on these terms are so extreme as to enkindle doubt whether a flaw may not exist in the implicating of a duty that exposes to these consequences." *Id.* at 444. The ascertainment of a universal and inviolate formula for defining the parameters of duty in the abstract has proven evasive.

Perhaps the most acclaimed declaration of the concept of duty was announced by Justice Cardozo in *Palsgraf v. Long Island Railroad Co.*, 248 N.Y. 339, 162 N.E. 99 (1928), three years prior to the decision quoted above. . . .

The United States Supreme Court has also recognized the need to draw a line to prevent unfettered imposition of unlimited exposure to liability. The Supreme Court reasoned that the doctrine of remoteness is a component of proximate cause, which in turn embraces the concept that "the judicial remedy cannot encompass every conceivable harm that can be traced to alleged wrongdoing." *Associated Gen. Contractors v. California State Council of Carpenters*, 459 U.S. 519, 536, 103 S.Ct. 897, 74 L.Ed.2d 723 (1983).

The need to restrict the spatial concept of duty to something less than the limits of logical connection was cogently stated as follows in *In re Exxon Valdez*, No. A89-0095-CV, 1994 WL 182856 (D.Alaska March 23, 1994):

> There is no question but that the Exxon Valdez grounding impacted, in one fashion or another, far more people than will ever recover anything in these proceedings. There is an understandable public perception that if one suffers harm which is perceived to be a result of the conduct of another, the harmed person should be compensated. That perception does not always square up with the institutional guidelines (statutes and case law) under which the court must operate. It is the function of both Congress and the courts (principally the courts of appeal and supreme courts) to determine the extent to which public expectations with respect to financial responsibility are to be realized. Legal liability does not always extend to all of the foreseeable consequences of an accident. In the area of harm to one's body, the reach of what is recoverable is very great. Where one's property is injured, the extent of legal liability is considerable, but not to the same extent as with bodily injury. Where pure economic loss is at issue — not connected with any injury to one's body or property, and especially where that economic loss occurs in a marine setting — the reach of legal liability is quite limited except as to commercial fishermen.[2]

---

[2] The Ninth Circuit, in *Union Oil Co. v. Oppen*, 501 F.2d 558 (9th Cir.1974), found that the routine reliance by commercial fishermen upon an ability to fish in unpolluted waters satisfied the foreseeability requirement and justified an award of economic damages as an exception to the general rule. The Ninth Circuit emphasized that offshore oil producers have a duty to commercial fishermen to conduct their operations in a reasonably prudent manner designed to avoid any diminution in marine life. *Id.* at 570; *see also Pruitt v. Allied Chemical Corp.*, 523 F.Supp. 975 (E.D.Va.1981) (commercial fishermen were permitted to recover

> . . . *Were it otherwise, we would have a form of organized anarchy in which no one could count on what rule would apply at any given time or in any given situation.*

Id. at 8–9 (footnote and emphasis added).

While the holding of the majority in *Harris* is not in conflict with our decision in the present case, we underscore the reasoning of Justice Maynard in his insightful dissent in *Harris [v. R.A. Martin, Inc.,* 204 W.Va. 397, 513 S.E.2d 170 (1998)]. Justice Maynard cautioned against the limitless expansion of the element of duty, postulating that the majority had "so expand[ed] the element of duty, that its existence now becomes almost a given in any tort case. If a party is injured by the conduct of another, there must have been a duty to avoid such conduct." 204 W.Va. at 403, 513 S.E.2d at 176. In his dissent, Justice Maynard quoted, with approval, the following language from 57A Am.Jur.2d *Negligence* § 87:

> A line must be drawn between the competing policy considerations of providing a remedy to everyone who is injured and of extending exposure to tort liability almost without limit. It is always tempting to impose new duties and, concomitantly, liabilities, regardless of the economic and social burden. Thus, the *courts have generally recognized that public policy and social considerations, as well as foreseeability, are important factors in determining whether a duty will be held to exist in a particular situation.*

204 W.Va. at 403, 513 S.E.2d at 176 (emphasis supplied).

The obvious question: Who draws the line demarcating tort liability? Who, in our society, has the burden of defining the existence and extent of the element of "duty" in tort actions? It necessarily falls to the courts to consider all relevant claims of the competing parties; to determine where and upon whom the burden of carrying the risk of injury will fall; and to draw the line, to declare the existence or absence of "duty," in every case, as a matter of law. The temptation is to accede to the arguments of logical connection in every instance of resulting harm while, in fact, the consequences of pure logic would be socially and economically ruinous.

V. Traditional Approach-No Economic Damages in the Absence of Physical Impact

The sole issue presented for our resolution is whether economic loss from an interruption in commerce in the absence of damage to a plaintiff's person or property is recoverable in a tort action. While this Court has never directly addressed this issue, other jurisdictions, almost without exception, have concluded that economic loss alone will not warrant recovery in the absence of some special relationship between the plaintiff and the tortfeasor. In the seminal decision of *Robins Dry Dock & Repair Co. v. Flint*, 275 U.S. 303, 48 S.Ct. 134, 72 L.Ed. 290

---

economic damages as an exception to the general rule prohibiting economic damages). The rationale for this limited exception for commercial fishermen was explained in *Burgess v. M/V Tamano*, 370 F.Supp. 247 (D.Me.1973), *aff'd per curiam*, 559 F.2d 1200 (1st Cir.1977). In *Tamano*, the court reasoned that while fishermen and clammers have no individual property rights to the aquatic life harmed by oil pollution, the fishermen could sue for tortious invasion of a public right, having suffered damages greater in degree than the general public. 370 F.Supp. at 250. The court recognized the oil spill as an interference with the "direct exercise of the public right to fish and to dig clams" which was, in fact, a special interest different from that of the general public. *Id.*

(1927), the United States Supreme Court refused to permit recovery from the dry dock owner when plaintiffs were denied use of a vessel for two weeks because of a third party's act of negligence during the ship's refurbishing. In establishing this long-standing rule of denying recovery in tort for indirect economic injury, Justice Holmes articulated the rationale, based upon English and American precedent, that continues to justify the nonexistence of a legally cognizable or compensable claim for such attenuated injuries even today:[3] "The law does not spread its protection so far." *Id.* at 309, 48 S.Ct. 134. In writing *Robins Dry Dock*, Justice Holmes relied upon the reasoning of the English case of *Elliott Steam Tug Co. v. The Shipping Controller*, 1 K.B. 127 (1922), in which recovery was refused for negligent interference with contractual rights.

Where the factual scenario involves a plaintiff's contractual right to use property damaged by a tortfeasor, courts have invoked the Restatement of Torts as a basis for denying causes of action limited to economic damages. In *Philip Morris, Inc. v. Emerson*, 235 Va. 380, 368 S.E.2d 268 (1988), the plaintiff sought recovery of lost profits to his campground business due to the negligent release of gases from the defendant's property. Citing the well-recognized principle in the Restatement of Torts[5] which recognizes that interference with the ability to contract with third persons is too remote to permit recovery, the court refused to permit recovery of the profits plaintiffs allegedly sustained from his inability to contract with campers for overnight stays.

In denying economic damages in the absence of physical impact, courts frequently refer to this element of remoteness between the injury and the act of negligence that is the source of such injury. In *Rickards v. Sun Oil Co.*, 23 N.J. Misc. 89, 41 A.2d 267 (N.J.Sup.1945), a case remarkably similar to the one under scrutiny by this Court, plaintiff business owners sought to recover "losses from expectant gains" from a defendant whose barge negligently damaged a drawbridge which served as the only means of access to the island on which plaintiffs' business premises were situated. *Id.* at 268. In granting the defendant's motions to strike the complaints, the court held that "[defendant's] negligent action may be a cause of injury to the plaintiffs, but it is not the natural and proximate effect of such negligence and therefore [is] not actionable." *Id.* The court observed:

> The entire doctrine assumes the defendant is not necessarily to be held for all consequences of his acts. Professor McLaughlin, Article 39 Harvard Law Review (Dec.1925) 149 at 155. It is fundamental that there must be some reasonable limitation of liability for the commission of the tort. The wrongdoer is not liable in

---

[3] In *Robins Dry Dock*, the court stated: "[A]s a general rule, at least, a tort to the person or property of one man does not make the tortfeasor liable to another merely because the injured person was under a contract with that other unknown to the doer of the wrong." 275 U.S. at 309, 48 S.Ct. 134.

[5] Section 766, Negligent Interference with Contract or Prospective Contractual Relation, provides that "[o]ne is not liable to another for pecuniary harm not derived from physical harm to the other, if that harm results from the actor's negligently

> (a) causing a third person not to perform a contract with the other, or
> (b) interfering with the other's performance of his contract or making the performance more expensive or burdensome, or
> (c) interfering with the other's acquiring a contractual relation with a third person."

> the eyes of the law for all possible consequences. He is thus responsible in damages only for the natural and probable consequence of his negligent act.

The court recognized that "[n]o rule embraces within its scope all the resulting consequences of the given act. The effect would be to impose a liability entirely disproportionate to the act committed or to the failure to perform the duty assumed."

In *General Foods Corp. v. United States*, 448 F.Supp. 111 (D.Md.1978), the plaintiff manufacturer sought to recover economic damages from the defendant bridge owner for economic damages allegedly arising from the closing of the Penn Central Railroad Bridge over the Chesapeake and Delaware Canal caused by a ship wreck. Citing *Robins Dry Dock* for the proposition that economic losses suffered by the plaintiff in conducting its business, even if proven, are not recoverable damages as a matter of law, the court dismissed plaintiff's complaint, explaining:

> Courts which have addressed this issue have repeatedly expressed concern that a contrary rule would open the door to virtually limitless suits, often of a highly speculative and remote nature. Such suits would expose the negligent defendant to a severe penalty, and would produce serious problems in litigation, particularly in the areas of proof and apportionment of damages.

448 F.Supp. at 113.

In an analogous case, *Nebraska Innkeepers, Inc. v. Pittsburgh-Des Moines Corp.*, 345 N.W.2d 124 (Iowa 1984), the Iowa Supreme Court considered the viability of an action brought by various business owners to recover purely economic losses resulting from the closure of a bridge to repair certain structural defects. Affirming the lower court's grant of summary judgment to defendants, the court recognized, as "uniform[,]" the position of rejecting negligence actions seeking pure economic damages "regardless of how vital to the claimant be the flow of commerce that is interrupted." *Id.* at 126. Critical to the court's ruling was its conclusion that "[e]xceptions to that general rule such as ownership of the bridge, physical injury or direct damages to the claimant's property or person, or a direct contractual relation with the alleged wrongdoer [we]re not factually present here." *Id.*

The recognized necessity of imposing a line of demarcation on actionable theories of recovery serves as another rationale for the denial of purely economic damages. In *Stevenson v. East Ohio Gas. Co.*, 73 N.E.2d 200 (Ohio Ct.App.1946), the Ohio court held that employees of a neighboring company could not recover lost wages incurred after they were evacuated due to an explosion and fire allegedly caused by the defendant's negligence. The *Stevenson* court reasoned as follows:

> While the reason usually given for the refusal to permit recovery in this class of cases is that the damages are "indirect" or are "too remote" it is our opinion that the principal reason that has motivated the courts in denying recovery . . . is that *to permit recovery of damages in such cases would open the door to a mass of litigation which might very well overwhelm the courts so that in the long run while injustice might result in special cases, the ends of justice are conserved . . .*

Id. at 203 (emphasis added).

In similar fashion, the Seventh Circuit, in affirming the district court's dismissal of an action seeking economic damages arising from a bridge closing, reasoned that extension of liability in the absence of harm to a plaintiff's person or property would thrust courts into "a field with no sensible or just stopping point." *Leadfree Enterprises, Inc. v. United States Steel Corp.*, 711 F.2d 805, 808 (7th Cir.1983) (citing *Hass v. Chicago & North Western Ry. Co.*, 48 Wis.2d 321, 179 N.W.2d 885, 888 (1970)). The court observed further in *Leadfree Enterprises*, that "[i]n the economic injury case, there is less a fear of fraudulent claims than a sense of wanting to have a sensible stopping point in order to preclude open-ended, crushing liability on a tortfeasor." 711 F.2d at 808; *see also Dundee Cement Co. v. Chemical Labs., Inc.*, 712 F.2d 1166, 1172 (7th Cir.1983) (discussing policy reasons advocating against permitting third party recovery of economic losses and "conclud[ing] that there is a legitimate fear that a crushing burden of litigation would result from allowing recovery for economic damages like this").

Astutely anticipating the economic chaos that would result from permitting theoretically limitless recovery of economic injury, the court in *Aikens v. Baltimore & Ohio R.R. Co.*, 348 Pa.Super. 17, 501 A.2d 277 (1985), denied recovery for indirect economic losses incurred by employees who lost wages due to the defendant's alleged negligence in causing a train derailment which damaged the plaintiffs' employer's plant. The court affirmed the dismissal of the complaint and opined:

> that allowance of a cause of action for negligent interference with economic advantage would create an undue burden upon industrial freedom of action, and would create a disproportion between the large amount of damages that might be recovered and the extent of the defendant's fault. To allow a cause of action for negligent cause of purely economic loss would be to open the door to every person in the economic chain of the negligent person or business to bring a cause of action. Such an outstanding burden is . . . a danger to our economic system.

Id. at 279 (citation omitted).

In analyzing the development of legal theories regarding the efficacy of permitting economic damages in the absence of physical harm, the United States Court of Appeals for the Fifth Circuit in *State of Louisiana v. M/V Testbank*, 752 F.2d 1019 (5th Cir.1985), reexamined the authority and scope of *Robins Dry Dock.* Two vessels had collided in the Mississippi River Gulf Outlet, resulting in a chemical spill. Fearing widespread contamination, authorities closed the outlet to navigation for approximately twenty days. Forty-one plaintiffs, including commercial fishermen, operators of marinas, bait and tackle shops, cargo terminal operators, and restaurant owners filed suit, and those actions were consolidated. In its canvass of relevant case law, the *M/V Testbank* court acknowledged the opposition to the exclusionary policy prohibiting recovery of economic damages in the absence of physical impact and noted that "[t]he push to delete the restrictions on recovery for economic loss lost its support and by the early 1940's had failed." *Id.* at 1023. The majority of the court reasserted the traditional interpretation of *Robins Dry Dock* and concluded that all claims for economic loss in the absence of physical injury should be excluded:

> After extensive additional briefs and oral argument, we are unpersuaded that we ought to drop physical damage to a proprietary interest as a prerequisite to recovery for economic loss. To the contrary, our reexamination of the history and central purpose of this pragmatic restriction on the doctrine of foreseeability heightens our

> commitment to it. Ultimately we conclude that without this limitation foreseeability loses much of its ability to function as a rule of law.

. . .

VI. The Minority View: Recovery of Economic Damages Under Limited Circumstances

A few jurisdictions have permitted recovery of economic damages without damage to person or property under certain limited circumstances. The New Jersey Supreme Court's approach to this concept is recognized as the leading authority for the minority view and represents a departure from a substantial collection of American and British cases. In *People Express Airlines, Inc. v. Consolidated Rail Corp.*, 100 N.J. 246, 495 A.2d 107 (1985), the New Jersey court permitted economic recovery where a leak of toxic chemicals from a railway car forced a twelve-hour evacuation of a commercial airline office building adjacent to the site of the leak. *Id.* at 115. The plaintiff sought to recover expenses incurred for flight cancellations, lost bookings and revenue, and certain operating expenses. In permitting the action, the court applied a special foreseeability rule, reasoning that the defendant would be liable only for damages proximately caused and requiring that the defendant must have "knowledge or special reason to know of the consequences of the tortious conduct in terms of the persons likely to be victimized and the nature of the damages likely to be suffered. . . ." *Id.*

Narrowly crafting its decision to apply to a limited and particularized group, the court held:

> that a defendant owes a duty of care to take reasonable measures to avoid the risk of causing economic damages, aside from physical injury, to particular plaintiffs or plaintiffs comprising an identifiable class with respect to whom defendant knows or has reason to know are likely to suffer such damages from its conduct. A defendant failing to adhere to this duty of care may be found liable for such economic damages proximately caused by its breach of duty.

495 A.2d at 116. In further explaining its rationale for departure from established doctrine, the New Jersey court noted:

> the close proximity of the North Terminal and People Express Airlines to the Conrail freight yard; the obvious nature of the plaintiff's operations and particular foreseeability of economic losses resulting from an accident and evacuation; the defendants' actual or constructive knowledge of the volatile properties of ethylene oxide; and the existence of an emergency response plan prepared by some of the defendants (alluded to in the course of oral argument), which apparently called for the nearby area to be evacuated to avoid the risk of harm in case of an explosion.

Id. at 118. In fashioning its test, the court in *People Express* determined that liability and foreseeability "stand in direct proportion to one another[:] The more particular is the foreseeability that economic loss will be suffered by the plaintiff as a result of defendant's negligence, the more just is it that liability be imposed and recovery allowed." *Id.* at 116.

An analysis of the facts involved in the *People Express* decision supports the conclusion that the New Jersey court traversed a logical path more closely akin to that navigated in cases involving physical damage to property. Subsequent to the Three Mile Island nuclear incident, plaintiffs similarly asserted claims of temporary loss of use of property and "damage to property" as a result of the intrusion of radioactive materials through the ambient air. In resolving their claims in *Commonwealth of Pennsylvania v. General Public Utilities Corp.*, 710 F.2d 117 (3rd Cir.1983), the United States Court of Appeals for the Third Circuit acknowledged that the complaints did not contain any claim of damages for direct physical damage to any of the plaintiffs' property. *Id.* at 120–21. While the lower court had concluded that the losses claimed were purely economic in nature and unrecoverable, the plaintiffs contended that "increased radioactivity and radioactive materials emitted during the nuclear incident permeated the entire area, and this rendered the public buildings unsafe for a temporary period of time, and constituted a physical intrusion upon the plaintiffs' properties." *Id.* at 122. The plaintiffs maintained that the gaseous intrusion satisfied the requirement of physical harm to justify the recovery of damages in tort. The Third Circuit found that the plaintiffs' contentions were sufficient to defeat a motion for summary judgment, permitting the plaintiffs an opportunity to prove that an invasion by an invisible substance may still constitute a physical damage warranting recovery of economic loss. Similar to the inhabitability problems experienced by the Three Mile Island plaintiffs, the plaintiff's building in *People Express* was rendered uninhabitable by the negligent release of toxic gases. Thus, in *People Express*, the New Jersey court could have reached its decision by reasoning that to render a building uninhabitable by releasing poison gas against it constitutes a direct physical damage to that building.

Analysts of the *People Express* rationale have also criticized the wisdom of that approach by emphasizing that the "Court itself noted the contradictory and inconsistent nature of its reasoning" by acknowledging the inherent limitations to predicating recovery on a principle of particular foreseeability. The *People Express* court stated that "there will arise many similar cases that cannot be resolved by our decision today." The court further recognized that some cases will present circumstances that defy the categorization here devised to circumscribe a defendant's orbit of duty, limit otherwise boundless liability and define an identifiable class of plaintiffs that may recover. In these cases, the courts will be required to draw upon notions of fairness, common sense and morality to fix the line limiting liability as a matter of public policy, rather than an uncritical application of the principle of particular foreseeability.

. . .

VII. Conclusion

After thoroughly considering the intricacies of a potential rule permitting the recovery of economic damages absent physical or personal injury, we conclude that an individual who sustains purely economic loss from an interruption in commerce caused by another's negligence may not recover damages in the absence of physical harm to that individual's person or property, a contractual relationship with the alleged tortfeasor, or some other special relationship between the alleged tortfeasor and the individual who sustains purely economic damages sufficient to compel the conclusion that the tortfeasor had a duty to the particular plaintiff and that the injury complained of was clearly foreseeable to the tortfeasor. The existence of a special relationship will be determined largely by the extent to which the particular plaintiff is affected differently from society in general. It may be evident from the defendant's knowledge or specific reason to know of the potential consequences of the wrongdoing, the persons likely to be injured, and the damages likely to be suffered. Such special relationship may be proven through evidence of foreseeability of the nature of the harm to be suffered by the particular plaintiff or an identifiable class and can arise from contractual privity or other close nexus. As observed by the Maryland court in *L & P Converters v. Alling & Cory Co.*, 100 Md.App. 563, 642 A.2d 264 (Md.1994), a civil action in which the tort of negligent misrepresentation was asserted, "Where failure to exercise due care only creates a risk of economic loss, an intimate nexus between the parties is generally required. The requirement of an intimate nexus is satisfied by contractual privity or its equivalent." *Id.* at 267 (citations omitted). The Maryland court continued, "In the absence of contractual privity, its equivalent has been found and a tort duty imposed when 'a sufficiently close nexus or relationship' is shown." *Id.* (quoting *Weisman v. Connors*, 312 Md. 428, 540 A.2d 783, 793 (1988)). Any attempt by this Court to more specifically define the parameters of circumstances which may be held to establish a "special relationship" would create more confusion than clarity.

We base our holding upon our analysis of the complexities of this area of tort law, demonstrated through both historical evolvement and current concerns, and our belief that a hybrid approach must be fabricated to authorize recovery of meritorious claims while simultaneously providing a barrier against limitless liability. The common thread which permeates the analysis of potential economic recovery in the absence of physical harm is the recognition of the underlying concept of duty. Absent some special relationship, the confines of which will differ depending upon the facts of each relationship, there simply is no duty. A thorough examination of the cases comprising what has been referenced as the minority view reveals reasoning similar to ours, which provides the opportunity for recovery only upon a showing of a special relationship between the plaintiff and alleged tortfeasor and narrowly tailors the recovery to conform to the facts of the case under scrutiny.

Our decision under the limited factual scenario presented in this certified question has no impact upon our prior rulings permitting recovery of purely economic damages in negligence actions where a special relationship exists between the plaintiff and the alleged tortfeasor. Our holding in the case sub judice is, in fact, consistent with the rationale underlying such rulings, and we affirm our previous recognition that where a special and narrowly defined relationship can be established between the tortfeasor and a plaintiff who was deprived of an economic benefit, the tortfeasor can be held liable. In cases of that nature, the duty exists because of the special relationship. The special class of plaintiffs involved in those cases were particularly foreseeable to the tortfeasor, and the economic losses were proximately caused by the tortfeasor's negligence.

For example, auditors have been held liable to plaintiffs who bought stock in reliance upon a financial statement negligently prepared for a corporation; surveyors and termite inspectors liable to remote purchasers of property; engineers and architects liable to contractors who relied upon plans negligently prepared for property owners who later hired the contractors; attorneys and notaries public liable to beneficiaries of negligently prepare wills; real estate brokers for failure to disclose defects; and telegraph companies liable to individuals who failed to secure a contract due to the negligent transmission of a message.

. . .

The resolution of this matter of restrictions on tort liability is ultimately a matter of "practical politics." *Palsgraf*, 162 N.E. at 103 (Andrews, J., dissenting). The "law arbitrarily declines to trace a series of events beyond a certain point." *Id.* In other words, it is a question of public policy. The purely economic damages sought by a plaintiff may be indistinguishable in terms of societal entitlement from those damages incurred by the restaurant owner in the next block, the antique dealer in the next town, and all the ripple-effect "losses" experienced by each employer and each resident of every town and village surrounding the location of the initial act of negligence. In crafting a rule to address the issue of economic damages, we have attempted to avoid the expression of a judicial definition of duty which would permit the maintenance of a class action as a result of almost every car wreck and other inconvenience that results to our state's citizenry.

In determining questions of duty and extension of duty to particular plaintiffs, the court in *Stevenson* echoed widespread speculation concerning the ripple effects of a negligence claim based upon pure economic loss and observed:

> Cases might well occur where a manufacturer would be obliged to close down his factory because of the inability of his supplier due to a fire loss to make prompt deliveries; the power company with a contract to supply a factory with electricity would be deprived of the profit which it would have made if the operation of the factory had not been interrupted by reason of fire damage; a man who had a contract to paint a building may not be able to proceed with his work; a salesman who would have sold the products of the factory may be deprived of his commissions; the neighborhood restaurant which relies on the trade of the factory employees may suffer a substantial loss. The claims of workmen for loss of wages who were employed in such a factory and cannot continue to work there because of a fire, represent only a small fraction of the claims which would arise if recovery is allowed in this class of cases.

73 N.E.2d at 203–04.

In an endeavor to focus upon the rights of other innocent parties not typically considered, a commentator reconstructs the *Stevenson* paradigm, as follows:

> Cases might well occur where a manufacturer would be obliged to close down his factory [and the manufacturer's employees would be obliged to spend days idle and without income] because of the inability of [the manufacturer's] supplier due to a fire loss to make prompt deliveries; the [employees of a] power company with a contract to supply a factory with electricity would be deprived of [their income] which [they] would have made if the operations of the factory had not been interrupted by reason of fire damage; a [person] who had a contract to paint [the worker's house] may not be able to proceed with [the] work; a [travel agent] who would have sold [the workers vacation packages] may be deprived of [her] commissions; the [teen-age gardener, the grocer's delivery person, the piano teacher, and the weekly housekeeper who serviced the worker's home and family] may [each] suffer a substantial loss.

Silverstein, Eileen, *On Recovery in Tort for Pure Economic Loss*, 32 U.Mich.J.L.Ref. 403, 437 (1999).

Tort law is essentially a recognition of limitations expressing finite boundaries of recovery. Using the absurdity of these chain-of-reaction but purely logical examples, courts and commentators have expressed disdain for limitless liability and have also cautioned against the potential injustices which might result. This Court's obligation is to draw a line beyond which the law will not extend its protection in tort, and to declare, as a matter of law, that no duty exists beyond that court-created line. It is not a matter of protection of a certain class of defendants; nor is it a matter of championing the causes of a certain class of plaintiffs. It is a question of public policy. Each segment of society will suffer injustice, whether situated as plaintiff or defendant, if there are no finite boundaries to liability and no confines within which the rights of plaintiffs and defendants can be determined. We accept the wise admonition expressed over a century ago, in language both simple and eloquent, proven by the passage of time and the lessons of experience: "There would be no bounds to actions and litigious intricacies, if the ill effects of the negligences of men could be followed down the chain of results to the final effect." *Kahl*, 37 N.J.L. at 8.

Certified question answered. . . .

Notes and Questions

1. Are modern courts more or less willing to recognize claims for emotional harm than for economic harm? How do you account for the difference?

2. Would contract law be as useful as an alternative to tort law to set liability limits in emotional harm cases as it is in the context of economic harm?

3. The law assumes that prospective plaintiffs in economic harm cases can contract *ex ante* to address eventual economic harm. Is this assumption viable?

4. Develop a statement of the majority and minority rules applicable to claims for stand-alone economic loss, apply them to the economic loss problem that follows, and note the difference in outcomes.

Problem Five: Stranded at O'Hare

The following Associated Press article appeared in *The Washington Post* on April 16, 2013:

American Airlines Grounds Flights, Passengers Stranded as Reservations System Fails

> Dallas — American Airlines grounded flights across the country Tuesday because of an outage of its main reservations system. Thousands of passengers were stranded at airports and on airplanes.
>
> A spokesman for the Federal Aviation Administration said American asked to halt all of its flights until 6 p.m. EDT. Flights into American's five biggest cities — New York, Dallas, Los Angeles, Chicago and Miami — are stopped until 6:30 p.m. EDT. "Any American plane sitting on the ground anywhere in the U.S." won't be taking off, said FAA spokesman Lynn Lunsford.
>
> Flight-tracking service FlightAware estimated that about 900 flights would be delayed if American resumed flying at 6 p.m., and the cascading effect would cause

another 800 delays Tuesday evening because planes and crews wouldn't be where they were needed.

Customers couldn't make reservations or rebook if their flight was cancelled. Passengers described long airport lines and frustration at the lack of information from airline employees.

"Tensions are high. A lot of people are getting mad. I've seen several yelling at the American agents," said Julie Burch, a business-meeting speaker who was stuck at Dallas-Fort Worth International Airport waiting for a flight to Denver. . . ."

Terry Anzur, a TV news consultant from Los Angeles who was also stranded at DFW, said American Airlines gate employees were doing everything the old-fashioned, manual way because their computers were useless.
"No one at the counter can do anything. They can't check people in," Anzur said. "The airline is at a dead halt."

American's problems on Tuesday were reminiscent of what United Airlines passengers endured on several days last year. United experienced computer glitches after combining its reservations system with that of Continental after the two airlines merged. On one day in August, 580 United flights were delayed and its website was shut down for two hours. Another outage in November delayed 636 flights.

As with the United meltdowns last year, American Airlines passengers used social media to flood the airline with complaints.

"We are working to resolve this issue as quickly as we can, and we apologize to our customers for this inconvenience," said Andrea Huguely, a spokeswoman for the airline.

Huguely said all flights would be held on the ground until Tuesday afternoon, when she promised the airline would provide an update.

The airline, which conceded in a press release that the outage was the result of the company's negligent failure to keep its system up-to-date, was offering free reservations changes and refunds for stranded passengers. But Huguely said American couldn't process those changes until the reservations system was fixed.

About a week before the outage, P went online to CheapTickets.com[**] and bought a one-way ticket to fly from Chicago-O'Hare to London-Heathrow. The flight he selected was on American Airlines (AA), leaving O'Hare at 5:15 p.m. and arriving at Heathrow at 6:50 a.m. P was especially happy with the price on CheapTickets because he had been on AA's site and had seen the same flight for a lot more money; indeed, several airlines had a daily flight from Chicago to London, but they were all much more expensive than the ticket P purchased on CheapTickets. On the day of the outage, P's flight was among the many that AA cancelled. As a result of the cancellation, P missed the auction Sotheby's held the next day in part to sell a

[**] Editors' note: according to its website, "CheapTickets is a leading seller of discounted leisure travel products online . . . CheapTickets provides consumers access to its collection of airfares on hundreds of airlines."

lot of Picasso's drawings; the drawings were of keen interest to P's client who sought to acquire as many original Picassos as he could, and who would have paid P a $150,000 commission had P managed to purchase them for him. P's client, a venture capitalist said to be worth several billion dollars, had authorized P to "pay as much as it takes" to get the drawings. When P called to let his client know that he had failed because of the cancelled AA flight and his inability to rebook on another airline, his client fired him. Both the lost commission and the firing were devastating to P who had for many years worked as an agent mostly for this client. P sues AA in negligence.

AA is our firm's biggest client. We handle both their corporate and litigation matters. We've just been asked to help with this case in particular. Our goal is to file and win a motion to dismiss for failure to state a claim. Please prepare a one-page memo outlining the basis or bases for a successful motion.

D. Premises Liability

Premises liability is the term used to capture the different duties that owners and occupiers have to entrants who are injured on land. These special duty rules apply whether the injuries are the result of misfeasance or nonfeasance — and thus the distinction is generally irrelevant in this context — because the policy goals at issue concern (or at common law concerned) the relative sanctity of private property. The two cases that follow exemplify the evolution of this common law across the relevant entrant categories.

NELSON v. FREELAND
507 S.E.2D 882 (N.C. 1998)

WYNN, Justice.

The sole issue arising out of the case *sub judice* is whether defendant Dean Freeland's ("Freeland") act of leaving a stick on his porch constituted negligence. Indeed, this case presents us with the simplest of factual scenarios — Freeland requested that plaintiff John Harvey Nelson ("Nelson") pick him up at his house for a business meeting the two were attending, and Nelson, while doing so, tripped over a stick that Freeland had inadvertently left lying on his porch. Nelson brought this action against Freeland and his wife seeking damages for the injuries he sustained in the fall. The trial court granted summary judgment for the defendants, and the Court of Appeals affirmed.

Although the most basic principles of tort law should provide an easy answer to this case, our current premises-liability trichotomy — that is, the invitee, licensee, and trespasser classifications — provides no clear solution and has created dissension and confusion amongst the attorneys and judges involved. Thus, once again, this Court confronts the problem of clarifying our enigmatic premises — liability scheme — a problem that we have addressed over fourteen times.

. . . [W]e have repeatedly waded through the mire of North Carolina premises — liability law. Nonetheless, despite our numerous attempts to clarify this liability scheme and transform it into a system capable of guiding North Carolina landowners toward appropriate conduct, this case and its similarly situated predecessors convincingly demonstrate that our current premises-liability scheme has failed to establish a stable and predictable system of laws. Significantly, despite over one hundred years of utilizing the common-law trichotomy, we still are unable to determine unquestionably whether a man who trips over a stick at a friend/business partner's house is entitled to a jury trial — a question ostensibly answerable by the most basic tenet and duty under tort law: the reasonable-person standard of care.

Given that our current premises-liability scheme has confounded our judiciary, we can only assume that it has inadequately apprised landowners of their respective duties of care. Thus, it befalls us to examine the continuing utility of the common-law trichotomy as a means of determining landowner liability in North Carolina. In analyzing this question, we will consider the effectiveness of our current scheme of premises-liability law, the nationwide trend of abandoning the common-law trichotomy in favor of a reasonable-care standard, and the policy reasons for and against abandoning the trichotomy in this state.

I. Analysis

A. Current North Carolina Premises-Liability Law

Under current North Carolina law, the standard of care a landowner[***] owes to persons entering upon his land depends upon the entrant's status, that is, whether the entrant is a licensee, invitee, or trespasser. An invitee is one who goes onto another's premises in response to an express or implied invitation and does so for the mutual benefit of both the owner and himself. The classic example of an invitee is a store customer. A licensee, on the other hand, "is one who enters onto another's premises with the possessor's permission, express or implied, solely for his own purposes rather than the possessor's benefit. The classic example of a licensee is a social guest. Lastly, a trespasser is one who enters another's premises without permission or other right.

In a traditional common-law premises-liability action, the threshold issue of determining the plaintiff's status at the time of the injury is of substantial import. The gravity of this determination stems from the fact that there is a descending degree of duty owed by a landowner based upon the plaintiff's status.

The highest degree of care a landowner owes is the duty of reasonable care toward those entrants classified as invitees. Specifically, a landowner owes an invitee a duty to use ordinary care to keep his property reasonably safe and to warn of hidden perils or unsafe conditions that could be discovered by reasonable inspection and supervision.

A landowner's duty toward a licensee, on the other hand, is significantly less stringent. The duty of care owed to a licensee by an owner or possessor of land ordinarily is to refrain from doing the licensee willful injury and from wantonly and recklessly exposing him to danger. Thus, a licensee enters another's premises at his own risk and enjoys the license subject to its concomitant perils.

Finally, with respect to trespassers, a landowner need only refrain from the willful or wanton infliction of injury. Willful injury constitutes actual knowledge of the danger combined with a

[***] Editors' note: The term "landowner" as used in this opinion refers to owners and occupiers of land.

design, purpose, or intent to do wrong and inflict injury. Similarly, a wanton act is performed intentionally with a reckless indifference to the injuries likely to result.

B. Premises-Liability Nationwide-The Modern Trend Of Abolishing The Common-Law Trichotomy In Favor Of A Reasonable-Person Standard

Although the common-law trichotomy has been entrenched in this country's tort-liability jurisprudence since our nation's inception, over the past fifty years, many states have questioned, modified, and even abolished it after analyzing its utility in modern times. At first, states believed that although the policies underlying the trichotomy — specifically those involving the supremacy of land ownership rights — were no longer viable, they nonetheless could find means to salvage it. In particular, states attempted to salvage the trichotomy by engrafting into it certain exceptions and subclassifications which would allow it to better congeal with our present-day policy of balancing land-ownership rights with the right of entrants to receive adequate protection from harm. Accordingly, North Carolina, along with the rest of the country, witnessed the burgeoning of novel jurisprudence involving entrant-protection theories such as the active-negligence and attractive-nuisance doctrines. Unfortunately, these exceptions and subclassifications ultimately forced courts to maneuver their way through a dizzying array of factual nuances and delineations.

Additionally, courts were often confronted with situations where none of the exceptions or subclassifications applied, yet if they utilized the basic trichotomy, unjust and unfair results would emerge. Therefore, these courts were forced to define terms such as "invitee" and "active conduct" in a broad or strained manner to avoid leaving an injured plaintiff deserving of compensation without redress. Although these broad or strained definitions may have led to just and fair results, they often involved rationales teetering on the edge of absurdity. . . .

. . .

The first significant move toward abolishing the common-law trichotomy occurred in 1957 when England-the jurisdiction giving rise to the trichotomy-passed the Occupier's Liability Act which abolished the distinction between invitees, licensees and so-called contractual visitors. Shortly thereafter, the United States Supreme Court decided not to apply the trichotomy to admiralty law after concluding that it would be inappropriate to hold that a visitor is entitled to a different or lower standard of care simply because he is classified as a "licensee." *See Kermarec*, 358 U.S. at 630, 79 S.Ct. at 409–10, 3 L.Ed.2d at 554. In so ruling, the Court noted that "[t]he distinctions which the common law draws between licensee and invitee were inherited from a culture deeply rooted to the land, a culture which traced many of its standards to a heritage of feudalism." *Id.* The Court continued:

> In an effort to do justice in an industrialized urban society, with its complex economic and individual relationships, modern common-law courts have found it necessary to formulate increasingly subtle verbal refinements, to create subclassifications among traditional common-law categories, and to delineate fine gradations in the standards of care which the landowners owe to each. Yet even within a single jurisdiction, the classifications and subclassifications bred by the common law have produced confusion and conflict.

Id. at 631, 79 S.Ct. at 410, 3 L.Ed.2d at 554–55 (footnote omitted). Ultimately, the Court concluded that the numerous exceptions and subclassifications engrafted into the trichotomy have obscured the law, thereby causing it to move unevenly and with hesitation toward "'imposing on owners and occupiers a single duty of reasonable care in all the circumstances.'" *Id.* at 631, 79 S.Ct. at 410, 3 L.Ed.2d at 555 (quoting *Kermarec v. Compagnie Generale Transatlantique*, 245 F.2d 175, 180 (Clark, C.J., dissenting)).

Nine years later, the Supreme Court of California decided the seminal case of *Rowland v. Christian*, 69 Cal.2d 108, 443 P.2d 561, 70 Cal.Rptr. 97, which abolished the common-law trichotomy in California in favor of modern negligence principles. Specifically, the court in *Rowland* held that the proper question to be asked in premises-liability actions is whether "in the management of his property [the landowner] has acted as a reasonable man in view of the probability of injury to others." Moreover, the court followed both England's and the United States Supreme Court's lead by noting that "[w]hatever may have been the historical justifications for the common law distinctions, it is clear that those distinctions are not justified in the light of our modern society." The court continued by stating that the trichotomy was "contrary to our modern social mores and humanitarian values . . . [, and it] obscure[s] rather than illuminate[s] the proper considerations which should govern determination of the question of duty."

The *Rowland* decision ultimately served as a catalyst for similar judicial decisions across the country. Indeed, since *Rowland*, twenty-five jurisdictions have either modified or abolished their common-law trichotomy scheme — seven within the last five years.

. . .

In summation, nearly half of all jurisdictions in this country have judicially abandoned or modified the common-law trichotomy in favor of the modern "reasonable-person" approach that is the norm in all areas of tort law.

C. The Advantages And Disadvantages Of Abolishing The Common-Law Trichotomy

1. History and Purpose Behind the Trichotomy

To assess the advantages and disadvantages of abolishing the common-law trichotomy, we first consider the purposes and policies behind its creation and current use.

Additionally, the trichotomy was created at a time when principles of negligence were not in existence. Indeed, when English common law was articulating the trichotomy, the principle that a man should be held responsible for foreseeable damages was only hesitatingly recognized in a limited number of cases. Therefore, the trichotomy was perfected at a time when our modern tenet and pillar of tort law — the legal concept of negligence — was largely unrecognized.[3] It was not until the beginning of this country's industrial revolution that the community and the judiciary undertook a greater acceptance of fault-based liability which led to the creation of our modern era of tort law and the law of negligence.

---

[3] Indeed, negligence principles were first enunciated in the 1883 case of *Heaven v. Pender*, 11 Q.B.D. 503 (1883), a case decided more than forty years after the common-law trichotomy emerged.

Almost immediately, the emergence of negligence law conflicted with the immunity conferred upon landowners under the trichotomy. Common-law courts, however, decided not to replace the trichotomy with modern principles of negligence law, as they did in almost all other tort areas, but rather "superimposed the new [negligence] principles upon the existing framework of entrant categories." This combination resulted in our current scheme of premises-liability law which allows judges to maintain control over jury discretion while, at the same time, utilizing "duty of care" principles set forth in negligence theory.

2. Reasons for and Against Abolishing the Trichotomy

Although the modern trend of premises-liability law in this country has been toward abolishing the trichotomy in favor of a reasonable-person standard, there are some jurisdictions that have refused to modify or abolish it. One of the primary reasons that some jurisdictions have retained the trichotomy is fear of jury abuse — a fear similar to the reason it was created in the first place. Specifically, jurisdictions retaining the trichotomy fear that plaintiff-oriented juries — like feudal juries composed mostly of land entrants — will impose unreasonable burdens upon defendant-landowners. This argument, however, fails to take into account that juries have properly applied negligence principles in all other areas of tort law, and there has been no indication that defendants in other areas have had unreasonable burdens placed upon them. Moreover, given that modern jurors are more likely than feudal jurors to be landowners themselves, it is unlikely that they would be willing to place a burden upon a defendant that they would be unwilling to accept upon themselves.

Another fear held by jurisdictions retaining the trichotomy is that by substituting the negligence standard of care for the common-law categories, landowners will be forced to bear the burden of taking precautions such as the expensive cost associated with maintaining adequate insurance policies. This argument, however, ignores the fact that every court which has abolished the trichotomy has explicitly stated that its holding was not intended to make the landowner an absolute insurer against all injuries suffered on his property.

Lastly, opponents of abolishing the trichotomy argue that retention of the scheme is necessary to ensure predictability in the law. For example, prior to abolishing its common-law trichotomy, the Kansas Supreme Court declined an invitation to do so because it believed that the replacement of its stable and established system would result in one that is devoid of standards for liability. See *Britt v. Allen County Community Jr. College*, 230 Kan. 502, 638 P.2d 914 (1982). Kansas, however, eventually recognized that the trichotomy and its accompanying exceptions and subclassifications were more complex and confusing than the negligence standard of reasonableness.

The jurisdictions eliminating the trichotomy address the aforementioned concerns and provide well-articulated reasons for their decision to abandon the trichotomy. First, these jurisdictions note that the trichotomy was created during feudal times when land formed the principal basis of wealth and when it was desirable to provide a landowner free reign to use and exploit his land, without need for vigilant protection of those who entered his property. In following this reasoning, the Supreme Court of New Hampshire noted that "'the consensus of modern opinion is that the special privilege these rules accord to the occupation of land sprang from the high place which land has traditionally held in English and American thought.'" *Ouellette*, 116 N.H. at 554, 364 A.2d at 632 (quoting 2 Fowler V. Harper & Fleming James, Jr., *The Law of Torts*

1432 (1956)). Similarly, the District of Columbia Circuit Court noted that "[t]he prestige and dominance of the landowning class in the nineteenth century contributed to the common law's emphasis on the economic and social importance of free use and exploitation of land over and above [an entrant's] personal safety." *Smith*, 469 F.2d at 101.

After noting the trichotomy's origins, abolishing courts expressed apprehension about applying it in modern times. For example, the Supreme Court of Massachusetts stated:

> Perhaps, in a rural society with sparse land settlements and large estates, it would have been unduly burdensome to obligate the owner to inspect and maintain distant holdings for a class of entrants who were using the property "for their own convenience" but the special immunity which the licensee rule affords landowners cannot be justified in an urban industrial society.

Mounsey, 363 Mass. at 706, 297 N.E.2d at 51 (citation omitted). Likewise, when the Supreme Court of Florida abolished the common-law trichotomy, it noted that it was

> aware of the contiguous property of others which demands concern for the welfare of our neighbor. Life in these United States is no longer as simple as in the frontier days of broad expanses and sparsely settled lands. Inexorably our peoples, gregarious in nature, have magnetized to limited and congested areas. With social change must come change in the law, for as President Woodrow Wilson observed, "The first duty of the law is to keep sound the society it serves."

Wood, 284 So.2d at 696. Moreover, in *Smith v. Arbaugh's Restaurant, Inc.*, the District of Columbia Circuit Court noted that it did "not believe the rules of liability imposed by courts in the eighteenth century are today the proper tools with which to allocate the costs and risk of loss for human injury." 469 F.2d at 99. Thus, these courts determined that the social and policy considerations underlying the creation of the common-law trichotomy were no longer viable, and therefore they concluded that it was proper to lay it to rest.

On a more practical level, the trichotomy has been criticized for creating a complex, confusing, and unpredictable state of law. The United States Supreme Court, for example, stated that the trichotomy "bred by the common law [has] produced confusion and conflict." *Kermarec*, 358 U.S. at 631, 79 S.Ct. at 410, 3 L.Ed.2d at 555. Similarly, the California Supreme Court noted that "[t]he common law rules obscure rather than illuminate the proper considerations which should govern determination of the question of duty . . . [, and] continued adherence to the common law distinctions can only lead to injustice or, if we are to avoid injustice, further fictions with the resulting complexity and confusion." *Rowland*, 69 Cal.2d at 118, 443 P.2d at 567, 70 Cal.Rptr. at 104; *see also Peterson*, 294 Minn. at 166, 199 N.W.2d at 643 (stating that "judges have been highly critical of the common-law straitjacket of highly technical and arbitrary classifications which have often led to confusion in the law and inequity in the cases decided").

The complexity and confusion associated with the trichotomy is twofold. First, the trichotomy itself often leads to irrational results not only because the entrant's status can change on a whim, but also because the nuances which alter an entrant's status are undefinable. Consider, for example, the following scenario: A real-estate agent trespasses onto another's land to determine the value of property adjoining that which he is trying to sell; the real-estate agent is discovered by the landowner, and the two men engage in a business conversation with respect to the landowner's willingness to sell his property; after completing the business conversation, the two men realize that they went to the same college and have a nostalgic conversation about school while the landowner walks with the man for one acre until they get to the edge of the property; lastly, the two men stand on the property's edge and speak for another ten minutes about school. If the real-estate agent was injured while they were walking off the property, what is his classification? Surely, he is no longer a trespasser, but did his status change from invitee to licensee once the business conversation ended? What if he was hurt while the two men were talking at the property's edge? Does it matter how long they were talking?

The Supreme Court of Wisconsin made a similar argument in *Antoniewicz* when it asked whether there is any reason why one who invites a guest to a party should have less concern for that individual's well-being than he has for the safety of an insurance salesman delivering a policy to his home. See *Antoniewicz*, 70 Wis.2d at 854, 236 N.W.2d at 10. The court then inquired whether the life or welfare of the guest should be regarded in a more sacred manner. *Id.* Moreover, it queried whether we realistically can say that reasonable people vary their conduct based upon the status of the entrant. *Id.*

The preceding illustrations demonstrate the complexity associated with the trichotomy. Moreover, they demonstrate that the trichotomy often forces the trier of fact to focus upon irrelevant factual gradations instead of the pertinent question of whether the landowner acted reasonably toward the injured entrant. For instance, in the real-estate agent hypothetical posed above, the trier of fact would be focused on determining the agent's purpose for being on the land at the time of injury instead of addressing the pertinent question of whether the landowner acted as a reasonable person would under the circumstances.

Corresponding to this argument is the fact that "[i]n many instances, recovery by an entrant has become largely a matter of chance, dependent upon the pigeonhole in which the law has put him, e.g., 'trespasser,' 'licensee,' or 'invitee' — each of which has radically different consequences in law." Significantly, this pigeonholing is essentially an attempt to transmute propositions of fact into propositions of law — a transmutation that has only distracted the jury's vision away from the proper consideration of whether the defendant acted reasonably. For instance, the three experienced Court of Appeals judges who initially decided this case — Judge Smith, Chief Judge Arnold, and Judge Walker — disagreed not only with respect to whether plaintiff was an invitee or a licensee, but also as to whether this case involved a question of law or fact.

Lastly, we note that the trichotomy has been criticized because its underlying landowner-immunity principles force many courts to reach unfair and unjust results disjunctive to the modern fault-based tenets of tort law. For example, the Kansas Supreme Court noted that "modern times demand a recognition that requiring all to exercise reasonable care for the safety of others is the more humane approach." *Jones*, 254 Kan. at 504, 867 P.2d at 307. Likewise, the California Supreme Court noted that using the trichotomy to determine whether a landowner owed the injured plaintiff a duty of care "is contrary to our modern social mores and humanitarian values." *Rowland*, 69 Cal.2d at 118, 443 P.2d at 567, 70 Cal.Rptr. at 104. Indeed, modern thought dictates that "[a] man's life or limb does not become less worthy of protection by the law nor a loss less worthy of compensation . . . because he has come upon the land of another without permission or with permission but without a business purpose." *Id.* Simply put,

> the traditional rule confers on an occupier of land a special privilege to be careless which is quite out of keeping with the development of accident law generally and is no more justifiable here than it would be in the case of any other useful enterprise or activity.

Antoniewicz, 70 Wis.2d at 851, 236 N.W.2d at 8–9 (quoting 2 Fowler V. Harper & Fleming James, Jr., *The Law of Torts* § 27.3, at 1440 (1956)).

The aforementioned complexity, confusion, and harshness associated with the trichotomy's application is evidenced in North Carolina's dealings with the question of whether a licensee turns into an invitee when he provides the landowner with some benefit. For example, in *Crane v. Caldwell*, 113 N.C.App. 362, 438 S.E.2d 449, our Court of Appeals determined that the injured plaintiff was an invitee when, at his neighbor's request, he helped his neighbor move a boat from his backyard dock. In making this ruling, the Court stated that the act of helping a neighbor move a boat from his yard was not one "which one neighbor customarily performs for another in the ordinary course of friendly relations." *Id.* at 366, 438 S.E.2d at 452. Yet, at the same time, the Court stated that "[p]laintiff received no benefit from any of the services he performed for defendant." *Id.* Reading these statements together creates an inconsistency-that is, if the plaintiff received nothing for his acts, yet did not do them as a friendly neighbor, then how should we classify his conduct?

The issue of benefit becomes more perplexing when the preceding case is read in light of some other North Carolina decisions. For example, in *Beaver v. Lefler*, 8 N.C.App. 574, 174 S.E.2d 806 (1970), our Court of Appeals classified the plaintiff as a licensee when he was injured helping his neighbor carry meat into his home. Apparently, reading *Beaver* in conjunction with *Crane* leads one to believe that neighbors regularly carry meat into each others' homes, but do not help each other move things. This decision is even more baffling when read in light of *Briles v. Briles*, 43 N.C.App. 575, 259 S.E.2d 393 (1979), *disc. rev. denied*, 299 N.C. 329, 265 S.E.2d 394 (1980), where our Court of Appeals held that the plaintiff-parents were invitees when, at their son's request, they went to his house to check on his freezer. Logically, this case cannot be reconciled with *Crane* and *Beaver.* Indeed, looking at all three cases as a whole, North Carolina premises-liability jurisprudence appears to stand for the proposition that a friend who carries meat into his neighbor's house is a licensee because he performs a neighborly or friendly act, while a parent who checks her son's freezer is an invitee because she performs some duty which thereby mandates that the parent receive a higher degree of care.

Further, our cases show that the trichotomy is no longer viable because of the complexity and confusion surrounding the numerous exceptions and subclassifications engrafted into it. Indeed, our Court of Appeals noted that "the relevant cases tend to illustrate exceptions to the general rule rather than the rule itself." *Hockaday v. Morse*, 57 N.C.App. 109, 111, 290 S.E.2d 763, 765, *disc. rev. denied*, 306 N.C. 384, 294 S.E.2d 209 (1982). . . . These exceptions and subclassifications have created a labyrinth of jurisprudence through which the trier of fact must make its way with difficulty to determine liability. Instead of clarifying premises-liability law, these exceptions and subclassifications have created such subtle nuances that a typical landowner can never be sure what constitutes actionable conduct.

Significantly, the fact that judges and justices cannot agree as to whether a landowner's conduct is actionable — as evidenced by dissents in prior cases — evidences that the trichotomy fails to clearly articulate a landowner's standard of care. . . . This confusion is most disturbing when considered in light of the comparatively simplistic approach set forth in the modern tort principle of negligence and its accompanying standard of reasonable care under the circumstances.

In sum, there are numerous advantages associated with abolishing the trichotomy. First, it is based upon principles which no longer apply to today's modern industrial society. Further, the preceding cases demonstrate that the trichotomy has failed to elucidate the duty a landowner owes to entrants upon his property. Rather, it has caused confusion amongst our citizens and the judiciary-a confusion exaggerated by the numerous exceptions and subclassifications engrafted into it. Lastly, the trichotomy is unjust and unfair because it usurps the jury's function either by allowing the judge to dismiss or decide the case or by forcing the jury to apply mechanical rules instead of focusing upon the pertinent issue of whether the landowner acted reasonably under the circumstances. Thus, we conclude that North Carolina should join the twenty-four other jurisdictions which have modified or abolished the trichotomy in favor of modern negligence principles.

II. The New Approach to Premises Liability in North Carolina

Given the numerous advantages associated with abolishing the trichotomy, this Court concludes that we should eliminate the distinction between licensees and invitees by requiring a standard of reasonable care toward all lawful visitors. Adoption of a true negligence standard eliminates the complex, confusing, and unpredictable state of premises-liability law and replaces it with a rule which focuses the jury's attention upon the pertinent issue of whether the landowner acted as a reasonable person would under the circumstances.

In so holding, we note that we do not hold that owners and occupiers of land are now insurers of their premises. Moreover, we do not intend for owners and occupiers of land to undergo unwarranted burdens in maintaining their premises. Rather, we impose upon them only the duty to exercise reasonable care in the maintenance of their premises for the protection of lawful visitors.

Further, we emphasize that we will retain a separate classification for trespassers. We believe that the status of trespasser still maintains viability in modern society, and more importantly, we believe that abandoning the status of trespasser may place an unfair burden on a landowner who has no reason to expect a trespasser's presence. Indeed, whereas both invitees and licensees enter another's land under color of right, a trespasser has no basis for claiming protection beyond refraining from willful injury.

Lastly, we note that we are well aware of the principle of *stare decisis* and the important role it plays in maintaining a stable, established, and predictable set of laws. Indeed, we undertake this exhaustive analysis to illustrate our reluctance to abolish parts of our common law. "This Court has never overruled its decisions lightly. No court has been more faithful to *stare decisis*." *Rabon v. Rowan Mem'l Hosp., Inc.*, 269 N.C. 1, 20, 152 S.E.2d 485, 498 (1967). Nonetheless, we also are aware that "[i]t is the tradition of common-law courts to reflect the spirit of their times and discard legal rules when they serve to impede society rather than to advance it." *Antoniewicz*, 70 Wis.2d at 855, 236 N.W.2d at 10. The doctrine is not inflexible, and therefore we will not hesitate to abandon a rule which has resulted in injustices, whether it be criminal or civil. *See Rabon*, 269 N.C. at 20, 152 S.E.2d at 498. "There is no virtue in sinning against light or in persisting in palpable error, for nothing is settled until it is settled right."

Sidney Spitzer & Co. v. Commissioners of Franklin County, 188 N.C. 30, 32, 123 S.E. 636, 638 (1924). As appropriately stated by Judge Cardozo,

> I think that when a rule, after it has been duly tested by experience, has been found to be inconsistent with the sense of justice or with the social welfare, there should be less hesitation in frank avowal and full abandonment. There should be greater readiness to abandon an untenable position when the rule to be discarded may not reasonably be supposed to have determined the conduct of the litigants, and particularly when in its origins it was the product of institutions or conditions which have gained a new significance or development with the progress of the years.

Benjamin Cardozo, *The Nature of the Judicial Process* 120 (1921).

Given that we are convinced that the common-law trichotomy is no longer viable, we should put it to rest. By so doing, we align North Carolina premises-liability law with all other aspects of tort law by basing liability upon the pillar of modern tort theory: negligence. Moreover, we now join twenty-four other jurisdictions which have carefully examined and analyzed this issue, ultimately determining that the trichotomy is no longer applicable in the modern world.

Having adopted a new rule in premises-liability cases, we are obliged to balance countervailing factors to determine whether it should be applied retroactively. *See Cox v. Haworth*, 304 N.C. 571, 573, 284 S.E.2d 322, 324 (1981). These factors include the "reliance on the prior decision, the degree to which the purpose behind the new decision can be achieved solely through prospective application, and the effect of retroactive application on the administration of justice." *Id.* In considering these factors, we begin with a presumption of retroactivity, a presumption which can only be rebutted by compelling reasons. *Id.* After balancing the aforementioned factors, we do not find compelling reasons to apply this rule prospectively only and therefore give it both prospective and retrospective application.

Accordingly, plaintiff Nelson is entitled to a trial at which the jury shall be instructed under the new rule adopted by this opinion. Specifically, the jury must determine whether defendant Freeland fulfilled his duty of reasonable care under the circumstances. This case is therefore remanded to the Court of Appeals for further remand to the Superior Court, Guilford County, for proceedings consistent with this opinion.

REVERSED AND REMANDED.

MITCHELL, Chief Justice, concurring in the result.

In the present case the trial court entered summary judgment in favor of defendants. The majority in the Court of Appeals affirmed the trial court. I am convinced that a jury could find that plaintiff entered defendants' premises as an invitee and defendants violated the duty of care owed an invitee. That being the case, the Court of Appeals erred in affirming the trial court's order of summary judgment for defendants. Accordingly, I find it unnecessary for this Court to consider whether our prior holdings in this area of the common law have been erroneous and must be modified. Further, I think it inadvisable to render an opinion of the magnitude of that entered by the majority in this case when, as here, no party has suggested such a modification of the common law and this Court has not had the benefit of briefs and arguments on the issues decided by the majority.

For the foregoing reasons, I concur only in the result reached by the majority.

LAKE and ORR, JJ., join in this concurring opinion.

Notes and Questions

1. Because following precedent is critical to the stability of the rule of law, courts are generally reluctant to abolish especially longstanding legal rules. Rather, as *Nelson* illustrates, when a rule is believed to be unfair or unjust as applied in particular circumstances, the courts prefer to maintain the rule while carving out specific exceptions to meet those circumstances. Over time, however, the resulting patchwork of exceptions may effectively swallow the rule, make it exceedingly difficult to apply, or simply mask the fact that significant changes in social conditions and community norms (sometimes described as "great social upheaval") have rendered the traditional rule unfair and unjust. It is in these conditions that appellate courts may be willing to abolish and replace the precedent with a new rule that is more consistent with modern conditions and norms. The North Carolina Supreme Court's opinion in *Nelson* is a paradigm example of appellate courts' traditional methodology in this context, regardless of the subject-matter: (1) The court describes the original rule and its traditional justification. (2) The court sets out the exceptions to the rule that over time were carved out to ameliorate its harsh effects in particular circumstances. (3) The court explores the new and different social conditions that obtain in the current period that make it difficult (taking into consideration fairness and justice) to justify retaining the old rule. (4) The court abolishes or significantly modifies the precedent accordingly.

2. Most jurisdictions have abolished the common law "trichotomy." Some have abolished it completely in favor of a duty of reasonable care in all circumstances, and others have abolished the distinction between invitees and licensees but have retained the special rules and exceptions that apply to trespassers. Note, however, that even where a jurisdiction has abolished all three categories in favor of a duty of reasonable care, the traditional status of the entrant may influence the determination what is reasonable care.

3. One of the first exceptions to be carved out to the original rules was for child trespassers. The following case describes the evolution of this exception, which remains salient in those jurisdictions that retain the traditional trichotomy and in those that, like North Carolina, have not abolished the special rules for trespassers. The latter approach remains the majority rule.

BENNETT v. STANLEY
748 N.E.2D 41 (Oh. 2001)

In this case we are called upon to determine what level of duty a property owner owes to a child trespasser. We resolve the question by adopting the attractive nuisance doctrine set forth in Restatement of the Law 2d, Torts (1965), Section 339. We also hold that an adult who attempts to rescue a child from an attractive nuisance assumes the status of the child, and is owed a duty of ordinary care by the property owner.

Factual and Procedural Background

When Rickey G. Bennett, plaintiff-appellant, arrived home in the late afternoon of March 20, 1997, he found his two young daughters crying. The three-year-old, Kyleigh, told him that "Mommy" and Chance, her five-year-old half-brother, were "drowning in the water." Bennett ran next door to his neighbors' house to find mother and son unconscious in the swimming pool. Both died.

The Bennetts had moved next door to defendants-appellees, Jeffrey and Stacey Stanley, in the fall of 1996. The Stanleys had purchased their home the previous June. At the time of their purchase, the Stanleys' property included a swimming pool that had gone unused for three years. At that time, the pool was enclosed with fencing and a brick wall. After moving in, the Stanleys drained the pool once but thereafter they allowed rainwater to accumulate in the pool to a depth of over six feet. They removed a tarp that had been on the pool and also removed the fencing that had been around two sides of the pool. The pool became pond-like: it contained tadpoles and frogs, and Mr. Stanley had seen a snake swimming on the surface. The pool contained no ladders, and its sides were slimy with algae.

Rickey and Cher Bennett were married in 1995. They had two daughters, born in 1993 and 1995. Cher brought her son, Chance Lattea, into the marriage. The Bennetts rented the house next to the Stanleys. The houses were about one hundred feet apart. There was some fencing with an eight-foot gap between the two properties.

The Stanleys were aware that the Bennetts had moved next door and that they had young children. They had seen the children outside unsupervised. Stacey Stanley had once called Chance onto her property to retrieve a dog. The Stanleys testified, however, that they never had any concern about the children getting into the pool. They did not post any warning or "no trespassing" signs on their property.

Rickey Bennett testified that he had told his children to stay away from the pool on the Stanleys' property. He also stated that he had never seen the children playing near the pool.

Kyleigh told her father that she and Chance had been playing at the pool on the afternoon of the tragedy. The sheriff's department concluded that Chance had gone to the pool to look at the frogs and somehow fell into the pool. His mother apparently drowned trying to save him.

Bennett, in his capacity as Administrator of the Estate of Cher D. Bennett, as Administrator of the Estate of Chance C. Lattea, and as custodial parent of Kyleigh D. Bennett, filed a wrongful death and personal injury suit against the Stanleys. The complaint alleged that appellees had negligently maintained an abandoned swimming pool on their property and that appellees' negligence proximately caused the March 20, 1997 drowning of Chance and Cher. Appellant averred that appellees had created a dangerous condition by negligently maintaining the pool and that appellees reasonably should have known that the pool posed an unreasonable risk of serious harm to others. Appellant specifically alleged that appellees' pool created an unreasonable risk of harm to children who, because of their youth, would not realize the potential danger. Appellant further asserted that appellees' conduct in maintaining the pool constituted willful and wanton misconduct such as to justify an award of punitive damages. Appellant sought damages for the beneficiaries of the deceased, for Kyleigh's mental anguish for witnessing the drownings, for mental anguish for Cher before her death, and for punitive damages. Appellees denied any negligence and asserted affirmative defenses of contributory negligence and assumption of the risk.

Appellees filed a motion for summary judgment, which the trial court granted on September 4, 1998. The trial court found that Chance and Cher were trespassers on appellees' property and that appellees therefore owed them only a duty to refrain from wanton and willful misconduct. The trial court further rejected appellant's argument that appellees' maintenance of the swimming pool amounted to a dangerous active operation that would create for them a duty of ordinary care pursuant to *Coy v. Columbus, Delaware & Marion Elec. Co.* (1932), 125 Ohio St. 283, 181 N.E. 131. As the complaint alleged that appellees had violated a duty of ordinary care, the court found for the Stanleys as a matter of law.

On appeal, the appellate court affirmed the trial court's granting of summary judgment. It, too, held that appellees owed the decedents only a duty to refrain from wanton and willful misconduct, and added that there was no evidence of such misconduct. The appellate court also addressed the issue of appellees' duty to Cher Bennett. The court held that even if she were on the Stanleys' property in an attempt to rescue Chance, she would still have the status only of a licensee, who is owed no greater duty of care than a trespasser.

The cause is now before this court upon the allowance of a discretionary appeal.

Law and Analysis

Ohio has long recognized a range of duties for property owners vis-à-vis persons entering their property. A recent discussion of Ohio's classification system can be found in *Gladon v. Greater Cleveland Regional Transit Auth.* (1996), 75 Ohio St.3d 312, 315, 662 N.E.2d 287, 291. Currently, to an invitee the landowner owes a duty "to exercise ordinary care and to protect the invitee by maintaining the premises in a safe condition." *Light v. Ohio Univ.* (1986), 28 Ohio St.3d 66, 68, 28 OBR 165, 167, 502 N.E.2d 611, 613. To licensees and trespassers, on the other hand, "a landowner owes no duty * * * except to refrain from willful, wanton or reckless conduct which is likely to injure [the licensee or trespasser]." *Gladon*, 75 Ohio St.3d at 317, 662 N.E.2d at 293. Today, we face the issue of whether child trespassers should become another class of users who are owed a different duty of care.

This court has consistently held that children have a special status in tort law and that duties of care owed to children are different from duties owed to adults:

> [T]he amount of care required to discharge a duty owed to a child of tender years is necessarily greater than that required to discharge a duty owed to an adult under the same circumstances. This is the approach long followed by this court and we see no reason to abandon it. "Children of tender years, and youthful persons generally, are entitled to a degree of care proportioned to their inability to foresee and avoid the perils that they may encounter. * * * The same discernment and foresight in discovering defects and dangers cannot be reasonably expected of them, that older and experienced persons habitually employ; and therefore the greater precaution should be taken, where children are exposed to them."

Di Gildo v. Caponi (1969), 18 Ohio St.2d 125, 127, 47 O.O.2d 282, 283, 247 N.E.2d 732, 734, quoting Ohio Jurisprudence 2d 512 (1959), Negligence, Section 21.

Recognizing the special status of children in the law, this court has even accorded special protection to child trespassers by adopting the "dangerous instrumentality" doctrine:

> The dangerous instrumentality exception [to nonliability to trespassers] imposes upon the owner or occupier of a premises a higher duty of care to a child trespasser when such owner or occupier actively and negligently operates hazardous machinery or other apparatus, the dangerousness of which is not readily apparent to children.

McKinney v. Hartz & Restle Realtors, Inc. (1987), 31 Ohio St.3d 244, 247, 31 OBR 449, 452, 510 N.E.2d 386, 390.

That doctrine was developed in *Coy v. Columbus, Delaware & Marion Elec. Co.* (1932), 125 Ohio St. 283, 181 N.E. 131, a case where a six-year-old boy was injured when he touched a high voltage transformer owned by the defendant and located in a vacant lot known to be frequented by children. The court applied a negligence standard to the behavior of the company, despite the fact that the child had been trespassing. This court quoted with favor the court in *Haywood v. S. Hill Mfg. Co.* (1925), 142 Va. 761, 765–766, 128 S.E. 362, 363–364:

> "'Certainly a deadly, hidden force, as in this case, should not be left easily accessible to children whose frequent presence in this vicinity was known to the defendant, and acquiesced in by it, and this without so much as a danger sign anywhere thereabout.
>
> * * * The care must be commensurate with the danger.'"

Thus, the court adopted as early as 1932 some of the hallmarks of the attractive nuisance doctrine. Elements such as knowledge of children's presence, the maintenance of a potentially dangerous force, and an exercise of care by the owner commensurate with the danger are a part of the attractive nuisance doctrine in most states, as reflected in Section 339 of the Restatement of Torts.

Despite the fact that in premises liability cases a landowner's duty is defined by the status of the plaintiff, and that children, even child trespassers, are accorded special protection in Ohio tort law, this court has never adopted the attractive nuisance doctrine. The doctrine as adopted by numerous states is set forth in Restatement of the Law 2d, Torts (1965), Section 339:

> A possessor of land is subject to liability for physical harm to children trespassing thereon caused by an artificial condition upon land if:
>
> "(a) the place where the condition exists is one upon which the possessor knows or has reason to know that children are likely to trespass, and
>
> "(b) the condition is one of which the possessor knows or has reason to know and which he realizes or should realize will involve an unreasonable risk of death or serious bodily harm to such children, and
>
> "(c) the children because of their youth do not discover the condition or realize the risk involved in intermeddling with it or in coming within the area made dangerous by it, and

"(d) the utility to the possessor of maintaining the condition and the burden of eliminating the danger are slight as compared with the risk to children involved, and

"(e) the possessor fails to exercise reasonable care to eliminate the danger or otherwise to protect the children.

This court has never explicitly rejected the Restatement version of the doctrine, which was adopted in 1965. Instead, Ohio's tradition in this area of the law is based upon this court's rejection in 1907 of the "turntable doctrine" in *Wheeling & Lake Erie RR. Co. v. Harvey* (1907), 77 Ohio St. 235, 83 N.E. 66, paragraph two of the syllabus. In *Harvey*, this court held in paragraph one of the syllabus that "[i]t is not the duty of an occupier of land to exercise care to make it safe for infant children who come upon it without invitation but merely by sufferance."

The "turntable doctrine" was a somewhat controversial doctrine wherein railroads could be liable to children for injuries suffered on unguarded railroad turntables. The theory of liability was established in *Sioux City & Pacific RR. Co. v. Stout* (1873), 84 U.S. (17 Wall.) 657, 21 L.Ed. 745, and had been adopted by many states as of 1907. The burning question for many years was whether to apply the doctrine to non-turntable cases. Many of the states that adopted the turntable doctrine refused to apply it to cases not involving turntables.

However, the theory of liability has evolved since 1907. The Restatement of the Law, Torts (1934) and Restatement of the Law 2d, Torts (1965) removed legal fictions and imposed balancing factors to consider on behalf of landowners. Ohio's refusal to recognize the turntable doctrine in 1907 was not a serious anomaly at the time; today, our failure to adopt the attractive nuisance doctrine is.

Ohio is one of only three states that have not either created a special duty for trespassing children or done away with distinctions of duty based upon a person's status as an invitee, licensee, or trespasser.

In more recent years, this court has failed to address the issue of attractive nuisance head-on. In *Elliott v. Nagy* (1986), 22 Ohio St.3d 58, 22 OBR 77, 488 N.E.2d 853, this court avoided the opportunity to adopt the attractive nuisance doctrine, stating that the case at hand "present[ed] no compelling reasons meriting the adoption of the attractive nuisance doctrine." *Id.* at 61, 22 OBR at 79, 488 N.E.2d at 855. *Elliott* was a swimming pool case. However, in that case, the child who perished in the pool was visiting her grandparents, who lived one hundred to three hundred feet from the neighbor who owned the pool. Rather than rejecting the doctrine of attractive nuisance, this court simply declined to apply it in *Elliott*, finding that the neighbors could not have foreseen that a nineteen-month-old child would be visiting her grandparents and wander into their yard. The court held in its syllabus:

> The attractive nuisance doctrine will not extend tort liability to the owner of a residential swimming pool where the presence of a child who was injured or drowned therein was not foreseeable by the property owner.

That ruling is not contradictory to the attractive nuisance doctrine as set forth in the Restatement of Torts. One of the key elements of the doctrine as defined in the Restatement is that "the place where the condition exists is one upon which the possessor knows or has reason to know that children are likely to trespass." Section 339(a). The Elliott court quite obviously withheld from ruling on whether the attractive nuisance doctrine would apply where the presence of a child is foreseeable.

The court recognized that fact later that same year in *Wills v. Frank Hoover Supply* (1986), 26 Ohio St.3d 186, 191, 26 OBR 160, 164, 497 N.E.2d 1118, 1122, holding that the "linchpin was foreseeability" in this court's refusal to adopt the attractive nuisance doctrine in *Elliott.* The *Wills* court also avoided adopting the attractive nuisance doctrine, concluding that that case involved a dangerous instrumentality.

In this case, there is at least a genuine issue of fact regarding the foreseeability of one of the Bennett children entering onto the Stanley property. In *Elliott*, the injured child was a visitor; here, the child resided next door. Reasonable minds could conclude that it was foreseeable that one of the Bennett children would explore around the pool.

Thus, in this case we cannot decline to adopt the attractive nuisance doctrine because of a lack of foreseeability. Any failure to adopt attractive nuisance would be to reject its philosophical underpinnings and would keep Ohio in the small minority of states that do not recognize some form of the doctrine.

Adopting the attractive nuisance doctrine would be merely an incremental change in Ohio law, not out of line with the law that has developed over time. It is an appropriate evolution of the common law. While the present case is by no means a guaranteed winner for the plaintiff, it does present a factual scenario that would allow a jury to consider whether the elements of the cause of action have been fulfilled.

We therefore use this case to adopt the attractive nuisance doctrine contained in Restatement of the Law 2d, Torts (1965), Section 339. In doing so, we do not abandon the differences in duty a landowner owes to the different classes of users. In this case we simply further recognize that children are entitled to a greater level of protection than adults are. We remove the "distinctions without differences" between the dangerous instrumentality doctrine and the attractive nuisance doctrine. See *Wills*, 26 Ohio St.3d at 192, 26 OBR at 165, 497 N.E.2d at 1123, A.W. Sweeney, J., concurring. Whether an apparatus or a condition of property is involved, the key element should be whether there is a foreseeable, "unreasonable risk of death or serious bodily harm to * * * children." Restatement, Section 339(b).

The Restatement's version of the attractive nuisance doctrine balances society's interest in protecting children with the rights of landowners to enjoy their property. Even when a landowner is found to have an attractive nuisance on his or her land, the landowner is left merely with the burden of acting with ordinary care. A landowner does not automatically become liable for any injury a child trespasser may suffer on that land.

The requirement of foreseeability is built into the doctrine. The landowner must know or have reason to know that children are likely to trespass upon the part of the property that contains the dangerous condition. See Section 339(a). Moreover, the landowner's duty "does not extend to those conditions the existence of which is obvious even to children and the risk of which should be fully realized by them." *Id.* at Comment *i.* Also, if the condition of the property that poses the risk is essential to the landowner, the doctrine would not apply:

"The public interest in the possessor's free use of his land for his own purposes is of great significance. A particular condition is, therefore, regarded as not involving unreasonable risk to trespassing children unless it involves a grave risk to them which could be obviated without any serious interference with the possessor's legitimate use of his land." *Id.* at Comment *n.*

We are satisfied that the Restatement view effectively harmonizes the competing societal interests of protecting children and preserving property rights. In adopting the attractive nuisance doctrine, we acknowledge that the way we live now is different from the way we lived in 1907, when *Harvey* was decided. We are not a rural society any longer, our neighbors live closer, and our use of our own property affects others more than it once did.

Despite our societal changes, children are still children. They still learn through their curiosity. They still have developing senses of judgment. They still do not always appreciate danger. They still need protection by adults. Protecting children in a changing world requires the common law to adapt. Today, we make that change.

Finally, we add that on remand should the facts establish that the attractive nuisance doctrine applies in this case, that finding would also affect the duty of care the appellees owed to Cher Bennett if Cher entered the property to rescue her son. The appellate court held that even if it is assumed that Cher entered the Stanleys' property to rescue Chance, her status was still that of a licensee. The court reasoned that in that instance, Cher would possess a privilege to enter the property, and that a person privileged to enter the land is owed the same duties as a licensee.

On remand, the evidence may establish that Cher's status was that of a rescuer. This court has held pertaining to rescuers that "if the rescuer does not rashly and unnecessarily expose himself to danger, and is injured, the injury should be attributed to the party that negligently, or wrongfully, exposed to danger, the person who required assistance." While the attractive nuisance doctrine is not ordinarily applicable to adults, it "may be successfully invoked by an adult seeking damages for his or her own injury if the injury was suffered in an attempt to rescue a child from a danger created by the defendant's negligence." 62 American Jurisprudence 2d (1990), Premises Liability, Section 288. Therefore, we hold that if Cher Bennett entered the Stanleys' property to rescue her son from an attractive nuisance, the Stanleys owed her a duty of ordinary care.

Accordingly, we reverse the judgment of the court of appeals and remand the cause to the trial court.

Judgment reversed and cause remanded.

Notes and Questions

1. Why did the Ohio Supreme Court adopt the attractive nuisance doctrine when it had declined to do so over the years? What changed over time in Ohio's social conditions and norms that made adoption of the doctrine appropriate finally in 2001?

2. Does the Restatement 2d's version of the attractive nuisance doctrine appropriately balance property rights with child protection? Imagine you represent a property owner. Are there aspects of the rule that might not adequately protect your client's interests?

3. Swimming pools are a classic attractive nuisance according to the caselaw. However, their status as such has been abrogated by statutes or municipal ordinances in many jurisdictions. These codifications effectively immunize property owners from negligence liability for injuries to trespassers (including children) so long as certain conditions — usually involving required fencing — are met. In effect, these provisions establish that providing the required fencing is reasonable care as a matter of law. Does this mean that a property owner who has a pool and fences it according to the terms of the relevant local ordinance or statute does not need to purchase liability insurance in connection with the pool?

4. As we saw in *Nelson*, at common law no duty was owed to trespassers; an owner or occupier of land could only be liable for intentional (willful) injury to a trespasser. This rule was ameliorated in most jurisdictions so that an owner or occupier of land who willfully or wantonly (recklessly) injured a trespasser could be liable. Over time, the courts carved out three exceptions to this rule. The first was the attractive nuisance doctrine. This doctrine originated in the turntable rule described in *Bennett*. Specifically, children who were attracted onto private property to play on train turntables were owed a duty of care by the owners and occupiers. Again as we saw in *Bennett,* many jurisdictions came to apply this turntable rule to other attractive nuisances — hence the name of the doctrine. The second and third exceptions to the traditional rule that trespassers were owed no duty of care were developed for known and constant trespassers, who (because they were foreseeable) came to be treated like licensees. Note that, at most, licensees and known or constant trespassers were owed a duty to refrain from gross negligence; in other words, mostly the duty to entrants in these categories was not a negligence duty. In jurisdictions which retain the traditional distinctions among entrants or which continue to treat trespassers according to the common law rules and their exceptions, this result still obtains.

5. Premises liability includes the subcategory of landlord-tenant liability. These rules vary substantially by jurisdiction and today are mostly codified in local ordinances or state statutes. Contracts (in the form of rental/lease agreements) may also substantially dictate the terms of landlord-tenant liability. Thus, the traditional common law rules in this area have mostly been abrogated or altered by the contracting parties. However, to the extent they are still relevant, their highlights include the rules that landlords are responsible for the design, construction, maintenance, and repair of common areas but not for the leasehold, e.g., the inside of the apartment; but if landlords do make repairs, they assume a duty to do so with reasonable care. Finally, states that have eliminated the common law categories of entrants onto land in favor of a duty of reasonable care for all entrants may have also have abolished their special landlord-tenant rules in favor of the same duty.

CHAPTER FOUR
BREACH

Establishing a duty of care in negligence necessarily begs the question, "What care?" As we will see in this chapter, the standard of care (the measure by which a person's conduct is judged) is reasonable prudence in the circumstances. Proof that the defendant violated this standard — that is, proof of unreasonableness — is proof of breach.

The chapter is in three parts. The first part focuses on defining the standard of care for adults and children. The second part discusses the roles played by the legislature, the judge, and the jury in determining the standard of care in particular cases. The third part provides instruction on how plaintiffs go about arguing and proving that the standard of care was breached by the defendant, and how defendants can refute the plaintiff's proof.

I. DEFINING THE STANDARD OF CARE

A. Adults

VAUGHAN v. MENLOVE
3 Bing. (N.C.) 468, 132 Eng.Rep. 490 (1837)

At the trial, before PATTESON, J, it appeared that the rick had been made by the defendant near the boundary of his own premises; that the hay was in such a state when put together, as to give rise to discussions on the probability of fire: that although there were conflicting opinions on the subject, yet during a period of five weeks, the defendant was repeatedly warned of his peril; that his stock was insured and that on one occasion, being advised to take the risk down to avoid all danger, he said "he would chance it." He made an aperture or chimney through the rick but in spite, or perhaps in consequence of this precaution, the rick at length burst into flames from the spontaneous heating of its materials; the flames communicated to the defendant's barn and stables and thence to the plaintiff's cottages, which were entirely destroyed. PATTESON, J, told the jury that the question for them to consider was whether the fire had been occasioned by gross negligence on the part of the defendant; adding that he was bound to proceed with such reasonable caution as a prudent man would have exercised under such circumstances.

A verdict having been found for the plaintiff, [the defendant appealed] on the ground that the jury should have been directed to consider not whether the defendant had been guilty of gross negligence with reference to the standard of ordinary prudence, a standard too uncertain to afford any criterion, but whether he had acted bona fide to the best of his judgment; that if he had, he ought not to be responsible for the misfortune of not possessing the highest order of intelligence.

[The plaintiff's lawyer argued:]

The pleas having expressly raised issues on the negligence of the Defendant, the learned Judge could not do otherwise than leave that question to the jury. The declaration alleges that the Defendant knew of the dangerous state of the rick, and yet negligently and improperly allowed it to stand. The plea of not guilty, therefore, puts in issue the scienter, it being of the substance of the issue. And the action, though new in specie, is founded on a principle fully established, that a man must so use his own property as not to injure that of others. On the same circuit a defendant was sued a few years ago, for burning weeds so near the extremity of his own land as to set fire to and destroy his neighbours' wood. The plaintiff recovered damages, and no motion was made to set aside the verdict. Then, there were no means of estimating the defendant's negligence, except by taking as a standard, the conduct of a man of ordinary prudence: that has been the rule always laid down, and there is no other that would not be open to much greater uncertainties.

[The defendant's lawyer argued:]

First, there was no duty imposed on the Defendant, as there is on carriers or other bailees, under an implied contract, to be responsible for the exercise of any given degree of prudence: the Defendant had a right to place his stack as near to the extremity of his own land as he pleased: under that right, and subject to no contract, he can only be called on to act bonâ fide to the best of his judgment: if he has done that, it is a contradiction in terms, to inquire whether or not he has been guilty of gross negligence. At all events what would have been gross negligence ought to be estimated by the faculties of the individual, and not by those of other men. The measure of prudence varies so with the varying faculties of men, that it is impossible to say what is gross negligence with reference to the standard of what is called ordinary prudence. In *Crook v. Jadis* (5 B. & Adol. 910), Patteson J. says, "I never could understand what is meant by parties taking a bill under circumstances which ought to have excited the suspicion of a prudent man:" and Taunton J., "I cannot estimate the degree of care which a prudent man should take."

TINDAL CJ: I agree that this is a case primae impressionis; but I feel no difficulty in applying to it the principles of law as laid down in other cases of a similar kind . . . ; but there is a rule of law which says you must so enjoy your own property as not to injure that of another, and according to that rule the defendant is liable for the consequence of his own neglect; and though the defendant did not himself light the fire, yet mediately, he is as much the cause of it as if he had himself put a candle to the rick, for it is well known that hay will ferment and take fire if it be not carefully stacked. It has been decided that if an occupier burns weeds so near the boundary of his own land that damage ensues to the property of his neighbour, he is liable to an action for the amount of injury done, unless the accident were occasioned by a sudden blast which he could not foresee. But put the case of a chemist making experiments with ingredients singly innocent, but when combined, liable to ignite; if he leaves them together and injury is thereby occasioned to the property of his neighbour, can any one doubt that an action on the case would lie?

It is contended, however, that the judge was wrong in leaving this to the jury as a case of gross negligence, and that the question of negligence was so mixed up with reference to what would be the conduct of a man of ordinary prudence that the jury might have thought the latter the rule by which they were to decide; that such a rule would be too uncertain to act on; and that the question ought to have been whether the defendant had acted honestly and bona fide to the best of his own judgment. That, however, would leave so vague a line as to afford no rule at all, the degree of judgment belonging to each individual being infinitely various; and although it has been urged that the care which a prudent man would take, is not an intelligible proposition as a rule of law, yet such has always been the rule adopted in cases of bailment.

The care taken by a prudent man has always been the rule laid down; and as to the supposed difficulty of applying it, a jury has always been able to say, whether, taking that rule as their guide, there has been negligence on the occasion in question. Instead, therefore, of saying that the liability for negligence should be co-extensive with the judgment of each individual, which would be as variable as the length of the foot of each individual, we ought rather to adhere to the rule which requires in all cases a regard to caution such as a man of ordinary prudence would observe. That was, in substance, the criterion presented to the jury in this case and, therefore, the present [appeal] must be discharged.

PARK J: I entirely concur in what has fallen from TINDAL, CJ. Although the facts in this case are new in specie, they fall within a principle long established, that a man must so use his own property as not to injure that of others.

As to the direction of the judge, it was perfectly correct. In the circumstances of the case it was proper to leave it to the jury whether, with reference to the caution which would have been observed by a man of ordinary prudence, the defendant had not been guilty of gross negligence. After he had been warned repeatedly during five weeks as to the consequences likely to happen, there is no colour for altering the verdict, unless it were to increase the damages.

GASELEE, J: Concurred in discharging the rule.

VAUGHAN J: The principle on which this action proceeds, is by no means new. It has been urged that the defendant in such a case, takes no duty on himself but I do not agree in that position. Everyone takes on himself the duty of so dealing with his own property as not to injure the property of others. It was, if anything, too favourable to the defendant to leave it to the jury whether he had been guilty of gross negligence; for when the defendant, on being warned as to the consequences likely to ensue from the condition of the rick, said, "he would chance it," it was manifest [he was referring to his insurance coverage]. The conduct of a prudent man has always been the criterion for the jury in such cases but it is by no means confined to them. In insurance cases, where a captain has sold his vessel after damage too extensive for repairs, the question has always been whether he has pursued the course which a prudent man would have pursued in the same circumstances. Here, there was not a single witness whose testimony did not go to establish gross negligence in the defendant. He had repeated warnings of what was likely to occur, and the whole calamity was occasioned by his procrastination.

[Appeal dismissed.]

Notes and Questions

1. *Vaughan* was decided in 1837 in the period where negligence (at the time usually known as "trespass on the case") was emerging as a tort distinct from "trespass." (Go back to Chapter 1 if you need to refresh your recollection about this history and the distinction between the two torts.) To the extent there was room for argument about what a defendant's duty was, and about

what the standard of care was once a duty was established, it is because the action took place in that formative period. At the same time, notice which long-established precedents from other contexts the appellate judges relied on to articulate the rule that would apply in this context. This mode of analysis made their decisions appear to be a seamless move, as though nothing particularly revolutionary was going on.

2. The plaintiff claimed that the defendant was grossly negligence and was ultimately successful on that count. What facts supported this charge?

3. The defendant contested the plaintiff's allegations on both duty and breach. Both challenges were about the law, not the facts. What were his arguments?

4. Most of the appellate judges agreed that the trial judge had no choice but to send the case to the jury. Why was that? Specifically, why is the jury the right institution to decide the breach question?

5. The last appellate judge (Vaughan) suggested that the case need not have been sent to the jury — that it could have been decided for the plaintiff as a matter of law. What facts would have supported this different procedural result?

OLIVER WENDELL HOLMES
The Common Law
107–111 (1881)

. . .

Supposing it now to be conceded that the general notion upon which liability to an action is founded is fault or blameworthiness in some sense, the question arises, whether it is so in the sense of personal moral shortcoming. . . . Suppose that a defendant were allowed to testify that, before acting, he considered carefully what would be the conduct of a prudent man under the circumstances, and, having formed the best judgment he could, acted accordingly. If the story was believed, it would be conclusive against the defendant's negligence judged by a moral standard which would take his personal characteristics into account. But supposing any such evidence to have got before the jury, it is very clear that the court would say, Gentlemen, the question is not whether the defendant thought his conduct was that of a prudent man, but whether you think it was.

. . .

The standards of the law are standards of general application. The law takes no account of the infinite varieties of temperament, intellect, and education which make the internal character of a given act so different in different men. It does not attempt to see men as God sees them, for more than one sufficient reason. In the first place, the impossibility of nicely measuring a man's powers and limitations is far clearer than that of ascertaining his knowledge of law, which has been thought to account for what is called the presumption that every man knows the law. But a more satisfactory explanation is, that, when men live in society, a certain average of conduct, a sacrifice of individual peculiarities going beyond a certain point, is necessary to the general welfare. If, for instance, a man is born hasty and awkward, is always having accidents and hurting himself or his neighbors, no doubt his congenital defects will be allowed for in the courts of Heaven, but his slips are no less troublesome to his neighbors than if they sprang from guilty neglect. His neighbors accordingly require him, at his proper peril, to come up to their standard, and the courts which they establish decline to take his personal equation into account.

The rule that the law does, in general, determine liability by blameworthiness, is subject to the limitation that minute differences of character are not allowed for. The law considers, in other words, what would be blameworthy in the average man, the man of ordinary intelligence and prudence, and determines liability by that. If we fall below the level in those gifts, it is our misfortune; so much as that we must have at our peril, for the reasons just given. But he who is intelligent and prudent does not act at his peril, in theory of law. On the contrary, it is only when he fails to exercise the foresight of which he is capable, or exercises it with evil intent, that he is answerable for the consequences.

There are exceptions to the principle that every man is presumed to possess ordinary capacity to avoid harm to his neighbors, which illustrate the rule, and also the moral basis of liability in general. When a man has a distinct defect of such a nature that all can recognize it as making certain precautions impossible, he will not be held answerable for not taking them. A blind man is not required to see at his peril; and although he is, no doubt, bound to consider his infirmity in regulating his actions, yet if he properly finds himself in a certain situation, the neglect of precautions requiring eyesight would not prevent his recovering for an injury to himself, and, it may be presumed, would not make him liable for injuring another. So it is held that, in cases where he is the plaintiff, an infant of very tender years is only bound to take the precautions of which an infant is capable; the same principle may be cautiously applied where he is defendant. Insanity is a more difficult matter to deal with, and no general rule can be laid down about it. There is no doubt that in many cases a man may be insane, and yet perfectly capable of taking the precautions, and of being influenced by the motives, which the circumstances demand. But if insanity of a pronounced type exists, manifestly incapacitating the sufferer from complying with the rule which he has broken, good sense would require it to be admitted as an excuse.

Taking the qualification last established in connection with the general proposition previously laid down, it will now be assumed that, on the one hand, the law presumes or requires a man to possess ordinary capacity to avoid harming his neighbors, unless a clear and manifest incapacity be shown; but that, on the other, it does not in general hold him liable for unintentional injury, unless, possessing such capacity, he might and ought to have foreseen the danger, or, in other words, unless a man of ordinary intelligence and forethought would have been to blame for acting as he did. The next question is, whether this vague test is all that the law has to say upon the matter, and the same question in another form, by whom this test is to be applied.

Notwithstanding the fact that the grounds of legal liability are moral to the extent above explained, it must be borne in mind that law only works within the sphere of the senses. If the external phenomena, the manifest acts and omissions, are such as it requires, it is wholly indifferent to the internal phenomena of conscience. A man may have as bad a heart as he chooses, if his conduct is within the rules. In other words, the standards of the law are external standards, and, however much it may take moral considerations into account, it does so only for the purpose of drawing a line between such bodily motions and rests as it permits, and such as it does not. What the law really forbids, and the only thing it forbids, is the act on the wrong side of the line, be that act blameworthy or otherwise.

Again, any legal standard must, in theory, be one which would apply to all men, not specially excepted, under the same circumstances. It is not intended that the public force should fall upon an individual accidentally, or at the whim of any body of men. The standard, that is, must be fixed. In practice, no doubt, one man may have to pay and another may escape, according to the different feelings of different juries. But this merely shows that the law does not perfectly accomplish its ends. The theory or intention of the law is not that the feeling of approbation or blame which a particular twelve may entertain should be the criterion. They are supposed to leave their idiosyncrasies on one side, and to represent the feeling of the community. The ideal average prudent man, whose equivalent the jury is taken to be in many cases, and whose culpability or innocence is the supposed test, is a constant, and his conduct under given circumstances is theoretically always the same.

. . .

Notes and Questions

1. What is Holmes's preferred rationale for the reasonable prudent person standard? Is this more convincing to you than the rationale provided by the court in *Vaughan*?

2. Holmes writes of insanity that it "is a more difficult matter to deal with, and no general rule can be laid down about it." Why might insanity be more complex than poor intelligence or poor judgment, for which negligence law makes no allowances? At what point might insanity be like blindness?

3. Should personal characteristics be taken into account when they involve special or extra knowledge and skill? For example, should a defendant who is a professional race car driver be required to use her driving expertise when she uses her personal car on city streets, or should it be sufficient for tort law purposes if her conduct is at least consistent with that of the average person? How would the law rationalize requiring her to use her special knowledge and skill in these off-track circumstances?

4. How does Holmes describe the jury and why does he believe that it is the appropriate institution to establish responsibility in negligence? What do you think a jury consultant would say to the expression of this ideal?

5. Notice that the law is designed to reflect "the feeling of the community" about what is and isn't reasonable behavior. Holmes makes clear that the community's view isn't necessarily the same as that of the individuals involved in the litigation; rather, the individuals who comprise the jury find their community's "ideal average prudent man" in their deliberations with their fellow jurors. Given how jury venires are selected — from voter rolls or in combination with driver license lists — this means that "the feelings of the community" are only partly captured by the design, and that they are not necessarily the same as those of the country or even the region as a whole. In other words, the "ideal average prudent person" can differ based both on the locale and on who is in the jury pool and available to serve. With respect to the former,

what is reasonable in Scottsdale, Arizona, may not be the same as in Brooklyn, New York, or Birmingham, Alabama. With respect to the latter, notice that Holmes assumed only men would serve, which left out the views of the women in the community. It was only in our lifetimes that the United States Supreme Court finally held that the Constitution protects the right of women to be included without sex-linked conditions in venires and on juries. See Women Serving on Juries, the Library of Congress, 2020 (featuring Ruth Bader Ginsberg's notes in preparation of her oral argument in Duren v. Missouri, 439 U.S. 357 (1979)). And although he left this unsaid, at the time Holmes was writing, African-Americans would also have been excluded from venires and/or service in most jurisdictions. Since the Supreme Court's decision in Batson v. Kentucky, 476 U.S. 79 (1986), striking prospective jurors on the basis of race has been unconstitutional, but the practice nevertheless continues on pretextual grounds. See, e.g., Flowers v. Mississippi, 588 U.S. (2019) (applying *Batson*); State v. Hobbs, 841 S.E.2d 492 (N.C. 2020) (same).

6. Make sure you can identify the objective and subjective aspects of the reasonable person standard. Why does it make sense to pair these two aspects?

MCCALL v. WILDER
913 S.W.2d 150 (Tenn. 1995)

WHITE, Justice.

In this negligence action seeking damages for personal injury and property damage, Lisa A. McCall, appellant, appeals from the decision of the Court of Appeals affirming the trial court's grant of summary judgment in favor of appellee, Edgar A. Wilder, administrator of the estate of James Robert Ratley, Sr., deceased. We granted plaintiff's application for permission to appeal to decide an issue not previously faced by this Court: whether, and under what circumstances, the driver of a motor vehicle who suddenly loses control of the vehicle because of physical incapacitation caused by a known medical condition may be liable for personal injury or property damages. We hold that liability may be imposed upon the driver who knows of the medically incapacitating disorder, and who poses an unreasonable risk of harm to others by driving under circumstances such that a reasonably prudent person could foresee an accident. For the reasons set forth below, the judgment of the Court of Appeals is reversed and the case remanded for trial.

I. Facts and Background

Plaintiff sued defendant in the Blount County General Sessions Court alleging that defendant's decedent hit plaintiff's vehicle head-on damaging the vehicle and injuring plaintiff. Following the entry of a default against defendant, the case was appealed to the Blount County Circuit Court where defendant moved for summary judgment. The basis for defendant's motion was that the accident was an unavoidable consequence of a sudden emergency created when the decedent suffered a seizure while driving. Defendant's motion was supported by the affidavit of a board certified physician practicing in the field of neurosurgery who treated decedent from the day of the accident until his death approximately three months later. According to the affidavit, a CT scan performed on the decedent after the accident revealed evidence of a brain tumor. Further evaluation and testing revealed that the tumor was located in a "very highly epileptogenic region of [the] brain." Surgery confirmed the presence of the brain tumor. The doctor opined that the tumor was present in decedent's brain on the day of the accident and that it made him susceptible to seizures. Therefore, the doctor concluded, within a reasonable degree of medical certainty, "that it is very likely that [decedent] suffered a seizure while driving his vehicle . . . which in turn caused the motor vehicle accident of December 12, 1990."

In response to defendant's motion for summary judgment, plaintiff filed the affidavit of a board certified physician concentrating in the fields of pathology and laboratory medicine. The affidavit reflected the parties' stipulations that decedent had experienced seizures prior to the day of the accident and that decedent knew he had a seizure disorder which caused loss of consciousness. The affidavit concluded, based upon independent research, including a review of decedent's medical records, consultation with a neurologist, a neuropathologist, and a family practitioner, that decedent "took an unreasonable risk by driving his vehicle knowing he suffered from a seizure disorder which caused a loss of consciousness. It was certainly foreseeable that an accident might occur if [decedent] experienced a seizure while driving his vehicle."

The trial court granted defendant's motion for summary judgment. In a divided decision, the Court of Appeals affirmed. The majority of the court reasoned that the case fell within the "established principles in this state that an automobile accident resulting from an unavoidable sudden emergency, such as an epileptic seizure, negates negligence." Summary judgment was appropriate, the majority concluded, based upon the affidavit filed by defendant which established that the accident was caused by the seizure. Additionally, the majority rejected the affidavit filed by plaintiff as a legal conclusion insufficient to establish a material issue of fact.

The dissenting judge, Judge Crawford, concluded that the affidavit filed by defendant likewise contained a legal, rather than medical, opinion pertaining to the cause of the accident. The dissent viewed the issue in the case as "whether the driver acted unreasonably in that he should have foreseen the accident." Accordingly, the dissent concluded that summary judgment should have been reversed and the matter remanded for trial.

We granted plaintiff's application for permission to appeal to address the question of whether, and under what circumstances, liability may be imposed upon the driver of a car who suddenly loses control because the driver is rendered physically incapacitated by a medical disorder known to the driver.

II. Background

A. Principles related to Summary Judgment

Since this case is before the Court on the trial court's grant of summary judgment, we are guided by well-established legal principles. We must review the record without attaching any presumption of correctness to the trial court's judgment to determine whether the absence of genuine issues of material facts entitle the movant to judgment as a matter of law. In reviewing the record, we must view the evidence in the light most favorable to the non-moving party drawing all inferences in that party's favor. If the facts and conclusions permit a reasonable person to reach only one conclusion, summary judgment should be granted.

B. Principles related to Negligence

Guided by these well-established principles, we turn to the controlling substantive law of negligence. A claim of negligence requires proof of the following elements: (1) a duty of care owed by defendant to plaintiff; (2) conduct below the applicable standard of care that amounts to a breach of that duty; (3) an injury or loss; (4) cause in fact; and (5) proximate, or legal, cause. Our resolution of this case focuses on the first two elements: duty of care and breach.

. . .

Once it is determined that defendant owed plaintiff a legal obligation to conform to a reasonable person standard of conduct, i.e., a duty — the question becomes whether defendant failed to exercise reasonable care under the circumstances, i.e., whether defendant breached the duty. "What the defendant must do, or must not do, is a question of the standard of conduct required to satisfy the duty." *Prosser and Keeton on the Law of Torts, supra,* at § 356.

In a negligence action, the standard of conduct is always the same. It is a standard of reasonable care in light of the apparent risk. *Id. See also Pittman v. Upjohn Co.,* 890 S.W.2d at 428 ("As in all cases, there is a duty to exercise reasonable care under the circumstances."); *Bradshaw v. Daniel,* 854 S.W.2d at 870 ("All persons have a duty to use reasonable care to refrain from conduct that will foreseeably cause injury to others."). If defendant does not exercise reasonable care, defendant has breached the duty. *Doe v. Linder Const. Co., Inc.,* 845 S.W.2d 173, 178 (Tenn.1992).

C. Negligence in Physical Incapacity Circumstances

Perhaps surprisingly, this Court has not previously dealt with the liability of one who suddenly loses consciousness or control from a known medical disorder while driving. The Court of Appeals has faced the issue, but in only a limited number of cases, many of which are unpublished. In the earliest case, *Wishone v. Yellow Cab Co.,* 20 Tenn.App. 229, 97 S.W.2d 452, *cert. denied,* (Tenn.1936), a passenger in a taxicab was injured when the driver suddenly, and without warning, suffered an epileptic seizure. The driver had been experiencing such attacks, which caused unconsciousness, for several years prior to the accident. *Wishone v. Yellow Cab Co.,* 97 S.W.2d at 453. With little analysis, the Court of Appeals merely concluded that "there was no negligence immediately connected with the accident." *Id.*

In the only other relevant reported Tennessee decision, *Robinson v. Moore,* 512 S.W.2d 573 (Tenn.App.), *cert. denied,* (Tenn.1974), a bus driver, who had slipped into a diabetic coma, ran a red light and caused an accident, The Court of Appeals found in favor of the employer and noted that the driver had been driving the bus for twenty-one years, had received numerous driving safety awards, and had never experienced a sudden blackout, although he knew he had diabetes and was receiving treatment for it. *Robinson v. Moore,* 512 S.W.2d at 577. Additionally, the court focused on the absence of medical proof finding that plaintiff "adduced no medical testimony to the effect that the physical diseased condition of [defendant] rendered [defendant] incompetent [to drive.]" *Id.* at 578.

The unreported cases focus similarly on the substance of the medical evidence. In one, a driver experienced an epileptic seizure while driving. Though he knew he had epilepsy, the driver was under a physician's care, faithfully took his medication, had not had a seizure in the last two and one-half years, and had been advised by his physician that there was no reason to refrain from driving. A finding of no liability was affirmed.

In another case involving an accident caused by an epileptic seizure, the injured plaintiff relied on the fact that defendant had not taken her prescribed medication and had not asked her physician what the effect might be. Nonetheless, the judgment for plaintiff was reversed because plaintiff had not established that defendant's failure to take her medication had caused plaintiff's damages nor that defendant's driving with the epileptic condition was an unreasonable risk.

The court deemed the absence of medical testimony establishing a foreseeable risk of danger by driving as critical because of the impossibility of evaluating the reasonableness of the risk without a medical evaluation of the severity of the condition, the effectiveness of the medication, and the likelihood of seizures with or without medication.

Our case law, as reflected in these few opinions, is generally consistent with the approach of other jurisdictions faced with similar situations. The generally accepted approach is to accept as a defense the sudden loss of physical capacity or consciousness while driving provided that the loss of capacity or consciousness was unforeseeable.

The rule recognized by th[e] cases has been succinctly summarized as follows:

> The operator of a motor vehicle is not ordinarily chargeable with negligence because he becomes suddenly stricken by a fainting spell or loses consciousness from an unforeseen cause, and is unable to control the vehicle. In other words, fainting or momentary loss of consciousness while driving is a complete defense to an action based on negligence if such loss of consciousness was not foreseeable.
>
> . . .
>
> If the operator of a motor vehicle knows that he [or she] is subject to attacks in the course of which he [or she] is likely to lose consciousness, such a loss of consciousness does not constitute a defense in an action brought by a person injured as a result of the operator's conduct.

7A Am.Jur.2d *Automobiles and Highway Traffic,* § 773 (1980). *See also* Travers, Annotation, *Liability for Automobile Accident Allegedly Caused By Driver's Blackout, Sudden Unconsciousness, or the Like,* 93 A.L.R.3d 326 (1979) ("[C]ases decided under negligence theories have uniformly held that a sudden loss of consciousness while driving is a complete defense to an action based on negligence . . . if such loss of consciousness was not foreseeable."). The rule covers accidents caused by, among other incapacitating events, actual loss of consciousness, dizziness, temporary loss of vision, stroke, heart attack, or seizure.

The key to establishing the physical capacity or loss of consciousness defense is foreseeability. Consequently, the defense would be inappropriate if the driver was aware of facts sufficient to cause a reasonably prudent person to anticipate that his or her driving might likely lead to an accident. Courts differ, however, in the strictness of the approach. For example, some courts hold that any driver suffering from a medical disorder capable of producing a seizure or unconsciousness is liable, as a matter of law, for driving at all. Other courts recognize that such knowledge creates a question for the jury as to whether there was a breach of the standard of care. Still other courts hold that the mere knowledge of past incapacitating medical episodes or a history of an incapacitating medical condition is insufficient notice to warrant a finding of negligence. These courts often require symptoms on the day of or immediately before the accident.

III. Rule Established in Physical Incapacitation Cases

Our careful consideration of the jurisprudence of other jurisdictions and our own leads us to adopt the following rule: A sudden loss of consciousness or physical capacity experienced while driving which is not reasonably foreseeable is a defense to a negligence action. To constitute a defense, defendant must establish that the sudden loss of consciousness or physical capacity to control the vehicle was not reasonably foreseeable to a prudent person. As a result, the defense is not available under circumstances in which defendant was made aware of facts sufficient to lead a reasonably prudent person to anticipate that driving in that condition would likely result in an accident.

In determining whether the loss of capacity or consciousness was foreseeable, pertinent, nonexclusive considerations would include: the extent of the driver's awareness or knowledge of the condition that caused the sudden incapacity; whether the driver had sought medical advice or was under a physician's care for the condition when the accident occurred; whether the driver had been prescribed, and had taken, medication for the condition; whether a sudden incapacity had previously occurred while driving; the number, frequency, extent, and duration of incapacitating episodes prior to the accident while driving and otherwise; the temporal relationship of the prior incapacitating episodes to the accident; a physician's guidance or advice regarding driving to the driver, if any; and medical opinions regarding the nature of the driver's condition, adherence to treatment, foreseeability of the incapacitation, and potential advance warnings which the driver would have experienced immediately prior to the accident. These factors, and any other relevant ones under the circumstances, would tend to establish whether the duty to exercise reasonable care was breached.

We agree with the Court of Appeals' reluctance to adopt a rule that would exclude individuals who had once suffered an incapacitating episode from ever driving again. Nonetheless, we can envision without much difficulty situations in which driving at all might constitute negligence. One who is ill or incapacitated at times may be negligent in driving at all when he or she is aware that a sudden incapacitation could likely occur at any moment. *Restatement (Second) of Torts,* § 283C, comment c (1965).

2. "[A]n automobile driver who suddenly and quite unexpectedly suffers a heart attack does not become negligent when [the driver] loses control of [the] car and drives it in a manner which would otherwise be unreasonable; but one who knows that he [or she] is subject to such attacks may be negligent in driving at all." *Restatement of Torts,* § 283C, comment c (1965).

IV. Application of Rule to Facts in Present Case

Here, plaintiff contends that disputed issues of material fact exist as to whether decedent took an unreasonable risk by driving knowing that he suffered from a seizure disorder which caused loss of consciousness, and whether it was reasonably foreseeable that an accident might occur in the event he experienced a seizure while driving. In addition to the affidavit filed by plaintiff,

plaintiff relies on two stipulated facts. First, plaintiff relies on the fact that decedent suffered seizures prior to the date of the accident. Second, plaintiff relies on the fact that decedent was aware that he suffered seizure disorders that caused, at times, a loss of consciousness.

Conversely, defendant contends that the fact that the accident was caused by a suddenly occurring disability negates liability as a matter of law. Specifically it is defendant's contention that the record contains no facts from which a reasonable juror could find negligence. There is no evidence that decedent was prescribed medication or that he failed to follow a physician's recommendations. Further, there is no evidence of decedent's history or frequency of incapacitation and whether any debilitating episodes had occurred while he was driving.

In light of the stipulated facts that decedent had suffered seizures prior to the accident and was aware of the medical condition causing unconsciousness, we have no difficulty concluding that a jury could find that an accident with resulting injury to others was reasonably foreseeable. Even without the stipulated facts, decedent, under the law of this state, would owe a duty to act reasonably in light of the inherent dangers associated with driving. Unquestionably, decedent owed plaintiff a duty to act as a reasonably prudent person would act in light of the inherent dangers associated with driving and exacerbated by his known incapacitating medical condition.

Our second inquiry is whether the duty of reasonable care was breached. We are persuaded that defendant's argument that liability is negated as a matter of law sweeps too broadly and is inconsistent with the weight of authority from other jurisdictions. Additionally, defendant's assertion that he is entitled to summary judgment because plaintiff did not establish facts from which the jury could find negligence is equally unpersuasive. To survive the summary judgment motion filed by defendant, plaintiff was obliged to demonstrate that reasonable persons might draw differing conclusions from the facts. Plaintiff was not required to prove her case by a preponderance of the evidence in order to successfully counter defendant's summary judgment motion. Viewing the evidence in a light most favorable to plaintiff, and drawing all reasonable inferences in her behalf, as we must, we conclude that reasonable jurors could reach different conclusions as to whether decedent was acting as a reasonably prudent person in driving at the time the accident occurred.

We base our holding not only on the stipulated facts, but also on the affidavit filed by plaintiff in which the physician opined that defendant took an unreasonable risk in driving. We recognize the very good argument that this medical opinion offered on foreseeability is actually a legal conclusion. Nonetheless, we think it is also correctly viewed as a medical opinion given by one uniquely qualified to evaluate the effect of a brain tumor on one's abilities to safely operate a vehicle. Additionally, this issue of foreseeability, recognized initially in this opinion as the key to the duty issue, is generally a question of fact for the jury, unless no reasonable person could dispute the only reasonable outcome. This is not a case where all reasonable minds are compelled to reach one conclusion on the crucial issue of foreseeability.

Finally, defendant's reliance on the sudden emergency doctrine is misplaced. The sudden emergency doctrine, which has now been subsumed into Tennessee's comparative fault scheme, *Eaton v. McLain,* 891 S.W.2d 587, 592 (Tenn.1995), recognizes that a person confronted with a sudden or unexpected emergency which calls for immediate action is not expected to exercise the same accuracy of judgment as one acting under normal circumstances who has time for reflection and thought before acting.

3. "[T]he basis of the rule is merely that the actor is left no time for adequate thought, or is reasonably so disturbed or excited that the actor cannot weigh alternative courses of action, and must make a speedy decision, based very largely upon impulse or guess. Under such circumstances, the actor cannot reasonably be held to the same accuracy of judgment or conduct as one who has had the full opportunity to reflect, even though it later appears that the actor made the wrong decision, one which no reasonable person could possible have made after due deliberation." *Prosser and Keeton on the Law of Torts,* § 196.

The doctrine no longer constitutes a defense as a matter of law but, if at issue, must be considered as a factor in the total comparative fault analysis. Accordingly, the doctrine of sudden emergency does not negate defendant's liability in the case before us as a matter of law.

Therefore, summary judgment was improper. For these reasons, the judgment of the Court below granting and affirming summary judgment for defendant is vacated. The case is remanded to the trial court for proceedings consistent with this opinion. Costs are taxed to defendant.

ANDERSON, C.J., and DROWOTA, REID and BIRCH, JJ., concur.

Notes and Questions

1. The standard of care is the reasonably prudent person in the circumstances. Explain how the *McCall* court's holding fits squarely within this standard, including in both its objective and quasi-subjective or "flexible" aspects.

2. How is foreseeability relevant to the standard of care in general and as applied to the rule from *McCall*?

3. What is the sudden emergency doctrine? Explain how it fits squarely within the reasonable person standard.

4. What work does the qualifier "sudden" do in the "sudden emergency doctrine"? Think of different scenarios that might develop in a pandemic like Covid — which would be "emergencies" and which would be "sudden emergencies"?

5. Describe *McCall*'s procedural history. Why was the defendant's motion for summary judgment granted by the trial court and affirmed by the intermediate appellate court? Why were these courts overruled by the Tennessee Supreme Court?

B. Children

PETERSON v. TAYLOR
316 N.W.2d 869 (Iowa 1982)

An unfortunate combination of gasoline, matches and a seven-year-old boy resulted in the lawsuit which underlies this appeal. Badly burned as a result of his experimentation with fire, the minor plaintiff David Peterson, by his mother as next friend, brought a negligence suit against his neighbors, the Taylors, from whose storage shed he obtained the gasoline. The jury returned a verdict for the defendants, and plaintiff appeals.

Evidence at trial showed that the Taylors and the Petersons lived on neighboring small acreages just outside the Des Moines city limits and that David Peterson frequently played with the Taylors' son Greg. On Sunday, August 7, 1977, David and his three-year-old sister Molly stopped at the Taylor place on their way home from another neighbor's house. Finding no one home, David decided to gather some twigs and build a fire on a concrete slab in the Taylors' back yard, using some matches he had taken from his uncle's car earlier that day. When the wind blew that fire out, David "got mad." He then went to the Taylors' storage shed, removed a can of gasoline, opened it, smelled it to confirm that it was gasoline, threw a lighted match into it and stood back to watch the fire come out of the can. When that fire appeared to have died out, he went to the shed, removed a second can of gasoline, and accidentally spilled some of it on his pants. Then he dropped the second can and either lit another match or knocked over the first can which was still flaming inside; in any event, David's gasoline-soaked pants somehow became ignited, and he rolled on the ground to put out the fire. As a result of the incident, David received serious burns on the lower half of his body and superficial burns on portions of the upper half.

The shed from which David removed the gasoline cans was a small brick building with a single wooden door, held shut by a sliding bolt located approximately fifty-seven inches above the ground. When David approached the shed on August 7, the door was bolted as usual, and he stood on his "tippy-toes" to unlatch it. Although David had never been in the shed prior to the day of his injury, he knew the Taylors stored cans of gasoline there.

David also testified that he had been told not to go onto the Taylors' property when they weren't home, and that he knew the Taylors would not have allowed him to enter the shed had they been present. He knew that gasoline would burn and might even explode when ignited with a match. When he put the match into the first gasoline can, he thought about the possibility that he would be burned. His mother testified that David had previously been caught playing with fire on a few other occasions and had been punished and sternly warned about the dangers involved.

Plaintiff presented expert testimony to the effect that David was of average intelligence, that he was mildly hyperactive, and that hyperactive children tend to be somewhat more attracted to playing with fire than other children. The expert also testified that a child having David's characteristics probably would not realize the full extent of the danger involved in playing with matches and gasoline; for instance, he probably would not realize that a gasoline fire cannot be put out with water. The same expert did testify, however, that such a child "would certainly know that he'd get burned" if he played with gasoline and matches.

On appeal, plaintiff presents for our review questions concerning the sufficiency of the evidence of his contributory negligence, the adequacy of the jury instructions, and the denial of a motion to amend his petition. We turn now to those issues.

I. Contributory Negligence

A. Sufficiency of Evidence

Plaintiff's first argument on appeal is that trial court erred in submitting the question of David's contributory negligence to the jury. He contends that defendants failed to present sufficient evidence to rebut the presumption that a child under the age of fourteen is incapable of contributory negligence. In response to that contention, defendants assert as an initial matter that the presumption referred to by plaintiff is no longer an appropriate part of Iowa negligence law. We agree.

In Doggett v. Chicago, Burlington & Quincy Railway, 134 Iowa 690, 696–97, 112 N.W. 171, 173 (1907), this court adopted a presumption that children under the age of fourteen are incapable of contributory negligence, the presumption being conclusive for children under seven and rebuttable for those between seven and fourteen. A defendant could overcome the rebuttable presumption by showing that the child plaintiff failed to "exercis[e] such care to avoid danger as may fairly and reasonably be expected from persons of [his] age and capacity." Id. at 697, 112 N.W. at 173. Although some later cases applied a rebuttable rather than a conclusive presumption to children under seven, the rule regarding children between seven and fourteen appears to have remained unchanged since Doggett.

The presumptions adopted in Doggett were expressly based upon an analogy to rules regarding the age at which criminal responsibility attaches. 134 Iowa at 695, 112 N.W. at 172. That analogy, however, has come under a good deal of criticism, such as the following:

> Some courts have attempted to fix a minimum age, below which the child is held to be incapable of all negligence. Although other limits have been set, those most commonly accepted are taken over from the arbitrary rules of the criminal law, as to the age at which children are capable of crime. Below the age of seven, the child is arbitrarily held to be incapable of any negligence; between seven and fourteen he is presumed to be incapable, but may be shown to be capable; from fourteen to twenty-one he is presumed to be capable, but the contrary may be shown. These multiples of seven are derived originally from the Bible, which is a poor reason for such arbitrary limits; and the analogy of the criminal law is certainly of dubious value where neither crime nor intent is in question.

W. Prosser, Handbook of the Law of Torts 155–56 (4th ed. 1971) (footnotes omitted). See also 2 F. Harper & F. James, The Law of Torts § 16.8, at 926 (1956).

We further observe that the presumptions based on age became a part of our law at a time when the plaintiff in a negligence suit had the burden of pleading and proving his freedom from contributory negligence. By legislative enactment in 1965, however, the burden of pleading and proving contributory negligence, if any, was assigned to the defendant. 61st G.A., ch. 430, § 1 (1965); see § 619.17, The Code 1981. As a result, the rebuttable presumption of a child's incapacity for contributory negligence no longer serves any useful purpose, because the defendant has the burden of proving the child's capacity by a preponderance of the evidence in any event. Cf. Froman v. Perrin, 213 N.W.2d 684, 686–88 (Iowa 1973) (abrogating rule that in absence of eyewitness, plaintiff was rebuttably presumed to be free of contributory negligence; aid of presumption no longer necessary now that defendant has burden of proof on issue of plaintiff's contributory negligence). When a rebuttable presumption operates against the party which already bears the burden of proof, instructing on the presumption serves only to confuse the jury and may cause it to "subjectively . . . require a stronger preponderance than in a case where no presumption was present." Note, Presumptions in Iowa, 44 Iowa L.Rev. 147, 160 (1958). See also E. Cleary, McCormick's Handbook of the Law of Evidence § 346, at 829 (2d ed. 1972).

Finally, we note that the majority of courts have rejected the arbitrary presumptions of incapacity for contributory negligence based on a child's age. The trend is to view the question of a child's capacity for negligence as an issue of fact. Under this approach, a particular child's incapacity for negligence may be determined by the court as a matter of law only if the child is so young or the evidence of incapacity so overwhelming that reasonable minds could not differ on that issue. If reasonable minds could differ, the question of the child's contributory negligence is submitted to the jury with instructions to apply a standard of care similar to that set forth in § 283A of the Restatement, supra:

> If the actor is a child, the standard of conduct to which he must conform to avoid being negligent is that of a reasonable person of like age, intelligence, and experience under like circumstances.

In applying this standard, the jury must initially make a subjective determination of the particular child's capacity to perceive and avoid the specific risk involved, based on evidence of his age, intelligence and experience.

We have articulated a standard of care for children similar to that in the Restatement, see, e.g., Ruby v. Easton, 207 N.W.2d 10, 20 (Iowa 1973) ("standard of reasonable behavior of children of similar age, intelligence and experience"); Rosenau, 199 N.W.2d at 129 (same); however, that standard has been applied in conjunction with presumptions of incapacity where the child was below the age of fourteen. See, e.g., Webster, 219 Iowa at 1056, 258 N.W. at 689; Brekke, 196 Iowa at 1296–97, 196 N.W. at 88. We now bring Iowa in line with the majority position by holding that we no longer recognize any presumptions regarding the capacity of children for negligence or contributory negligence; rather, the question of a particular child's capacity is an issue of fact to be determined on the basis of evidence of the child's age, intelligence and experience, as outlined in the preceding paragraph. This holding shall be applicable to all actions in which a final judgment has not been entered on the date of the filing of this opinion, and to adjudicated cases in which error was preserved and the time for appeal has not expired.

Having established the appropriate legal framework, we return to plaintiff's contention that there was insufficient evidence for the issue of his contributory negligence to be submitted to the jury. Plaintiff argues that defendants had the burden of establishing the appropriate standard of care by which David's actions should be judged, and that they failed to meet that burden as a matter of law. Specifically, he asserts that evidence at trial showed David was generally a normal seven-year-old child, and that defendants presented no evidence that a normal seven-year-old child would have acted differently than David did. Therefore, it is argued, there was no evidence from which the jury could find that David did not exercise that degree of care which may be expected of a seven-year-old child. We believe this argument reflects a basic misunderstanding concerning the evidentiary showing which must be made in regard to the standard of care for children.

In applying the standard of care, as noted above, the jury's first inquiry is a subjective one: What was the capacity of this particular child — given what the evidence shows about his age, intelligence and experience — to perceive and avoid the particular risk involved in this case? Once this has been determined, the focus becomes objective: How would a reasonable child of like capacity have acted under similar circumstances? The particular child in question can be found negligent only if his actions fall short of what may reasonably be expected of children of similar capacity. See 2 F. Harper & F. James, supra, § 16.8, at 924–25; Shulman, The Standard of Care Required of Children, 37 Yale L. J. 618, 625 (1928).

Regarding the subjective inquiry, there must be evidence adduced at trial concerning the child's age, intelligence and experience so that the jury may determine the child's capacity, if any, to perceive and avoid the risk. We find there was ample evidence of that nature in this case, and the evidence was not such that David could be found incapable of contributory negligence as a matter of law. Plaintiff appears to complain, however, that no witness testified that a reasonable child of like capacity would not have acted as plaintiff did in this case. We hold that such testimony need not, and indeed may not, be presented. Determining how a reasonable person would have acted under the circumstances is clearly the function of the jury. The "reasonable child" inquiry differs from the "reasonable man" inquiry only in that the "circumstances" in the former case are broadened to include consideration of the child's age, intelligence and experience. In neither case should a witness, expert or otherwise, be permitted to express an opinion on what a reasonable person would have done in a similar situation, because such testimony would be tantamount to an opinion on whether the person in question was negligent.

We conclude that there was sufficient evidence for trial court to submit the question of David's contributory negligence to the jury.

. . .

Having found no merit in any of plaintiff's assignments of error, we affirm trial court's judgment.

AFFIRMED.

HARRY SHULMAN
THE STANDARD OF CARE REQUIRED OF CHILDREN
37 Yale L.J. 618 (1928)

It is undoubtedly true that the law of torts does not generally hold children to the exercise of the same degree of care and intelligence that it requires of adults. To do otherwise, would be to shut its eyes, ostrich-like, to the facts of life and to burden unduly the child's growth to majority. Similar concessions to immaturity are made in other branches of the law. The same realism, however, necessitates the recognition of the fact that at some age prior to twenty-one, and in some situations, a minor is fully as competent as a person over twenty-one and should be held to the same standard of conduct.

There are very few cases in which the problem is raised in an issue of direct negligence for which the infant is sought to be held liable. Most of the cases discussing the problem are concerned with the child's alleged contributory negligence, or assumption of risk or some other disabling contributory fault. In many cases where the child's conduct is considered, the only issue relates to the negligence of the defendant, and the infant's conduct is important only in determining whether or not the defendant discharged his duty of reasonable care under the circumstances.[3]

The standard of conduct to which an infant is to be held when his own liability is in question may properly be quite different from that to which he is to be held when he seeks to recover from an admittedly negligent defendant.[4] It is apparent that different considerations may be involved in these several types of cases. There is a strong policy in favor of protecting children from losses attributable to their immaturity. It would be quite plausible, therefore, for a court to be more lenient toward children whose injuries are attributable, not only to their immaturity, but also to conceded tortious conduct on the part of the defendant, than toward children who are the sole responsible causes of injury to others. Yet the cases do not enter into niceties. The opinions are replete with loose language, sometimes altogether unnecessary, sometimes equivocal, sometimes incomplete, and sometimes even contradictory of statements in the very same opinion. A law review editor has recently concluded that, for the purpose of determining contributory negligence, "the acts of a child are tested by the individual capacity of the child himself. . . . [The standard] is subjective, depending entirely upon the individual capacity of the child."

---

[3] It is obvious that an actor is required to be more careful when his conduct is likely to endanger children than when it is likely to endanger only adults. In general, unless a defendant has reason to know otherwise, he is entitled to assume that persons and things will react as they are commonly supposed to react under the circumstances. Children do generally exercise a lesser caution for their own safety than do adults. Since this is common knowledge, a defendant is not only entitled to assume it, but he is charged with the knowledge of it, and must act with a view to it. In determining a defendant's negligence toward a child, it may, therefore, become important to ascertain whether or not the defendant should have foreseen a particular kind of conduct on the part of the child.

[4] This may be true in the case of adults as well as in the case of children. Accepting the doctrine of contributory negligence, it does not at all necessarily follow that the care used by *X* to prevent injury to others, or his duty to perceive the possibility of, and provide against, injury to others is to be measured by the same standard as that employed to measure the care that *X* used to prevent injury to himself or his duty to foresee, and provide against, injury to himself by an admittedly negligent person.

It will be shown that such statements are not entirely true. There is some objective standard even in the case of children.

There are cases in which it is said that the care required of children is that care which is ordinarily exercised under similar circumstances by children of the same age. But it is apparent that such statements are not intended to be complete and that age is not the only individualized quality even in those cases.

Judicial opinion is overwhelmingly to this effect. Thus: "the sounder doctrine seems to be that age is an important but not decisive factor" "It is the capacity, not the age of an infant that is the criterion. . . ." "The average child of its own age is not the standard by which to measure its legal diligence. . . ." "Age is of no significance except as a mark of capacity." "Age is not the true test in such cases." Most of the plethora of cases on this point, . . . individualize some other qualities in addition to age. In one case or another, the courts have named, in diverse combinations the following qualities which are to be individualized: age, ability, alertness, appreciation, capability, capacity, comprehension, discernment, discretion, development, education, experience, intelligence, judgment, knowledge, maturity, reason, sex, understanding. Age is included in all the combinations. Usually the combination consists of three qualities; and the combination, — age, intelligence and experience is the most frequent one.

If a child is unusually intelligent, or experienced, or well informed for one of his age, he is held to the exercise of greater caution than the ordinary child with the intelligence, experience, and knowledge common to that age. The quality of his conduct must be commensurate with his superiority. Many of the cases found really go no further than that (though their language is general to the effect that the qualities of intelligence, experience and knowledge are always to be individualized in the case of children). An increase in the requirements on the ground of superiority does not, however, negative the existence of a minimum standard to which children must conform. Nor is the principle peculiar to cases of infants. If an adult has greater knowledge or experience than an ordinary person in his position would have, he is required to exercise that greater knowledge and experience. Instances of superiority are not important in determining a minimum standard.

Deficiencies of a particular individual are, however, of primary importance. On the whole, adults cannot defend imputations of negligence on the ground that in mental capacity, experience or knowledge they fall below the standard of the reasonable man. In the case of infants, on the contrary, deficiencies in mental capacity, experience or knowledge are to be considered in determining whether or not their conduct is negligent. Thus, the Delaware court has stated that the ordinary rule "is to be modified according to the maturity and capacity of the infant, his ability to understand and appreciate the danger and his familiarity with all the surroundings. . . . While a particular act committed by an infant of discerning age might clearly constitute contributory negligence, yet, if the same act should be committed by an infant of less discernment, it might not constitute contributory negligence."

So also, an Arkansas court held that where there was testimony to the effect that the plaintiff (16 years old) "was of inferior intelligence . . . was not bright and did not have good understanding," the jury should have been instructed to consider the plaintiff's "intelligence" and "capacity." Similar holdings are implicit in cases which refuse to make allowances for backwardness in the particular child on the ground that there was no evidence, or insufficient evidence, of such backwardness. The burden of raising the issue of, and proving, backwardness is on the child. If no claim of inferiority is made it is properly presumed that the child has the intelligence and experience common to children of its age.

With all the above-named qualities individualized, even if they are not mutually exclusive, it is difficult to see what is left for standardization. The mere fact that there is such a great diversity of expression and so much periphrasis on this point is sufficient evidence to raise a strong doubt as to the existence of a standard.

Yet there seems to be some standardization. No court ever says that a child is to be held to the measure of care which the particular child in question ordinarily exercises. On the contrary, the courts always state the measure with some objectivity. The usual statement is that a child is held to the exercise of the degree of care which ordinary children of his age, intelligence and experience (or whatever combination is used) ordinarily exercise under similar circumstances. Sometimes it is the care which is reasonably to be expected of children of his age, experience and intelligence. . . . In the words of the Maine court, "The standard is the conduct of boys who are ordinarily careful." . . .

It cannot fairly be said that this persistence in expression is mere logomachy, or that such statements are euphemisms for expressions like "the care which this particular child ordinarily exercises." If a child has the capacity to appreciate danger and is sufficiently experienced to avoid it, but is regularly more reckless or daring than ordinary children of his age, intelligence and experience, he will be held to the standard of conduct established by such ordinary children rather than by his own usually reckless conduct. Evidence of particular trends towards recklessness and impetuosity on the part of a particular child is not admissible on an issue of his contributory negligence.

. . .

Is there, then, any objective standard with which an infant's conduct must be compared? As to liability-creating conduct a conclusion cannot here be drawn. But as to contributory fault, at least, there is sufficient data for a conclusion. The mental capacity, the knowledge and experience of the particular child, are to be taken in consideration in each case. These qualities are individualized — subjective — but only for the purpose of determining whether or not the child was capable of perceiving the risk of injury to himself and of avoiding the danger. Beyond that, there is an objective standard. In determining whether or not his conduct was proper in view of his intelligence, knowledge and experience, his conduct is to be compared with that of the careful and prudent child of similar qualities. Just as in the case of adults, one of the qualities of the standard "reasonable man" is consistent carefulness or prudence, so in the case of infants, the element of prudence is standardized. A definition of the term will not be attempted. In this connection, at least, prudence does connote a certain selfishness — a proper regard for one's own safety. It includes more. It conveys an idea of proper evaluation of interests, of proper choice of conduct. At any rate, it is a conveniently vague term to admit of adjustment to particular situations in a field of law where certainty in advance is not all-important.

Notes and Questions

1. What is the standard of care in negligence for children? In particular, what are its objective and subjective components?

2. Why did it make sense to move away from the old "Rule of 7s" to this partly-objective, partly-subjective standard of care?

3. The child standard of care is typically justified on fairness and welfare grounds. Why is it unfair to hold children to the adult standard of care? As you consider this question, review a summary of typical human brain development, for example, The Child's Developing Brain, The New York Times, Sept. 15, 2008, available at http://www.nytimes.com/interactive/2008/09/15/health/20080915-brain-development.html. These facts of human biology aside, does the fairness rationale make sense in a legal scheme that otherwise makes no allowances for mental deficiencies? That is, why should it matter that a defendant is a child or an adult? The welfare rationale provides that it is in everyone's (society's) interests that children are given a legal "bye" corresponding with their age, intelligence, and experience. Is this right? What is the argument that this interest outweighs society's interest in providing compensation to tort victims? Related to this welfare rationale is the idea that children are adults in training and that training necessarily involves trial and error. Does this additional explanation help to support the welfare rationale?

NEUMANN v. SHLANSKY
294 N.Y.S.2d 628 (Westchester County Court 1968)

JOHN C. MARBACH, Justice.

Defendant moves to set aside the verdict and for a new trial on the grounds that the verdict was contrary to the law of the case since the charge given by me, as trial judge, was erroneous as a matter of law.

The question presented here is, as far as can be determined, a case of first impression not only in this state but also in the nation. The issue is the standard of care which must be exercised by an eleven year old infant defendant when he is playing golf.

The facts are relatively simple and may be summarized as follows: Defendant, an 11 year old boy was playing in a foursome at the Harrison Country Club with his mother, and two other adults. The infant defendant was on the tee of a par three hole of about 170 yards. Plaintiff had just left the green on the par 3 hole and was crossing a foot bridge, which his caddy was about to cross, about 150–160 yards from the tee in plain view of the tee when he was hit in the knee by the ball driven from the tee by the infant defendant. The infant testified that he saw the plaintiff before he hit. There was testimony that indicated that infant had yelled 'fore', the traditional warning given on the golf course when a golfer sees that someone may be hit by a golf ball. Plaintiff testified he did not hear the warning. There was further testimony which indicated that the infant was a boy who had been playing golf two to three times a week during the season for the past two years. It was apparent on the trial from the shot hit by the infant that he had at least some proficiency in hitting the golf ball.

The Court charged the jury that the infant in this case was to be held to the standard of care of an adult and not to the usual standard of care of a child. The jury returned with a verdict for the plaintiff.

At the outset it should be established that a golfer owes a duty to use reasonable care to avoid injuring other players on the golf course. Furthermore, a golf ball is a dangerous missile which can cause serious injury if it hits someone while in flight. Povanda v. Powers, 152 Misc. 75, 272 N.Y.S. 619 (Sup.Ct.N.Y.County 1934). See also Ratcliffe v. Whitehead, 3 West Week.Rep. 447, Manitoba, 1933, where the Court stated that in some ways hitting a golf ball can be more dangerous than firing a gun or throwing a stone since one is likely to have more control over the direction of a gunshot or a thrown stone than a golf ball. The ordinary rules of negligence apply to games and in playing of games as in other transactions in life a person must exercise reasonable care. It is for this Court to determine based upon all the factors involved whether this infant defendant while he was on the golf course is to be held to the standard of care of the reasonably prudent infant or the reasonably prudent man.

This Court holds that this infant should be held to the standard of care of the reasonable man. This raises several questions and the Court will proceed to discuss the relevant considerations.

I

The mere fact that there is lack of precedent on this question is not controlling since the real issue is not whether there is precedent for this type of a situation but whether the defendant should be held liable for the wrong inflicted on the plaintiff. Courts sometimes are called upon to sustain a recovery upon legal principles clearly applicable to a new set of facts although there is no direct precedent for it. The law is not static. It must adapt and change as new situations dictate. If a court were to refuse to consider novel questions it would be shirking its responsibilities to itself, to the Bar and above all to the administration of justice.

II

The ancient and honorable game of golf has been with us since around 1100. It is only within the last few decades that it has evolved into a game which is either played or played at by some eight million people throughout the world. The pastime that was at one time 'indulged in by only kings and the nobility' Gleason v. Hillcrest Golf Course, Inc., 148 Misc. 246 at p. 248, 265 N.Y.S. 886 at p. 889, and was described by Andrew Carnegie as an 'indispensable adjunct of high civilization'. (The Complete Golfer, edited by Herbert Warren Wind, Simon and Schuster, New York, 1954 at XVI of Preface), has now become a game which is played by people of all classes from all walks of life. Hand in hand with the increasing popularity of the sport has been a rise in the number and type of accidents occurring on the golf course. One of the most common accidents results when one of the participants, or a person in the gallery is struck by an errant golf ball projected from the club of a competitor who never dreamed he or she would ever hit anyone with that shot.

All golfers assume the ordinary risks incident to the game when they venture onto the course. This is inherent in a game which has few players able to accurately and consistently control the flight of a golf ball. Indeed, as Judge Lauer indicates in Povanda v. Powers, supra, 152 Misc. at p. 78, 272 N.Y.S. at p. 622, it is this very uncertainty which makes golf intriguing and which undoubtedly has contributed greatly to its phenomenal growth. A competitor or for that matter a member of the gallery does not, however, assume the risk of someone's negligent conduct while on the golf course. While the rule is sometimes loosely stated that a person who hits a golf ball must give timely and adequate warning to any persons in the general direction of his drive, that rule applies only to shots initially played under non-negligent circumstances. The shouting of 'fore' does not exculpate careless or reckless conduct. All persons on the golf course have a right to rely on the players' adherence to a standard of care, based upon the avoidance of reasonably foreseeable risks. All courts would hold every adult to the standard of the reasonably prudent man under all the circumstances. Our inquiry here is directed solely to the question of whether it is reasonable to hold this defendant infant to the same standard of care.

III

An infant may be held civilly liable for damages occasioned by his tortious acts. The general rule is that, if the actor is a child, the standard of conduct to which he must conform to avoid being negligent is that of a reasonable person of like age, intelligence and experience under the like circumstances. Restatement of Torts Second s 283–A. The theory behind the general rule is that there is a general interest in the welfare and protection of infants and if a question of the infant's liability arises the Courts can draw upon a wealth of community experience from which it is possible to determine what standard the infant should be held to in a particular situation. It has been recognized that the standards of conduct which apply to infants when his own liability is in question may be different from that to which he is to be held when he seeks to recover from an admittedly negligent defendant. Stated another way he may be held to a higher standard when he actively exposes others to hazards than when he is protecting himself against hazards. While most of the cases, such as all those cited by the defendant, referring to infant's standard of care are questions of the infant's contributory negligence, in the case at bar the infant is a party defendant, along with his father who was not present on the links at the time of the occurrence.

IV

There is an exception to the general rules for infants who engage in adult activities. Restatement of Torts, Second Section 283A, Sub. Section C provides:

> 'Child engaging in adult activity. An exception to the rule * * * may arise where the child engages in an activity which is normally undertaken only by adults, and for which adult qualifications are required. As in the case of one entering upon a professional activity which requires special skill * * *, he may be held to the standard of adult skill, knowledge, and competence, and no allowance may be made for his immaturity.'

It has been held that an infant must exercise the same standard of care as an adult when he is driving a motorboat or airplane, Dellwo v. Pearson, 259 Minn. 452, 107 N.W.2d 859, 97 A.L.R.2d 866 (1961); a go-cart, Ewing v. Biddle, Ind.App., 216 N.E.2d 863; a motor vehicle or motorcycle, Daniels v. Evans, 107 N.H. 407, 224 A.2d 63. There are several other cases in various jurisdictions concerning infants driving power operated machines such as the above. The rationale for these decisions is that when a minor engages in such activities as the operation of an automobile or similar power-driven device, he forfeits his rights to have the reasonableness of his conduct measured by a standard commensurate with his age and is thenceforth held to the same standard as all other persons. (Ann. 97 A.L.R.2d 872 at 875). The underlying theory for this view would seem to be that the very nature of a power-driven vehicle makes it a dangerous instrument whether driven by an adult or a child since it obviously makes little difference to the maimed pedestrian or occupant of a vehicle that his mechanized nemesis was a minor.

This Court cannot adopt the theory advocated by some in support of this standard, that licensing statutes automatically impose the adult standard on the driver. If this were so, the unlicensed minor driver who would, presumably, be an even greater menace on the highways would be held only to the mitigated standard, (Ann. 97 A.L.R.2d, supra at 876), the absence of a license being then only a portion of the proof of the infant's lack of experience. Likewise, compliance with the administrative and quasi criminal requirements of licensing laws are not controlling on the issue of negligence as between adult drivers and it is equally unimportant in the case of a minor and therefore should not be the criterion determining the standard by which the minor is to be judged. (7 Am.Jur.2d Automobiles and Highway Traffic #367 and the cases cited therein).

V

As applied to the instant case one of the critical elements in the opinion of the Court is the risk involved when a dangerous missile is hit by a golfer. Just as a motor vehicle or other power-driven vehicle is dangerous, so is a golf ball hit with a club. Driving a car, an airplane or powerboat has been referred to as adult activity even though actively engaged in by infants. (Dellwo v. Pearson, supra). Likewise, golf can easily be determined to be an adult activity engaged in by infants. Both involve dangerous instruments. No matter what the age of a driver of a car or a driver of a golf ball, if he fails to exercise due care serious injury may result. Driving a car, it is true, is not a game as golf may be. However, golf is not a game in the same way that football, baseball, basketball or tennis is a game. It is a game played by an individual which in order to be played well demands an abundance of skill and personal discipline, not to mention constant practice and dedication. Custom, rules and etiquette play an important role in this game. Foremost among these is the fact, as is indicated on many scorecards, that one does not hit a ball when it is likely that the ball could or will hit someone else for the obvious reason that someone could get hurt. In the definitive work on the subject the rule of etiquette is stated as follows: 'No player should play until the party in front is out of range'. 'Golf, Its Rules and Decisions', Richard S. Francis, Norwood Press, Norwood, Massachusetts, p. 369.

The risks attendant in the game of golf have long been recognized. As early as 1905 the Scottish Court in Andrew v. Stevenson, 13 Scot.L.T. 581, 582 (1905) stated that the risks of accident in golf are such, that no one is entitled to take part in the game without paying attention to what is going on around and near him. No mention was made of this not applying to people under 21, or under 18 or 15 or 10. The nature of the game is the same, even if the age of the participant varies. In the case at bar we have an 11 year old boy playing in the company of three adults. He has taken lessons and plays regularly at his club. On a par three hole of about 170 yards he sees the plaintiff within the realm of foreseeable danger and he hits a golf ball, a dangerous missile, 150–160 yards where it hits the plaintiff. Had it hit the plaintiff in the head it may have seriously injured or even killed him. The boy knew or should have known that a golf ball can inflict serious injury. He could have waited for a few seconds until plaintiff was clear yet he chose to hit in breach of his duty and injury resulted. This particular infant defendant was for all purposes on the golf course as an adult golfer. He was playing in a foursome with adults; he had played this course in the company of adults before and he hit the ball, as well as, if not better than many adults. If this Court were to say that the standard of care which defendant must bring to a golf course is only that of an infant it would be ignoring the realities of the game as well as the situation applicable to this case.

It might be argued that the applicable standard should be that of an 11 year old boy who possesses the experience or intelligence of one who has played a great deal of golf. This subjective standard does not adequately consider the objective nature of the game, the inherent risks involved and the undisputed fact that a golf ball is a dangerous missile capable of inflicting grievous harm no matter who hits it.

It is not uncommon today that teenagers are outstanding amateur golfers. Indeed, the 1968 U.S. Amateur Championship was won by Bruce Fleisher, a 19 year old, and youths of varying ages were at the top of the leader boards all during this tournament. Craig Harmon was the amateur champion of this county at a young age. Members of high school teams in this area regularly shoot scores of championship caliber, as do competitors in 'junior' golf. These facts are well known, and are not only particular to this county but are also applicable to other areas throughout the state and nation.

Should this Court say that all of these competitors are to be held to a different standard than adults playing golf? Even if we adopted a subjective standard based on the experience and intelligence of a 16 year old infant tournament golfer, is his experience and intelligence on the golf course less than that of an adult? Is the cutoff point a matter of age? I think not. When you have, as we have here, a situation where there is potentially an inherently dangerous object hit by someone who despite his age is for all practical purposes just like an adult on the golf course then it is this Court's opinion that he should be treated like an adult and held to an adult standard of care. It may be true that, hypothetically, a six year old could appear on the course for the first time and hit a ball which would hurt someone and the objective standard might not be applicable, but that would be the exception rather than the rule. People who play golf on a golf course know or should know that a golf ball can cause serious injury just as a car may cause serious injury and they should exercise the same degree of care.

In conclusion, this Court holds that golf involves special factors which when considered together in the abstract and in conjunction with the fact situation in this particular case require this infant be held to the standard of the reasonable man on the golf course. Motion denied.

Notes and Questions

1. Duke Law Professor Jim Coleman, a proud holder of three hole-in-one trophies, provides this explanation in support of the plaintiff's case:

> Any golfer will tell you that the kid hit the ball out of arrogance: he assumed he would hit the ball well enough to land it on the green. In fact, he overestimated his skill. The other situation in which a golfer would hit the ball in these circumstances is where he thought he could not hit 160 yards. But even in that case, nothing is gained by hitting before the people ahead of you have cleared and most golfers would wait. An eleven-

> year-old girl recently played in the Women's U.S. Open. She shot a 78 both days, better than some pros. She would have waited for the people ahead to clear.

Not all golfers would agree with Professor Coleman's analysis. For example, Victoria Morgan (J.D. 2022), one of our former students who had been on the women's professional golf tour, suggested that it was more likely the eleven-year-old underestimated his ability to reach the green and believed the ball would fall short. Could you see this debate taking place in the jury room? How might it affect the outcome of the jury's deliberations about breach?

2. Consistent with the Restatement's position, the adult activities exception is generally applied to "activit[ies] which [are] normally undertaken only by adults, and for which adult qualifications are required." Restatement (Second) of Torts § 283. Does the Neumann court analyze the issue whether golf is such an activity? Is its focus consistent with the rationales underlying the child standard of care?

3. Judges and jurisdictions disagree about whether it makes sense to base the exception either importantly or in part on the dangerousness of the activity. This discussion from the Arkansas Supreme Court illustrates the problem:

> We have no doubt that deer hunting is a dangerous sport. We cannot say, however, either on the basis of the record before us or on the basis of common knowledge, that deer hunting is an activity normally engaged in by adults only. To the contrary, all the indications are the other way. A child may lawfully hunt without a hunting license at any age under sixteen. Arkansas Game & Fish Commission's 1971–1972 Hunting Regulations, p. 4. We know, from common knowledge, that youngsters only six or eight years old frequently use .22 caliber rifles and other lethal firearms to hunt rabbits, birds, and other small game. We cannot conscientiously declare, without proof and on the basis of mere judicial notice, that only adults normally go deer hunting.
>
> In refusing to apply an adult standard of care to a minor engaged in hunting deer, we do not imply that a statute to that effect would be unwise. Indeed, we express no opinion upon that question. As judges, we cannot lay down a rule with the precision and inflexibility of a statute drafted by the legislature. If we should declare that a minor hunting deer with a high-powered rifle must in all instances be held to an adult standard of care, we must be prepared to explain why the same rule should not apply to a minor hunting deer with a shotgun, to a minor hunting rabbits with a high-powered rifle, to a twelve-year-old shooting crows with a .22, and so on down to the six-year-old shooting at tin cans with an air rifle. Not to mention other dangerous activities, such as the swinging of a baseball bat, the explosion of firecrackers, or the operation of an electric train. All we mean to say in this case is that we are unwilling to lay down a brand-new rule of law, without precedent and without any logical or practical means of even surmising where the stopping point of the new rule might ultimately be reached.

Purtle v. Shelton, 474 S.W.2d 123, 125–26 (Ark. 1971).

4. It should come as no surprise that judges and jurisdictions also disagree about which activities are normally undertaken only by adults and require adult qualifications. Where might you find judges disagreeing with the Neumann court about the status of golf in this regard? See also, Goss v. Allen, 360 A.2d 388 (N.J. 1976) (state supreme court disagreeing with its appellate bretheren about whether skiing is an adult activity and providing in dicta that the use of a firearm would be an adult activity).

II. WHO DECIDES WHAT IS "REASONABLE" IN THE CIRCUMSTANCES?

A. The Legislature's Role

At common law, it was unusual for the standard of care to be established by the legislature; indeed, it was unusual for the legislature to attend itself to tort law beyond promulgating statutes of limitations, and wrongful death and survival statutes. In contrast, in the current period statutes are increasingly influential, either directly to dictate the terms of tort law — for for example, as we saw in Chapter 3, by expressly precluding negligence actions against good Samaritans — or indirectly, to establish breach through the doctrine of negligence per se.

Negligence per se means negligence as a matter of law. The doctrine applies when a judge in a torts case borrows the terms of a statute, regulation, or ordinance in lieu of its own or the jury's determination of breach. The most commonly borrowed enactments for this purpose are highway (vehicular) safety statutes. *See, e.g.*, Martin v. Herzog, 126 N.E. 814 (N.Y. 1920) (borrowing a law that required drivers to turn on their headlights at dusk); Tedla v. Ellman, 19 N.E.2d 987 (1937) (borrowing a law that provided that pedestrians who walk on the road must do so facing traffic); Barnum v. Williams, 504 P.2d 122 (Or. 1972) (borrowing a law that disallowed riding on or crossing the center dividing lane of a highway). These laws were not developed for tort law and they do not provide for a private right of action when they are violated, but at least in principle they reflect the consensus of those who have studied highway safety about the specific conduct that is reasonable in the circumstances.

Consistent with this analysis, courts draw a standard of care from an enactment when (1) it specifies particular conduct beyond merely providing that reasonable care is required; (2) the plaintiff is a member of the class of individuals the legislative body had in mind to protect when it acted; and (3) the harm that occurred was the kind the legislative body intended to address.

Negligence per se can have different procedural effects depending on the jurisdiction, the enactment at issue, and the facts of the case:

In the classic negligence per se situation, the plaintiff pleads the statute as the defendant's duty and standard of care. Assuming that the judge determines as a matter of law that the statute meets the three requirements outlined above, the plaintiff has no burden to offer evidence on either issue, and contrary evidence will not be received from the defendant. Instead, all the plaintiff must do to prevail is persuade the jury that the defendant violated the enactment; that the violation was the cause of the plaintiff's injury; and what compensation is due. In these jurisdictions, the defendant may escape the effect of negligence per se only if the facts involve an emergency or some other special situation that makes following the terms of the statute unreasonable. *See, e.g.,* Tedla v. Ellman, 19 N.E.2d 987 (1937) (plaintiffs, walking with traffic, violated highway safety law requiring them to walk facing traffic; their violation was excused because walking facing traffic was more dangerous — less reasonable — at that time of day than walking with traffic).

Some jurisdictions hold that statutes are "prima facie" or presumptive evidence of duty and the standard of care, but that this evidence is always rebuttable. In such jurisdictions, proving a violation of the statute plus causation and injury will get a plaintiff to a jury, but if the defendant succeeds in establishing the reasonableness of his or her actions despite the statutory violation, the plaintiff will lose. *See, e.g.*, Barnum v. Williams, 504 P.2d 122 (Or. 1972) (rejecting the standard per se formulation requiring the defendant to point to an established exception to the rule and permitting instead general arguments about reasonableness in the circumstances).

A final group of jurisdictions views statutes as evidence of what the standard of care might be; their evidentiary weight — dispositive, presumptive, or of only some significance — depends on the circumstances.

Some jurisdictions use only statutes and not regulations or ordinances to set the duty and standard of care. Others use regulations and/or ordinances. Jurisdictions that use all three may only give true "per se" weight to statutes — in other words, only statutes will replace the trier of fact's role in setting the standard of care applicable in the particular circumstances. In such jurisdictions, regulations and/or ordinances will be simply evidence for the jury to evaluate in determining what reasonable care required.

B. The Judge and the Jury

AKINS v. GLENS FALLS CITY SCHOOL DISTRICT
424 N.E.2d 531 (N.Y. 1981)

JASEN, Judge.

On this appeal, we are called upon to define the scope of the duty owed by a proprietor of a baseball field to the spectators attending its games. The specific question presented is whether such an owner, having provided protective screening for the area behind home plate, is liable in negligence for the injuries sustained by a spectator as a result of being struck by a foul ball while standing in an unscreened section of the field. . . .

In the early afternoon of April 14, 1976, plaintiff attended a high school baseball game that was being played on a field owned and maintained by defendant Glens Falls City School District. The field was equipped with a backstop 24 feet high and 50 feet wide. This backstop was located 60 feet behind home plate and was positioned in front of bleachers that could seat approximately 120 adults. There was additional standing room behind the backstop as well. Two chain link fences, three feet in height, ran from each end of the backstop along the base lines to a distance approximately 60 feet behind first and third base.

Plaintiff arrived while the game was in progress and elected to view the contest from a position behind the three-foot fence along the third base line, approximately 10 to 15 feet from the end of the backstop and 60 feet from home plate. As there were no seating facilities for spectators along the base lines, plaintiff had to stand in order to watch the game. At the time, other spectators were also standing along the base lines behind the three-foot fence. There was, however, no proof that the screened bleachers behind home plate were filled or that plaintiff was prevented from watching the game from behind the backstop. Approximately 10 minutes after arriving at the baseball field, plaintiff was struck in the eye by a sharply hit foul ball, causing her serious and permanent injury.

The present action was then commenced by the plaintiff against the defendant school district. Alleging that the school district was negligent in failing to provide safe and proper screening devices along the base lines of its field, plaintiff sought judgment against the school district in the sum of $250,000. After trial, the jury returned a verdict in plaintiff's favor, assessing damages in the amount of $100,000 and apportioning fault at 65% to the school district and 35% to plaintiff.

On appeal, a divided Appellate Division affirmed the judgment rendered in plaintiff's favor, one Justice concurring in result and two Justices dissenting. The majority held that there was no error of law which warranted disturbing the jury's verdict. The dissenters were of the view that, as a matter of law, there was no showing of any negligence on the school district's part. According to the dissent, "[h]aving adequately screened the area of its ball park behind home plate, the defendant fulfilled its duty to the plaintiff and cannot be held in negligence when she herself selected a position that was outside the area screened." We agree.

. . .

At the outset, it should be stated that an owner of a baseball field is not an insurer of the safety of its spectators. Rather, like any other owner or occupier of land, it is only under a duty to exercise "reasonable care under the circumstances" to prevent injury to those who come to watch the games played on its field. The perils of the game of baseball, however, are not so imminent that due care on the part of the owner requires that the entire playing field be screened. Indeed, many spectators prefer to sit where their view of the game is unobstructed by fences or protective netting and the proprietor of a ball park has a legitimate interest in catering to these desires. Thus, the critical question becomes what amount of screening must be provided by an owner of a baseball field before it will be found to have discharged its duty of care to its spectators.

Other jurisdictions addressing this question have adopted various standards in defining the duty of a ball park proprietor to protect its spectators from stray balls. Some courts have held that an owner merely has a duty to screen such seats as are adequate to provide its spectators with an opportunity to sit in a protected area if they so desire. Other courts have stated that a proprietor of a baseball field need only screen as many seats as may reasonably be expected to be applied for on an ordinary occasion by those desiring such protection. Most courts, however, have adopted a two-prong standard in defining the scope of an owner's duty to provide protective screening for its patrons. Under the majority rule, the owner must screen the most dangerous section of the field — the area behind home plate — and the screening that is provided must be sufficient for those spectators who may be reasonably anticipated to desire protected seats on an ordinary occasion. We believe this to be the better rule and adopt this definition of the duty owed by an owner of a baseball field to provide protective screening for its spectators.

We hold that, in the exercise of reasonable care, the proprietor of a ball park need only provide screening for the area of the field behind home plate where the danger of being struck by a ball is the greatest. Moreover, such screening must be of sufficient extent to provide adequate protection for as many spectators as may reasonably be expected to desire such seating in the course of an ordinary game. In so holding, we merely recognize the practical realities of this sporting event. As mentioned earlier, many spectators attending such exhibitions desire to watch the contest taking place on the playing field without having their view obstructed or obscured by a fence or a protective net. In ministering to these desires, while at the same time providing adequate protection in the most dangerous area of the field for those spectators who wish to avail themselves of it, a proprietor fulfills its duty of reasonable care under such circumstances.

This is not to say that, by adequately screening the area of the field where the incidence of foul balls is the greatest, the risks inherent in viewing the game are completely eliminated. Rather, even after the exercise of reasonable care, some risk of being struck by a ball will continue to exist. Moreover, contrary to the supposition of the dissent, we do not attempt to prescribe precisely what, as a matter of law, are the required dimensions of a baseball field backstop. Nor do we suggest that where the adequacy of the screening in terms of protecting the area behind home plate properly is put in issue, the case should not be submitted to the jury. We merely hold that where a proprietor of a ball park furnishes screening for the area of the field behind home plate where the danger of being struck by a ball is the greatest and that screening is of sufficient extent to provide adequate protection for as many spectators as may reasonably be expected to desire such seating in the course of an ordinary game, the proprietor fulfills the duty of care imposed by law and, therefore, cannot be liable in negligence. Indeed, to adopt the view urged by the dissent would mean that every spectator injured by a foul ball, no matter where he is seated or standing in the ball park, would have an absolute right to go to the jury on every claim of negligence, regardless of the owner's efforts to provide reasonable protection and despite the spectator's failure to utilize the protection made available.

. . .

In this case, it is undisputed that the school district equipped its field with a backstop which was 24 feet high and 50 feet wide. Plaintiff presented no evidence that this backstop was inadequate in terms of providing protection for the area behind home plate where there was a substantial likelihood of spectators being struck by misguided balls or that there was an insufficient number of screened seats for those who might reasonably be expected to desire such protection. Under these circumstances, having provided adequate protection for those spectators seated, or standing, in the area behind home plate, liability may not be imposed on the school district for failing to provide additional screening along the baselines of its field where the risk of being struck by a stray ball was considerably less.

As the dissent correctly notes, what constitutes reasonable care under the circumstances ordinarily is a question for the jury. This is not to say, however, that in every case involving a landowner's liability in negligence the question whether reasonable care was exercised must be determined by the jury. As we have only recently stated, "before it becomes appropriate for the jury to consider * * * such questions, the court, as it would in the usual negligence action, must make the threshold determination as to whether the plaintiff, by introducing adequate evidence on each element, has made out a case sufficient in law to support a favorable jury verdict. Only in those cases where there arises a real question as to the landowner's negligence should the jury be permitted to proceed. In all others, where proof of any essential element falls short, the case should go no further." In short, a court always is required to undertake an initial evaluation of the evidence to determine whether the plaintiff has established the elements necessary to a cause of action in negligence, to wit: (1) the existence of a duty on defendant's part as to plaintiff; (2) a breach of this duty; and (3) injury to the plaintiff as a result thereof. (See Prosser, Torts [4th ed.], § 30, p. 143.) In this regard, this court, on more than one occasion, has held that a defendant fulfilled its duty of care notwithstanding a jury verdict to the contrary. Similarly, on the record before us and the undisputed facts of this case, the school district fulfilled its duty of reasonable care to plaintiff as a matter of law and, therefore, no question of negligence remained for the jury's consideration.

. . .

Accordingly, the order of the Appellate Division should be reversed, with costs, and the complaint dismissed.

COOKE, Chief Judge (dissenting).

The majority today engages in an unfortunate exercise in judicial rule making in an area that should be left to the jury. This attempt to precisely prescribe what steps the proprietor of a baseball field must take to fulfill its duty of reasonable care is unwarranted and unwise. . . . I therefore dissent and vote to affirm.

As the majority recognizes, the proprietor of a baseball field owes the same duty to spectators that any landowner owes to a person who comes onto the owner's property — "reasonable care under the circumstances." This duty requires that the landowner "must act as a reasonable man in maintaining his property in a reasonably safe condition in view of all the circumstances, including the likelihood of injury to others, the seriousness of the injury, and the burden of avoiding the risk."

The majority errs, however, in deciding as a matter of law exactly what steps by a baseball field proprietor will constitute reasonable care under the circumstances. Such a determination, by its very dependence upon the "circumstances," hinges upon the facts of the individual situation and should be left for the jury. Indeed, those exceptions to this rule that have been made by courts occur only in those narrow classes of cases where an identical set of facts is likely to recur with regularity, and "[s]uch holdings today are rare" (2 Harper and James, Torts, p. 977).

This court has made clear that "[w]hat safety precautions may reasonably be required of a landowner is almost always a question of fact for the jury." This is not to say that every case of alleged negligence by the proprietor of a baseball field must go to the jury. But it is just as unreasonable to declare with such absolutism that, outside narrow and artificial limits, *no* such case can go to the jury.

The majority has in effect undertaken the task of prescribing the size, shape and location of backstops and other protective devices that will satisfy a baseball field owner's duty of reasonable care under the circumstances. This attempt to impose a straightjacket upon the relationship between a baseball field proprietor and spectators, regardless of the particular circumstances, is arbitrary and unrealistic. . . . It is reminiscent of the [United States] Supreme Court's attempt, in the early years of the automobile, to impose upon the operator the duty of leaving the vehicle and examining each railroad grade crossing on foot, if necessary for a better view of the tracks (*Baltimore & Ohio R. R. v. Goodman*, 275 U.S. 66, 48 S.Ct. 24, 72 L.Ed. 167 [per Holmes, J.]). This standard enjoyed little favor among State courts, engendered confusion among lower Federal courts attempting to apply it and was quickly repudiated by the Supreme Court (*Pokora v. Wabash Ry. Co.*, 292 U.S. 98, 54 S.Ct. 580, 78 L.Ed. 1149).

In *Pokora*, Justice Cardozo noted that the problems springing from the grade-crossing rule emphasized "the need for caution in framing standards of behavior that amount to rules of law." Indeed, railroad crossing cases provide a good example of this court's reluctance to impose blanket rules of conduct divorced from actual events. More than a century ago, this court stated that "[i]t is a general rule that care commensurate with the danger must be exercised, and it is also a general rule that it is the province of the jury, and not of the court, to determine whether such care has been exercised." The court has expressed this reluctance to take negligence questions from the jury in a variety of other contexts, as well.

The wisdom of eschewing such blanket rules where negligence is concerned is obvious. In the present context, the majority has held as a matter of law that the proprietor of the baseball field fulfilled his duty of reasonable care by erecting a backstop that was 24 feet high and 50 feet wide. The court issues this rule with no more expertise available to it than Justice Holmes had in 1927 when he recommended that motorists venture on foot onto railroad grade crossings for a better view. It has selected one of a variety of forms of protection currently in use at professional ballparks and school playgrounds — what in reality is nothing more than a straight, high fence behind home plate — and has designated it as sufficient protection as a matter of law.

Such a ruling robs the jury of its ability to pass on whether the circumstances here might have made this type of backstop inadequate. In the present case, the majority has taken from the jury its ability to consider the following evidence: that the cost of placing "wings" on the backstop extending to first and third base would have been only $209 when the backstop was built; that other baseball diamonds do have such wings; that the type of game being played at the field was not a softball game between young tykes but rather a varsity high school hardball game involving players such as the batter in this incident, who was six-foot two-inches tall, weighed 190 pounds and was advanced enough in ability to later play professional ball; that school authorities were aware that line drives "frequently" went over the low fence that ran along the base lines, and that there were no signs or other warnings of the dangers of standing behind this fence. Because of public familiarity with the "national pastime", no expert testimony would generally be required to make out a showing of failure to exercise due care in such a case. In this case, however, the jury even had before it the testimony of a civil engineer as to the feasibility and minimal cost of ensuring greater safety for spectators. This makes an even stronger argument for sending this case to the jury.

The court's ruling will also foreclose juries in the future from considering the wide range of circumstances of individual cases, as well as new developments in safety devices or procedures. Unless the court plans to periodically take up such cases in the future to adjust its rule, it has frozen a position that is certain to become outdated, if it is not already. It would make as much sense for the court to decree, as a matter of law, what sort of batting helmet or catcher's mask a school district should supply to its baseball team. Baseball may be a sport steeped in tradition, but it is hardly immune from technological change and shifts in public perception of what constitute reasonable safety measures. It has traditionally been the jury that reflects these shifts and changes.

. . .

Accordingly, the order of the Appellate Division should be affirmed.

GABRIELLI, JONES and WACHTLER, JJ., concur with JASEN, J.

COOKE, C. J., dissents and votes to affirm in a separate opinion in which FUCHSBERG and MEYER, JJ., concur.

Restatement (Third) of Torts: Liability for Physical and Emotional Harm
§ 8. Judge and Jury

(a) When, in light of all the evidence, reasonable minds can differ as to the facts relating to the actor's conduct, it is the function of the jury to determine those facts.

(b) When, in light of all the facts relating to the actor's conduct, reasonable minds can differ as to whether the conduct lacks reasonable care, it is the function of the jury to make that determination.

Comment:

a. Background. In tort cases involving physical or emotional harm, trial by jury is almost always requested by one of the parties. Many of the rules in this Restatement concern, explicitly or implicitly, the respective roles of judge and jury — for example, whether the judge should decide the case under the heading of no duty, and whether certain evidence is merely evidence of negligence (or nonnegligence) or is instead negligence (or nonnegligence) per se of the sort that would justify a directed verdict. Accordingly, this Section clarifies the general rules as to the allocation of function between judge and jury.

. . .

In light of the facts relating to the actor's conduct, the question arises whether that conduct is negligent — whether it lacks reasonable care under all the circumstances. Because this is a matter of the law's evaluation of the legal significance of the actor's conduct, such a question could be characterized as a question of law that should be decided by the court. More precisely, it can be characterized as a mixed question of law and fact. Yet this characterization is not itself sufficient to determine whether the question should be given its answer by the court or instead by the jury. The longstanding American practice has been to treat the negligence question as one that is assigned to the jury; to this extent, the question is treated as one that is equivalent to a question of fact. Accordingly, so long as reasonable minds can differ in evaluating whether the actor's conduct lacks reasonable care, the responsibility for making this evaluation rests with the jury. To be sure, in some cases reasonable minds can reach only one conclusion. Accordingly, the rule recognized in this Section permits a directed verdict or judgment as a matter of law — that the actor's conduct must be found negligent, or free of negligence. Yet most of the time, the rule set forth in this Section calls for a jury decision on the negligence issue. . . . The jury is assigned the responsibility of rendering such judgments partly because several minds are better than one, and also because of the desirability of taking advantage of the insight and values of the community, as embodied in the jury, rather than relying on the professional knowledge of the judge.

. . .

c. Implications and problems. A jury decision on the negligence issue is not a precedent for later cases involving different parties and is not even admissible in such later cases as a possible guide to later juries. Jury decisions, then, are generally ad hoc. Most of the time, this ad hoc quality seems inevitable, since the actor's conduct is sufficiently unique as to render largely irrelevant whatever precedent the jury's verdict might set.

Some of the time, however, the conduct that is immediately before the court is conduct that is likely to be repeated by large numbers of other parties in later cases. In such situations, there can be important advantages in having the negligence issue decided once and for all by the court. This would reduce litigation costs in later cases, avoid different outcomes in apparently equal cases, and provide better guidance to parties as to what conduct they should (and need not) avoid in order to escape liability.

By and large, however, American courts have decided that the advantages of allowing courts to decide the negligence issue in cases of this sort do not justify removing the issue from the jury. For one thing, what looks at first to be a constant or recurring issue of conduct in which many parties engage may reveal on closer inspection many variables that can best be considered on a case-by-case basis. Tort law has thus accepted an ethics of particularism, which tends to cast doubt on the viability of general rules capable of producing determinate results and which requires that actual moral judgments be based on the circumstances of each individual situation. Tort law's affirmation of this requirement highlights the primary role necessarily fulfilled by the jury.

Occasionally, however, the need for providing a clear and stable answer to the question of negligence is so overwhelming as to justify a court in withdrawing the negligence evaluation from the jury. In highway-accident cases, for example, the question recurrently arises whether it is contributory negligence not to wear an available seat belt. Granted, the advantages of wearing a seat belt vary to some extent from case to case; the advantage, for example, is greater when the person is riding in a more vulnerable subcompact car. Still, the benefits of having the contributory-negligence question settled in advance are of such force as to make it acceptable for a state's highest court to reach a final, general decision as to whether not wearing seat belts is or is not contributory negligence.

Notes and Questions

1. Is the activity of spectating at a baseball game sufficiently like wearing a seat belt that an appellate court is warranted in deciding the parameters of reasonableness as a matter of law?

2. Note that there are generally three circumstances in which a court will take the reasonableness question away from the jury: when the evidence in the particular case record so clearly favors one side that a judge would inevitably have to overturn a nonconforming verdict; when a judge recognizes that over time juries have repeatedly addressed the same reasonableness question and have always or typically resolved it similarly so that it is, in effect, a waste of judicial resources to continue to send the same question to subsequent juries; and when as a normative matter, the court believes that there is only one way that the reasonableness question *should* be decided. Which of these circumstances best describes the basis for the New York Court of Appeal's decision in *Akins*?

3. Resolving reasonableness as normative matter violates the convention that this is usually a question of fact for the jury; however, doing so is consistent with boundaries of the court's authority since reasonableness is formally a "mixed question of fact and law" and the court is always responsible for law. How is reasonableness a question of fact? How is it a question of law? What kinds of cases might trigger a court's sense that the reasonableness question is best pulled from the jury to assure that the "right" result is reached?

4. The dissent in *Akins* refers to a famous dispute between Oliver Wendell Holmes and Benjamin Cardozo, on the subject of the reasonable course of action when coming onto a railroad crossing in a car. Holmes, who was a proponent of the view that reasonableness is a question of law and that judges abdicate their responsibility to determine the law when they send the question to the jury, believed that the reasonable course of action was to stop, get out of the car, and look most carefully for an oncoming train before returning to the car and proceeding across the tracks. This view was ensconced in a decision of the United States Supreme Court he authored, Baltimore & Ohio R. R. v. Goodman, 275 U.S. 66 (1927). It was overturned just a few years later in Pokora v. Wabash Ry. Co., 292 U.S. 98, 105-106 (1934), Justice Cardozo writing for the majority:

> Standards of prudent conduct are declared at times by courts, but they are taken over from the facts of life. To get out of a vehicle and reconnoitre is an uncommon precaution, as everyday experience informs us. Besides being uncommon, it is very likely to be futile, and sometimes even dangerous. If the driver leaves his vehicle when he nears a cut or curve, he will learn nothing by getting out about the perils that lurk beyond. By the time he regains his seat and sets his car in motion, the hidden train may be upon him. Often the added safeguard will be dubious though the track happens to be straight, as it seems that this one was, at all events as far as the station, about five blocks to the north. A train traveling at a speed of thirty miles an hour will cover a quarter of a mile in the space of thirty seconds. It may thus emerge out of obscurity as the driver turns his back to regain the waiting car, and may then descend upon him suddenly when his car is on the track. Instead of helping himself by getting out, he might do better to press forward with all his faculties alert. So a train at a neighboring station, apparently at rest and harmless, may be transformed in a few seconds into an instrument of destruction. At times the course of safety may be

different. One can figure to oneself a roadbed so level and unbroken that getting out will be a gain. Even then the balance of advantage depends on many circumstances and can be easily disturbed.

Illustrations such as these bear witness to the need for caution in framing standards of behavior that amount to rules of law. The need is the more urgent when there is no background of experience out of which the standards have emerged. They are then, not the natural flowerings of behavior in its customary forms, but rules artificially developed, and imposed from without. Extraordinary situations may not wisely or fairly be subjected to tests or regulations that are fitting for the commonplace or normal. In default of the guide of customary conduct, what is suitable for the traveler caught in a mesh where the ordinary safeguards fail him is for the judgment of a jury. The opinion in Goodman's Case has been a source of confusion in the federal courts to the extent that it imposes a standard for application by the judge, and has had only wavering support in the courts of the states. We limit it accordingly.

III. PROVING BREACH

This last part of the chapter considers how plaintiffs go about proving a departure from the standard of care (that is, proving breach) beyond simply alleging unreasonableness. (Recall from the Introduction's discussion of the burden of proof that a successful claim requires the plaintiff to satisfy the burden of pleading breach of the standard of care; the burden of producing evidence to support the allegation; and the burden of persuasion, that is, of convincing the trier of fact that the evidence meets the preponderance of the evidence requirement.) The focus here is on the burdens of production and persuasion, on how the plaintiff meets those burdens, and on how the defendant responds.

A. The "BPL" Formula

UNITED STATES v. CARROLL TOWING, INC.
159 F.2d 169 (2d Cir. 1947)

L. HAND, Circuit Judge.

These appeals concern the sinking of the barge, 'Anna C,' on January 4, 1944, off Pier 51, North River. The Conners Marine Co., Inc., was the owner of the barge, which the Pennsylvania Railroad Company had chartered; the Grace Line, Inc., was the charterer of the tug, 'Carroll,' of which the Carroll Towing Co., Inc., was the owner. The decree in the limitation proceeding held the Carroll Company liable to the United States for the loss of the barge's cargo of flour, and to the Pennsylvania Railroad Company, for expenses in salving the cargo and barge; and it held the Carroll Company also liable to the Conners Company for one half the damage to the barge; these liabilities being all subject to limitation. The decree in the libel suit held the Grace Line primarily liable for the other half of the damage to the barge, and for any part of the first half, not recovered against the Carroll Company because of limitation of liability; it also held the Pennsylvania Railroad secondarily liable for the same amount that the Grace Line was liable. The Carroll Company and the Pennsylvania Railroad Company have filed assignments of error.

The facts, as the judge found them, were as follows. On June 20, 1943, the Conners Company chartered the barge, 'Anna C.' to the Pennsylvania Railroad Company at a stated hire per diem, by a charter of the kind usual in the Harbor, which included the services of a bargee, apparently limited to the hours 8 A.M. to 4 P.M. On January 2, 1944, the barge, which had lifted the cargo of flour, was made fast off the end of Pier 58 on the Manhattan side of the North River, whence she was later shifted to Pier 52. At some time not disclosed, five other barges were moored outside her, extending into the river; her lines to the pier were not then strengthened. At the end of the next pier north (called the Public Pier), lay four barges; and a line had been made fast from the outermost of these to the fourth barge of the tier hanging to Pier 52. The purpose of this line is not entirely apparent, and in any event it obstructed entrance into the slip between the two piers of barges. The Grace Line, which had chartered the tug, 'Carroll,' sent her down to the locus in quo to 'drill' out one of the barges which lay at the end of the Public Pier; and in order to do so it was necessary to throw off the line between the two tiers. On board the 'Carroll' at the time were not only her master, but a 'harbormaster' employed by the Grace Line. Before throwing off the line between the two tiers, the 'Carroll' nosed up against the outer barge of the tier lying off Pier 52, ran a line from her own stem to the middle bit of that barge, and kept working her engines 'slow ahead' against the ebb tide which was making at that time. The captain of the 'Carroll' put a deckhand and the 'harbormaster' on the barges, told them to throw off the line which barred the entrance to the slip; but, before doing so, to make sure that the tier on Pier 52 was safely moored, as there was a strong northerly wind blowing down the river. The 'harbormaster' and the deckhand went aboard the barges and readjusted all the fasts to their satisfaction, including those from the 'Anna C.' to the pier.

After doing so, they threw off the line between the two tiers and again boarded the 'Carroll,' which backed away from the outside barge, preparatory to 'drilling' out the barge she was after in the tier off the Public Pier. She had only got about seventy-five feet away when the tier off Pier 52 broke adrift because the fasts from the 'Anna C,' either rendered, or carried away. The tide and wind carried down the six barges, still holding together, until the 'Anna C' fetched up against a tanker, lying on the north side of the pier below- Pier 51- whose propeller broke a hole in her at or near her bottom. Shortly thereafter: i.e., at about 2:15 P.M., she careened, dumped her cargo of flour and sank. The tug, 'Grace,' owned by the Grace Line, and the 'Carroll,' came to the help of the flotilla after it broke loose; and, as both had syphon pumps on board, they could have kept the 'Anna C' afloat, had they learned of her condition; but the bargee had left her on the evening before, and nobody was on board to observe that she was leaking. The Grace Line wishes to exonerate itself from all liability because the 'harbormaster' was not authorized to pass on the sufficiency of the fasts of the 'Anna C' which held the tier to Pier 52; the Carroll Company wishes to charge the Grace Line with the entire liability because the 'harbormaster' was given an over-all authority. Both wish to charge the 'Anna C' with a share of all her damages, or at least with so much as resulted from her sinking. The Pennsylvania Railroad Company also wishes to hold the barge liable. The Conners Company wishes the decrees to be affirmed.

. . .

We cannot, however, excuse the Conners Company for the bargee's failure to care for the barge, and we think that this prevents full recovery. First as to the facts. As we have said, the deckhand and the 'harbormaster' jointly undertook to pass upon the 'Anna C's' fasts to the pier; and even though we assume that the bargee was responsible for his fasts after the other barges were added outside, there is not the slightest ground for saying that the deckhand and the 'harbormaster' would have paid any attention to any protest which he might have made, had he been there. We do not therefore attribute it as in any degree a fault of the 'Anna C' that the flotilla broke adrift. Hence she may recover in full against the Carroll Company and the Grace Line for any injury she suffered from the contact with the tanker's propeller, which we shall speak of as the 'collision damages.' On the other hand, if the bargee had been on board, and had done his duty to his employer, he would have gone below at once, examined the injury, and called for help from the 'Carroll' and the Grace Line tug. Moreover, it is clear that these tugs could have kept the barge afloat, until they had safely beached her, and saved her cargo. This would have avoided what we shall call the 'sinking damages.' Thus, if it was a failure in the Conner Company's proper care of its own barge, for the bargee to be absent, the company can recover only one third of the 'sinking' damages from the Carroll Company and one third from the Grace Line. For this reason the question arises whether a barge owner is slack in the care of his barge if the bargee is absent.

As to the consequences of a bargee's absence from his barge there have been a number of decisions;

. . .

It appears . . . that there is no general rule to determine when the absence of a bargee or other attendant will make the owner of the barge liable for injuries to other vessels if she breaks away from her moorings. However, in any cases where he would be so liable for injuries to others obviously he must reduce his damages proportionately, if the injury is to his own barge. It becomes apparent why there can be no such general rule, when we consider the grounds for such a liability. Since there are occasions when every vessel will break from her moorings, and since, if she does, she becomes a menace to those about her; the owner's duty, as in other similar situations, to provide against resulting injuries is a function of three variables: (1) The probability that she will break away; (2) the gravity of the resulting injury, if she does; (3) the burden of adequate precautions. Possibly it serves to bring this notion into relief to state it in algebraic terms: if the probability be called P; the injury, L; and the burden, B; liability depends upon whether B is less than L multiplied by P: i.e., whether B less than PL. Applied to the situation at bar, the likelihood that a barge will break from her fasts and the damage she will do, vary with the place and time; for example, if a storm threatens, the danger is greater; so it is, if she is in a crowded harbor where moored barges are constantly being shifted about. On the other hand, the barge must not be the bargee's prison, even though he lives aboard; he must go ashore at times. We need not say whether, even in such crowded waters as New York Harbor a bargee must be aboard at night at all; it may be that the custom is otherwise . . . ; and that, if so, the situation is one where custom should control. We leave that question open; but we hold that it is not in all cases a sufficient answer to a bargee's absence without excuse, during working hours, that he has properly made fast his barge to a pier, when he leaves her. In the case at bar the bargee left at five o'clock in the afternoon of January 3rd, and the flotilla broke away at about two o'clock in the afternoon of the following day, twenty-one hours afterwards. The bargee had been away all the time, and we hold that his fabricated story was affirmative evidence that he had no excuse for his absence. At the locus in quo- especially during the short January days and in the full tide of war activity- barges were being constantly 'drilled' in and out. Certainly it was not beyond reasonable expectation that, with the inevitable haste and bustle, the work might not be done with adequate care. In such circumstances we hold — and it is all that we do hold — that it was a fair requirement that the Conners Company should have a bargee aboard (unless he had some excuse for his absence), during the working hours of daylight.

The decrees will be modified as follows. In the libel of the Conners Company against the Pennsylvania Railroad Company in which the Grace Line was impleaded, since the Grace Line is liable in solido, and the Carroll Company was not impleaded, the decree must be for full 'collision damages' and half 'sinking damages,' and the Pennsylvania Railroad Company will be secondarily liable. In the limitation proceeding of the Carroll Company (the privilege of limitation being conceded), the claim of the United States and of the Pennsylvania Railroad Company will be allowed in full. Since the claim of the Conners Company for 'collision damages' will be collected full in the libel against the Grace Line, the claim will be disallowed pro tanto. The claim of the Conners Company for 'sinking damages' being allowed for one half in the libel, will be allowed for only one sixth in the limitation proceeding. The Grace Line has claimed for only so much as the Conners Company may recover in the libel. That means that its claim will be one half the 'collision damages' and for one sixth the 'sinking damages.' If the fund be large enough, the result will be to throw one half the 'collision damages' upon the Grace Line and one half on the Carroll Company; and one third of the 'sinking damages' on the Conners Company, the Grace Line and the Carroll Company, each. If the fund is not large enough, the Grace Line will not be able altogether to recoup itself in the limitation proceeding for its proper contribution from the Carroll Company.

Decrees reversed and cause remanded for further proceedings in accordance with the foregoing.

HALEY v. LONDON ELECTRICITY BOARD
[1965] A.C. 778, [1964] 3 W.L.R. 479, 3 All E.R. 185

LORD REID. My Lords, the appellant became blind many years ago as a result of an accident. He conquered his disability to such an extent that for some years before 1956 he was employed as a telephonist by the London County Council. He lived in a street in South East London and it was his habit to walk unaccompanied from his home for about 100 yards along the pavement and then to get someone to help him to cross the main road where he boarded a bus. With the aid of his white stick he had learned to avoid all ordinary obstacles. On the morning of October 29, 1956, he had walked some 50 yards from his house. On that morning, unknown to him, the respondents' workmen had begun excavating a trench in the pavement, and they had placed an obstacle, which I shall describe in a moment, near the end of the trench. The appellant tripped over it and fell heavily. As a result of his head striking the pavement he has become deaf. He now sues the respondents on the ground of negligence. The case was decided against him by the trial judge and by the Court of Appeal and he now appeals to this House.

The respondents had authority to make this excavation under the Public Utilities Street Works Act, 1950. That Act requires that any such excavation shall be adequately fenced and guarded but the respondents argue that there is no civil liability under that Act for breach of a statutory duty. I need not consider that question because I am of opinion that the appellant is entitled to succeed at common law.

The respondents gave no instructions to their men as to how they were to guard this excavation and gave them no apparatus for that purpose except two notice boards. What the men did was to put the notice boards in such a position in the roadway as to prevent vehicles coming near the kerb and so enable pedestrians to avoid the excavation by walking past it on the roadway. At one end of the excavation they put a pick and shovel on the pavement, and at the end, to which the appellant came, they put a punner. This implement consists of a long handle like a broomstick to one end of which is attached a heavy weight. They put the heavy end on the pavement near the kerb and put the other end on to a railing, which runs along the inside of the pavement, so that it was some two feet above the ground. The handle was therefore sloping up from ground level at the outside to a height of about two feet at the inside of the pavement.

The appellant approached using his stick in the proper way — keeping it in front of him more or less vertical and moving it about so as to detect anything in his way. But he missed the punner handle and his leg caught it about 4½ inches above his ankle or about 8 or 9 inches above the ground. It is not alleged that he was negligent. He gave evidence that he had more than once detected with his stick the railing which the Post Office always use to guard their excavations. A senior Post Office engineer gave evidence that they always guard their excavations with a light fence like a towel rail about two feet high, and that they take into account the protection of blind people. He said that he knew of cases of blind people coming into contact with their fences. Unfortunately he was not asked whether this fence was effective to protect blind people, but I think that one can infer that it is seeing that the Post Office do have regard to their needs. Certainly the appellant's view, based on his own experience, is that a fence like that would have prevented his accident.

The trial judge held that what the respondents' men did gave adequate warning to ordinary people with good sight, and I am not disposed to disagree with that. The excavation was shallow and was to be filled in before nightfall, and the punner (or the pick and shovel) together with the notice boards and the heap of spoil on the pavement beside the trench were, I think, sufficient warning to ordinary people that they should not try to pass along the pavement past the trench . . .

On the other hand, if it was the duty of the respondents to have in mind the needs of blind or infirm pedestrians I think that what they did was quite insufficient. Indeed, the evidence shows that an obstacle attached to a heavy weight and only 9 inches above the ground may well escape detection by a blind man's stick and is for him a trap rather than a warning.

So the question for your Lordships' decision is the nature and extent of the duty owed to pedestrians by persons who carry out operations on a city pavement. The respondents argue that they were only bound to have in mind or to safeguard ordinary able-bodied people and were under no obligation to give particular consideration to the blind or infirm. If that is right, it means that a blind or infirm person who goes out alone goes at his peril. He may meet obstacles which are a danger to him but not to those with good sight because no one is under any obligation to remove or protect them. And if such an obstacle causes him injury he must suffer the damage in silence.

I could understand the respondents' contention if it was based on an argument that it was not reasonably foreseeable that a blind person might pass along that pavement on that day; or that, although foreseeable, the chance of a blind man coming there was so small and the difficulty of affording protection to him so great that it would have been in the circumstances unreasonable to afford that protection. Those are well recognised grounds of defence. But in my judgment neither is open to the respondents in this case.

In deciding what is reasonably foreseeable one must have regard to common knowledge. We are all accustomed to meeting blind people walking alone with their white sticks on city pavements. No doubt there are many places open to the public where for one reason or another one would be surprised to see a blind person walking alone, but a city pavement is not one of them. And a residential street cannot be different from any other. The blind people we meet must live somewhere and most of them probably left their homes unaccompanied. It may seem surprising that blind people can avoid ordinary obstacles so well as they do, but we must take account of the facts. There is evidence in this case about the number of blind people in London and it appears from Government publications that the proportion in the whole country is near one in 500. By no means all are sufficiently skilled or confident to venture out alone but the number who habitually do so must be very large. I find it quite impossible to say that it is not reasonably foreseeable that a blind person may pass along a particular pavement on a particular day.

No question can arise in this case of any great difficulty in affording adequate protection for the blind. In considering what is adequate protection again one must have regard to common knowledge. One is entitled to expect of a blind person a high degree of skill and care because none but the most foolhardy would venture to go out alone without having that skill and exercising that care. We know that in fact blind people do safely avoid all ordinary obstacles on pavements; there can be no question of padding lamp posts as was suggested in one case. But a moment's reflection shows that a low obstacle in an unusual place is a grave danger: on the other hand, it is clear from the evidence in this case and also, I think, from common knowledge that quite a light fence some two feet high is an adequate warning. There would have been no difficulty in providing such a fence here. The evidence is that the Post Office always provide one, and that the respondents have similar fences which are often used. Indeed the evidence suggests that the only reason there was no fence here was that the accident occurred before the necessary fences had arrived. So if the respondents are to succeed it can only be on the ground that there was no duty to do more than safeguard ordinary able-bodied people.

. . .

We were also referred to American authorities. . . . Most are in reports not available here, but it seems clear that widely differing views are expressed. We were informed that there is nothing in the American Restatement on the question we have to decide, and I am unable to determine whether any view on the question can now be said to prevail in the United States.

I can see no justification for laying down any hard-and-fast rule limiting the classes of persons for whom those interfering with a pavement must make provision. It is said that it is impossible to tell what precautions will be adequate to protect all kinds of infirm pedestrians or that taking such precautions would be unreasonably difficult or expensive. I think that such fears are exaggerated. . . . It appears to me that the ordinary principles of the common law must apply in streets as well as elsewhere, and that fundamentally they depend on what a reasonable man, careful of his neighbour's safety, would do having the knowledge which a reasonable man in the position of the defendant must be deemed to have. I agree with the statement of law at the end of the speech of Lord Sumner in *Glasgow Corporation v. Taylor*: "a measure of care appropriate to the inability or disability of those who are immature or feeble in mind or body is due from others, who know of or ought to anticipate the presence of such persons within the scope and hazard of their own operations." I would therefore allow this appeal. The assessment of damages has been deferred and the case must be remitted for such assessment.

. . . Appeal allowed.

Notes and Questions

1. What facts (evidence) did the parties in *Carroll Towing* offer to support the allegation that the Connors Company was unreasonable and imprudent (that is, in breach of the standard of care) not to have a bargee aboard the Anna C. in the circumstances? What facts did the Connors Company proffer in response? How would you characterize those facts in general?

2. What facts (evidence) did the plaintiff in *Haley* offer to support the allegation that the Electricity Board was unreasonable and imprudent in how it fenced its excavation? Was this the same kind of evidence that the parties in *Carroll Towing* proffered in support of their breach argument? How did this evidence fit into the Hand formula? Did the parties have an argument from social utility about how the breach issue should be resolved?

3. How do you think the evidence in *Carroll Towing* and *Haley* was introduced into evidence? If you were a lawyer in the cases, how would you make the relevant facts available to the court and to the triers of fact?

4. Judge Hand's "BPL formula" for establishing the standard of care and breach appears to be mathematical in nature, but he did not intend it to be so. Rather, Hand believed that he was merely codifying a process we all engage in (lawyers and laypersons alike) when we analyze situations to determine what it means to be careful and careless. Richard Posner, A Theory of Negligence, 1 J. Legal Studies 29, 32–34 (1972). Was Judge Hand correct? Consider the point of decision as you are turning off of a main road into a residential area; what facts do you consider as you choose how fast you will drive, and how do you relate them to each other? Is your mode of analysis consistent with Hand's formula?

5. Proponents of an economic approach to the establishment of breach appreciate the Hand formula because it provides some assurances that breach analysis will be consistent and rigorous, and that outcomes will be correct — defendants will only be considered unreasonable and thus subject to liability when, on balance, the burden of alternative precautions is lower than the risk of the particular loss that occurred.

6. The burden of alternative precautions has a flip side: the benefit of the defendant's conduct. It is in this context that the relative social utility of the defendant's actual conduct and the plaintiff's proposed conduct can be considered. Social utility analysis adds a "macro" or policy dimension to breach analysis, which usually focuses on the particulars of the case at issue. This policy analysis is not always relevant, but it might be; for example, in the case of an automobile manufacturer whose design lacks some safety feature (for example, rear-seat, side-impact air bags) that would have predictably saved a certain number of lives, but that would have priced the design out of the low-income market for which it was intended. Imagine that you are the

lawyer for the automobile manufacturer which has just been sued by the widow of a man who died in part because there were no rear-seat, side-impact airbags in the car in which he was a rear-seat passenger. How would you argue and support your argument that burden of alternative precautions — redesigning the car with rear-seat, side-impact airbags — is too high in relation to the probability and gravity of loss? How would argue this issue from the plaintiff's side of the case?

B. Custom Evidence

1. Business Custom

THE T.J. HOOPER v. NORTHERN BARGE CORPORATION
60 F.2d 737 (2d Cir. 1932)

L. HAND, Circuit Judge.

The barges No. 17 and No. 30, belonging to the Northern Barge Company, had lifted cargoes of coal at Norfolk, Virginia, for New York in March, 1928. They were towed by two tugs of the petitioner, the 'Montrose' and the 'Hooper,' and were lost off the Jersey Coast on March tenth, in an easterly gale. The cargo owners sued the barges under the contracts of carriage; the owner of the barges sued the tugs under the towing contract, both for its own loss and as bailee of the cargoes; the owner of the tug filed a petition to limit its liability. All the suits were joined and heard together, and the judge found that all the vessels were unseaworthy; the tugs, because they did not carry radio receiving sets by which they could have seasonably got warnings of a change in the weather which should have caused them to seek shelter in the Delaware Breakwater en route. He therefore entered an interlocutory decree holding each tug and barge jointly liable to each cargo owner, and each tug for half damages for the loss of its barge. The petitioner appealed, and the barge owner appealed and filed assignments of error.

Each tug had three ocean going coal barges in tow, the lost barge being at the end. The 'Montrose,' which had the No. 17, took an outside course; the 'Hooper' with the No. 30, inside. The weather was fair without ominous symptoms, as the tows passed the Delaware Breakwater about midnight of March eighth, and the barges did not get into serious trouble until they were about opposite Atlantic City some sixty or seventy miles to the north. The wind began to freshen in the morning of the ninth and rose to a gale before noon; by afternoon the second barge of the Hooper's tow was out of hand and signalled the tug, which found that not only this barge needed help, but that the No. 30 was aleak. Both barges anchored and the crew of the No. 30 rode out the storm until the afternoon of the tenth, when she sank, her crew having been meanwhile taken off. The No. 17 sprang a leak about the same time; she too anchored at the Montrose's command and sank on the next morning after her crew also had been rescued.

[The court's discussion of the barges' seaworthiness is omitted.]

A more difficult issue is as to the tugs. We agree with the judge that once conceding the propriety of passing the Breakwater on the night of the eighth, the navigation was good enough. It might have been worse to go back when the storm broke than to keep on. The seas were from the east and southeast, breaking on the starboard quarter of the barges, which if tight and well found should have lived. True they were at the tail and this is the most trying position, but to face the seas in an attempt to return was a doubtful choice; the masters' decision is final unless they made a plain error. The evidence does not justify that conclusion; and so, the case as to them turns upon whether they should have put in at the Breakwater.

The weather bureau at Arlington broadcasts two predictions daily, at ten in the morning and ten in the evening. Apparently there are other reports floating about, which come at uncertain hours but which can also be picked up. The Arlington report of the morning read as follows: 'Moderate north, shifting to east and southeast winds, increasing Friday, fair weather to-night.' The substance of this, apparently from another source, reached a tow bound north to New York about noon, and, coupled with a falling glass, decided the master to put in to the Delaware Breakwater in the afternoon. The glass had not indeed fallen much and perhaps the tug was over cautious; nevertheless, although the appearances were all fair, he thought discretion the better part of valor. Three other tows followed him, the masters of two of which testified. Their decision was in part determined by example; but they too had received the Arlington report or its equivalent, and though it is doubtful whether alone it would have turned the scale, it is plain that it left them in an indecision which needed little to be resolved on the side of prudence; they preferred to take no chances, and chances they believed there were. Courts have not often such evidence of the opinion of impartial experts, formed in the very circumstances and confirmed by their own conduct at the time.

Moreover, the 'Montrose' and the 'Hooper' would have had the benefit of the evening report from Arlington had they had proper receiving sets. This predicted worse weather; it read: 'Increasing east and southeast winds, becoming fresh to strong, Friday night and increasing cloudiness followed by rain Friday.' The bare 'increase' of the morning had become 'fresh to strong.' To be sure this scarcely foretold a gale of from forty to fifty miles for five hours or more, rising at one time to fifty-six; but if the four tows thought the first report enough, the second ought to have laid any doubts. The master of the 'Montrose' himself, when asked what he would have done had he received a substantially similar report, said that he would certainly have put in. The master of the 'Hooper' was also asked for his opinion, and said that he would have turned back also, but this admission is somewhat vitiated by the incorporation in the question of the statement that it was a 'storm warning,' which the witness seized upon in his answer. All this seems to us to support the conclusion of the judge that prudent masters, who had received the second warning, would have found the risk more than the exigency warranted; they would have been amply vindicated by what followed. To be sure the barges would, as we have said, probably have withstood the gale, had they been well found; but a master is not justified in putting his tow to every test which she will survive, if she be fit. There is a zone in which proper caution will avoid putting her capacity to the proof; a coefficient of prudence that he should not disregard. Taking the situation as a whole, it seems to us that these masters would have taken undue chances, had they got the broadcasts.

They did not, because their private radio receiving sets, which were on board, were not in working order. These belonged to them personally, and were partly a toy, partly a part of the equipment, but neither furnished by the owner, nor supervised by it. It is not fair to say that there was a general custom among coastwise carriers so to equip their tugs. One line alone did it; as for the rest, they relied upon their crews, so far as they can be said to have relied at all. An adequate receiving set suitable for a coastwise tug can now be got at small cost and is reasonably reliable if kept up; obviously it is a source of great protection to their tows. Twice every day they can receive these predictions, based upon the widest possible information, available to every vessel within two or three hundred miles and more. Such a set is the ears of the tug to catch the spoken word, just as the master's binoculars are her eyes to see a storm signal ashore. Whatever may be said as to other vessels, tugs towing heavy coal laden barges, strung out for half a mile, have little power to manoeuvre, and do not, as this case proves, expose themselves to weather which would not turn back stauncher craft. They can have at hand protection against dangers of which they can learn in no other way.

Is it then a final answer that the business had not yet generally adopted receiving sets? There are, no doubt, cases where courts seem to make the general practice of the calling the standard of proper diligence; we have indeed given some currency to the notion ourselves. Indeed in most cases reasonable prudence is in fact common prudence; but strictly it is never its measure; a whole calling may have unduly lagged in the adoption of new and available devices. It never may set its own tests, however persuasive be its usages. Courts must in the end say what is required; there are precautions so imperative that even their universal disregard will not excuse their omission. But here there was no custom at all as to receiving sets; some had them, some did not; the most that can be urged is that they had not yet become general. Certainly in such a case we need not pause; when some have thought a device necessary, at least we may say that they were right, and the others too slack. The statute (section 484, title 46, U. S. Code [46 USCA § 484]) does not bear on this situation at all. It prescribes not a receiving, but a transmitting set, and for a very different purpose; to call for help, not to get news. We hold the tugs therefore because had they been properly equipped, they would have got the Arlington reports. The injury was a direct consequence of this unseaworthiness.

Decree affirmed.

Notes and Questions

1. Judge Hand's opinion in *The T.J. Hooper* predates his opinion in *Carroll Towing*. Can you nevertheless see his BPL formula at work? Why is it that the defendants were unreasonable not to have receiving sets on board their tugs?

2. *The T.J. Hooper* is the classic case on the issue of the relevance of business custom evidence to establish breach or reasonableness: this evidence is relevant, and perhaps even persuasive in most instances, but it is never dispositive as a matter of law. In Hand's words, "[c]ourts must in the end say what is required; there are precautions so imperative that even their universal disregard will not excuse their omission." Why is it usually the case that the business custom is persuasive on the standard of care? What business error did *The T.J. Hooper* defendants make?

3. How do you think custom evidence is typically introduced to the court and to the trier of fact? If you were a lawyer in a case in which such evidence was relevant, how would you imagine doing this work?

2. Medical and Other Professional Custom

Medical custom evidence is treated differently than ordinary business custom evidence: the former is dispositive as to what constitutes reasonable care; that is, the medical profession, not the court or the jury, dictates the "degree of care and skill which is expected of the average practitioner in the class to which [the defendant] belongs, acting in the same or similar circumstances." Why might the law give physicians this bye? What is it about the medical profession that makes sense of this important exception to the rule in *The T.J. Hooper*? As you consider this question, read Atul Gawande, *Personal Best*, The New Yorker, Oct. 3, 2011 (available online).

As applied, this professional custom rule requires the plaintiff in an ordinary medical malpractice case to proffer one or more medical experts who will testify as to the relevant professional standard of care and that the defendant deviated from it. The defendant is a medical expert by definition; because of this and because the plaintiff has the burden of proof, if the defendant testifies on the standard of care he or she is not required to retain additional testifying experts on that point. However, the defendant may choose to do so to corroborate the defense's position. On the issue of standard of care and deviation from it, the jury must either accept the judgment of at least one of the medical experts, or find that none of the experts are credible. (In the latter case, the plaintiff loses because the burden of proof was not sustained.) Interestingly, the law's approach to establishing reasonableness in medical malpractice cases risks adopting a standard that is beneath that which expected by the medical profession itself. For example, because of the way the case is litigated, the jury may find for the defendant in circumstances where the relevant accrediting bodies may have rejected the approach as antiquated or inappropriately experimental. How might the law explain and then justify such a result?

The question of who qualifies as an expert on the standard of care in medical malpractice cases incorporates three separate inquiries: How "expert" must the person be? Must the expert be familiar with the locality where the defendant practiced? And if a medical specialty is involved, must the expert practice within the same specialty?

As to "expertness," the Federal Rules of Evidence, followed in most jurisdictions, require that the proposed witness be "qualified as an expert by knowledge, skill, experience, training, or education. . . ." Fed. R. Evid. 702. If there is a challenge to the witness's expertise, the court decides if the expert meets these qualifications before the witness testifies. While some states have modified their expert qualification rules to address the related questions of locality and specialization, most have not and those matters have been resolved by common law development or statutes.

The original common law rule on locality required all experts to know the standard of care in the community where the defendant doctor practiced. As a practical matter, this required a witness from that place. As the Washington Supreme Court noted in *Pederson v. Dumouchel*, 491 P.2d 973, 977 (1967),

> [t]he original reason for the 'locality rule' is apparent. When there was little intercommunity travel, courts required experts who testified to the standard of care that should have been used to have a personal knowledge of the practice of physicians

> in that particular community where the patient was treated. It was the accepted theory that a doctor in a small community did not have the same opportunities and resources as did a doctor practicing in a large city to keep abreast of advances in his profession; hence, he should not be held to the same standard of care and skill as that employed by doctors in other communities or in larger cities.

The locality rule was not without its problems, as the *Pederson* court went on to note:

> The 'locality rule' had two practical difficulties: first, the scarcity of professional men in the community who were qualified or willing to testify about the local standard of care; and second, the possibility of a small group, who, by their laxness or carelessness, could establish a local standard of care that was below that which the law requires. The fact that several careless practitioners might settle in the same place cannot affect the standard of diligence and skill which local patients have a right to expect. Negligence cannot be excused on the ground that others in the same locality practice the same kind of negligence. No degree of antiquity can give sanction to usage bad in itself.

Id. at 977.

The court's mention of "scarcity" fails adequately to convey the problem. Doctors in a small town were for reasons of comity or fear of retribution unwilling to testify against their local colleagues. In the absence of a witness to testify to the standard of care, the plaintiff's claim necessarily failed. Over time, this problem was addressed by common law expansions of the locality rule from requiring experts from the "same community" to requiring experts from "the same or similar communities" to allowing a broader search for willing experts. This did help with the scarcity issue but it did nothing to address the problem that an entire community might have lagged in the adoption of a reasonable standard of care. The latter is particularly troublesome given that in the modern period, there is no lack of opportunity for a physician or surgeon to keep abreast of the advances made in his profession and to be familiar with the latest methods and practices adopted.

> The comprehensive coverage of the Journal of the American Medical Association, the availability of numerous other journals, the ubiquitous 'detail men' of the drug companies, closed circuit television presentations of medical subjects, special radio networks for physicians, tape recorded digests of medical literature, and hundreds of widely available postgraduate courses all serve to keep physicians informed and increasingly to establish nationwide standards. Medicine realizes this, so it is inevitable that the law will do likewise.

Id. at 977–78. As a result, in most jurisdictions,

> [t]he 'locality rule' has no present-day vitality except that it may be considered as one of the elements to determine the degree of care and skill which is to be expected of the average practitioner of the class to which he belongs. The degree of care which must be observed is, of course, that of an average, competent practitioner acting in the same or similar circumstances. In other words, local practice within geographic proximity is one, but not the only factor to be considered. No longer is it proper to limit the definition of the standard of care which a medical doctor or dentist must

> meet solely to the practice or custom of a particular locality, a similar locality, or a geographic area.

Id. at 978.

The modern standard of care is thus that degree of care and skill which is to be expected of the average[1] practitioner of the class to which the defendant belongs, acting in the same or similar circumstances. Most jurisdictions have adopted a "national" (as opposed to same or similar locality) standard of care for specialists because they are nationally certified and accredited. See, e.g., Thierfelder v. Wolfert, 52 A.3d 1251 (Penn. 2012). This requires them to practice up to that standard and allows plaintiffs to compare their professional decisions to those of other specialists in their class wherever they practice in the United States. How might local circumstances nevertheless influence the reasonableness of specialists' decision making in particular cases? Similarly, the standard for hospitals, clinics, and other institutional providers is almost universally a national standard since all are subject to national accreditation standards. For general practitioners, the trend is also towards a national standard but the movement has been slower. The modified locality rule still prevails in many jurisdictions, reflecting a continued sense in those places that general practitioners have fewer resources for keeping abreast of developments across the specialties that inform their work.

The only standard exception to the rule that the medical profession sets its own standard of care is in the case of clear medical errors. Examples of clear medical errors include wrong-sided or wrong-site surgeries and leaving tools in the patient's body after surgery. Plaintiffs do not need a medical expert to testify that these are a breach of the medical standard of care. *See, e.g.,* Hestbeck v. Hennepin County, 212 N.W.2d 361 (Minn. 1973). How is this exception consistent with the rationales underlying the general rule?

The medical community itself has sought to establish lists of clear medical errors and to develop and implement systems to prevent such errors. These lists go well beyond wrong-sided surgeries and "retained" surgical implements, although these particular events remain the most publicized. See Sarah Kliff, Surgeons left 4,857 objects in patients over the past two decades, The Washington Post, Dec. 20, 2012 (describing medical research documenting phenomenon of medical errors and "checklist" approach to prevention); Hospital Repeats Wrong-Sided Brain Surgery, ABC News, Nov. 28, 2007. This movement began as a response to a series of internal (to the profession) studies and reports documenting the incidence of errors and suggesting other-than-legal solutions to address the problem. See, e.g., David M. Studdert, Michelle M. Mello, and Troyen A. Brennan, Health Policy Report: Medical Malpractice, 350 New Eng. J. of Med. 283, 285–86 (Jan. 15, 2004); To Err Is Human: Building a Safer Health System, The Institute of Medicine (Nov. 1999). In this respect, the law and courts have lagged significantly: the only modern case to hold that at least some diagnostic and treatment decisions are subject to the *T.J. Hooper* doctrine was quickly corrected by the state's legislature and saw no traction in other states. Helling v. Carey, 519 P.2d 981 (Wa. 1974) (finding unreasonable as a matter of law the standard of care among ophthalmologists not to subject younger patients to routine eye pressure tests). See also, Philip M. Rosoff & Doriane Lambelet Coleman, The Case for Legal Regulation of Physicians' Off-Label Prescribing, 86 Notre Dame L. Rev. 649, 666-

[1] Jurisdictions differ on whether the comparison is between the defendant's conduct and that of an "average" practitioner or a "minimally competent" practitioner.

74 (2011) (describing medical malpractice law's deference to physicians' own standards, even when these standards contravene AMA and related proscriptions).

Whether medical malpractice law serves tort law's compensatory and deterrent functions is much debated. Statistically speaking, or in terms of social utility broadly, it appears to be relatively clear that the law is at least somewhat ineffective and inefficient in both respects. *See supra*, Studdert, Mellow, and Brennan, *Health Policy Report: Medical Malpractice*, 350 New Eng. J. of Med. at 283-86. On the other hand, malpractice law clearly continues to serve an important role in individual cases, especially in a context where more effective and efficient approaches to compensation and regulation remain elusive.

At least formally, the standard of care for legal and other professional malpractice mirrors the medical malpractice standard. Thus, "a lawyer must exercise that degree of reasonable care and skill expected of lawyers acting under similar circumstances." Morrison v. MacNamara, 407 A.2d 555, 561 (D.C. App. 1979). And while the plaintiff is generally required to proffer a relevant (by expertise and geography) expert to testify to the applicable standard of care, this "is not necessary where the negligence is so grossly apparent that a lay person would have no difficulty recognizing it." Asphalt Engineers, Inc. v. Galusha, 770 P.2d 1180, 1181–82 (Ariz. App.1989). However, judges are a lot more comfortable finding apparent negligence or clear error by lawyers than they are by doctors; in other words, as applied, the rule for legal professionals is much less deferential than the rule for medical professionals. Why is this not surprising? What would you expect of judges reviewing architectural or engineering malpractice cases?

HARNISH v. CHILDREN'S HOSPITAL MEDICAL CENTER
439 N.E.2d 240 (Mass. 1982)

O'CONNOR, Justice.

The plaintiff underwent an operation to remove a [benign] tumor in her neck. During the procedure, her hypoglossal nerve was severed, allegedly resulting in a permanent and almost total loss of tongue function.

The plaintiff's complaint charges the defendant physicians and hospital with misrepresentation and negligence in failing to inform her before surgery of the risk of loss of tongue function. The complaint alleges that the purpose of the operation was cosmetic, that the loss of tongue function was a material and foreseeable risk of the operation, and that, had the plaintiff been informed of this risk, she would not have consented to the operation. There is no claim that the operation was negligently performed.

A medical malpractice tribunal, convened pursuant to G.L. c. 231, § 60B, concluded that the plaintiff's offer of proof was insufficient to raise a question appropriate for judicial inquiry. The action was dismissed after the plaintiff failed to post a bond in accordance with G.L. c. 231, § 60B. The plaintiff appeals from the judgment of dismissal, claiming that her offer of proof satisfied the requirements of the directed verdict test, as defined in *Kapp v. Ballantine*, 380 Mass. 186, 402 N.E.2d 463 (1980), and *Little v. Rosenthal*, 376 Mass. 573, 578, 382 N.E.2d 1037 (1978). She argues that her offer of proof was sufficient to raise a question of liability under the doctrine of lack of informed consent.[2] We reverse so much of the judgment of dismissal as applies to Drs. Holmes and Mulliken, and affirm the dismissal of the complaint against Dr. Gilman and Children's Hospital Medical Center.

1. *The rule of liability.* A medical malpractice tribunal has jurisdiction over actions for "malpractice, error or mistake against a provider of health care." G.L. c. 231, § 60B, inserted by St. 1975, c. 362, § 5. The performance of a surgical procedure by a physician without the patient's consent constitutes professional misconduct, is malpractice within G.L. c. 231, § 60B, and is subject to the procedures established by this statute.

"There is implicit recognition in the law of the Commonwealth, as elsewhere, that a person has a strong interest in being free from nonconsensual invasion of his bodily integrity. . . . In short, the law recognizes the individual interest in preserving 'the inviolability of his person.' *Pratt v. Davis*, 118 Ill.App. 161, 166 (1905), aff'd, 224 Ill. 300, 79 N.E. 562 (1906). One means by which the law has developed in a manner consistent with the protection of this interest is through the development of the doctrine of informed consent." *Superintendent of Belchertown State School v. Saikewicz*, 373 Mass. 728, 738-739, 370 N.E.2d 417 (1977). See also . . . *Schloendorff v. Society of the New York Hosp.*, 211 N.Y. 125, 129-130, 105 N.E. 92 (1914). "[I]t is the prerogative of the patient, not the physician, to determine . . . the direction in which . . . his interest lie." *Cobbs v. Grant, supra*, 8 Cal.3d at 242, 104 Cal.Rptr. 505, 502 P.2d 1. *Canterbury v. Spence*, 464 F.2d 772, 781 (D.C.Cir.), cert. denied, 409 U.S. 1064, 93 S.Ct. 560, 34 L.Ed.2d 518 (1972). Every competent adult has a right "to forego treatment, or even cure, if it entails what for him are intolerable consequences or risks however unwise his sense of values may be in the eyes of the medical profession." *Wilkinson v. Vesey*, 110 R.I. 606, 624, 295 A.2d 676 (1972). Knowing exercise of this right requires knowledge of the available options and the risks attendant on each. *Canterbury v. Spence, supra* at 780. *Cobbs v. Grant, supra* 8 Cal.3d at 242–243, 104 Cal.Rptr. 505, 502 P.2d 1. We hold, therefore, that a physician's failure to divulge in a reasonable manner to a competent adult patient sufficient information to enable the patient to make an informed judgment whether to give or withhold consent to a medical or surgical procedure constitutes professional misconduct and comes within the ambit of G.L. c. 231, § 60B.

While we recognize that a patient ordinarily cannot make an intelligent decision whether to undergo a medical or surgical procedure without receiving from the physician information significant to the decision, we also recognize that there are limits to what society or an individual can reasonably expect of a physician in this regard. Medical matters are often complex. Recommendations of treatment frequently require the application of considerable medical knowledge gained through extensive training and experience. Communication of scientific information by the trained physician to the untrained patient may be difficult. The remotely possible risks of a proposed treatment may be almost without limit. The patient's right to know must be harmonized with the recognition that an undue burden should not be placed on the physician. These interests are accommodated by the rule that we adopt today, that a physician owes to his patient the duty to disclose in a reasonable manner all significant

---

[2] In her brief, the plaintiff asserts that her claim is based solely on the doctrine of lack of informed consent. Since she does not present argument on the propriety of the tribunal's ruling as it relates to her claims of misrepresentation, we do not address this issue on appeal. *Commonwealth v. Horton*, 376 Mass. 380, 388, 380 N.E.2d 687 (1978), cert. denied, 440 U.S. 923, 99 S.Ct. 1252, 59 L.Ed.2d 477 (1979).

medical information that the physician possesses or reasonably should possess that is material to an intelligent decision by the patient whether to undergo a proposed procedure. The information a physician reasonably should possess is that information possessed by the average qualified physician or, in the case of a specialty, by the average qualified physician practicing that specialty. What the physician should know involves professional expertise and can ordinarily be proved only through the testimony of experts. However, the extent to which he must share that information with his patient depends upon what information he should reasonably recognize is material to the plaintiff's decision. *Wilkinson v. Vesey, supra* at 627-628, 295 A.2d 676. "Materiality may be said to be the significance a reasonable person, in what the physician knows or should know is his patient's position, would attach to the disclosed risk or risks in deciding whether to submit or not to submit to surgery or treatment." *Id.* at 627, 295 A.2d 676. The materiality determination is one that lay persons are qualified to make without the aid of an expert. Appropriate information may include the nature of the patient's condition, the nature and probability of risks involved, the benefits to be reasonably expected, the inability of the physician to predict results, if that is the situation, the irreversibility of the procedure, if that be the case, the likely result of no treatment, and the available alternatives, including their risks and benefits. The obligation to give adequate information does not require the disclosure of all risks of a proposed therapy, or of information the physician reasonably believes the patient already has, such as the risks, like infection, inherent in any operation.

Many jurisdictions have adopted the rule that a physician must disclose to his patient only such information as is customarily disclosed by physicians in similar circumstances. We think that the better rule is the one we adopt today. The customary practice standard overlooks the purpose of requiring disclosure, which is protection of the patient's right to decide for himself.

We recognize that despite the importance of the patient's right to know, there may be situations that call for a privilege of nondisclosure. For instance, sound medical judgment might indicate that disclosure would complicate the patient's medical condition or render him unfit for treatment. "Where that is so, the cases have generally held that the physician is armed with a privilege to keep the information from the patient. . . . The physician's privilege to withhold information for therapeutic reasons must be carefully circumscribed, however, for otherwise it might devour the disclosure rule itself. The privilege does not accept the paternalistic notion that the physician may remain silent simply because divulgence might prompt the patient to forego therapy the physician feels the patient really needs" (footnotes omitted). *Canterbury v. Spence, supra* at 789. A full discussion of the privilege is neither required nor attempted here, because the burden of proving it must rest with the physician, and thus the question of privilege is inappropriate to the directed verdict standard to be applied to the plaintiff's offer of proof before the medical malpractice tribunal.

2. *Causation.* We turn to the question of causation. "An unrevealed risk that should have been made known must materialize, for otherwise the omission, however unpardonable, is legally without consequence." *Canterbury v. Spence, supra* at 790. *Schroeder v. Lawrence*, 372 Mass. 1, 5, 359 N.E.2d 1301 (1977). Whether the alleged undisclosed risk materialized is a medical question appropriate to the tribunal's inquiry. At trial, the plaintiff must also show that had the proper information been provided neither he nor a reasonable person in similar circumstances would have undergone the procedure. *Id.* at 5, 359 N.E.2d 1301. *Wilkinson v. Vesey, supra* 110 R.I. at 628–629, 295 A.2d 676. Such proof, not relating to medical questions, is not appropriate to the tribunal's inquiry.

3. *The offer of proof.* The plaintiff's offer of proof, which we accept as true, consisted of her affidavit, an opinion letter from two oral surgeons, and various hospital reports. We summarize the offer of proof, relying principally on the surgeons' letter. In April, 1978, a subtotal excision of a cystic hygroma was performed on the plaintiff's neck at the defendant hospital. Over a course of several years the plaintiff had required several surgical procedures for this disorder. Although the disease had in the past been life threatening, the April, 1978, procedure was done purely for cosmetic reasons. The procedure resulted in severance of the hypoglossal nerve with resulting severe dysfunctions in speech, mastication, saliva management, and swallowing. The severance of the nerve, with the ensuing consequences, was foreseeable as a probability despite proper performance of the surgery. Standard and acceptable medical practice required that the plaintiff be informed before the operation of the risk of nerve severance and the consequences of severance. The plaintiff was not given that information. If she had been, she would have declined the operation.

According to the offer of proof, Dr. Mulliken was the admitting physician and surgeon in charge of the operation. Dr. Holmes and Dr. Gilman assisted at the operation. In addition, before the operation Dr. Holmes discussed with the plaintiff the potential consequences, risks and side effects of the surgery, but he never informed her of the risk of loss of tongue function and its consequences. He told the plaintiff that he would perform the operation successfully.

It is apparent that the offer of proof was sufficient to raise a question appropriate for judicial inquiry with respect to the defendants, Mulliken and Holmes. The only mention of Dr. Gilman in the offer of proof is found in the operative report, where he is listed as an assistant. The plaintiff asserts that Dr. Gilman's participation as an assistant is sufficient to create a doctor-patient relationship with a concomitant duty of disclosure. The plaintiff does not present any case law to support this proposition, and we have found no authority that would impose such a duty on a surgical assistant. It would not be reasonable to require all of the individuals who only assist in the operating room to obtain the informed consent of the patient.

The plaintiff claims that the hospital is vicariously liable for the alleged negligence of the surgeons. In her brief, the plaintiff argues that the doctors were servants of the hospital. The offer of proof does not show the surgeons' affiliation with the hospital. Even if we were to assume staff affiliation, there is nothing to show that the hospital had power of control over the surgeons' professional conduct.

The judgment as to the defendants Mulliken and Holmes is reversed. The judgment as to defendants Gilman and Children's Hospital Medical Center is affirmed.

Notes and Questions

1. What are the two main jurisdictional approaches to the use of experts in informed consent cases? Which of the two is most consistent with the personal (decisional) autonomy rationale underlying the doctrine? Which approach best balances patients' and doctors' interests?

2. Finding the right balance between respecting patient autonomy and doing one's job can sometimes be difficult for medical professionals. For example, in an effort to provide patients with all of the information they need to make an informed decision about their medical care,

doctors may give patients too much unfiltered information either orally or in an overly complex and comprehensive consent form. Does the informed consent standard provide guidance or a solution in this respect?

3. As we saw in Chapter Two, where there is no valid consent at all, the patient-plaintiffs claim is in battery. In contrast, where there is consent but it is claimed to be under- or misinformed, the claim is in negligence.

4. In *Harnish* the court refers to a "medical malpractice tribunal" that is tasked with conducting an initial merits screening of the case. The Illinois Supreme Court explained the history of such pre-suit procedures in a different case:

> It is generally agreed that in the early 1970's what has been termed a medical malpractice insurance crisis existed in most jurisdictions in this country. The crisis resulted from the increasing reluctance of insurance companies to write medical malpractice insurance policies and the dramatic rise in premiums demanded by those companies which continued to issue policies. The difficulty in obtaining insurance at reasonable rates forced many health-care providers to curtail or cease to render their services. The legislative response to this crisis sought to reduce the cost of medical malpractice insurance and to insure its continued availability to the providers of health care. By October 1975, 39 States had commissioned studies of the medical malpractice problem and 22 States had revised civil practice laws and rules in an attempt to remedy the problem. Redish, *Legislative Response to the Medical Malpractice Insurance Crisis: Constitutional Implications,* 55 Tex. L. Rev. 759, 761 n. 14 (1977).
>
> Legislative efforts dealing with the malpractice crisis included a variety of changes in tort law principles. In many instances direct limits were placed on the amount of recovery. The use of screening panels and arbitration was broadly recommended and followed, and certain procedural changes such as altering the statute of limitations were made.

Anderson v. Wagner, 402 N.E.2d 560, 560-61 (Ill. 1979). Most states did not take away the plaintiff's right to sue after an adverse decision by the panel, but some allowed an adverse decision on the merits of the case to be introduced at trial. See, e.g., Indiana Code § 34-189.10. A related pre-suit merits screening requirement in some states was requiring the plaintiff to have a qualified expert certify the merits before a case could be filed. See, e.g., N.C.G.S. 1A-1, Rule 9(j).

Other legislative measures enacted in that period included abolition of the collateral source rule or its modification, see, e.g., Conn. Gen. Stat. §52-225a; caps on contingent fees for plaintiffs' lawyers, see, e.g., Mass. Ann. Laws Chap.231. § 601; and caps on non-economic damages, see, e.g., Cal. Civ. Code, § 3333.1 subds. (a), (b) (limiting damages "for pain, suffering, inconvenience, physical impairment, disfigurement and other nonpecuniary damage" to no more than "two hundred fifty thousand dollars ($250,000)"). We will discuss the collateral source rule and non-economic damages when we study injuries and damages later in the course.

5. Covid-related medical malpractice claims will raise issues throughout the negligence prima facie case: Immunities and liability limitations developed by courts and legislatures may alter the duty medical professionals and their affiliated institutions have to patients and their families. Establishing reasonable care in circumstances involving a novel, highly contagious disease and the allocation of scare resources in emergencies and near emergencies will be difficult, thus ensuring that breach will be a litigated issue in those cases where immunities and special duty rules are not threshold bars to recovery. Finally, as we will see when we discuss the material in the following chapters, proving causation and damages will also be difficult and expensive in virtually all Covid cases, particularly those involving plaintiffs with pre-existing conditions or co-morbidities. As a result, it will be difficult for potential plaintiffs to find lawyers who will agree to take on such cases. What is the argument that this is the right outcome? And if it is the right outcome, should the goals of tort law be met differently?

Problem Six: The Nose

Cosmetic surgeon Dr. Defendant specializes in rhinosplasty—she "fixes" noses. She advertises widely, her ads hinting that she can go almost anywhere in town and see the product of her 30 years in practice. Indeed, the striking uniformity of local noses despite the area's wide ethnic diversity suggests that lots of people in town have had their noses fixed by the good doctor, who is apparently not very flexible in her work.

Our Plaintiff is a conformist. He had seen Defendant's signature nose around town and he wanted one for himself. And so he made an appointment to meet with her. At this appointment, Defendant explained the risks of the procedure, including that "rhinoplasty risks scarring and damaging proximate underlying structures." She told Plaintiff that these potential complications have to be balanced against the procedure's benefits, including for him the psychological benefits of getting *the* nose. Plaintiff listened, said he understood, and agreed to have the doctor do the work. (He really, really wanted the nose, which was everywhere, and he hadn't heard of any complaints. Defendant's warnings were, in his view, simply pro forma and otherwise obvious.) Per the doctor's requirements, Plaintiff signed a consent form memorializing their discussion and agreement, and paid for the surgery and his post-operative care in advance.

After a few weeks of recovery, Plaintiff looked in the mirror and there it was! The nose! He was very happy. The only problem was that he had difficulty breathing through it. Defendant told Plaintiff that this was because of swelling from the surgery that would diminish in time, he just had to be patient. She was right about the swelling, but apparently not about its connection to Plaintiff's breathing difficulties. According to Dr. Kate Chopin, his family physician to whom he went next, the surgery had caused scarring that, together with the particularly narrow nose at issue, was causing the breathing difficulties. She said that he had "keloid scars" from the surgery and provided a printout from the National Institutes' of Health's MedlinePlus website, which explains that "[a] keloid is a growth of extra scar tissue where the skin has healed after an injury [including] after skin injuries from surgery." She said that the risk of keloids is tied to melanin levels so that, although anyone can get them, they are more likely to occur in people with darker skin. Because of this and given Plaintiff's olive-to-medium-brown skin, Dr. Chopin concluded that Defendant should have cautioned Plaintiff against such a narrow nose and been specific about the risk of keloid scarring. And if Plaintiff had nevertheless insisted on the nose, Defendant should have sculpted wider nostrils as a way to mitigate the risk of blockage should keloid scarring occur. Plaintiff asked her about his options, and Dr. Chopin responded, "revision surgery"—which is exactly what it sounds like. Finally, she also suggested that Plaintiff check Defendant's professional status. Lo and behold, although Defendant was up-to-date with her specialists' certification, her state medical license had expired the week before she performed Plaintiff's surgery and it had not been renewed until the following month. (She is a busy woman.) State law is clear that "practicing medicine without a license is a crime."

P believes that breathing out of his nose is more important to him than the particular nose, even though he still loves it. And so he wants to have the revision surgery but he exhausted his discretionary resources on the original surgery. In any event, he thinks that D who did this to him should pay. How would the litigation go if he sued the D—what would be his claim(s), D's strategy in response, his rebuttals?

C. When There Is No Evidence of Breach: Res Ipsa Loquitur

BYRNE v. BOADLE
2 H. & C. 722, 159 Eng.Rep. 299 (1863)

Declaration. For that the defendant, by his servants, so negligently and unskillfully managed and lowered certain barrels of flour by means of a certain jigger-hoist and machinery attached to the shop of the defendant, situated in a certain highway, along which the plaintiff was then passing, that by and through the negligence of the defendant, by his said servants, one of the said barrels of flour fell upon and struck against the plaintiff, whereby the plaintiff was thrown down, wounded, lamed, and permanently injured, and was prevented from attending to his business for a long time, to wit, thence hitherto, and incurred great expense for medical attendance, and suffered great pain and anguish, and was otherwise damnified.

Plea. Not guilty.

At the trial before the learned Assessor of the Court of Passage at Liverpool, the evidence adduced on the part of the plaintiff was as follows: —A witness named Critchley said: "On the 18th July, I was in Scotland Road, on the right side going north, defendant's shop is on that side. When I was opposite to his shop, a barrel of flour fell from a window above in defendant's house and shop, and knocked the plaintiff down. He was carried into an adjoining shop. A horse and cart came opposite the defendant's door. Barrels of flour were in the cart. I do not think the barrel was being lowered by a rope. I cannot say: I did not see the barrel until it struck the plaintiff. It was not swinging when it struck the plaintiff. It struck him on the shoulder and knocked him towards the shop. No one called out until after the accident." The plaintiff said: "On approaching Scotland Place and defendant's shop, I lost all recollection. I felt no blow. I saw nothing to warn me of danger. I was taken home in a cab. I was helpless for a fortnight." (He then described his sufferings.) "I saw the path clear. I did not see any cart opposite defendant's shop." Another witness said: "I saw a barrel falling. I don't know how, but from defendant's." The only other witness was a surgeon, who described the injury which the plaintiff had received. It was admitted that the defendant was a dealer in flour.

It was submitted, on the part of the defendant, that there was no evidence of negligence for the jury. The learned Assessor was of that opinion, and nonsuited the plaintiff, reserving leave to him to move the Court of Exchequer to enter the verdict for him with 50*l*. damages, the amount assessed by the jury.

Littler, in the present term, obtained a rule nisi to enter the verdict for the plaintiff, on the ground of misdirection of the learned Assessor in ruling that there was no evidence of negligence on the part of the defendant; against which Charles Russell now shewed cause. First, there was no evidence to connect the defendant or his servants with the occurrence. It is not suggested that the defendant himself was present, and it will be argued that upon these pleadings it is not open to the defendant to contend that his servants were not engaged in lowering the barrel of flour. But the declaration alleges that the defendant, by his servants, so negligently lowered the barrel of flour, that by and through the negligence of the defendant, by his said servants, it fell upon the plaintiff. That is tantamount to an allegation that the injury was caused by the defendant's negligence, and it is competent to him, under the plea of not guilty, to contend that his servants were not concerned in the act alleged. . . . Then, assuming the point is open upon these pleadings, there was no evidence that the defendant, or any person for whose acts he would be responsible, was engaged in lowering the barrel of flour. It is consistent with the evidence that the purchaser of the flour was superintending the lowering of it by his servant, or it may be that a stranger was engaged to do it without the knowledge or authority of the defendant. [Pollock, C.B. The presumption is that the defendant's servants were engaged in removing the defendant's flour; if they were not it was competent to the defendant to prove it.] Surmise ought not to be substituted for strict proof when it is sought to fix a defendant with serious liability. The plaintiff should establish his case by affirmative evidence.

Secondly, assuming the facts to be brought home to the defendant or his servants, these facts do not disclose any evidence for the jury of negligence. The plaintiff was bound to give affirmative proof of negligence. But there was not a scintilla of evidence, unless the occurrence is of itself evidence of negligence. There was not even evidence that the barrel was being lowered by a jigger-hoist as alleged in the declaration. [Pollock, C.B. There are certain cases of which it may be said res ipsa loquitur, and this seems one of them. In some cases the Courts have held that the mere fact of the accident having occurred is evidence of negligence, as, for instance, in the case of railway collisions.] On examination of the authorities, that doctrine would seem to be confined to the case of a collision between two trains upon the same line, and both being the property and under the management of the same Company. Such was the case of *Skinner v. The London, Brighton and South Coast Railway Company* (5 Exch. 787), where the train in which the plaintiff was ran into another train which had stopped a short distance from a station, in consequence of a luggage train before it having broken down. In that case there must have been negligence, or the accident could not have happened. . . . Later cases have qualified the doctrine of presumptive negligence. In *Cotton v. Wood* (8 C.B.N.S. 568) it was held that a Judge is not justified in leaving the case to the jury where the plaintiff's evidence is equally consistent with the absence as with the existence of negligence in the defendant. In *Hammack v. White* (11 C.B.N.S. 588, 594), Erle, J., said that he was of opinion "that the plaintiff in a case of this sort was not entitled to have the case left to the jury unless he gives some affirmative evidence that there has been negligence on the part of the defendant." [Pollock, C.B. If he meant that to apply to all cases, I must say, with great respect, that I entirely differ from him. He must refer to the mere nature of the accident in that particular case. Bramwell, B. No doubt, the presumption of negligence is not raised in every case of injury from accident, but in some it is. We must judge of the facts in a reasonable way; and regarding them in that light we know that these accidents do not take place without a cause, and in general that cause is negligence.] The law will not presume that a man is guilty of a wrong. It is consistent with the facts proved that the defendant's servants were using the utmost care and the best appliances to lower the barrel with safety. Then why should the fact that accidents of this nature are sometimes caused by negligence raise any presumption against the defendant? There are many accidents from which no presumption of negligence can arise. [Bramwell, B. Looking at the matter in a reasonable way it comes to this — an injury is done to the plaintiff, who has no means of knowing whether it was the result of negligence; the defendant, who knows how it was caused, does not think fit to tell the jury.] Unless a plaintiff gives some evidence which ought to be submitted to the jury, the defendant is not bound to offer any defence. The plaintiff cannot, by a defective proof of his case, compel the defendant to give evidence in explanation. [Pollock, C.B. I have frequently observed that a defendant has a right to remain silent unless a primâ facie case is established against him. But here the question is whether the plaintiff has not shewn such a case.] In a case of this nature, in which the sympathies of a jury are with the plaintiff, it would be dangerous to allow presumption to be substituted for affirmative proof of negligence.

Littler appeared to support the rule, but was not called upon to argue.

POLLOCK, C.B. We are all of opinion that the rule must be absolute to enter the verdict for the plaintiff. The learned counsel was quite right in saying that there are many accidents from which no presumption of negligence can arise, but I think it would be wrong to lay down as a rule that in no case can presumption of negligence arise from the fact of an accident. Suppose in this case the barrel had rolled out of the warehouse and fallen on the plaintiff, how could he possibly ascertain from what cause it occurred? It is the duty of persons who keep barrels in a warehouse to take care that they do not roll out, and I think that such a case would, beyond all doubt, afford primâ facie evidence of negligence. A barrel could not roll out of a warehouse without some negligence, and to say that a plaintiff who is injured by it must call witnesses from the warehouse to prove negligence seems to me preposterous. So in the building or repairing a house, or putting pots on the chimneys, if a person passing along the road is injured by something falling upon him, I think the accident alone would be primâ facie evidence of negligence. Or if an article calculated to cause damage is put in a wrong place and does mischief, I think that those whose duty it was to put it in the right place are primâ facie responsible, and if there is any state of facts to rebut the presumption of negligence, they must prove them. The present case upon the evidence comes to this, a man is passing in front of the premises of a dealer in flour, and there falls down upon him a barrel of flour. I think it apparent that the barrel was in the custody of the defendant who occupied the premises, and who is responsible for the acts of his servants who had the controul of it; and in my opinion the fact of its falling is primâ facie evidence of negligence, and the plaintiff who was injured by it is not bound to shew that it could not fall without negligence, but if there are any facts inconsistent with negligence it is for the defendant to prove them.

BRAMWELL, B. I am of the same opinion.

CHANNELL, B. I am of the same opinion. The first part of the rule assumes the existence of negligence, but takes this shape, that there was no evidence to connect the defendant with the negligence. The barrel of flour fell from a warehouse over a shop which the defendant occupied, and therefore primâ facie he is responsible. Then the question is whether there was any evidence of negligence, not a mere scintilla, but such as in the absence of any evidence in answer would entitle the plaintiff to a verdict. I am of opinion that there was. I think that a person who has a warehouse by the side of a public highway, and assumes to himself the right to lower from it a barrel of flour into a cart, has a duty cast upon him to take care that persons passing along the highway are not injured by it. I agree that it is not every accident which will warrant the inference of negligence. On the other hand, I dissent from the doctrine that there is no accident which will in itself raise a presumption of negligence. In this case I think that there was evidence for the jury, and that the rule ought to be absolute to enter the verdict for the plaintiff.

PIGOTT, B. I am of the same opinion.

Rule absolute.

MAYER v. ONCE UPON A ROSE, INC.
58 A.3d 1221 (N.J. App. 2013)

SABATINO, J.A.D.

This negligence case arises from the personal injuries that a caterer sustained when a glass vase shattered and his hands were struck and cut by the propelled fragments. The vase contained a floral arrangement, which a florist working at the same catered event had been carrying across the room. The injured caterer sued the florist and the floral company, contending that either the florist had been gripping the vase in a dangerous manner or that the vase had not been adequately inspected for cracks before it was brought to the site.

The trial court granted defendants a directed verdict at the close of the caterer's proofs before the jury, mainly because the caterer had not retained a liability expert to explain why the vase had shattered. We reverse, concluding that it was not essential for this plaintiff to have retained a liability expert in these circumstances.

I.

We describe the facts in a light most favorable to plaintiff. On February 15, 2009, plaintiff Martin Mayer, a professional caterer, was setting up for an engagement party at a synagogue in Passaic. Defendant Samuel Grunwald, a florist employed by co-defendant, Once Upon a Rose, Inc., also was at the synagogue with his wife, getting the floral arrangements in place for that same engagement party.

Plaintiff arrived at the synagogue at approximately 3:00 p.m. With the help of his assistant, plaintiff started bringing the food inside. He also moved tables around the banquet room under the direction of the party planner.

Meanwhile, Mr. Grunwald and his wife were setting up the floral arrangements in the room. Mrs. Grunwald is the sole owner of Once Upon a Rose, Inc., and Mr. Grunwald is an employee of the company. Mr. and Mrs. Grunwald brought all the floral materials to the synagogue, and they assembled the arrangements at the event.

The floral vases were stored in individual boxes, which had then been placed in milk crates. The Grunwalds used two similar types of vases, which were both made of glass and had the same width, except some were a couple of inches taller than the others. They assembled five or six arrangements at the synagogue.

According to Mrs. Grunwald's testimony, the same glass vases had previously been used between ten and thirty times. Mrs. Grunwald stated that she had checked all the vases that day for chips and cracks and found none. She did not remove any vases while making the floral arrangements that day. However, she insisted that she would have removed any vase if it had been found chipped or cracked.

During the course of setting up for the engagement party, Mr. Grunwald began to move a floral vase from one table to another. The tables were ten to fifteen feet apart. The vase in question was a tall glass square, which was flat on all sides. It had bamboo and flowers extending a few feet over the top and was nearly filled with water.

From about ten to twelve feet away, plaintiff observed Mr. Grunwald hold the vase with outstretched arms. According to plaintiff, Mr. Grunwald appeared to be applying pressure with the palms of his hands on the sides of the vase, about halfway up on opposite sides.

No one else was touching the vase as Mr. Grunwald lifted it. He testified that he felt the vase "caving in" and a sensation of the vase pressing inwards.

Upon observing Mr. Grunwald attempting to carry the vase on his own, plaintiff ran towards Mr. Grunwald to help him. According to plaintiff, as he approached, he said in an undertone, "you're going to hurt yourself."

As plaintiff reached his hands under the vase, the glass vase shattered. Shards of broken glass fell into plaintiff's hands.

The glass shards severely cut plaintiff's hands, which began bleeding. He was in "excruciating pain." Plaintiff was transported to a local hospital with Mr. Grunwald, who also had been injured.

Plaintiff suffered multiple tendon cuts and nerve damage from the glass shards. He underwent emergency surgery that same day. Plaintiff had physical therapy for over six months to restore movement to his hands. His injuries from this incident have caused him permanent scarring, a loss of grip strength, and various alleged lifestyle restrictions.

In this ensuing lawsuit, plaintiff invoked the doctrine of res ipsa loquitur. He argued that he was blameless in connection with the incident, that the vase had been in defendants' exclusive control, and that it was not likely to have exploded in the absence of defendants' fault. Defendants, meanwhile, took the position that this was a spontaneous accident that they could not have reasonably prevented.

At trial, plaintiff testified about the events at the synagogue and his resulting injuries. He also presented testimony from the Grunwalds, who were called as adverse parties, and from an orthopedic surgeon who gave expert testimony about the hand injuries.

After plaintiff rested his case, defendants moved for a directed verdict. The trial court granted their motion. In the course of his oral ruling, the judge observed that he had "two problems" with plaintiff's theory of recovery:

> *Number one, with regard to pressure having any part whatsoever in the implosion or collapse of this vase, the [c]ourt determines that that is an issue that would require expert testimony.* It would be extremely speculative and impermissible to allow the jury to speculate as to whether the way the vase was being carried somehow played a part in its failure. If in fact that is a theory to be pursued, *that theory would require expert testimony in order to deal with the issue of . . . how much pressure, what type of pressure, thickness of glass, . . . [and] other factors and variables that would impact or support such a theory.* And we do not have that . . . in this case.
>
> *The second problem that the [c]ourt has is . . . as to whether it is more probable under these circumstances in order to invoke the res ipsa doctrine whether in fact the accident bespeaks negligence.* And that is whether it is more probable than not that [Mr. Grunwald's] negligence was a proximate cause of the mishap. *We don't know what happened.* And the issue is . . . is it more probable than not that [Mr. Grunwald's] negligence was the proximate cause of the mishap?
>
> *There are other potential explanations.* And as [plaintiff's counsel] points out, he need not rule out those other explanations, but there are other explanations. *One looming explanation is that there could have been a product defect. . . .*
>
> . . . .
>
> It's also possible that [the Grunwalds] were negligent. *It's possible that there was something that they did with regard to this vase that would have resulted in this accident. But the [c]ourt can't rely on possibilities.* It must be that it's probable that there was negligence on the part of [Mr. Grunwald] sufficient to invoke the doctrine of *res ipsa loquitur.*

[Emphasis added.]

Based on this analysis, the judge discharged the jury and entered final judgment in defendants' favor.

Plaintiff now appeals. He principally argues that the trial court erred in faulting plaintiff for not calling a liability expert. As a secondary point, plaintiff contends that the court was improperly swayed by the mere possibility of other explanations for what may have caused the glass explosion.

II.

A motion for involuntary dismissal [directed verdict] at the end of a plaintiff's case is governed by *Rule* 4:37–2(b). The rule instructs that "such [a] motion shall be denied if the evidence, together with the legitimate inferences therefrom, could sustain a judgment in plaintiff's favor." *Ibid.* "[I]f, accepting as true all the evidence which supports the position of the party defending against the motion and according him the benefit of all inferences which can reasonably and legitimately be deduced therefrom, reasonable minds could differ, the motion must be denied." *Dolson v. Anastasia,* 55 *N.J.* 2, 5, 258 *A.*2d 706 (1969).

"[T]he judicial function [in evaluating a motion for a directed verdict] is quite a mechanical one." *Ibid.* "The trial court is not concerned with the worth, nature or extent (beyond a scintilla) of the evidence, but only with its existence, viewed most favorably to the party opposing the motion." *Id.* at 5–6, 258 *A.*2d 706; *see also Quinlan v. Curtiss–Wright Corp.,* 204 *N.J.* 239, 276–77, 8 *A.*3d 209 (2010) (noting that "the appropriate focus for the trial court and the Appellate Division [is] not whether there was some contrary evidence; instead the focus [should be] on whether there [is] too little evidence . . . presented by plaintiff to get to the jury on the issue at all").

Defendants' motion for a directed verdict in the present case challenged plaintiff's invocation of the doctrine of res ipsa loquitur. Our Supreme Court has described that doctrine as follows:

> In any case founded upon negligence, the proofs ultimately must establish that defendant breached a duty of reasonable care, which constituted a proximate cause of the plaintiff's injuries. *Res ipsa loquitur,* a Latin phrase meaning "the thing speaks for itself," is a rule that governs the availability and adequacy of evidence of negligence in special circumstances. The rule creates an allowable inference of the defendant's want of due care when the following conditions have been shown: (a) the occurrence itself ordinarily bespeaks negligence; (b) the instrumentality [causing the injury] was within the defendant's exclusive control; and (c) there is no indication in the circumstances that the injury was the result of the plaintiff's own voluntary act or neglect.

The res ipsa loquitur doctrine is based upon considerations of public policy, allowing a blameless injured plaintiff to obtain an inference of negligence where certain required factors are present. In essence, the doctrine "plac[es] the duty of producing evidence on the party who has superior knowledge or opportunity for explanation of the causative circumstances." *Buckelew v. Grossbard,* 87 *N.J.* 512, 526, 435 *A.*2d 1150 (1981). Res ipsa loquitur "in effect creates a permissive presumption that a set of facts furnish reasonable grounds for the inference that if due care had been exercised by the person having control of the instrumentality causing the injury, the mishap would not have occurred." *Szalontai, supra,* 183 *N.J.* at 398, 874 *A.*2d 507 (quoting *Brown, supra,* 95 *N.J.* at 288–89, 471 *A.*2d 25). The jury is free to accept or reject that permissible inference. *Ibid.*

An important aspect of the res ipsa loquitur doctrine is its role at trial in repelling a defendant's motion for a directed verdict. "Once res ipsa loquitur is established, the case should go to the jury *unless defendant's countervailing proof is so strong as to admit of no reasonable doubt as to the absence of negligence.*" *Id.* at 398, 874 *A.*2d 507 (emphasis added) (quoting *Brown, supra,* 95 *N.J.* at 289, 471 *A.*2d 25). "In a case in which res ipsa loquitur applies, a directed verdict against the plaintiff can occur *only if the defendant produces evidence which will destroy any reasonable inference of negligence, or so completely contradict it that reasonable men could no longer accept it.*" *Id.* at 399, 874 *A.*2d 507 (emphasis added) (quoting *Brown, supra,* 95 *N.J.* at 289, 471 *A.*2d 25).

The res ipsa loquitur doctrine has been successfully applied on several occasions to cases involving exploding glass bottles. *See Bornstein v. Metro. Bottling Co.,* 26 *N.J.* 263, 274–75,

139 *A.*2d 404 (1958); *see also Stolle v. Anheuser–Busch, Inc.*, 307 *Mo.* 520, 271 *S.W.* 497, 499–500 (1925); *Can. Dry Ginger Ale Co. v. Jochum,* 43 *A.*2d 42, 43–44 (D.C.1945). Although those bottling cases are somewhat distinguishable from the present case because they involved pressurized glass, they do illustrate the fundamental proposition that the res ipsa doctrine can apply to accidents involving a glass vessel that had been in a defendant's exclusive control.

Here, the trial court declined to allow the jury to consider any inference of negligence on the part of defendants. A focal point of the court's decision was its belief that plaintiff was obligated to present a liability expert to explain why the glass vase shattered. We disagree that such an expert witness was required.

In *Jerista v. Murray,* 185 *N.J.* 175, 195, 883 *A.*2d 350 (2005), a leading case in which the plaintiff invoked the res ipsa loquitur doctrine, the Supreme Court concluded that expert testimony was not required for a " *res ipsa* inference" to be made with respect to injuries caused by an automatic door. The plaintiffs in *Jerista* brought a malpractice claim against their prior attorney, whose inaction had allegedly led to the dismissal of their negligence complaint against a supermarket. The defendant attorney argued that he had not caused his former clients harm, because their lack of supporting expert testimony on liability would have prevented them anyway from obtaining a res ipsa inference, and consequently they did not have a provable claim in the underlying suit. The Supreme Court rejected this court's "sweeping suggesti[on] . . . that in almost all complex instrumentality cases a *res ipsa* inference will be conditioned on the production of expert testimony." Instead, the Court determined that the pertinent question is "whether based on *common knowledge* the balance of probabilities favors negligence, thus rendering fair the drawing of a *res ipsa* inference." *Id.* at 199, 883 *A.*2d 350 (emphasis added).

As to the necessity of liability experts, the Court instructed in *Jerista* that "[o]nly when the *res ipsa* inference falls outside of the common knowledge of the factfinder and depends on scientific, technical, or other specialized knowledge is expert testimony required." *Ibid.; see also N.J.R.E.* 702 (limiting the admission of expert testimony to evidence or issues requiring "specialized knowledge" for a factfinder to understand). "A jury does not need an expert to tell it what it already knows." *Jerista, supra,* 185 *N.J.* at 197, 883 *A.*2d 350.

The Court concluded in *Jerista* that the plaintiffs could have obtained a res ipsa inference absent expert testimony because, even though automatic doors are complex machines, "based on common knowledge" it is improbable that such a door would close unexpectedly on a person unless it was negligently maintained. *Ibid.* "When the average juror can deduce what happened without resort to scientific or technical knowledge, expert testimony is not mandated." *Id.* at 200, 883 *A.*2d 350.

Similarly, in *Rosenberg v. Otis Elevator Co.,* 366 *N.J.Super.* 292, 305, 841 *A.*2d 99 (App.Div.2004), no expert testimony was required to assist the jury in evaluating an incident where an elevator had dropped at least three floors in a freefall before coming to a sudden stop. This court reasoned that the jurors could make a rational inference, unaided by expert testimony, that an elevator would not have fallen in such a precipitous manner unless the defendant had breached its duty and caused the malfunction. *Ibid.*

By contrast, in *Buckelew, supra,* 87 *N.J.* at 527, 435 *A.*2d 1150, a liability expert was needed where the defendant physician had cut into the plaintiff's bladder during surgery. An expert was required in that professional liability context to address the relevant standard of care for such surgery because the Court "[could] not say, *as a matter of common understanding,* the injury to plaintiff's bladder raises an inference of negligence." *Ibid.* (emphasis added).

Applying these principles here, we conclude that the trial court erred in insisting that plaintiff had to present a liability expert to the jury before a res ipsa inference could be permitted. A jury does not need an expert to tell it that excessive pressure placed on glass can cause it to shatter. That basic notion lies within the common knowledge of jurors and does not require scientific or technical knowledge. Glass does not typically shatter on its own. The average juror should readily appreciate that too much pressure applied to glass can cause it to break. It is also common knowledge that glass is fragile, as evidenced by how glass is customarily transported with protective material to prevent breakage.

To be sure, expert testimony in this case might have been helpful, but it was not essential to plaintiff's case. The shattering of the vase was an incident arguably bespeaking negligence, and one that fell within a juror's common knowledge. This is not a professional liability case where a nuanced or complex standard of care is implicated. Moreover, it is undisputed that plaintiff himself did not cause the vase to shatter as he attempted to intercede. In addition, the vase had been in defendants' exclusive control up until the moment it exploded.

We also disagree with the trial court that the theoretical possibility that the glass was defectively manufactured foreclosed plaintiff's invocation of res ipsa loquitur. As defendants noted, they had used the vase many times before without incident. Such repetitive previous use of the vase makes it highly conjectural that the vessel had been fabricated with defective glass. Although we cannot totally rule out the possibility of a product defect, defendants failed to provide evidential support for such a counter-theory that "destroy[ed] any reasonable inference of negligence, or so completely contradict[ed] it that reasonable men could no longer accept it." *Szalontai, supra,* 183 *N.J.* at 399, 874 *A.*2d 507.

In sum, although the jurors rationally could have ruled against plaintiff on the merits, the circumstances here did not warrant the trial court's outright dismissal of plaintiff's case before they had a fair opportunity to consider it.

The directed verdict for defendants is reversed and the matter is remanded for a new trial.

Notes and Questions

1. From the text of the declaration (complaint) in *Byrne*, state the facts the plaintiff alleged to satisfy his burden of pleading each element of the negligence prima facie case. Then review the rest of the opinion to see which of these allegations he was able to prove — what was the evidence he used to support each of the allegations?

2. How did the *Byrne* court reach the conclusion that the defendant was more likely than not unreasonable in how he managed the barrel that hit the plaintiff? Were there not other explanations for how the barrel might have fallen out of the window?

3. According to a defense lawyer in *Mayer,* the vase at issue was three to three-and-a-half feet tall and rectangular in cross section. It was heavy enough filled with water that it took two hands to lift it.

4. *Mayer* describes the modern doctrine of *res ipsa loquitur* including its procedural aspects. Using the court's discussion of the law and analysis of the *Mayer* facts, try to answer the following questions:

a. When does the plaintiff's need for the doctrine arise?

b. When does the court likely first rule on the issue?

c. Can a defendant get a directed verdict at the close of the plaintiff's case if the court has ruled that the doctrine applies?

d. What does the possibility of an alternative explanation for the accident, for example a product defect, do for the defendant?

e. Can the plaintiff get a directed verdict at the close of the defendant's case if the court has ruled that the doctrine applies?

f. If the case goes to the jury, what is the weight of the plaintiff's evidence of breach?

Defense counsel recalls that after the case was remanded, he expected the jury would deliberate for quite some time. He was surprised (and also happy) when the jury returned a defense verdict after only fifteen minutes.

5. The *Mayer* court references a medical malpractice case in which *res ipsa* was an issue. The doctrine was most famously used in this context in Ybarra v. Spangard, 154 P.2d 687, 689 (Cal.1944), involving a plaintiff who was injured while he was unconscious in an operating room; because he was unconscious at the time of the injury, he was unable to describe either the instrumentality that caused his injury or (obviously) to attribute exclusive custody or control of the instrumentality to any one person who was in the room at the time. The California Supreme Court nevertheless permitted the plaintiff to proceed:

> The present case is of a type which comes within the reason and spirit of the doctrine more fully perhaps than any other. The passenger sitting awake in a railroad car at the time of a collision, the pedestrian walking along the street and struck by a falling object or the debris of an explosion, are surely not more entitled to an explanation than the unconscious patient on the operating table. Viewed from this aspect, it is difficult to see how the doctrine can, with any justification, be so restricted in its statement as to become inapplicable to a patient who submits himself to the care and custody of doctors and nurses, is rendered unconscious, and receives some injury from instrumentalities used in his treatment. Without the aid of the doctrine a patient who received permanent injuries of a serious character, obviously the result of some one's negligence, would be entirely unable to recover unless the doctors and nurses in attendance voluntarily chose to disclose the identity of the negligent person and the facts establishing liability. If this were the state of the law of negligence, the courts, to avoid gross injustice, would be forced to invoke the principles of absolute

liability, irrespective of negligence, in actions by persons suffering injuries during the course of treatment under anesthesia. But we think this juncture has not yet been reached, and that the doctrine of res ipsa loquitur is properly applicable to the case before us.

Problem Seven: Driving While Distracted

At the age of nineteen, Belinda Balint works hard at her job in the county courthouse mailroom, bakes a mean apple pie, loves to play with her rescued retriever-mix, and, along with her father, coaches a baseball team for underprivileged youth. She is not without her flaws, however. As she is wont to say, "We're all a work-in-progress, right?" Her own major life's work is her severe attention deficit disorder (ADD), which, since childhood, has made even simple conceptual tasks harder for her than they are for people without ADD. Mostly, she has trouble focusing and then re-focusing as required in many important situations. This is the correct and also nice way of describing her functional impairment. When she was younger, she was picked on relentlessly by her meaner, ignorant classmates for being "mental," "a retard," or just "stupid." Because her parents were both trained in child development science, they spotted her problem early on and so she was formally diagnosed and treated throughout her time in school. That is, her pediatric neurologist diagnosed her with ADD, described its etiology as biochemical in nature – specifically, an imbalance in the neurotransmitters dopamine and acetylcholine – and prescribed a regimen of drugs and occupational therapy. As a young adult, though, Belinda has mostly managed her problem herself, by recognizing the situations in which she is "good" and "bad," and minimizing the extent to which she is in bad ones.

Driving home from work one day on a two-lane back road, Belinda encountered a dead deer in the middle of her lane. Because the deer was just on the other side of a sharp turn, Belinda had to brake hard and swerve into the other lane to avoid it. She just managed to get back into her own lane as an oncoming car crossed her path. Worried that the next driver in her lane wouldn't be so lucky — Belinda imagined the awful, head-on collision she had just managed to avoid — she decided to text her mother so that her mother could notify the police about the dead deer and the safety hazard it posed for other drivers. This may seem like a strange choice, texting her mother instead of calling the police directly, but Belinda had always relied on her parents, especially her mother, in stressful situations. And having come of age in the era of texting, this mode of communication was her (and her generation's) default, including when behind the wheel: surveys show that approximately 37% of people aged 18-34 text while driving. Belinda was aware that her state had recently criminalized "driving while distracted" (DWD), including by texting, sexting, reading stock reports, applying cosmetics, etcetera, because these distractions significantly increase the risk of vehicular accidents. (Doing any of these activities while driving is now a "ticketable offense" subject to a fine of up to $750.00.) But in the moment, all Belinda could think about was being a good Samaritan. (The view that texting is compatible with safe driving is widely-held, despite the statistics that show that distractions, including texting, account for approximately 80% of car accidents. Indeed, surveys show that up to 83% of people believe they are safe drivers, including when they are distracted.) In any event, as Belinda texted her mother, she became distracted, lost control of her car, and collided head-on into a car driven non-negligently by a young father of two-year-old triplets.

Plaintiff's estate files a wrongful death action against Belinda based in negligence. Analyze the likely focus of that litigation.

CHAPTER FIVE
CAUSATION

Causation is the third element of the prima facie case for negligence. It is comprised of two distinct sub-elements: cause-in-fact and proximate cause. As we discussed earlier in the course, causation is also part of the intentional torts and strict liability prima facie cases: before a defendant can be liable for any tort, the plaintiff must prove that their actions or omissions caused the injury at issue. Thus, while we will be focusing in this chapter on causation in negligence, remember that the same principles apply across the board.

Cause-in-fact is mostly what it appears to be: an inquiry into the factual cause of the plaintiff's injury or damages. The plaintiff's job is to show that the defendant's breach caused that injury or damage, or at least that the breach was an important contributing cause. Although this is typically a factual inquiry, we will see that in some circumstances, the courts relax the burden of proof on the plaintiff so that cause-in-fact is effectively established in plaintiff's favor (at least initially) as a policy matter.

Proximate cause assumes that cause-in-fact has been established; in other words, that the defendant had a duty of care to the plaintiff that was breached, and that this breach in fact caused (or contributed to causing) the plaintiff's qualifying injury or property damage. It seeks to ensure that imposing liability on the defendant for that injury or damage is fair and just in the circumstances, in other words, that there is not something about the facts that suggests the defendant ought not be required to pay. As we will see, proximate cause is primarily litigated in circumstances where the defendant believes that liability is out of proportion to fault and where the facts leading up to the plaintiff's damages were unexpected.

I. CAUSE-IN-FACT

A. The Straightforward Cases

1. The "But For" and "Substantial Factor" Tests

SHRINERS HOSPITALS FOR CRIPPLED CHILDREN v. GARDINER
733 P.2d 1110 (Ariz. 1987)

HAYS, Justice (Retired).

Laurabel Gardiner established a trust to provide income to her daughter, Mary Jane Gardiner; her two grandchildren, Charles Gardiner and Robert Gardiner; and a now-deceased daughter-in-law, Jean Gardiner. The remainder of the estate passes to Shriners Hospitals for Crippled Children (Shriners) upon the death of the life income beneficiaries. Laurabel appointed Mary Jane as trustee, Charles as first alternate trustee, and Robert as second alternate trustee. Mary Jane was not an experienced investor, and she placed the trust assets with Dean Witter Reynolds, a brokerage house. Charles, an investment counselor and stockbroker, made all investment decisions concerning the trust assets. At some point in time, Charles embezzled $317,234.36 from the trust. Shriners brought a petition to surcharge Mary Jane for the full $317,234.36. The trial court denied the petition, but a divided court of appeals reversed.

We granted review on three issues:

1) Whether Mary Jane's delegation of investment power to Charles was a breach of Mary Jane's fiduciary duty.

2) Whether Mary Jane's delegation to Charles of investment power was the proximate cause of the loss of $317,234.36.

3) Whether Robert can properly continue to act as successor trustee and as guardian and conservator for the predecessor trustee Mary Jane.

. . .

1. BREACH OF FIDUCIARY DUTY

In Arizona, a trustee has the duty to "observe the standard in dealing with the trust assets that would be observed by a prudent man dealing with the property of another." A.R.S. § 14–7302. If the trustee breaches that responsibility, he is personally liable for any resulting loss to the trust assets. Restatement (Second) of Trusts §§ 201, 205(a). A trustee breaches the prudent man standard when he delegates responsibilities that he reasonably can be expected personally to perform. Restatement (Second) of Trusts § 171.

We believe that Mary Jane breached the prudent man standard when she transferred investment power to Charles. Mary Jane argues, and we agree, that a trustee lacking investment experience must seek out expert advice. Although a trustee must seek out expert advice, "he is not ordinarily justified in relying on such advice, but must exercise his own judgment." Restatement (Second) of Trusts § 227. *In re Will of Newhoff,* 107 Misc.2d 589, 595, 435 N.Y.S.2d 632, 637 (1980) (a trustee must not only obtain information concerning investment possibilities but also is "under a duty to use a reasonable degree of skill in selecting an investment"). Mary Jane, though, did not evaluate Charles' advice and then make her own decisions. Charles managed the trust fund, not Mary Jane. A prudent investor would certainly participate, to some degree, in investment decisions.

The dissent in the court of appeals stated that "there is nothing to indicate the trustee 'gave up her trusteeship' or 'delegated' the 'complete management' of trust assets to Charles." *Shriners Hospitals for Crippled Children,* 152 Ariz. at 525, 733 P.2d at 1108, (Froeb, C.J., dissenting). While we agree that the record on appeal is meager, Mary Jane unquestionably transferred trustee discretion to Charles.

Mary Jane's second accounting of the Gardiner trust states:

> From time to time the Trustee made investments ("investments") in the money market and also in the purchase and sale of shares of stock listed on the New York Stock Exchange, the American Stock Exchange and the Over-the-Counter Markets. . . . *All*

> *of said investments were made on behalf of the Trust Estate by a person qualified in that business,* [Charles] *who was selected by and in whom the Trustee justifiably had the utmost trust and confidence.*

(emphasis added)

Most damning, however, are the admissions of Mary Jane's own attorney.

> Now, we can show, if the Court pleases, by way of evidence if counsel will not accept my avowal, we can show that Charles Gardiner for the past many years, including several years prior to and since these assets were placed in his hands for investment, was in the business of a consultant and in the business of investing and selecting investments in the stock market, and this he did. And it was only natural that Mary Jane would turn to him to make that selection, to invest those funds and to account in an appropriate proceeding if, as and when required. So the prudent man rule has been adhered to here. She got a man who is capable and fortunately he was a man who was designated as an alternate trustee *and for all practical purposes really served as trustee.*

(emphasis added)

Together, the accounting and admissions establish that Charles was functioning as a surrogate trustee. Mary Jane was not exercising any control over the selection of investments. She clearly breached her duties to act prudently and to personally perform her duties as a trustee. *In re Kohler's Estate,* 348 Pa. 55, 33 A.2d 920 (1943) (fiduciary may not delegate to another the performance of a duty involving discretion and judgment).

Even on appeal, Mary Jane does not argue that she, in fact, exercised any discretionary investment power. Instead, she argues that her lack of investment experience made it prudent for her to delegate her investment power. She relies on the Restatement (Second) of Torts § 171.

> § 171. Duty Not To Delegate
>
> The trustee is under a duty to the beneficiary not to delegate to others the doing of acts which the trustee can reasonably be required personally to perform.

Mary Jane asserts that her lack of investment experience prevented her from personally exercising investment power and consequently permitted delegation of that power. The standard of care required, however, is measured objectively. *In re Mild's Estate,* 25 N.J. 467, 480–81, 136 A.2d 875, 882 (1957) (the standard of care required of a trustee does not take into account the "differing degrees of education or intellect possessed by a fiduciary"). The trustee must be *reasonable* in her delegation. A delegation of investment authority is unreasonable and therefore Mary Jane's delegation is a breach of trust. *See Estate of Baldwin,* 442 A.2d 529 (Me.1982) (bank trustee liable for losses incurred when it failed to monitor management of grocery store despite bank's lack of expertise in grocery store management).

It is of no import that Charles was named as alternate trustee. A trustee is not permitted to delegate his responsibilities to a co-trustee. Restatement (Second) of Trusts § 224(2)(b); *see also id.*, comment a (improper for co-trustee A to direct co-trustee B to invest trust funds without consulting A). Certainly, then, a trustee is subject to liability when she improperly delegates her investment responsibility to an alternate trustee. *Bumbaugh v. Burns*, 635 S.W.2d 518, 521 (Tenn.App.1982) (impermissible for trustee to delegate discretion as to investment of funds to co-trustee).

Mary Jane also argues that broad language in the trust document permitted her to delegate her investment authority to Charles. A trust document may allow a trustee to delegate powers ordinarily nondelegable. The Gardiner Trust permits the trustee "to employ and compensate attorneys, accountants, agents and brokers." This language does not bear on Mary Jane's delegation of investment authority. Mary Jane did not simply employ Charles; she allowed him to serve as surrogate trustee. We view this language as merely an express recognition of the trustee's obligation to obtain expert advice, not as a license to remove herself from her role as a trustee.

2. PROXIMATE CAUSE

Mary Jane next argues that there is no causal connection between her breach and the loss suffered by the trust. The court of appeals rejected this argument in a summary fashion, stating that "the trustee offers no evidence to meet this burden of showing that the loss would have occurred anyway." *Shriners Hospitals for Crippled Children*, 152 Ariz. at 523, 733 P.2d at 1106. We disagree.

The very nature of the loss indicates that the breach was not causally connected to the loss. The accounting indicates that Charles embezzled the funds.

> Without the knowledge or consent of the Trustee, said person received from said investments, and diverted to his own use, a total believed by the Trustee to aggregate \$317,234.36 (\$116,695.55 on January 16, 1981 and \$200,537.81 on March 4, 1981). The trustee did not learn of said diversions until long after they occurred. No part of the amount so diverted had been returned or paid to the Trustee or the Trust Estate.
> . . .

If the trust had suffered because poor investments were made, the delegation of investment authority would unquestionably be the cause of the loss. Otherwise, a causal connection between Charles' diversion of funds and Mary Jane's breach is absent unless the delegation of investment authority gave Charles control and dominion over the trust fund that permitted the defalcation.

A causal connection does not exist simply because "but for" Mary Jane's opening of the account at Dean Witter Reynolds, no loss would have occurred. A trustee is not personally liable for losses not resulting from a breach of trust. Restatement (Second) of Trusts § 204; *Citizens & Southern Nat'l Bank v. Haskins*, 254 Ga. 131, 134, 327 S.E.2d 192, 197 (1985). Mary Jane did not breach her duty by establishing an account at Dean Witter Reynolds, a major brokerage house. Charles was not only the type of person Mary Jane was obliged to seek out for investment advice, but he was a person whom Laurabel Gardiner indicated was trustworthy by naming him as second alternate trustee. Furthermore, the Dean Witter Reynolds account was apparently in Mary Jane's name. If Dean Witter Reynolds wrongfully allowed

Charles access to the fund, Mary Jane is not personally liable. Restatement (Second) of Trusts § 225 (trustee not generally liable for wrongful acts of agents employed in administration of estate).

Unfortunately, the record does not reveal the nature of the diversion. The relative culpability of Charles, Mary Jane and Dean Witter Reynolds is unclear. The trial court found that Mary Jane was without fault and, therefore, did not consider the causal connection between Mary Jane's breach and Charles's defalcation. The inadequacy of the record demands a remand for a determination of the relationship between Mary Jane's delegation of investment authority and Charles' diversion of funds.

3. ROBERT GARDINER AS TRUSTEE

If, after remand, the trial court determines that Mary Jane is personally liable for the diversion of funds, Robert must be removed as trustee.[12] A trustee is liable to a beneficiary if he fails to "redress a breach of trust committed by the predecessor [trustee]." Restatement (Second) of Trusts § 223(2). Robert would, therefore, have a duty to enforce the surcharge against his aunt and ward, Mary Jane. The conflict between personal responsibilities and trust obligations is obvious and great. *Estate of Rothko,* 43 N.Y.2d 305, 319, 401 N.Y.S.2d 449, 454, 372 N.E.2d 291, 296 (1977) (while a trustee is administering the trust he must refrain from placing himself in position where his personal interest does or may conflict with interest of beneficiaries). Another trustee, without such conflicts, would have to be appointed.

The decision of the court of appeals is vacated, and the case is remanded for further proceedings consistent with this opinion.

GORDON, C.J., and FELDMAN, V.C.J., and HOLOHAN, J., concur.

JAMES DUKE CAMERON, Justice, recused himself from participation in the determination of the foregoing case.

Notes and Questions

1. The first paragraph of the case describes a simple trust situation: income to A, B, and C for life, remainder to D. The settlor funds the trust with some property, names beneficiaries, describes its purpose, and designates a trustee to effect it. The trust in *Shriners* involved significant assets and investments and thus a relatively complex situation for the trustee, but trusts can be and often are much simpler. For example, a trust instrument can be a note written on a napkin by a settlor letting a friend know how to allocate funds on deposit in a savings account. The trustee does not have to accept the job, but once they do, they become a fiduciary with responsibilities to the beneficiaries.

2. The court described the fiduciary's duty as the obligation to make decisions as a "prudent man" would in "dealing with the property of another." In contrast, it is sometimes said that a fiduciary must act as a reasonable, prudent, unmarried person would with their own property.

[12] Robert Gardiner is currently serving as trustee because Mary Jane is an invalid and Charles is untrustworthy. Robert is also Mary Jane's guardian-conservator.

How would you describe the difference between the two standards? Which is most consistent with the premise that fiduciary relationships are positions of trust?

3. Shriners and Mary Jane disagreed about whether she had breached her fiduciary duty. Make sure you can describe their respective positions and the different rule choices they reflect. Shriners wins the argument in this case. Given what you know about the standard of care, do you agree with the decision?

4. This case is here in the book as a bridge between the last chapter on breach and this chapter on causation, and so be sure to focus closely on the relationship between Mary Jane's breach of fiduciary duty and the causation inquiry. Specifically, be prepared to describe her contribution to the embezzlement that caused Shriners' loss. What does the court mean when it says that "[a] causal connection does not exist simply because 'but for' Mary Jane's opening of the account at Dean Witter Reynolds, no loss would have occurred"?

5. The court titles its causation discussion "proximate cause" even though it is only concerned with cause-in-fact. This loose and informal use of the term "proximate cause" is commonplace. You should be attentive to it and careful in your own word choice.

FEDORCZYK v. CARIBBEAN CRUISE LINES, LTD.
82 F.3d 69 (3rd Cir. 1996)

COWEN, Circuit Judge.

This case arises from a slip and fall incident in a bathtub aboard the M/V Sovereign, a vessel operated by defendants Caribbean Cruise Lines, Ltd. and Royal Caribbean Cruises, Ltd., et al. ("Royal Caribbean"). The district court granted Royal Caribbean's motion for summary judgment, holding that plaintiff Elizabeth Fedorczyk did not provide any evidence to support her claim that Royal Caribbean's failure to provide adequate abrasive strips in its bathtub was the proximate cause of her injuries. Because we agree with the district court that the evidence presented does not create a material issue of fact as to causation, which is an essential element of the tort of negligence, we will affirm the June 26, 1995 order of the district court.

I.

The following facts are not disputed. Fedorczyk sailed from Miami aboard the Sovereign, a cruise ship operated by Royal Caribbean. While on board she went to the pool area, applied sunscreen to her body, sunned herself, and swam in the pool. After approximately two hours Fedorczyk returned to her cabin to take a shower. She turned on the water, stepped into the middle of the bathtub and started to soap herself, at which time she slipped and fell onto the floor of the tub.

The tub in her cabin was about five and one-half feet long and two-feet, four-inches wide. It had four anti-skid strips, each running from the middle to the back of the tub. Fedorczyk has no recollection whether her feet were on or off the abrasive strips at the time of her fall. The tub was also equipped with a grab rail which Fedorczyk made a failed attempt to reach when she fell. After the accident she returned to the bathtub to ascertain the cause of the accident. She re-entered the tub and discovered that there was sufficient space between the abrasive strips so that her feet could just fit in between them. However, she does not know where her feet were at the time of the accident.

Fedorczyk's expert, an architect, testified that at the time he examined the bathtub, there were seven as opposed to four abrasive strips. Even with the seven abrasive strips, according to the expert, Royal Caribbean failed to provide a sufficiently large area of non-slip surface to permit its safe use. He based his finding on the fact that the tub failed to comply with the Consumer Products Safety Commission's standard for slip-resistent bathing facilities. This standard specifies that for any surface that is textured or treated with appliques, the pattern shall be such that a one and one-half by three inch rectangular template placed anywhere thereon shall cover some textured or treated area.

The expert also testified that beyond certain safety measures, there is no definite way of preventing slips altogether, and that falls can happen under any circumstances. He stated that the presence of bath oils and soap are large variables that can skew the correlation between the amount of textured surface area and safety. He concluded that Royal Caribbean deviated from an acceptable standard of care in failing adequately to treat or texturize the tub, and that the spacing between the nonslip strips was the direct cause of Fedorczyk's injuries.

II.

The district court had jurisdiction pursuant to 28 U.S.C. § 1332. We have appellate jurisdiction under 28 U.S.C. § 1291. "When reviewing an order granting summary judgment we exercise plenary review and apply the same test the district court should have applied." *Armbruster v. Unisys Corp.*, 32 F.3d 768, 777 (3d Cir.1994). "Under Federal Rule of Civil Procedure 56(c), that test is whether there is a genuine issue of material fact and, if not, whether the moving party is entitled to judgment as a matter of law." *Id.* (quoting *Gray v. York Newspapers, Inc.*, 957 F.2d 1070, 1078 (3d Cir.1992)). "In so deciding, the court must view the facts in a light most favorable to the nonmoving party and draw all reasonable inferences in that party's favor. Fed.R.Civ.P. 56(c)." *Id.* (quoting *Gray*, 957 F.2d at 1078.)

. . .

B.

For Fedorczyk to prevail on her negligence claim, in addition to proving that Royal Caribbean was negligent, she must also prove that the Royal Caribbean's negligence caused her injury. Causation includes cause in fact and legal causation, which is often referred to as proximate cause. Courts have often conflated cause in fact and legal causation into "proximate cause," but the two are conceptually distinct. W. PAGE KEETON ET AL., *Prosser and Keeton on the Law of Torts* § 41, at 263 (5th ed. 1984) ("PROSSER") ("There is perhaps nothing in the entire field of law which has called forth more disagreement . . . [and] confusion.").

Causation in fact depends on whether an act or omission played a material part in bringing about an event. An act or omission is not regarded as a cause in fact of an event if the particular event would have occurred without it. When more than one act or omission could have caused an event, then the negligent conduct must be shown to have been a substantial factor in causing the harm. RESTATEMENT (SECOND) OF TORTS § 432(2) (1965). The New Jersey Supreme Court has adopted these principles.

On the issue of causation, as on any other essential element of the tort of negligence, the plaintiff has the burden of proof. It is axiomatic that "the mere showing of an accident causing injuries is not sufficient from which to infer negligence. Negligence is a fact which must be proved; it will not be presumed." *Hansen,* 84 A.2d at 284. The plaintiff must introduce evidence which provides a reasonable basis for the conclusion that it was more likely than not that the negligent conduct of the defendant was a cause in fact of the injury.

The core problem for Fedorczyk is she is unable to prove that the negligence of Royal Caribbean in fact caused her injury. Fedorczyk's expert testified that a person may fall in a bathtub under ordinary circumstances and the presence of bath oil and soap are "great variables" that could have caused the fall. Fedorczyk could have fallen in the bathtub for reasons other than Royal Caribbean's negligence. Therefore, Fedorczyk must show that Royal Caribbean's negligence was a substantial factor in causing her injury. Fedorczyk concedes that if she had been standing on any of the four abrasive strips at the time of the accident, she could not establish Royal Caribbean's failure to provide adequate stripping was the cause of her injuries.

Fedorczyk has not provided any direct evidence that the lack of abrasive surface in the bathtub caused her accident. Instead, Fedorczyk relies solely upon what she asserts is circumstantial proof of causation. Circumstantial evidence when used to reason deductively in civil cases is defined as "a preponderance of probabilities according to the common experience of mankind." *Bornstein v. Metropolitan Bottling Co.,* 26 N.J. 263, 139 A.2d 404, 411 (1958); *Hansen,* 84 A.2d at 284. The circumstances must be strong enough "that a jury might properly, on the grounds of probability rather than certainty, exclude the inferences favorable to the defendant." *Jackson v. Delaware, L. & W. R.R. Co.,* 111 N.J.L. 487, 170 A. 22, 24 (1933). *See Hansen,* 84 A.2d at 284 ("the evidence must be such as to justify an inference of probability as distinguished from . . . mere possibility") (citing *Callahan v. National Lead Co.,* 4 N.J. 150, 72 A.2d 187, 189 (1950)); *see also Kulas,* 196 A.2d at 773 ("[Causation] may rest upon legitimate inference, so long as the proof will justify a . . . logical inference as distinguished from mere speculation.") (internal quotation marks and citation omitted); *Kahalili v. Rosecliff Realty,* 26 N.J. 595, 141 A.2d 301, 307 (1958) (" 'Reasonable probability' is the standard of persuasion"); PROSSER, *supra,* § 41, at 269.

. . .

Fedorczyk presents the following circumstantial evidence. After the accident, she discovered that her feet could fit between the strips. Fedorczyk also testified that she was in the middle of the tub at the time of the accident. Finally, her expert opined that based on his inspection of the tub and the evidence in the record, Royal Caribbean's failure to adequately strip the tub caused Fedorczyk's injuries.

Even though we must draw all legitimate inferences in Fedorczyk's favor, the inference that she was standing between the strips at the time of the accident, because her feet could fit between the strips, is not an appropriate inference to be drawn. The possibility of the existence of an event does not tend to prove its probability. *See Dombrowska v. Kresge-Newark, Inc.,* 75 N.J.Super. 271, 183 A.2d 111 (App.Div.1962) (evidence that worn wheel could cause accident insufficient to take to a jury the issue of whether an injury was likely to have been caused by wheel malfunction); *see also Dziedzic v. St. John's Cleaners and Shirt Launderers Inc.,* 53 N.J. 157, 249 A.2d 382 (1969) (since no evidence introduced on the issue of how plaintiff's positioning in a truck increased her injury in resulting from an automobile accident, jury could only speculate as to whether plaintiff's contributory negligence caused her injuries).

The testimony that Fedorczyk was standing in the middle of the tub also says nothing about whether it was more probable than not that she was standing between the strips when she fell. The four strips were placed parallel to the long dimension of the tub, running one and one-half feet from the back end of the tub to the middle. Standing in the middle of the tub does not provide any relevant information on whether she was standing on or between the strips.

Finally, the expert's conclusion that the failure to adequately strip the tub caused Fedorczyk's accident was not legally admissible. An expert opinion is not admissible if the court concludes that an opinion based upon particular facts cannot be grounded upon those facts. 1 MCCORMICK ON EVIDENCE, § 13, at 56 (John William Strong, ed.1992). In order for an expert opinion to be admissible, the technique the expert employs in formulating an opinion must be reliable. *In re Paoli R.R. Yard PCB Lit.,* 35 F.3d 717, 741 (3d Cir.1994), *cert. denied, sub nom., General Elec. Co. v. Ingram,* 513 U.S. 1190, 115 S.Ct. 1253, 131 L.Ed.2d 134 (1995). In contrast, if an expert opinion is based on speculation or conjecture, it may be stricken. 1 MCCORMICK, *supra,* § 13, at 56 n.15.

Fedorczyk's expert testified that if there had been more stripping, it would be more likely that she would not have fallen. He went on to conclude that the absence of strips caused her to fall. We agree that the more stripping there is in the tub, the less likely it is a person would fall because of inadequate stripping. However, the expert's opinion that inadequate stripping caused Fedorczyk's injuries is not based on any direct or circumstantial evidence of where she was standing when she fell. It is speculative to conclude that the inadequate stripping caused Fedorczyk's injuries when no evidence in the record indicates where Fedorczyk was standing in the tub. It is also speculative to infer that Fedorczyk was standing between the strips at the time of the accident solely from the fact that she fell. Because the expert's conclusion is based on pure speculation, rather than a reasonable inference, it is without foundation and is inadmissable.

A portion of the bathtub had nonskid stripping and a portion of it did not have the stripping. No evidence presented tends to prove Fedorczyk was standing either on or off the stripping at the time she fell. Without such evidence, the jury is left to speculate whether Royal Cruise's negligence was the cause in fact of her injury. "A mere possibility of causation is not enough; and when the matter remains one of pure speculation or conjecture, or the probabilities are at best evenly balanced, it becomes the duty of the court to direct a verdict for the defendant." *Restatement (Second) of Torts* § 433B (1965).

A hypothetical illustrates the point. A company provides a stairway in which some of the stairs are defective and some are in fine condition. A person falls on the steps, but does not know which step she fell on. No evidence is introduced that tends to prove she stepped on the defective step. The injured party simply testified that she walked down the steps and fell. We may not reasonably infer that the defective steps probably caused her injury merely because she may have stepped on a defective stair. Without evidence establishing a likelihood that the injured party stepped on the defective stair, a jury would be left to speculate as to the cause of the injury. Simply put, increased risk of harm due to a defendant's negligence, standing alone, does not permit an inference that an injury, more probably than not, was caused by the negligence.

IV.

Fedorczyk has failed to provide any direct or circumstantial evidence of how Royal Caribbean's admitted failure to adequately strip the bathtub caused her injury. Without providing any evidence tending to show where Fedorczyk was standing when she fell, she is unable to create a material issue of fact regarding causation. Based on the evidence presented, a jury could only speculate whether Fedorczyk's injuries were caused by the inadequate stripping. We will affirm the order of the district court granting summary judgment for the defendant.

STAPLETON, Circuit Judge, Dissenting:

Because I conclude that Fedorczyck has produced sufficient evidence to allow a reasonable jury to infer causation, I would reverse and remand for trial.

Comment b to *Restatement (Second) of Torts* § 433B (1965) is directly on point:

> The fact of causation is incapable of mathematical proof, since no man can say with absolute certainty what would have occurred if the defendant had acted otherwise. If, as a matter of ordinary experience, a particular act or omission might be expected to produce a particular result, and if that result has in fact followed, the conclusion may be justified that the causal relationship exists. In drawing that conclusion, the triers of fact are permitted to draw upon ordinary human experience as to the probabilities of the case.

Illustration 3, which provides an example of the application of this principle, is similar to the present case:

> The A Railroad Company fails to use reasonable care to light a steep and winding stairway leading from its waiting room to the train platform. B, an elderly and corpulent woman, is in the room waiting for a train. The attendant calls out the train. B hurries down the steps, and misses her footing in the dusk on the unlighted stair, falls, and is injured. On the basis of common experience that absence of light increases the likelihood of such a fall, and that people do not ordinarily fall on properly lighted stairs, it may be found that the absence of light was a substantial factor in causing the fall.

Id. More specifically, *Prosser and Keeton on the Law of Torts* § 41 (5th ed.1984) explains that a conclusion of causation is permissible where "the injury which has in fact occurred is precisely the sort of thing that proper care on the part of the defendant would be intended to prevent." *Id.* at 270.

I would resolve this appeal using these basic principles. Fedrorczyck's expert testified that the bathtub was too slippery to be reasonably safe because it had insufficient abrasive strips. Fedorczyck was standing in the bathtub and she fell. Her fall is precisely the type of injury that adequate abrasive strips were designed to prevent. Moreover, one could conclude based on everyday experience that while falls do occur in bathtubs that are not too slippery, they are not routine. Accordingly, a reasonable jury could infer that Fedorczyk's fall was caused by the unsafe condition of the tub. . . .

Notes and Questions

1. Both the majority and the dissent in *Fedorczyk* were correct on the law: mere speculation or a possibility of causation will not suffice; but inferences about the probabilities based on ordinary human experience are permissible. Why then did they disagree about whether the plaintiff had satisfied her burden of producing evidence on actual causation? What was it about the plaintiff's facts that made the court rule that no reasonable juror could view the probabilities in her favor? Do you think the majority disagreed with the Restatement (Second) on the outcome of Illustration 3 above or can Comment b be distinguished from *Fedorczyk*?

2. The "easy" actual cause cases are, of course, simpler than *Fedorczyk* in that they don't require an exploration of the possibilities and a weighing of inferences. The paradigmatic car accident in the intersection with a negligent defendant who crashes into a non-negligent plaintiff is but one example of such a simple case.

Restatement (Third) of Torts: Liability for Physical and Emotional Harm
§ 26. Factual Cause

Tortious conduct must be a factual cause of harm for liability to be imposed. Conduct is a factual cause of harm when the harm would not have occurred absent the conduct. . . .

Comment:

. . .

b. "But-for" standard for factual cause. The standard for factual causation in this Section is familiarly referred to as the "but-for" test, as well as a *sine qua non* test. Both express the same concept: an act is a factual cause of an outcome if, in the absence of the act, the outcome would not have occurred. With recognition that there are multiple factual causes of an event, see Comment *c*, a factual cause can also be described as a necessary condition for the outcome.

. . .

An act can also be a factual cause in accelerating an outcome that otherwise would have occurred at a later time. Thus, an electrocution due to a faulty ground-fault interrupter causes an acceleration in the death of the victim from natural causes. The loss of the victim's remaining years of life caused by the electrocution provides the framework for determining the damages that would be recoverable in a wrongful-death action. Acceleration may occur for harms other than death as well.

c. Tortious conduct need only be one of the factual causes of harm. An actor's tortious conduct need only be *a* factual cause of the other's harm. The existence of other causes of the harm does not affect whether specified tortious conduct was a necessary condition for the harm to occur. Those other causes may be innocent or tortious, known or unknown, influenced by the tortious conduct or independent of it, but so long as the harm would not have occurred absent the tortious conduct, the tortious conduct is a factual cause. Recognition of multiple causes does not require modifying or abandoning the but-for standard in this Section. Tortious conduct by an actor need be only one of the causes of another's harm. . . .

A useful model for understanding factual causation is to conceive of a set made up of each of the necessary conditions for the plaintiff's harm. Absent any one of the elements of the set, the plaintiff's harm would not have occurred. Thus, there will always be multiple (some say, infinite) factual causes of a harm, although most will not be of significance for tort law and many will be unidentified. That there are a large number of causes of an event does not mean that everything is a cause of an event. The vast majority of acts, omissions, and other factors play no role in causing any discrete event.

This causal-set model does not imply any chronological relationship among the causal elements involved, although all causes must precede the plaintiff's harm. An actor's tortious conduct may occur well before the other person suffers harm and may require a number of subsequent events to produce the harm. Thus, a gas valve negligently constructed may not fail for many years. Toxic substances may be sold without adequate warnings but not produce harm for decades. Conversely, the tortious conduct may occur after a number of other necessary events have already occurred, but close in time to the occurrence of harm. Nor does this model imply any relationship among the causal elements; causal elements may operate independently, as when a property owner neglects a patch of ice on a sidewalk and a careless pedestrian fails to notice the condition, producing a fall.

In some cases, two causal sets may exist, one or the other of which was the cause of harm. Thus, for example, in a case in which the plaintiff claims that a vaccination caused subsequent seizures, and the defendant claims that the seizures were caused not by the vaccination, but by a preexisting traumatic injury to the plaintiff, the causal set including the vaccination and the causal set including the traumatic injury are such alternative causes. If sufficient evidence to support each of these causal sets is introduced, the factfinder will have to determine which one is better supported by the evidence. On the other hand, if the evidence revealed that a traumatic injury and a vaccination can interact and cause seizures, then the vaccination and the trauma may each be a factual cause (both elements of the causal set) of the plaintiff's seizures. . . .

d. Causes and conditions. Because many of the causes necessary for an outcome regularly exist as background conditions and are unimportant for legal or other purposes, some would distinguish them from causes and describe them as conditions. Historically, many courts sought to distinguish certain events that were thought to be unimportant or inappropriate for the imposition of liability as conditions rather than causes. This distinction is common also in nonlegal discourse, and there is thus some awkwardness in describing oxygen and fuel as causes of the destruction of a building, along with the arsonist who provided the source of ignition. Nevertheless, providing criteria to distinguish causes from conditions, which inevitably entails ambiguity and uncertainty, is unnecessary for legal purposes. Further, to emphasize the empirical nature of factual causal determinations, all necessary elements for an outcome are described as causes in this Restatement. Thus, this Restatement refers to tortious conduct as *a* cause of harm and refers to a causal set, of which the tortious conduct was one necessary condition, as *the* cause of harm. On occasion, this Restatement refers to all of the routine, background causes that complete the necessary causal set as "background causes."

e. Counterfactual inquiry for factual cause. The requirement that the actor's tortious conduct be necessary for the harm to occur requires a counterfactual inquiry. One must ask what would have occurred if the actor had not engaged in the tortious conduct. In some cases, in which the tortious conduct consists of the entirety of an act, this inquiry may not be difficult. Thus, if a driver falls asleep and that driver's car crashes into another's home, assessing what would have occurred if the actor had not fallen asleep poses little difficulty. In other cases, especially those in which the tortious conduct consisted of marginally more risky conduct than is acceptable or in which the actor failed to take a precaution that would have reduced the risk to another, such as by warning of a danger, the counterfactual inquiry may pose difficult problems of proof.

. . .

l. Burden of proof. The burden of proof in civil actions requires proof by a preponderance of the evidence. . . . a plaintiff must prove that it is more likely than not that, if the defendant had not acted tortiously, the plaintiff's harm would not have occurred. Consistent with Comment *c*, the plaintiff need not prove that the defendant's tortious conduct was the predominant or primary cause of the harm. So long as the defendant's tortious conduct was more likely than not *a* factual cause of the harm, the plaintiff has established the element of factual cause.

Notes and Questions

1. What might the authors of the Restatement mean by the point in Comment c that "there will always be multiple (some say, infinite) factual causes of a harm, although most will not be of significance for tort law and many will be unidentified"? What might some of these insignificant (for tort law) causes be?

2. Some jurisdictions developed the "substantial factor" test as an alternative to the "but for" test to apply in more complicated circumstances where two or more forces either combined or were sufficient standing alone to produce the plaintiffs injuries or damage. Thus, as provided in the Restatement (Second) of Torts § 431,

> The actor's negligent conduct is a legal cause of harm to another if
>
> (a) his conduct is a substantial factor in bringing about the harm, and
>
> (b) there is no rule of law relieving the actor from liability because of the manner in which his negligence has resulted in harm.

As one court recently explained, however, "[t]he 'substantial factor' test has not turned out to be the hoped for panacea for all causation in fact problems. Over the years, it has taken on several distinct and conflicting meanings." Waste Management, Inc., of Tennessee v. South Central Bell Telephone Company, 15 S.W.3d 425 (Tenn. App. 1997). Because of these concerns and its reconceptualization of the traditional "but for" test, the Restatement Third no longer espouses the "substantial factor" alternative. *See* Restatement (Third) of Torts: Liability For Physical and Emotional Harm, § 26 Factual Cause, Comment j ("The substantial-factor test has not . . . withstood the test of time, as it has proved confusing and been misused.")

2. Cases in Which There Are Multiple Sufficient Causes

Restatement (Third) of Torts: Liability for Physical and Emotional Harm § 27. Multiple Sufficient Causes

If multiple acts occur, each of which under § 26 alone would have been a factual cause of the physical harm at the same time in the absence of the other act(s), each act is regarded as a factual cause of the harm.

Comment:

a. Multiple sufficient causes generally. This Section applies whenever there are two or more competing causes, each of which is sufficient without the other to cause the harm and each of which is in operation at the time the plaintiff's harm occurs. When an actor's tortious conduct is such a cause, it nevertheless would not be a factual cause if factual causes were limited to the definition in § 26: even without that tortious conduct, the harm would still have occurred because of the competing cause. Nevertheless, courts have long imposed liability when a tortfeasor's conduct, while not necessary for the outcome, would have been a factual cause if the other competing cause had not been operating.

Illustration:

1. Rosaria and Vincenzo were independently camping in a heavily forested campground. Each one had a campfire, and each negligently failed to ensure that the fire was extinguished upon retiring for the night. Due to unusually dry forest conditions and a stiff wind, both campfires escaped their sites and began a forest fire. The two fires, burning out of control, joined together and engulfed Centurion Company's hunting lodge, destroying it. Either fire alone would have destroyed the lodge. Each of Rosaria's and Vincenzo's negligence is a factual cause of the destruction of Centurion's hunting lodge.

In many cases, multiple sufficient causes will each, along with background causes, be capable of causing the harm, as in Illustration 1. This Restatement thus refers to causes such as Rosaria's and Vincenzo's negligence as multiple sufficient causes. However, in some cases, the tortious conduct will not be sufficient with background causes to be capable of causing the harm. This situation is addressed in Comments *f* and *g*. The cases addressed in those Comments include agents, such as a fraction of a lethal dose of a poison, that requires additional nonbackground causes in order to be capable of causing the harm. For those cases, "multiple sufficient causal sets" is a more accurate description of the factual circumstance.

As with causes under § 26, multiple sufficient causes may accelerate the time of the occurrence of a harm that would have occurred at some later point in the absence of the multiple sufficient causes. See § 26, Comment *b*. The period of time reflected by the acceleration of the harm forms the basis for determining damages in the case.

. . .

c. Rationale. A number of justifications exist for the rule in this Section. A defendant whose tortious act was fully capable of causing the plaintiff's harm should not escape liability merely because of the fortuity of another sufficient cause. That justification is not entirely satisfactory. Tortious acts occur, with some frequency, that fortuitously do not cause harm. Nevertheless, the actors committing these acts are not held liable in tort. When two tortious multiple sufficient causes exist, to deny liability would make the plaintiff worse off due to multiple tortfeasors than would have been the case if only one of the tortfeasors had existed. Perhaps most significant is the recognition that, while the but-for standard provided in § 26 is a helpful method for identifying causes, it is not the exclusive means for determining a factual cause. Multiple sufficient causes are also factual causes because we recognize them as such in our common understanding of causation, even if the but-for standard does not. Thus, the standard for causation in this Section comports with deep-seated intuitions about causation and fairness in attributing responsibility.

d. One cause tortious, the other innocent. This Section applies in a case of multiple sufficient causes, regardless of whether the competing cause involves tortious conduct or consists only of innocent conduct. So long as each of the competing causes was sufficient to produce the same harm as the defendant's tortious conduct, this Section is applicable. Conduct is a factual cause of harm regardless of whether it is tortious or innocent and regardless of any other cause with which it concurs to produce overdetermined harm.

When one of multiple sufficient causes is not tortious, the question of damages is a different matter from the causal question. The question of what (if any) damages should be awarded against these tortfeasors properly belongs to the law of damages and is not addressed in this Restatement.

. . .

e. Alternative causes. In some cases, a defendant may contend that the acts of another were the cause of the plaintiff's harm and thus that defendant's tortious conduct was not a cause of the plaintiff's harm. Whether that claim implicates the rule in this Section depends on whether the other forces were operating and sufficient to cause the harm contemporaneously with the defendant's tortious conduct or, alternatively, were the factual cause of the harm *instead of* the defendant's tortious conduct. If the evidence supports the former finding, then this Section is applicable. If the evidence supports the latter finding, then the applicable standard for factual causation is that stated in § 26.

. . .

f. Multiple sufficient causal sets. In some cases, tortious conduct by one actor is insufficient, even with other background causes, to cause the plaintiff's harm. Nevertheless, when combined with conduct by other persons, the conduct overdetermines the harm, i.e., is more than sufficient to cause the harm. This circumstance thus creates the multiple-sufficient-causal-set situation addressed in this Comment. The fact that an actor's conduct requires other conduct to be sufficient to cause another's harm does not obviate the applicability of this Section. See § 26, Comment *c*. Moreover, the fact that the other person's conduct is sufficient to cause the harm does not prevent the actor's conduct from being a factual cause of harm pursuant to this Section, if the actor's conduct is necessary to at least one causal set. Sometimes, one actor's contribution may be sufficient to bring about the harm while another actor's contribution is only sufficient when combined with some portion of the first actor's contribution. Whether the second actor's contribution can be so combined into a sufficient causal set is a matter on which this Restatement takes no position and leaves to future development in the courts. See Comment *i*.

. . .

i. Special cases involving multiple sufficient causal sets and preempted conditions. Results in some cases are difficult to explain under the rules stated in this Section and its Comments. Sometimes, one candidate for a multiple sufficient cause appears de minimis, as when a match is thrown into an already raging fire. Another such situation occurs when an element of a potentially sufficient set, see Comment *f*, requires additional elements and the additional contribution that occurs is greater than necessary to cause the harm. For example, a negligently constructed dam that would have collapsed in an ordinary flood may be overwhelmed by a flood so large and unforeseeable that no dam would have controlled it. Other times, two candidates for multiple sufficient causes may be two omissions that fail to prevent harm and each is dependent on the nonexistence of the other to be a but-for cause, as when a motorist fails to apply brakes that, because of earlier failures during repair, would not have worked, or when a consumer fails to read a product label that omitted a warning.

Both the match and the negligent construction of the dam could be characterized as causes if one conceptualizes them as combining with something less than the actual events that occurred. Thus, a fire that needed just the additional amount of heat of a match to destroy a home and a flood of normal proportions make the match and dam factual causes. Nevertheless, courts often decline to hold the de minimis candidate a cause and thus dismiss the negligent construction of the dam as not a cause of any flooding damage. That conclusion may be affected by the fact that the flood is a nontortious competing cause. See Comment *d*. Similarly, courts often conclude that the earlier of two multiple-sufficient-cause candidates, separated in time, that failed to prevent harm was not a cause. Indeed, courts routinely hold that an inadequate warning, which would not have prevented an injury even if read, is not a cause of an injury if an adequate warning would not have been read. Those courts may also be tempted to dismiss the later candidate as noncausal because it is not a but-for cause of the harm; they may also be influenced when the later candidate does not involve tortious conduct. These results seem to depend on intuitions that are not captured in the purely conceptual general rule that each of two sufficient sets of conditions to bring about an injury is treated as a cause.

. . .

Notes and Questions

1. Is the Restatement correct that "[m]ultiple sufficient causes are also factual causes because we recognize them as such in our common understanding of causation" and that "the standard for causation in this Section comports with deep-seated intuitions about causation and fairness in attributing responsibility"? Is the rationale it provides for this rule convincing?

2. Many of the early American cases on this point involved multiple fires, any of which would have been sufficient on their own to cause the damage for which the plaintiff sought recovery. Sometimes, one of two fires was caused by the defendant's negligence and the other was caused "innocently," for example by lightning. In that early period, some courts held that the defendant

could not be found liable in such circumstances because this would bring a windfall to the plaintiff who would not have otherwise been able to recover for damages caused by lightning and because it would be unfair to the defendant who would have no one with whom to share the responsibility for the loss. *See* Kingston v. Chicago & Northwest Railway Col, 211 N.W. 913 (Wis. 1927). If you represented the plaintiff on similar facts, how would you counter these explanations?

3. As the Restatement suggests, characterizing a cause as *de minimis* suggests that its contribution to the damage was legally insignificant. Courts sometimes characterize such a cause as being superseded or overwhelmed by other more important causes. *See, e.g., id.* ("there is no intimation or suggestion that the northeast fire was enveloped and swallowed up by the northwest fire.") Where the facts allow it, this strategy may be helpful for both defendants whose causal contributions join with others to produce harm, and for plaintiffs who are charged with contributory negligence in similar circumstances.

B. Establishing Cause-in-Fact on Policy Grounds

As we saw in *Fedorczyk,* satisfying the burden of proof on actual causation can be difficult. In most cases, the plaintiff's failure to meet this burden results in dismissal of the suit. However, there are occasions where, for policy reasons, the courts will permit the plaintiff to proceed notwithstanding a lack of evidence on actual cause. The notion of such a policy-based bye should be familiar to you from your work on duty (see Strauss v. Belle Realty Company) and on breach (see Byrne v. Boadle and Mayer v. Once Upon A Rose, Inc.).

SUMMERS v. TICE
199 P.2d 1 (Cal. 1948)

CARTER, Justice.

Each of the two defendants appeals from a judgment against them in an action for personal injuries. Pursuant to stipulation the appeals have been consolidated.

Plaintiff's action was against both defendants for an injury to his right eye and face as the result of being struck by bird shot discharged from a shotgun. The case was tried by the court without a jury and the court found that on November 20, 1945, plaintiff and the two defendants were hunting quail on the open range. Each of the defendants was armed with a 12 gauge shotgun loaded with shells containing 7 1/2 size shot. Prior to going hunting plaintiff discussed the hunting procedure with defendants, indicating that they were to exercise care when shooting and to 'keep in line.' In the course of hunting plaintiff proceeded up a hill, thus placing the hunters at the points of a triangle. The view of defendants with reference to plaintiff was unobstructed and they knew his location. Defendant Tice flushed a quail which rose in flight to a ten foot elevation and flew between plaintiff and defendants. Both defendants shot at the quail, shooting in plaintiff's direction. At that time defendants were 75 yards from plaintiff. One shot struck plaintiff in his eye and another in his upper lip. Finally it was found by the court that as the direct result of the shooting by defendants the shots struck plaintiff as above mentioned and that defendants were negligent in so shooting and plaintiff was not contributorily negligent.

. . .

The problem presented in this case is whether the judgment against both defendants may stand. It is argued by defendants that they are not joint tortfeasors, and thus jointly and severally liable, as they were not acting in concert, and that there is not sufficient evidence to show which defendant was guilty of the negligence which caused the injuries the shooting by Tice or that by Simonson. Tice argues that there is evidence to show that the shot which struck plaintiff came from Simonson's gun because of admissions allegedly made by him to third persons and no evidence that they came from his gun. Further in connection with the latter contention, the court failed to find on plaintiff's allegation in his complaint that he did not know which one was at fault did not find which defendant was guilty of the negligence which caused the injuries to plaintiff.

Considering the last argument first, we believe it is clear that the court sufficiently found on the issue that defendants were jointly liable and that thus the negligence of both was the cause of the injury or to that legal effect. It found that both defendants were negligent and 'That as a direct and proximate result of the shots fired by defendants, and each of them, a birdshot pellet was caused to and did lodge in plaintiff's right eye and that another birdshot pellet was caused to and did lodge in plaintiff's upper lip.' In so doing the court evidently did not give credence to the admissions of Simonson to third persons that he fired the shots, which it was justified in doing. It thus determined that the negligence of both defendants was the legal cause of the injury or that both were responsible. Implicit in such finding is the assumption that the court was unable to ascertain whether the shots were from the gun of one defendant or the other or one shot from each of them. The one shot that entered plaintiff's eye was the major factor in assessing damages and that shot could not have come from the gun of both defendants. It was from one or the other only.

It has been held that where a group of persons are on a hunting party, or otherwise engaged in the use of firearms, and two of them are negligent in firing in the direction of a third person who is injured thereby, both of those so firing are liable for the injury suffered by the third person, although the negligence of only one of them could have caused the injury. The same rule has been applied in criminal cases, and both drivers have been held liable for the negligence of one where they engaged in a racing contest causing an injury to a third person. These cases speak of the action of defendants as being in concert as the ground of decision, yet it would seem they are straining that concept and the more reasonable basis appears in Oliver v. Miles, [110 So. 666 (Miss. 1926)]. There two persons were hunting together. Both shot at some partridges and in so doing shot across the highway injuring plaintiff who was travelling on it. The court stated they were acting in concert and thus both were liable. The court then stated: 'We think that * * * each is liable for the resulting injury to the boy, although no one can say definitely who actually shot him. *To hold otherwise would be to exonerate both from liability, although each was negligent, and the injury resulted from such negligence.*' (Emphasis added.) It is said in the Restatement: 'For harm resulting to a third person from the tortious conduct of another, a person is liable if he * * * (b) knows that the other's conduct constitutes a breach of duty and gives substantial assistance or encouragement to the other so to conduct himself, or (c) gives substantial assistance to the other in accomplishing a tortious result and his own conduct, separately considered, constitutes a breach of duty to the third person.' (Rest., Torts, sec. 876(b)(c).) Under subsection (b) the example is given: 'A and B are members of a hunting party. Each of them in the presence of the other shoots across a public road at an animal this being negligent as to persons on the road. A hits the animal. B's bullet strikes C, a traveler on the road. A is liable to C.' (Rest., Torts, Sec. 876(b), Com., Illus. 3.) An illustration given under subsection (c) is the same as above except the factor of both defendants shooting is missing and joint liability is not imposed. It is further said that: 'If two forces are actively operating, one because of the actor's negligence, the other not because of any misconduct on his part, and each of itself sufficient to bring about harm to another, the actor's negligence may be held by the jury to be a substantial factor in bringing it about.' (Rest., Torts, sec. 432.) Dean Wigmore has this to say: 'When two or more persons by their acts are possibly the sole cause of a harm, or when two or more acts of the same person are possibly the sole cause, and the plaintiff has introduced evidence that the one of the two persons, or the one of the same person's two acts, is culpable, then the defendant has the burden of proving that the other person, or his other act, was the sole cause of the harm. (b) * * * The real reason for the rule that each joint tortfeasor is responsible for the whole damage is the practical unfairness of denying the injured person redress simply because he cannot prove how much damage each did, when it is certain that between them they did all; let them be the ones to apportion it among themselves. Since, then, the difficulty of proof is the reason, the rule should apply whenever the harm has plural causes, and not merely when they acted in conscious concert. * * *' (Wigmore, Select Cases on the Law of Torts, sec. 153.) Similarly Professor Carpenter has said: '(Suppose) the case where A and B independently shoot at C and but one bullet touches C's body. In such case, such proof as is ordinarily required that either A or B shot C, of course fails. It is suggested that there should be a relaxation of the proof required of the plaintiff * * * where the injury occurs as the result of one where more than one independent force is operating, and it is impossible to determine that the force set in operation by defendant did not in fact constitute a cause of the damage, and where it may have caused the damage, but the plaintiff is unable to establish that it was a cause.' (20 Cal.L.Rev. 406.)

When we consider the relative position of the parties and the results that would flow if plaintiff was required to pin the injury on one of the defendants only, a requirement that the burden of proof on that subject be shifted to defendants becomes manifest. They are both wrongdoers both negligent toward plaintiff. They brought about a situation where the negligence of one of them injured the plaintiff, hence it should rest with them each to absolve himself if he can. The injured party has been placed by defendants in the unfair position of pointing to which defendant caused the harm. If one can escape the other may also and plaintiff is remediless. Ordinarily defendants are in a far better position to offer evidence to determine which one caused the injury. This reasoning has recently found favor in this Court. In a quite analogous situation this Court held that a patient injured while unconscious on an operating table in a hospital could hold all or any of the persons who had any connection with the operation even though he could not select the particular acts by the particular person which led to his disability. Ybarra v. Spangard, 25 Cal.2d 486, 154 P.2d 687, 162 A.L.R. 1258. There the Court was considering whether the patient could avail himself of res ipsa loquitur, rather than where the burden of proof lay, yet the effect of the decision is that plaintiff has made out a case when he has produced evidence which gives rise to an inference of negligence which was the proximate cause of the injury. It is up to defendants to explain the cause of the injury. It was there said: 'If the doctrine is to continue to serve a useful purpose, we should not forget that 'the particular force and justice of the rule, regarded as a presumption throwing upon the party charged the duty of producing evidence, consists in the circumstance that the chief evidence of the true cause, whether culpable or innocent, is practically accessible to him but inaccessible to the injured person.'' 25 Cal.2d at page 490, 154 P.2d at page 689, 162 A.L.R. 1258. Similarly in the instant case plaintiff is not able to establish which of defendants caused his injury.

. . .

Cases are cited for the proposition that where two or more tort feasors acting independently of each other cause an injury to plaintiff, they are not joint tort feasors and plaintiff must establish the portion of the damage caused by each, even though it is impossible to prove the portion of the injury caused by each. See, Slater v. Pacific American Oil Co., 212 Cal. 648, 300 P. 31; Miller v. Highland Ditch Co., 87 cal. 430, 25 P. 550, 22 Am.St.Rep. 254; People v. Gold Run D. & M. Co., 66 Cal. 138, 4 P. 1152, 56 Am.Rep. 80; Wade v. Thorsen, 5 Cal.App.2d 706, 43 P.2d 592; California Orange Co. v. Riverside P. C. Co., 50 Cal.App. 522, 195 P. 694; City of Oakland v. Pacific Gas & E. Co., 47 Cal.App.2d 444, 118 P.2d 328. In view of the foregoing discussion it is apparent that defendants in cases like the present one may be treated as liable on the same basis as joint tort feasors, and hence the last cited cases are distinguishable inasmuch as they involve independent tort feasors.

In addition to that, however, it should be pointed out that the same reasons of policy and justice shift the burden to each of defendants to absolve himself if he can relieving the wronged person of the duty of apportioning the injury to a particular defendant, apply here where we are concerned with whether plaintiff is required to supply evidence for the apportionment of damages. If defendants are independent tort feasors and thus each liable for the damage caused by him alone, and, at least, where the matter of apportionment is incapable of proof, the innocent wronged party should not be deprived of his right to redress. The wrongdoers should be left to work out between themselves any apportionment. Some of the cited cases refer to the difficulty of apportioning the burden of damages between the independent tort feasors, and say that where factually a correct division cannot be made, the trier of fact may make it the best it can, which would be more or less a guess, stressing the factor that the wrongdoers are not a position to complain of uncertainty.

It is urged that plaintiff now has changed the theory of his case in claiming a concert of action; that he did not plead or prove such concert. From what has been said it is clear that there has been no change in theory. The joint liability, as well as the lack of knowledge as to which defendant was liable, was pleaded and the proof developed the case under either theory. We have seen that for the reasons of policy discussed herein, the case is based upon the legal proposition that, under the circumstances here presented, each defendant is liable for the whole damage whether they are deemed to be acting in concert or independently.

The judgment is affirmed.

GIBSON, C. J., and SHENK, EDMONDS, TRAYNOR, SCHAUER, and SPENCE, JJ., concur.

Notes and Questions

1. Why was the plaintiff unable to prove that the defendants actually caused his facial injuries, and what was the California Supreme Court's explanation for permitting the plaintiff to proceed notwithstanding this failure of proof?

2. Based on the court's opinion, can you distinguish between the plaintiff's two causation theories, concerted action and joint action? How would the result have been different for the defendants had the court decided that they were independent actors?

3. The Restatement (Third) of Torts: Liability for Physical and Emotional Harm § 28, provides that

> (a) Subject to Subsection (b), the plaintiff has the burden to prove that the defendant's tortious conduct was a factual cause of the plaintiff's harm.
>
> (b) When the plaintiff sues all of multiple actors and proves that each engaged in tortious conduct that exposed the plaintiff to a risk of harm and that the tortious conduct of one or more of them caused the plaintiff's harm but the plaintiff cannot reasonably be expected to prove which actor or actors caused the harm, the burden of proof, including both production and persuasion, on factual causation is shifted to the defendants.

Describe how this rule (in effect the rule from Summers v. Tice) is different from the rule of *res ipsa loquitur*.

4. There are related fact patterns that test the boundaries of the rule from Summers v. Tice because they involve more than two defendants. *See, e.g.*, Hall v. E. I. Du Pont De Nemours & Co., 345 F.Supp. 353 (E.D. N.Y. 1972) (suit against six manufacturers of blasting caps); Sindell v. Abbott Laboratories, 607 P.2d 924 (Cal. 1980) (suit against eleven manufacturers of DES); Case v. Fibreboard Corp., 743 P.2d 1062 (Okl. 1987) (suit against manufacturers of asbestos). The equities involved in shifting the burden to the defendants in *Summers* were relatively comfortable because there was a fifty percent chance that Simonson was responsible for the plaintiff's most expensive (eye) injury, and a fifty percent chance that Tice was responsible for that injury. As the number of defendants increases beyond two, this likelihood drops and the equities of assuming causation become correspondingly less comfortable. On the other hand, the plaintiff remains in the same circumstances: injured and unable to prove which of a number of negligent defendants caused the damage at issue. Over time, courts have developed different policy-based approaches to the problem posed by this special category of cases. These approaches are nicely cataloged *supra* in *Hall*, *Sindell*, and *Case*. *See also* Restatement (Third) of Torts: Liability for Physical and Emotional Harm, § 28, Comment on Subsection (b), Rest 3d Torts-PEH § 28.

5. Another line of cases in which it is difficult for plaintiffs to establish actual cause in circumstances where there are good policy arguments for allowing them nevertheless to proceed involve the "lost chance" doctrine. The generic "lost chance" fact pattern has a plaintiff with a pre-existing condition entering into a relationship with a physician who commits malpractice that may or may not have caused the condition to worsen, so that it's not clear whether the condition or the malpractice caused the ultimate injury, e.g., the plaintiff's permanent injury or death. Where the plaintiff has evidence tending to show that it's more likely than not that the malpractice caused the injury, the doctrine is not invoked—the plaintiff is able to develop a "regular" causation argument. However, the lost chance doctrine is used and can be very helpful where the plaintiff has less evidence than this, e.g., where their best evidence tends only to show that it was possible the malpractice caused the injury. Depending on the jurisdiction's approach to the doctrine, a successful plaintiff might recover for the value

of the lost chance or for the whole injury. The former is called "damages theory" on the view that the doctrine alters the theory of the injury itself; what's lost is not the plaintiff's life, for example, but rather a 10% chance at avoiding death. The latter is called "causation theory" on the view that the doctrine doesn't alter the theory of the injury, that's still "death", rather, it gives the plaintiff a "bye" on the causation element of the prima facie case—it allows them to establish causation with less than a preponderance of the evidence. Illustrative fact patterns include plaintiffs who come into the emergency room having sustained collision injuries that are improperly diagnosed on intake as minor when they are actually major, and plaintiffs who see an oncologist for tumors that are improperly diagnosed as being at an earlier stage when they are actually at a later stage. In both instances, the likelihood of a full recovery or avoiding death are less than 50%, which is insufficient to meet the "regular" burden of proof. Why might the law make an exception to that burden in medical malpractice cases? For an example of a case reviewing the doctrine, see Mahue v. Sparkman, 563 N.E.2d 1384 (Indiana 1995).

6. Even apart from the lost chance cases, actual cause cases arising on medical facts often highlight the difference between the medical and legal communities' views on causation. Thus, "[f]or science and medicine, causation is established only if a high threshold of proof is met." Doriane Lambelet Coleman and Philip M. Rosoff, *The Legal Authority of Mature Minors to Consent to General Medical Treatment*, 131 PEDIATRICS 1, 4 (April 2013). This is because for science and medicine, the objective of the causation inquiry is exclusively factual. In contrast, "[f]or law, causation is established with this same high threshold if the matter is criminal, but if the case is civil, a 51% likelihood will do because the objective is compensation and because society is said to be willing to bear a 49% error rate if the penalty involves money (as opposed to liberty)." *Id.* The effect of this difference is that a court can, for example, find that a physical trauma "caused" the development of cancer at the point of the trauma if the evidence and balance of probabilities suggests that this is the case, even if the medical community largely rejects this explanation. *See, e.g.*, Daly v. Bergstedt, 126 N.W.2d 242 (Minn. 1964).

II. PROXIMATE CAUSE

A. The Concept and Its History

Courts have long included a corrective element in the negligence prima facie case. That is, they have required plaintiffs to allege and prove that those whom they chose to hold liable were not only the actual but also the proximate cause of their injuries and damages. And they have permitted defendants to rebut this allegation and proof on the basis that on the facts, it would be unfair and unjust to make them pay the plaintiffs' damages. Generally, arguments over proximate cause have arisen in circumstances where the plaintiff or the losses were somehow different (for example, in kind, degree, or etiology) than expected at the moment of the defendant's breach.

Because "correcting injustices" and ensuring "fairness" are loose terms subject to much interpretation, judges have used proxies and related descriptions that are less susceptible to subjective judgment but that accomplish the same ends. Indeed, the term "proximate" along with its frequent descriptor "natural and continuous sequence" (also framed as "natural and probable consequence") is an original proxy for this purpose. As described in Laidlaw v. Sage, 52 N.E. 679, 688 (N.Y. 1899):

> The doctrine of proximate cause is a fundamental rule of the law of damages, to the effect that damages are to be allowed in general only for the proximate consequences of the wrong . . . there may be a degree of uncertainty as to the plain signification of the term 'proximate cause,' or rather in its application to various cases, . . . Bishop, in his work on Noncontract Law (section 42), in discussing this question, after remarking as to the uncertainty with which the term 'proximate cause' may have been used and applied, and after defining the terms 'proximate' and 'remote' cause, says: 'If, after the cause in question has been in operation, some independent force comes in, and produces an injury not its natural or probable effect, the author of the cause is not responsible.' In Shear. & R. Neg. § 26, it is said: 'The breach of duty upon which an action is brought must be not only the cause, but the proximate cause, of the damage to the plaintiff. * * * The proximate cause of an event must be understood to be that which, in a natural and continuous sequence, unbroken by any new cause, produces that event, and without which that event would not have occurred.' Wharton thus discusses the question: 'Supposing that, if it had not been for the intervention of a responsible third party, the defendant's negligence would have produced no damage to the plaintiff, is the defendant liable to the plaintiff? This question must be answered in the negative, for the general reason that causal connection between negligence and damage is broken by the interposition of independent responsible human action.

Among other things, *Laidlaw* exemplifies the courts' struggles to define the difference between a proximate and a remote cause and to defend the use of these terms as proxies for the corrective justice enterprise. These struggles inevitably led judges and academics in search of a better proxy. The 1921 British case Polemis and Furness Withy & Co Ltd, Re, 3 K.B. 560 (Court of Appeal 1921), famously cataloged the weaknesses inherent in the term "proximate cause" and provided an historically important alternative, "direct cause":

> '[T]he legal distinction between what is proximate and what is remote is not a logical one, nor does it depend upon relations of time and space; it is purely practical, the reason for distinguishing between the proximate and remote causes and consequences being a purely practical one'; and again, to use the words of an eminent English jurist (Sir F. Pollock), 'In whatever form we state the rule of "natural and probable consequences," we must remember that it is not a logical definition, but only a guide to the exercise of common sense. The Lawyer cannot afford to adventure himself with philosophers in the logical and metaphysical controversies that beset the idea of cause.' " In [another] case Lord Sumner said:
>
> "What are 'natural, probable and necessary' consequences? Everything that happens, happens in the order of nature and is therefore 'natural.' Nothing that happens by the free choice of a thinking man is 'necessary,' except in the sense of predestination. To speak of 'probable' consequence is to throw everything upon the jury. It is tautologous to speak of 'effective' cause or to say that damages too remote from the cause are irrecoverable, for an effective cause is simply that which causes, and in law what is ineffective or too remote is not a cause at all. I still venture to think that direct cause is the best expression. Proximate cause has acquired a special connotation through its use in reference to contracts of insurance. Direct cause excludes what is indirect, conveys the essential distinction, which causa causans and causa sine qua non rather cumbrously indicate, and is consistent with the possibility of the

> concurrence of more direct causes than one, operating at the same time and leading to a common result . . .

Id. at 570–71. Most notably and controversially, despite its historical basis in "natural and probable consequences," the direct cause test rejected any role for foreseeability in proximate cause analysis. *Polemis* itself stands for the proposition that "[w]hat the defendants might reasonably anticipate is only material with reference to the question, whether the defendants were negligent or not, and cannot alter their liability if they were guilty of negligence." *Id.* at 570 (internal citations omitted).

Meanwhile, because the term "proximate cause" literally read did not capture the intent of the inquiry, the American Law Institute sought to garner support among lawyers and judges for the more-descriptive term "legal cause." As Professor Richard Cupp has explained:

> The basic principles of proximate cause have not changed much since the 1930s, but the ALI's restatements of it have. Indeed, in each of the three efforts the ALI has made at restating proximate cause, it has employed different approaches. The first, second, and proposed third Restatements all seem to agree that the phrase "proximate cause" is undesirable, but they take different paths in seeking to identify appropriate labels and tests. The First Restatement adopted the phrase "legal cause" as a substitute for proximate cause language. Although the courts did not respond favorably to this effort, the Second Restatement continued utilization of "legal cause" language. The Second Restatement introduced some changes to the proximate cause formulation, such as adding language . . . indicating that a highly-extraordinary-in-hindsight test is appropriate in determining foreseeability of harm—another concept that has not fared well with the courts. Neither the first nor the second Restatements faithfully reflected the language or, in some respects, the approaches utilized by the courts, and the Restatements' efforts to steer the courts to new language and approaches met with failure.

Richard L. Cupp, Jr., *Proximate Cause, The Proposed Basic Principles Restatement, and Products Liability*, 53 SO. CAR. L. REV. 1085, 1086-87 (2002)

Ultimately, as we will see, the proxy term of art "proximate cause" has withstood the test of time as have some of its original aspects; but the precise focus of the courts' analysis has continued to evolve. The distinction between a proximate and a remote cause still finds its way into modern opinions as a descriptor, but it is no longer itself the test for proximate cause. Direct cause has suffered a similar fate. Indeed, as *Palsgraf* foretells, modern courts seeking to establish proximate cause mostly focus on the foreseeability of the plaintiff and of the injuries and losses.

Notes and Questions

1. Courts sometimes use the locution "proximate cause" as shorthand for both actual and proximate cause. It is important to remember that the inquiries are separate even though (depending on the test for proximate cause) they may have elements in common.

2. Older cases like *Laidlaw* and *Polemis* sometimes define proximate or direct cause using examples in which the defendant's breach is followed by an intervening cause or causes that might be said to supersede the defendant's responsibility. Although the direct cause test is mostly defunct as a proxy for proximate cause, the doctrine of superseding cause itself survives in many jurisdictions as a basis to find that the plaintiff has not satisfied the proximate cause requirement; that is, it continues to be the sense that it is unfair and unjust to hold a defendant responsible whose breach is followed by an act or event that by its nature or effect "breaks the chain of causation." We consider superseding causes in additional detail below.

3. Consider why proximate cause might be formally applicable in all tort cases whether they are based in intent, negligence, or no-fault liability principles. Then consider why it is more likely to be applicable in negligence cases than in those based on an intent theory. Finally, consider why, as Professor Leon Green famously noted, "[i]n the overwhelming majority of suits brought and defenses interposed, this element is not only present, *but so clearly so* that no issue is raised for a jury's determination." Leon Green, Contributory Negligence and Proximate Cause, 6 N.C. L. Rev. 3, 7 (1927) (emphasis in original).

B. The Move from Direct Cause to Foreseeability

PALSGRAF v. LONG ISLAND RAILROAD
162 N.E. 99 (N.Y. 1928)

CARDOZO, C. J.

Plaintiff was standing on a platform of defendant's railroad after buying a ticket to go to Rockaway Beach. A train stopped at the station, bound for another place. Two men ran forward to catch it. One of the men reached the platform of the car without mishap, though the train was already moving. The other man, carrying a package, jumped aboard the car, but seemed unsteady as if about to fall. A guard on the car, who had held the door open, reached forward to help him in, and another guard on the platform pushed him from behind. In this act, the package was dislodged, and fell upon the rails. It was a package of small size, about fifteen inches long, and was covered by a newspaper. In fact it contained fireworks, but there was nothing in its appearance to give notice of its contents. The fireworks when they fell exploded. The shock of the explosion threw down some scales at the other end of the platform many feet away. The scales struck the plaintiff, causing injuries for which she sues.

The conduct of the defendant's guard, if a wrong in its relation to the holder of the package, was not a wrong in its relation to the plaintiff, standing far away. Relatively to her it was not negligence at all. Nothing in the situation gave notice that the falling package had in it the potency of peril to persons thus removed. Negligence is not actionable unless it involves the invasion of a legally protected interest, the violation of a right. 'Proof of negligence in the air, so to speak, will not do.' Pollock, Torts (11th ed.) p. 455 . . . The plaintiff, as she stood upon the platform of the station, might claim to be protected against intentional invasion of her bodily security. Such invasion is not charged. She might claim to be protected against unintentional invasion by conduct involving in the thought of reasonable men an unreasonable hazard that such invasion would ensue. These, from the point of view of the law, were the bounds of her immunity, with perhaps some rare exceptions, survivals for the most part of ancient forms of liability, where conduct is held to be at the peril of the actor. If no hazard was apparent to the eye of ordinary vigilance, an act innocent and harmless, at least to outward seeming, with reference to her, did not take to itself the quality of a tort because it happened to be a wrong, though apparently not one involving the risk of bodily insecurity, with reference to some one else. 'In every instance, before negligence can be predicated of a given act, back of the act must be sought and found a duty to the individual complaining, the observance of which would have averted or avoided the injury.' McSherry, C. J., in West Virginia Central & P. R. Co. v. State, 96 Md. 652, 666, 54 A. 669, 671 (61 L. R. A. 574). 'The ideas of negligence and duty are strictly correlative.' Bowen, L. J., in Thomas v. Quartermaine, 18 Q. B. D. 685, 694. The plaintiff sues in her own right for a wrong personal to her, and not as the vicarious beneficiary of a breach of duty to another.

A different conclusion will involve us, and swiftly too, in a maze of contradictions. A guard stumbles over a package which has been left upon a platform. It seems to be a bundle of newspapers. It turns out to be a can of dynamite. To the eye of ordinary vigilance, the bundle is abandoned waste, which may be kicked or trod on with impunity. Is a passenger at the other end of the platform protected by the law against the unsuspected hazard concealed beneath the waste? If not, is the result to be any different, so far as the distant passenger is concerned, when the guard stumbles over a valise which a truckman or a porter has left upon the walk? The passenger far away, if the victim of a wrong at all, has a cause of action, not derivative, but original and primary. His claim to be protected against invasion of his bodily security is neither greater nor less because the act resulting in the invasion is a wrong to another far removed. In this case, the rights that are said to have been violated, are not even of the same order. The man was not injured in his person nor even put in danger. The purpose of the act, as well as its effect, was to make his person safe. It there was a wrong to him at all, which may very well be doubted it was a wrong to a property interest only, the safety of his package. Out of this wrong to property, which threatened injury to nothing else, there has passed, we are told, to the plaintiff by derivation or succession a right of action for the invasion of an interest of another order, the right to bodily security. The diversity of interests emphasizes the futility of the effort to build the plaintiff's right upon the basis of a wrong to some one else. The gain is one of emphasis, for a like result would follow if the interests were the same. Even then, the orbit of the danger as disclosed to the eye of reasonable vigilance would be the orbit of the duty. One who jostles one's neighbor in a crowd does not invade the rights of others standing at the outer fringe when the unintended contact casts a bomb upon the ground. The wrongdoer as to them is the man who carries the bomb, not the one who explodes it without suspicion of the danger. Life will have to be made over, and human nature transformed, before prevision so extravagant can be accepted as the norm of conduct, the customary standard to which behavior must conform.

The argument for the plaintiff is built upon the shifting meanings of such words as 'wrong' and 'wrongful,' and shares their instability. What the plaintiff must show is 'a wrong' to herself; i.e., a violation of her own right, and not merely a wrong to some one else, nor conduct 'wrongful' because unsocial, but not 'a wrong' to any one. We are told that one who drives at reckless speed through a crowded city street is guilty of a negligent act and therefore of a wrongful one, irrespective of the consequences. Negligent the act is, and wrongful in the sense that it is unsocial, but wrongful and unsocial in relation to other travelers, only because the eye of vigilance perceives the risk of damage. If the same act were to be committed on a speedway or a race course, it would lose its wrongful quality. The risk reasonably to be perceived defines the duty to be obeyed, and risk imports relation; it is risk to another or to others within the range of apprehension. This does not mean, of course, that one who launches a destructive force is always relieved of liability, if the force, though known to be destructive, pursues an unexpected path. 'It was not necessary that the defendant should have had notice of the particular method in which an accident would occur, if the possibility of an accident was clear to the ordinarily prudent eye.' Munsey v. Webb, 231 U. S. 150, 156, 34 S. Ct. 44, 45 (58 L. Ed. 162). . . . acts, such as shooting are so imminently dangerous to any one who may come within reach of the missile however unexpectedly, as to impose a duty of prevision not far from that of an insurer. Even to-day, and much oftener in earlier stages of the law, one acts sometimes at one's peril. Under this head, it may be, fall certain cases of what is known as transferred intent, an act willfully dangerous to A resulting by misadventure in injury to B. These cases aside, wrong is defined in terms of the natural or probable, at least when unintentional. The range of reasonable apprehension is at times a question for the court, and at times, if varying inferences are possible, a question for the jury. Here, by concession, there was nothing in the situation to suggest to the most cautious mind that the parcel wrapped in newspaper would spread wreckage through the station. If the guard had thrown it down knowingly and willfully, he would not have threatened the plaintiff's safety, so far as appearances could warn him. His conduct would not have involved, even then, an unreasonable probability of invasion of her bodily security. Liability can be no greater where the act is inadvertent.

Negligence, like risk, is thus a term of relation. Negligence in the abstract, apart from things related, is surely not a tort, if indeed it is understandable at all. Negligence is not a tort unless it results in the commission of a wrong, and the commission of a wrong imports the violation of a right, in this case, we are told, the right to be protected against interference with one's bodily security. But bodily security is protected, not against all forms of interference or aggression, but only against some. One who seeks redress at law does not make out a cause of action by showing without more that there has been damage to his person. If the harm was not willful, he must show that the act as to him had possibilities of danger so many and apparent as to entitle him to be protected against the doing of it though the harm was unintended. Affront to personality is still the keynote of the wrong. Confirmation of this view will be found in the history and development of the action on the case. Negligence as a basis of civil liability was unknown to mediaeval law. For damage to the person, the sole remedy was trespass, and trespass did not lie in the absence of aggression, and that direct and personal. Liability for other damage, as where a servant without orders from the master does or omits something to the damage of another, is a plant of later growth. When it emerged out of the legal soil, it was thought of as a variant of trespass, an offshoot of the parent stock. This appears in the form of action, which was known as trespass on the case. The victim does not sue derivatively, or by right of subrogation, to vindicate an interest invaded in the person of another. Thus to view his cause of action is to ignore the fundamental difference between tort and crime. He sues for breach of a duty owing to himself.

The law of causation, remote or proximate, is thus foreign to the case before us. The question of liability is always anterior to the question of the measure of the consequences that go with liability. If there is no tort to be redressed, there is no occasion to consider what damage might be recovered if there were a finding of a tort. We may assume, without deciding, that negligence, not at large or in the abstract, but in relation to the plaintiff, would entail liability for any and all consequences, however novel or extraordinary. There is room for argument that a distinction is to be drawn according to the diversity of interests invaded by the act, as where conduct negligent in that it threatens an insignificant invasion of an interest in property results in an unforeseeable invasion of an interest of another order, as, e. g., one of bodily security. Perhaps other distinctions may be necessary. We do not go into the question now. The consequences to be followed must first be rooted in a wrong.

The judgment of the Appellate Division and that of the Trial Term should be reversed, and the complaint dismissed, with costs in all courts.

ANDREWS, J. (dissenting).

Assisting a passenger to board a train, the defendant's servant negligently knocked a package from his arms. It fell between the platform and the cars. Of its contents the servant knew and could know nothing. A violent explosion followed. The concussion broke some scales standing a considerable distance away. In falling, they injured the plaintiff, an intending passenger.

Upon these facts, may she recover the damages she has suffered in an action brought against the master? The result we shall reach depends upon our theory as to the nature of negligence. Is it a relative concept — the breach of some duty owing to a particular person or to particular persons? Or, where there is an act which unreasonably threatens the safety of others, is the doer liable for all its proximate consequences, even where they result in injury to one who would generally be thought to be outside the radius of danger? This is not a mere dispute as to words. We might not believe that to the average mind the dropping of the bundle would seem to involve the probability of harm to the plaintiff standing many feet away whatever might be the case as to the owner or to one so near as to be likely to be struck by its fall. If, however, we adopt the second hypothesis, we have to inquire only as to the relation between cause and effect. We deal in terms of proximate cause, not of negligence.

. . .

In the well-known Polemis Case, [1921] 3 K. B. 560, Scrutton, L. J., said that the dropping of a plank was negligent, for it might injure 'workman or cargo or ship.' Because of either possibility, the owner of the vessel was to be made good for his loss. The act being wrongful, the doer was liable for its proximate results. Criticized and explained as this statement may have been, I think it states the law as it should be and as it is.

. . .

The right to recover damages rests on additional considerations. The plaintiff's rights must be injured, and this injury must be caused by the negligence. We build a dam, but are negligent as to its foundations. Breaking, it injures property down stream. We are not liable if all this happened because of some reason other than the insecure foundation. But, when injuries do result from our unlawful act, we are liable for the consequences. It does not matter that they are unusual, unexpected, unforeseen, and unforeseeable. But there is one limitation. The damages must be so connected with the negligence that the latter may be said to be the proximate cause of the former.

These two words have never been given an inclusive definition. What is a cause in a legal sense, still more what is a proximate cause, depend in each case upon many considerations, as does the existence of negligence itself. Any philosophical doctrine of causation does not help us. A boy throws a stone into a pond. The ripples spread. The water level rises. The history of that pond is altered to all eternity. It will be altered by other causes also. Yet it will be forever the resultant of all causes combined. Each one will have an influence. How great only omniscience can say. You may speak of a chain, or, if you please, a net. An analogy is of little aid. Each cause brings about future events. Without each the future would not be the same. Each is proximate in the sense it is essential. But that is not what we mean by the word. Nor on the other hand do we mean sole cause. There is no such thing.

Should analogy be though helpful, however, I prefer that of a stream. The spring, starting on its journey, is joined by tributary after tributary. The river, reaching the ocean, comes from a hundred sources. No man may say whence any drop of water is derived. Yet for a time distinction may be possible. Into the clear creek, brown swamp water flows from the left. Later, from the right comes water stained by its clay bed. The three may remain for a space, sharply divided. But at last inevitably no trace of separation remains. They are so commingled that all distinction is lost.

As we have said, we cannot trace the effect of an act to the end, if end there is. Again, however, we may trace it part of the way. A murder at Serajevo may be the necessary antecedent to an assassination in London twenty years hence. An overturned lantern may burn all Chicago. We may follow the fire from the shed to the last building. We rightly say the fire started by the lantern caused its destruction.

A cause, but not the proximate cause. What we do mean by the word 'proximate' is that, because of convenience, of public policy, of a rough sense of justice, the law arbitrarily declines to trace a series of events beyond a certain point. This is not logic. It is practical politics. Take our rule as to fires. Sparks from my burning haystack set on fire my house and my neighbor's. I may recover from a negligent railroad. He may not. Yet the wrongful act as directly harmed the one as the other. We may regret that the line was drawn just where it was, but drawn somewhere it had to be. We said the act of the railroad was not the proximate cause of our neighbor's fire. Cause it surely was. The words we used were simply indicative of our notions of public policy. Other courts think differently. But somewhere they reach the point where they cannot say the stream comes from any one source.

Take the illustration given in an unpublished manuscript by a distinguished and helpful writer on the law of torts. A chauffeur negligently collides with another car which is filled with dynamite, although he could not know it. An explosion follows. A, walking on the sidewalk nearby, is killed. B, sitting in a window of a building opposite, is cut by flying glass. C, likewise sitting in a window a block away, is similarly injured. And a further illustration: A nursemaid, ten blocks away, startled by the noise, involuntarily drops a baby from her arms to the sidewalk. We are told that C may not recover while A may. As to B it is a question for court or jury. We will all agree that the baby might not. Because, we are again told, the chauffeur had no reason to believe his conduct involved any risk of injuring either C or the baby. As to them he was not negligent.

But the chauffeur, being negligent in risking the collision, his belief that the scope of the harm he might do would be limited is immaterial. His act unreasonably jeopardized the safety of any one who might be affected by it. C's injury and that of the baby were directly traceable to the collision. Without that, the injury would not have happened. C had the right to sit in his office, secure from such dangers. The baby was entitled to use the sidewalk with reasonable safety.

The true theory is, it seems to me, that the injury to C, if in truth he is to be denied recovery, and the injury to the baby, is that their several injuries were not the proximate result of the negligence. And here not what the chauffeur had reason to believe would be the result of his conduct, but what the prudent would foresee, may have a bearing — may have some bearing, for the problem of proximate cause is not to be solved by any one consideration. It is all a question of expediency. There are no fixed rules to govern our judgment. There are simply matters of which we may take account. We have in a somewhat different connection spoken of 'the stream of events.' We have asked whether that stream was deflected — whether it was forced into new and unexpected channels. This is rather rhetoric than law. There is in truth little to guide us other than common sense.

There are some hints that may help us. The proximate cause, involved as it may be with many other causes, must be, at the least, something without which the event would not happen. The court must ask itself whether there was a natural and continuous sequence between cause and effect. Was the one a substantial factor in producing the other? Was there a direct connection between them, without too many intervening causes? Is the effect of cause on result not too attenuated? Is the cause likely, in the usual judgment of mankind, to produce the result? Or, by the exercise of prudent foresight, could the result be foreseen? Is the result too remote from the cause, and here we consider remoteness in time and space. Bird v. St. Paul & M. Ins. Co., 224 N. Y. 47, 120 N. E. 86, 13 A. L. R. 875, where we passed upon the construction of a contract — but something was also said on this subject. Clearly we must so consider, for the greater the distance either in time or space, the more surely do other causes intervene to affect the result. When a lantern is overturned, the firing of a shed is a fairly direct consequence. Many things contribute to the spread of the conflagration — the force of the wind, the direction and width of streets, the character of intervening structures, other factors. We draw an uncertain and wavering line, but draw it we must as best we can.

Once again, it is all a question of fair judgment, always keeping in mind the fact that we endeavor to make a rule in each case that will be practical and in keeping with the general understanding of mankind.

Here another question must be answered. In the case supposed, it is said, and said correctly, that the chauffeur is liable for the direct effect of the explosion, although he had no reason to suppose it would follow a collision. 'The fact that the injury occurred in a different manner than that which might have been expected does not prevent the chauffeur's negligence from being in law the cause of the injury.' But the natural results of a negligent act — the results which a prudent man would or should foresee — do have a bearing upon the decision as to proximate cause. We have said so repeatedly. What should be foreseen? No human foresight would suggest that a collision itself might injure one a block away. On the contrary, given an explosion, such a possibility might be reasonably expected. I think the direct connection, the foresight of which the courts speak, assumes prevision of the explosion, for the immediate results of which, at least, the chauffeur is responsible.

It may be said this is unjust. Why? In fairness he should make good every injury flowing from his negligence. Not because of tenderness toward him we say he need not answer for all that follows his wrong. We look back to the catastrophe, the fire kindled by the spark, or the explosion. We trace the consequences, not indefinitely, but to a certain point. And to aid us in fixing that point we ask what might ordinarily be expected to follow the fire or the explosion.

This last suggestion is the factor which must determine the case before us. The act upon which defendant's liability rests is knocking an apparently harmless package onto the platform. The act was negligent. For its proximate consequences the defendant is liable. If its contents were broken, to the owner; if it fell upon and crushed a passenger's foot, then to him; if it exploded and injured one in the immediate vicinity, to him also as to A in the illustration. Mrs. Palsgraf was standing some distance away. How far cannot be told from the record — apparently 25 or 30 feet, perhaps less. Except for the explosion, she would not have been injured. We are told by the appellant in his brief, 'It cannot be denied that the explosion was the direct cause of the plaintiff's injuries.' So it was a substantial factor in producing the result — there was here a natural and continuous sequence — direct connection. The only intervening cause was that, instead of blowing her to the ground, the concussion smashed the weighing machine which in turn fell upon her. There was no remoteness in time, little in space. And surely, given such an explosion as here, it needed no great foresight to predict that the natural result would be to injure one on the platform at no greater distance from its scene than was the plaintiff. Just how no one might be able to predict. Whether by flying fragments, by broken glass, by wreckage of machines or structures no one could say. But injury in some form was most probable.

Under these circumstances I cannot say as a matter of law that the plaintiff's injuries were not the proximate result of the negligence. That is all we have before us. The court refused to so charge. No request was made to submit the matter to the jury as a question of fact, even would that have been proper upon the record before us.

The judgment appealed from should be affirmed, with costs.

POUND, LEHMAN, and KELLOGG, JJ., concur with CARDOZO, C. J., ANDREWS, J., dissents in opinion in which CRANE and O'BRIEN, JJ., concur.

Notes and Questions

1. Although Justice Cardozo found that duty was the rule of decision in *Palsgraf*, and thus that "the law of causation [was] . . . foreign to the case," over time his methodology for analyzing the scope of the defendant's duty has become a principal methodology for analyzing the scope of the defendant's liability, or proximate cause. Draft a statement explaining this methodology. Apply it to the facts of Barker v. City of Philadelphia, *supra*. What is the best argument that the decedent in *Barker* was within Cardozo's range of reasonable apprehension? What is the best argument that he was not within the range?

2. What is Justice Andrews's approach to proximate cause analysis and how does it differ from Justice Cardozo's approach?

3. In its Comment f, Section 29 (Scope of Liability) of the Restatement (Third) of Torts: Liability for Physical and Emotional Harm provides additional context to the relationship between duty and proximate cause:

> There are two primary legal doctrines for limiting liability: duty and scope of liability. Some courts use duty in situations in which other courts would use proximate cause. The classic case of Palsgraf v. Long Island Railroad Co., revealed the potential for interchangeability between duty and scope of liability, although proximate cause was

> the term employed at the time. Judge Cardozo employed duty, while Judge Andrews employed proximate cause, to determine whether the defendant was liable for harm to a particular plaintiff. *Palsgraf*'s legacy has been a tension in tort law about the proper balance between duty rules and proximate-cause limits to circumscribe appropriately the scope of liability.
>
> One significant difference between these two doctrines is helpful in determining their appropriate spheres of application. Duty is a question of law for the court, see § 7, while scope of liability, although very much an evaluative matter, is treated as a question of fact for the factfinder. Hence, duty is a preferable means for addressing limits on liability when those limitations are clear, when they are based on relatively bright lines, when they are of general application, when they do not usually require resort to disputed facts in a case, when they implicate policy concerns that apply to a class of cases that may not be fully appreciated by a jury deciding a specific case, and when they are employed in cases in which early resolution of liability is particularly desirable. See § 7. Duty is usefully employed when a court seeks to make a telling pronouncement about when actors may or, on the other hand, may not be held liable. Thus, the liability of social hosts for providing alcohol to their guests is best treated as a duty issue, rather than as a matter of scope of liability. On the other hand, when the limits imposed require careful attention to the specific facts of a case, and difficult, often amorphous evaluative judgments for which modest differences in the factual circumstances may change the outcome, scope of liability is a more flexible and preferable device for placing limits on liability. Its use is also consistent with the role of the jury in tort cases.

Given these distinctions, do you understand why Justice Cardozo's methodology in *Palsgraf* has been less useful in discussions of duty and more useful in discussions of proximate cause?

4. Following (but not necessarily because of) *Palsgraf*, courts in the United Kingdom and then in the United States began to abandon the "direct cause" test in favor of a "foreseeability" test. The point of litigation and debate thus moved from whether the plaintiff's losses directly flowed from the defendant's breach to whether those losses were foreseeable. But this move immediately begged the question, "What needs to be foreseeable?" *Palsgraf* stood for the proposition that a foreseeable plaintiff was essential; and Justice Cardozo's opinion in that case suggested further that "[t]here is room for argument that a distinction is to be drawn according to the diversity of interests invaded by the act, [for example between] . . . an interest in property [and] . . . one of bodily security." *Id.* at 347. The U.K. courts narrowed this last suggestion so that differences among kinds of property damage and personal injuries were relevant to proximate cause determinations. *See* Overseas Tankship (U.K.) Ltd. v. Mort's Dock & Engineering Co., Ltd., [1961] A.C. 388, 2 W.L.R. 126, 1 All E.R. 404 (Privy Council 1961) (permitting recovery for foreseeable property damage caused by oil spill but not for unforeseeable property damage caused by fire from the same spill); Hughes v. Lord Advocate, [1963] A.C. 837, 2 W.L.R. 779, 1 All E.R. 705 (House of Lords 1963) (permitting recovery for foreseeable burn injuries notwithstanding that neither their extent nor the manner in which they happened was foreseeable); Doughty v. Turner Manufacturing Co., [1964] 1 Q.B. 518, 2 W.L.R. 240, 1 All. E.R. 98 (Court of Appeal 1963) (disallowing recovery for burn injuries caused by unforeseeable explosion notwithstanding that burn injuries caused by splashing were foreseeable). As we will see below, other courts, particularly those in the U.S., have declined to interpret foreseeability so narrowly.

WILLIAMSON v. LIPTZIN
539 S.E.2d 313 (N.C. App. 2000)

TIMMONS–GOODSON, Judge.

This case arises out of the tragic events of 26 January 1995, when Wendell Williamson ("plaintiff") shot and killed two people in downtown Chapel Hill, North Carolina. Plaintiff brought suit against Myron B. Liptzin ("defendant"), [his former] psychiatrist at Student Psychological Services of the University of North Carolina at Chapel Hill ("Student Services") who treated plaintiff, on the grounds that he was damaged by the negligence of defendant.

The evidence presented at trial tended to show the following. Student Services operates only on a voluntary, outpatient basis. In May 1990, as an undergraduate student, plaintiff visited Student Services as a "walk-in," and received counseling for relationship issues and academic problems. The doctor who reviewed plaintiff's intake form concluded that plaintiff's problems were "fairly normative."

In September 1992, when plaintiff was a twenty-four-year-old law student at the University of North Carolina at Chapel Hill ("UNC"), he screamed at students on campus and struck himself about the face. Plaintiff was referred to Student Services. As a result, Student Services further referred him to the UNC Hospitals, where he was involuntarily committed. During his stay, plaintiff disclosed that he had been hearing a voice talking to him for eight months and that he believed he was telepathic. The hospital staff recorded that plaintiff possessed a gun in his apartment.

. . . The final primary diagnosis was "rule/out schizophrenia." One of plaintiff's expert psychiatrists explained at trial that the term "rule/out schizophrenia" means that either: (a) "it's [schizophrenia] until proven otherwise, but we haven't had enough time to prove otherwise yet [,]" or (b) "you should keep [schizophrenia] first and foremost in your mind until a less serious condition is shown to be causing the problem."

On 2 March 1994, plaintiff was again referred to Student Services after he disrupted class at the law school by announcing that he was a "telepath." Plaintiff completed an intake form on which he denied any urge "to hit, injure or harm someone" or any "[s]uicidal thoughts or concerns." Intake psychologists assessed that involuntary hospitalization was "not appropriate as student denies danger to self or others." Plaintiff was again diagnosed with "rule/o[ut] schizophrenia." The staff recommended treatment and medication, which plaintiff refused. However, after a law school dean informed plaintiff that he might not be recommended as a candidate for the bar exam unless he received counseling, plaintiff agreed to seek treatment.

During a ten-week period beginning on 8 March 1994, plaintiff had six counseling sessions with defendant at Student Services, each of which lasted between twenty minutes and one hour. Defendant prepared for the treatment by reviewing plaintiff's chart from Student Services, which included an intake form from plaintiff's May 1990 visit to Student Services and a "discharge summary" from his 1992 hospital stay. However, defendant did not review the complete medical records from plaintiff's 1992 treatment. During the first session with defendant, plaintiff stated that he had believed he was a "telepath" for two years, he consumed approximately six beers each night, and he used marijuana occasionally. Defendant suggested that plaintiff begin taking an antipsychotic drug, Navane, and diagnosed plaintiff with "delusional disorder grandiose." While defendant recognized that plaintiff exhibited some symptoms of schizophrenia, he decided to record the more "generous" diagnosis, so as not to deprive plaintiff of the opportunity to practice law.

On 5 April 1994, during the fourth counseling session, defendant informed plaintiff that defendant would be leaving Student Services in June, and suggested that plaintiff "consider the possibility of seeing somebody on a regular basis in therapy, and that [defendant] would be happy to make a referral for him; that it would probably make sense to do this sooner rather than later."

The last counseling session between plaintiff and defendant occurred on 25 May 1994. Plaintiff informed defendant that he was not sure whether he would stay in Chapel Hill for the summer or whether he would stay with his family in Clyde, North Carolina. Defendant recorded in plaintiff's medical chart that plaintiff knew defendant would be leaving Student Services and that plaintiff would be seeing his replacement in the fall semester. Defendant told plaintiff that he needed to contact defendant's replacement so that he could have his prescriptions filled.

During plaintiff's final counseling session, defendant supplied plaintiff with a prescription for thirty Navane capsules. Defendant recorded that plaintiff was "content to stay on [Navane]." As plaintiff's plans for the summer were uncertain, defendant instructed plaintiff that if he returned to Clyde, he was to visit the community health center or see his family doctor. If, on the other hand, plaintiff remained in Chapel Hill, he was to return to Student Services for counseling with defendant's replacement.

During the course of his treatment, plaintiff followed virtually all of defendant's instructions concerning the regularity with which he was to take his medication. Plaintiff testified that he did on one occasion "voluntarily [go] off his medication," but reported it to defendant. Plaintiff reported that he was no longer hearing voices, his "telepathy" and delusions were completely gone, and his hallucinations were either completely gone or virtually gone. Although he still used alcohol and recreational drugs, his usage had decreased. Plaintiff attended all of his classes without incident, sat for his law school exams, improved his grades, and took part in a law school writing competition. Friends reported that plaintiff was "more 'like his old self.' " While he was under defendant's care, plaintiff had no thoughts of harming or killing himself or anyone else. His first thoughts of harming others occurred "much later" or "some number of months" after he last saw defendant.

Plaintiff believed that his mental illness was temporary and that the medication was a short-term measure. According to plaintiff, defendant told him "that in his opinion, [plaintiff] was probably not really schizophrenic or psychotic." Plaintiff further stated that defendant told him that "if someday [he] wanted to go off the medication, that [he] could do that if [he] told someone [he] trust[ed]."

Plaintiff spent the summer at his parents' home in Clyde. He did not visit the community health center or Student Services. Plaintiff decided to stop taking Navane for a few days, as the drug made him susceptible to the sun and he had become sunburned. After he discontinued his medication, plaintiff felt physically better. He determined that he would stop taking his medication indefinitely and informed his parents of that decision.

Plaintiff returned to Chapel Hill in August of 1994 for the fall semester. He attended virtually all of his classes and did not disrupt any of them. He passed all of his courses, managed his finances, and took care of his day-to-day needs, such as grooming, eating, and shopping. He took trips alone in his car, including trips to Connecticut and New York City over Christmas break.

In January 1995, plaintiff returned to Chapel Hill and began living out of his car. He stopped attending classes and purchased guns and ammunition. In addition, plaintiff returned to Clyde to retrieve a M–1 rifle, the gun UNC Hospital staff noted he possessed. This weapon had been in Clyde since plaintiff's hospital stay in 1992. On 26 January 1995, eight months after his last session with defendant, plaintiff randomly fired the M–1 rifle at unarmed people in downtown Chapel Hill, killing two of them. In an effort to stop plaintiff, police officers shot him in the legs. Plaintiff required surgery for the leg wounds. Plaintiff was charged with two counts of first-degree murder. In November of 1995, he was found not guilty by reason of insanity.

Psychiatrist Stephen Kramer ("Dr. Kramer") testified as an expert witness on behalf of plaintiff. Doctor Kramer stated that defendant violated the standard of care for a psychiatrist with similar training and experience practicing in Chapel Hill, North Carolina, or similar communities, in 1994. Doctor Kramer specified that defendant failed "to pursue a proper diagnosis, including review of old records available and assessing risk for potential deterioration and violence[,]" failed "to develop a program for continuing care [for plaintiff] once [defendant] retired and left the Student Health Center," failed to address the issue of noncompliance, and failed to properly manage the use of antipsychotic medication. Dr. Kramer noted that the discharge summary from plaintiff's hospital stay indicated that he had no insight into his illness and that he had a history of noncompliance. Dr. Kramer stated that especially in this context, if defendant advised plaintiff that he could go off his medication if he told a responsible adult, such advice would have been improper and an "invitation to not comply with the recommended therapy."

According to Dr. Kramer, the correct diagnosis was chronic paranoid schizophrenia rather than delusional disorder grandiose, and defendant's failure to review the medical records from plaintiff's inpatient stay at UNC Hospitals in 1992 contributed to the misdiagnosis. Dr. Kramer further noted that there was a marked difference between plaintiff's diagnosis of delusional disorder and schizophrenia. Dr. Kramer explained that schizophrenia is a long-term, lifelong illness requiring long-term care, while delusional disorder was more intermittent in nature.

Dr. Kramer testified that it was "harder to answer" whether defendant could have reasonably foreseen that plaintiff would become violent to himself or others. Dr. Kramer further testified:

> First was, what's foreseeable is noncompliance with treatment, which would directly lead to exacerbation or increase in the psychotic symptoms, especially that of his thought processes. His insight and judgment would remain poor or get worse. He would continue abusing substances. . . . That access to a gun might not be cut off for him but might be reunited with him, and that dangerous behavior might occur.

Those elements regarding dangerousness may come together at a point in time.

When asked whether he was "prepared to say . . . a part of foreseeability would be dangerousness . . . to himself or others[,]" Dr. Kramer answered, "I'm not sure that I can go that far with it. I can say that the foreseeable elements are those that when they come together in time would lead to dangerousness." Had plaintiff received a proper diagnosis and treatment, his delusions and acting out could have been kept under control, according to Dr. Kramer.

James Bellard ("Dr. Bellard"), a psychiatrist, also testified as an expert witness on behalf of plaintiff. Dr. Bellard agreed that defendant violated the applicable standard of care by misdiagnosing plaintiff and failing to ensure that plaintiff received ongoing care, especially given plaintiff's history of noncompliance. Dr. Bellard stated that it was foreseeable that plaintiff would again believe he was a "telepath." When asked where that would lead, Dr. Bellard answered, "If I may, that's not what's foreseeable. What's foreseeable is that he would believe [he was a "telepath"] again. But what he would do with that, I don't think—nobody's crystal ball is that good, that they could predict that." Dr. Bellard further stated that if defendant had given plaintiff the name of a specific doctor to visit during the summer of 1994, Dr. Bellard still could not predict what would have happened. Dr. Bellard stated that "it was foreseeable that [plaintiff] would deteriorate and eventually decompensate, that he would really fall apart mentally, eventually." Once he began to deteriorate, plaintiff would certainly become dangerous to himself, according to Dr. Bellard. Both Drs. Kramer and Bellard acknowledged that plaintiff improved under defendant's care and stated that plaintiff made no expressions of violence and was not committable at any point during his treatment.

Psychologist John Warren, III ("Dr.Warren") testified on behalf of plaintiff as an expert witness in psychology and the treatment of paranoid schizophrenia. Dr. Warren stated that plaintiff was not competent to take charge of his medical treatment at the time his therapy with defendant ended. Dr. Warren testified that

> there's nothing in the record that suggests that [plaintiff] got that information that he needed in order to make decisions about whether or not he had a major mental illness, whether or not he needed to take medication on a long-term basis, what he needed to do in case the symptoms got worse.

Plaintiff reported to Dr. Warren on the day following the shootings that defendant had advised him that he could discontinue his medication if he told someone he trusted.

Concerning schizophrenia, Dr. Warren echoed the testimony of Dr. Kramer stating that it was a very serious, major mental disorder, requiring lifelong treatment. Dr. Warren also testified that "[a]s a group, people with schizophrenia, paranoid type, are among the most likely to hurt themselves or hurt other people." Dr. Warren believed that because plaintiff did not understand the seriousness of his illness, he could not make competent decisions concerning treatment.

When asked whether it was foreseeable that defendant "might" degenerate and become dangerous to himself or others, Dr. Warren responded by stating that plaintiff would become sicker, which "might" result in violence to himself or others. Both Drs. Kramer and Warren testified that plaintiff exhibited risk factors for dangerous behavior such as being a young male, living alone, and having access to a gun.

Holly Rogers ("Dr. Rogers"), a psychiatrist at Duke University's Student Counseling Center, testified as an expert on behalf of defendant. Dr. Rogers indicated that student mental health centers provide "short-term treatment." Dr. Rogers stated that "[m]ost psychotic people aren't dangerous." Similarly, Jeffrey Janofsky ("Dr. Janofsky"), a psychiatrist at Johns Hopkins

University stated that "because the base rate of violence is so low, and most schizophrenics aren't violent and most normal people aren't violent either, that demographic data does not get you anywhere in predicting dangerousness."

Bruce Berger ("Dr. Berger"), a psychiatrist who previously worked as a student health counselor at East Carolina University, testified on behalf of defendant. He stated that in the student health setting, psychiatrists are only able to work with students for a short time "before [the students] have to make plans with or without [the psychiatrists'] assistance to get further treatment, or at least make choices in their life."

Plaintiff filed suit against defendant on 16 May 1997, alleging that defendant had been negligent and that the negligence caused him to be shot in the legs, endure a murder trial, and be confined indefinitely to a mental institution. Defendant moved for summary judgment. On 4 September 1998, the trial court entered an order denying defendant's motion, concluding that "a genuine issue of material facts exist[ed] to show that [defendant] breached the applicable standard of care and that [defendant's] treatment proximately caused injury to [plaintiff]." The court further found that defendant failed to prove that there was no triable issue concerning contributory negligence.

The case was tried in the Superior Court, Orange County, before a jury. Defendant moved for directed verdict at the close of plaintiff's evidence and at the close of all the evidence. The trial court denied the motions and submitted the case to the jury, which determined that plaintiff was damaged by the negligence of defendant and that plaintiff was not contributorily negligent. Based on the jury verdict, the trial court entered judgment ordering defendant to pay $500,000 with interest and the court costs of the action to plaintiff. Defendant moved for a new trial or judgment notwithstanding the verdict. On 31 March 1999, the trial court entered an order denying the motions. Defendant appeals.

Defendant argues that the trial court erred in denying his dispositive motions. Defendant first contends that the trial court erred in denying his motions for directed verdict and for judgment notwithstanding the verdict ("JNOV"). *See* N.C.Gen.Stat. § 1A–1, Rule 50 (1999). A motion for JNOV is a renewal of a motion for directed verdict made after the jury has returned its verdict. As such, a JNOV "shall be granted if it appears that the motion for directed verdict could properly have been granted." N.C.G.S. § 1A–1, Rule 50(b)(1).

In deciding whether to grant or deny either motion, the trial court must accept the non-movant's evidence as true and view all the evidence "in the light most favorable to [him], giving [him] the benefit of every reasonable inference which may be legitimately drawn therefrom, with conflicts, contradictions, and inconsistencies being resolved in the [non-movant's] favor." *Bryant v. Thalhimer Brothers,* Inc., 113 N.C.App. 1, 6, 437 S.E.2d 519, 522 (1993) (citation omitted), *dismissal allowed and disc. review denied,* 336 N.C. 71, 445 S.E.2d 29 (1994). "If there is more than a scintilla of evidence supporting each element of the non-movant's claim, the motion should be denied." *Poor v. Hill,* 138 N.C.App. 19, 26, 530 S.E.2d 838, 843 (2000) (citation omitted). An appellate court's review of a denial of these motions is limited to a consideration of "whether the evidence viewed in the light most favorable to [the non-movant] is sufficient to support the jury verdict." *Suggs v. Norris,* 88 N.C.App. 539, 543, 364 S.E.2d 159, 162 (1988) (citation omitted).

To prevail on a claim of negligence, the plaintiff must establish that the defendant owed him a duty of reasonable care, "that [the defendant] was negligent in his care of [the plaintiff,] and that such negligence was the proximate cause of [the plaintiff's] injuries and damage." *Beaver v. Hancock,* 72 N.C.App. 306, 311, 324 S.E.2d 294, 298 (1985) (citation omitted). While we recognize that this case presents a variety of novel issues concerning virtually every facet of negligence, we have chosen to focus our discussion on the element of proximate cause. Defendant's main contention on appeal is, in fact, that his alleged negligence was not the proximate cause of plaintiff's injuries, and therefore he was entitled to a directed verdict and JNOV. With this, we must agree.

North Carolina appellate courts define proximate cause as

> a cause which in natural and continuous sequence, unbroken by any new and independent cause, produced the plaintiff's injuries, and without which the injuries would not have occurred, and one from which a person of ordinary prudence could have reasonably foreseen that such a result, or consequences of a generally injurious nature, was probable under all the facts as they existed.

Hairston v. Alexander Tank & Equipment Co., 310 N.C. 227, 233, 311 S.E.2d 559, 565 (1984) (citations omitted). The element of foreseeability is a requisite of proximate cause. To prove that an action is foreseeable, a plaintiff is required to prove that "in 'the exercise of reasonable care, the defendant might have foreseen that some injury would result from his act or omission, or that consequences of a generally injurious nature might have been expected.' " *Hart v. Curry,* 238 N.C. 448, 449, 78 S.E.2d 170, 170 (1953) (citation omitted). Thus, the plaintiff does not have to prove that the defendant foresaw the injury in its precise form. *Hairston,* 310 N.C. at 233–34, 311 S.E.2d at 565; *see also Palsgraf v. Long Island R. Co.,* 248 N.Y. 339, 162 N.E. 99, 103 (1928) (Andrews, J., dissenting) ("It does not matter that [the actual injuries] are unusual, unexpected, unforeseen, and unforeseeable.") However, the law does not require that the defendant "foresee events which are *merely possible* but only those which are reasonably foreseeable." *Hairston,* 310 N.C. at 234, 311 S.E.2d at 565 (emphasis added) (citations omitted).

> A man's responsibility for his negligence must end somewhere. If the connection between negligence and the injury appears unnatural, unreasonable and improbable in the light of common experience, the negligence, if deemed a cause of the injury at all, is to be considered remote rather than a proximate cause. It imposes too heavy a responsibility for negligence to hold the [tort-feasor] responsible for what is unusual and unlikely to happen or for what was only remotely and slightly possible.

Phelps v. Winston–Salem, 272 N.C. 24, 30, 157 S.E.2d 719, 723 (1967) (citation omitted); *accord Sutton v. Duke,* 277 N.C. 94, 108, 176 S.E.2d 161, 169 (1970) (quoting William L. Prosser, *Law of Torts* § 50, at 303 (3d ed.1964)) ("it is 'inconceivable that any defendant should be held liable to infinity for all the consequences which flow from his act,' [thus] some boundary must be set").

Foreseeability is but one element of proximate cause. *Wyatt v. Gilmore,* 57 N.C.App. 57, 290 S.E.2d 790 (1982). Other "equally important considerations" include:

> whether the cause is, in the usual judgment of mankind, likely to produce the result; whether the relationship between cause and effect is too attenuated; whether there is a direct connection without intervening causes; whether the cause was a substantial factor in bringing about the result; and whether there was a natural and continuous sequence between the cause and the result.

Id. at 59, 290 S.E.2d at 791 (citation omitted).

Plaintiff alleged that he was injured as a result of defendant's actions, in that he was wounded during the 26 January 1995 shoot-out, tried for capital murder, and confined to a mental institution. An examination of the evidence, construed in the light most favorable to the plaintiff, reveals that defendant could not foresee plaintiff's injuries. There was absolutely no evidence that plaintiff posed a threat of violence to others which would in turn lead to injury. When asked whether dangerousness to others or to plaintiff himself was foreseeable, plaintiff's own expert, Dr. Kramer stated, "I'm not sure that I can go that far with it." Another one of plaintiff's experts, Dr. Bellard, likewise testified that it was not foreseeable that plaintiff would kill others. In fact, in the most telling testimony at trial, Dr. Bellard further responded, "[N]obody's crystal ball is that good[.]"

Plaintiff's own behavior prior to or at the time of defendant's retirement in no way indicated that he would become violent. Other than striking himself about the face, plaintiff never exhibited violent behavior. On his 2 March 1994 intake form, plaintiff noted that he had no urge to harm others and that he had no suicidal thoughts.

Plaintiff even noticed an improvement in his condition. Plaintiff informed defendant that he no longer heard voices and his hallucinations were virtually gone. Plaintiff further noted that he had decreased his use of alcohol and recreational drugs, had attended his law school classes without incident, and had improved his grades. Furthermore, although plaintiff testified that he contemplated suicide in 1992, he admitted that he never seriously thought of harming himself between the 1992 hospitalization and 1994, including the period in which he saw defendant. Plaintiff further affirmed that thoughts of harming others only occurred "some number of months" after his last visit with defendant. In his notes from the last visit with plaintiff, defendant wrote that plaintiff stated "his friends have been giving him feedback that he's more 'like his old self, and the guy they used to know and like.' "

In addition to being unforeseeable, plaintiff's injuries were too remote in time, and the chain of events which lead to plaintiff's injuries was too attenuated for defendant's actions to be the proximate cause of plaintiff's injuries. It was eight months between plaintiff's last visit with defendant and the incident which led to his injuries. Plaintiff was, by all accounts, functioning normally when he last visited defendant in May 1994. Plaintiff spent the summer with his parents in Clyde, at which time he discontinued his medication and failed to visit a mental health center or to have his prescriptions refilled. In August 1994, plaintiff returned to law school and began his fall classes. Plaintiff testified that his hallucinations began to resurface gradually and achieved fruition sometime in August or September. However, plaintiff attended virtually all of his classes during the fall semester, without disruption, and passed every course. He maintained his daily needs, including eating, grooming, shopping, and managing his financial affairs. Furthermore, after completing the semester, plaintiff took two long trips alone, after which time he returned to his parents' home in Clyde.

In January 1995, plaintiff returned to Chapel Hill. Only at this time did plaintiff begin living out of his car, stop attending classes, and purchase guns and ammunition. Eight months after his last visit with defendant, plaintiff shot and killed two individuals in Chapel Hill, despite never expressing any intent to do so. Defendant simply could not have foreseen that as a result of this attenuated chain of events, eight months after his last appointment, plaintiff, who expressed no violent intentions or threats, would be wounded during a shoot-out, tried for capital murder, committed to a mental institution, and not able to continue his legal studies or pursue a possible career.

Despite this attenuated chain of events, plaintiff contends that the testimony of his experts was tantamount to the issue of foreseeability and was more than sufficient to establish that "some" injury was foreseeable. With this argument, we cannot agree.

In his testimony, Dr. Kramer expressed difficulty in concluding that plaintiff's dangerousness to others was foreseeable. Dr. Kramer then testified as follows:

> [W]hat's foreseeable is noncompliance with treatment, which would directly lead to exacerbation or increase in the psychotic symptoms, especially that of his thought processes. His insight and judgment would remain poor or get worse. He would continue abusing substances. . . . That access to a gun *might* not be cut off for him but *might* be reunited with him, and that dangerous behavior *might* occur.
>
> Those elements regarding dangerousness *may* come together at a point in time. (Emphasis added.)

Dr. Kramer later testified that although he could not go so far as to say that plaintiff's dangerousness was foreseeable, "[he could] say that the foreseeable elements are those that when they come together in time would lead to dangerousness."

Dr. Bellard testified that it was foreseeable that plaintiff would again believe he was a "telepath" and "it was foreseeable that [plaintiff] would deteriorate and eventually decompensate, that he would really fall apart mentally, eventually." Dr. Bellard further testified that no one could predict "what [plaintiff] would do with that." Dr. Bellard stated that certain "risk factors" such as plaintiff's "self-injurious behavior, a history of psychosis, a history of being resistant to treatment, and an ongoing history of substance abuse," would place plaintiff at a "[c]onsiderably greater risk" for violence against himself. Dr. Bellard could not definitively say that being at risk for violence to oneself was a "risk factor" for violence to others. Both Doctors Kramer and Warren stated that plaintiff's age, gender, his living alone, and his owning a gun were "risk factors" for violence.

The experts' testimony does not establish foreseeability but evinces a situation similar to those in which our appellate courts hesitate to find an individual liable for a possible breach of duty. . . . North Carolina courts are reluctant to hold a person liable where the chain of events which led to the resulting injuries is unforeseeable, remote, and attenuated, even though "some" injury to plaintiff was "possible." *See Hairston,* 310 N.C. at 234, 311 S.E.2d at 565 (citations omitted). The contemplation of what "might" happen, which leads to what "might" or "may" potentially be the outcome, and the consideration of "risk factors" for violence to oneself which may or may not lead to a risk of violence to others, is simply not sufficient as a matter of law to establish the foreseeability of plaintiff's injuries or the circumstances in which the alleged injuries arose. Furthermore, evidence of "risk factors" for potential violence, such as gun ownership, being under a certain age, or being of a certain gender, implicates a large portion of our population and is simply insufficient in and of itself to prove foreseeability. Given the lack of evidence of violence or any threats of violence on plaintiff's behalf, "the connection between negligence and the injury appears unnatural, unreasonable, and improbable." *Phelps,* 272 N.C. at 30, 157 S.E.2d at 723 (citation omitted). We therefore conclude that the expert testimony presented by plaintiff established what was merely possible and not what was reasonably foreseeable.

Plaintiff also argues that evidence of foreseeability in the instant case far surpasses the evidence presented in *Hairston,* 310 N.C. 227, 311 S.E.2d 559, and in other cases in which our appellate courts have deemed proximate cause an issue for the jury. Plaintiff contends that like the defendant in *Hairston,* defendant in the case *sub judice* should have foreseen an injury would result from his actions. We find *Hairston* distinguishable from the present case.

In *Hairston,* our Supreme Court examined the liability of a car dealership in a wrongful death suit by a deceased motorist's wife against the dealer and a truck driver. On the same day as the accident which led to the suit, the motorist purchased an automobile from defendant dealer. While the motorist waited, the dealer changed the tires on the vehicle, but failed to tighten the lug nuts on one of the wheels. The motorist drove the car out of the dealer's lot and within minutes, the loose wheel fell off. The motorist stopped the car, and a van pulled up behind the disabled vehicle. As the motorist stood between his car and the van, the defendant truck driver struck the van, killing the motorist.

Our Supreme Court held that proximate cause existed to hold the dealer liable for the motorist's death. *Id.* at 235, 311 S.E.2d at 566. The court found that the dealer could have foreseen the accident which led to plaintiff's injuries. *Id.* The Court noted that defendant dealer was on "notice of the exigencies of traffic, and he must take into account the prevalence of the 'occasional negligence which is one of the incidents of human life.' " *Id.* at 234, 311 S.E.2d at 565 (citations omitted).

In the case at bar, plaintiff's violent rampage occurred eight months after his final session with defendant, while the time between the dealer's negligence and the motorist's harm in *Hairston* was "barely six minutes." *Id.* at 238, 311 S.E.2d at 567. More importantly, treating plaintiff's mental illness and predicting future human behavior are vastly different than maintaining an automobile and predicting traffic. Indeed, this Court as well as courts in other jurisdictions have previously recognized the difficulties inherit in the treatment and diagnosis of mental illness. In *Pangburn v. Saad,* 73 N.C.App. 336, 326 S.E.2d 365 (1985), this Court stated:

> "The uncertainties inherent in analyzing and treating the human mind, let alone the decision of when a person is 'cured' and no longer a danger, renders the decisions of skilled doctors highly discretionary and subject to rebuke only for the most flagrant, capricious, and arbitrary abuse."

73 N.C.App. at 344–45, 326 S.E.2d at 371 (quoting *Leverett v. State,* 61 Ohio App.2d 35, 399 N.E.2d 106, 110 (1978)); *see also Lee v. Corregedore,* 83 Hawai'i 154, 925 P.2d 324, 338 (1996) (quoting *Seibel v. Kemble,* 63 Haw. 516, 631 P.2d 173, 176–77 (1981) (footnote omitted)) (" 'There is much uncertainty in the diagnosis and treatment of mental illness and in the prediction of future behavior.' "); *Hicks v. United States,* 511 F.2d 407, 415 (D.C.Cir.1975)

("A claim of negligence must be considered in light of the elusive qualities of mental disorders and the difficulty of analyzing and evaluating them."); *Tarasoff v. Regents of Univ. of California,* 17 Cal.3d 425, 131 Cal.Rptr. 14, 551 P.2d 334, 345 (1976) ("We recognize the difficulty that a therapist encounters in attempting to forecast whether a patient presents a serious danger of violence.")

The uncertainties in diagnosing diseases of the human mind and predicting future behavior were further hampered in the instant case by the setting in which defendant observed plaintiff. Defendant treated plaintiff not in a hospital or private out-patient facility, but in an out-patient student health care facility. Dr. Rogers, a university student counseling center psychiatrist, testified that student health centers provide only "short-term treatment." Dr. Berger, a former counselor at a university facility, likewise testified that a psychiatrist in a student health care setting provides short-term care "before [the student has] to make plans with or without [the psychiatrist's] assistance to get further treatment, or at least make choices in his life." There is no doubt that such a limited setting, coupled with the few number of times defendant observed plaintiff, impeded defendant's ability to predict and foresee plaintiff's actions eight months after their last meeting.

Our conclusions concerning the foreseeability of plaintiff's injuries and the unpredictability of mental illness are further supported by public policy concerns. A court must "evaluate [the plaintiff's] allegations in light of the goal of treatment, recovery and rehabilitation of those afflicted with a mental disease, defect or disorder." *Seibel,* 631 P.2d at 176. Imposing liability on a psychiatrist in an outpatient, short-term care setting for the actions of a patient that were at most based on risk factors and not foreseeability would have adverse effects on psychiatric care. It would encourage psychiatrists and other mental health providers to return to paternalistic practices, such as involuntary commitment, to protect themselves against possible medical malpractice liability. Despite public perceptions to the contrary, the vast majority of the mentally ill are not violent or are no more violent than the general population and thus, such rigid measures as involuntary commitment are rarely a necessity. *See generally* John Monahan, *Mental Disorder and Violent Behavior: Perceptions and Evidence,* 47 Am. Psychol. 511, 519 (1992) ("None of the data give any support to the sensationalized caricature of the mentally disordered served up by the media, the shunning of former patients by employers and neighbors in the community, or regressive 'lock 'em all up' laws [based on] public fears.' "); Linda A. Teplin, *The Criminality of the Mentally Ill: A Dangerous Misconception,* 142 Am. J. Psychiatry 593, 598 (1985) ("stereotype [s] of the mentally ill as dangerous [are] not substantiated by our data"). "If a liability were imposed on the physician . . . each time the prediction of future course of mental disease was wrong, few releases would ever be made and the hope of recovery and rehabilitation of a vast number of patients would be impeded and frustrated." *Taig v. State,* 19 A.D.2d 182, 241 N.Y.S.2d 495, 496–97 (1963).

In the instant case, plaintiff functioned well under defendant's less-restrictive outpatient care, despite having what his experts termed a very serious mental illness. He passed all of his law school courses, took his medication on a regular basis, and even noted his friends' positive comments on his improved behavior. This improvement came without the need for involuntary commitment. In fact, plaintiff's own experts' testimony established that at the time he was being treated by defendant, plaintiff, like the majority of the mentally ill, was not a candidate for involuntary commitment.

Furthermore, North Carolina's policy on the mentally ill promotes less restrictive methods of treatment and more patient autonomy.

> The policy of the State is to assist individuals with mental illness, development disabilities, and substance abuse problems in ways consistent with the dignity, rights, and responsibilities of all North Carolina citizens. Within available resources, [the State is to provide] services to eliminate, reduce, or prevent the disabling effects of mental illness . . . through a service delivery system designed to meet the needs of clients in the least restrictive available setting, if the least restrictive setting is therapeutically most appropriate, and to maximize their quality of life.

N.C.Gen.Stat. § 122C–2 (1999); *see also Cobo v. Raba,* 347 N.C. 541, 546, 495 S.E.2d 362, 366 (1998) (citation omitted) ("a patient has an active responsibility for his own care and well-being"). It would therefore be irrational to promote unnecessary, more restrictive practices in affirming the judgment below.

We recognize that our jurisprudence in the area of proximate cause is quite varied. *See generally Sutton,* 277 N.C. 94, 176 S.E.2d 161; David A. Logan & Wayne A. Logan, *North Carolina Torts,* § 7.30, at 169 (1996) ("Many of the [North Carolina proximate cause] cases could have been decided differently.") We further recognize that it is only in the rarest of cases that our appellate courts find proximate cause is lacking as a matter of law. *See Hairston,* 310 N.C. at 235, 311 S.E.2d at 566. However, the law of proximate cause " 'cannot be reduced to absolute rules.' " *Sutton,* 277 N.C. at 108, 176 S.E.2d at 169 (quoting Prosser, *supra,* § 50, at 288). This is one of those rare cases where "because of convenience, of public policy, of a rough sense of justice, the law arbitrarily declines to trace a series of events beyond a certain point." *Palsgraf,* 162 N.E. at 103 (Andrews, J., dissenting), quoted in *Wyatt,* 57 N.C.App. at 59, 290 S.E.2d at 791; *Westbrook,* 105 N.C.App. at 68, 411 S.E.2d at 654 (citation omitted) ("proximate cause is to be determined on the facts of each case upon mixed considerations of logic, common sense, justice, policy and precedent").

We conclude that given the very specific and novel factual scenario presented by this case, defendant's alleged negligence was not the proximate cause of plaintiff's injuries. Therefore, the trial court should have granted defendant's directed verdict motion made at the close of all the evidence.

Having determined that the trial court erred in failing to grant a directed verdict in defendant's favor based on the issue of proximate cause, we need not address defendant's remaining assignments of error.

Because we find that the trial court erred in failing to grant defendant's directed verdict motion, we reverse the order of the trial court denying a JNOV and remand with directions for the trial court to enter judgment in defendant's favor.

Reversed and remanded.

Notes and Questions

1. At what level of generality does the North Carolina Supreme Court focus in its evaluation of the foreseeability of plaintiff's injury and losses? Is it foreseeability of any sort of harm? Of the particular harms that occurred?

2. Given the purposes of the proximate cause inquiry, what are the arguments for focusing on foreseeability most generally? Most specifically? Somewhere in between?

3. In its foreseeability discussion, the court emphasizes that "the law does not require that the defendant 'foresee events which are *merely possible* but only those which are reasonably foreseeable.' " How much foreseeability is involved in circumstances where an event is "merely possible"? What is the difference between "merely possible" events and "reasonably foreseeable" ones? What additional work does this aspect of the foreseeability test do for the corrective justice enterprise? Imagine that the plaintiff and the kind of harm suffered are both foreseeable, but only slightly?

4. Consistent with the decisions in *Palsgraf* and *Barker*, among others, it is generally held that neither the manner in which the plaintiff's' losses occur nor their extent are relevant to proximate cause analysis. *See* Restatement (Third) of Torts: Liability for Physical and Emotional Harm, § 29, Scope of Liability (Proximate Cause), Comments *o* and *p*. The former is generally rejected as a tool for establishing proximate cause because it tends to overcorrect in the defendant's favor. *See* Hughes v. Lord Advocate, *supra*. The latter is rejected for the different policy reasons that underlie the thin-skulled plaintiff rule more generally. *See* Camille A. Nelson, *Considering Tortious Racism*, 9 DEPAUL J. HEALTH CARE L. 905, 956-57 (2005) (explaining that the thin-skulled plaintiff rule is rationalized on the ground that vulnerable individuals are foreseeable and on the separate ground that unexpected losses, if they are such, should be borne by the wrongdoer).

5. Notice that the court focuses its analysis on foreseeability, but not exclusively. What else goes into its proximate cause calculus? Are these additional inquiries useful to doing fairness and justice by the defendant? Did the court reach the right result on liability?

6. Causes of natural or human—also called "responsible"—origin that "intervene" between an original defendant's negligence and a plaintiff's injury are sometimes found to be "superseding", as in superseding that original negligence. The effect of this finding is to let the original defendant off the hook for the claim entirely rather than, for example, to permit the plaintiff to proceed against multiple defendants.

By now you shouldn't be surprised to learn that the most common superseding cause test is also foreseeability-based, i.e., the question is whether the intervening cause was foreseeable to the original defendant; if so, the claim against them is good, but if not, they are off the hook. An alternative test asks whether the original defendant's negligence is still "actively and continuously operating" through the intervening causes to the injury. Were there intervening causes in *Williamson* that might have been described as superseding according to either analysis? Can you see why modern courts might prefer to collapse superseding cause analysis into the proximate cause inquiry?

Traditionally, superseding cause doctrine only applied in cases of simple, not aggravated negligence. The notion was that subsequent reckless or intentional acts, especially crimes, were unforeseeable as a matter of law. See Restatement (Second) of Torts, § 448. The significance if this rule has been largely eroded by the exception, also codified in the Restatement Second, that such acts will be superseding unless they were in fact foreseeable or foreseen. *See also* Britton v. Wooten, 817 S.W.443 (Ky. 1991) ("'The intervention of a criminal act . . . does not necessarily interrupt the relation of cause and effect between negligence and an injury. If at the time of the negligence, the criminal act might reasonably have been foreseen, the causal chain is not broken by the intervention of such act.' ")

Other acts and occurrences have been considered superseding as a matter of law, including voluntary intoxication, suicide, and acts of God or nature. As in the case of more than merely negligent acts, however, these too may be subject to exceptions. *See, e.g.*, McGuigan v. New England Tel. & Tel. Co., 496 N.E.2d 141 (Mass. 1986) (voluntary intoxication and social host liability); Exxon Corp. v. Brecheen, 526 S.W.2d 519 (Tex. 1975) (suicide); Ransome v. Wisconsin Elec. Power Co., 275 N.W.2d 641 (Wis. 1979) (lightning strike as act of God).

The Restatement (Third) of Torts: Liability for Physical and Emotional Harm § 29. Scope of Liability (Proximate Cause)

An actor's liability is limited to those harms that result from the risks that made the actor's conduct tortious.

Notes and Questions

1. Comment *d* following section 29 explains that "[t]his limit on liability serves the purpose of avoiding what might be unjustified or enormous liability by confining liability's scope to the reasons for holding the actor liable in the first place." How well does the risk standard serve this intended purpose? What if the negligent act is the failure properly to dock and anchor a boat, and the risks posed by that negligence are that the boat will collide with other boats downstream and also in the end dam the river and cause substantial local and upstream flood damages? Are additional tools necessary beyond the risk standard to do fairness and justice by the owner who carelessly docked his boat? Comment *m* acknowledges that the risk standard is not perfect in this regard:

> [T]here are cases in which the scope of liability would be too vast, in light of the circumstances of the tortious conduct, if a risk standard governed liability. One example of this situation would be a negligent jailer who permitted a dangerous criminal to escape. While liability might extend to some of the escaped criminal's immediate victims, courts would be loathe to extend the jailer's liability to include hundreds or thousands of victims across the country over a period of decades, if the criminal were not recaptured. Another example is the risk that a drug like DES, while posing a foreseeable risk of causing harm to the fetus of a woman taking the drug, also poses a risk of a genetic defect that could replicate itself generation after generation, the possibility of which was raised in the third-generation DES cases. Courts have used a variety of techniques to cabin liability in such circumstances, including no-duty rules, unforeseeable-plaintiff rules (see Comment *n*) constricting

> the risk standard to exclude victims some distance in time or geography from the escape, and declaring that, at some point, the actor's negligence was no longer "operating." Whatever verbal formulation is employed in these rare cases of unacceptably overwhelming liability in light of the tortious conduct, courts should appreciate that there are such occasions when the risk principle may require supplementation.

How would you restate the risk standard in light of these qualifications?

2. Comment *d* provides that:

> Tortious conduct may be wrongful because of a variety of risks to a number of different classes of persons. Thus, driving a vehicle negligently poses risks to persons and property who might foreseeably be harmed in a number of ways — by a collision with another vehicle or pedestrian, by the vehicle leaving the road, by the consequences of a narrowly averted collision, by the confusion and distraction of an accident scene, or by other consequences. Some of those risks may be more prominent than others, but all are relevant in determining whether the harm is within the scope of liability of the actor's tortious conduct.

Compare this formulation of the "scope of liability" with Justice Cardozo's methodology in *Palsgraf*. How are they similar and different? Would Mrs. Palsgraf fare better under the Third Restatement than she did with Cardozo?

3. Comment *d* also explains that "if the harms risked by th[e] tortious conduct include the general sort of harm suffered by the plaintiff, the defendant is subject to liability for the plaintiff's harm." An accompanying illustration provides:

> Richard, a hunter, finishes his day in the field and stops at a friend's house while walking home. His friend's nine-year-old daughter, Kim, greets Richard, who hands his loaded shotgun to her as he enters the house. Kim drops the shotgun, which lands on her toe, breaking it. Although Richard is negligent for giving Kim his shotgun, the risk that makes Richard negligent is that Kim might shoot someone with the gun, not that she would drop it and hurt herself (the gun was neither especially heavy nor unwieldy). Kim's broken toe is outside the scope of Richard's liability, even though Richard's tortious conduct was a factual cause of Kim's harm.

What was the "general sort of harm" risked by Richard's negligence? At what level of generality is the Restatement operating? Recall that Justice Cardozo in *Palsgraf* suggested that we might distinguish between general sorts of harm like personal injury and property damage. Has the Restatement adopted his suggestion or has it narrowed the inquiry further? Comment *i* provides this additional explanation:

> No rule can be provided about the appropriate level of generality or specificity to employ in characterizing the type of harm for purposes of this Section. Nevertheless, some guidance can be obtained by careful reference to the risks that made the actor's conduct tortious. . . . Courts often respond to efforts by advocates to employ excessive detail in characterizing the type of harm in order to make it appear more unforeseeable with the dictum that the manner of harm is irrelevant. Factfinders, no doubt, respond

> to these efforts with their own judgment and common sense to decide the appropriate specificity with which to assess the scope of liability. Conversely, in Illustration 3, characterizing the type of harm as merely physical harm and therefore arising from the risks posed by negligently entrusting a gun to a child fails to acknowledge the more limited risks posed by the negligent act — namely, those that might occur due to an accidental firing of the gun within the geographic range in which any bullet might travel. Different types of harm may be threatened by different tortious acts; a risk of a gunshot wound is different from a risk of a chemical burning, a traumatic collision, an electrical shock, or a snarling pit bull.
>
> In addition to the difficulty of determining the appropriate level of generality with which to describe the type of harm, courts also confront the problem that the risks that are encompassed within the actor's tortious conduct may not be readily apparent. To be sure, some legal rules make the specific evils with which they are concerned readily apparent. Thus, some negligence per se cases, in which the actor's conduct violated a safety statute directed at preventing a specific, identifiable kind of harm, present much easier contexts in which to decide whether the harm that occurred was produced by a risk that the statute was intended to avoid. However, the negligence standard is quite general in the risks that it addresses. Thus, greater uncertainty and difficulty occur in negligence cases in determining whether the harm that resulted arose from the risks that made the actor's conduct unreasonable.
>
> Many cases will pose straightforward or manageable determinations of whether the type of harm that occurred was one of those risked by the tortious conduct. Yet in others, there will be contending plausible characterizations that lead to different outcomes and require the drawing of an evaluative and somewhat arbitrary line. Those cases are left to the community judgment and common sense provided by the jury.

Is the flexibility inherent in this explanation a strength or a weakness of the new risk standard?

4. Consistent with the historical search for the best proxy for doing corrective justice, the Third Restatement asserts that "[l]imiting liability to harm arising from the risks created by the tortious conduct . . . provides a more refined analytical standard than a foreseeability standard or an amorphous direct-consequences test." Section 29, Comment *e*. With respect to the foreseeability standard in particular, Comment *j* provides the following:

> Many jurisdictions employ a "foreseeability" test for proximate cause, and in negligence actions such a rule is essentially consistent with the standard set forth in this Section. Properly understood, both the risk standard and a foreseeability test exclude liability for harms that were sufficiently unforeseeable at the time of the actor's tortious conduct that they were not among the risks — potential harms — that made the actor negligent. Negligence limits the requirement of reasonable care to those risks that are foreseeable. See § 3, Comment *g*. Thus, when scope of liability arises in a negligence case, the risks that make an actor negligent are limited to foreseeable ones, and the factfinder must determine whether the type of harm that occurred is among those reasonably foreseeable potential harms that made the actor's conduct negligent.

> Although the risk standard in this Section is comparable to the foreseeability standard in actions based on negligence, the risk standard contained in this Section is preferable because it provides greater clarity, facilitates clearer analysis in a given case, and better reveals the reason for its existence. The risk standard provides greater clarity and facilitates analysis because it focuses attention on the particular circumstances that existed at the time of the actor's conduct and the risks that were posed by that conduct. Risks may be foreseeable in context, as when an extraordinary storm is forecast, requiring precautions against the risks posed by it, that might otherwise be thought of, out of context, as exceedingly unlikely and therefore unforeseeable. The risk standard focuses on the appropriate context, although a foreseeability standard, properly explained, could do this also. The risk standard provides better understanding about the reasons for its existence by appealing to the intuition that it is fair for an actor's liability to be limited to those risks that made the conduct wrongful. Thus, factfinders can apply the risk standard with more sensitivity to the underlying rationale than they might muster with an unadorned foreseeable-harm standard.
>
> A foreseeability test for negligence cases risks being misunderstood because of uncertainty about what must be foreseen, by whom, and at what time. When courts pose the foreseeability inquiry as whether the harm was foreseeable at the time the defendant acted or as whether an intervening act was foreseeable, attention is deflected from the crux of the risk-standard inquiry. Moreover, the risk standard deals more comfortably with scope of liability when the defendant is an actor for whom the law modifies the objective standard of care. Thus, the risk standard would adapt the scope of liability for a child who is not expected to anticipate the same scope of harms as an adult.

Do you agree with the Restatement that the risk standard is better than the foreseeability standard?

Problem Eight: An Accident in the Intersection

Brad, who was 19 and a high school senior, got drunk at a party at his classmate Aaron's house. Aaron was also 19. Aaron's parents, Don and Megan Draper, weren't home at the time. Before they left at about 7 p.m. that night, they told Aaron and his 22-year-old brother Tony that they could have friends over but that "if any of our beer or whiskey is missing when we return, it will have to be replaced." Aaron's and Tony's friends, including Brad, arrived between 9 and 10 p.m. A lot of alcohol was consumed, all of which belonged to Don and Megan Draper.

As he was driving to his girlfriend's house from the Drapers at about midnight, Brad ran a red light at an intersection. At the time, he was texting his girlfriend and so never saw the light. Isaac, who was driving a Hummer (a civilian military-style SUV) through the same intersection at the same time but who had the right of way (on a green light), had to swerve to avoid being hit by Brad. This caused Isaac to jump the curb and to crash into a utility pole. Brad, who continued to be oblivious to the effects of his distractions, kept driving. Neither Isaac nor his vehicle suffered harm/damage (the Hummer did its job) but the force of the impact (it is an especially powerful machine) toppled the pole. Paul, who was walking his dog on the sidewalk nearby, was electrocuted as he stepped on downed live wire that had previously been suspended by the pole; because it was pitch black out — the pole had provided electricity to the intersection itself, among other places — Paul had no way of seeing the wire before he stepped on it. Isaac saw and recorded everything, including Brad's license plate number.

There is a statute in the jurisdiction establishing 18 as the age of majority. Various provisions of state's the criminal code provide that it is unlawful to provide alcohol to individuals under the age of 21; for persons under the age of 21 to consume alcohol; and for anyone to drive under the influence of alcohol. In a recent opinion upholding a plaintiff's dramshop liability claim, the Supreme Court of the jurisdiction indicated (in dicta) that under the right conditions, it would be amenable to social host liability.

We work in-house for Don and Megan Draper's insurance company. Paul's estate has written to the company indicating "the estate's interest in settling its clear-cut negligence claim against Mr. and Mrs. Draper out of court." Do we counsel our employer to write a check, or are there issues we might litigate to avoid a payout?

Problem Nine: #NousSommesTousAlpinistes (We Are All Mountain Climbers)

Selfie challenges are a thing on Instagram. Some are boring, some are funny, some are dumb. This is a Torts exam so of course this one falls into the latter category. The names of real people and real companies were used to develop this fact pattern, but in all other respects, the following is fiction:

Several months ago, a French company called Black Diamond hired a couple of influencers to promote their brand and products on Instagram. Ashima Shiraishi (aka "Rock Star") and Adam Ondra (aka "Rock God") are the best female and male rock climbers in the world, respectively. Shiraishi is from New York City but both of her parents are originally from Japan. Ondra is Czech. Both have a global fan base and many of these fans are not rock climbers. Black Diamond's strategy depended on this last group of fans in particular because its hope was to develop crossover appeal for its brand and products and thereby significantly to expand its customer base. It had seen what the Moncler company had been able to accomplish and it wanted in on that market. (It too makes really expensive quilted jackets.) Associating Black Diamond with Ondra and Shiraishi, especially in an Olympic year when they are widely expected to win Gold, would be to associate the company with the characteristics their fans associate with them. As described in the company's marketing plan, the two are "cool, athletic, edgy, thrilling." And so the hashtags #BlackDiamondChallenge™ and #NousSommesTousAlpinistes™ (we are all mountain climbers) were born.

The Black Diamond Challenge was heavily promoted by Shiraishi and Ondra on their Instagram. Their instructions to fans were to take and post a cool, athletic, edgy, thrilling selfie on Instagram using #BlackDiamondChallenge and #NousSommesTousAlpinistes and tagging Shiraishi, Ondra, and Black Diamond. Once a week, a winning selfie would be selected, nominally by Shiraishi and Ondra but actually by Black Diamond. The winning selfie would be announced and posted on all of their Instagrams and the winner would be gifted one of the company's best quilted jackets.

You probably know what happened next. People who had no business doing this took selfies in increasingly precarious circumstances including on rock faces and cliff edges, but also on rooftops and — my favorite — the tops of skyscrapers under construction. (Who does that?) Many of these selfies went viral so that even in Black Diamond's wildest dreams the company couldn't have imagined the numbers of people who would be somehow engaged with the challenge and their product, either as active participants or simply as voyeurs. Because of Instagram's algorithms which are designed to push popular posts — no matter how ridiculous they are — to the top of people's feeds, and then to link them up to related advertising, the implications for the company were tremendous. Visits to Black Diamond's website and sales of its clothing increased dramatically. As they did, more and more people took the challenge. It went exactly as advertising theory would have it in the most optimal conditions, which in this case included the boost provided by the digital drug that is social media. Mad Men meets neuromarketing. This was great for all concerned.

Until people started falling. At first it was just one person and seemingly a fluke, but then it was a lot of people. And because they died literally in the moments after they posted their selfies with the company's trademarked hashtags, the previously lucrative associations lost their luster for everyone involved. Instagram users reposted those selfies with the hashtag #NousSommeTousMorts (we are all dead). It was a real mess. Among other obvious consequences: Black Diamond's sales plummeted and Ondra and Shiraishi lost pending sponsorship deals with other companies.

Identify and work through the issues prompted by this fact pattern.

CHAPTER SIX
INJURY AND DAMAGES

However a claim is styled, injury is the final element of the prima facie case. As we saw in Chapter Two, the term "injury" refers to a legally recognized and thus compensable harm. And, of course, damages flow from injuries. Injury and damages together answer the plaintiff's question, "How much will I get?" and the defendant's question, "What will I have to pay?" The fact finder's answer to the jury verdict form's damages issues is the parties' bottom line for the trial. Long before the jury completes that form, and after the facts and law are sufficiently well understood, the parties' respective anticipated answers drive much of the analysis that determines whether the plaintiff will sue, what time and money will be spent pursuing or defending the case, and whether to settle and for how much.

I. DEFINITIONS AND EXPLANATIONS

A. Injury and Damages Distinguished

Courts and practicing lawyers often interchange the terms injury, harm, and damages, and throw in others like "loss" to add to the confusion. To the extent possible, we use only the legal terms and apply only their formal definitions. Thus, again in summary, injury is a legally recognized harm and damages are the amounts, expressed in dollars, that a judge, jury, or arbitral panel requires the wrongdoer to pay the plaintiff for that injury. To ensure that you are comfortable distinguishing between the these concepts, review the discussion of "injury" in the beginning of Chapter Two, including as it is distinguished from "harm" and "damages."

B. The Single Recovery Rule and Its Consequences

A plaintiff can sue a defendant for a tort only once. Any other result would be an inefficient use of judicial resources and unduly burdensome for the defendant. This "one bite at the apple" rule poses no problem for harms whose consequences are fully realized by the time at trial. But what about the plaintiff who has not fully recovered before the trial? Or the plaintiff who because of the nature of his injury — for example to his elbow — probably will develop a new condition in the future — for example arthritis? The general rule in these situations is that the plaintiff is entitled to recover damages for likely future consequences of the original injury. So, in our arthritis example, if the plaintiff can prove she is more likely than not to have arthritis due to the joint injury, she can recover damages for that harm and its consequences, including the cost of treatment, pain and suffering, and lost wages if the condition is debilitating.

C. Major Categories of Damages

1. Nominal Damages

A plaintiff who establishes an intentional tort but suffers only dignitary harm is entitled to a symbolic or nominal amount of compensation, typically one dollar. For example, you will recall from our work in Chapter Two that offensive batteries and trespasses to land that are unaccompanied by physical harm may be the basis for nominal damages. Nominal damages are also available for violations of the federal "constitutional torts" statute, 42 U.S.C §1983:

> Every person who under color of any statute, ordinance, regulation, custom, or usage, of any State or Territory or the District of Columbia, subjects, or causes to be subjected, any citizen of the United States or other person within the jurisdiction thereof to the deprivation of any rights, privileges, or immunities secured by the Constitution and laws, shall be liable to the party injured in an action at law, Suit in equity, or other proper proceeding for redress, except that in any action brought against a judicial officer for an act or omission taken in such officer's judicial capacity, injunctive relief shall not be granted unless a declaratory decree was violated or declaratory relief was unavailable.

See, e.g., Floyd v. Laws, 929 F.2d 1390 (9th Cir. 1991) ("even if jury awards zero actual damages in § 1983 action [involving assault, battery, false arrest, and IIED], judgment and $1 nominal damage award are mandatory if jury finds constitutional violation").

Although state tort law and constitutional tort claims for nominal damages may seem anachronistic, they continue to be useful both generally, as a way for the law to signal that a harm is legally cognizable even if it does not qualify for compensatory damages on particular facts, and specifically, to plaintiffs for whom a formal acknowledgment that their rights have been violated is important. The former is consistent with the law's deterrence function. The latter is consistent with the law's goal of preventing private retribution. Importantly, claims for nominal damages may also provide the basis for punitive damages. *See, e.g.,* Jacque v. Steenberg Homes, Inc., 563 N.W.2d 154 (Wis. 1997) (plaintiffs recovered both nominal and punitive damages against defendant company whose employees ignored plaintiffs' objections and trespassed on plaintiffs' land to deliver a mobile home to a neighbor); Williams v. Kaufman County, 352 F.3d 994 (5th Cir. 2003) (upholding award of nominal and punitive damages to plaintiffs who were strip searched by sheriff at night club in violation of their Fourth Amendment rights).

Note that the United States Supreme Court's punitive damages cases appear thus far to have excepted from its (non-binding) single-digit ratio rule punitive damages awards that are based in nominal damages. *See, e.g.,* State Farm Mutual Automobile Insurance Company v. Campbell, 538 U.S. 408, 425 (2003) ("Nonetheless, because there are no rigid benchmarks that a punitive damages award may not surpass, ratios greater than those we have previously upheld may comport with due process where 'a particularly egregious act has resulted in only a small amount of economic damages.'") You will read part of the *State Farm* decision in the punitive damages section of this Chapter.

2. Punitive Damages

Punitive damages are what the English called "the sting of the shilling." These are damages to punish the defendant, to deter the defendant and others from again engaging in the conduct, and to prevent retribution by the plaintiff or his family or friends. Under the common law, punitive damages are available in conjunction with nominal and compensatory damages for intentional torts. In negligence cases, punitive damages accompany compensatory damages only when the defendant's conduct rises to a level beyond ordinary negligence. This level is generally set by statute at willful or wanton misconduct or, in some jurisdictions, recklessness. We consider punitive damages in additional detail at the end of this Chapter.

3. Compensatory Damages

Compensatory damages are the most commonly awarded damages in tort cases. They are available for all categories of torts: intentional, negligence, and strict liability, and for both personal injuries and property damage. To the extent this can be accomplished with money, compensatory damages are designed to make the plaintiff "whole" again, or, more specifically, to put the plaintiff back in the position he or she occupied before the tort. We consider compensatory damages in detail immediately below.

II. COMPENSATORY DAMAGES

A. Property Damages

Compensatory damages are available to the plaintiff when the defendant has caused actual harm to real or personal property. Depending on the results of the harm, compensatory damages may be measured in one of two ways. The first approach treats the property as an asset with a fair market value. After the harm, that value is typically less than it was before. In this context, the compensatory damages award is the difference between the fair market value before and after the loss. The second approach focuses on the cost of restoring the property to its former condition, i.e., the cost of repair. For example, in the case of a wrecked car, the defendant's responsibility for damages may be calculated using one or the other approach depending on the circumstances:

If a car worth $5,000 sustains $1,200 in damages, the plaintiff typically seeks the costs of repairs. This gives the plaintiff the option of pocketing the money or repairing the car.

However, if the car worth $5,000 would cost $7,000 to repair, the jury would not ordinarily be given the choice of damages measures. It would instead be told to award damages for the loss in fair market value of the car; this would ordinarily be $5,000 minus the salvage value of the car to the plaintiff. The economic inefficiency of spending $7,000 to repair a $5,000 car that will again be worth $5,000 after the repair precludes using the repair cost measure of damages.

Similarly, if a classic car in perfect condition and worth millions sustains $50,000 in damages on the way to a car show, the plaintiff would likely seek compensation according to the fair market value or loss in value approach. This is because a $50,000 repair might leave the car visually and mechanically perfect again, but it might not sufficiently compensate for the car's loss in value on the classic car market. In this instance, a jury might find the more accurate and acceptable damages measure of damages to be the loss in value rather than the cost of repairs.

When only property is damaged, the traditional rule has long been that the plaintiff cannot recover for other harms that flow from that property damage. Thus, for example, the plaintiff who suffers the loss of personal property — a chattel — with significant sentimental value can only recover the repair costs or diminution in value of that personal property, which may be relatively insignificant; the plaintiff cannot also recover for the emotional distress or pain and suffering that might flow from the loss. Although this rule is quite firm and firmly established across the jurisdictions, plaintiffs have sought to make an exception for beloved pets, with some success. For a discussion of this movement and the related cases, *see, e.g.,* Richard James Tracy III, *Fido is One of a Kind: Looking Beyond Fair Market Value in Damages Against Pets*, Seton Hall Law eRespository: Student Scholarship (2013), *available at* http://scholarship.shu.edu/cgi/viewcontent.cgi?article=1318&context=student_scholarship; Phil Goldberg, *Courts and Legislatures Have Kept the Proper Leash on Pet Injury Lawsuits: Why Rejecting Emotion-Based Damages Promotes The Rule of Law, Modern Values, and Animal Welfare*, Stan. J. Animal L. & Pol'y 6 (2013).

B. Personal Injury Damages

Courts and lawyers generally categorize personal injury damages as either "special" or "general." Special damages are also known as economic loss damages and include losses such as past and future lost wages, past medical bills, and future care needs. The common thread of special damages is that outside the courtroom their value is calculated in dollars. General damages are also known as non-economic loss damages and include such losses as pain and suffering, loss of consortium, and emotional distress. These damages are also designed to compensate for real injuries, but these are not normally described in monetary terms outside the courtroom.

1. Special Damages for Economic Losses

As we have seen, tort law disfavors claims involving standalone economic loss—that is, where no person or property was physically damaged. When we use the term economic loss here in conjunction with damages, we consider only economic loss as a consequence of injury to person or property. In this damages context, economic losses are generally favored; although some "tort reform" legislation has limited or "capped" damages for non-economic losses, damages for economic losses have largely survived intact.

Economic losses typically fall into two categories: out of pocket expenses and lost wages and earning capacity. Out of pocket expenses are monies that are paid by, or on behalf of, the plaintiff that were necessitated by the defendant's negligence. These may include, for example, past and future hospital and doctor bills, medications, health care services, and home modifications. Lost wages and earning capacity are calculated based on past and future losses. Not surprisingly, this calculation is often more complicated with respect to earning capacity. Consider this discussion from Andler v. Clear Channel Broadcasting, Inc.:

A tort plaintiff can recover future economic damages for any loss of earning capacity caused by her injury. A plaintiff claiming lost earning capacity must offer sufficient proof of (1) future impairment and (2) the extent of prospective damages flowing from the impairment. The measure of damages in the second step is the difference between the amount which the plaintiff was capable of earning before his injury and that which he is capable of earning thereafter. Because predictions about future earning potential are necessarily somewhat speculative, an exact calculation of what the plaintiff could have earned but for the injury is not required; a plaintiff must prove damages with "reasonable certainty."

The damages are awarded for loss of earning *power,* not simply loss of earnings. The proper focus is thus what the injured plaintiff could have earned over the course of her working life without the injury versus what she will now earn, not what she earned or will earn in any given year. Accordingly, the fact that a plaintiff earns a higher annual salary after an injury than she did prior to the injury does not bar her from recovering for loss of earning capacity. In such situations, the plaintiff can still recover if she can show that she would have earned even more over the course of her working life if she had not been injured.

Similarly, the jury may consider the earnings of the plaintiff at the time of the injury, but the jury is not bound to accept such earnings as conclusive of his future earning power. A plaintiff who is unemployed or otherwise earning below her potential at the time of injury, for example, can recover damages for lost earning capacity, as can an injured child, student, or homemaker.

Departures from actual pre-injury earnings must be justified and cannot be unduly speculative. Like all expert testimony, an expert witness's calculations of future earning capacity are inadmissible under Federal Rule of Evidence 702 if based on "unsupported speculation." *Daubert v. Merrell Dow Pharms., Inc.,* 509 U.S. 579, 589-90, 113 S.Ct. 2786, 125 L.Ed.2d 469 (1993). Such testimony should be excluded if it is based on "unrealistic assumptions regarding the plaintiff's future employment prospects," *Boucher v. U.S. Suzuki Motor Corp.,* 73 F.3d 18, 21 (2d Cir.1996), or "facts that [a]re clearly contradicted by the evidence," *Boyar v. Korean Air Lines Co.,* 954 F.Supp. 4, 8–9 (D.D.C.1996). In *Boucher,* for example, the court held that an expert's figures for pre-injury earning capacity based on full-time employment, fringe benefits, and annual raises should have been excluded because the plaintiff's actual employment history had been "seasonal and intermittent." 73 F.3d at 22.

Testimony regarding what an injured plaintiff could have earned should take into account factors such as the plaintiff's age, employment record, training, education, ability to work, and opportunities for advancement. Further, an expert may reasonably depart from historical earning patterns in light of changed circumstances that occurred prior to the injury but were not yet reflected in the plaintiff's actual salary.

When calculating earning-capacity factors such as projected salary and years in the workforce, experts often consult actuarial tables, Bureau of Labor Statistics figures, or other averages along with the plaintiff's historical earnings. We held in *Cappello v. Duncan Aircraft Sales of Florida, Inc.* that calculating lost earning capacity based on the plaintiff's actual average income for the previous five years was unreasonable, in part, because that figure was inconsistent with the average lifetime earnings profile for someone in the plaintiff's position.

670 F.3d 717, 726–28 (C.A. 6, 2012) (most internal quotations and citations omitted).

DAVIS v. FOREMOST DAIRIES, et al., 58 So. 3d 977 (La. App. 2011)

CARAWAY, J.

. . .

Facts

On the morning of April 11, 2005, the 24-year-old plaintiff, Kristin Davis, was traveling to an elementary school for her first day of professional block student teaching. Davis's car was struck by a Foremost Dairy truck which ran a stop sign and struck the front passenger side of her Dodge Stratus. Davis's vehicle sustained damage to the right front window, right mirror and two front tires. Some time after the impact, Davis realized that she "was having a headache" and "pain in [her] neck and shoulders." After she went home to get cleaned up, Davis's parents took her to the emergency room at Glenwood Regional Medical Center in West Monroe, where she reported a headache and pain in her upper back and between her shoulder blades. At the time, Davis was diagnosed with neck strain by Dr. Edward Calvert and given a work excuse through April 18, 2005. She was prescribed pain medication.

In the four years between the accident and the time of trial in May of 2009, Davis sought the medical advice of numerous physicians and other medical personnel and made a large number of emergency room visits for complaints of pain. . . .

In 2005, she saw chiropractor Greg Mayfield and family physicians Drs. David Hebert, Doyle Hamilton and Warren Daniel, for pain in her upper and lower back and headaches. Both Drs. Hebert and Hamilton expressed concern over Davis's prescription drug use.[2] Davis also returned to the Glenwood emergency room two weeks after the accident with complaints of head and neck pain and made two visits to the St. Francis Medical Center emergency room in November and December of 2005, after falling down eight stairs and a fainting episode. In 2006, Davis reported to the St. Francis Medical Center emergency room eight times with complaints of neck and back pain.

Davis began seeing Dr. Doug Brown, an orthopedist, in January of 2006. Dr. Brown diagnosed Davis with a bulging disc at C6–7 after an MRI in January of 2006 and a myelogram and CT scan in June of 2006 which revealed the condition. During 2006, Davis also consistently saw Dr. Doyle Hamilton seeking pain medication for neck and back pain. Dr. Hamilton ultimately discontinued Davis as a patient in October of 2006 due to his concerns over her prescription drug use. Davis began physical therapy in February of 2006 but stopped by May of 2006.

---

[2] In fact, Dr. Hebert discontinued Davis as a patient by October 2005.

In January of 2007, Davis reported to Dr. Brown that a school child had grabbed her by the neck, causing the onset of pain in the left arm and fingers. A second MRI was performed in January of 2007 and showed a progression of the degenerative disc disease. Davis also continually saw Dr. Warren Daniel during 2007, and reported to the St. Francis emergency room two times with complaints of neck, arm and back pain. In March of 2007, she also saw neurosurgeon, Dr. Bernie McHugh, who referred her to pain specialist Dr. Vincent Forte. Davis began seeing Dr. Forte in April of 2007.

After undergoing various procedures, Dr. Forte ultimately diagnosed Davis with C6–7 nerve impingement and facet joint problems. The facet joints are joints located in the posterior part of the neck that frequently cause pain. According to the physicians, it was literally through the process of elimination, by diagnostic procedures, that both of these diagnoses were made.

Accordingly, during 2007, Davis received three steroid injections at C6–7, underwent a medial nerve block of the facet joint nerves, a discogram and a rhizotomy involving five facet joint nerves (C3, 4, 5, 6 and 7).[3] In 2008, Davis underwent two more rhizotomy procedures. In 2009, Dr. Forte administered a trigger point injection upon Davis and performed a fourth rhizotomy in May.

The diagnosis of Davis's condition, which she asserted at trial, is described in the opinions of Dr. Doug Brown, an orthopedic surgeon, and Dr. Vincent Forte, the pain management specialist. As noted above, Dr. Brown diagnosed the disc bulge at C6–7 and Dr. Forte diagnosed Davis with C6–7 nerve impingement and facet joint pain.

Davis's work history after the accident was equally eventful. Davis was able to complete her college education and student teaching in November of 2005 and graduated in December of 2005. Davis took a permanent job with the Ouachita Parish School Board on January 5, 2006. By February 15, 2006, work records document that Davis applied for sick days through March 17, 2006, due to cervical pain. Although Davis requested unspecified sick leave on two days in October and November of 2006, she worked full-time through December of 2006. A 2006 federal tax return shows that Davis reported $24,586 in income for 2006.

After the child incident in January of 2007, Davis was granted extended leave from work from January 27 through May 24, 2007, the end of the school year. Davis did not return to teaching in the fall semester of 2007 or the spring semester of 2008. Her 2007 tax records show an income of $7,926. By the summer of 2008 after moving to Lafayette, Louisiana, Davis obtained a part-time job as a swim instructor at a rehabilitation center. In October of 2008, Davis secured a part-time administrative position at a private school in Lafayette where she continued to work through 2009. Documentation showed that Davis performed both administrative work at $12.50/hour and substitute teacher work at $45/day. A check stub dated October 15–30, 2008, shows that Davis worked 56 hours at a rate of $12.50/hr. The 2008 tax records show that Davis earned $2,994 at the school and $1,060 at the rehabilitation clinic. Documentation showed that with a full-time administrative position at the private school, Davis would make approximately $25,000 a year.

---

[3] A rhizotomy is the cauterization of the nerves near the facet joints. The physician places a needle near the nerve which is stimulated with an electrical current. The physician then "burns" the nerve. Records from Dr. Forte's office indicated the cost of one rhizotomy procedure in June of 2008 was $10,400.

On April 10, 2006, Davis filed suit against the truck driver, Johnny Richardson, Dean Foods, Foremost Dairies and Southern Foods Group, L.P., seeking damages for injuries she allegedly sustained in the accident. Defendants admitted liability and the case proceeded to a bench trial on the issue of causation and damages. The defense raised the issue of whether Davis exaggerated her symptoms due to a prescription drug addiction. Additionally, the defense claimed that intervening and/or superseding events caused Davis's long-term injuries.

A two-day trial occurred in May of 2009. Live testimony included that of Kristin, her mother, a friend and an emergency room physician. Otherwise, the plaintiff submitted the deposition testimony of eight physicians, one addictionologist, a physical therapist and an economist as well as Davis's medical and work records. The defendants presented no evidence, but relied on the cross-examination of plaintiff's witnesses. After the submission of several post-trial briefs to the court, judgment was rendered in favor of Davis awarding $300,000 general damages and $100,000 loss of enjoyment of life. The court also awarded Davis special damages as follows:

Past Medical Damage	$ 120,337.88
Car Rental	$ 676.11
Past Lost Wages	$ 157,370.00
Future Lost Wages	$ 734,795.00
Past Household Services	$ 9,984.00
Future Household Services	$ 84,766.00
Future Medical Expenses	$1,146,321.00

Defendants appeal the $2,654,249.99 judgment raising arguments regarding causation of Davis's injuries, the award of past and future lost wages, past and future household services and future medical expenses.

Discussion

. . .

II.

Past Special Damages Lost Wages and Household Services

Defendants assign as error the trial court's award for lost wages and lost household services occurring before trial. They assert that Davis presented no medical testimony that she was disabled from any occupation or from performing household duties. They cite Davis's work history and claim that her non-teaching position in school administration at the time of trial was of her own choosing.

To recover for actual wage loss, a plaintiff must prove that she would have been earning wages but for the accident in question. In other words, it is the plaintiff's burden to prove past lost earnings and the length of time missed from work due to the accident.

Awards for past lost wages are not susceptible to the great discretion given the fact finder, because lost income is subject to mathematical calculation. Past lost income can be computed on an amount the plaintiff would in all probability have been earning at the time of trial and damages for loss of past income are not necessarily limited to a multiplier of the amount earned at the time of injury.

The jurisprudence has allowed as an element of damages, reasonable housekeeping expenses necessitated by the incapacity of an injured person. These awards have been rejected in cases where the plaintiff employed a housekeeper prior to the accident or injury, and the evidence failed to show that plaintiff would be unable to perform substantially all of the usual household duties.

Proof of lost wages included the testimony of Davis who asserted that she could not return to teaching first grade because of its physical demands and her pain. She also discussed her inability to perform high intensity cardio or lifting, although she is able to walk. Davis submitted her employment records from the Ouachita Parish School board which documented the time she was off of work. The sole expert testimony regarding the issue of Davis's ability to work was that of Dr. Brown. He explained that the 10% impairment of the body rating he gave Davis in May of 2006 was an anatomic impairment, not a functional impairment. At the time of the rating, he stated there was nothing that would have prevented Davis from teaching. Additionally, the evidence regarding Davis's lost earnings included the expert report and testimony of economist Dr. Melvin Harju, the documentation supporting his conclusions and Davis's tax returns.

We find that this evidence is sufficient proof of Davis's entitlement to past lost wages. As discussed above, Davis's testimony proved that she consistently experienced pain after the April 2005 accident which caused her to miss work and ultimately accept an administrative position. The documentation of her work history corroborates this testimony. Thus, Davis established that she would have been earning the lost wages but for the accident in question. As noted above, Dr. Harju obtained his salary figures from documentation provided by the Ouachita Parish School Board, including salary and supplemental check information. His total past earnings calculation from January 31, 2006 until May 20, 2009, was $131,093. Because these calculations were provided by Davis's employer, they are sufficient proof of salary information. However, for the years 2006–2007, Dr. Harju failed to deduct certain income earned by Davis as shown on her tax returns for those years as he erroneously concluded that Davis stopped working completely on January 31, 2006. The evidence, including Davis's tax returns and W–2s, shows that she in fact earned more income than Dr. Harju documented in both 2006 and 2007. Thus, Dr. Harju's calculations for 2006 and 2007 are in error. Accordingly, Davis's lost earnings calculation from the date of the accident until trial will be reduced by the sum of $17,858 ($9,932 in 2006 and $7,926 in 2007).

The documentation supporting Dr. Harju's fringe benefit calculations, moreover, was unsupported by any testimony of officials from the Ouachita Parish School Board. Additionally, there are clear inaccuracies in the data, e.g., the inclusion of social security benefits for the state employee. Without proof from the subject school board regarding any actual fringe benefits paid by the board to its employees, the evidence is insufficient to establish Davis's entitlement to these additional sums. On this basis we exclude any fringe benefit calculation.

After deducting these sums from the lost earnings calculation, the past lost earnings award is adjusted to the sum of $113,235.

Regarding past household services, the only evidence presented by the plaintiff included Davis's testimony and Dr. Harju's report. Davis testified that she had great difficulty with housework because it aggravates her neck. She estimated that after the accident, she would spend 6–7 hours per week longer on housework than before. Nevertheless, she testified that since she has received the rhizotomy procedures with Dr. Forte, she has been able to "resume normal activities." Further in a verified economic loss, household services statement submitted to her economist on May 22, 2008, and admitted into evidence, Davis made the following statement:

> All of my home care tasks such as cleaning, laundry, and cooking were done by my family as I was unable to complete simple household chores. Since having the procedures, I am currently able to complete these duties.

Dr. Harju calculated the replacement cost per hour for a maid or housekeeping services in Monroe at $6.68 per hour. He concluded that the replacement cost of one hour of work per week from April 11, 2005 until May 20, 2009, would be $1,536, and the trial court award of $9,984 represents 6.5 hours per week. Nevertheless, the above-referenced verified document submitted to Dr. Harju, Davis indicated that by May 22, 2008, she was able to complete these household tasks without any indicated restriction. Thus, Davis's need for these household services was only supported by the evidence prior to May of 2008, and we reduce the past household services award to $7,548.

. . .

IV.

Future Wages and Household Services

The defendants next argue that the trial court erred in awarding lost future wages and household services due to the complete lack of expert evidence that Davis was disabled from any occupation or from performing household duties. Defendants further contend that Davis's occupational decisions were "based upon choice, not disability."

A plaintiff bears the burden of proving his claim for lost earnings. For purposes of determining this type of damages, the amount of lost earnings need not be proved with mathematical certainty, but by such proof as reasonably establishes the claim. Since awards for future lost income are inherently speculative and intrinsically insusceptible of being calculated with mathematical certainty, the courts must exercise sound judicial discretion to determine these awards. The awards should be consistent with the record and not work a hardship upon either party. Purely conjectural or uncertain future lost earnings will not be allowed.

To ascertain whether a personal injury plaintiff should recover for lost earning capacity, the trial court should consider whether and how much the plaintiff's current condition disadvantages her in the work force. Among the factors to be considered are her physical condition before and after her injury, her age and life expectancy, work life expectancy, discount and inflation rates, and past work record. Lost income awards are speculative and cannot be calculated with absolute certainty. Therefore, the trial court is given broad discretion in setting an award for lost earning capacity. However, there must be a factual basis in the record.

The testimony of an economist is entitled to great weight, but since it is necessarily based on uncertain future events, it is not conclusive.

In computing loss of future income, it is first necessary to determine whether and for how long a plaintiff's disability will prevent her from engaging in work of the same or similar kind that she was doing at the time of his injury; it is necessary to ascertain whether she has been disabled from work for which she is fitted by training and experience.

In order to obtain an award for impaired earning capacity or future loss of wages, a plaintiff must present medical evidence which indicates with reasonable certainty that there exists a residual disability causally related to the accident. Lay testimony simply serves to complement and corroborate the medical evidence.

For Davis's future lost wages, the trial court awarded her the sum of $734,795, which according to Dr. Harju's calculations represented the amount of projected future income lost by Davis as a teacher in her expected worklife of 30.8 years with offset earnings of $25,000 per year. Defendants urge error in this award based upon the "complete absence in the record of any expert testimony that plaintiff was disabled from any occupation." We agree with defendants.

The sole evidence relating to Davis's inability to continue teaching first grade was that of Davis. In sum, Davis testified that while she can perform administrative duties in the school where she works, teaching in the future was "far too much that I can foresee right now to undertake." She explained that given the opportunity to substitute teach, "it's been so physically demanding just for the one day that it's hard to imagine a whole year of bending and pulling and doing all those things." Unfortunately, however, Davis presented no medical testimony establishing that she is disabled as the result of her injuries. As noted above, Dr. Brown gave her no functional impairment and concluded in May of 2006 that there was nothing that would have prevented Davis from teaching. This was before the time that Davis began receiving the rhizotomy and other procedures which significantly improved her condition. No physician offered any further testimony on the issue. Thus, with no medical evidence establishing her disability with reasonable certainty, Davis cannot recover future lost wages. We amend the judgment to delete the future lost wage award.

As discussed above, the jurisprudence has allowed as an element of damages, reasonable housekeeping expenses necessitated by the incapacity of an injured person. These awards have been rejected in cases where the plaintiff employed a housekeeper prior to the accident or injury, and the evidence failed to show that plaintiff would be unable to perform substantially all of the usual household duties.

The judgment in this case awarded Davis $84,766 in future household services for the remainder of Davis's life based upon Dr. Harju's calculations and Davis's testimony that it took her an extra 6.5 hours per week to complete her household chores. Davis did not testify that she was unable to do any housework. In fact, as discussed above, Davis admitted her ability to complete these chores after the rhizotomy procedures, although at a slower pace.

A review of the jurisprudence from 1962, first discussing the award of reasonable and necessary expenditures for past and future household services, shows that these awards have historically been limited to repayment for domestic help which was secured to perform domestic chores because of total incapacity of the injured party. Only in one case did the court award future damages for maid services even though the family did not hire a maid when the plaintiff was unable to perform any household chores. Thus, the cases awarding past and future lost household services limited recovery to situations where substitute housekeepers were actually utilized or would be necessary because of the plaintiff's total incapacity to perform housekeeping services.

In addition to the lack of legal authority for such an award, no medical testimony established that Davis was physically incapable of performing such duties. In fact, there is no evidence on the record that Drs. Brown and Forte assigned any permanent disability to Davis. As discussed above, Davis conceded that she was able to complete her housework. The record also lacks proof that Davis utilized maid services or that the services were or would be necessary for the remainder of her life. Thus, Davis did not prove the need for the services or the extent and duration they would be required. On these grounds, we reverse the award of future lost household services. Ultimately, Davis's receipt of $100,000 in general damages for loss of enjoyment of life serves to compensate her for any alterations to her lifestyle and activities which can be attributed to her neck injuries.

Conclusion

For the foregoing reasons, the judgment of the trial court is affirmed as to the causation determination, amended to reduce the past lost wage award from $157,370 to $113,235, past household services from $9,984 to $7,548, and the future medical awards from $1,146,321 to $229,515 and reversed as to the award of future lost wages and future household services for a total judgment of $871,301.99. Costs of appeal are assessed equally to the parties.

Judgment affirmed in part, reversed in part and amended in part.

Notes and Questions

1. Although the plaintiff's proof of fringe benefits in *Davis* was wanting, with proper evidence, the plaintiff is entitled to damages for benefits that did not accrue because of missed work. These losses can include the value of non-accrued vacation days, sick or personal leave days, and pension and other employer-provided benefits linked to the number of hours, days, weeks, or months actually worked by an employee.

2. Ms. Davis's past housekeeping responsibilities were assumed by volunteers from her family. In other words, these services were gifts; she paid nothing for them. Despite that, she received damages for these past losses. The same result obtains when an injured person has disability or health insurance that defrays the plaintiff's lost wages or medical and hospital bills.

These situations are traditionally resolved under the "collateral source" rule. This rule provides that the defendant's liability is not offset by gifts, insurance, or other benefits obtained by a plaintiff as a result of an injury. The premise of the rule is that where there is a choice to be made between double compensating the innocent plaintiff and passing the benefit instead on to the negligent defendant, fairness dictates deciding in favor of the plaintiff. Of course, in many instances, the plaintiff would pay the family members who provided the services or would owe back to the insurer amounts received under a disability or health insurance plan. These amounts would be due because the plan included in its contract with the subscriber a subrogation clause allowing recovery by the insurer of amounts previously paid for an injury if the injured person recovers from a third party. This works no hardship on the plaintiff because the plaintiff was paid twice, once from the insurer and once from the defendant, but only pays the insurer what it paid, leaving the plaintiff fully compensated by the defendant assuming the jury's verdict was adequate.

Many jurisdictions have enacted "tort reform" measures that modify or abolish the collateral source rule to prevent double compensation of the plaintiff in circumstances where either the services were performed by volunteers or the plaintiff has no subrogation obligation. Is this a fair result in the situation where the plaintiff paid for the insurance but the defendant benefits from that payment? If the claim involves future medical bills, should the fact that the plaintiff presently has insurance or is eligible for insurance under a guaranteed national insurance program be considered in calculating damages?

A related "tort reform" measure involves medical and hospital bills. Formerly, according to the same rationale as that which supports the collateral source rule, the defendant was liable for the provider's standard charge for a service, even if the plaintiff's insurer had negotiated a lower charge and actually paid less than the standard charge. This is known as a charge that is "billed but not paid." Many jurisdictions by statute now allow the plaintiff to seek only what was actually paid by the plaintiff and/or that person's insurer. Can you see any negative consequences of this change?

3. Most jurisdictions recognize that there is a relationship between time and money. Because of this, they generally require that damages for future losses be discounted to their present value. For example, if the plaintiff will have to pay a $1,000 medical bill in ten years, paying the plaintiff that amount now would probably overcompensate him because, even very conservatively invested, the $1,000 should be worth more then. The present value of a future sum is generally calculated by an economist, taking into account historic interest and inflation rates. The parties often disagree about these calculations and thus the jury is left to decide on the correct number as a question of fact. A few jurisdictions simply assume that the inflation and earnings rate will, on average, counteract each other and do not require the jury to find a present value for future damages.

4. Since 1918, the Internal Revenue Code has excluded from income subject to taxation any compensatory damages received due to personal injury or sickness. 6 U.S.C. §104(a)(2). This means that lost wages are not taxable by the Internal Revenue Service (IRS) even though they would have been taxed if they had actually been earned. Punitive damages and interest on compensatory damages awards are included in taxable income. *Id.* This statute only addresses how the Internal Revenue Service treats damages awards. In federal cases, jurors are required to reduce damages for lost wages by the amount that would have been paid in taxes. *See* Jones & Laughlin Steel Corp. v. Pfeifer, 462 U.S. 523, 534, 536 (1983); Norfolk & W. Ry. Co. v. Liepelt, 444 U.S. 490, 493 (1980). Many states have taken this approach, which seeks to the extent possible to approximate the plaintiff's real losses. It is essentially this same desire for accuracy that has other states taking the opposite position, on the view that this calculation cannot be done with sufficient precision because tax rates fluctuate as do the availability of deductions and reductions.

5. After the trial judge enters the judgment, the defendant is obliged to pay interest on the amount of the judgment until it is paid assuming it is not reversed. This is called post-judgment

interest. The interest rate varies wildly from jurisdiction to jurisdiction; some rates are fixed and some fluctuate with a tracked interest rate. Some jurisdictions also provide for pre-judgment interest at the same or a different interest rate as the post-judgment rate. This interest is paid on the amount of the judgment ultimately obtained and is calculated on that amount from the time the suit is filed until the verdict is entered. Post-judgment interest discourages frivolous appeals by defendants interested in postponing the day on which they must pay the judgment; prejudgment interest discourages delays in settlement of meritorious cases.

6. Review the discussion of respondeat superior liability in Chapter 1. Now assume that Ms. Davis sued both Foremost Dairies and its driver. Davis' theory against the driver was negligence; her theory against Foremost was both respondeat superior and negligent hiring of the company's driver. What is the effect on the negligent hiring claim if Foremost admits it is liable for the negligence of the driver?

7. The *Davis* court noted that when considering future lost wages, life expectancy and work life expectancy should be considered. Life expectancy can be determined from actuarial tables published by various sources including the United States Government. Many states have presumptive mortality tables that, barring contrary evidence, will be presumed to be accurate. For example, the current table in North Carolina presumes the following:

Age completed	Years remaining
21	56.0
22	55.1
23	54.1
24	53.2
25	52.2
26	51.3
27	50.4
28	49.4
29	48.5
30	47.5

N.C. G.S. §8-46. Individual life expectancies can vary widely from the median numbers expressed in such a table. Family history, ongoing medical issues, demographic factors, and health and life habits can all be used to prove the life expectancy for a specific plaintiff. Juries typically determine life expectancy from some combination of statutory tables, information provided through records, lay witnesses, and the opinions of expert witnesses.

As noted in the *Andler* case, work life expectancy calculations can be done in the same manner as life expectancy calculations. Tables available from various sources predict, based on a person's current age, how much longer they are expected to work. Work life expectancy is different from life expectancy in that the former is by definition continuous, while work life is expressed in a number of years but takes into account that people will be out of work for periods of time. Work life expectancy may vary based on demographic factors, particularly education and sex. Here is a work life expectancy table looking at sex:

Age	Worklife Male	Worklife Female
25	33.5	24.8
26	32.7	24.2
27	31.8	23.6
28	30.9	22.9
29	30.1	22.3
30	29.2	21.7
31	28.3	21.1
32	27.5	20.5
	***	
40	20.4	15.5
	***	
50	12.3	9.8
	***	
60	5.7	5.0
	***	
70	3.2	3.0

https://www.econedlink.org/resources/how-long-is-your-life/

As the following case illustrates, work life expectancy can also vary by race.

MCMILLAN v. CITY OF NEW YORK
253 F.R.D. 247 (E.D. NY 2008)

I. Introduction

James McMillan, the claimant, was rendered a quadriplegic in the crash of a ferryboat operated negligently by the City of New York. *In re City of New York,* 475 F.Supp.2d 235 (E.D.N.Y.2007), *aff'd,* 522 F.3d 279 (2d Cir.2008). He sued for pain, suffering and cost of necessary medical care. *See McMillan v. City of New York,* 2008 WL 4287573 (E.D.N.Y. amended Sept. 19, 2008) (findings of fact and law assessing damages).

A critical factor in determining claimant's damages is his estimated life expectancy. In a trial before the court and an advisory jury, statistical evidence was introduced suggesting that a spinal cord-injured "African-American" was likely to survive for fewer years than persons of other "races" with similar injuries. *See* Trial Tr. pages 723–24. The parties characterized claimant as an "African-American."

The question posed is whether such "racially" based statistics and other compilations may be relied upon to find a shorter life expectancy for a person characterized as an "African-American," than for one in the general American population of mixed "ethnic" and "racial" backgrounds. The answer is "no." "Racially" based life expectancy and related data may not be utilized to find a reduced life expectancy for a claimant in computing damages based on predictions of life expectancy. As indicated below, the unreliability of "race" as a predictor of life expectancy as well as normative constitutional requirements of equal treatment and due process support this conclusion.

The court's findings of fact and conclusions of law disregarded all "race"-based computations of life expectancy and applied predictions for the general male population, and particularly those suffering from quadriplegia. Properly rejected in predicting life expectancy were "racially" based statistics.

II. Factual Unreliability of "Race"-Based Statistics

In the United States, there has been "racial mixing" among "Whites," "Africans," "Native Americans," and individuals of other "racial" and "ethnic" backgrounds for more than three and a half centuries. *See, e.g.*, Annette Gordon-Reed, *The Hemingses of Monticello: An American Family* 660 (2008) (Thomas Jefferson fathered children with his "mixed blood" slave Sally Hemings. "[T]he choices the children of Sally Hemings and Thomas Jefferson made would separate their lines forever. Three would live in the white world, and one would remain in the black world."); Gregory Howard Williams, *Life on the Color Line: The True Story of a White Boy Who Discovered He Was Black* (1996). In *Plessy v. Ferguson,* 163 U.S. 537 (1896) (approving separation of "Whites" and "Blacks" on the grounds of "social" inferiority) the plaintiff was apparently 7/8th "White" and 1/8th "Black." *See also Dred Scott v. Sandford,* 60 U.S. 393, 19 How. 393, 15 L.Ed. 691 (1856) ("racial" inferiority of "Blacks," who could not be citizens). Clear-eyed observers of the American scene scoff at the use of "blood" in characterizing "race." *See, e.g.*, Mark Twain, *Pudd'nhead Wilson* (1894) ("White" and "Black" babies who looked "White" taken home by wrong mothers and raised inadvertently in "wrong 'racial' categories").

Statistical reliance on "race" leads to such questions as whether Plessy would have been categorized today as "African-American" for life expectancy purposes. In a more recent example, "racially" characterizing for statistical purposes in a negligence lawsuit the current Democrat Party presidential candidate, born of a "White" American mother and an "African" citizen of Kenya, would be considered absurd by most Americans. *See* Colm Tóibín, *James Baldwin & Barack Obama,* N.Y. Rev., Oct. 23, 2008, at 18 ("When Obama was a child, he wrote, 'my father . . . was black as pitch, my mother white as milk.' "). Reliance on "race"-based statistics in estimating life expectancy of individuals for purposes of calculating damages is not scientifically acceptable in our current heterogeneous population. As indicated below, "race" is largely a social construct inappropriate in assessing damages in a negligence suit.

A. "Race" as Biological Fiction

Franz Boas, the great Columbia University Anthropologist, pointed out that "[e]very classification of mankind must be more or less artificial;" he exposed much of the false cant of "racial" homogeneity when he declared that "no racial group is genetically 'pure.' " *Quoted in* Keay Davidson, *Franz Boas* in 3 American National Biography 83 (1999). *See also The Shaping of American Anthropology, 1883–1911, A Franz Boas Reader* 273 (George W. Stocking, Jr., ed., 1974) ("if we base our inferences entirely on the results of anatomical study, it would seem that there is no reason to believe that the bulk of the people constituting two distinct races might not be approximately on the same level" as to mental ability); Scott L. Malcomson, *One Drop of Blood: The American Misadventure of Race* 277 (2000) ("within the premodern written records of, globally speaking, light-skinned people, references to white people as white people, as a race, are remarkably scarce"); Orlando Patterson, *Rituals of Blood: Consequences of Slavery in Two American Centuries* 155–58, 165–66 (1998) (intermarriage); *The Concept of Race* xi (Ashley Montagu, ed., 1964) ("the biological concept of race has become unacceptable to a growing number of biologists"); Douglas S. Massey & Nancy A. Denton, *American Apartheid, Segregation and the Making of the Underclass* 9 (1993) ("Our fundamental argument is that racial segregation — and its characteristic institutional form, the black ghetto — are the key structural factors responsible for the perpetuation of black poverty in the United States."); James C. King, *The Biology of Race* 146 (2d ed.1981) ("estimates of the proportion of genetic material from white ancestry in American blacks range all the way from a few per cent [*sic*] to more than 50 percent").

An anthropologist who has written extensively on "race" and its evolution in American society notes:

> Despite legal and social attempts to prohibit intermarriage or intermating, some genetic mixture still occurred. In response, the United States had to resort to a fiction to help preserve the distinctiveness of the White/Black racial (and social) dichotomy. North Americans define as Black anyone who has known African ancestors, a phenomenon known and introduced by historians over half a century ago as the "one drop rule." . . . There is mounting historical evidence that this modern ideology of race took on a life of its own in the latter half of the 19th century . . . [a]s a paradigm for portraying the social reality of permanent inequality as something that was natural.

Audrey Smedley & Brian D. Smedley, *Race as Biology Is Fiction, Racism as a Social Problem is Real,* 60:1 Am. Psychologist 16, 20 (2005) (internal citations omitted) (referred to herein as an article by Professor Smedley). Professor Smedley finds that "[t]he ideology [of "race"] arose as a rationalization and justification for human slavery at a time when Western European societies were embracing philosophies promoting individual and human rights, liberty, democracy, justice, brotherhood, and equality." Smedley, *supra,* at 22. She cites Robert Moore, a sociologist from the University of Liverpool, who "observed that in the mid–1800s, a consensus emerged that human cultural differences were of a permanent kind, expressing underlying natural differences." *Id.* at n. 15. Professor Moore quotes Alexis de Tocqueville, who as an early observer of American life was among the first to recognize this conception of "race," writing that "the existence of innate and immutable racial characteristics is to be regarded with skepticism and theories founded upon such doctrine are mere rationalizations for slavery and other forms of racial oppression." *Id.* (internal citations omitted).

Professor Smedley cautions against scientific investigations that focus on justifying the differences between "racial" groups:

> Racialized science, with its emphasis on identifying immutable differences between racial groups, can be expected only to maintain and reinforce existing racial inequality, in that its adherents indirectly argue that no degree of government intervention or social change will alter the skills and abilities of different racial groups. The disproportionate representation of some "racial" groups (e.g., African Americans, American Indians) among lower socioeconomic tiers can therefore be

> explained as an unavoidable byproduct of human evolution. Yet reinforcing this widely held social stereotype of racial inferiority risks limiting individual human potential, in that individuals' abilities and opportunities would likely be assessed in relation to their racial group.

Id. at 24.

DNA technology finds little variation among "races" (humans are genetically 99.9% identical), and it is difficult to pinpoint any "racial identity" of an individual through his or her genes. *Id.* at 19. International gene mapping projects have only "revealed variations in strings of DNA that correlate with geographic differences in phenotypes among humans around the world," the reality being that the diversity of human biology has little in common with socially constructed "racial" categories. *Id.* at 21–22.

While "race" may be a social construct, many policymakers and courts insist that it "remains a significant predictor of . . . access to societal goods and resources." *Id.* at 22. "Racial" and "ethnic" disparities in quality of health care, for example, remain substantial across a broad range of medical services. *Id.* at 23. But those "disparities are associated with socioeconomic differences and tend to diminish significantly and, in a few cases, to disappear altogether when socioeconomic factors are controlled." *Id.* By allowing the use of "race"-based life expectancy tables, which are based on historical data, courts are essentially reinforcing the underlying social inequalities of our society rather than describing a significant biological difference.

B. Unreliability of "Racial" Categories

In 1977, the Office of Management and Budget (OMB) issued Statistical Policy Directive Number 15, "Race and Ethnic Standards for Federal Statistics and Administrative Reporting." *See* U.S. Census Bureau, Population Division, Racial and Ethnic Classifications Used in Census 2000 and Beyond. The directive established four "racial" categories ("American Indian or Alaskan Native," "Asian or Pacific Islander," "Black," and "White") for federal legislative, programmatic and administrative purposes. *Id.*The OMB revised these standards in October of 1997, creating five groups instead of four by splitting "Asian" and "Native Hawaiian or Other Pacific Islander." *Id.* The 2000 census also added a sixth "racial" set, "Some Other Race," and allowed responders to choose more than one category. *Id.* The catch-all of "Some Other Race," which was meant to "capture responses such as Mulatto, Creole, and Mestizo," also included a write-in option. *Id.*

Despite the 2000 census' more detailed self-categorization system, demographic studies that use pre–2000 census data continue to define "race" by using the 1977 OMB directive. *See, e.g.,* Christopher J.L. Murray et al., *Eight Americas: Investigating Mortality Disparities across Races, Counties, and Race–Counties in the United States,* 3:9 PLoS Med. 1513, 1515 (2006); Martha Chamallas, *Questioning the Use of Race–Specific and Gender–Specific Economic Data in Tort Litigation: A Constitutional Argument,* 63 Fordham L.Rev. 73, 82–83 (1994) ("The tables presented in [a practitioner's text for calculating lost earning capacity] are the P–60 Series (for 1977–90) from the Current Population Reports published by the United States Bureau of the Census . . . As was the case for most government data collections for these periods, race is reduced to either black or white; there is no separate breakdown for other racial/ethnic groups.").

Life expectancy tables are based on historical data and thus largely rely on the OMB's former archaic "racial" analysis. This means that the tables frequently employed by courts in determining tort damages fail to account for the nuanced reality of "racial" heritage in the United States today.

After hundreds of years of sexual mixings, there continues to be "no socially sanctioned in-between classification" of "race" in America. Smedley, *supra,* at 20. Even researchers investigating the differences between the life expectancies of "Black" and "White" Americans admit that the "presently available summary measures such as age-adjusted mortality and estimated life expectancy are crude" and "may mask special successes and/or problems for specific age categories/diseases or in specific local populations." Robert S. Levine et al., *Black–White Inequalities in Mortality and Life Expectancy, 1933–1999: Implications for Healthy People 2010,* 116 Pub. Health Rep. 474, 482 (Sept.-Oct.2001). *See also* Murray, *supra,* at 1521 ("The most important limitation of the data used for our analysis is that reported race in the census, used for population estimates, may be different from race in mortality statistics, where race may be reported by the family, the certifying physician, or the funeral director."). Even if reliance on "race"-based statistical projections made factual sense in the United States, available statistics do not appear to account for what might be called "blood ratios," in view of the American reality of long-term "racial" mixing.

C. Socio-Economic Status and "Race"

Putting aside the question of the fallacy of treating all "dark-skinned" Americans as completely different from "light-skinned" Americans in predicting life expectancy, socio-economic factors have a large role in influencing length of life. While many sociologists, epidemiologists, and other researchers have noted "[t]he broad influence of race/ethnicity and socioeconomic position on functional status, active life expectancy, and mortality," Arline T. Geronimus et al., *Inequality in Life Expectancy, Functional Status, and Active Life Expectancy across Selected Black and White Populations in the United States,* 38:2 Demography 227, 227 (2001), the influence of socio-economic factors is often masked by "race." *See* Levine, *supra,* at 482 ("race itself may be largely a surrogate for other factors, especially differences in environmental exposures"). Reliable studies have found that "[t]he relationships between socioeconomic position or race/ethnicity and health may be modified by geographic influence and community conditions that contextualize and structure these relationships." Geronimus, *supra,* at 227. As one group of researchers has cautioned, "while race-based mortality ratios and absolute risks are important, there are clear limitations to their use as indicators of health," including the appropriateness and reliability of the "racial" and "ethnic" categories used in statistical analysis. Levine, *supra,* at 481–82.

The impact of socio-economic status (SES) on life expectancy has long been recognized. *See* Joseph J. Sudano & David W. Baker, *Explaining U.S. racial/ethnic disparities in health declines and mortality in late middle age: The roles of socioeconomic status, health behaviors, and health insurance,* 62 Soc. Sci. & Med. 909, 918 (2006) ("Our results are also consistent with previous studies that have found large 'direct' (or residual) effects of SES on health that were not explained by differences in health behaviors."). Aside from "baseline health," the next "dominant explanation for the worse health outcomes for blacks and Hispanics was SES." *Id.* "In contrast, health insurance and health behaviors explained little of the racial/ethnic differences in health outcomes." *Id.; see also* Murray, *supra,* at 1522 ("Important research in the past few decades has illustrated the critical role of individual and community-level socio-economic factors, be it in absolute or relative terms, in health outcomes"); Lloyd B. Potter, *Socioeconomic Determinants of White and Black Males' Life Expectancy Differentials, 1980,* 28:2 Demography 303, 304 (1991) ("There is a long-standing consensus that a negative relationship exists between socioeconomic conditions and the levels of mortality experienced by a population.").

More detailed investigations into the life expectancy gap between "White" and "Black" Americans have shown that life expectancy varies within "racial" groups by economic characteristics and geography. *See* Geronimus, *supra,* at 244 ("Our analyses revealed heterogeneity in length and quality of life *within* the black and the white populations with respect to their communities' economic characteristics and, to some extent, the location of their residence."). Given the significant impact of socio-economic factors, it is natural for courts to be concerned with the use of life expectancy tables that ignore important distinctions such as education, place of residency, and employment, collapsing all members of a "racial" group into a single number. Gross statistical tables do not answer the question: how does the life expectancy of well-off or middle-class "African-Americans" compare to that of poor "African-Americans?"

In a national study of twenty-three local areas, researchers found that "African American residents of advantaged urban areas have substantially higher life expectancies than their poor urban counterparts; in some cases their life expectancies approach the white national average." Geronimus, *supra,* at 241. That study also found that "White residents of urban poor areas have mortality profiles comparable to those of black residents of poor rural areas and blacks nationwide," and "somewhat worse than residents of relatively advantaged black urban areas." *Id.* at 234–35. In fact, "African-Americans" residing "in the advantaged population of New York City fare as well as whites nationwide." *Id.* at 233.

In studies targeting cardiovascular diseases (CVD), researchers found that after controlling for risk level, "there was no consistent pattern in CVD mortality differences for Black and White men according to income level. As shown in other research, the higher overall CVD mortality rate among Black men than among White men was largely explained by differences in zip code area incomes and risk factor levels." Avis J. Thomas et al., *Race/Ethnicity, Income, Major Risk Factors, and Cardiovascular Disease Mortality,* 95:8 Am. J. Pub. Health 1417, 1421 (2005).

When determining tort damages based upon an injured individual's future life span and potential needs, consideration must be given to the fact that changing a person's socio-economic status may have an impact upon his or her life expectancy. While studies have found that expanding health insurance alone would not greatly impact the life expectancy or morbidity of individuals, it may well be that elevating a group of individuals from a lower socio-economic class to a higher one would change their overall cause-of-death structure and enhance their health and lifespan. Major causes of death in "African-American" populations include homicide, HIV, unintentional injuries, and other factors associated with poverty and low socio-economic status. *See generally*Sam Harper et al., *Trends in the Black–White Life Expectancy Gap in the United States, 1983–2003,* 297:11 J. Am. Med. Ass'n 1224 (2007); *see also* Potter, *supra,* at 304 ("Improvement of socioeconomic conditions is associated with a change from a cause-of-death structure characterized by infectious and parasitic diseases toward one characterized by degenerative disease . . . such a shift will lead to higher life expectancy.").

The findings of the studies cited above reinforce the conclusion that despite a documented gap in life expectancy between "Black" and "White" Americans, the simple characterization of individuals as "Black" or "White" is not only misleading, it risks masking the complex interactions between a host of genetic and socio-economic factors. While some researchers have suggested that higher socio-economic position may not impact "African-American" health as directly as other populations (due to stress-related diseases potentially linked to structural racism), Geronimus, *supra,* at 228, this is not reason for courts to enforce the negative impacts of lower socio-economic status while ignoring the diversity within populations.

D. Legal Decisions on "Race"

A 1905 decision by a federal court in New York relied on "race"-based statistics and "racial" categories in reducing damages in an admiralty case. *The Saginaw and The Hamilton,* 139 F. 906 (S.D.N.Y.1905); *see* Jennifer B. Wriggins, *Damages in Tort Litigation: Thoughts on Race and Remedies, 1865–2007,* 27 Rev. Litig. 37, 53–57 (2007) (discussing the case). Two steamships collided, resulting in the deaths of some passengers and crewmembers. *See In re Clyde S.S. Co.,* 134 F. 95 (S.D.N.Y.1904) (decision on limitation of liability in the same case). Wrongful death actions were brought for six "Colored" and two "White" persons killed in the accident. *The Saginaw* at 139 F. 910. Rejecting the use of standard mortality tables to predict the life expectancies of all the deceased, the court cited census data summarizing differences in "White" and "Colored" life expectancies in justifying its reduction of awards. *The Saginaw* at 139 F. 913–14. At that time census respondents did not have the option of selecting more than one "race" to identify themselves. *See* Part II.B, *supra.* Professor Jennifer B. Wriggins found that "on average [the *Saginaw* court] lowered the awards for the deaths of blacks ten percent more than the awards for the deaths of whites and [the court] slashed three of the awards for blacks by forty percent or more." Wriggins, *supra,* at 56. *See also* Marc Galanter, *Bhopals, Past and Present: The Changing Legal Response to Mass Disaster,* 10 Windsor Yearbook of Justice 151, 157–59 (1990) (describing the Hawk's Nest Tunnel disaster in early 1930s West Virginia in which over 700 unprotected laborers were victims of acute silicosis and settlements ranged from $30 for a single "Black" to $1600 for a "White" Family); Monograph, *Individual Justice in Mass Tort Litigation* 7 (1995) (same).

It should be noted in assessing *The Saginaw* that the case was decided shortly after *Plessy, supra,* approving "racial" segregation of "African-Americans." *Plessy's* "racial" basis was entirely rejected by *Brown v. Board of Education,* 347 U.S. 483, 74 S.Ct. 686, 98 L.Ed. 873 (1954). *The Saginaw* has no precedential value.

1. Future Earnings

Courts are increasingly troubled by "race"- and gender-based figures for calculating loss of future income. The district court in *United States v. Bedonie* noted that "surprisingly the reported cases have almost completely neglected the question" of whether to use sex- and "race"-neutral statistics. 317 F.Supp.2d 1285, 1315 (D.Utah 2004), *aff'd sub nom, United States v. Serawop,* 505 F.3d 1112 (10th Cir. 2007). After receiving an expert report (for restitution purposes) that reduced the estimate of lost income based on the fact that a victim was "Native American," that court directed recalculation without regard to "race" or gender. *Id.* at 1313–14. Avoiding reaching any constitutional questions, the court chose to "exercise its discretion in favor of victims of violent crime and against the possible perpetuation of inappropriate stereotypes," especially "where the defendants have deprived their victims of the chance to excel in life beyond predicted statistical averages." *Id.* at 1319. The court ultimately utilized gender-and "race"-neutral figures in its findings. *Id.* at 1321–22.

One court refused to use "racial" statistics in calculating tort damages for loss of future income when the plaintiff was half "Black" and half "White." *Wheeler Tarpeh–Doe v. United States,* 771 F.Supp. 427 (D.D.C.1991). The defendant argued that the wage earnings projections for "Black" men were the appropriate figures for the plaintiff, whose mother was "White" and father was "Black." *Id.* at 455. Apparently "race"-based life expectancy figures were not introduced in the case. *Id.* at 456. The court held it "inappropriate to incorporate current discrimination resulting in wage differences between the sexes or races or the potential for any future such discrimination into a calculation for damages resulting from lost wages." *Id.* at 455. It used "the average earnings of all persons." *Id.* at 456; *see also* Laura Greenberg, *Compensating the Lead Poisoned Child: Proposals for Mitigating Discriminatory Damage Awards,* 28 B.C. Envtl. Aff. L.Rev. 429, 447 (2001) (arguing that "race"-based economic statistics "reinforce the status quo of racial disparities" and "propel[ ] race to the forefront of predictions about individual achievement"; advocating use of "race"-neutral statistics).

Canadian courts have refused to use gender-specific wage calculations in determining damages. *See, e.g., Walker v. Ritchie,* 119 A.C.W.S. (3d) (Ont.Sup.Ct. J. Jan. 3, 2003) (using statistical figures which reflected the entire population).

2. Work–Life Expectancy

In an action for damages by an injured seaman, the plaintiff presented statistics on work-life expectancy modified to exclude "race" as a factor; the defendant challenged the increased work-life expectancy that resulted. *Theodile v. Delmar Systems, Inc.,*2007 WL 2491808 at *8 (W.D.La.2007). The district court refused to upset the jury's award in the "race"-neutral amount suggested by plaintiff's expert. *Id.* Another district court rejected an expert calculation that reduced a female tort victim's estimated working life by 40% based on a historical statistic about the number of years females average in the workforce. *Reilly v. United States,* 665 F.Supp. 976, 997 (D.R.I.1987), *aff'd,* 863 F.2d 149, 167 (1st Cir.1988).

In administering the September 11th Victim Compensation Fund, Special Master Kenneth R. Feinberg based estimations of remaining years of work-life on the victim's age, using statistics for the general population of active males in the United States for all claimants and ignoring "racial" differences. September 11th Victim Compensation Fund of 2001, 67 Fed.Reg. 11,233, 11,238 (Mar. 13, 2002) (codified at 28 C.F.R. pt. 104); *see generally* Kenneth R. Feinberg, *What is Life Worth?* (2005).

3. Life Expectancy

In the context of Title VII, the Supreme Court noted that while "[a]ctuarial studies could unquestionably identify differences in life expectancy based on race or national origin, as well as sex," Congress has outlawed classifications based on "race," national origin, and sex. *City of Los Angeles, Dep't of Water and Power v. Manhart,* 435 U.S. 702, 709, 98 S.Ct. 1370, 55 L.Ed.2d 657 (1978). Thus, "[e]ven a true generalization about the class is an insufficient reason for disqualifying an individual to whom the generalization does not apply." *Id.* at 708, 98 S.Ct. 1370. *See also* Jill Gaulding, *Race, Sex, and Genetic Discrimination in Insurance: What's Fair?,* 80 Cornell L.Rev. 1646, 1659 & n. 86 (collecting state statutes forbidding "race" classifications by insurers). "Racial" statistics present an especially strong argument for exclusion, since, as already noted, the question of "race" is ambiguous, whereas gender is generally conceded.

III. Unconstitutionality of "Race" as a Criterion for Assessing Damages

A. Equal Protection

For half a century the Supreme Court has rejected on equal protection grounds "race"-based discrimination. *See, e.g., Parents Involved in Community Schools v. Seattle School Dist. No. 1,* 551 U.S. 701, 127 S.Ct. 2738, 168 L.Ed.2d 508 (2007) (allocating students to particular schools based on "race" unconstitutional); *Shaw v. Reno,* 509 U.S. 630, 113 S.Ct. 2816, 125 L.Ed.2d 511 (1993) (redistricting based on "race" impermissible); *Palmore v. Sidoti,* 466 U.S. 429, 104 S.Ct. 1879, 80 L.Ed.2d 421 (1984) (consideration of "race" in child custody decision unconstitutional despite possibility that societal "racial" biases might affect child); *Loving v. Virginia,* 388 U.S. 1, 87 S.Ct. 1817, 18 L.Ed.2d 1010 (1967) ("race"-based restrictions on marriage unconstitutional); *Brown, supra* (abolishing segregation in public schools); *Bolling v. Sharpe,* 347 U.S. 497, 74 S.Ct. 693, 98 L.Ed. 884 (1954) (applying rationale of *Brown* to federal government). *See also, e.g.,* Richard Kluger, *Simple Justice* (2d ed.2004); Jack Greenberg, *Crusaders in the Courts* (1994); Jack Greenberg, *Race Relations and American Law* (1959); Benjamin N. Cardozo Lecture: *The Role of Judges In A Government Of, By, and For the People* at 477–541 (2007).

As Professor Martha Chamallas notes, "when experts rely on race or gender-based statistics to calculate tort damages, we tend not to notice the discrimination and to accept it as natural and unproblematic." *Civil Rights in Ordinary Tort Cases: Race, Gender, and the Calculation of Economic Loss,* 38 Loy. L.A. L.Rev. 1435, 1442 (2005). "Racial" classifications of individuals are "suspect categories," *see United States v. Carolene Products Co.,* 304 U.S. 144, 152 n. 4, 58 S.Ct. 778, 82 L.Ed. 1234 (1938), meaning that state action in reliance on "race"-based statistics triggers strict scrutiny. *See, e.g.,* Chamallas, *Civil Rights in Ordinary Tort Cases: Race, Gender, and the Calculation of Economic Loss, supra,* at 1441; *cf.* Charleen Hsuan, *Note Medicaid Coverage for Race-Based Drugs,* 41 Colum. J. L. & Soc. Probs. 443 (2008) (arguing that strict scrutiny under equal protection would apply to state Medicaid agency decisions to deny off-label coverage for FDA-approved "race"-based drugs). Judicial reliance on "racial" classifications constitutes state action. *See Edmonson v. Leesville Concrete Co.,* 500 U.S. 614, 620–28, 111 S.Ct. 2077, 114 L.Ed.2d 660 (1991) (permitting peremptory jury challenges based on "race" is state action violating equal protection); *Shelley v. Kraemer,* 334 U.S. 1, 14–21, 68 S.Ct. 836, 92 L.Ed. 1161 (1948) (state action in judicial enforcement of restrictive covenants based on "race"); *see also* Chamallas, *Questioning the Use of Race-Specific and Gender-Specific Economic Data in Tort Litigation: A Constitutional Argument, supra,* at 106 ("By conceding the relevance of race-based or gender-based data through its admission into evidence . . . the judge necessarily leads the jury to believe that gender and race are legally permissible factors and thus cannot be said to be neutral on the issue.") Equal protection in this context demands that the claimant not be subjected to a disadvantageous life expectancy estimate solely on the basis of a "racial" classification.

B. Due Process

There is a right—in effect a property right—to compensation in cases of negligently caused damage to the person under state and federal law. *See Martinez v. State of California,* 444 U.S. 277, 282, 100 S.Ct. 553, 62 L.Ed.2d 481 (1980) ("[a]rguably" a tort cause of action created by a State constitutes "a species of 'property' protected by the Due Process Clause" and there is a federal "interest in protecting the individual citizen from state action that is wholly arbitrary or irrational"); *see also* John C.P. Goldberg, *The Constitutional Status of Tort Law: Due Process and the Right to a Law for the Redress of Wrongs,* 115 Yale L.J. 524 (2005) (constitutional right to a body of tort law for the purpose of redressing private wrongs); Benjamin N. Cardozo Lecture: *The Role of Judges In A Government Of, By, and For the People* at 495–506 (2007) (same).

By allowing use of "race"-based statistics at trial, a court would be creating arbitrary and irrational state action. "[T]he form and content of statistical evidence is shaped by the requirements of the substantive law." David C. Baldus & James W.L. Cole, *Statistical Proof of Discrimination* 10 (1980). Were the court to apply an ill-founded assumption, automatically burdening on "racial" grounds a class of litigants who seek compensation, there would be a denial of due process. *Cf. Brinkerhoff–Faris Trust & Savings Co. v. Hill,* 281 U.S. 673, 680, 50 S.Ct. 451, 74 L.Ed. 1107 (1930) ("federal guaranty of due process extends to state action through its judicial . . . branch of government").

The legal system does not work fairly and with due process if one class of litigants is unduly burdened in litigation through the application of inappropriate "race"-based statistics. Where, as in the instant case, no attempt was made to justify the use of "racial" statistics by the City, the due process rights of the defendant cannot be said to have been affected. *See McMillan v. City of New York,* 2008 WL 4181695 (E.D.N.Y. Sept.3, 2008) (City was given the opportunity to brief and address the issue and did not do so).

IV. Application of Law to Facts

There is no factual basis for discriminating against this claimant by finding a reduced life expectancy based upon "race." That conclusion is particularly sound in the instant case where the damages awarded are designed to extend claimant's life by providing him with the best medical and other care—more than the equivalent of what the average American quadriplegic could expect.

Constitutional normative doctrine also supports excluding "race"-based statistics. "[A]ny decision to use a group-based projection into the future as the basis for a damage remedy also involves normative judgments about the relevant frame of reference and the rate of future change." Wriggins, *supra,* at 56. The American reality reflects that "people do not fall naturally into discrete racial groupings" and "[l]egal classifications of race tend to be unrefined and often reflect ignorance of differences within a given category." Chamallas, *Questioning the Use of Race–Specific and Gender–Specific Economic Data in Tort Litigation: A Constitutional Argument, supra,* at 113.

V. Conclusion

Reliance on "race"-based statistics in estimating life expectancy for purposes of calculating damages in this case is rejected in computing life expectancy and damages.

SO ORDERED.

Notes and Questions

1. Derive the outline of the court's analysis from the headings and summarize the point of each section. Then, to the best of your ability based on your background knowledge and experience, assess the strengths and weaknesses of each point.

2. Judge Weinstein extended the reasoning in *McMillan* to ethnicity in *G.M.M. ex rel. Hernandez-Adams v. Kimpson*, 116 F. Supp. 3d 126, 152 (E.D.N.Y. 2015); and scholars since Professor Martha Chamallas did the seminal work featured in *McMillan* have further examined and developed its analysis, including, as she did originally, by applying it to sex. See, e.g., Martha Chamallas and Jennifer B. Wriggins, The Measure of Injury: Race, Gender, and Tort Law (NYU Press 2010); Kimberly A. Yuracko & Ronen Avraham, Valuing Black Lives: A Constitutional Challenge to the Use of Race-Based Tables in Calculating Tort Damages, 106 Cal. L. Rev. 325 (2018); Ronen Avraham and Kimberly Yuracko, Torts and Discrimination, 78 Ohio St. L.J. 661 (2017). However, to date, only one state — California — has banned the use race- and sex-based tables in the calculation of tort damages. Cal. Civ. Code § 3361 (Deering, LEXIS through Ch. 9 of 2021 Reg. Sess.). That date — 2021 — is relevant, as is the state, of course: The date marks the moment in this general period when policymakers began working actively to ferret out and address instances of structural racism in the law; and it is often said that as California goes, so goes the nation. The first sign of movement along these lines comes from New Jersey, which introduced legislation modeled after California's later that same year.

3. That very few courts and legislatures have picked up on McMillan's analysis since 2008 does not mean that the use of race in calculating life and work life expectancy continues unabated, or that nothing has changed on the ground. Many decisions are made by judges that go unreported and unchallenged. However, the dearth of action does suggest that, at least until recently, the practice was acceptable enough that no major reforms were deemed necessary. Which of its rationales is most likely to explain its ongoing acceptability? As you consider this question, think about both factual and political rationales, including political rationales from the left and the right.

4. Race and sex are both ways that we sort each other, and that the government classifies us. Focusing on the goals of tort damages in particular, and using the analysis in McMillan as your guide, consider how race and sex are the same and how they are different.

5. According to the "List of U.S. states and territories by life expectancy" on Wikipedia, what we call "race" or "ethnicity" and "sex" intersect with "domicile at birth" so that the longest lived people on average in this period are Asian females in the District of Columbia (#1), followed by Asian females in Colorado and Hawaii (tied for #2). Go to the table on Wikipedia and play around with it; see what interests you and think about why. Then, focusing again on

the goals of tort damages, consider the arguments for and against an evidentiary rule that allows the parties in litigation to operate at this level of detail.

2. Non-economic Losses

Outside of litigation, non-economic losses are not normally expressed in monetary terms. Although a person may talk about their $1,000 medical bill, when they talk about their pain, they use non-financial descriptions, for example, "on a scale of one to ten, it was a nine," or "it felt like my head was going to explode." The job of a lawyer at trial is to translate these injuries into monetary numbers for the jury.

In most jurisdictions, a lawyer can expressly suggest an amount of compensation for the non-economic injury to the jury. In some jurisdictions, the lawyer can go further and use a "per diem" argument to quantify the damages. For example, if the plaintiff lost a leg and will have continuous phantom pain in the future, the lawyer can suggest that the jury consider awarding $50 a day for each future day of the person's life. Some jurisdictions even permit calculations broken down to the hour or minute.

A minority of jurisdictions prohibit lawyers from suggesting the dollar value of non-economic losses. Lawyers may argue about what the non-economic losses are, and they may argue about the facts in connection with those losses, but they may not propose a number for the jury. Juries must arrive at this number themselves.

Every jurisdiction provides for compensation for the mental effects of a physical injury. Some call these mental effects "pain and suffering," others call them "mental anguish," and still others describe them as "loss of enjoyment of life." Compensation is also due for scarring and disfigurement, and for the loss of the use of a body part either because it is missing or because it no longer fully functions.

MEALS EX REL. MEALS v. FORD MOTOR CO.,
417 S.W.3d 414 (Tenn. 2013)

SHARON G. LEE, J.,

A six-year-old boy's spine was fractured in a car wreck when the force of the impact caused him to jackknife over his lap seatbelt and pushed the seatbelt into his stomach and against his spine. The child's mother filed suit on his behalf against Ford Motor Company ("Ford"), alleging that the defective design of the seatbelt and Ford's failure to warn of a potential danger caused the child's permanent paralysis and other enhanced injuries. A jury returned a $43.8 million verdict for compensatory damages, finding Ford to be 15% at fault and two non-parties 85% at fault. Ford's share of the verdict, based on its degree of fault, was $6,570,000. The jury awarded no punitive damages. Ford moved for a new trial, arguing that the verdict was excessive. The trial court denied the motion for new trial and affirmed the verdict in its capacity as thirteenth juror. The Court of Appeals, in a divided opinion, ruled that the verdict was excessive and remanded to the trial court with a suggestion of remittitur from $43.8 million to $12.9 million, a 70.55% reduction. The suggested remittitur, if the plaintiff accepted it, would reduce Ford's share of the verdict to $1,935,000. *Meals ex rel. Meals v. Ford Motor Co.*, No.

W2010-01493-COA-R3-CV, 2012 WL 1264454, at *18–21 (Tenn.Ct.App. Apr. 13, 2012). We hold that the Court of Appeals had the authority to suggest a remittitur even though Ford did not request a remittitur. We further hold that the Court of Appeals erred in remitting the verdict to $12.9 million. Having taken the strongest legitimate view of all the material evidence in favor of the verdict, assuming the truth of all that supports it, allowing all reasonable inferences, and discarding any to the contrary, we hold that the jury's verdict was supported by material evidence and was within the range of reasonableness. The judgment of the Court of Appeals is reversed and the jury's verdict is reinstated.

I.

Around 6:30 p.m. on January 18, 2002 in Memphis, Tennessee, six-year-old William ("Billy") Meals was riding with his father and grandfather to visit a family member in the hospital. Billy's grandfather was driving his 1995 Mercury Grand Marquis, which was manufactured by Ford. Billy's father was seated in the front passenger seat, and Billy was seated in the back seat behind his grandfather. Billy's father had buckled him into the back seat, using the vehicle's three-point restraint system that included both a lap and a shoulder strap. Because the shoulder strap ran directly across Billy's face, his father placed the shoulder strap behind Billy's back, leaving him restrained only by the lap seatbelt.

As the Meals family was traveling down Covington Pike, Memphis Police Department Officer Bridgette King observed a vehicle moving at a high rate of speed on Raleigh LaGrange Road. Officer King turned on her cruiser's blue lights and began following the vehicle. The vehicle's operator, John Harris, was driving under the influence of alcohol and cocaine. After turning onto Covington Pike and crossing the median into oncoming traffic, the Harris vehicle collided head-on with the Meals vehicle. The violent impact killed Billy's father and grandfather, and Mr. Harris. Billy, the sole survivor, was seriously injured when he jackknifed over the lap seatbelt. His upper torso was thrust forward, but his lower body was stopped by the seatbelt. The force of the collision caused the lap seatbelt to move up across his stomach, propel into his body, and damage his spine. Emergency medical responders removed Billy from the vehicle and took him to LeBonheur Children's Medical Center.

The seatbelt fractured Billy's lumbar spine and caused serious internal injuries. Billy's injuries included a closed head injury, a fractured and dislocated second lumbar vertebra, a collapsed lung, internal bleeding, injuries to the abdominal wall and small intestine, bruises, and abrasions. He was hospitalized for fifty-four days and underwent numerous medical and surgical procedures. Billy was paralyzed from the waist down and for a period of time, needed a ventilator to support his breathing. About two-thirds of his small intestine had no blood supply, and a significant portion had to be removed and the bowel resectioned. Two surgeries were required to drain blood from his abdomen and remove necrotic tissue. A large abscess in his abdomen had to be drained. He underwent a cystoscopy to evacuate bladder sediment. He had multiple infections with high fevers and required intravenous antibiotics. After his discharge from the hospital, he was transferred to the Scottish Rite Pediatric Hospital in Atlanta, Georgia, for rehabilitation. He spent twenty-five days in the rehabilitation facility and then returned home. He was subsequently hospitalized on several occasions for surgeries to remove kidney stones and to receive treatment for a scrotal abscess and urinary tract infections. He also had to undergo a surgical spinal fusion, which required the placement of rods, screws, and wires to straighten his back.

On January 15, 2003, Aundrey Meals ("Plaintiff") filed suit on behalf of her son against Ford and other defendants in the Circuit Court for Shelby County. As to Ford, Plaintiff alleged negligence, comparative fault, gross negligence, misrepresentation, breach of express and implied warranties of merchantability and fitness for a particular purpose, and strict liability. Plaintiff sought compensatory and punitive damages. When the case went to trial, Ford was the sole defendant.

The trial began on September 28, 2009, and lasted approximately seven weeks. After closing arguments, the jury deliberated for three days and returned a verdict in Plaintiff's favor, concluding that Ford was 15% at fault; Mr. Harris, a non-party, 70% at fault; and Billy's deceased father, a non-party, 15% at fault. The jury awarded Plaintiff $43.8 million in compensatory damages. No punitive damages were awarded. The amount of the verdict attributable to Ford, based on the jury's allocation of fault, was $6,570,000.

In its motion for new trial, Ford argued, among other things, that the verdict was excessive, the result of passion, prejudice, or bias, and not supported by material evidence. Ford did not seek a remittitur, arguing that the necessary remittitur to bring the verdict within a reasonable range would destroy the verdict. The trial court denied the motion for new trial and approved the jury's verdict as thirteenth juror.

In the Court of Appeals, Ford argued that the verdict was excessive and asked the court to order a new trial, but did not request a remittitur. In a split decision, the court ruled that the verdict was excessive and remitted the verdict by 70.55%, reducing the total award to $12.9 million and Ford's liability to $1,935,000. *Meals ex rel. Meals v. Ford Motor Co.,* No. W2010-01493-COA-R3-CV, 2012 WL 1264454, at *21 (Tenn.Ct.App. Apr. 13, 2012). The majority explained that the non-economic damages awarded were reduced to "$8.6 million, an amount that is approximately equal to twice the proven quantifiable economic damages."

We granted Plaintiff's application for permission to appeal to review the remittitur suggested by the Court of Appeals and the reasonableness of the jury's award of damages.

II.

A.

We entrust the responsibility of resolving questions of disputed fact, including the assessment of damages, to the jury. An award of damages, which is intended to make a plaintiff whole, compensates the plaintiff for damage or injury caused by a defendant's wrongful conduct. A plaintiff may be compensated for any economic or pecuniary losses that naturally result from the defendant's wrongful conduct. *Id.* Economic damages include out-of-pocket medical expenses, future medical expenses, lost wages, and lost earning potential. The plaintiff bears the burden of proving damages to such a degree that, while perhaps not mathematically precise, will allow the jury to make a reasoned assessment of the plaintiff's injury and loss.

A plaintiff is also entitled to recover compensatory damages for non-economic loss or injury. *Elliott v. Cobb,* 320 S.W.3d 246, 247 (Tenn.2010). "Non-economic damages include pain and suffering, permanent impairment and/or disfigurement, and loss of enjoyment of life." *Id.* at 248 n. 1. Damages for pain and suffering are awarded for the physical and mental suffering that accompany an injury. Damages awarded for loss of enjoyment of life are intended to compensate a plaintiff for the impairment of the ability to enjoy the normal pleasures of living. Assigning a compensable, monetary value to non-economic damages can be difficult. The assessment of non-economic damages is not an exact science, nor is there a precise mathematical formula to apply in determining the amount of damages an injured party has incurred. Thus, a plaintiff is generally not required to prove the monetary value of non-economic damages.

The trial judge, charged with ensuring a fair trial, serves as an important check on a jury's discretion to award damages. One way the trial judge does this is by serving as the thirteenth juror. As thirteenth juror, the trial judge must independently weigh and review the evidence presented at trial to determine whether it preponderates in favor of the verdict and decide whether he or she agrees with and is satisfied with the jury's verdict. No verdict is valid unless approved by the trial judge acting as the thirteenth juror.

Generally, if the trial judge is not satisfied with the jury's verdict, the judge must set aside the verdict and order a new trial. If the trial judge's dissatisfaction, however, is based only upon the jury's award of damages, the trial judge may suggest a remittitur, which, if accepted by the plaintiff, would reduce the award to an amount the judge deems appropriate.[8] Tennessee Code Annotated section 20-10-102(a) (2009) authorizes the trial judge to suggest a remittitur:

> In all jury trials had in civil actions, after the verdict has been rendered and on motion for a new trial, *when the trial judge is of the opinion that the verdict in favor of a party should be reduced and a remittitur is suggested by the trial judge on that account,* with the proviso that in case the party in whose favor the verdict has been rendered refuses to make the remittitur, a new trial will be awarded, the party in whose favor such verdict has been rendered may make such remittitur under protest, and appeal from the action of the trial judge to the [C]ourt of [A]ppeals.
>
> (Emphasis added). Due to concerns of cost and efficiency, we have encouraged trial courts to cure excessive verdicts, whenever feasible, through the practice of remittitur, rather than by ordering a new trial. * * * A request for remittitur is implicit in a motion for a new trial and is a valid alternative to a new trial.

Trial judges may suggest adjustments to a jury's verdict even if the verdict is within the range of reasonableness. The range of reasonableness is determined by establishing the upper and lower limits of an award of damages that can be supported by material proof. *Ellis v. White Freightliner Corp.,* 603 S.W.2d 125, 126–27 (Tenn.1980). To determine whether a verdict is within the range of reasonableness, the trial judge must consider the credible proof at trial regarding the nature and extent of the injuries, pain and suffering, economic losses including past and future medical bills, lost wages and loss of earning capacity, age, and life expectancy. "When remittitur is the issue in a personal injury . . . case, the question is whether the amount of money awarded is excessive, which requires ascertainment of a figure that represents the point at which excessiveness begins." *Ellis,* 603 S.W.2d at 126. This will establish the upper limit of the range of reasonableness. An excessive verdict may be cured by remitting the sum by which the award exceeds that figure. The trial court may consider the amount awarded in

---

[8] The trial court's authority to suggest a remittitur of a jury's verdict rather than grant a new trial when it disagrees solely with the award of damages is not absolute. A suggested remittitur should not be so substantial as to destroy the jury's verdict. * * *

similar cases in determining whether a verdict is excessive. When the trial judge suggests a remittitur, the plaintiff has three options: accept the remittitur, refuse the remittitur and opt for a new trial, or accept the remittitur under protest and seek relief from the Court of Appeals.

The appellate court's standard of review depends on whether the trial judge suggested a remittitur or affirmed the verdict in his or her role as thirteenth juror. Where the trial court has suggested a remittitur,

> [t]he [C]ourt of [A]ppeals shall review the action of the trial court suggesting a remittitur using the standard of review provided for in [Tennessee Rule of Appellate Procedure] 13(d) applicable to decisions of the trial court sitting without a jury. If, in the opinion of the [C]ourt of [A]ppeals, the verdict of the jury should not have been reduced, but the judgment of the trial court is correct in other respects, the case shall be reversed to that extent, and judgment shall be rendered in the [C]ourt of [A]ppeals for the full amount originally awarded by the jury in the trial court.

Tenn.Code Ann. § 20-10-102(b). Where the trial court approves the verdict as thirteenth juror, the appellate courts maintain the statutory authority to suggest or require a remittitur on appeal. *See* Tenn. Code Ann. § 20-10-103(a) (2009). Specifically,

> if after the case was tried in the lower court with a jury and no remittitur was suggested by the trial judge, *a remittitur is first suggested or required in the [C]ourt of [A]ppeals,* on penalty of granting a new trial, then . . . the party in whose favor the verdict or judgment has been rendered may make the remittitur under protest in the [C]ourt of [A]ppeals, and take the case, by application for permission to appeal, for review upon that point, to the [S]upreme [C]ourt.

Id. § 20-10-103(a) (emphasis added).

Where the trial judge has approved the verdict in its role as thirteenth juror — as the trial court did in this case — the Court of Appeals' review of the verdict and its ability to suggest a remittitur is limited to a review of the record to determine whether the verdict is supported by material evidence. Material evidence is "evidence material to the question in controversy, which must necessarily enter into the consideration of the controversy and by itself, or in connection with the other evidence, be determinative of the case." *Knoxville Traction Co. v. Brown,* 115 Tenn. 323, 331, 89 S.W. 319, 321 (1905). An appellate court is required to take "the strongest legitimate view of all the evidence in favor of the verdict, assume the truth of all evidence that supports the verdict, allowing all reasonable inferences to sustain the verdict, and to discard all countervailing evidence." *Akers v. Prime Succession of Tenn., Inc.,* 387 S.W.3d 495, 501-02 (Tenn.2012) (quoting *Barkes v. River Park Hosp., Inc.,* 328 S.W.3d 829, 833 (Tenn.2010)). The material evidence analysis is very deferential to the award by the jury and the judgment of the trial court when it affirms the verdict as the thirteenth juror. ("[W]hen the trial judge has approved the verdict, the review in the Court of Appeals is subject to the rule that if there is *any* material evidence to support the award, it should not be disturbed." (emphasis added)). "It matters not a whit where the weight or preponderance of the evidence lies under a material evidence review." *Hohenberg Bros. Co. v. Mo. Pac. R.R. Co.,* 586 S.W.2d 117, 119-20 (Tenn.Ct.App. 1979). "It is simply a search of the record to ascertain if material evidence is present to support the verdict." *Id.* Because the material evidence standard lies at the foundation of the right to trial by jury, if there is material evidence to support a jury verdict, the appellate courts must affirm it. *See* Tenn. Const. art. I, § 6; *see also Grandstaff v. Hawks,* 36 S.W.3d 482, 497 (Tenn.Ct.App.2000) ("We have a duty to uphold a jury's verdict whenever possible.").

The Court of Appeals' authority to suggest a remittitur when the trial court has affirmed the verdict is far more circumscribed than that of the trial court. If the Court of Appeals suggests a remittitur, the plaintiff may either accept the remitted amount, opt for a new trial, or accept the remitted amount under protest and apply to this Court for permission to appeal.

B.

In this case, the Court of Appeals reduced the jury's award of damages by 70.55% based on its conclusion that the award of non-economic damages of $39.5 million demonstrated sympathy and was excessive. The Court of Appeals reached this conclusion without discussing the evidence regarding Plaintiff's damages and by relying on the amount of the verdict in *Potter v. Ford Motor Co.,* 213 S.W.3d 264 (Tenn.Ct.App.2006). We respectfully disagree with the conclusion reached by the Court of Appeals.

In our review of the material evidence supporting the award of compensatory damages, we first consider the nature and extent of Billy's injuries. It is not disputed that he suffered a serious, life-altering, permanent injury. He had a fractured and dislocated lumbar vertebra, which caused him to be permanently paralyzed from the waist down. He sustained a closed head injury, a collapsed lung, internal bleeding, and severe abdominal and intestinal injuries. He spent fifty-four days in the hospital and underwent a number of surgical procedures, including surgery to remove a significant portion of his small intestine and resection the bowel, surgeries to drain blood from the abdomen and remove necrotic tissue, and a cystoscopy to evacuate bladder sediment. He developed an abdominal abscess which had to be drained and had multiple infections which required the administration of antibiotics. He spent twenty-five days in a rehabilitation center learning how to adapt to his impairment and receiving physical therapy.

After his discharge from the hospital and rehabilitation center, Billy's medical issues and treatment did not end. To treat his condition of progressive kyphosis, he had to have rods, screws, and wires surgically installed in his back and a spinal fusion performed. His paraplegia causes him to suffer from pressure sores, which on occasion become infected and require medical treatment. He requires physical therapy to protect against contractures in his ankles, knees, and hips. He suffers from atrophy in his legs, and his toes are misshapened and claw-like. He occasionally suffers from kidney stones; he has had to undergo two surgeries to remove kidney stones. He sometimes gets burned or cut, but cannot feel the pain associated with the injuries and does not know he needs to seek treatment. As he ages, his shoulders and wrists will require medical treatment due to overuse. He also has a weakened immune system and is therefore more susceptible to illness and slower to recover.

Likewise, there is no question that Billy has experienced a significant amount of mental and physical pain and suffering as a result of these serious injuries. He was conscious when emergency workers arrived at the wreck scene, removed him from the vehicle, and rushed him to the hospital. While he was hospitalized, he complained of pain, cried, moaned, and was restless and irritable. He became withdrawn and depressed. He did not socialize as he once did. He would have outbursts "over the littlest things" and be angry with his mother.

Plaintiff's economic damages totaled approximately $4.3 million. Medical bills incurred were $552,920.28. Future medical bills were calculated, when reduced to present day value, as being between $1,300,000 and $1,479,340.80. Lost earning capacity, when reduced to present day value, was determined to be $1,429,000, if Billy entered the workforce with a high school diploma, or $2,262,789, if he received a college degree.

The next element of damages to be considered is the impact of Billy's injuries on his enjoyment of life. The impact is clearly substantial. Before the wreck, he was a happy, active, normal six-year-old boy who enjoyed playing outside and going fishing. He was a good student and an all-star baseball player; he enjoyed school and his friends. After the wreck, he was paralyzed from the waist down and confined to a wheelchair, without the ability to ever run, walk, or play baseball again. He has no control over his bowel or bladder. He must use a catheter in order to urinate and experiences frequent urinary tract infections. His bowel regimen takes up to an hour a day and requires a suppository and manual stimulation. He is likely impotent and his sexual functioning impaired. Following the wreck, he was not able to finish the school year and had to repeat the first grade. His grades dropped and he had little interest in his studies. He has received psychiatric treatment and will likely need more counseling in the future to assist with the emotional issues caused by his paralysis. As a testament to his determination and resilience, and with the support of his mother and medical professionals, Billy has gradually adapted to his impaired condition. The Meals family moved to Murfreesboro, Tennessee, so that they could be closer to family members and so that Billy could have access to more opportunities. He enjoys participating in a wheelchair basketball league.

Billy, who was six years old at the time of the wreck, was fourteen years old at the time of trial and had a life expectancy of 55.79 years.

Our review of the evidence leads us to the conclusion that Plaintiff is entitled to a substantial award of damages. Billy suffered a catastrophic injury and will never recover the ability to walk or engage in the activities he participated in prior to the wreck. He spent fifty-four days in the hospital and twenty-five days in a rehabilitation facility. He underwent numerous surgical procedures, including removal and resection of part of his small intestine and a spinal fusion with the insertion of rods and screws. He has had frequent urinary tract infections and other conditions that required medical attention and the administration of antibiotics. He will continue to have medical problems and require medical treatment. He no longer has control over his bowel or bladder. Much of his small intestine has been removed. He will likely never father a child or have normal sexual functioning. His economic damages, including past medical bills, future medical bills, and lost earning capacity total $4.3 million. Non-economic damages, including pain and suffering, permanent impairment or disfigurement, and loss of enjoyment of life, past and future, are not as easy to determine. The jury returned a general verdict of $43.8 million in damages.[11] Because this was a general verdict, with no

---

[11] In closing argument, Plaintiff's counsel did not ask for a specific amount, but itemized the economic damages and reiterated the ways in which Billy was affected by the wreck. Plaintiff's counsel argued that Ford paid one of its expert witnesses $1,110.75 per day for her work, suggesting that Billy's remaining days were worth just as much. For his life expectancy of 20,363.35 days, this would total $22,618,591.01. Counsel for Ford, however, took an "all-or-nothing" approach and gave the jury little direction in assessing damages, arguing in closing:

> Now, I don't believe that you will get to this question with regard to damages. It's Question Number 6 [on the verdict form]. It's on Page 3. But if you do, *I have nothing to say.* We have never in this

apportionment between economic and non-economic damages, we can only presume that the jury awarded the Plaintiff $39.5 million in non-economic damages.[12]

A jury has wide latitude in assessing non-economic damages. We trust jurors to use their personal experiences and sensibilities to value the intangible harms such as pain, suffering, and the inability to engage in normal activities. This task is made more difficult in a catastrophic injury case. It is not our role to second-guess the jury and to substitute our judgment; but it is our role to protect against a verdict that is excessive. When determining whether a damage award is excessive and should be reduced, we carefully review the material evidence supporting the damage award. In addition, we can look to verdicts in similar cases. Our review of verdicts in similar cases must be approached with some caution. First, we recognize that by reviewing verdicts in published opinions, we are not reviewing the entire pool of damage awards. Cases resolved by settlement and/or mediation are not included in the pool of damage awards, and their absence can skew the results. Second, we must take care to only consider cases that are "similar" — presumably involving a similar plaintiff with similar injuries. Third, courts should take inflation and the reduced value of the dollar into account when considering these verdicts. Finally, courts should be mindful that when looking at other jury verdicts, each case must be judged on its own particular facts.

The Court of Appeals relied on *Potter,* 213 S.W.3d 264, as a similar case to support its decision to suggest a remittitur; however, we do not find *Potter* to be similar. In *Potter,* a forty-two-year-old woman's vehicle slid off a wet roadway and struck a tree. She sustained a spinal fracture when her seat-back collapsed, and she was paralyzed from the waist down. The jury returned a $10 million verdict, finding the automobile manufacturer to be 70% at fault. The issue on appeal was liability, not damages. There was no discussion in *Potter* as to the amount of economic or non-economic damages, nor of the forty-two-year-old plaintiff's life expectancy, which we presume was much shorter than Billy's life expectancy.

Ford cites to other Tennessee cases involving lower jury verdicts. In *Flax v. DaimlerChrysler Corp.,* 272 S.W.3d 521, 525, 527 (Tenn.2008), a jury awarded a $5 million verdict for the wrongful death of an infant. But a wrongful death case involves different elements of damages, and is therefore not comparable. Moreover, the amount of compensatory damages was not challenged on appeal and there is no discussion of the evidence which supported the award.

In *Palanki ex rel. Palanki v. Vanderbilt University,* 215 S.W.3d 380, 384 (Tenn.Ct.App.2006), a jury awarded a $16.4 million verdict in a case where a doctor negligently removed 90% of a child's bladder. The trial judge suggested a remittitur to $6.5 million, which was accepted

---

> case questioned that Billy is hurt and that he has limitations in his life that are tragic and that should never have happened to him as a result of John Harris running like an idiot into his family on the day of this accident. We have never questioned that.

So if you get to this, you have the information about how he is hurt. And you have heard from [a witness] about how people with limitations also have opportunities. You have all that information. *I have nothing else to say about it.* (Emphasis added.)

[12] Effective October 1, 2011, the Tennessee Civil Justice Act of 2011, Tennessee Code Annotated section 29-39-101 to -104 (2012), limits recovery of non-economic damages in a civil suit where the injury or loss is catastrophic in nature — including a spinal cord injury resulting in paraplegia or quadriplegia, *see id.* § 29-39-102(c) — to $1 million, *id.* § 29-39-102(c).

under protest and appealed. The Court of Appeals applied a preponderance of the evidence standard and affirmed the trial court's suggestion of remittitur. *Palanki* did not involve a spinal cord injury. Although the child was unable to urinate on his own and had to self-catheterize, his injury did not limit his ability to engage in normal life activities, have friends, get married, have a normal sex life, father children, receive an education, or earn a living. The child's economic damages totaled approximately $417,000, whereas Billy's economic damages totaled $4.3 million. In addition, Billy's injuries had a much greater impact on his daily activities and prospects for the future. *Palanki* also involved the trial court's suggestion of remittitur, *id.* at 385, which presents a different standard of review for the appellate courts than a case where the trial court affirmed the verdict as the thirteenth juror. *See* Tenn.Code Ann. § 20-10-102(b).

In *Duran v. Hyundai Motor America, Inc.*, 271 S.W.3d 178 (Tenn.Ct.App.2008), a fifty-year-old woman who suffered second and third-degree burns and an inhalation injury after her vehicle left the roadway and caught fire was awarded a $3 million verdict against the vehicle manufacturer. The trial judge suggested remitting the verdict to $2 million based on the facts that the plaintiff's medical bills were only $41,456.86, yet she was awarded $200,000 in medical expenses, and that the plaintiff had only sued for $2 million, yet was awarded $3 million. The Court of Appeals ruled that the reduced verdict was supported by material evidence and affirmed the suggestion of remittitur. The court explained that "whether [it] would have awarded [the plaintiff] $1,958,543.14 in non-economic damages is not the point. The assessment of these subjective damages was for the jury to decide in the first instance and then for the trial judge." *Id.* The court also noted that the remitted verdict consisted of $1,958,543.14 in noneconomic damages, which was not unreasonable given that the plaintiff's lung condition and decreased lung capacity interfered with her ability to work and engage in regular daily activities and would continue for the rest of her life expectancy of twenty-seven years. A lung injury, while serious, is not similar to a spinal cord injury resulting in paraplegia.

Ford also cited to cases from other jurisdictions in support of its argument that the verdict in this case is excessive. Only two of these cases involve a spinal cord injury. In *Auer ex rel. Auer v. New York,* 289 A.D.2d 626, 733 N.Y.S.2d 784, 785-86 (N.Y.App.Div.2001), an eighteen-year-old woman, paralyzed in a car wreck, was awarded $18,952,486 in compensatory damages. The appellate court increased the award for pain and suffering to $1.5 million for a total award of $20,456,486. In *Simon v. American Crescent Elevator Co.,* 767 So.2d 64, 67 (La.Ct.App. 2000), a man, rendered a paraplegic after he was injured at work, was awarded $6.4 million for pain and suffering, $1 million for medical and rehabilitation expenses, and $1.2 million of lost wages — totaling $8.6 million in compensatory damages. Additionally, his wife was awarded $900,000 and each of his five children was awarded $250,000 for loss of consortium. The trial court denied the defendant's motion for remittitur, and the appellate court affirmed the awards of damages.

Our research reveals other cases that involved spinal cord injuries and resulted in substantial verdicts. *See, e.g., Gutierrez ex rel. Gutierrez v. United States,* 323 Fed.Appx 493, 493–94 (9th Cir.2009) (awarding $31 million in non-economic damages to a four-year-old child who was rendered a quadriplegic as a result of a car wreck); *Foradori v. Harris,* 523 F.3d 477, 481, 484-85, 501 (5th Cir.2008) (awarding a verdict of $20,881,884.41 to a fifteen-year-old boy with a life expectancy of fifty-three years who became a quadriplegic after sustaining injuries during an altercation); *Okraynets v. Metro. Transp. Auth.,* 555 F.Supp.2d 420, 438, 454 (S.D.N.Y.2008) (suggesting a reduction of a compensatory damages award from $44,706,444 to $30,471,710 for a man who was paralyzed after an on-the-job injury and had a life expectancy of thirty-nine years); *Karlsson v. Ford Motor Co.,* 140 Cal.App.4th 1202, 45 Cal.Rptr.3d 265, 268-69 (2006) (awarding $30.45 million in compensatory damages to a five-year-old boy who sustained a spinal cord injury during a car wreck and the parties stipulated to reduce the total verdict to $30,341,636.50 based on findings of comparative fault); *Toe v. Cooper Tire & Rubber Co.,* 834 N.W.2d 8, No. 11-1588, 2013 WL 1749739, at *3 (Iowa Ct.App. Apr. 24, 2013) (awarding $28.4 million in compensatory damages to a woman who was paralyzed due to injuries sustained in a car wreck).

After carefully reviewing the evidence in the light most favorable to Plaintiff, assuming the truth of all that supports it, allowing all reasonable inferences and discarding any inferences to the contrary, affording all due respect for the life-changing injuries Billy suffered, and considering verdicts in similar cases, we conclude that this verdict was supported by material evidence and is within the range of reasonableness. We recognize, however, that the amount of this verdict rests at the high end of the range of reasonableness but is not excessive. This amount reflects an award of $4.3 million in economic damages and $39.5 million in non-economic damages for a young man who, at the age of six, sustained catastrophic injuries and has a life expectancy of 55.79 years. The Court of Appeals erred in its analysis of the material evidence and its reliance on *Potter.* We therefore reverse the judgment of the Court of Appeals and reinstate the jury's verdict.

Conclusion

The judgment of the Court of Appeals is reversed and the jury's verdict of $43.8 million is reinstated, with Ford's share of the verdict being $6,570,000. The case is remanded to the Circuit Court for Shelby County for further proceedings as necessary. Costs of this appeal are taxed to Ford Motor Company and its surety, execution for which may issue if necessary.

Notes and Questions

1. In comparative negligence jurisdictions, the jury allocates responsibility for paying the verdict between those found to be negligent in proportion to their percentage of the negligence. Where a portion of the fault is allocated to the plaintiff, the plaintiff's share necessarily goes uncollected, but in *Meals* the portion allocated to the plaintiff's father's estate might be at least partially covered by his car's liability insurance.

But what happens when a party cannot pay his share? In this case, assume that Mr. Harris's estate was insolvent. Any unpaid share is a "defaulting share." Jurisdictions that do not have comparative negligence have "joint and several liability" — an allocation rule we first saw in the causation chapter when we read Summers v. Tice. Under this regime, every defendant found liable is responsible for the entire amount of a judgment, so the plaintiff will typically elect to collect from the most solvent of the defendants until the judgment is satisfied. Any defendant paying more that that defendant's per capita share can then seek "contribution" from non-paying or underpaying defendants in an amount sufficient so that the paying defendant ends up out only its per capita share — if they can pay. If they cannot, risk of the defaulted shares rests entirely on the solvent defendants.

Comparative negligence jurisdictions have various rules for allocating these amounts which are called "defaulting shares." One system is the application of joint and several liability but only to parties whose initial negligence share exceeded a statutorily set percentage, commonly 50%. Another system involves reallocation of the share of the defaulting defendant among the remaining parties according to their respective percentage shares of the negligence. So, if four parties each are 25% negligent and one is the plaintiff and another defaults, the 25% defaulted share is equally allocated among the remaining parties, with each getting 8 1/3% added to their share. The result leaves the non-defaulting parties each responsible for one-third of the verdict, and the plaintiff able to collect two thirds of the verdict from the two solvent defendants, and unable to collect the remaining third assigned to the plaintiff after the reallocated amount was added to the initial 25% the plaintiff would not be able to collect. In some comparative negligence jurisdictions, only economic damages are subject to reallocation and the non-economic damages are allowed to default. Considering these various systems, what are the arguments for and against them? Would another system strike you as fairer?

2. Some claims for non-economic losses are commonly but not universally recognized. For example, most if not all jurisdictions permit the injured plaintiff's spouse to recover "loss of consortium" damages when the injuries interfere with conjugal relations and the companionship and services formerly provided by the injured partner. Generally, these are seen as derivative claims and must be brought at the same time and in the same case as the injured spouse's claims. Because the loss of consortium claim arose in the context of the spousal relationship, claims arising from injuries to other family members were traditionally rejected. However, states are increasingly recognizing loss of consortium claims arising out of the parent-child relationship. These may also be called loss of companionship claims. *See, e.g.*, Mass. Gen. L. Ann. 231 §85x, Loss of consortium of a dependent child; cause of action ("the parents of a minor child or an adult child who is dependent on his parents for support shall have a cause of action for loss of consortium of the child who has been seriously injured against any person who is legally responsible for causing such injury); Rolf v. Tri State Motor Transit Company, 745 N.E.2d 424 (Oh. 2001) (adult emancipated children can recover for loss of parental consortium). *Cf.*, Fernandez v. Walgreen Hastings Co., 968 P.2d 774 (N.M. 1998) (grandparent can recover for loss of consortium of minor child). Claims for damages for loss of filial (sibling) consortium are not faring as well. *See, e.g.*, Bobick v. United States Fidelity and Guaranty Company, 790 N.E.2d 653 (Mass. 2003) ("We have never recognized the right of a sibling to bring a loss of consortium claim and, in fact, have repeatedly rejected attempts to extend such claims past an actual spouse or parent-child relationship); Ford Motor Co. v. Miles, 967 S.W.2d 377, 383-84 (Tex.1998) (allowing spousal and parent-child consortium claims but rejecting filial loss of consortium). *Cf.*, McMorris v. McMorris, 654 So.2d 742 (La. App. 1995) (explaining that loss of consortium claims may be brought by anyone entitled to sue under state's wrongful death statute including "spouse and children, then parents, and then siblings").

Problem Ten: Working Compensatory Damages

Your firm does insurance defense work. You've received this fact memo from the adjustor who investigated the case. She says that the only contested issue will be damages. She asks for a report, based on what she has given you, analyzing the damages potentially available to the plaintiff and identifying any other information that would be helpful to finalizing that analysis.

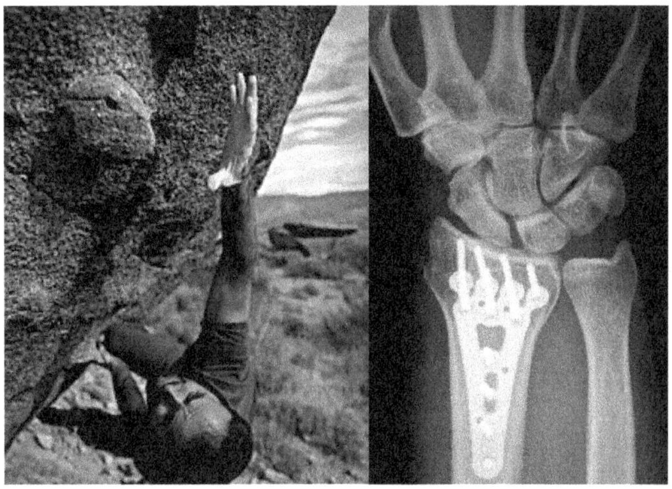

A year and a half ago, Rice was home for his tenth high school reunion. After finishing high school, he decided college was not for him even though his SATs put him in the top 1% of test takers, he had excellent grades, and he was being recruited by Division I schools for track.

Instead, according to his business's web site, he spent two years wandering the planet – visiting over 80 countries. He ended that journey in Spain where he studied with a master Spanish guitar maker until he returned to the U.S. Once back, Rice set up a small shop where only he worked. According to *Guitar Magazine*, Rice sold all the custom acoustic guitars he could make for upwards of $15,000 a guitar. Before the accident, he made about two guitars a month. His tax return, provided by his lawyer, indicates he netted over $120,000 every year. Rice had not married and had no children. His main hobby was free climbing sheer rock faces. See his photo below.

Driving his pickup truck to the reunion dance, our insured ran a stop sign and hit Rice's side of the car. Medical records provided by Rice's attorney quote Rice as having seen the pickup coming just before impact and putting his hands up to protect himself. The impact of his hands with the door of the car fractured his right (dominant) wrist. Glass from the shattered car door window left an obvious but not deep one inch scar on his left cheek about half way between the corner of his mouth and his ear lobe. No plastic surgery is recommended.

The fracture required one surgery to set the bones with hardware and screws (see photo below) and physical therapy three times a week for two months. At the end of his physical therapy, Rice was told that he had reached maximum medical improvement — his wrist was as good as it was going to get. Rice's health insurer paid $147,000 for his care and Rice had a $3,000 co-pay.

Even though the surgery was a success, Rice's hand will never be as flexible as it once was. Again according to his web site, the lack of flexibility in his wrist affected both the quality and quantity of guitars he could make to the point that he shut down his business four months after he finished therapy. He is currently looking for work and considering college but petrified by the expense. Rock climbing, even with ropes, is now impossible.

The medical records assign Rice 35% permanent partial impairment of his right upper extremity (arm) based on the impairment to his wrist. His discharge summary from orthopedic care says he might need to have the hardware in his wrist removed if the screws loosen, and that he will likely have arthritis in that wrist joint.

III. WRONGFUL DEATH DAMAGES

DiDONATO v. WORTMAN
358 S.E.2d 489 (N.C. 1987)

EXUM, Chief Justice.

This is an action for the wrongful death of a stillborn child. Plaintiff administrator alleges that defendant doctors provided prenatal care to the child's mother, Norma DiDonato. Defendants estimated that the child would be born on 10 October 1982. On 26 October 1982 the child had not yet been born, and Mrs. DiDonato underwent an examination that revealed a healthy fetal heartbeat. Four days later the heartbeat had stopped and Mrs. DiDonato delivered a stillborn baby by cesarean section. Plaintiff alleges that defendants' negligence was a proximate cause of the child's stillbirth.

The sole question presented by this appeal is whether N.C.G.S. § 28A-18-2, North Carolina's Wrongful Death Act, allows recovery for the death of a viable but unborn child. We conclude that it does, and we therefore reverse the decision of the Court of Appeals. We hold, however, that the damages available in any such action will be limited to those that are not purely speculative. In addition, we hold that the action for wrongful death of a viable fetus must be joined with any action based on the same facts brought by the decedent's parents.

I.

In North Carolina, as in most states, actions for wrongful death exist solely by virtue of statute. This Court's primary task, therefore, is to determine whether the state's wrongful death statute permits recovery for the death of a viable fetus.

. . .

A.

The Wrongful Death Act states, in pertinent part:

> (a) When the death of a person is caused by a wrongful act, neglect or default of another, such as would, if the injured person had lived, have entitled him to an action

for damages therefor, the person or corporation that would have been so liable . . . shall be liable to an action for damages. . . . The amount recovered in such action . . . shall be disposed of as provided in the Intestate Succession Act.

(b) Damages recoverable for death by wrongful act include:

(1) Expenses for care, treatment and hospitalization incident to the injury resulting in death;

(2) Compensation for pain and suffering of the decedent;

(3) The reasonable funeral expenses of the decedent;

(4) The present monetary value of the decedent to the persons entitled to receive the damages recovered, including but not limited to compensation for the loss of the reasonably expected:

a. Net income of the decedent,

b. Services, protection, care and assistance of the decedent, whether voluntary or obligatory, to the persons entitled to the damages recovered,

c. Society, companionship, comfort, guidance, kindly offices and advice of the decedent to the persons entitled to the damages recovered;

(5) Such punitive damages as the decedent could have recovered had he survived, and punitive damages for wrongfully causing the death of the decedent through maliciousness, willful or wanton injury, or gross negligence;

(6) Nominal damages when the jury so finds.

N.C.G.S. § 28A-18-2 (1984).

In plain English, an action for wrongful death exists if the decedent could have maintained an action for negligence or some other misconduct if he had survived. The real party in interest in any wrongful death action is the beneficiary for whom the recovery is sought. In the case of a stillborn fetus, the beneficiaries of a wrongful death action will necessarily be the child's parents, unless they too are dead.

The facts in this case require us to determine whether the word "person" in the Wrongful Death Act includes a viable fetus. The statute does not provide a clear-cut answer to this question, but case law regarding recovery by children for fetal injuries is instructive. Tort claims brought by children to recover for fetal injuries are recognized in virtually every state, including North Carolina. It would be logical and consistent with these decisions, and would further the policy of deterring dangerous conduct that underlies them, to allow such claims when the fetus does not survive. Courts construing wrongful death statutes similar to N.C.G.S. § 28A-18-2 generally have concluded that a viable fetus is among the class of "persons" contemplated by the statute's authors.

It is unlikely that the legislature would want to preclude recovery for the death of a fetus when recovery for a fetal injury not resulting in death is permitted. The unborn child's parents are the real parties in interest here, and they seek compensation for the complete loss of, rather than mere injury to, their offspring. Surely the legislature would find their claim as compelling as that of a child who seeks to recover for a prenatally inflicted but nonfatal injury, the consequences of which could vary from moderate to severe.

The legislature, moreover, has indicated that for purposes of the wrongful death statute, a "person" is someone who possesses "human life." The preamble to the most recent revision of N.C.G.S. § 28A-18-2 stated:

> WHEREAS, *human life* is inherently valuable; and
>
> WHEREAS, the present statute is so written and construed that damages recoverable from a person who has caused death by a wrongful act are effectively limited to such figure as can be calculated from the expected earnings of the deceased, which is far from an adequate measure of the value of *human life;* Now, therefore, [the damages available for the wrongful death of a person were redefined].

1969 N.C.Sess.Laws ch. 215, preamble (emphasis added). A viable fetus, whatever its legal status might be, is undeniably alive and undeniably human. It is, by definition, capable of life independent of its mother. A viable fetus is genetically complete and can be taxonomically distinguished from non-human life forms. Again, this is some evidence that a viable fetus is a person under the wrongful death statute.

We conclude that although the face of the wrongful death statute does not conclusively answer the question before us, case law concerning recovery for fetal injuries and the amending legislation quoted above both point toward acknowledging fetal personhood.

B.

The Anglo-American history of wrongful death actions begins with the English case of *Baker v. Bolton,* 170 Eng.Rep. 1033 (1808), which held that at common law there was no right to an action for wrongful death. Parliament responded to this holding — albeit somewhat belatedly — by enacting a wrongful death statute known as Lord Campbell's Act in 1846. All fifty American legislatures have since followed suit. Prosser & Keeton on Torts 945 (1984).

North Carolina adopted its first wrongful death statute shortly before the Civil War. At that time, this Court probably would not have recognized an action to recover for the death of a stillborn child. Until 1946, nearly all states denied recovery to persons who had suffered prenatal injuries, whether they survived or not. Following World War II, however, there occurred "'the most spectacular abrupt reversal of a well settled rule in the whole history of the law of torts.'" *Id.* (quoting Prosser on Torts § 56 (1964)). Courts everywhere began allowing children to bring actions for injuries they suffered prior to birth. In 1949, Minnesota became the first state to recognize an action for wrongful death brought on behalf of a stillborn child. Since then, more than thirty other states and the District of Columbia have recognized a cause of action for infants negligently or intentionally killed *in utero.* Comment, *Wrong Without a Remedy—North Carolina and the Wrongful Death of a Stillborn,* 9 Campbell L.Rev. 93, 110-11 (1986).

Before 1969, plaintiffs in North Carolina wrongful death actions could recover only "such damages as are a fair and just compensation for the pecuniary injury resulting from such death." N.C.G.S. § 28-174 (superseded by N.C.G.S. § 28A-18-2(b)). The amount recoverable for this "pecuniary injury" was determined by deducting the probable cost of the decedent's living expenses from his probable gross income during the years he would have been expected to live had it not been for the defendant's tort. This income-focused measure of damages severely limited recovery in many cases and eliminated it altogether in others. Often, evidence of pecuniary loss was unobtainable where the decedent was a child, homemaker or handicapped person. Wrongful death actions brought on behalf of stillborn infants were denied because the pecuniary injuries stemming from the prenatal death of a viable child were "sheer speculation." *Gay v. Thompson,* 266 N.C. 394, 402, 146 S.E.2d 425, 429 (1966).

The legislature amended the Wrongful Death Act in 1969 by passing what was popularly known as "The Wife Bill." The purpose of the amendment was to permit recovery for losses unrelated to the decedent's actual monetary income. Since 1969 the wrongful death statute has permitted beneficiaries to recover, in addition to lost income, compensation for the decedent's medical and funeral expenses, his pain and suffering, and loss of the decedent's services, protection, care, assistance, society, companionship, comfort, guidance, kindly offices and advice, among other things. Punitive and nominal damages are also available.

The legislature's 1969 expansion of the recovery permitted in wrongful death actions substantially undercut the rationale for this Court's earlier decision in *Gay.* Actions for the wrongful death of a fetus were disallowed in that case because the plaintiff could not prove "pecuniary injury" — that is, loss of income — without resorting to excessive speculation. Damages available under the amended statute are no longer limited, however, to lost income. The statute now permits recovery for such things as funeral expenses, which can be precisely calculated. Thus, it is plain that *Gay* should not control the outcome of this case.

The original purpose of our Wrongful Death Act was to change the common law rule of no recovery for the deaths of persons victimized by tortfeasors. The statute provides compensation to beneficiaries of the decedent's estate for their loss, and helps to deter dangerous conduct. As Justice Cardozo said fifty years ago:

> Death statutes have their roots in dissatisfaction with the archaisms of the [common law rule of no liability]. It would be a misfortune if a narrow or grudging process of construction were to exemplify and perpetuate the very evils to be remedied. There are times when uncertain words are to be wrought into consistency and unity with a legislative policy which is itself a source of law, a new generative impulse transmitted to the legal system.

Van Beeck v. Sabine Towing *Co.,* 300 U.S. 342, 350-51, 57 S.Ct. 452, 456, 81 L.Ed. 685, 690 (1937) (quoted in *O'Grady,* 654 S.W.2d at 909).

The language of our wrongful death statute, its legislative history, and recognition of the statute's broadly remedial objectives compel us to conclude that any uncertainty in the meaning of the word "person" should be resolved in favor of permitting an action to recover for the destruction of a viable fetus *en ventre sa mere*. . . .

II.

Although the Court has determined that N.C.G.S. § 28A-18-2 permits plaintiff to maintain an action for wrongful death in this case, the matter does not end there. Damages available under the statute are not automatic; they are what the legislature will permit the beneficiaries to recover *provided those damages can be proved.* The law disfavors — and in fact prohibits — recovery for damages based on sheer speculation. Damages must be proved to a reasonable level of certainty, and may not be based on pure conjecture. *Norwood v. Carter,* 242 N.C. 152, 156, 87 S.E.2d 2, 5 (1955) ("No substantial recovery may be based on mere guesswork or inference . . . without evidence of facts, circumstances, and data justifying an inference that the damages awarded are just and reasonable compensation for the injury suffered."). Damage awards based on sheer speculation would render the wrongful death statute punitive in its effect, which is not what the legislature intended.

This Court has said that the "pecuniary injury" suffered by a stillborn child — that is, its loss of income — could be determined only through sheer speculation. Before 1969 this was sufficient reason to deny the action entirely; the wrongful death statute, as it was then construed, did not permit recovery of any other damages. Now that the damages available under the statute have been expanded, the rationale for denying the action in *Gay* has largely evaporated — *but the lesson of that case concerning the income-related losses of stillborn children remains valid.* As another court has said in this context:

> On the death of a very young child . . . at least some facts can be shown to aid in estimating damages as, for example, its mental and physical condition.
>
> But not even these scant proofs can be offered when the child is stillborn. It is virtually impossible to predict whether the unborn child, but for its death, would have been capable of giving pecuniary benefit to its survivors. We recognize that the damages in any wrongful death action are to some extent uncertain and speculative. But our liberality in allowing substantial damages where the proofs are relatively speculative should not preclude us from drawing a line where the speculation becomes unreasonable.

Graf, 43 N.J. at 310, 204 A.2d at 144. When a child is stillborn we can know nothing about its intelligence, abilities, interests and other factors relevant to the monetary contribution it might — or might not — someday have made to the beneficiaries in a wrongful death action. A jury attempting to calculate an award for such damages would be reduced to "sheer speculation." *Gay,* 266 N.C. at 402, 146 S.E.2d at 429. We therefore hold that lost income damages normally available under N.C.G.S. § 28A-18-2(b)(4)a. cannot be recovered in an action for the wrongful death of a stillborn child. To hold otherwise would require us to overrule *Gay,* which we believe was correctly decided.

We also hold that damages normally recovered under N.C.G.S. § 28A-18-2(b)(4)b. & c. — loss of services, companionship, advice and the like — will not be available in an action for the wrongful death of a viable fetus. The reasons are the same as in the case of pecuniary loss. When a child is stillborn we simply cannot know anything about its personality and other traits relevant to what kind of companion it might have been and what kind of services it might have provided. An award of damages covering these kinds of losses would necessarily be based on speculation rather than reason.

Recovery for the mother's mental anguish at having lost her child presumably will be available in a personal injury action brought in her own right.

The Court is not convinced that the pain and suffering of a fetus can ever be satisfactorily proved, but given recent advances in medical technology relating to the observation and treatment of life *in utero,* we cannot foreclose the possibility as a matter of law. Thus, damages for the pain and suffering of a decedent fetus are recoverable if they can be reasonably established. Medical and funeral expenses, as well as punitive and nominal damages, are just as susceptible of proof here as in any other tort case, and should be allowed where appropriate.

. . .

IV.

To summarize: The legislature does not appear to have directly considered the question presented in this case when it adopted and amended North Carolina's wrongful death statute. Therefore, it is the Court's obligation to construe the statute in a way that is consistent with both its language and the broad purposes it was intended to serve. An examination of that language and those purposes leads us to conclude that the death of a viable fetus falls within the purview of N.C.G.S. § 28A-18-2, and that this action must be allowed insofar as plaintiff seeks to recover damages that are not based on sheer speculation. Plaintiff's action for wrongful death must, however, be joined with any action based on the same facts brought by the decedent's parents.

REVERSED AND REMANDED.

MARTIN, Justice, concurring in part and dissenting in part.

I concur in the holding of the majority that a viable unborn child is a "person" within the meaning of the wrongful death statute, N.C.G.S. § 28A-18-2(b). . . .

. . .

I must dissent, however, from the opinion of the majority with respect to damages. The majority correctly holds that a viable unborn fetus is a "person" within the meaning of the wrongful death statute, then inexplicably attempts to cut away part of the statutory damages provided within the statute. This the Court cannot do. The plaintiff in this wrongful death action is no different from any other plaintiff; the plaintiff is entitled to recover such damages as are proved in accordance with the law. The trial judge *may* rule that plaintiff has failed to prove one or more elements of damages as a matter of law, but it is not for this Court to bar plaintiff from *trying* to prove all damages recoverable under the statute.

As I stated with regard to the limitation of damages in *Jackson v. Bumgardner,* 318 N.C. 172, 347 S.E.2d 743 (1986):

> The better practice would be to allow the trial court in the first instance to address the issue of what damages are recoverable. The appellate division would then have a full evidentiary record upon which to make a proper analysis as to damages rather than attempting to formulate an abstract rule. The majority has decided damage issues that have not been presented to us upon an evidentiary record and which may never be so

> presented. Sound judicial discipline would dictate withholding such momentous decisions until all available evidence and arguments can be presented to the Court. Precipitous judgments are to be avoided.

Id. at 189, 347 S.E.2d at 753 (Martin, J., concurring in part and dissenting in part). The legislature has defined the possible elements of damage recoverable in a wrongful death action and must have intended that the same rule of damages apply to all such actions. It is not the prerogative [*sic*]of this Court to usurp a legislative function by rewriting the statute to change the rule of damages.

Nor can I adhere to the rule announced in the majority opinion that a wrongful death action based upon the death of a viable unborn fetus *must* be tried with any action the parents may have arising out of the fetal death. This is a matter better left to the discretion of the trial judge. There are many factors to be considered in deciding this question, such as the identity of parties and the negligent act or acts involved. Defenses available to defendant or defendants as to each plaintiff, time constraints within which to institute the different actions, the measurement of damages, and other factors, may vary. Protecting a defendant from paying double punitive damages on the same evidence can be accomplished on a case-by-case basis. The blanket rule required in the majority opinion would be at best unworkable and at worst unjust.

MITCHELL, J., joins in this concurring and dissenting opinion.

WEBB, Justice, dissenting. [Omitted]

Notes and Questions

1. In *DiDonato* both the defendants' negligence and the plaintiff's death were before birth. If the death occurred a day after birth as a result of the same negligence, would the damages available to the plaintiff be different? If you were a legislator and disagreed with how the majority ruled on this issue, what changes would you propose and why?

2. There are two causes of action to be considered when discussing wrongful death claims. The first is the "survival action" — the decedent's own claim for damages up to the time of his death. Such damages include, for example, medical bills and pain and suffering, just as they would have had the decedent survived. The second is the wrongful death claim — the action for the losses of those other than the decedent caused by the decedent's death. These two actions are joined in North Carolina and many other states and are generically called "wrongful death actions."

3. Two critical questions in wrongful death cases are: who can bring the claim and who gets the money that is recovered. On the former standing issue, some jurisdictions allow the claim to be brought directly by the individuals entitled to recover and others require that the claim be brought by the decedent's estate on their behalf. On the latter damages issue, some jurisdictions allocate funds to specific survivors based on their individual losses and others provide that the money passes by intestate succession, as though the decedent died without a will. This means the legislature has decided who should be taken care of when someone dies — typically spouses and children if there are any. Take a look at the wrongful death statute in your state and see if you understand what would happen if you or a family member died due to negligence.

Does the system reflect what you or they would want to happen? Why would it make sense for the legislature to ignore the person's will and pass this money by intestate succession even if the rest of the person's estate passed by will?

4. Another important question concerns what damages can be recovered. The North Carolina enactment seen in *DiDonato* is quite broad in allowing for a range of damages. Other states have quite severe limits, such as allowing only economic losses and nothing for the loss of the relationship with the decedent. What arguments can you make for and against the breadth or limitation of damages in wrongful death cases?

5. There are other negligence claims that arise from conception, gestation, and birth: Perhaps the simplest claim, recognized in almost every state, is one for *wrongful conception*. Here, a woman who becomes pregnant with a child sues the health care provider whose negligence caused her pregnancy. Examples of direct cause cases include those for improperly inserting an IUD, or for improperly filling a contraceptives prescription. Indirect case cases include those in which the health care provider's negligent advice about the safety of becoming pregnant or having a healthy child results in the woman choosing to become pregnant. See, e.g., Gallagher v. Duke University, 852 F. 2d 733 (1988) (misdiagnosis of stillborn child's genetic condition caused mother to have a second child who survived with the same problems as the first). Jurisdictions vary as to recoverable damages in wrongful conception cases. Some limit the damages to the costs related to being pregnant, others add full child rearing costs, and still others allow only the childrearing costs associated with a child born with special needs that would have been avoided had the provider's advice been non-negligent. The rules for recovery of emotional distress damages are more diverse.

Wrongful birth claims allege that the negligence of a doctor deprived the mother of the opportunity to terminate a pregnancy. Typically, these claims involve situations where the child should have been diagnosed in utero with a permanent disabling medical condition in time for the mother to choose to have an abortion. Wrongful birth claims differ from wrongful conception claims in that the negligence in a wrongful birth claim occurs after conception. Depending on the jurisdiction, damages for wrongful birth claims may include the costs of rearing the child beyond those a health child would have required. And again here, emotional distress damages are treated in varying ways. Azzolino v. Dingfelder, 377 S.E. 2d (1985), exemplifies a common wrongful birth fact pattern albeit with an uncommon result.

Wrongful life claims feature the child with special needs born after wrongful birth or wrongful conception as plaintiff, alleging that they too were injured by the health care provider's negligence. *Azzolino* was a wrongful birth case and a wrongful life case. Wrongful life cases have found limited acceptance in the courts because of judges' unwillingness to decide the difficult question whether a person should be compensated for a disability in a situation where their only other option was not to exist at all.

IV. PUNITIVE DAMAGES

STATE FARM MUTUAL v. CAMPBELL ET AL.
538 U.S. 408 (2003)

Certiorari to the Supreme Court of Utah.

Kennedy, J., delivered the opinion of the Court, in which Rehnquist, C. J., and Stevens, O'Connor, Souter, and Breyer, JJ., joined. Scalia, J., Thomas, J., and Ginsburg, J., filed dissenting opinions.

Justice Kennedy delivered the opinion of the Court.

We address once again the measure of punishment, by means of punitive damages, a State may impose upon a defendant in a civil case. The question is whether, in the circumstances we shall recount, an award of $145 million in punitive damages, where full compensatory damages are $1 million, is excessive and in violation of the Due Process Clause of the Fourteenth Amendment to the Constitution of the United States.

I

In 1981, Curtis Campbell (Campbell) was driving with his wife, Inez Preece Campbell, in Cache County, Utah. He decided to pass six vans traveling ahead of them on a two-lane highway. Todd Ospital was driving a small car approaching from the opposite direction. To avoid a head-on collision with Campbell, who by then was driving on the wrong side of the highway and toward oncoming traffic, Ospital swerved onto the shoulder, lost control of his automobile, and collided with a vehicle driven by Robert G. Slusher. Ospital was killed, and Slusher was rendered permanently disabled. The Campbells escaped unscathed.

In the ensuing wrongful death and tort action, Campbell insisted he was not at fault. Early investigations did support differing conclusions as to who caused the accident, but "a consensus was reached early on by the investigators and witnesses that Mr. Campbell's unsafe pass had indeed caused the crash." 65 P. 3d 1134, 1141 (Utah 2001). Campbell's insurance company, petitioner State Farm Mutual Automobile Insurance Company (State Farm), nonetheless decided to contest liability and declined offers by Slusher and Ospital's estate (Ospital) to settle the claims for the policy limit of $50,000 ($25,000 per claimant). State Farm also ignored the advice of one of its own investigators and took the case to trial, assuring the Campbells that "their assets were safe, that they had no liability for the accident, that [State Farm] would represent their interests, and that they did not need to procure separate counsel." *Id.,* at 1142. To the contrary, a jury determined that Campbell was 100 percent at fault, and a judgment was returned for $185,849, far more than the amount offered in settlement.

At first State Farm refused to cover the $135,849 in excess liability. Its counsel made this clear to the Campbells: "'You may want to put for sale signs on your property to get things moving.'" *Ibid.* Nor was State Farm willing to post a supersedeas bond to allow Campbell to appeal the judgment against him. Campbell obtained his own counsel to appeal the verdict. During the pendency of the appeal, in late 1984, Slusher, Ospital, and the Campbells reached an agreement whereby Slusher and Ospital agreed not to seek satisfaction of their claims against the

Campbells. In exchange the Campbells agreed to pursue a bad-faith action against State Farm and to be represented by Slusher's and Ospital's attorneys. The Campbells also agreed that Slusher and Ospital would have a right to play a part in all major decisions concerning the bad-faith action. No settlement could be concluded without Slusher's and Ospital's approval, and Slusher and Ospital would receive 90 percent of any verdict against State Farm.

In 1989, the Utah Supreme Court denied Campbell's appeal in the wrongful-death and tort actions. State Farm then paid the entire judgment, including the amounts in excess of the policy limits. The Campbells nonetheless filed a complaint against State Farm alleging bad faith, fraud, and intentional infliction of emotional distress. The trial court initially granted State Farm's motion for summary judgment because State Farm had paid the excess verdict, but that ruling was reversed on appeal. On remand State Farm moved *in limine* to exclude evidence of alleged conduct that occurred in unrelated cases outside of Utah, but the trial court denied the motion. At State Farm's request the trial court bifurcated the trial into two phases conducted before different juries. In the first phase the jury determined that State Farm's decision not to settle was unreasonable because there was a substantial likelihood of an excess verdict.

Before the second phase of the action against State Farm we decided *BMW of North America, Inc.* v. *Gore,* 517 U. S. 559 (1996), and refused to sustain a $2 million punitive damages award which accompanied a verdict of only $4,000 in compensatory damages. Based on that decision, State Farm again moved for the exclusion of evidence of dissimilar out-of-state conduct. The trial court denied State Farm's motion.

The second phase addressed State Farm's liability for fraud and intentional infliction of emotional distress, as well as compensatory and punitive damages. The Utah Supreme Court aptly characterized this phase of the trial:

> "State Farm argued during phase II that its decision to take the case to trial was an 'honest mistake' that did not warrant punitive damages. In contrast, the Campbells introduced evidence that State Farm's decision to take the case to trial was a result of a national scheme to meet corporate fiscal goals by capping payouts on claims company wide. This scheme was referred to as State Farm's 'Performance, Planning and Review,' or PP & R, policy. To prove the existence of this scheme, the trial court allowed the Campbells to introduce extensive expert testimony regarding fraudulent practices by State Farm in its nation-wide operations. Although State Farm moved prior to phase II of the trial for the exclusion of such evidence and continued to object to it at trial, the trial court ruled that such evidence was admissible to determine whether State Farm's conduct in the Campbell case was indeed intentional and sufficiently egregious to warrant punitive damages." 65 P. 3d, at 1143.

Evidence pertaining to the PP&R policy concerned State Farm's business practices for over 20 years in numerous States. Most of these practices bore no relation to third-party automobile insurance claims, the type of claim underlying the Campbells's complaint against the company. The jury awarded the Campbells $2.6 million in compensatory damages and $145 million in punitive damages, which the trial court reduced to $1 million and $25 million respectively. Both parties appealed.

The Utah Supreme Court sought to apply the three guideposts we identified in *Gore,* and it reinstated the $145 million punitive damages award. Relying in large part on the extensive evidence concerning the PP&R policy, the court concluded State Farm's conduct was reprehensible. The court also relied upon State Farm's "massive wealth" and on testimony indicating that "State Farm's actions, because of their clandestine nature, will be punished at most in one out of every 50,000 cases as a matter of statistical probability," 65 P. 3d, at 1153, and concluded that the ratio between punitive and compensatory damages was not unwarranted. Finally, the court noted that the punitive damages award was not excessive when compared to various civil and criminal penalties State Farm could have faced, including $10,000 for each act of fraud, the suspension of its license to conduct business in Utah, the disgorgement of profits, and imprisonment. We granted certiorari.

II

We recognized in *Cooper Industries, Inc.* v. *Leatherman Tool Group, Inc.*, 532 U. S. 424 (2001), that in our judicial system compensatory and punitive damages, although usually awarded at the same time by the same decisionmaker, serve different purposes. *Id.*, at 432. Compensatory damages "are intended to redress the concrete loss that the plaintiff has suffered by reason of the defendant's wrongful conduct." *Ibid.* (citing Restatement (Second) of Torts § 903, pp. 453-454 (1979)). By contrast, punitive damages serve a broader function; they are aimed at deterrence and retribution; . . .

While States possess discretion over the imposition of punitive damages, it is well established that there are procedural and substantive constitutional limitations on these awards. The Due Process Clause of the Fourteenth Amendment prohibits the imposition of grossly excessive or arbitrary punishments on a tortfeasor. The reason is that "[e]lementary notions of fairness enshrined in our constitutional jurisprudence dictate that a person receive fair notice not only of the conduct that will subject him to punishment, but also of the severity of the penalty that a State may impose." *Id.*, at 574. To the extent an award is grossly excessive, it furthers no legitimate purpose and constitutes an arbitrary deprivation of property.

Although these awards serve the same purposes as criminal penalties, defendants subjected to punitive damages in civil cases have not been accorded the protections applicable in a criminal proceeding. This increases our concerns over the imprecise manner in which punitive damages systems are administered. . . . Our concerns are heightened when the decisionmaker is presented, as we shall discuss, with evidence that has little bearing as to the amount of punitive damages that should be awarded. Vague instructions, or those that merely inform the jury to avoid "passion or prejudice," App. to Pet. for Cert. 108a-109a, do little to aid the decisionmaker in its task of assigning appropriate weight to evidence that is relevant and evidence that is tangential or only inflammatory.

In light of these concerns, in *Gore, supra,* we instructed courts reviewing punitive damages to consider three guideposts: (1) the degree of reprehensibility of the defendant's misconduct; (2) the disparity between the actual or potential harm suffered by the plaintiff and the punitive damages award; and (3) the difference between the punitive damages awarded by the jury and the civil penalties authorized or imposed in comparable cases. *Id.*, at 575. We reiterated the importance of these three guideposts in *Cooper Industries* and mandated appellate courts to conduct *de novo* review of a trial court's application of them to the jury's award. 532 U. S. 424. Exacting appellate review ensures that an award of punitive damages is based upon an "application of law, rather than a decisionmaker's caprice." *Id.*, at 436 (quoting *Gore, supra,* at 587 (BREYER, J., concurring)).

III

Under the principles outlined in *BMW of North America, Inc.* v. *Gore,* this case is neither close nor difficult. It was error to reinstate the jury's $145 million punitive damages award. We address each guidepost of *Gore* in some detail.

A

"[T]he most important indicium of the reasonableness of a punitive damages award is the degree of reprehensibility of the defendant's conduct." *Gore,* 517 U. S., at 575. We have instructed courts to determine the reprehensibility of a defendant by considering whether: the harm caused was physical as opposed to economic; the tortious conduct evinced an indifference to or a reckless disregard of the health or safety of others; the target of the conduct had financial vulnerability; the conduct involved repeated actions or was an isolated incident; and the harm was the result of intentional malice, trickery, or deceit, or mere accident. The existence of any one of these factors weighing in favor of a plaintiff may not be sufficient to sustain a punitive damages award; and the absence of all of them renders any award suspect. It should be presumed a plaintiff has been made whole for his injuries by compensatory damages, so punitive damages should only be awarded if the defendant's culpability, after having paid compensatory damages, is so reprehensible as to warrant the imposition of further sanctions to achieve punishment or deterrence.

Applying these factors in the instant case, we must acknowledge that State Farm's handling of the claims against the Campbells merits no praise. The trial court found that State Farm's employees altered the company's records to make Campbell appear less culpable. State Farm disregarded the overwhelming likelihood of liability and the near-certain probability that, by taking the case to trial, a judgment in excess of the policy limits would be awarded. State Farm amplified the harm by at first assuring the Campbells their assets would be safe from any verdict and by later telling them, post-judgment, to put a for-sale sign on their house. While we do not suggest there was error in awarding punitive damages based upon State Farm's conduct toward the Campbells, a more modest punishment for this reprehensible conduct could have satisfied the State's legitimate objectives, and the Utah courts should have gone no further.

This case, instead, was used as a platform to expose, and punish, the perceived deficiencies of State Farm's operations throughout the country. The Utah Supreme Court's opinion makes explicit that State Farm was being condemned for its nationwide policies rather than for the conduct directed toward the Campbells. This was, as well, an explicit rationale of the trial court's decision in approving the award, though reduced from $145 million to $25 million. App. to Pet. for Cert. 120a ("[T]he Campbells demonstrated, through the testimony of State Farm employees who had worked outside of Utah, and through expert testimony, that this pattern of claims adjustment under the PP&R program was not a local anomaly, but was a consistent, nationwide feature of State Farm's business operations, orchestrated from the highest levels of corporate management").

The Campbells contend that State Farm has only itself to blame for the reliance upon dissimilar and out-of-state conduct evidence. The record does not support this contention. From their opening statements onward the Campbells framed this case as a chance to rebuke State Farm for its nationwide activities. App. 208 ("You're going to hear evidence that even the insurance commission in Utah and around the country are unwilling or inept at protecting people against abuses"); *id.*, at 242 ("[T]his is a very important case. . . . [I]t transcends the Campbell file. It involves a nationwide practice. And you, here, are going to be evaluating and assessing, and hopefully requiring State Farm to stand accountable for what it's doing across the country, which is the purpose of punitive damages"). This was a position maintained throughout the litigation. In opposing State Farm's motion to exclude such evidence under *Gore,* the Campbells' counsel convinced the trial court that there was no limitation on the scope of evidence that could be considered under our precedents. App. to Pet. for Cert. 172a ("As I read the case *[Gore],* I was struck with the fact that a clear message in the case . . . seems to be that courts in punitive damages cases should receive more evidence, not less. And that the court seems to be inviting an even broader area of evidence than the current rulings of the court would indicate"); *id.,* at 189a (trial court ruling).

A State cannot punish a defendant for conduct that may have been lawful where it occurred. Nor, as a general rule, does a State have a legitimate concern in imposing punitive damages to punish a defendant for unlawful acts committed outside of the State's jurisdiction. Any proper adjudication of conduct that occurred outside Utah to other persons would require their inclusion, and, to those parties, the Utah courts, in the usual case, would need to apply the laws of their relevant jurisdiction.

Here, the Campbells do not dispute that much of the out-of-state conduct was lawful where it occurred. They argue, however, that such evidence was not the primary basis for the punitive damages award and was relevant to the extent it demonstrated, in a general sense, State Farm's motive against its insured. Brief for Respondents 46-47 ("[E]ven if the practices described by State Farm were not malum in se or malum prohibitum, they became relevant to punitive damages to the extent they were used as tools to implement State Farm's wrongful PP&R policy"). This argument misses the mark. Lawful out-of-state conduct may be probative when it demonstrates the deliberateness and culpability of the defendant's action in the State where it is tortious, but that conduct must have a nexus to the specific harm suffered by the plaintiff. A jury must be instructed, furthermore, that it may not use evidence of out-of-state conduct to punish a defendant for action that was lawful in the jurisdiction where it occurred. A basic principle of federalism is that each State may make its own reasoned judgment about what conduct is permitted or proscribed within its borders, and each State alone can determine what measure of punishment, if any, to impose on a defendant who acts within its jurisdiction.

For a more fundamental reason, however, the Utah courts erred in relying upon this and other evidence: The courts awarded punitive damages to punish and deter conduct that bore no relation to the Campbells' harm. A defendant's dissimilar acts, independent from the acts upon which liability was premised, may not serve as the basis for punitive damages. A defendant should be punished for the conduct that harmed the plaintiff, not for being an unsavory individual or business. Due process does not permit courts, in the calculation of punitive damages, to adjudicate the merits of other parties' hypothetical claims against a defendant under the guise of the reprehensibility analysis, but we have no doubt the Utah Supreme Court did that here. 65 P. 3d, at 1149 ("Even if the harm to the Campbells can be appropriately characterized as minimal, the trial court's assessment of the situation is on target: 'The harm is minor to the individual but massive in the aggregate'"). Punishment on these bases creates the possibility of multiple punitive damages awards for the same conduct; for in the usual case nonparties are not bound by the judgment some other plaintiff obtains.

The same reasons lead us to conclude the Utah Supreme Court's decision cannot be justified on the grounds that State Farm was a recidivist. Although "[o]ur holdings that a recidivist may be punished more severely than a first offender recognize that repeated misconduct is more reprehensible than an individual instance of malfeasance," *Gore, supra,* at 577, in the context of civil actions courts must ensure the conduct in question replicates the prior transgressions.

The Campbells have identified scant evidence of repeated misconduct of the sort that injured them. Nor does our review of the Utah courts' decisions convince us that State Farm was only punished for its actions toward the Campbells. Although evidence of other acts need not be identical to have relevance in the calculation of punitive damages, the Utah court erred here because evidence pertaining to claims that had nothing to do with a third-party lawsuit was introduced at length. Other evidence concerning reprehensibility was even more tangential. For example, the Utah Supreme Court criticized State Farm's investigation into the personal life of one of its employees and, in a broader approach, the manner in which State Farm's policies corrupted its employees. The Campbells attempt to justify the courts' reliance upon this unrelated testimony on the theory that each dollar of profit made by underpaying a third-party claimant is the same as a dollar made by underpaying a first-party one. Brief for Respondents 45; see also 65 P. 3d, at 1150 ("State Farm's continuing illicit practice created market disadvantages for other honest insurance companies because these practices increased profits. As plaintiffs' expert witnesses established, such wrongfully obtained competitive advantages have the potential to pressure other companies to adopt similar fraudulent tactics, or to force them out of business. Thus, such actions cause distortions throughout the insurance market and ultimately hurt all consumers"). For the reasons already stated, this argument is unconvincing. The reprehensibility guidepost does not permit courts to expand the scope of the case so that a defendant may be punished for any malfeasance, which in this case extended for a 20-year period. In this case, because the Campbells have shown no conduct by State Farm similar to that which harmed them, the conduct that harmed them is the only conduct relevant to the reprehensibility analysis.

B

Turning to the second *Gore* guidepost, we have been reluctant to identify concrete constitutional limits on the ratio between harm, or potential harm, to the plaintiff and the punitive damages award. We decline again to impose a bright-line ratio which a punitive damages award cannot exceed. Our jurisprudence and the principles it has now established demonstrate, however, that, in practice, few awards exceeding a single-digit ratio between punitive and compensatory damages, to a significant degree, will satisfy due process. In *Haslip,* in upholding a punitive damages award, we concluded that an award of more than four times the amount of compensatory damages might be close to the line of constitutional impropriety. 499 U. S., at 23-24. We cited that 4-to-1 ratio again in *Gore.* 517 U. S., at 581. The Court further referenced a long legislative history, dating back over 700 years and going forward to today, providing for sanctions of double, treble, or quadruple damages to deter and punish. While these ratios are not binding, they are instructive. They demonstrate what should be obvious: Single-digit multipliers are more likely to comport with due process, while still achieving the State's goals of deterrence and retribution, than awards with ratios in range of 500 to 1, *id.,* at 582, or, in this case, of 145 to 1.

Nonetheless, because there are no rigid benchmarks that a punitive damages award may not surpass, ratios greater than those we have previously upheld may comport with due process where "a particularly egregious act has resulted in only a small amount of economic damages." *Ibid.;* see also *ibid.* (positing that a higher ratio *might* be necessary where "the injury is hard to detect or the monetary value of noneconomic harm might have been difficult to determine"). The converse is also true, however. When compensatory damages are substantial, then a lesser ratio, perhaps only equal to compensatory damages, can reach the outermost limit of the due process guarantee. The precise award in any case, of course, must be based upon the facts and circumstances of the defendant's conduct and the harm to the plaintiff.

In sum, courts must ensure that the measure of punishment is both reasonable and proportionate to the amount of harm to the plaintiff and to the general damages recovered. In the context of this case, we have no doubt that there is a presumption against an award that has a 145-to-1 ratio. The compensatory award in this case was substantial; the Campbells were awarded $1 million for a year and a half of emotional distress. This was complete compensation. The harm arose from a transaction in the economic realm, not from some physical assault or trauma; there were no physical injuries; and State Farm paid the excess verdict before the complaint was filed, so the Campbells suffered only minor economic injuries for the 18-month period in which State Farm refused to resolve the claim against them. The compensatory damages for the injury suffered here, moreover, likely were based on a component which was duplicated in the punitive award. Much of the distress was caused by the outrage and humiliation the Campbells suffered at the actions of their insurer; and it is a major role of punitive damages to condemn such conduct. Compensatory damages, however, already contain this punitive element. See Restatement (Second) of Torts § 908, Comment *c,* p. 466 (1977) ("In many cases in which compensatory damages include an amount for emotional distress, such as humiliation or indignation aroused by the defendant's act, there is no clear line of demarcation between punishment and compensation and a verdict for a specified amount frequently includes elements of both").

The Utah Supreme Court sought to justify the massive award by pointing to State Farm's purported failure to report a prior $100 million punitive damages award in Texas to its corporate headquarters; the fact that State Farm's policies have affected numerous Utah consumers; the fact that State Farm will only be punished in one out of every 50,000 cases as a matter of statistical probability; and State Farm's enormous wealth. Since the Supreme Court of Utah discussed the Texas award when applying the ratio guidepost, we discuss it here. The Texas award, however, should have been analyzed in the context of the reprehensibility guidepost only. The failure of the company to report the Texas award is out-of-state conduct that, if the conduct were similar, might have had some bearing on the degree of reprehensibility, subject to the limitations we have described. Here, it was dissimilar, and of such marginal relevance that it should have been accorded little or no weight. The award was rendered in a first-party lawsuit; no judgment was entered in the case; and it was later settled for a fraction of the verdict. With respect to the Utah Supreme Court's second justification, the Campbells' inability to direct us to testimony demonstrating harm to the people of Utah (other than those directly involved in this case) indicates that the adverse effect on the State's general population was in fact minor.

The remaining premises for the Utah Supreme Court's decision bear no relation to the award's reasonableness or proportionality to the harm. They are, rather, arguments that seek to defend a departure from well-established constraints on punitive damages. While States enjoy considerable discretion in deducing when punitive damages are warranted, each award must comport with the principles set forth in *Gore.* Here the argument that State Farm will be punished in only the rare case, coupled with reference to its assets (which, of course, are what other insured parties in Utah and other States must rely upon for payment of claims) had little to do with the actual harm sustained by the Campbells. The wealth of a defendant cannot justify an otherwise unconstitutional punitive damages award. The principles set forth in *Gore* must be implemented with care, to ensure both reasonableness and proportionality.

C

The third guidepost in *Gore* is the disparity between the punitive damages award and the "civil penalties authorized or imposed in comparable cases." *Id.,* at 575. We note that, in the past, we have also looked to criminal penalties that could be imposed. The existence of a criminal penalty does have bearing on the seriousness with which a State views the wrongful action. When used to determine the dollar amount of the award, however, the criminal penalty has less utility. Great care must be taken to avoid use of the civil process to assess criminal penalties that can be imposed only after the heightened protections of a criminal trial have been observed, including, of course, its higher standards of proof. Punitive damages are not a substitute for the criminal process, and the remote possibility of a criminal sanction does not automatically sustain a punitive damages award.

Here, we need not dwell long on this guidepost. The most relevant civil sanction under Utah state law for the wrong done to the Campbells appears to be a $10,000 fine for an act of fraud, an amount dwarfed by the $145 million punitive damages award. The Supreme Court of Utah speculated about the loss of State Farm's business license, the disgorgement of profits, and possible imprisonment, but here again its references were to the broad fraudulent scheme drawn from evidence of out-of-state and dissimilar conduct. This analysis was insufficient to justify the award.

IV

An application of the *Gore* guideposts to the facts of this case, especially in light of the substantial compensatory damages awarded (a portion of which contained a punitive element), likely would justify a punitive damages award at or near the amount of compensatory damages. The punitive award of $145 million, therefore, was neither reasonable nor proportionate to the wrong committed, and it was an irrational and arbitrary deprivation of the property of the defendant. The proper calculation of punitive damages under the principles we have discussed should be resolved, in the first instance, by the Utah courts.

The judgment of the Utah Supreme Court is reversed, and the case is remanded for further proceedings not inconsistent with this opinion.

It is so ordered.

JUSTICE SCALIA, dissenting.

I adhere to the view expressed in my dissenting opinion in *BMW of North America, Inc.* v. *Gore,* 517 U. S. 559, 598-599 (1996), that the Due Process Clause provides no substantive protections against "excessive" or "'unreasonable'" awards of punitive damages. I am also of the view that the punitive damages jurisprudence which has sprung forth from *BMW* v. *Gore* is insusceptible of principled application; accordingly, I do not feel justified in giving the case *stare decisis* effect. I would affirm the judgment of the Utah Supreme Court.

JUSTICE THOMAS, dissenting.

I would affirm the judgment below because "I continue to believe that the Constitution does not constrain the size of punitive damages awards." *Cooper Industries, Inc.* v. *Leatherman Tool Group, Inc.,* 532 U. S. 424, 443 (2001) (THOMAS, J., concurring) (citing *BMW of North America, Inc.* v. *Gore,* 517 U. S. 559, 599 (1996) (SCALIA, J., joined by THOMAS, J., dissenting)). Accordingly, I respectfully dissent.

JUSTICE GINSBURG, dissenting.

. . .

It was not until 1996, in *BMW of North America, Inc.* v. *Gore,* 517 U. S. 559, that the Court, for the first time, invalidated a state-court punitive damages assessment as unreasonably large. See *id.,* at 599 (SCALIA, J., dissenting). If our activity in this domain is now "well established," see *ante,* at 416, 427, it takes place on ground not long held.

In *Gore,* I stated why I resisted the Court's foray into punitive damages "territory traditionally within the States' domain." 517 U. S., at 612 (dissenting opinion). I adhere to those views, and note again that, unlike federal habeas corpus review of state-court convictions under 28 U. S. C. § 2254, the Court "work[s] at this business [of checking state courts] alone," *unaided* by the participation of federal district courts and courts of appeals. 517 U. S., at 613. It was once recognized that "the laws of the particular State must suffice [to superintend punitive damages awards] until judges or legislators authorized to do so initiate system-wide change." *Haslip,* 499 U. S., at 42 (KENNEDY, J., concurring in judgment). I would adhere to that traditional view.

I

The large size of the award upheld by the Utah Supreme Court in this case indicates why damages-capping legislation may be altogether fitting and proper. Neither the amount of the award nor the trial record, however, justifies this Court's substitution of its judgment for that of Utah's competent decisionmakers. . . .

CAMPBELL v. STATE FARM MUTUAL AUTOMOBILE INSURANCE COMPANY
98 P.3d 409 (Utah 2004)

NEHRING, Justice:

We take up this case after remand from the United States Supreme Court, which held that the imposition of a $145 million punitive damages award against State Farm Mutual Automobile Insurance Company in favor of State Farm's insured, Curtis B. Campbell, and his wife, Inez Preece Campbell, was excessive and violated the due process clause of the Fourteenth Amendment to the Constitution of the United States. The Supreme Court directed us to recalculate the punitive damages award under principles articulated in its decision. We have performed this task and reduced the jury's award to $9,018,780.75 in punitive damages, a figure nine times the amount of compensatory and special damages awarded to the Campbells.

. . .

II. DUTY ON REMAND

State Farm suggests that our duty in the face of a remand order demands unwavering fidelity to the letter and spirit of the mandate. We agree. State Farm further argues that the letter and spirit of the mandate erect an impenetrable ceiling on the punitive damages award of $1,002,086.75, based on a 1–to–1 ratio of punitive damages to compensatory damages.

State Farm makes two arguments in aid of this contention. First, it invokes what it characterizes as the "mandate rule" which, it claims, elevates all of the statements in the Supreme Court's opinion to the status of a holding, thereby binding us to what would otherwise be properly deemed dicta. Second, having identified and broadly defined a "mandate rule," State Farm then turns to the text of Campbell II which states that "[a]n application of the [relevant] guideposts to the facts of this case . . . likely would justify a punitive damages award at or near the amount of compensatory damages." Campbell II, 538 U.S. at 429, 123 S.Ct. 1513. State Farm claims that, when given the dignity required by the mandate rule, this language limits our punitive damages award to the amount of compensatory damages.

We are both sensitive to our responsibility as an inferior court to honor the Supreme Court's remand order with utmost fidelity and skeptical of claims that our duties can be reduced to an enumerated task list imposed by a "mandate rule." We do not, therefore, interpret the Supreme Court's mandate to be as restrictive as State Farm claims. Had the letter of the Supreme Court's mandate included an express punitive damages award, our responsibilities would be easily discharged. The Supreme Court declined, however, to fix a substitute award, choosing instead to entrust to our judgment the calculation of a punitive award which both achieves the legitimate objectives of punitive damages and meets the demands of due process. We take seriously the Supreme Court's direction that "[t]he proper calculation of punitive damages under the principles we have discussed should be resolved, in the first instance, by the Utah courts." Id.

By assigning to us the duty to resolve the issue of punitive damages by fixing an award, the Supreme Court signaled its intention to vest in us some discretion to exercise our independent judgment to reach a reasonable and proportionate award. To faithfully exercise our discretion, we must properly identify and apply the Supreme Court's principles announced in Campbell II. These principles restated and refined the analytical tools first announced in BMW of North America, Inc. v. Gore, 517 U.S. 559, 116 S.Ct. 1589, 134 L.Ed.2d 809 (1996). In Gore, the Supreme Court issued an invitation to the Alabama Supreme Court to undertake on remand an "independent determination" of an appropriate punitive damages award consistent with the guideposts erected by the Supreme Court. Id. at 586, 116 S.Ct. 1589. We understand our duties to mirror those assigned to the Alabama Supreme Court, supplemented by the evolving principles of punitive damages jurisprudence announced in Campbell II.

It is within this delegated responsibility that the "spirit" of the Supreme Court's order of remand resides, presenting the greater challenge to us to honor that mandate. Accordingly, our view of the limits of our discretion to award punitive damages relies little on the "mandate rule" or any similar interpretive aid. Rather, the text of Campbell II provides us with clear direction.

The Supreme Court has long held the view that, except when they transgress due process guarantees, punitive damages awards are properly the province of the states. Cooper Indus., Inc. v. Leatherman Tool Group, Inc., 532 U.S. 424, 433, 121 S.Ct. 1678, 149 L.Ed.2d 674 (2001) ("Despite the broad discretion that States possess with respect to the imposition of criminal penalties and punitive damages, the Due Process Clause of the Fourteenth Amendment to the Federal Constitution imposes substantive limits on that discretion."); Browning–Ferris Indus. of Vt., Inc. v. Kelco Disposal, Inc., 492 U.S. 257, 278, 109 S.Ct. 2909, 106 L.Ed.2d 219 (1989) ("[T]he propriety of an award of punitive damages for the conduct in question, and the factors the jury may consider in determining their amount, are questions of state law.").

Reinforcing our conclusion that we may properly exercise our judgment in fixing the punitive damages award are certain themes prominently featured in Campbell II and Gore. In both cases, the Supreme Court resisted the impulse to draw bright lines or create categorical classifications in fixing punitive damages awards, electing instead to adopt general standards and guideposts. The Supreme Court has also consistently recognized punitive damages as a means to "further a State's legitimate interests in punishing unlawful conduct and deterring its repetition." Gore, 517 U.S. at 568, 116 S.Ct. 1589. Taken together, these themes create a logical underpinning to an interpretation of the Supreme Court's remand order which sanctions and expects us to exercise a considerable measure of independent judgment in fixing the punitive damages award.

Even the Supreme Court's observation that this case "likely would justify a punitive damages award at or near the amount of compensatory damages" does not cause us to retreat from our view that we have been granted discretion to determine the amount of punitive damages. Campbell II, 538 U.S. at 429, 123 S.Ct. 1513. Contrary to State Farm's assertions, this language cannot reasonably be interpreted as a conclusive determination that the magnitude of State Farm's blameworthiness merits a punitive damages award no greater than the compensatory award. These are words of prediction, not direction, and are wholly compatible with a remand order which both instructs us to apply the Supreme Court's standards with fidelity and recognizes that Utah courts are best able to address our state's legitimate interests. Consistent with that view, the Supreme Court has clearly communicated its intention to cede to us the responsibility to assess the reprehensibility of State Farm's conduct, to identify Utah's legitimate interests, and to exercise reasoned judgment in fixing punitive damages.

III. ANALYSIS LIMITED TO ACTIVITY IN UTAH

While authorizing us to determine the amount of the punitive damages award, the Supreme Court leashed us more tightly to the established analytical guideposts of Gore in two ways: by narrowing the scope of relevant evidence which we may consider in evaluating the reprehensibility of State Farm's conduct, and by providing more detailed guidance for determining the relationship between compensatory and punitive damages.

The Supreme Court chided us for basing our reinstatement of the jury's $145 million punitive damages award on State Farm's "nationwide policies rather than for the conduct direct [sic] toward the Campbells." Id. at 420, 123 S.Ct. 1513. The Supreme Court found impermissible our reliance on State Farm's conduct outside Utah in measuring the reprehensibility of the company's conduct. Drawing on views expressed in Gore, the Supreme Court limited evidence that can properly be weighed in the reprehensibility scale to behavior which took place within our borders and was directed at the Campbells. We are mindful that it was our consideration of irrelevant extra-territorial evidence concerning reprehensibility which attracted most of the Supreme Court's criticism in Campbell II. We therefore reevaluate State Farm's conduct based solely on its behavior that affected the Campbells and took place within Utah.

The Supreme Court stopped well short, however, of punctuating its disagreement with the evidence we considered in our analysis by pinning State Farm's behavior to a particular location along the reprehensibility continuum. It instead simply issued the mandate that "a more modest punishment for this reprehensible conduct could have satisfied the State's legitimate objectives, and the Utah courts should have gone no further." Id. at 419–20, 123 S.Ct. 1513.

Had the Supreme Court injected into Campbell II its own conclusive findings concerning the degree of State Farm's blameworthiness, it would have announced a federal standard measuring reprehensibility. By creating such a national reprehensibility standard, however, the Supreme Court would have collided with its own rationale for limiting the scope of relevant reprehensibility evidence to intra-state conduct. The Supreme Court's rejection of our consideration of State Farm's conduct in other states was grounded in the recognition that much of the out-of-state conduct was lawful where it occurred. The Supreme Court respected states' autonomy to make policy choices about the lawfulness of human and corporate behavior within their own borders, and used that deference to justify disallowing out-of-state conduct as an indicator of reprehensibility.

Just as behavior may be unlawful or tortious in one state and not in another, the degree of blameworthiness assigned to conduct may also differ among the states. As long as the Supreme Court stands by its view that punitive damages serve a legitimate means to satisfy a state's objectives to punish and deter behavior which it deems unlawful or tortious based on its own values and traditions, it would seemingly be bound to avoid creating and imposing on the states a nationwide code of personal and corporate behavior.

In this instance, we find the blameworthiness of State Farm's behavior toward the Campbells to be several degrees more offensive than the Supreme Court's less than condemnatory view that State Farm's behavior "merits no praise." Id. at 419, 123 S.Ct. 1513. We reach this conclusion after applying the relevant reprehensibility standards to the facts approved for consideration of State Farm's reprehensibility in Campbell II, and in light of Utah's values and traditions. We now turn to explaining how we exercised the discretion granted us by the Supreme Court to award the Campbells $9,018,780.75 in punitive damages.

IV. FEDERAL DUE PROCESS GUIDEPOSTS

In Gore, the Supreme Court established three guideposts for punitive damages awards in Gore: (1) the degree of reprehensibility of the defendant's misconduct; (2) the disparity between the actual or potential harm suffered by the plaintiff and the punitive damages award; and (3) the difference between the punitive damages awarded by the jury and the civil penalties authorized or imposed in comparable cases. Campbell II, 538 U.S. at 418, 123 S.Ct. 1513 (citing Gore, 517 U.S. at 574–75, 116 S.Ct. 1589). The Supreme Court structured its constitutional review of our reinstatement of the jury's $145 million punitive damages award in Campbell I within the framework of these guideposts.

In Campbell I, we conducted two separate reviews of the trial court's punitive damages award, under both state and federal law.[3] In Campbell II, the Supreme Court limited its review of the constitutionality of our award to the Gore guideposts. Since Campbell II, we have continued to apply our state standards, recognizing that they substantially reflect the Supreme Court's directives and modifying them as necessary to fully meet the federal requirements. See, e.g., Smith v. Fairfax Realty, 2003 UT 41, ¶ 31, 82 P.3d 1064. However, in this case we follow the lead of the Supreme Court and restrict our review to the guideposts set forth in Gore.

A. Reprehensibility

Just as we reinstated the jury's $145 million punitive damages award primarily because of our assessment of the reprehensibility of State Farm's conduct, Campbell I, 2001 UT 89, ¶¶ 27–36, 53, 65 P.3d 1134 (analyzing reprehensibility under Crookston standards), so do we again look primarily to Gore's reprehensibility guidepost to fix those damages on remand. We do so in recognition of the Supreme Court's reaffirmation in Campbell II that reprehensibility is " '[t]he most important indicium of the reasonableness of a punitive damages award.' " 538 U.S. at 419, 123 S.Ct. 1513 (quoting Gore, 517 U.S. at 575, 116 S.Ct. 1589).

Because any determination of reprehensibility inevitably implicates moral judgments and is therefore susceptible to an arbitrary, inexplicable, and disproportionate outcome, the Supreme Court has fashioned certain measuring tools. These include consideration of whether

> the harm caused was physical as opposed to economic; the tortious conduct evinced an indifference to or a reckless disregard of the health or safety of others; the target of the conduct had financial vulnerability; the conduct involved repeated actions or was an isolated incident; and the harm was the result of intentional malice, trickery, or deceit, or mere accident.

Id.

First, we consider whether the harm was economic or physical. We are mindful of the Supreme Court's observation that "the harm [in this case] arose from a transaction in the economic realm, not from some physical assault or trauma." Id. at 426, 123 S.Ct. 1513. Wedo not, however, read this comment to foreclose our value-based assessment of the type of injuries which may flow from the abuse of transactions in the economic realm, nor to bar us from judging the reprehensibility of such abusive conduct. The Supreme Court's observation is

[3] In Utah, punitive damages are analyzed under a seven-factor test commonly known as the Crookston standards. The Crookston factors are:

> (i) the relative wealth of the defendant; (ii) the nature of the alleged misconduct; (iii) the facts and circumstances surrounding such conduct; (iv) the effect thereof on the lives of the plaintiff and others; (v) the probability of future recurrence of the misconduct; (vi) the relationship of the parties; and (vii) the amount of actual damages awarded.

Crookston v. Fire Ins. Exch., 817 P.2d 789, 808 (Utah 1991); see also Crookston v. Fire Ins. Exch., 860 P.2d 937 (Utah 1993).

carefully phrased. It does not classify the injury inflicted on the Campbells by State Farm as "economic." Rather, it notes that the transaction which gave rise to the injury was in the "economic realm."

If we were to hold the view that insurance has no purpose beyond providing economic compensation for loss, there would be little reason to dwell on this first reprehensibility factor. So interpreted, not only would the harm caused by State Farm be purely economic in nature, but the economic harm sustained by the Campbells would be minimal. State Farm ultimately paid the entire judgment which was awarded against the Campbells, including amounts in excess of the policy limits. However, we do not believe that the Campbells' injuries were limited to their economic loss.

Instead, we recognize that the gravity of harm which an insurer may potentially inflict on an insured is unique to the nature of the product and service that insurance provides. Life is fraught with uncertainty and risk. In Utah alone, our citizens pay nearly $1 billion annually in automobile insurance premiums in an effort to ameliorate the anxiety caused by uncertainty and risk.

We have shaped our law relating to first party insurance contracts to recognize the practical reality "that insurance frequently is purchased not only to provide funds in case of loss, but to provide peace of mind for the insured or his beneficiaries." Beck v. Farmers Ins. Exch., 701 P.2d 795, 802 (Utah 1985). Peace of mind clearly plays a central role in accounting for the appeal of liability insurance.

In insurance each party must take a risk. But it is inaccurate to assert that if the insured event does not occur then the insured receives nothing in return for the premium payment made. Each insured receives at the time of contract formation present assurance of compensation if the loss occurs which is a valuable peace-of-mind protection.

1–1 Holmes' Appleman on Insurance 2d § 1.3.

An allegation that one's negligent conduct has caused the injury or death of another inevitably triggers fear and apprehension that insurance succors.

Insureds buy financial protection and peace of mind against fortuitous losses. They pay the requisite premiums and put their faith and trust in their insurers to pay policy benefits promptly and fairly when the insured event occurs. Good faith and fair dealing is their expectation. It is the very essence of the insurer-insured relationship. In some instances, however, insurance companies refuse to pay the promised benefits when the underwritten harm occurs. When an insurer decides to delay or to deny paying benefits, the policyholder can suffer injury not only to his economic well-being but to his emotional and physical health as well. Moreover, the holder of a policy with low monetary limits may see his whole claim virtually wiped out by expenses if the insurance company compels him to resort to court action.

2–8 Holmes' Appleman on Insurance 2d § 8.7.

As the facts of this case make clear, misconduct which occurs in the insurance sector of the economic realm is likely to cause injury more closely akin to physical assault or trauma than to mere economic loss.[5] When an insurer callously betrays the insured's expectation of peace of mind, as State Farm did to the Campbells, its conduct is substantially more reprehensible than, for example, the undisclosed repainting of an automobile which spawned the punitive damages award in Gore.

State Farm expressly assured the Campbells that their assets would not be placed at risk by the negligence and wrongful death lawsuit brought against them. The company then unnecessarily subjected the Campbells to the risks and rigors of a trial. State Farm disregarded facts from which it should have concluded that the Campbells faced a near-certain probability of having a judgment entered against them in excess of policy limits. When this probability came to pass, State Farm withdrew its expressions of assurance and told the Campbells to place a "for sale" sign on their house. These acts, all of which the Supreme Court conceded that State Farm had committed, Campbell II, 538 U.S. at 419, 123 S.Ct. 1513, and for which State Farm has not voiced so much as a whisper of apology or remorse, caused the Campbells profound noneconomic injury.

It simply will not do to classify this injury as solely "economic" for the purposes of evaluating it under the first prong of the Gore reprehensibility test, and we decline to do so. We turn now to the remaining Gore indicia for evaluating reprehensibility.

The second factor in assessing reprehensibility is whether State Farm showed indifference or reckless disregard for the health and safety of the Campbells. There is little doubt that State Farm could reasonably have known that its conduct would cause stress and trauma to a policyholder. State Farm was clearly indifferent to this result, evincing a reckless disregard for the Campbells' peace of mind.

The third factor is whether the victims were financially vulnerable. It remains obvious to us that not only were the Campbells financially vulnerable, but their vulnerability enabled, if not motivated, State Farm's conduct. We need stray no further into the record than to the post-judgment advice given to the Campbells by State Farm's attorney that they put a "for sale" sign on their house to make this point. It is difficult to imagine State Farm making this statement to a sophisticated insured whom State Farm believed to have the wherewithal to protect himself from its predations.

Fourth, we consider whether the reprehensible conduct was repeated or merely an isolated incident. We take up this measure of reprehensibility with considerable caution because, although Gore instructs us to consider whether "the conduct involved repeated actions or was an isolated incident," id. (citing Gore, 517 U.S. at 576–77, 116 S.Ct. 1589), the Supreme Court expressly found that we erred in determining that State Farm was a recidivist. Id. at 423, 123 S.Ct. 1513. Repeated misconduct justifies a more severe sanction both because it minimizes the likelihood that the conduct was a unique aberration and because it justifies the imposition

---

[5] In Campbell II, the Supreme Court articulated bipolar injury categories of "economic" and "physical." 538 U.S. at 419, 123 S.Ct. 1513 (citing Gore, 517 U.S. at 576–77, 116 S.Ct. 1589). These categories are well suited to highlight the Supreme Court's view that the injury suffered by a misled and disappointed BMW purchaser could not reasonably justify the moral outrage which ought properly be reserved for conduct that results in physical harm. State Farm has sought to exploit, unhelpfully in our view, an exaggerated economic versus physical dichotomy. For example, as we observed in Campbell I, State Farm attempted to diffuse the odious nature of its conduct by claiming that it did not "after all, involve murder, torture, or deliberate poisoning of the environment." 2001 UT 89 at ¶ 33, 65 P.3d 1134.

of punitive damages as a deterrent. Although we are bound by the Supreme Court's finding that State Farm was not a recidivist, absence of prior bad acts does not mean that State Farm has forsworn the conduct that caused the Campbells' injury, and that the citizens of Utah therefore have no reason to deter State Farm's future conduct. State Farm's obdurate insistence that its treatment of the Campbells was proper clearly calls out for vigorous deterrence.

In Campbell I, we voiced our incredulity over State Farm's protestations of blamelessness. We noted:

> State Farm refuses in its brief on appeal to concede any error or impropriety in the handling of the Campbell case. Rather, testimony at trial indicated that State Farm was "proud" of the way it treated the Campbells. Further, State Farm asserts that it is in fact a "victim" in this case because it is the target of the secret "conspiracy" perpetrated by the Campbells, Ospital, Slusher, and their attorneys to bring this bad faith lawsuit and to share any recovery received.

2001 UT 89 at ¶ 35, 65 P.3d 1134 (internal citations omitted). The Supreme Court did not take issue with this observation. Since Campbell I, State Farm has directed us to no evidence suggesting that it has gained insight into the wrongfulness of its behavior or has reconsidered its feelings of pride and victimization.

We will not and, consistent with our duty on remand, cannot invoke deterrence as a justification for punitive damages based on conduct dissimilar to that which State Farm inflicted on the Campbells. We can, however, find ample grounds to defend an award of punitive damages in the upper range permitted by due process based on our concern that State Farm's defiance strongly suggests that it will not hesitate to treat its Utah insureds with the callousness that marked its treatment of the Campbells.

Lastly, we consider whether the substantial emotional damages sustained by the Campbells were the result of State Farm's intentional malice, trickery, and deceit. We conclude that the damages sustained by the Campbells were no mere accident. At trial, Ray Summers, the adjuster who handled the Campbell case, testified that State Farm resorted to various tactics to create prejudice in the event the case ever went before a jury. Campbell I, 2001 UT 89 at ¶ 29, 65 P.3d 1134. For example, State Farm manager Bob Noxon instructed Summers to manufacture the false story that Todd Ospital, who was killed in the automobile accident for which Mr. Campbell was found to be at fault, was speeding because he was on his way to see a pregnant girlfriend. Id. In truth, there was no pregnant girlfriend, nor was Mr. Ospital even speeding; this story was invented only to cause prejudice in the record. Id. This deceitful conduct can only be explained as part of a scheme to reduce State Farm's economic exposure. The possibility that its dissembling would expose the Campbells to an excess judgment must have been apparent to State Farm. To react as it did when the excess judgment became a reality only confirms the toxicity of State Farm's behavior.

B. Ratio of Compensatory Damages to Punitive Damages

We turn now to the second Gore guidepost: the ratio between actual and punitive damages awarded. State Farm focuses its attention on the Supreme Court's statement that "[w]hen compensatory damages are substantial, then a lesser ratio [of compensatory to punitive damages], perhaps only equal to compensatory damages, can reach the outermost limit of the due process guarantee." Campbell II, 538 U.S. at 425, 123 S.Ct. 1513. The compensatory damages award to the Campbells was substantial and, in the Supreme Court's view, provided them "complete compensation." Id. at 426, 123 S.Ct. 1513. This is due at least in part to the possibility, recognized by the Supreme Court, that the compensatory damages award for emotional distress incorporated within it a punitive component.[7] Id.

Such a conclusion, though plausible as an abstract proposition, does not account for the circumstances of the compensatory damages award in this case. The jury awarded the Campbells $2.6 million in compensatory damages. The trial court granted State Farm's motion for remittitur and reduced the award to $1 million: $600,000 for Mr. Campbell and $400,000 for Mrs. Campbell. The trial court's ruling was supported by extensive and detailed findings explaining the basis for the reduced compensatory damages award. Based on this thorough record, we conclude that the trial court's compensatory damages award was purged of elements which may have been more properly placed in the category of punitive damages. We are convinced that the combined efforts of the jury and the trial judge ensured that the compensatory damages award was what it purported to be: compensation based on considered evaluation of the degree of emotional harm inflicted on the Campbells by State Farm. Because it is exclusively for actual harm sustained by the Campbells, the compensatory damages award supports a punitive damages award exceeding $1 million.

In its discussion of the relationship between compensatory and punitive damages, the Supreme Court reaffirmed that ratios exceeding single-digits, which it strongly implied mark the outer limits of due process, may be appropriate only where " 'a particularly egregious act has resulted in only a small amount of economic damages,' " or where " 'the monetary value of noneconomic harm may have been difficult to determine.' " Id. at 425, 123 S.Ct. 1513 (quoting Gore, 517 U.S. at 582, 116 S.Ct. 1589). These circumstances are not present here. But, neither is this a proper case to limit a punitive damages award to the amount of compensatory damages. The 1–to–1 ratio between compensatory and punitive damages is most applicable where a sizeable compensatory damages award for economic injury is coupled with conduct of unremarkable reprehensibility. This scenario, likewise, does not describe this case.

Here, the Campbells were awarded substantial noneconomic damages for emotional distress. As the Supreme Court noted, "Much of the distress was caused by the outrage and humiliation the Campbells suffered at the actions of their insurer; and it is a major rule of punitive damages to condemn such conduct." Id. at 426, 123 S.Ct. 1513. The trial court valued the extent of the Campbells' injury at $1 million. We have no difficulty concluding that conduct which causes $1 million of emotional distress and humiliation is markedly more egregious than conduct which results in $1 million of economic harm. Furthermore, such conduct is a candidate for the imposition of punitive damages in excess of a 1–to–1 ratio to compensatory damages. Simply put, the trial court's determination that State Farm caused the Campbells $1 million of emotional distress warrants condemnation in the upper single-digit ratio range rather than the 1–to–1 ratio urged by State Farm.

---

[7] Campbell II, 538 U.S. at 426, 123 S.Ct. 1513 (" 'In many cases in which compensatory damages include an amount for emotional distress, such as humiliation or indignation aroused by the defendant's act, there is no clear line of demarcation between punishment and compensation and a verdict for a specified amount frequently includes elements of both.' ") (quoting Restatement (Second) of Torts § 908, cmt. c (1977)).

When considered in light of all of the Gore reprehensibility factors, we conclude that a 9–to–1 ratio between compensatory and punitive damages, yielding a $9,018,780.75 punitive damages award, serves Utah's legitimate goals of deterrence and retribution within the limits of due process.

C. Comparable Civil and Criminal Penalties

The application of Gore's final guidepost, the difference between the punitive damages awarded by the jury and the civil penalties authorized or imposed in comparable cases, to State Farm's conduct does not cause us to retreat from our determination that a punitive damages award nine times greater than the compensatory damages is called for here.

In Campbell II, the Supreme Court pointed to a potential $10,000 fine for fraud as "the most relevant civil sanction" to which State Farm was exposed for its conduct toward the Campbells.[8] 538 U.S. at 428, 123 S.Ct. 1513; see also Utah Code Ann. § 31A–26–303 (2003). According to the Supreme Court, this fine was "dwarfed" by the $145 million punitive damages jury award. Id. It is unclear, however, what amount of punitive damages would be supported by a $10,000 fine. The Supreme Court endorsed a punitive damages award of $1 million, which is one hundred times greater than the $10,000 fine. Presumably, then, this 100–to–1 ratio does not offend due process. Thus, somewhere between $1 million and $145 million, the difference between the $10,000 civil penalty and the punitive damages award becomes so great that the latter "dwarfs" the former. State Farm claims in its brief that the Supreme Court impliedly found that the civil penalty would be dwarfed by a $17 million punitive damages award. Whether or not this is true, we hold fast to our conviction that a punitive damages award of $9,018,780.75 is in line with the third Gore guidepost.

The nature of a civil or criminal penalty provides some useful guidance to courts when fixing punitive damages because it reflects "legislative judgments concerning appropriate sanctions for the conduct at issue." Browning–Ferris, 492 U.S. at 301, 109 S.Ct. 2909 (O'Connor, J., concurring in part and dissenting in part). However, the quest to reliably position any misconduct within the ranks of criminal or civil wrongdoing based on penalties affixed by a legislature can be quixotic. For example, while a $10,000 fine for fraud may appear modest in relationship to a multi-million dollar punitive damages award, it is identical to the maximum fine which may be imposed on a person in Utah for the commission of a first degree felony, the classification assigned our most serious crimes. Utah Code Ann. § 76–3–301 (2003).

The Campbells invite us to conduct anew an analysis of the potential penalties to which State Farm may be exposed, based on the narrowed range of conduct deemed relevant by the Supreme Court. While we agree that the Supreme Court opened the door to such a reassessment, we believe that it is unnecessary in light of our conclusion that $9,018,780.75 is amply supported by the $10,000 civil penalty.

In sum, the Supreme Court affirmed the authority of a state to "make its own reasoned judgment about what conduct is permitted or proscribed within its borders." Campbell II, 538 U.S. at 422, 123 S.Ct. 1513 (citing Gore, 517 U.S. at 569, 116 S.Ct. 1589). It follows, therefore, that each state retains the right and the responsibility to draw on its own values and traditions when assessing the reprehensibility of tortious conduct for the purpose of reviewing the propriety of a punitive damages award, so long as that review conforms to the Gore guidelines and the demands of due process. To the extent that our conclusions about what size punitive damages award best serves the legitimate interests of Utah exceeds an award suggested by the Supreme Court, we are exercising what we interpret to be a clear grant of discretion to do so. We have carefully considered the scope of the Supreme Court's mandate and have endeavored scrupulously to confine ourselves to it.

V. ATTORNEY FEES, EXCESS VERDICT, AND SPECIAL DAMAGES

Finally, we turn to the Campbells' claim that costs and attorney fees incurred in this action, as well as the excess portion of the verdict not covered by insurance, should be included as part of the denominator in calculating a ratio between compensatory and punitive damages. We disagree.

We believe that fairly read, the Supreme Court's opinion forecloses consideration of a compensatory damages number other than the $1,000,000 awarded by the jury. The Supreme Court's analysis of the reasonableness and proportionality of the punitive damages award was grounded in its conviction "that there is a presumption against an award that has a 145–to–1 ratio." Campbell II, 538 U.S. at 426, 123 S.Ct. 1513. While that analysis may not have been different had the denominator been $1,939,518.10 (the amount of the compensatory damages, special damages, excess verdict, and attorney fees combined), and the ratio thereby reduced to 75–to–1, the considerable attention given by the Supreme Court to the issue of compensatory damages and the methodology for arriving at a constitutionally permissible ratio of compensatory to punitive damages convinces us that we would not be at liberty to consider a substitute denominator. We do, however, include the award of special damages as part of our punitive damages award as both parties agree it is part of the overall damages assessment.

To consider attorney fees and expenses in awarding punitive damages also invites unnecessary conceptual and practical complications to an already complex enterprise. In almost every case, including this one, the attorney fees and expense damage component would require its own independent reprehensibility assessment using the Gore standards. The manner in which a defendant conducts litigation bears a rational relationship to the conduct giving rise to the claim for punitive damages and would inevitably lead to an unseemly and time-consuming appendage to the trial.

The incorporation of attorney fees and expenses into the compensatory damages award would substantially alter the manner in which trials are conducted in this state. Under our general practice, the issues of whether attorney fees are available to a party and the reasonableness of the requested fees are reserved for determination by the judge after the conclusion of the trial or other proceedings. We have little doubt that the interests of justice would be subverted by sidetracking the focus of a trial away from the central claims of the parties and onto issues relating to attorney fees and expenses.

VI. CONCLUSION

In conclusion, we hold that State Farm's behavior toward the Campbells was so egregious as to warrant a punitive damages award of $9,018,780.75, an amount nine times greater than the amount of compensatory and special damages.

Chief Justice DURHAM, Justice WILKINS, Justice PARRISH, and Judge BILLINGS concur in Justice NEHRING'S opinion. Having disqualified himself, Associate Chief Justice DURRANT does not participate herein; Utah Court of Appeals Judge JUDITH BILLINGS sat.

Notes and Questions

1. Because torts is a state law subject, it is relatively unusual for the United States Supreme Court to address cases arising out of tort claims. However, because the federal Constitution preempts inconsistent state law, where that law and related decisions out of state courts implicate constitutional constraints, it may become a federal issue. This is what happened in the *State Farm* case: the amount of punitive damages awarded by the jury and upheld by the state courts was found to violate the federal Constitution's due process requirements and thus was rejected by the Supreme Court.

2. What is the test the United States Supreme Court used in *State Farm* to determine the due process fairness of the state's punitive damages award? Do you agree with the Court that this test ensures that "a person [will] receive fair notice not only of the conduct that will subject him to punishment, but also of the severity of the penalty that a State may impose"?

3. How did the Utah State Supreme Court respond to the United States Supreme Court's remand of its prior decision? Was it properly constrained by the latter's formula for establishing constitutional punitive damages awards? What flexibility did it find within that formula? Finally, how would you characterize the principal tensions between the two courts over the course of the litigation?

4. The aspects of the *State Farm* litigation we have presented here all centered on a question of federal constitutional law. As we have seen, lower state courts generally avoid such issues and instead decide questions presented on the basis of state law. Given this, how would a lower state court today decide a challenge to the size of a punitive damages award?

5. Punitive damages have been extensively studied. *See, e.g.,* Neil Vidmar and Mirya Holman, *The Frequency, Predictability, and Proportionality of Jury Awards of Punitive Damages in State Courts in 2005: A New Audit,* 43 SUFFOLK U. L. REV. 855 (2010); Michael L. Rustad, *Unraveling Punitive Damages: Current Data and Further Inquiry,* 1998 WIS. L. REV. 15 (1998). Professors Vidmar, Rustad, and others reach similar conclusions and two of their judgments are worth considering:

First, they find that punitive damage awards are infrequent. The public hears about the occasional huge verdict, but in actuality, most cases settle and settlements almost never include payments for punitive damages because of the tax implications for both parties. Even in the increasingly small number of cases that go to trial, punitive damages are awarded in very few cases and in considerably fewer do the awards survive appellate scrutiny.

Second, the amount of punitive damage awards varies significantly from case-to-case even when the cases appear to be similar on their facts, leading the United States Supreme Court to lament "the[ir] stark unpredictability." Exxon Shipping Co. v. Baker, 554 U.S. 471, 499 (2008). For example, *Gore* (discussed in *State Farm)* was not the only Alabama case arising out of BMW's repainting practices. The plaintiffs in those cases received similar compensatory damage awards but Dr. Gore's jury awarded punitive damages and the other plaintiffs' juries did not. What might account for this unpredictability? And is it a sufficient basis for curtailing the range of punitive damages a jury can award?

6. Curtailing the range of punitive damages a jury can award implicates the jury's and ultimately tort law's ability to use punitive damages as a tool to punish especially wealthy corporate defendants. As an English judge wrote in 1814, in a simpler but analogous context:

> I wish to know, in a case where a man disregards every principle which actuates the conduct of gentlemen, what is to restrain him except large damages? To be sure, one can hardly conceive worse conduct than this. What would be said to a person in a low situation of life, who should behave himself in this manner? I do not know upon what principle we can grant a rule in this case, unless we were to lay it down that the jury are not justified in giving more than the absolute pecuniary damage that the Plaintiff may sustain. Suppose a gentleman has a paved walk in his paddock, before his window, and that a man intrudes and walks up and down before the window of his house, and looks in while the owner is at dinner, is the trespasser to be permitted to say, "here is a halfpenny for you, which is the full extent of all the mischief I have done?" Would that be a compensation? I cannot say that it would be.

Merest v. Harvey, 128 E. R. 761, 5 Taunt. 442 (1814). Because punishment is a way to regulate behavior, this means that tort law's deterrence function is also necessarily limited. Would it make sense, as some have suggested, for a jurisdiction to abolish punitive damages and leave it to the criminal justice system to provide any punishment or deterrence beyond compensatory damages?

CHAPTER SEVEN
AFFIRMATIVE DEFENSES TO NEGLIGENCE

The classic affirmative defenses in negligence cases are contributory negligence and assumption of the risk. At common law, both defenses were absolute bars to recovery. As the cases in this chapter reflect, this bar has been ameliorated in many instances.

I. CONTRIBUTORY NEGLIGENCE

The term "contributory negligence" is used in two different ways: to state the argument or the fact that a plaintiff's own negligence has contributed to the injuries or damages, and to describe the rule still extant in a few jurisdictions that provides that when a plaintiff's negligence contributes to the injuries or damages, they are barred from recovery. The following case focuses on this second, formal usage. As you read it, in addition to gaining an understanding of the ways in which courts deal with a plaintiff's negligence, observe the competing arguments for and against common law development and legislative action.

COLEMAN v. SOCCER ASSOCIATION OF COLUMBIA
69 A. 3d 1149, 2013 (Md. App. 2013)

ELDRIDGE, J.

. . .

I.

The petitioner and plaintiff below, James Kyle Coleman, was an accomplished soccer player who had volunteered to assist in coaching a team of young soccer players in a program of the Soccer Association of Columbia, in Howard County, Maryland. On August 19, 2008, Coleman, at the time 20 years old, was assisting the coach during the practice of a team of young soccer players on the field of the Lime Kiln Middle School. While the Soccer Association of Columbia had fields of its own, it did not have enough to accommodate all of the program's young soccer players; the Association was required to use school fields for practices. At some point during the practice, Coleman kicked a soccer ball into a soccer goal. As he passed under the goal's metal top rail, or crossbar, to retrieve the ball, he jumped up and grabbed the crossbar. The soccer goal was not anchored to the ground, and, as he held on to the upper crossbar, Coleman fell backwards, drawing the weight of the crossbar onto his face. He suffered multiple severe facial fractures which required surgery and the placing of three titanium plates in his face. Coleman instituted the present action by filing a complaint, in the Circuit Court for Howard County, alleging that he was injured by the defendants' negligence. The defendant and respondent, the Soccer Association of Columbia, asserted the defense of contributory negligence.

At the ensuing jury trial, the soccer coach who had invited Coleman to help coach the soccer players testified that he had not inspected or anchored the goal which fell on Coleman. The coach also testified that the goal was not owned or provided by the Soccer Association, and he did not believe that it was his responsibility to anchor the goal. During the trial, the parties disputed whether the goal was located in an area under the supervision and control of the Soccer Association and whether the Soccer Association was required to inspect and anchor the goal. The Soccer Association presented testimony tending to show that, because the goal was not owned by the Soccer Association, the Soccer Association owed no duty to Coleman. The Soccer Association also presented testimony that the condition of the goal was open and obvious to all persons. The Association maintained that the accident was caused solely by Coleman's negligence.

Testimony was provided by Coleman to the effect that players commonly hang from soccer goals and that his actions should have been anticipated and expected by the Soccer Association. Coleman also provided testimony that anchoring goals is a standard safety practice in youth soccer. At the close of evidence, Coleman's attorney proffered a jury instruction on comparative negligence.[2] The judge declined to give Coleman's proffered comparative negligence instruction and, instead, instructed the jury on contributory negligence.

The jury was given a verdict sheet posing several questions. The first question was: "Do you find that the Soccer Association of Columbia was negligent?" The jury answered "yes" to this question. The jury also answered "yes" to the question: "Do you find that the Soccer Association of Columbia's negligence caused the Plaintiff's injuries?" Finally, the jury answered "yes" to the question: "Do you find that the Plaintiff was negligent and that his negligence contributed to his claimed injuries?"

In short, the jury concluded that the Soccer Association of Columbia was negligent and that the Soccer Association's negligence caused Coleman's injuries. The jury also found that Coleman was negligent, and that his negligence contributed to his own injuries. Because of the contributory negligence finding, Coleman was barred from any recovery. The trial court denied Coleman's motion for judgment notwithstanding the verdict and subsequently entered judgment in favor of the Soccer Association of Columbia.

Coleman filed a notice of appeal, and the Soccer Association filed a notice of cross-appeal. Before briefing and argument in the Court of Special Appeals, Coleman filed in this Court a petition for a writ of certiorari, which was granted. In his petition, Coleman posed only one question: whether this Court should retain the standard of contributory negligence as the common law standard governing negligence cases in the State of Maryland.

. . .

---

[2] The proffered jury instruction read as follows: "If you find that more than one party has established his/her burden of proof as to negligence, as defined by the court, you must then compare the negligence of those parties. The total amount of negligence is 100%. The figure that you arrive at should reflect the total percentage of negligence attributed to each party with respect to the happening of the accident. A comparison of negligence is made only if the negligence of more than one party proximately caused the accident."

II.

This Court last addressed the continuing viability of the contributory negligence doctrine in *Harrison v. Montgomery County Bd. of Educ., supra,* 295 Md. 442, 456 A.2d 894. In *Harrison,* the Court held that the contributory negligence principle remained the valid standard in Maryland negligence cases and that "any change in the established doctrine [was for] the Legislature."

Chief Judge Murphy, for the Court in *Harrison,* began his review of the contributory negligence standard by tracing the standard's historical origins to Lord Chief Justice Ellenborough's opinion in *Butterfield v. Forrester,* 11 East 60, 103 Eng. Rep. 926 (K.B.1809).[4]

As *Harrison* explained the case,

> "Butterfield left a public inn at dusk, mounted his horse and rode off 'violently' down the street. Forrester, who was effecting some repairs to his house, had placed a pole in the roadway. Although Butterfield could have seen and avoided the obstruction, he did not and was injured. The [English] court there noted:
>
> > 'One person being in fault will not dispense with another's using ordinary care for himself. Two things must concur to support this action, an obstruction in the road by the fault of the defendant, and no want of ordinary care to avoid it on the part of the plaintiff.' [11 East] at 61, 103 Eng. Rep. at 927."

The *Harrison* opinion explained that, when the contributory negligence standard was first judicially adopted in the United States, the courts at the time were concerned that juries would award to plaintiffs sums that had the potential to stifle "newly developing industry."[5] Early American courts were also concerned that they should not adopt a policy in which "courts . . . assist a wrongdoer who suffered an injury as a result of his own wrongdoing." *Harrison,* 295 Md. at 450, 456 A.2d at 898. *See also Smith v. Smith,* 2 Pick. 621, 19 Mass. 621, 624 (1824) (a leading early American case incorporating the contributory negligence bar as part of common law).

---

[4] Some commentators have claimed that the doctrine of contributory negligence originated even earlier, with the case of *Bayly v. Merrel,* 79 Eng. Rep. 331 (K.B.1606). Most authorities, however, take the position that the doctrine originated with *Butterfield v. Forrester,* 11 East 60, 103 Eng. Rep. 926 (K.B.1809). *See, e.g.,* William L. Prosser, *Comparative Negligence,* 41 Cal. L.Rev. 1, 3 (1953); Wex S. Malone, *The Formative Era of Contributory Negligence,* 41 Ill. L.Rev. 151 (1946).

[5] One commentator has written as follows (H. Woods, *The Negligence Case: Comparative Fault,* § 1:4, at 7–8 (1978), footnotes omitted):

> By 1850, [the country] had become heavily industrialized. This unprecedented development of industry and the general realization that it was related to Britain's continuance as the dominant world power brought out the protective instincts of her judiciary. The English courts eagerly seized upon Lord Ellenborough's holding in *Butterfield* as a most effective protective device. The American judiciary was no less enthusiastic. A Pennsylvania court in 1854 said this had been the 'rule from time immemorial and is not likely to be changed in all the time to come." '

This Court, relying on *Butterfield v. Forrester, supra,* first adopted the standard of contributory negligence in *Irwin v. Sprigg,* 6 Gill. 200, 205 (1847), stating:

> The established doctrine now is, that although the defendant's misconduct may have been the primary cause of the injury complained of, yet the plaintiff cannot recover in an action of this kind, if the proximate and immediate cause of the damage can be traced to a want of ordinary care and caution on his part. Under such circumstances he must bear the consequences of his own recklessness or folly.

The contributory negligence standard was later modified in part by this Court's adoption of the last clear chance doctrine, which allowed a plaintiff to recover "if the defendant might, by the exercise of care on its part, have avoided the consequences of the neglect or carelessness" of the plaintiff. The Court recognized another exception to the contributory negligence standard where the plaintiff is under five years old.

The *Harrison* Court examined the origins and impact of comparative negligence, noting that early in the 20th century, the Maryland General Assembly had adopted a form of comparative negligence for "certain perilous occupations," but had subsequently repealed the provisions. The Court in *Harrison* also pointed out that, as of 1983, of the thirty-nine states that had adopted comparative negligence, thirty-one had done so by statute, with the eight remaining states having adopted the principle by judicial action. The Court noted that it was "clear" that legal scholars "favored" the comparative negligence standard, as supported by "[a]n almost boundless array of scholarly writings."

Nevertheless, the *Harrison* Court pointed to other considerations involved in changing the standard from contributory negligence to comparative negligence:

> Also to be considered is the effect which a comparative fault system would have on other fundamental areas of negligence law. The last clear chance doctrine, assumption of the risk, joint and several liability, contribution, setoffs and counterclaims, and application of the doctrine to other fault systems, such as strict liability in tort, are several of the more obvious areas affected by the urged shift to comparative negligence. Even that change has its complications; beside the 'pure' form of comparative negligence, there are several 'modified' forms, so that abrogation of the contributory negligence doctrine will necessitate the substitution of an alternate doctrine. Which form to adopt presents its own questions and the choice is by no means clear. . . . That a change from contributory to comparative negligence involves considerably more than a simple common law adjustment is readily apparent.

Harrison also examined those states which had abrogated the contributory negligence standard, pointing out that "most of the states which have adopted comparative negligence have done so by statute in derogation of the common law." The Court observed that, in several of these states, the courts had refused to judicially abrogate the contributory negligence standard because they "expressly deferred on policy grounds to their respective legislatures." Only eight state supreme courts, as of 1983, had adopted a comparative negligence standard by judicial decision. The *Harrison* opinion further held that, when this Court is

> called upon, as here, to overrule our own decisions, consideration must be given to the doctrine of *stare decisis* — the policy which entails the reaffirmation of a

> decisional doctrine of an appellate court, even though if considered for the first time, the Court might reach a different conclusion.

Chief Judge Murphy in *Harrison* continued his assessment by explaining that the principle of *stare decisis* should not be construed to

> inhibit [this Court] from changing or modifying a common law rule by judicial decision where we find, in light of changed conditions or increased knowledge, that the rule has become unsound in the circumstances of modern life, a vestige of the past, no longer suitable to our people.

Nevertheless, *Harrison* concluded:

> [I]n considering whether a long-established common law rule — unchanged by the legislature and thus reflective of this State's public policy — is unsound in the circumstances of modern life, we have always recognized that declaration of the public policy of Maryland is normally the function of the General Assembly; that body, by Article 5 of the Maryland Declaration of Rights, is expressly empowered to revise the common law of Maryland by legislative enactment. The Court, therefore, has been particularly reluctant to alter a common law rule in the face of indications that to do so would be contrary to the public policy of the State.

In the years immediately prior to *Harrison,* from 1966 to 1982, the Maryland General Assembly had considered twenty-one bills seeking to change the contributory negligence standard. None of the bills had been enacted. The *Harrison* Court accorded a great deal of weight to the General Assembly's failure to enact any of these bills, stating:

> [T]he legislature's action in rejecting the proposed change is indicative of an intention to retain the contributory negligence doctrine.

The Court further pointed out that enactment of a comparative negligence standard is be made, beginning with the initial inquiry of what form of comparative negligence to adopt, "pure" or one "of the several types of modified comparative negligence," If Maryland's common law were to change, the *Harrison* opinion explained, the decision as to which form of comparative negligence to adopt "plainly involves major policy considerations" of the sort best left to the General Assembly.

III.

Since the time of *Harrison,* this Court has continued to recognize the standard of contributory negligence as the applicable principle in Maryland negligence actions.

Although the contributory negligence principle has been part of this State's common law for over 165 years, petitioners and numerous amici in this case urge this Court to abolish the contributory negligence standard and replace it with a form of comparative negligence. They argue contributory negligence is an antiquated doctrine, that it has been roundly criticized by academic legal scholars, and that it has been rejected in a majority of our sister states. It is also pointed out that contributory negligence works an inherent unfairness by barring plaintiffs from any recovery, even when it is proven, in a particular case, that a defendant's negligence was primarily responsible for the act or omission which resulted in a plaintiff's injuries. It is said that contributory negligence provides harsh justice to those who may have acted negligently, in minor ways, to contribute to their injuries, and that it absolves those defendants from liability who can find any minor negligence in the plaintiffs' behavior.

Petitioners correctly contend that, because contributory negligence is a court-created principle, and has not been embodied in Maryland statutes, this Court possesses the authority to change the principle. . . .

The Court's ability to modify the common law was further underscored in *Kelley v. R.G. Industries, Inc.*, 304 Md. 124, 140, 497 A.2d 1143. 1151 (1985):

> This Court has repeatedly said that 'the common law is not static; its life and heart is its dynamism — its ability to keep pace with the world while constantly searching for just and fair solutions to pressing societal problems.' The common law is, therefore, subject to judicial modification in light of modern circumstances or increased knowledge.

> . . .

Since the *Harrison* case, the General Assembly has continually considered and failed to pass bills that would abolish or modify the contributory negligence standard. The failure of so many bills, attempting to change the contributory negligence doctrine, is a clear indication of legislative policy at the present time. This Court in *Moore v. State,* 388 Md. 623, 641, 882 A.2d 256, 267 (2005), with regard to the failure of legislation, explained:

> Although the failure of a single bill in the General Assembly may be due to many reasons, and thus is not always a good indication of the Legislature's intent, under some circumstances, the failure to enact legislation is persuasive evidence of legislative intent.

The *Moore* opinion continued:

Legislative inaction is very significant where bills have repeatedly been introduced in the General Assembly to accomplish a particular result, and where the General Assembly has persistently refused to enact such bills.

The General Assembly's repeated failure to pass legislation abrogating the defense of contributory negligence is very strong evidence that the legislative policy in Maryland is to retain the principle of contributory negligence. Chief Judge Bell emphasized for the Court in *Baltimore v. Clark,* 404 Md. 13, 36, 944 A.2d 1122, 1135–1136 (2008), the following:

> It is well settled that, where the General Assembly has announced public policy, the Court will decline to enter the public policy debate, even when it is the common law that is at issue and the Court certainly has the authority to change the common law.

For this Court to change the common law and abrogate the contributory negligence defense in negligence actions, in the face of the General Assembly's repeated refusal to do so, would be totally inconsistent with the Court's long-standing jurisprudence.

JUDGMENT OF THE CIRCUIT COURT FOR HOWARD COUNTY AFFIRMED. COSTS TO BE PAID BY THE APPELLANT JAMES COLEMAN.

Concurring Opinion by GREENE, J., which BATTAGLIA, McDONALD and RAKER, JJ., join. Omitted.

Dissenting Opinion by HARRELL, J., which BELL, C.J., joins.

Paleontologists and geologists inform us that Earth's Cretaceous period (including in what is present day Maryland) ended approximately 65 million years ago with an asteroid striking Earth (the Cretaceous–Paleogene Extinction Event), wiping-out, in a relatively short period of geologic time, most plant and animal species, including dinosaurs. As to the last premise, they are wrong. A dinosaur roams yet the landscape of Maryland (and Virginia, Alabama, North Carolina and the District of Columbia), feeding on the claims of persons injured by the negligence of another, but who contributed proximately in some way to the occasion of his or her injuries, however slight their culpability. The name of that dinosaur is the doctrine of contributory negligence. With the force of a modern asteroid strike, this Court should render, in the present case, this dinosaur extinct. It chooses not to do so. Accordingly, I dissent.

My dissent does not take the form of a tit-for-tat trading of thrusts and parries with the Majority opinion. Rather, I write for a future majority of this Court, which, I have no doubt, will relegate the fossilized doctrine of contributory negligence to a judicial tar pit at some point.

I. The History of Contributory Negligence in Maryland

Under the doctrine of contributory negligence, a plaintiff who fails to exercise ordinary care for his or her own safety, and thus contributes proximately to his or her injury, "is barred from all recovery, regardless of the quantum of a defendant's primary negligence." *Harrison v. Montgomery Cnty. Bd. of Ed.,* 295 Md. 442, 451, 456 A.2d 894, 898 (1983). Contributory negligence is the "neglect of duty imposed upon all men to observe ordinary care for their own safety," *Potts v. Armour & Co.,* 183 Md. 483, 490, 39 A.2d 552, 556 (1944), and refers not to the breach of a duty owed to another, but rather to the failure of an individual to exercise that degree of care necessary to protect him or her self. *Baltimore Cnty. v. State, Use of Keenan,* 232 Md. 350, 362, 193 A.2d 30, 37 (1963). An "all-or-nothing" doctrine, contributory negligence operates in application as a total bar to recovery by an injured plaintiff.

The doctrine is of judicial "Big Bang" origin, credited generally to the 1809 English case of *Butterfield v. Forrester* (1809) 103 Eng. Rep. 926 (K.B.). In *Butterfield,* the court considered whether a plaintiff, injured while "violently" riding his horse on a roadway, by a pole negligently placed in the roadway, could recover damages. Denying recovery, Lord Ellenborough penned the first recognized incantation of contributory negligence, declaring, "One person being in fault will not dispense with another's using ordinary care for himself. Two things must concur to support this action, an obstruction in the road by the fault of the defendant, and no want of ordinary care to avoid it on the part of the plaintiff." *Id.* at 927, 193 A.2d 30.

Soon after *Butterfield,* American courts began to recognize the doctrine of contributory negligence. *See Smith v. Smith,* 19 Mass. (2 Pick.) 621 (1824); William L. Prosser, *Comparative Negligence,* 51 Mich. L.Rev. 465, 468 (1953). Although early courts explained rarely the reasons for their adoption of the doctrine, scholars set forth later multiple reasons for its widespread acceptance in the U.S. in the nineteenth and early twentieth centuries. For example, its ascendance was considered a means of encouraging potential plaintiffs to comply with the relevant standard of care, 4 Harper, James & Gray on Torts, § 22.2 at 340 (3d ed. 2006) (hereinafter "Harper, James & Gray"); requiring plaintiffs to enter court with clean hands, Prosser & Keeton on the Law of Torts, § 65 at 451 (5th ed. 1984) (hereinafter "Prosser & Keeton"); and, insulating developing industry from liability and fostering economic growth by keeping in check plaintiff-minded juries. *Id.* at 452; 4 Harper, James & Gray, *supra,* § 22.1 at 328–30. The doctrine was seen also as consistent with "several unwritten policies of the [nineteenth and early twentieth century] common law"—specifically, the idea that courts should not assist someone who contributes to causing his or her own injuries, and the "passion for a simple issue that could be categorically answered yes or no. . ." *Harrison,* 295 Md. at 450, 456 A.2d at 897–98; *see also* Edward S. Digges, Jr. & Robert Dale Klein, *Comparative Fault in Maryland: The Time Has Come,* 41 Md. L.Rev. 276, 278 (1982); Prosser & Keeton, *supra,* § 65 at 452.

Whatever the initial justifications attributed to its birth, contributory negligence has been a mainstay of Maryland law since its adoption in *Irwin v. Sprigg,* 6 Gill 200 (1847). Since that time, Maryland courts applied the doctrine of contributory negligence to bar recovery in negligence actions by at-fault plaintiffs. Exceptions evolved, however, to allow recovery in specific instances. For example, the defense of contributory negligence is not available against claimants under five years of age, in strict liability actions, and in actions based on intentional conduct. Additionally, the doctrine of last clear chance developed to allow a plaintiff to recover, despite his or her contributory negligence, if he or she establishes "something new or sequential, which affords the defendant a fresh opportunity (of which he fails to avail himself) to avert the consequences of his original negligence."

The all-or-nothing consequences of the application of contributory negligence have long been criticized nationally by scholars and commentators. Many have argued instead for, and most states have adopted a system of comparative negligence which apportions damages between a negligent plaintiff and a negligent defendant according to each party's relative degree of fault. Thus, under a comparative negligence system, a plaintiff's contributory negligence does not bar recovery, but rather reduces proportionately his or her damages in relation to his or her degree of fault.

This Court considered previously whether to replace the common law doctrine of contributory negligence with a system of comparative fault. We confronted this question most recently nearly thirty years ago. In *Harrison,* we considered whether to abrogate judicially contributory negligence in the midst of a nation-wide movement to transition to a system of comparative fault. We engaged first in a comparison of the historical and doctrinal principles of both contributory and comparative negligence. *Harrison,* 295 Md. at 449–53, 456 A.2d at 897–99. Although recognizing the growing trend toward adopting principles of comparative fault, we noted, on the other hand, Maryland's long history of applying the doctrine of contributory negligence.

Although acknowledging further that jurisdictions transitioning from contributory negligence to comparative fault regimes experienced little difficulty in doing so, we noted that making such a doctrinal change requires consideration of a multitude of options and implications. For example, this Court would have to choose between a pure or modified fault system, and consider "the effect which a comparative fault system would have on other fundamental areas of negligence law," such as the "last clear chance doctrine, assumption of the risk, joint and several liability, contribution, setoffs and counterclaims, and application of the doctrine to other fault systems, such as strict liability in tort. . . ." *Id.* at 455, 456 A.2d at 900. Noting the lack of uniformity among the systems adopted by new comparative fault jurisdictions in their treatment of these areas, we characterized the decision whether to adopt either pure or modified comparative fault as one "plainly involv[ing] major policy considerations." *Id.* at 462, 456 A.2d at 904.

Perhaps overawed by the difficult choices inherent in adopting comparative negligence, however, the *Harrison* court declined to ride atop the tsunami of states abandoning contributory negligence. Instead, the *Harrison* majority observed that "scant attention" had been paid by the Maryland Bench and Bar to the relative merits of contributory and comparative negligence, *id.* at 458, 456 A.2d at 902, and that, although the Legislature had considered numerous bills proposing to adopt comparative fault, none were enacted ultimately. Thus, ignoring the great societal change nationally demonstrating the unsuitability of contributory negligence principles to modern life, but finding no evidence of that groundswell in Maryland, we deferred instead to the Legislature, inferring from its inaction an "intention to retain the contributory negligence doctrine" as the public policy of the State of Maryland. *Id.* at 462, 456 A.2d at 904. We concluded:

> All things considered, we are unable to say that the circumstances of modern life have so changed as to render contributory negligence a vestige of the past, no longer suitable to the needs of the people of Maryland. In the final analysis, whether to abandon the doctrine of contributory negligence in favor of comparative negligence involves fundamental and basic public policy considerations properly to be addressed by the legislature. We therefore conclude . . . that while we recognize the force of the plaintiff's argument, in the present state of the law, we leave any change in the established doctrine to the Legislature.

Id. at 463, 456 A.2d at 905 (internal quotation marks and citations omitted). We are given straightforwardly in the present case another opportunity to replace the doctrine of contributory negligence with a system of comparative fault.

II. The Maryland Court of Appeals Has the Power to Abrogate Contributory Negligence

Unquestionably (as the Majority opinion agrees—see Maj. slip op. at 11–12), this Court has the power to change the doctrine of contributory negligence. Although the common law may be changed also by legislative act, Md. Const. Decl. of Rts. art. 5, we have stated frequently that it is "our duty to determine the common law as it exists in this State." Contributory negligence is, and has always been, a common law doctrine of judicial origin in this State. In the absence of codification by the Legislature, the defense of contributory negligence remains a dependent of the common law, and as such, is within the province of its parent, this Court, to abrogate or modify that to which it gave birth and nurtured.

In accordance with our authority to alter the common law, Petitioner James Coleman ("Coleman") urges this Court to abolish the doctrine of contributory negligence, arguing that it is a vestige of the past. In response, Respondent Soccer Association of Columbia ("SAC") and its Amici claim principally that this Court is bound by its decision in *Harrison* to retain the doctrine of contributory negligence; but, assuming that we are not bound by *Harrison,* Respondent contends that the abrogation of contributory negligence is more appropriate for legislative, rather than judicial, action, due to the complex policy considerations involved in adopting comparative negligence. I disagree. Principles of *stare decisis* do not require continued adherence to our decision in *Harrison,* nor does this Court owe continued deference to the General Assembly simply because of the difficult choices inherent in formulating a comparative negligence rule. Thus, I would abolish the doctrine of contributory negligence and replace it with comparative fault — "not because [it is] easy, but because [it is] hard." President John F. Kennedy, Address at Rice University on the Nation's Space Effort (12 Sept. 1962).

A. *Stare Decisis* Does Not Require Retention of the Doctrine of Contributory Negligence

Under the doctrine of *stare decisis,* changes in long-standing "decisional doctrine are left to the Legislature" for purposes of "certainty and stability." *Harrison,* 295 Md. at 458–59, 456 A.2d at 902 (quoting *Deems v. Western Md. Ry. Co.,* 247 Md. 95, 102, 231 A.2d 514, 518 (1967)). *Stare decisis,* meaning to stand by the thing decided, "promotes the evenhanded, predictable, and consistent development of legal principles, fosters reliance on judicial decisions, and contributes to the actual and perceived integrity of the judicial process." *Livesay v. Baltimore Cnty.,* 384 Md. 1, 14, 862 A.2d 33, 40–41 (2004) (quoting *Payne v. Tennessee,* 501 U.S. 808, 827, 111 S.Ct. 2597, 2609, 115 L.Ed.2d 720 (1991)). Notwithstanding the doctrine of *stare decisis,* the common law remains "subject to judicial modification in the light of modern circumstances or increased knowledge." *Ireland,* 310 Md. at 331, 529 A.2d at 366. As we stated in *Harrison,* we have never construed the doctrine of *stare decisis* "to inhibit us from changing or modifying a common law rule by judicial decision where we find, in light of changed conditions or increased knowledge, that the rule has become unsound in the circumstances of modern life, a vestige of the past, no longer suitable to our people." 295 Md. at 459, 456 A.2d at 903.

Although this Court has declined frequently to alter long-standing common law rules, we may depart from principles of *stare decisis* in two circumstances: (1) when a prior decision was "clearly wrong and contrary to established principles," *Tracey,* 427 Md. at 659, 50 A.3d at 1093 (quoting *State v. Adams,* 406 Md. 240, 259, 958 A.2d 295, 307 (2008)), or (2) "when precedent has been superseded by significant changes in the law or facts." *Id.* (citing *Harrison,* 295 Md. at 459, 456 A.2d at 903).

This Court has shown a willingness to depart from its stale decisions even where we expressed previously an intention to defer to legislative action on a longstanding, but widely-disfavored, common law rule. For example, we declined for decades to abrogate the common law interspousal immunity doctrine prohibiting married women from maintaining actions in tort against their husbands, in each instance deferring expressly to the Legislature.

Shortly after our decision in *Harrison,* however, we abrogated the common law doctrine of interspousal immunity in negligence actions. *Boblitz v. Boblitz,* 296 Md. 242, 462 A.2d 506 (1983). In so doing, we distanced ourselves from our prior cases and characterized the decision as one appropriate for judicial action. We considered persuasive the evolution of society's conceptions regarding women and the trend toward abrogation in other states, concluding that the foundation of the doctrine no longer coincided with modern values. . . . We distinguished *Harrison,* however, as both possessing a history of legislative inaction on proposed bills (lacking in the context of interspousal immunity) and involving necessarily more complex issues, stating that Harrison represented an attempt to grant judicially that which "the Legislature repeatedly had rejected efforts to achieve legislatively." Id. at 274, 462 A.2d 506, 462 A.2d at 521. Yet, we emphasized that, despite our decision in Harrison, it remains well within the authority of this Court to abrogate an outmoded rule of the common law.

. . .

Thus, as our abrogation of the interspousal tort immunity doctrine demonstrates, this Court has not only the power, but also the responsibility (*Harrison* notwithstanding) to abrogate the doctrine of contributory negligence if it concludes that the state of society and law have changed so that contributory negligence is a vestige of the past, unsuitable to the conditions of modern life. To that end, this Court reviews the foundation of the doctrine to determine its continued relevance in modern society, and considers persuasive, although not binding, the actions of other states on this issue. Additionally, we may analyze, to some degree (limited by the factual record before us), "the public policy concerns raised by the parties and by the other courts which have grappled with this issue." *State v. Wiegmann,* 350 Md. 585, 607, 714 A.2d 841, 851 (1998) (quoting *Gaver v. Harrant,* 316 Md. 17, 30, 557 A.2d 210, 217 (1989)).

As noted above, the widespread acceptance of contributory negligence as a complete defense is attributed principally to (1) the desire to protect the nations' newly-developing industry from liability and plaintiff-minded juries, E.A. Turk, *Comparative Negligence on the March,* 28 Chi.-Kent L.Rev. 189, 201 (1950); 4 Harper, James & Gray, *supra,* § 22.1 at 328–30; and (2) "the concept prevalent at the time that a plaintiff's irresponsibility in failing to use due care for his own safety erased whatever fault could be laid at defendant's feet for contributing to the injury." *Scott v. Rizzo,* 96 N.M. 682, 634 P.2d 1234, 1237 (N.M.1981) (citing F. Harper and F. James, Law of Torts, § 22.1 at 1198 (1956)). Neither of these justifications, however, carry weight in present-day Maryland. In today's society, there has been no need demonstrated to protect any "newly-developing" industry at the expense of injured litigants. Industry generally in this nation is no longer fledgling or so prone to withering at the prospect of liability. Moreover, tilting the scales to favor industry is inconsistent with modern conceptions of justice, which focus instead on proportional responsibility and fundamental fairness.

The evolution of society's conceptions of justice is exemplified by the move of tort law away from traditional "all-or-nothing" recovery rules and toward allocation of the burden of liability among at-fault parties. Contributory negligence is at odds with this fundamental premise. By barring recovery completely to a contributorily negligent plaintiff, the rule "visits the entire loss caused by the fault of two parties on one of them alone, and that one the injured plaintiff, least able to bear it, and quite possibly much less at fault than the defendant who goes scot-free." Prosser, *Comparative Negligence, supra,* at 469.

Respondent and its Amici count as a strength of the doctrine of contributory negligence its inflexibility in refusing to compensate any, even marginally, at-fault plaintiff. They argue that, in so doing, contributory negligence encourages personal responsibility by foreclosing the possibility of recovery for potential, negligent plaintiffs, and thus cannot possibly be outmoded.[11] To the contrary, that the doctrine of contributory negligence grants one party a

---

[11] As some scholars note, the deterrence rationale of contributory negligence (or comparative fault, for that matter) is dubious at best. "If the prospect of losing life and limb does not make a plaintiff careful, little further inducement to care will be added by speculations as to the outcome of a lawsuit. The same thing is

windfall at the expense of the other is, as courts and commentators alike have noted, unfair manifestly as a matter of policy. Prosser, *Comparative Negligence, supra,* at 469 (characterizing contributory negligence as "outrageous" and an "obvious injustice" that "[n]o one has ever succeeded in justifying . . , and no one ever will"). Moreover, if contributory negligence encourages would-be plaintiffs to exercise caution with respect to themselves, then so too does the doctrine of comparative fault by reducing the plaintiff's recoverable damages. Unlike contributory negligence, however, comparative fault deters also negligence on the part of the defendant by holding him or her responsible for the damages that he or she inflicted on the plaintiff. *See* Lande & MacAlister, *supra,* at 5–6 (noting that, although contributory negligence systems "burden[ ] only plaintiffs with the obligation to take precautions," comparative negligence provides a "mixture of responsibility" that is "the best way to prevent most accidents." . . . Thus, Respondent's contention that contributory negligence encourages personal responsibility, and is therefore preferable to comparative negligence, is unpersuasive.

Respondent contends also that the foundation of contributory negligence remains strong because, as we said in *Harrison,* "Maryland cases do not reflect any general dissatisfaction with the contributory negligence doctrine." 295 Md. at 458, 456 A.2d at 898. That the courts of this State have applied uniformly the doctrine, however, does not mean that we did not recognize along the way its flaws. For example, as Judge Eldridge noted recently, our retention of contributory negligence garnered extensive criticism — "few if any other legal principles have been criticized as much as this Court's continued adherence in negligence actions to the doctrine of contributory negligence and the Court's refusal to adopt comparative negligence." *State v. Adams,* 406 Md. 240, 332, 958 A.2d 295, 351 (2008) (Eldridge, J., dissenting), *overruled by Unger v. State,* 427 Md. 383, 48 A.3d 242 (2012). The Court of Special Appeals also noted similar criticism, calling the doctrine "harsh and pitiless," and noted that we are among the severe minority of states adhering still to it. *See Preston Carter v. Senate Masonry, Inc.,* 156 Md.App. 162, 175, 846 A.2d 50, 58 (2004); *see also Stewart v. Hechinger Stores Co.,* 118 Md.App. 354, 359, 702 A.2d 946, 949 (1997) ("Although we are aware of the often harsh consequences of Maryland's common law doctrine of contributory negligence, and that it has been abandoned by a vast majority of states in favor of some form of comparative negligence, we are in no position summarily to do so.").

Moreover, since our decision in *Harrison,* the doctrine of comparative negligence has continued to be accepted elsewhere as the superior legal principle. At the time *Harrison* was decided, thirty-nine states had replaced the doctrine of contributory negligence with some form of comparative negligence. This trend has continued unabated. Today, the number of states applying comparative negligence is forty-six, and not one jurisdiction adopting it has since retreated and re-adopted contributory negligence. Rather, seven additional states have enacted comparative negligence systems since *Harrison.* What was at the time of *Harrison* a quickening trend within the United States is today an established principle of law in nearly every right-thinking common law jurisdiction in the world with the exception of Maryland, Alabama, the District of Columbia, North Carolina, and Virginia.

---

often true of defendants. Yet today those who bear the burden of accident liability are increasingly absentee defendants — corporate and other employers or insurance companies, whose lives and limbs are not at stake in the accident. . . . Defendants, then, will often lack a powerful incentive to carefulness — self-preservation — that is virtually always present with plaintiffs." 4 Harper, James & Gray, *supra,* § 22.2 at 340–41.

Respondent argues, in effect, that there has not been a significant change in the state of law or society since *Harrison,* and therefore there is no reason to depart from *stare decisis* and reconsider whether the doctrine of contributory negligence should be retained in the State of Maryland. I could not disagree more. At the time *Harrison* was decided, the country was in the midst of a broad reform effort sweeping the nation. The doctrine of comparative fault was of fairly recent vintage at the time *Harrison* was filed, adopted in most states in the ten years prior to our decision. Essentially, Respondent contends that, because our decision in *Harrison* was made when the movement toward reform of negligence principles was well underway, this Court is constrained to retain the doctrine forever, having missed the single opportunity to get on board the train. Respondent's argument seems to suggest that, so long as there is some delay in abandoning an unjust law, the unjust law remains irretrievably an albatross tied around the neck of our common law, unless and until the Legislature decides to save us.[13] As our decision in *Bozman* demonstrates, however, our authority to modify the common law and overrule prior decisions is not so limited.

. . . Comparative fault is no longer a trend or a doctrine of recent vintage, but rather is an established and integral doctrine to the negligence systems of nearly every state in the country. Other jurisdictions, most notably those that abrogated contributory negligence judicially, have decades of experience applying comparative fault — experience that, in large part, was lacking at the time we decided *Harrison.* The twelve states to abrogate contributory negligence by judicial decision provide examples of how comparative negligence is applied, how it impacts collateral doctrines and fault systems, and how it is applied in reality. In essence, this Court may foresee more clearly today potential impacts and complications, as well as the value of a comparative fault system, than was possible in 1983. Maryland is no longer at the crest of a wave of reform — instead, it has been left behind, one of the last bastions of contributory negligence in a world which has discarded it as unjust and outmoded. In my estimation, this qualifies certainly as a significant change warranting reconsideration of *Harrison.*

Although I recognize certainly the value of the doctrine of *stare decisis,* I do not believe that in this instance, strict adherence is appropriate or warranted. I do not believe that because *Harrison* reaffirmed the vitality of contributory negligence in this State, absent legislative action, this Court is muted forever on the topic. The bounds of *stare decisis* are not so strict. Continued adherence to the doctrine of contributory negligence as rote obeisance to the principles of *stare decisis* and legislative deference "represents judicial inertia rather than a reasoned consideration of the intrinsic value of the rule." *Kaatz,* 540 P.2d at 1049. Contributory negligence is no longer justified, has been discarded by nearly every other jurisdiction, and is manifestly unjust. Thus, I conclude that contributory negligence is a vestige of the past, and that in considering whether to abrogate the doctrine of contributory negligence, we are not bound by our decision in *Harrison.*

B. This Court Need Not Defer to Continued Legislative Inaction

Respondent argues that, notwithstanding our decision in *Harrison,* whether to abrogate contributory negligence in favor of comparative fault is a matter more properly suited to the legislative, rather than judicial, process. In *Harrison,* we noted that "in considering whether a

[13] This would be like urging Dr. Wolf Frankenstein (portrayed by Basil Rathbone) to wait to see if the village's elected officials will kill his monster, before taking matters into his own hands. In the meantime, many villagers will be lost. *See* Son of Frankenstein (Universal Pictures 1939).

long-established common law rule—unchanged by the legislature and thus reflective of this State's public policy—is unsound in the circumstances of modern life, we have always recognized that declaration of the public policy of Maryland is normally the function of the General Assembly." 295 Md. at 460, 456 A.2d at 903. Because declaration of public policy is generally a matter for the Legislature, we declared our "particular[ ] reluctan[ce] to alter a common law rule in the face of indications that to do so would be contrary to the public policy of the State[,]" *id.,* and noted that we owe "initial deference to the legislature where change is sought in a long-established and well-settled common law principle." *Id.* at 461, 456 A.2d at 904.

In considering whether the doctrine of contributory negligence was declared the public policy of the State of Maryland, we placed particular emphasis on the Legislature's consideration of numerous bills proposing to adopt the doctrine of comparative negligence. Specifically, we noted that between 1966 and 1982, the General Assembly considered twenty-one bills proposing the adoption of comparative negligence, yet none passed. *Id.* "Although not conclusive," we stated, "the legislature's action in rejecting the proposed change is indicative of an intention [on the part of the Legislature] to retain the contributory negligence doctrine." *Id.*

Our statements in *Harrison* did not circumscribe, however, our authority to alter judicially-created common law rules in the face of repeated legislative inaction on the subject. Although we have declined frequently to effect changes in decisional doctrine upon observing repeated legislative inaction, we determined, on multiple occasions, that legislative inaction may not be a sufficient premise from which to draw a positive legislative intent in certain situations.

Although the *Harrison* court opted to defer to the Legislature, the opinion in that case gives no indication that such deference was unlimited. No acknowledgment was advanced that we lack the authority to alter a long-standing common law rule where the Legislature declines to enact proposed legislation. Rather, we expressed that we are "particularly reluctant" to do so, and that we give " *initial* deference" to the Legislature when considering a change to long-standing common law principles. *Harrison,* 495 Md. at 460–61, 456 A.2d at 903–04 (emphasis added). Further, we did not characterize the inaction of the General Assembly as a conclusive, definitive declaration of public policy—to the contrary, we specifically stated that legislative inaction is "not conclusive" and merely "indicative of an intention to retain the doctrine of contributory negligence." *Id* . at 461, 456 A.2d at 904.

I acknowledge, of course, that legislative consideration of comparative negligence did not cease with our decision in *Harrison.* The General Assembly considered numerous comparative negligence bills since *Harrison,* but has not to this date reached an agreement that comparative negligence should become the law of this State by legislative act.[16]

Declining to perpetuate unmindful deference to the Legislature on such a topic would not be without precedent. For example, as noted above, this Court stated repeatedly its intention to

---

[16] As the author of one tort law treatise noted in response to *Harrison,* "The history [of legislative attempts to abrogate contributory negligence] appears more nearly indicative, it is suggested with respect, of the superior ability of insurers' lobbyists to influence a committee or its chairman in a non-public decision-making than an entire legislative body in an open vote." The author goes on to note that, in the Senate's first opportunity to vote on a comparative negligence bill, it passed 45–1 on the floor before being defeated behind closed doors in the House Judiciary Committee. 4 Harper, James & Gray, *supra,* § 22.18 at 495 n.1.

defer to legislative action on the topic of interspousal immunity before acting. Decades later, after noting the Legislature's continued stasis on the subject, we rescinded our deference and modernized an outdated common law rule.

Other states, too, abrogated judicially the doctrine of contributory negligence in spite of legislative inaction on proposed bills of like objective. [Editor's note: Here the dissent looks at Kentucky, Missouri, New Mexico, and Illinois as examples.]

Respondent also contends that, the abstract principle of deference to legislative inaction notwithstanding, replacing the doctrine of contributory negligence is a task more appropriate for legislative action because that potential deliberative and comprehensive decision-making process is suited better to resolution of the complex policy considerations involved in adopting comparative fault and its collateral impacts. The *Harrison* court expressed a particular reluctance to abrogate contributory negligence due to the nature of comparative negligence as not being "a unitary doctrine[,] but one which has been adopted by other states in either a pure or modified form." 295 Md. at 462, 456 A.2d at 904. Characterizing the choice between pure and modified comparative fault as "a policy issue of major dimension," this Court opted in 1983 to leave the choice to the General Assembly. *Id.* at 463, 456 A.2d at 905. Respondent contends that, because this decision implicates policy considerations and this Court is limited in its consideration of the impact on collateral doctrines and principles by the facts of this case, we should continue to refrain from adopting comparative negligence and disrupting long-settled law to avoid confusion and disarray in our courts. Moreover, Respondent and its Amici argue that abolishing the doctrine of contributory negligence is bad public policy. They contend that in so doing, we would inject chaos and uncertainty into an area of settled law, and increase litigation, insurance rates, and taxes.[19]

It is recognized generally that no "good data" exists on whether comparative negligence increases insurance rates, due to the difficulty of controlling for all of the variables existing in state automobile insurance markets. As acknowledged in the 2004 Maryland Department of Legislative Services Report, "[i]n the absence of any comprehensive study, it is impossible to state with any certainty the direct and indirect consequences of changing to a comparative negligence system." *Id.* at 21. The possibility that comparative fault may increase insurance rates is insufficient to justify retention of what is certainly an unjust system. As the Supreme Court of Kentucky stated in response to this very argument, "there are no *good* economies in an *unjust* law." *Hilen,* 673 S.W.2d at 718 (emphasis in original).

Although the transition from contributory to comparative negligence systems is plainly "a policy issue of major dimension," I do not think that it is an issue on which awaiting legislative catharsis is appropriate any longer. Contributory negligence is a spawn of the court system—and as such, this Court is eminently able and uniquely situated to stay the course. Moreover, as the South Carolina Court of Appeals noted, the potential for a legislative body to affect comprehensively a doctrinal substitution has not proven out uniformly in execution. *Langley v. Boyter,* 284 S.C. 162, 325 S.E.2d 550, 560 (S.C.App.1984), *quashed,* 286 S.C. 85, 332 S.E.2d 100 (S.C.1984), *cited with approval, Nelson v. Concrete Supply Co.,* 303 S.C. 243, 399

[19] Respondent and its Amici cite to numerous studies bemoaning the potential for increased litigation, taxes, and insurance rates if Maryland were to adopt comparative negligence. The research on such topics, however, is highly conflicted, and studies concluding that insurance rates will increase are criticized roundly for "lack of academic rigor" and failing to consider and control for additional variables.

S.E.2d 783, 784 (S.C.1991) ("[T]he history of legislative action in the various states which have adopted the doctrine [of comparative negligence] by statute reveals that comprehensive statutes are not usually adopted."). Rather, most states adopting comparative negligence via legislative act have enacted short-form statutes that leave most doctrinal issues to be shaped and developed by the courts.

Additionally, deferring this issue to a future court or legislative session on grounds that the present case offers insufficient facts to reach binding declarations regarding all collateral doctrines and principles does not weigh so heavily as this Court's responsibility to administer justice. As this argument goes, "in essence, . . . where a court cannot correct all injustice, it should correct none." I am not persuaded that making the change by judicial decision, necessarily leaving some further development of the doctrine of comparative negligence to another day, will wreak havoc on our system of justice or the State's economy. To the contrary, the experiences of other states, having made an analogous change, "provide an accurate barometer of what can be expected after abrogation." *Bozman,* 376 Md. at 496, 830 A.2d at 471. In the twelve other states to abrogate by judicial decision the doctrine of contributory negligence, there is scant evidence that the judicial system was thrown into unmanageable disarray. In fact, other courts noted that "the fears of administering the doctrine are greater than the reality," and that the difficulties presumed inherent in the adoption of comparative negligence "are outweighed by the injustices attendant upon any delay in adopting the comparative negligence (fault) rule." *Scott,* 634 P.2d at 1239, 1241.

I recognize that a shift to comparative fault implicates numerous collateral doctrines. I expect fully that questions will arise about the application of comparative fault in practice in the State of Maryland that cannot be answered conclusively in the present case. This Court would be well-served, however, to place trust in the full array of the Judiciary of this State to administer faithfully the principles of comparative negligence in accordance with this Court's direction. Thus, I reject Respondent's contention that this matter is best left to a legislative enactment that *might* address all potential applications of the doctrine of comparative negligence in a single coup, rather than trusting to the incremental decisions that follow in the common law tradition, beginning with a seminal action by this Court.

III. This Court Should Adopt Pure Comparative Fault

Having concluded, as I have, that the doctrine of contributory negligence must fall, the question becomes: what form of comparative negligence should be adopted? Although the precise formulations of comparative fault systems may vary, there are essentially two basic forms: pure and modified.

Under a system of pure comparative fault, damages are apportioned among the parties according to the fact finder's determination of the percentage that each party's negligence contributed to the injury. A plaintiff is permitted to recover from the defendant (or defendants) the portion of his or her damages which the defendant (or defendants) caused — regardless of the quantum of the plaintiff's contributory negligence. Thus, even if the plaintiff's degree of fault exceeds that of the defendant (or defendants), the plaintiff may recover damages reduced by the proportion that the plaintiff is at fault.

Modified comparative fault, by contrast, considers relevant the proportion of the plaintiff's relative fault in varying degrees, depending on the standard adopted. Under such systems, a plaintiff "escapes the contributory negligence bar only if his share of the responsibility falls within a specified limitation." 4 Harper, James & Gray, *supra,* § 22.15 at 458. States that adopt a modified system generally choose one of two forms, allowing recovery of damages by a plaintiff reduced by the percentage of his or her own fault if either (1) the plaintiff's relative fault is less than the combined fault of all of the defendants; or (2) the plaintiff's relative fault is not greater than the combined fault of all of the defendants.

This Court should adopt for Maryland pure comparative negligence. Pure comparative negligence is favored almost universally by legal scholars and academics. It is "the fairest, most logical and simplest to administer of all available systems." *Goetzman,* 327 N.W.2d at 754. Because pure comparative negligence emphasizes the relationship of an individual's fault to the ultimate damages, "[n]either party is unjustly enriched[, and] [n]either party escapes liability resulting from his negligent acts or omissions." *Alvis,* 52 Ill.Dec. 23, 421 N.E.2d at 897. The shades of gray in jury determinations assigning proportions of fault is not, in a pure system, the difference between substantial recovery and no recovery at all. *See* Prosser, *Comparative Negligence, supra,* at 493–94 ("It is obvious that a slight difference in the proportionate fault [under a modified system] may permit a recovery; and there has been much quite justified criticism of a rule under which a plaintiff who is charged with 49 per cent of the total negligence recovers 51 percent of his damages, while one who is charged with 50 per cent recovers nothing at all."). Critics of pure comparative negligence call it a "radical break" from the principles of contributory negligence, and view a modified version instead as a logical evolution away from contributory negligence. Pure comparative negligence, however, more closely hews to the principle on which comparative fault systems are based — that liability should be commensurate with fault, and that individuals are responsible to the extent that their fault results in injury.

Moreover, although pure comparative negligence is the numerically minority choice nationally, it is the preferred version among states adopting comparative negligence by judicial decision. Nine of the twelve states adopting comparative negligence judicially have chosen a pure system, while three chose a modified version. Modified systems "reintroduce in large measure the very same all-or-nothing feature of contributory negligence that the remedy of comparative negligence is designed to overcome," by establishing a new set point at which recovery for a contributorily negligent plaintiff is barred. 4 Harper, James & Gray, *supra,* § 22.15 at 463; *see also Li,* 119 Cal.Rptr. 858, 532 P.2d at 1242 (criticizing a modified system as simply shifting the "lottery aspect" of contributory negligence to a different set point); *Alvis* 52 Ill.Dec. 23, 421 N.E.2d at 898 ("There is no better justification for allowing a defendant who is 49% at fault to completely escape liability than there is to allow a defendant who is 99% at fault under the old rule to escape liability."). Maryland courts should apply a system of pure comparative fault in negligence actions.

. . .

C.J. Bell has authorized me to state he joins in this opinion.

Notes and Questions

1. In an article commenting on the *Coleman* case, Donald G. Gifford, a torts professor at the University of Maryland said this: "A generation ago, singer-songwriter Don McLean sang of

'The Day the Music Died.' This summer, for many victims of negligently inflicted injuries, July 9, 2013, marked the day that the common law process in Maryland died." Donald G. Gifford, *The Death of the Common Law: Judicial Abdication and Contributory Negligence in Maryland*, 73 MD. L. REV. ENDNOTES 1 (2014). Putting aside the fact that a song from 1971 was sung much more than 'a' generation ago, do you agree with this comment? Which arguments for or against deference to the legislature do you find most compelling? Which of the primary purposes of tort law is most central to your position?

2. The dissent in *Coleman* suggests the adoption of pure comparative "fault" but describes the system as an allocation based on the percentage that each party's "negligence" contributed to the injury. Strictly speaking, the approach favored by the dissent was "comparative negligence" (which compares negligence to negligence) not "comparative fault (which compares different levels of fault, e.g., negligence and recklessness.) We will look at comparative fault at the end of this chapter.

3. As the *Coleman* opinion notes, only four states and the District of Columbia still retain the contributory negligence bar to recovery by a plaintiff whose negligence contributed in any way to his injury. All of the remaining jurisdictions have some form of allocation of responsibility between the negligent plaintiff and the negligent defendant. In the vast majority of these states, the system employed is comparative negligence of either the pure or modified variety. As you read the next case, compare its view of the virtues of the modified system with the virtues of the pure approach as described by the dissent in *Coleman* and consider which of these systems is most consistent with tort law's first principles, discussed in Chapter 1.

4. Contributory negligence and assumption of the risk are the only two affirmative defenses to negligence. However, most jurisdictions' civil procedure rules require affirmative pleading of other defensive strategies including duress, consent, statute of limitations, statute of repose, waiver, release, qualified or absolute immunity, and sovereign immunity. The most relevant of these for tort law were discussed in Chapter 1. For a reminder of the differences between affirmative defenses and rebuttals to prima facie case, see Chapter Two, Affirmative Defenses.

BRADLEY v. APPALACHIAN POWER COMPANY
256 S.E.2d 879 (W. Va. 1979)

MILLER, Justice:

[P]laintiff sought by way of an instruction to utilize the doctrine of comparative negligence to avoid the defense of contributory negligence. The tendered instruction was rejected and the usual contributory negligence instruction was given, with the jury returning a verdict for the defendant. . . .

[Editors' Note: The court began by determining that it had the authority to replace West Virginia's common law doctrine of contributory negligence with comparative negligence.]

I.

There have been several judicial modifications of the severity of contributory negligence. Under the doctrine of last clear chance, the plaintiff's contributory negligence is excused if it can be shown that the defendant had the last opportunity to avoid the accident.

The defense of contributory negligence is also not available where the defendant is found to be guilty of wanton and wilful misconduct. This result is justified on what is roughly a comparative negligence theory, whereby the intentional tort of the defendant makes trivial the simple negligence of the plaintiff. Perhaps this same explanation may also be the basis for barring contributory negligence where the defendant is subject to strict liability. . . .

In some instances the doctrine of contributory negligence is not available where the defendant violates a statute clearly designed for the protection of the plaintiff.

Legislatures in a number of states have enacted comparative negligence statutes of one variety or another. The basic framework of these statutes is to permit a negligent plaintiff to recover so long as his negligence does not exceed some established percentage, usually 50 percent.[5] Such statutes require that his recovery be reduced by the percentage of contributory negligence found to exist.

Four states Alaska, California, Florida, and Michigan have by judicial decision abolished the doctrine of contributory negligence and substituted in its place a "pure" comparative negligence concept. Under this principle, a plaintiff may recover regardless of the degree of his contributory negligence, but the jury is required to reduce his award in proportion to his contributory negligence.

Most commentators and the four courts which have adopted the pure comparative negligence position are critical of the 50 percent approach, primarily on the basis that it involves the drawing of an arbitrary line beyond which contributory negligence can still be asserted as a bar to the plaintiff's action. The basis of this criticism is expressed in Li v. Yellow Cab Co., 13 Cal.3d 804, 827-28, 119 Cal.Rptr. 858, 874-75, 532 P.2d 1226, 1242-43 (1975):

> "We have concluded that the 'pure' form of comparative negligence is that which should be adopted in this state. In our view the '50 percent' system simply shifts the lottery aspect of the contributory negligence rule to a different ground. As Dean Prosser has noted, under such a system '(i)t is obvious that a slight difference in the proportionate fault may permit a recovery; and there has been much justified criticism of a rule under which a plaintiff who is charged with 49 percent of a total negligence recovers 51 percent of his damages, while one who is charged with 50 percent recovers nothing at all.' "

The difficulty with the pure comparative negligence rule, however, is that it focuses solely on the hypothetical "plaintiff" without recognizing that once pure comparative negligence is

---

[5] Four states Mississippi, New York, Rhode Island and Washington have by statute adopted "pure" comparative negligence, whereby the plaintiff can recover so long as he is not 100 percent negligent.

embraced, all parties whose negligence or fault combined to contribute to the accident are automatically potential plaintiffs unless a particular party is found to be 100 percent at fault.

The fundamental justification for the pure comparative negligence rule is its fairness in permitting everyone to recover to the extent he is not at fault. Thus, the eye of the needle is "no fault," and we are asked not to think about the larger aspect the camel representing "fault." It is difficult, on theoretical grounds alone, to rationalize a system which permits a party who is 95 percent at fault to have his day in court as a plaintiff because he is 5 percent fault-free.

The practical result of such a system is that it favors the party who has incurred the most damages regardless of his amount of fault or negligence. To illustrate, a plaintiff who has sustained a moderate injury with a potential jury verdict of $20,000, and who is 90 percent fault-free, may be reluctant to file suit against a defendant who is 90 percent at fault, but who has received severe injuries and whose case carries a potential of $800,000 in damages from a jury verdict. In this situation, even though the defendant's verdict is reduced by his 90 percent fault to $80,000, it is still far in excess of the plaintiff's potential recovery of $18,000.[11]

While it can be conceded that there is an obvious injustice in the current contributory negligence rule which bars recovery no matter how slight the plaintiff's negligence, nevertheless the pure comparative negligence rule seems equally extreme at the other end of the spectrum. None of the courts which have adopted the pure comparative negligence rule have discussed the problems addressed above, and are content to rest their holdings on the following syllogism: (1) the contributory negligence rule is draconian in its operation; (2) the legislative solution of apportioning the plaintiff's fault up to 50 percent is an arbitrary line-drawing lottery;[12] (3) therefore, the pure comparative negligence rule is fairer.

. . .

The history of the common law is one of gradual judicial development and adjustment of the benefit to be gained by the radical break from the common law's tort-fault methodology that the pure comparative negligence rule requires. There are basic inequities inherent in the pure

---

[11] The courts which have adopted the pure comparative negligence rule have not discussed this type of result. They also appear to proceed on the unstated assumption that all accidents will be covered by sufficient insurance to pay all the verdicts stemming from a multi-party accident. This premise is never documented. If we consider the text illustration and assume the plaintiff has a modest insurance limit of $50,000 for any one injury, the potential exposure to an $80,000 net verdict in favor of the 90-percent-at-fault, but seriously damaged defendant, creates a substantial practical bar to a suit. It is doubtful that a competent attorney would advise the plaintiff to sue, since the plaintiff's claim has a maximum jury potential of $20,000, which nets $18,000 when reduced by his 10 percent fault or contributory negligence. This leaves the plaintiff with a potential $12,000 uninsured exposure even after he recovers his $18,000 and pays it to the defendant along with his $50,000 worth of insurance to satisfy the defendant's $80,000 net verdict.

[12] The argument that the difference between recovery at 49 percent contributory negligence and no recovery at 50 percent or above is an arbitrary line, is probably more theoretical than real. It is doubtful that any jury will be able to slice contributory negligence so thinly, a point which Prosser notes in his article Comparative Negligence in 41 Cal. L. Rev. at 25. In all probability, when the contributory negligence rises near the 50 percent level the jury will conclude that plaintiff is guilty of such substantial contributory negligence that it will fix his percentage at 50 or higher to bar his recovery.

comparative negligence rule and its resulting singular emphasis on the amount of damages and insurance coverage as the ultimate touchstone of the viability of instituting a suit.[15]

We do not accept the major premise of pure comparative negligence that a party should recover his damages regardless of his fault, so long as his fault is not 100 percent. Without embarking on an extended philosophical discussion of the nature and purpose of our legal system, we do state that in the field of tort law we are not willing to abandon the concept that where a party substantially contributes to his own damages, he should not be permitted to recover for any part of them. We do recognize that the present rule that prohibits recovery to the plaintiff if he is at fault in the slightest degree is manifestly unfair, and in effect rewards the substantially negligent defendant by permitting him to escape any responsibility for his negligence.

Our present judicial rule of contributory negligence is therefore modified to provide that a party is not barred from recovering damages in a tort action so long as his negligence or fault does not equal or exceed the combined negligence or fault of the other parties involved in the accident. To the extent that our prior contributory negligence cases are inconsistent with this rule, they are overruled.

II.

Some explanation is warranted as to how this new rule operates. We do not intend to consider exhaustively all the particular ramifications of the new rule, since they are best resolved within the particular factual framework of the individual case.

We do state what may be the obvious, that the sum of the negligence of all the parties to a given accident cannot exceed 100 percent. Furthermore, it will be the jury's obligation to assign the proportion or degree of this total negligence among the various parties, beginning with the plaintiff.

The requirements of proximate cause have not been altered by the new rule. Consequently, before any party is entitled to recover, it must be shown that the negligence of the defendant was the proximate cause of the accident and subsequent injuries. The same is true of contributory fault or negligence. Before it can be counted against a plaintiff, it must be found to be the proximate cause of his injuries.

The jury should be required by general verdict to state the total or gross amount of damages of each party whom they find entitled to a recovery, and by special interrogatory the percentage of fault or contributory negligence, if any, attributable to each party. After the verdicts have been accepted, the trial court will calculate the net amount by deducting the party's percentage of fault from his gross award. To this extent, we follow the mechanics of the jury verdict award employed by the courts which have adopted pure comparative negligence, which is compatible

[15] We acknowledge that in any legal system permitting recovery of damages, the amount actually recovered ultimately depends on the financial solvency of the defendant. To create, however, as does the pure comparative negligence rule, a system where plaintiff's decision to sue may depend not on the degree to which he is free from fault but on his financial ability to withstand the countersuit, is to emphasize unduly the damage aspect and to obscure the relative fault of the parties.

with most of the statutory approaches.[17] V. Schwartz, Comparative Negligence (1974), s 17.4, at 282, Et seq.

Our comparative negligence rule has no effect on the plaintiff's right to sue only one of several joint tortfeasors. However, as we pointed out in Haynes v. City of Nitro, W.Va., 240 S.E.2d 544 (1977), the joint tortfeasor so sued may implead the other joint tortfeasors as third-party defendants. Haynes established that there is an inchoate right of contribution between joint tortfeasors in advance of judgment except where the act is Malum in se. Thus, while the original defendant may have to respond only to the plaintiff for the latter's damages, the defendant in the third-party action can have these damages apportioned among the third-party defendants.

Haynes enables a joint tortfeasor to institute a third-party action before judgment in order to bring in the other joint tortfeasors to have them share in any liability that he may be found to have with regard to the plaintiff. Haynes is designed to moderate the inequity which existed in our law that enabled the plaintiff to cast the entire responsibility for an accident on one of several joint tortfeasors by deciding to sue only him.

Neither our comparative negligence rule nor Haynes is designed to alter our basic law which provides for joint and several liability among joint tortfeasors after judgment. Most courts which have considered the question after either a statutory or judicial adoption of some form of comparative negligence have held that the plaintiff can sue one or more joint tortfeasors, and if more than one is sued and a joint judgment is obtained, he may collect the entire amount from any one of the defendants. Under W.Va.Code, 55-7-13; joint tortfeasors may still obtain contribution after judgment.

Our comparative negligence rule does not change the right of a joint tortfeasor to obtain a Pro tanto credit on the plaintiff's judgment for monies obtained by the plaintiff in a settlement with another joint tortfeasor.

Since we have not completely abolished the doctrine of contributory negligence, we recognize that in appropriate circumstances the doctrine of last clear chance is still available. In the case of an intentional tort, contributory negligence is not a defense. Therefore, comparative negligence would not come into play, and the plaintiff would recover his damages undiminished by any contributory negligence.

---

[17] Both W.Va.Code, 56-6-5, and Rule 49 of the Rules of Civil Procedure permit the use of written interrogatories to accompany the general verdict. Obviously, by having the jury find the gross amount and the percentage of contributory negligence, the court has some ability to monitor the jury's conclusions. We anticipate that there may be occasions where the interrogatory answers returned by the jury are confusing or inconsistent. Rule 49(b) specifically provides:

> When the answers are consistent with each other but one or more is inconsistent with the general verdict, the (trial) court may direct the entry of judgment in accordance with the answers, notwithstanding the general verdict or may return the jury for further consideration of its answers and verdict or may order a new trial. When the answers are inconsistent with each other and one or more is likewise inconsistent with the general verdict, the court shall not direct the entry of judgment but may return the jury for further consideration of its answers and verdict or may order a new trial.

By way of summary, we believe that moderating the harshness of our contributory negligence rule achieves a more satisfactory balance in the allocation of fault as it relates to recovery in our tort system. Our comparative negligence rule still bars the substantially negligent plaintiff[19] from obtaining a recovery, but it does permit the plaintiff who is more than slightly at fault to recover his injuries diminished by his percentage of contributory negligence. The rule is an intermediate position between the absolute bar of the present contributory negligence rule and the almost total permissiveness of the pure comparative negligence rule. It represents a considerable improvement over the present rule without undertaking a radical change in our present fault-based tort system, as would be the case with pure comparative negligence.

III.

Finally, we address the question of the applicability of the rule here announced to cases now pending.

. . .

In a unanimous opinion by Justice Cardozo in Great Northern Railway v. Sunburst Oil & Refining Co., 287 U.S. 358, 364, 53 S.Ct. 145, 148, 77 L.Ed. 360, 366 (1932), the United States Supreme Court concluded from a federal constitutional standpoint:

> We think the federal constitution has no voice upon the subject. A state in defining the limits of adherence to precedent may make a choice for itself between the principle of forward operation and that of relation backward. It may say that decisions of its highest court, though later overruled, are law none the less for intermediate transactions. . . .

We do not find any provision in the West Virginia Constitution which addresses this point.

. . .

From a practical standpoint, it is perhaps unnecessary to refine the rules relating to retroactive application in great detail. It is an area of the law not frequently encountered, since the outright reversal of a prior case is a rather uncommon occurrence. While the need for accurate guidelines is important in the substantive areas of the law to provide trial courts and the practitioner with the essential element of predictability, it is of diminished importance with regard to the procedural question of whether an overruling case should be made fully retroactive.

We observe initially that retroactivity considerations in a criminal case presenting constitutional issues involve different policy judgments which may not be present in the ordinary civil case. . . .

In the present case, we are confronted with fashioning a retroactivity rule in regard to a civil case. These are various factors which should be taken into consideration in resolving the

[19] From a purely mechanical standpoint, our new rule of comparative negligence means that where plaintiff's contributory negligence is equal to or above 50 percent of the combined negligence of the parties to the accident, he is barred from recovery. This obviously is the meaning of the phrase, "substantially negligent plaintiff."

question of retroactivity. In any attempt to list factors, it should be stressed that not all factors always carry the same weight, for the weight of any given factor may vary with the facts of a given case.

Retroactivity of an overruling decision is designed to provide equality of application to the overruling decision because its new rule has been consciously designed to correct a flawed area of the law. The more egregious the error, the greater the need to extend the benefits of the overruling decision to others occupying the same status. . . .

Counterbalancing this factor are several considerations. First, the nature of the substantive issue overruled must be determined. If the issue involves a traditionally settled area of law, such as contracts or property as distinguished from torts, and the new rule was not clearly foreshadowed, then retroactivity is less justified. Second, where the overruled decision deals with procedural law rather than substantive, retroactivity ordinarily will be more readily accorded. Third, common law decisions, when overruled, may result in the overruling decision being given retroactive effect, since the substantive issue usually has a narrower impact and is likely to involve fewer parties. Fourth, where, on the other hand, substantial public issues are involved, arising from statutory or constitutional interpretations that represent a clear departure from prior precedent, prospective application will ordinarily be favored. Fifth, the more radically the new decision departs from previous substantive law, the greater the need for limiting retroactivity. Finally, we will also look to the precedent of other courts which have determined the retroactive/prospective question in the same area of the law in their overruling decisions.

In the present case, we have altered our judicially created rule that the slightest degree of contributory negligence bars recovery. We have not, however, completely abolished the defense of contributory negligence. The issue falls within the field of tort law, which historically has not been a settled area of the law such as property or contracts, but has been subject to continual change by the courts and legislatures to meet the evolving needs of an increasingly mobile, industrialized and technological society. The issue at hand primarily affects private parties and arises on a case-to-case basis with the cause of action controlled by the limited time period for actions for personal injuries, so that the beneficiaries of the new decision's retroactivity are a limited class.

In the four states which have adopted pure comparative negligence, a rule which we consider to be a much more radical departure than our new rule, two states have accorded what amounts to full retroactivity to their decision. [Editors' note: Florida and Michigan.]

California, in Li v. Yellow Cab Co., 13 Cal.3d 804, 119 Cal.Rptr. 858, 532 P.2d 1226 (1975), accorded retroactivity of its pure comparative negligence rule to cases which had not reached the trial stage prior to the date of the Li opinion, but denied it as to other cases on appeal.

We thus find that the cases have generally extended retroactivity to the pure comparative negligence rule. Under the foregoing analysis of retroactivity, we hold that the new rule of comparative negligence is fully retroactive.

For the foregoing reasons, the judgment in each case is reversed and the cases are remanded for further proceedings not inconsistent with this opinion.

Notes and Questions

1. "Last clear chance," mentioned in both *Coleman* and *Bradley*, is an ameliorative doctrine designed to reduce the harshness of the contributory negligence rule. Under last clear chance, when the plaintiff was in a position of peril and the defendant had ample time to know of the peril and act to avoid injury to the plaintiff, the plaintiff's own negligence was not a bar to the plaintiff's recovery. Different jurisdictions varied the rule depending on whether the plaintiff could have escaped from the peril and whether the defendant knew or should have known of the plaintiff's situation. Why does the *Bradley* court say that the last clear chance doctrine remains viable within its comparative negligence scheme? Would the viability of the last clear chance rule have been different if West Virginia had adopted the pure form of comparative negligence? In a pure comparative negligence jurisdiction, how could evidence that the defendant had the last clear chance to avoid a collision be used by the jury?

2. *Bradley* adds that the willful and wanton exception to the contributory negligence bar is also left intact by the decision. How would it be treated in a pure comparative negligence jurisdiction? In such a state, how could such evidence be used by the jury?

3. As between the pure comparative rule advocated by the dissent in *Coleman* and the modified comparative rule adopted in *Bradley*, which is most consistent with the first principles of the tort system discussed in Chapter 1?

4. Modified comparative negligence has two forms: that adopted by West Virginia, where the plaintiff who is at least 50% negligent is barred from recovery, and the more common form typified by this Massachusetts statute:

> Section 85. Contributory negligence shall not bar recovery in any action by any person or legal representative to recover damages for negligence resulting in death or in injury to person or property, if such negligence was not greater than the total amount of negligence attributable to the person or persons against whom recovery is sought, but any damages allowed shall be diminished in proportion to the amount of negligence attributable to the person for whose injury, damage or death recovery is made. In determining by what amount the plaintiff's damages shall be diminished in such a case, the negligence of each plaintiff shall be compared to the total negligence of all persons against whom recovery is sought. The combined total of the plaintiff's negligence taken together with all of the negligence of all defendants shall equal one hundred per cent.

7 M.G.L.A. 231 § 85(1973). Look closely at the statute for its answers to questions about what happens where there is more than one defendant. Also, observe how the Massachusetts statute handles the issue of potentially culpable parties who have not been sued in the case.

5. Even though the difference between the two forms of comparative negligence could be less than one percent in a given case, plaintiff-oriented organizations strongly support the form codified in the Massachusetts statute. Why would that be the case?

II. ASSUMPTION OF THE RISK

Assumption of the risk is the second traditional defense to a negligence claim. Assumption of the risk is to negligence what consent is to the intentional torts. As you consider the two doctrines, make sure to note both their similarities and their differences. And note that assumption of the risk is also a traditional defense to strict liability claims; in other words, that the policy common to consent and assumption of the risk is useful for defendants in all torts cases where the plaintiff is a responsible actor.

LaFRENZ v. LAKE COUNTY FAIR BOARD
360 N.E. 2d 605 (Ind. App. 1977)

HOFFMAN, Judge.

On August 19, 1972, Linda LaFrenz was fatally injured when an automobile participating in a demolition derby jumped a barrier striking her. At the time of the occurrence, the decedent was standing in the pit area. Before entering the pit area, decedent had executed an instrument entitled, 'WAIVER AND RELEASE FROM LIABILITY AND INDEMNITY AGREEMENT.' Appellant David LaFrenz, Administrator of the Estate of Linda LaFrenz, filed a complaint to recover damages from the various defendants. Defendants-appellees Lake County Fair Board and Variety Attractions, Inc. moved for summary judgment based on the release. Such motions were sustained by the trial court on October 24, 1974.

Appellant brings this appeal contending that there are genuine issues of material fact which preclude the entry of summary judgment. Appellant asserts that these fact issues involve the decedent's state of mind as to whether she knowingly and willingly assumed the risk and as to whether she knowingly and willingly signed the release.

In reviewing the propriety of a summary judgment, the materials on file are to be liberally construed in favor of the opponent of the motion, and any doubt as to the existence of a genuine issue of material fact must be resolved against the proponent of the motion.

Appellant David LaFrenz testified in his deposition that a demolition derby was to be held at the Lake County Fair on August 19, 1972. Approximately four to six weeks prior to August 19, 1972, Linda LaFrenz signed an entry blank to participate in the demolition derby. She had attended demolition derbies previously. In 1970 she observed a demolition derby from the grandstand, and in 1971 she worked in a booth selling tickets. She was aware of the nature of a demolition derby in that the cars would crash into each other.

On August 19, 1972, the demolition derby was scheduled for two sessions-one in the afternoon and another in the evening. Linda LaFrenz was in the pit area during both sessions. She signed documents to be in the pit area as opposed to the grandstand area. She executed a document entitled, 'WAIVER AND RELEASE FROM LIABILITY AND INDEMNITY AGREEMENT' which stated that in consideration of being permitted in the 'RESTRICTED

AREA[2] she agreed to release the appellees 'from all liability to the Undersigned, his personal representatives, assigns, heirs and next of kin for all loss or damage, and any claim or demands therefor, on account of injury to the person or property or resulting in death to the Undersigned, whether caused by the negligence of Releasees or otherwise while the Undersigned is upon the Restricted Area.' The agreement also contained a provision in which Linda LaFrenz agreed to indemnify and hold the Releasees harmless for 'any loss, liability, damage or cost they may incur due to the presence of the Undersigned in or about the Restricted Area and whether caused by the negligence of the Releasees or otherwise.

Linda LaFrenz was issued a pit pass for the evening session after signing in. She obtained the pit pass to assist her husband, David LaFrenz, as a helper or mechanic.

Later that evening, while standing in the pit area, an automobile participating in the demolition derby jumped the arena barrier striking Linda LaFrenz. She subsequently died from these injuries.

At the time of the occurrence, Linda LaFrenz was twenty-six years of age, had graduated from high school, and had attended two years as a part-time student at Indiana University Northwest.

Before considering whether the release bars recovery in the immediate case, the public policy ramifications of exculpatory agreements should be examined. In this respect, parties are generally permitted to agree in advance that one is under no obligation of care for the benefit of the other, and shall not be liable for the consequences of conduct which would otherwise be negligent.

Thus, in the absence of legislation to the contrary, there is ordinary no public policy which prevents parties from contracting as they see fit. Consequently, it is not against public policy to enter into an agreement which exculpates one from the consequences of his own negligence.

Other jurisdictions which have addressed the question in the context of race track release forms have upheld the validity of the releases as against challenges that such were against public policy.

However, there are several exceptions to the general rule that exculpatory clauses are not against public policy. For example, the Legislature has recently enacted a statute declaring all agreements in construction or design contracts (except highway contracts), which purport to indemnify the promisee against liability arising from the sole negligence or wilful misconduct of the promisee, void as against public policy.

Prosser, in his work on torts, notes several other exceptions to the general rule. One proviso is that the relationship of the parties must be such that their bargaining be free and open. Thus where one party is at such an obvious disadvantage in bargaining power that the effect of the contract is to put him at the mercy of the other's negligence, the contract is void as against public policy. This proviso is applicable on this basis between employer and employee. Prosser, Law of Torts, supra, s 68, at 442 (4th ed. 1971).

[2] The 'RESTRICTED AREA' was defined as being 'the area to which admission for the general public is prohibited, including but not limited to the pit area, racing surface and infield, including walkways, concessions and other appurtenances therein.'

A second exception noted by Prosser arises in transactions affecting the public interest, such as public utilities, common carriers, innskeepers, and public warehousemen. Id. at 443. Likewise it is against public policy in Indiana for a railway company, acting as a common carrier, to contract for indemnity against its own tort liability when it is performing either a public or quasi public duty such as that owing to a shipper, passenger, or servant.

This exception has been extended to other professional bailees who are under no public duty but who deal with the public, such as garagemen, owners of parking lots, and of parcel checkrooms, on the ground that the indispensable need for their services deprives the customer of all real equal bargaining power.

Prosser finally notes that exculpatory agreements are not construed to cover the more extreme forms of negligence or any conduct which constitutes an intentional tort. Prosser, Law of Torts, supra, at 444–45.

The leading case in Indiana on exculpatory provisions is Weaver v. American Oil Co., supra (1971), 257 Ind. 458, 276 N.E.2d 144, 49 A.L.R.3d 306, wherein our Supreme Court struck down an exculpatory clause in a commercial lease arrangement. The court, at 464 of 257 Ind., at 148 of 276 N.E.2d, stated:

When a party can show that the contract, which is sought to be enforced, was in fact an unconscionable one, due to a prodigious amount of bargaining power on behalf of the stronger party, which is used to the stronger party's advantage and is unknown to the lesser party, causing a great hardship and risk on the lesser party, the contract provision, or the contract as a whole, if the provision is not separable, should not be enforceable on the grounds that the provision is contrary to public policy. The party seeking to enforce such a contract has the burden of showing that the provisions were explained to the other party and came to his knowledge and there was in fact a real and voluntary meeting of the minds and not merely an objective meeting.

The court went on to explain that it did not mean to infer that parties may not make contracts exculpating one of his negligence, but that it must be done 'knowingly and willingly.'

In the case at bar, there was no unequal bargaining power between the parties. The decedent was under no compulsion, economic or otherwise, to be in the restricted pit area.

Likewise, the activity did not exhibit any of the characteristics of one affected with the public interest. In Winterstein v. Wilcom, supra, the court quoted from Tunkl v. Regents of University of California (1963), 60 Cal.2d 92, 32 Cal.Rptr. 33, 37-38, 383 P.2d 441, at 445-46, 6 A.L.R.3d 693, as listing the criteria for determining whether particular contracts are affected with the public interest, as follows:

> Thus the attempted but invalid exemption involves a transaction which exhibits some or all of the following characteristics. It concerns a business of a type generally thought suitable for public regulation. The party seeking exculpation is engaged in performing a service of great importance to the public, which is often a matter of practical necessity for some members of the public. The party holds himself out as willing to perform this service for any member of the public who seeks it, or at least for any member coming within certain established standards. As a result of the

> essential nature of the service, in the economic setting of the transaction, the party invoking exculpation possesses a decisive advantage of bargaining strength against any member of the public who seeks his services. In exercising a superior bargaining power the party confronts the public with a standarized adhesion contract of exculpation, and makes no provision whereby a purchaser may pay additional reasonable fees and obtain protection against negligence. Finally, as a result of the transaction, the person or property of the purchaser is placed under the control of the seller, subject to the risk of carelessness by the seller or his agents.

Winterstein v. Wilcom, supra, notes a further refinement in instances where a safety statute enacted for the protection of the public is violated. The rationale is that the obligation and the right created by the statute are public ones which are not within the power of any private individual to waive.

We must therefore turn to an examination of the release to determine whether such was 'knowingly and willingly' made. The 'WAIVER AND RELEASE FROM LIABILITY AND INDEMNITY AGREEMENT' clearly reveals that its sole purpose was to relieve the appellees of liability which may arise from permitting appellant's decedent to be in the restricted pit area. The release was to include all liability which may arise on account of injury to person or property whether caused by the negligence of appellees or otherwise. This situation is different from that which arose in Weaver in which the cause there in question 'was in fine print and contained no title heading which would have identified it as an indemnity clause.' (At 462 of 257 Ind., at 147 of 276 N.E.2d.) Moreover, in the case at bar, each and every signature line contains printing in bold, black print approximately 3/16th inch, stating 'THIS IS A RELEASE.' Such printing is placed upon the signature line in such a manner that one who signs the instrument is super-imposing his signature over such printing. Thus, the uncontroverted facts indicate that the decedent did execute the 'WAIVER AND RELEASE FROM LIABILITY AND INDEMNITY AGREEMENT'; the form and language of the agreement explicitly refers to the appellees' negligence; and the decedent could not have signed the instrument without seeing the wording 'THIS IS A RELEASE.' Thus the form and language is so conspicuous that reasonable men could not reach different conclusions on the question whether the deceased 'knowingly and willingly' signed the document.

Appellant asserts that decedent may have been misinformed concerning the nature of the agreement. In his deposition, Ronald Halcomb, Sr., the driver of the automobile which struck decedent, testified that someone, whom he assumed to be an official, stated that the form was an insurance form.

Appellant, however, was with decedent when she signed in for the evening session. He did not assert that such a representation was made.

Thus, we are faced with a situation in which appellant is attempting to raise an inference that such representations were made to the decedent by showing that similar representations were made to others.

However, this assertion alone would not be sufficient to establish a genuine issue of material fact involving misrepresentation. Generally proof of representations made by appellees to persons other than the decedent does not tend to establish that such representations were made to decedent.

In McCormick et al. on Evidence, s 197, at 468–69 (2d Ed. 1972), three alternative theories are recognized to support the admission of evidence of other misrepresentations of a party in order to raise an inference that such party probably engaged in the misconduct charged.

However, McCormick recognizes that misrepresentations made by defendants to persons other than plaintiff would not, standing alone, be sufficient to establish the issue that the misrepresentations charged were made to plaintiff.

Thus, Halcomb's statement does not raise a genuine issue of material fact which would preclude a summary judgment. The trial court therefore did not err in granting the appellees' respective motions for summary judgment.

Affirmed.

STATON, P.J., and GARRARD, J., concur.

Notes and Questions

1. *LaFrenz* is a classic express assumption of the risk case because the plaintiff explicitly agreed in advance of the injury to release the potential defendant from responsibility for negligence. So long as they satisfy the requirements described in the case, such agreements are recognized as valid by tort law. But they are also likely to be recognized as contracts so long as they are accompanied by lawful consideration. Like many contracts, express assumptions of the risk can be oral or in writing, as the agreement was in *LaFrenz.*

2. At common law, minors could not enter into legally enforceable agreements. The courts considered that as a matter of law, the would always be unequal bargaining power between adults who contracted with children and the children themselves, and so their agreements were void as against public policy. The standard exception was (and remains) that children can contract for necessaries, although their parents or guardians were ultimately responsible for the bills. Today in many jurisdictions, minors' contracts are voidable rather than void. As you process these rules, consider what the incentives might be in each instance.

3. Suppose that a patient alleges that she was injured two years ago by Dr. Smith's medical malpractice. Discovery reveals that when she first went to see Smith, she signed twelve documents of various sorts. In amongst the documents was a single page document entitled "RELEASE OF LIABILITY" in letters sized comparably to those in *LaFrenz*. That document was only one paragraph long and its key sentence said, "In exchange for the opportunity to have Dr. Smith as my physician, for non-emergency treatment I hereby release Dr. Smith from negligence, gross negligence and all other form of negligence in any treatment he provides me. Above the signature line signed by the patient were the words "YOU ARE GIVING UP IMPORTANT LEGAL RIGHTS, READ CAREFULLY BEFORE YOU SIGN." These words were printed in the same font size as the rest of the document. What would be your arguments for and against enforcement of the release in the malpractice suit against Dr. Smith based on the facts you have? What facts would you want to know that you do not yet have?

Problem Eleven: Torts Meets Contracts

P is in the 10th grade. She is an excellent student, captain of her high school's JV soccer team, and president of the tutoring club, which serves underprivileged elementary school children in her town. She is also especially mature and responsible for her age; in other words, from her parents' perspective, a dream teenager.

With their permission, P signed up to take state-mandated driving lessons from the Virginia Road Driving School (D). Several companies in her area provide this service, but P picked D because of how convenient it was for her given her schoolwork, sports, and other extracurricular activities. According to the company's website:

> We provide both the classroom phase and the behind the wheel phase of the Driver Education Program. The State of Virginia requires students who are under 18 years old to complete Driver Education before they can obtain their Learner's Permit. Virginia law requires all students to be 14 ½ years of age by the first date of driver education class. We will work with you to meet your schedule. Classroom sessions are offered on Saturday and there is no set start date. Students can start the Saturday class session on any Saturday as we rotate through the units of study. After five Saturdays, the student's classroom and behind the wheel training will be completed. For behind the wheel sessions, our instructor will pick the student up from a location of their choice and drop the student back off at that location. There is no additional charge for this service.

When P signed up for the lessons, she paid in full for both the classroom- and behind-the-wheel phases of the program — she had saved up her babysitting money to pay this herself. As required, she signed an agreement that included the following provision:

> In the operation of a motor vehicle, there are certain hazards and risks. The Student specifically assumes all such risks as may be incurred in the normal operation of a motor vehicle during the course of instruction. Each School vehicle is fully insured with liability coverage in the amount of $100,000/$300,000/$20,000.* The Student completely releases the School and its associates from any liability and all claims or courses of action resulting and arising from damages or injuries suffered by the Student during this course to the extent that claims shall not be covered by the School insurance coverage.

On the second day of P's behind-the-wheel phase of lessons, her instructor picked her up at her home and drove her to a low-traffic area where she could begin to practice parallel parking and three point turns. As they arrived at the designated location, the car had an engine fire and P suffered multiple severe and permanent injuries.

Accident reconstruction experts for both P and D agree that D's negligent maintenance of the car was the cause of the fire. All parties agree that it will take well over a million dollars to

* Editors' note: this is standard "insurance speak" which means that if there is an accident for which the insured is responsible, the insurance company will pay a maximum of $300,000 per accident, $100,000 per person injured, and $20,000 for property damage.

compensate P fully for her losses. In fact, the only thing P's and D's lawyers disagree about it whether D is liable for more than $100,000.

You are a law clerk for the trial court judge assigned to the case. The parties have jointly filed a motion asking the judge to declare as a matter of law on these facts whether the release limits P to a $100,000 recovery from D. The judge expects briefs from both sides but has asked you to get a head start on the issue. She has requested that you draft a one-page memorandum setting out the likely issues, rules, and arguments on both sides, as well as a preliminary view of how you believe she should rule.

COOMER v. KANSAS CITY ROYALS BASEBALL CORPORATION
437 S.W.3d 184 (Mo. 2014)

. . .

Background

Coomer is a longtime baseball fan and frequent spectator at Royals games in Kauffman Stadium. On September 8, 2009, he brought his father along to watch the Royals host the Detroit Tigers. Only about 12,000 people were on hand to watch the game because it had rained most of the day. With such a small crowd, Coomer and his father left their assigned seats early in the game and moved to empty seats six rows behind the visitor's dugout.

Shortly after Coomer changed seats, Sluggerrr mounted the visitor's dugout to begin the "Hotdog Launch," a feature of every Royals home game since 2000. The launch occurs between innings, when Sluggerrr uses an air gun to shoot hotdogs from the roof of the visitor's dugout to fans seated beyond hand-tossing range. When his assistants are reloading the air gun, Sluggerrr tosses hotdogs by hand to the fans seated nearby. Sluggerrr generally tossed the hotdogs underhand while facing the fans but sometimes throws overhand, behind his back, and side-armed.

Coomer estimates that he attended 175 Royals games before this game in September 2009. He admits that he frequently watched Sluggerrr toss hotdogs from the roof of the visitor's dugout and, on September 8, he saw Sluggerrr mount the dugout to begin the Hotdog Launch. Coomer and his father were seated approximately 15 to 20 feet from Sluggerrr, directly in his view. After employing his hotdog-shaped airgun to send hotdogs to distant fans, Sluggerrr began to toss hotdogs by hand to fans seated near Coomer. Coomer testified that he saw Sluggerrr turn away from the crowd as if to prepare for a behind-the-back throw, but, because Coomer chose that moment to turn and look at the scoreboard, he admits he never saw Sluggerrr throw the hotdog that he claims injured him. Coomer testified only that a "split second later . . . something hit me in the face," and he described the blow as "pretty forceful."

Coomer did not report this incident to the Royals when it happened because he did not realize he had been injured. Instead, he stayed for most of the rest of Tuesday's game (a thrilling 7–5 effort that snapped the first-place Tigers' six-game winning streak) and even returned to Kauffmann Stadium the following night to witness the Royals' further 5–1 drubbing of the Tigers. Thursday morning, however, Coomer felt he was "seeing differently" and something "wasn't right" with his left eye. The problem progressed until, approximately eight days after the incident, Coomer saw a doctor and was diagnosed with a detached retina. Coomer underwent surgeries to repair the retina and to remove a "traumatic cataract" in the same eye.

Coomer reported his injury to the Royals in September 2009, eight days after it occurred. In February 2010, Coomer filed this lawsuit alleging one count of negligence and one count of battery.[1] Regarding the negligence count, Coomer asserted that the Royals (through its employee, Sluggerrr) failed to exercise ordinary care in throwing hotdogs into the stands, that the team failed to adequately train Sluggerrr on how to throw hotdogs into the stand safely, and that the team failed to adequately supervise Sluggerrr's hotdog toss. In its answer, the Royals admitted responsibility for Sluggerrr's acts but denied he had been negligent. The Royals also asserted affirmative defenses of assumption of the risk and comparative fault.

The Royals employee who portrays Sluggerrr testified at trial he did not remember the throw that allegedly injured Coomer. He admitted that the Royals had given him no specific training on how to toss hotdogs, but testified that he was aware that fans could be hurt and that he was careful in making his tosses. For example, when a fan is seated nearby, Sluggerrr said he tries to make eye contact before tossing a hotdog so that the fan will know it is coming and—if the fan is seated near enough—tries to throw the hotdog in an arc to make it easier to catch. In addition to hearing Sluggerrr's testimony and Coomer's description of the incident, the jury heard testimony from another fan who claimed to have been injured by a hotdog toss from Sluggerrr under similar circumstances.

At the close of the evidence, Coomer moved for a directed verdict on the issues of comparative fault and assumption of the risk. He argued that implied primary assumption of the risk "only applies to risks that are inherent in the nature of the activity" and, in this case, "the harm of getting hit with a hotdog has absolutely no relationship to going to a baseball game." Regarding comparative fault, Coomer argued that, as a matter of law, he cannot have been negligent merely for not fleeing his seat during the Hotdog Launch. The trial court overruled Coomer's motion, holding that both (a) whether the risk of being injured by Sluggerrr's hotdog toss is one of the risks inherent in watching a Royals game and (b) the reasonableness of Coomer's actions were proper questions for the jury.

In preparing the jury instructions, the Royals proposed adding a "tail" to Instruction No. 9 (i.e., the verdict director for Coomer's negligence claim). This tail directs the jury to Instruction No. 11, which asks the jury to decide whether injury from Sluggerrr's hotdog toss is an inherent risk of watching the Royals play baseball. The Royals' proposed instructions, as given, read:

Instruction No. 9

In your verdict you must assess a percentage of fault to the defendant if you believe:

First, defendant's employee threw a hotdog that hit plaintiff; and

Second, defendant's employee was thereby negligence [*sic*], and

Third, as a direct result of such negligence plaintiff sustained damage,

[1] The trial court dismissed the battery claim in a partial summary judgment, and Coomer does not appeal that dismissal.

> unless you believe plaintiff is not entitled to recover by reason of Instruction No. 11.
>
> *Instruction No. 11:*
>
> In your verdict you must not assess a percentage of fault to defendant if you believe:
>
> First, the risk of suffering an injury by being struck by a hotdog thrown in a manner in which Sluggerrr threw the hotdog that plaintiff alleges struck him was a risk inherent in attending a game at Royals' Stadium, and
>
> Second, plaintiff comprehended the actual risk, and
>
> Third, plaintiff intelligently accepted the risk.

Coomer objected to Instruction No. 11 (and to the tail on Instruction No. 9 directing the jury to that instruction) on the same grounds raised in his directed verdict motion. In addition, Coomer objected to the Royals' proposed comparative fault instruction, arguing that there was insufficient evidence to submit this issue to the jury. The trial court overruled Coomer's objections.

The jury returned a verdict in favor of the Royals. The verdict form states that the jury assessed zero percent of fault to the Royals and 100 percent of fault to Coomer, but it does not disclose the basis for this decision. Coomer moved for judgment notwithstanding the verdict and for a new trial based on the arguments asserted in his directed verdict motion and in his objections to the jury instructions. The trial court overruled Coomer's motions and entered judgment for the Royals. Coomer appeals and, after granting transfer, this Court has jurisdiction.

Standard of Review

This Court reviews claims of instructional error *de novo. Hervey v. Missouri Dept. of Corrections,* 379 S.W.3d 159, 159 (Mo. Banc 2012). The Court will not vacate a judgment on the basis of such an error, however, unless that error materially affected the merits of the action.[**] Accordingly, "the party challenging the instruction must show that the offending instruction misdirected, misled, or confused the jury, resulting in prejudice to the party challenging the instruction." *Id.* (citation omitted).

Analysis

This case presents the question of whether the century-old affirmative defense commonly referred to as "assumption of the risk" survived this Court's adoption of comparative fault in *Gustafson v. Benda,* 661 S.W.2d 11 (Mo. banc 1983). To the extent it survives, Coomer claims that the application of this doctrine is to be decided by the court and not the jury. The Court agrees. Because the trial court erred in submitting the question of assumption of the risk to the jury, the judgment in this case must be vacated and the matter remanded.

[**] Editors' note: this is also sometimes called the harmless error rule.

I. Assumption of the Risk in a post-Gustafson World

It is safe to say that judicial analysis and application of assumption of the risk doctrine has not always achieved high marks for clarity and precision. Historically, courts often failed to draw or maintain important distinctions between this doctrine and defenses such as contributory negligence, which, though they may have seemed similar to assumption of the risk, were quite different. Simons, *Reflections on Assumption of Risk,* 50 UCLA L.Rev. 481, 486 (2002) ("*Reflections* "). Admittedly, those distinctions seldom made any difference as a practical matter because any of these often-overlapping defenses was sufficient to bar completely all recovery by the plaintiff. At least this was so before the advent of comparative fault. Because *Gustafson* rejects the complete defense of contributory negligence in favor of the partial defense of comparative fault, greater precision is required when analyzing claims of assumptions of the risk.

The assumption of the risk doctrine was a relative late-comer in the law of negligence. *See* William Prosser, *HANDBOOK OF THE LAW OF TORTS,* at 376 (1941) (hereinafter, "*PROSSER ON TORTS* ") (identifying 1809 as the earliest use of the defense in a negligence action). The basic principle of this defense is easily stated: if a person voluntarily consents to accept the danger of a known and appreciated risk, that person may not sue another for failing to protect him from it. *See Ross v. Clouser,* 637 S.W.2d 11, 14 (Mo. banc 1982) (recovery is barred when the plaintiff "comprehended the actual danger and intelligently acquiesced in it"). In practice, however, this principle proved easier to state than to apply.

The simplest application of this doctrine recognizes that, when a plaintiff makes an express statement that he is voluntarily accepting a specified risk, the plaintiff is barred from recovering damages for an injury resulting from that risk. This application (i.e., "express assumption of the risk") most often involves a written waiver or release by the would-be plaintiff, but it can be based on any form of any explicit acquiescence. *PROSSER ON TORTS,* at 376; *Reflections,* 50 UCLA L.Rev. at 486–87.

In most cases, however, the plaintiff's consent cannot be proved so easily. There, the defendant contends that the plaintiff's voluntary acceptance of a known and appreciated risk should be inferred from the plaintiff's conduct and the surrounding circumstances. *PROSSER ON TORTS,* at 376. Though the distinction seldom was noted before the adoption of comparative fault, this category of implied — rather than expressed — assumption of the risk includes two very different applications of this doctrine: "implied primary assumption of the risk" and "implied secondary assumption of the risk." The difference between these applications is the type — or, more precisely, the source — of the risk at issue. *Reflections,* 50 UCLA L.Rev. at 487–89.

When the risk arises from the circumstances (e.g., from a condition on the defendant's property or the inherent nature of the defendant's activity), "implied primary assumption of the risk" completely bars recovery by a plaintiff who knowingly and voluntarily encounters that risk. *Krause v. U.S. Truck Co., Inc.,* 787 S.W.2d 708, 711–12 (Mo. banc 1990); *Reflections,* 50 UCLA L.Rev. at 487–88. When the risk is created by defendant's negligence, on the other hand, this has been identified as "implied secondary assumption of the risk." *Lewis v. Snow Creek, Inc.,* 6 S.W.3d 388, 395 (Mo.App.1999); *Reflections,* 50 UCLA L.Rev. at 489. Understandably, courts were less willing to bar all recovery in the latter circumstance unless the plaintiff not only knowingly and voluntarily acquiesced in the risk created by the defendant's negligence but also acted unreasonably in doing so. *Id.*

Accordingly, prior to the advent of comparative fault, a plaintiff's claim was barred completely by assumption of the risk if the plaintiff (a) expressly consented to assume a known and understood risk (i.e., "express assumption of the risk"); (b) implicitly consented (based on his conduct and surrounding circumstances) to assume a known and understood risk that was not created by the defendant's own negligence (i.e., "implied primary assumption of the risk"); or (c) implicitly consented (based on his conduct and surrounding circumstances) to assume a known and understood risk that resulted from the defendant's own negligence, provided that the plaintiff acted unreasonably in doing so (i.e., "implied secondary assumption of the risk"). Though all three were lumped together under the heading of assumption of the risk and treated as affirmative defenses, only the latter application was properly viewed as such.

The version of comparative fault adopted by this Court in *Gustafson* fundamentally altered this landscape. Section 1(a) of the Uniform Comparative Fault Act (the "UCFA") provides that "any contributory fault chargeable to the claimant diminishes proportionately the amount awarded as compensatory damages for an injury attributable to the claimant's contributory fault, but does not bar recovery." *Gustafson,* 661 S.W.2d at 18 (quoting from the UCFA, which is set forth in full in an appendix to that opinion). Section 1(b) of the UCFA defines "fault" for purposes of section 1(a) to include "unreasonable assumption of risk not constituting an enforceable express consent." *Id.*

As a result, *Gustafson,* rejects any further application of "implied secondary assumption of the risk." When a plaintiff acts unreasonably in deciding to assume a risk created by a defendant's negligence, such "fault" may reduce-but not bar-the plaintiff's recovery under *Gustafson.* By the same token, when the plaintiff's decision was reasonable, it cannot be used to reduce his recovery because reasonable behavior does not constitute "fault" under the UCFA. *Reflections,* 50 UCLA L.Rev. at 489 (noting that the "predominant modern position" of most courts and the Restatement (Third) of Torts is that secondary implied assumption of the risk has be assimilated into comparative fault).

But *Gustafson* does not reject or abandon "express assumption of the risk." Though this application of the assumption of the risk doctrine always has been subject to certain limitations as a matter of public policy, *Gustafson* and the adoption of comparative fault have no effect on this application or its limitations. This is because, in an "express assumption of the risk" case, the plaintiff's consent relieves the defendant of any duty to protect the plaintiff from injury. As a result, the defendant cannot be negligent and there is no "fault" to which the jury can compare the plaintiff's fault. *Gustafson,* 661 S.W.2d at 18 ("fault" does not include "enforceable express consent").

By the same token, *Gustafson* has no effect on the continued viability of "implied primary assumption of the risk." *Gustafson,* 661 S.W.2d at 20 ("the term ["fault"] does not include . . . a lack of violation of duty by the defendant (as in the failure of a landowner to warn a licensee of a patent danger on the premises)"). This is because, under the law of Missouri and most other jurisdictions, implied primary assumption of the risk "is *not really an affirmative defense;* rather, it indicates that the defendant *did not even owe the plaintiff any duty of care.*" *Krause,* 787 S.W.2d at 711–12 (emphasis added). With no duty to protect the plaintiff, the defendant cannot be negligent and there is no "fault" for the jury to compare under comparative fault principles.

Missouri's characterization of the implied primary assumption of the risk doctrine in terms of "duty" is decidedly mainstream:

> Like express assumption of the risk, " 'primary' implied assumption of the risk . . . is really a principle of no duty, or no negligence, and so denies the existence of any cause of action."

W. Page Keeton, *PROSSER AND KEETON ON TORTS,* at 496–97 (5th ed.1984).

Accordingly, when the plaintiff is injured by the defendant's negligence, this Court holds that the adoption of comparative fault in *Gustafson* precludes any consideration of the plaintiff's conduct in assuming that risk (i.e., implied secondary assumption of the risk) except as a partial defense under a proper comparative fault instruction. Conversely, because the "express" and "implied primary" applications of assumption of the risk result in determinations that the defendant has no duty to protect the plaintiff, the form of comparative fault adopted in *Gustafson* does not preclude these applications as a complete—not merely a partial—bar to the plaintiff's recovery.

II. Implied Primary Assumption of the Risk and the "Baseball" Rule

One of the most interesting — and certainly the most relevant — applications of implied primary assumption of the risk involves certain risks assumed by spectators at sporting events. Long before the Kansas City Athletics moved to Oakland and the fledging Royals joined the Junior Circuit, an overwhelming majority of courts recognized that spectators at sporting events are exposed to certain risks that are inherent merely in watching the contest. Accordingly, under what is described above as implied primary assumption of the risk, these courts held that the home team was not liable to a spectator injured as a result of such risks. *See* Augustine, *Who Is Responsible When Spectators Are Injured While Attending Professional Sporting Events?,* 2008 Den. U. Sports & Ent. L.J. 39, 42–46 (2008) ("*When Spectators Are Injured* ").

The archetypal example of this application of implied primary assumption of the risk is when a baseball park owner fails to protect each and every spectator from the risk of being injured by a ball or bat flying into the stands. Just as Missouri teams have led (and continue to lead) professional baseball on the field, Missouri courts helped lead the nation in defining this area of the law off the field. More than 50 years ago, this Court was one of the first to articulate the so-called "Baseball Rule":

> [W]here a baseball game is being conducted under the customary and usual conditions prevailing in baseball parks, *it is not negligence to fail to protect all seats in the park by wire netting,* and that the special circumstances and specific negligence pleaded did not aid plaintiff or impose upon the defendant a duty to warn him against hazards which are necessarily incident to baseball and are perfectly obvious to a person in possession of his faculties.

> *Anderson v. Kansas City Baseball Club,* 231 S.W.2d 170, 172 (Mo .1950) (emphasis added).[6]

Anderson was based on this Court's earlier decision in *Hudson v. Kansas City Baseball Club,* 164 S.W.2d 318, 320 (Mo.1942), which used the "no duty" language of implied primary assumption of the risk to explain its holding:

> The basis of the proprietor's liability is his superior knowledge and if his invitee knows of the condition or hazard *there is no duty* on the part of the proprietor to warn him and there is no liability for resulting injury because the invitee has as much knowledge as the proprietor does and then by voluntarily acting, in view of his knowledge, assumes the risks and dangers incident to the known condition.

Hudson, 164 S.W.2d at 323 (emphasis added) (applying Restatement (Second) of Torts, § 343). *Hudson* involved a spectator with personal knowledge of the inherent risk of being injured by a foul ball while watching a baseball game. But, when the Court returned to this same issue eight years later in *Anderson,* it continued to rely on section 343 of the Restatement (Second) of Torts (i.e., the "open and obvious dangers" doctrine under the rules of premises liability) to extend Missouri's no-duty rule to cases involving baseball spectators with no prior knowledge of baseball or the risks inherent in watching it.

> All of the cases cited here and many others which are cited in *Hudson v. Kansas City Baseball Club, supra,* emphasize that when due care has been exercised to provide a reasonable number of screened seats, there remains a hazard that spectators in unscreened seats may be struck and injured by balls which are fouled or otherwise driven into the stands. *This risk is a necessary and inherent part of the game* and remains after ordinary care has been exercised to provide the spectators with seats which are reasonably safe. It is a risk which is assumed by the spectators because it remains after due care has been exercised and is not the result of negligence on the part of the baseball club. It is clearly *not an unreasonable risk to spectators which imposes a duty* to warn [or protect].

Anderson, 231 S.W.2d at 173 (emphasis added).[7]

---

[6] This "no duty" or "limited duty" rule for claims by baseball spectators has been dubbed the Baseball Rule and has been adopted by every court to consider it, save one. *Benejam v. Detroit Tigers, Inc.,* 635 N.W.2d 219, 221 (2001 (Mich.App.) ("review of precedents from other jurisdictions finds overwhelming, if not universal, support for the limited duty rule," and noting that the contrary decisions in Illinois were overruled by statute).

[7] This use of an objective standard based on what a defendant reasonably can expect, rather than a subjective standard based on what a plaintiff actually knew and understood, is one of the key distinctions between the primary and secondary varieties of implied assumption of the risk that went unnoticed until comparative fault. It also explains why, before comparative fault, the former was decided by the court as a question of the defendant's "duty," while the latter was usually decided by the jury as an affirmative defense. As noted above, *Gustafson* merges the latter into the jury's consideration of comparative fault but leaves the former to be decided by the court just as before. *See Harris,* 857 S.W.2d at 227 (notwithstanding Court's adoption of comparative fault, "open and obviousness of a condition [continues] as a consideration *for the court* in determining a possessor of land's standard of care") (emphasis added).

Anderson and *Hudson* are just two of the many dozens of cases around the country holding that, as long as some seats directly behind home plate are protected, the team owes "no duty" to spectators outside that area who are injured by a ball or bat while watching a baseball game.[9] Despite being decided by such different courts across so many decades, all of these cases reflect certain shared principles. First, it is not possible for baseball players to play the game without occasionally sending balls or bats (or parts of bats) into the stands, sometimes at unsafe speeds. Second, it is not possible for the home team to protect each and every spectator from such risks without fundamentally altering the game or the spectators' experience of watching it through such means as: (a) substituting foam rubber balls and bats that will not injure anyone (or be very fun to watch); (b) erecting a screen or other barrier around the entire field protecting all spectators while obstructing their view and making them feel more removed from the action; or (c) moving all spectators at least 600 feet away from home plate in all directions.[10] Third, ordinary negligence principles do not produce reliably acceptable results in these circumstances because the risk of injury (and the extent of the harm) to spectators is substantial,[11] yet the justification for not protecting spectators from that risk can be expressed only in terms of the amusement or entertainment value of watching the sport that brought the spectators to the stadium in the first place.[12]

Against this background, *Anderson* and *Hudson* (and dozens of Baseball Rule cases around the country) represent a conscious decision to favor the collective interests of all spectators by rejecting as a matter of law the individual claims of injured spectators. Using the rules of

---

[9] This "limited duty" to screen only certain seats is an anachronism, far less meaningful today than in the days before box seats, season tickets, and sellout crowds. As one court noted:

> Were we deciding this issue without the precedent . . . we would not be persuaded that there is a need to impose a duty to provide *any* screened seats. A person who fears injury always has the option of refraining from attending a baseball game or of sitting in a part of the park which is out of reach of balls traveling with sufficient velocity to cause harm. *In any event, the duty seems to be one of little practical value. The injured person is always going to be one who is seated in an unscreened area* and, who . . . would be precluded from recovering regardless of the reason why he or she elected to sit there.

Los Angeles Dodgers, 185 Cal.App.3d at 182 (emphasis added).

[10] *Los Angeles Dodgers,* 185 Cal.App.3d at 181 ("As we see it, to permit plaintiff to recover under the circumstances here would force baseball stadium owners to do one of two things: place all spectator areas behind a protective screen, thereby reducing the quality of everyone's view, and since players are often able to reach into the spectator area to catch foul balls, changing the very nature of the game itself; or continue the status quo and increase the price of tickets to cover the cost of compensating injured persons with the attendant result that persons of meager means might be 'priced out' of enjoying the great American pastime.")

[11] One study found injuries from foul balls in major league ballparks occur at a rate of 35.1 injuries per million spectator visits. *See When Spectators Are Injured,* 2008 Den. U. Sports & Ent. L.J. at 39 n. 3. For teams like the Royals, with more than 1.7 million in home attendance each season, this equates to approximately 60 injured fans per year.

[12] As one court noted, the "logical result of having these [baseball] cases governed by usual invitor-invitee principles of liability [without adjusting for "open and obvious" risks] would be that warned against in *Akins:* '[E]very spectator injured by a foul ball, no matter where he is seated or standing in the ball park, would have an absolute right to go to the jury on every claim of negligence.' " *Detroit Tigers, Inc.,* 635 N.W.2d 219, 224–25 (Mich.App.2001) (*quoting Akins v. Glen Falls City Sch. Dist.,* 424 N.E.2d at 534).

premises liability and the rationale now identified as implied primary assumption of the risk, these decisions protect the home team from liability for risks that are inherent in watching a baseball game based on the team's failure to take steps that could defeat the reason spectators are there at all, i.e., to get as close as they can to the action without interfering with the game they came to watch.[13]

But the rationale for this rule—and, therefore, the rule itself—extends only to those risks that the home team is powerless to alleviate without fundamentally altering the game or spectator's enjoyment of it. As a result, the solid wall of authority in support of the Baseball Rule is badly cracked in cases where a spectator is injured by a ball *when* the game is not underway or *where* fans ordinarily do expect to have to keep a careful lookout for balls or bats leaving the field. This Court has not had to address such a question and does not do so now.

Moreover, even though the "no duty" rationale of the Baseball Rule applies to risks inherent in watching a baseball game, the home team still owes a duty of reasonable care not to *alter or increase* such inherent risks.[15] One example, useful both for its facts and its analysis, is *Lowe v. California League of Prof. Baseball,* 56 Cal.App. 4th 112 (1997). There, the court began by explaining this "no duty" rationale:

> In the first instance, foul balls hit into the spectators' area clearly create a risk of injury. If such foul balls were to be eliminated, it would be impossible to play the game. Thus, foul balls represent an inherent risk to spectators attending baseball games. Under *Knight,* such risk is assumed.

Id. at 123 (*citing Knight v. Jewett,* 834 P.2d 696, 698 (Cal.1992)).

In *Lowe,* however, even though the plaintiff was struck by a foul ball, he claimed that his injuries were not caused by that inherent risk. Instead, the plaintiff claimed he was prevented from watching for foul balls because he was repeatedly jostled and distracted by the team's dinosaur mascot. The court agreed that the Baseball Rule did not bar such a claim:

> *[T]he key inquiry here is whether the risk which led to plaintiff's injury involved some feature or aspect of the game which is inevitable or unavoidable in the actual playing of the game.* . . . Can [this] be said about the antics of the mascot? *We think not.*

[13] *See Detroit Tigers,* 635 N.W.2d at 222 ("there is inherent value in having most seats unprotected by a screen because baseball patrons generally want to be involved with the game in an intimate way and are even hoping that they will come in contact with some projectile from the field (in the form of a souvenir baseball)."); *Rudnick v. Golden W. Broadcasters,* 156 Cal.App.3d 793, 802 (1984) ("Reasonable screening is defined in the expectations of the fans and the traditions of the national pastime itself" because "the chance to apprehend a misdirected baseball is as much a part of the game as the seventh inning stretch or peanuts and Cracker Jack"); *Akins,* 424 N.E.2d at 533 ("many spectators prefer to sit where their view of the game is unobstructed by fences or protective netting and the proprietor of a ball park has a legitimate interest in catering to these desires"); *Liability to Spectator,* 82 A.L.R.6th at 417 ("Part of the experience of attending a baseball game is that many of the dozens of baseballs used in each game are hit out of play into foul territory, into the backstop and screens, and into the stands. Most fans would love to return from a game with a souvenir of the actual play, and some even bring gloves with them in the hope of making a catch."). *See also Murphy v. Steeplechase Amusement Co.,* 166 N.E. 173, 174 (N.Y.1929) (Cardozo, C.J.) ("One who takes part in such a sport accepts the dangers that inhere in it so far as they are obvious and necessary, just as a fencer accepts the risk of a thrust by his antagonist or a spectator at a ball game the chance of contact with the ball. . . . The timorous may stay at home.").

> Actually, the . . . person who dressed up as Tremor, recounted that there were occasional games played when he was not there. In view of this testimony, as a matter of law, we hold that the antics of the mascot are not an essential or integral part of the playing of a baseball game. In short, the game can be played in the absence of such antics.

Id. (emphasis added).

Accordingly, even though implied primary assumption of the risk precludes recovery for injuries caused by the inherent risk of being hit by a foul ball while watching a baseball game, *Lowe* holds that the jury can hold the team liable for such injuries if the negligence of its mascot altered or increased that otherwise inherent risk and this negligence causes the plaintiff's injuries. *See also Sheppard,* 904 S.W.2d at 263–64 (even though the student cannot sue under implied primary assumption of the risk for injuries resulting from inherent risk of a bad landing in high school long-jump contest, the jury can hold the school district liable when the inherent risk of a bad landing was altered or increased by defendant's negligence in preparing the landing pit and this negligence caused the student's injuries).

Accordingly, the proper application of implied primary assumption of the risk in this case — unaffected by *Gustafson* — is this: if Coomer was injured by a risk that is an inherent part of watching the Royals play baseball, the team had no duty to protect him and cannot be liable for his injuries. But, if Coomer's injury resulted from a risk that is not an inherent part of watching baseball in person—or if the negligence of the Royals altered or increased one of these inherent risks and caused Coomer's injury — the jury is entitled to hold the Royals liable for such negligence and, to the extent the reasonableness of Coomer's actions are in dispute, the jury must apportion fault between the parties using comparative fault principles. This approach has been used in Missouri and around the country.

> Therefore, in the sports context, under comparative fault, if the plaintiff's *injury is the result of a risk inherent in the sport in which he was participating, the defendant is relieved from liability* on the grounds that by participating in the sport, the plaintiff assumed the risk and the defendant never owed the plaintiff a duty to protect him from that risk. *If on the other hand, the plaintiff's injury is the result of negligence on the part of the defendant,* the issue regarding the plaintiff's assumption of that risk and whether it was a reasonable assumption of risk, is *an element of fault to be compared to the defendant's negligence* by the jury.

Sheppard, 904 S.W.2d at 263–64 (emphasis added).

III. Implied Primary Assumption of the Risk is a Question of Law

To this point, it appears that the Royals are in at least tacit agreement with the Court's analysis. The Royals invoke the doctrine of implied primary assumption of the risk by name and contend that, under this doctrine, it owed no duty to protect Coomer from the risk of injury from Sluggerrr's hotdog toss because that is an inherent risk Coomer assumed by attending a Royals game at Kauffman Stadium. The Royals contend, however, that the question of which risks qualify as "inherent risks" for purposes of implied primary assumption of the risk is a question of fact for the jury to decide, not the court. The Court disagrees.

As explained above, the doctrine of implied primary assumption of the risk negates any duty the defendant otherwise may have owed the plaintiff. The question of whether and to what extent the defendant owes a duty to the plaintiff is always a question for the court, not the jury. *Hoffman v. Union Elec. Co.*, 176 S.W.3d 706, 708 (Mo. banc 2005). This principle is no less applicable when the question of duty arises in the context of implied primary assumption of the risk. . . .

This answer is even clearer when the doctrine of implied primary assumption of the risk arises in the context of claims by spectators at a sporting event. In such cases, this and others consistently have held that the question of whether a particular risk is or is not an inherent part of watching the event is to be decided by the court as a matter of law. *See Anderson,* 231 S.W.2d at 173 (holding as a matter of law that the risk of injury from a foul ball is "clearly not an unreasonable risk to spectators which imposes a duty to warn [or protect]"); *Hudson,* 164 S.W.2d at 323 (holding as a matter of law that, "if his invitee knows of the condition or hazard there is no duty on the part of the proprietor to warn him and there is no liability for resulting injury"). *See also Akins v. Glens Falls City Sch. Dist.,* 424 N.E.2d 531, 534 (N.Y.1981) (rejecting view that the extent of the team's duty should be left to the jury because it "would mean that every spectator injured by a foul ball, no matter where he is seated or standing in the ball park, would have an absolute right to go to the jury on every claim of negligence"); *When Spectators Are Injured,* 2008 Den. U. Sports & Ent. L.J. at 42–46 (collecting cases holding, as a matter of law, that the team owed no duty to injured spectators).[17]

. . . [I]mplied primary assumption of the risk cases around the country answer this "inherent risk" question as a matter of law because, if that question is left to each separate jury in each separate case, a team would never know for sure what duty it owes to its spectators. For example, under the Royals' approach, Sluggerrr could throw two consecutive hotdogs in precisely the same manner, hit two spectators causing precisely the same injuries, and the Royals could be held liable for all or some part of one spectator's damages and escape all liability for the other spectator's damages solely because the latter jury found the risk of injury from Sluggerrr's hotdog toss to be an "inherent risk" and the former jury did not. Such conflicting results are unacceptable.

The reason courts — not juries — decide what duty a defendant owes is to ensure that all similarly situated defendants are treated equally and, more importantly, to give notice of these duties so that potential defendants will have an opportunity to adjust their conduct accordingly. These principles of fair notice and equal treatment are fundamental values in our legal system. Courts are well positioned to serve and protect such values; juries are not. *See Prosser and Keeton on Torts,* at 236 (noting that "it is no part of the province of the jury" to weigh the considerations of precedent and sound public policy that inform decisions regarding the existence and extent of a defendant's duty of care).

The Royals' argument that juries should determine whether a particular risk is inherent simply in watching the game fails at an even more fundamental level. A question of fact is submitted to a jury in a civil case if, but only if, the evidence regarding that fact is such that reasonable jurors may reach contradictory conclusions. Here, the dispute between the Royals and Coomer

---

[17] When the court determines that the risk is not an inherent one and, therefore, that implied primary assumption of the risk does not apply, the question of whether the plaintiff was injured by the defendant's negligence remains a jury question.

concerning whether the risk of injury from Sluggerrr's hotdog toss is one of the risks that is inherent in watching the Royals play baseball is a policy debate, not an evidentiary one. To the extent there was any evidence at trial relevant to this debate, that evidence was not specific to Coomer, or to his decision whether to attend this specific game and where to sit, or to similar decisions made by the 12,000 other spectators in the park that day. Instead, the evidence — and, more importantly, the policy debate itself — will be the same in every case. The only thing that will change is the jury (and potentially, under the Royals' approach, the jury's answer).

Juries decide disputed questions of material fact, e.g., questions such as what the plaintiff or defendant (or others around them) did or did not do, what the circumstances surrounding this conduct were, and what the consequences of this conduct have been. Such questions may be difficult to answer, but there is a right and wrong answer for the jury to pursue. The question of whether being injured by Sluggerrr's hotdog toss is a risk inherent in watching a Royals home game, on the other hand, has no right or wrong answer. It is a conclusion *about* a fact, not a fact itself. Juries do not decide such questions; courts do.

Finally, even the word "inherent" defies the Royals' case-by-case approach. For a risk to be "inherent," it must be "*structural* or involved in the *constitution or essential character of* something: belonging *by nature or settled habit.*" *Webster's Third New International Dictionary* (1966), at 1163 (emphasis added). A particular risk cannot be "structural" or "involved in the constitution or essential character of something" one day but not the next. Under this definition, once a risk is determined to be "inherent" in something, it will remain so until there is a fundamental change in that thing's constitution or essential character.

In *Hudson* and *Anderson,* the Court decided that the risk of a spectator being injured by a foul ball at a baseball game was an inherent risk, i.e., that it was "structural" or "involved in the constitution or essential character" of watching baseball. This is why the Court's determinations in those cases were made as a matter of law, not fact, and this is why those determinations have properly been binding on all similar claims since they were made. As a result, the Court must approach the risk of being injured by Sluggerrr's hotdog toss the same way. Either that risk is "structural" and "involved in the constitution or essential character" of watching a Royals game or it is not. It cannot be both, any more than this Court can allow one jury to say it is and the next jury to say it is not.

Accordingly, this Court holds that the question of whether a risk is "inherent" for purposes of the doctrine of implied primary assumption of the risk is not a question for the jury. As a result, the question of whether being injured by Sluggerrr's hotdog toss is an "inherent risk" of watching a Royals home game must be answered as a matter of law.

IV. Being Injured by Sluggerrr's Hotdog Toss is Not a Risk Inherent in Watching Royals Baseball

The Royals admit that, "[s]trictly speaking, this is not a baseball rule case" because Coomer does not claim he was injured by a foul ball or loose bat. But, because it claims the Hotdog Launch is a "common sense" activity, the Royals contend that the same implied primary assumption of the risk rationale should apply and bar all recovery by Coomer. According to the Royals, the risk to a spectator of being injured by Sluggerrr's hotdog toss shares the same essential characteristics as the other risks that this Court (and many others) determined long ago were inherent in watching a baseball game in person, i.e., risks that a spectator will be injured by a flying ball or bat. The Court disagrees.

The rationale for barring recovery for injuries from risks that are inherent in watching a particular sport under implied primary assumption of the risk is that the defendant team owner cannot remove such risks without materially altering either the sport that the spectators come to see or the spectator's enjoyment of it. No such argument applies to Sluggerrr's hotdog toss. Millions of fans have watched the Royals (and its forebears in professional baseball) play the National Pastime for the better part of a century before Sluggerrr began tossing hotdogs, and millions more people watch professional baseball every year in stadiums all across this country without the benefit of such antics.

Some fans may find Sluggerrr's hotdog toss fun to watch between innings, and some fans may even have come to expect it, but this does not make the risk of injury from Sluggerrr's hotdog toss an "inherent risk" of watching a Royals game. As noted above, "inherent" means "*structural* or involved in the *constitution or essential character of* something: belonging *by nature or settled habit*," *Webster's Third New International Dictionary* (1966), at 1163 (emphasis added). There is nothing about the risk of injury from Sluggerrr's hotdog toss that is "structural" or involves the "constitution or essential character" of watching a Royals game at Kauffman Stadium.

The Royals concede that Sluggerrr's hotdog toss has nothing to do with watching the game of baseball but contend that the Hotdog Launch is a well-established (even customary) part of the overall stadium "experience." In support, the Royals cite cases that have applied the Baseball Rule to risks that were not created directly from the game. These cases do not support the Royals' argument.

In *Loughran v. The Phillies,* 888 A.2d 872 876–77 (Pa.2005), because a plaintiff was injured when a fielder tossed the ball into the stands after catching the last out of the inning, the court held that implied primary assumption of the risk barred the plaintiff's claims. In rejecting the plaintiff's claim that the Baseball Rule should not apply because the throw was not part of the game itself, *Loughran* holds that — even though the " 'no duty' rule applies only to 'common, expected, and frequent' risks of the game" — the link between the game and the risk of being hit with a ball tossed into the stands by a player is undeniable. *Id.* at 876. Baseball is the reason centerfielder Marlon Byrd was there, just as it was the reason the fans were in the stands (including the many who were yelling for Byrd to toss the ball to them). Here, on the other hand, there is no link between the game and the risk of being hit by Sluggerrr's hotdog toss. The Hotdog Launch is not an inherent part of the game; it is what the Royals do to entertain baseball fans when there is no game for them to watch. Sluggerrr may make breaks in the game more fun, but Coomer and his 12,000 rain-soaked fellow spectators were not there to watch Sluggerrr toss hotdogs; they were there to watch the Royals play baseball.

Somewhat closer to the mark—but still inapposite—is the Royals' reliance on *Cohen v. Sterling Mets, L.P,* 17 Misc.3d 218 (N.Y.Sup.Ct.2007), *aff'd* 870 N.Y.S.2d 914 (N.Y.App.Div.2009). A vendor sued the team for injuries caused by a fan who hit the vendor while diving for a souvenir T-shirt that had been tossed into the crowd. The court dismissed these claims, stating: "When a ball is tossed into the stands by a player many spectators rush toward the ball in hopes of getting a souvenir, just as what allegedly occurred here during the t-shirt launch." *Id.* at 220.

The Royals' reliance on *Cohen* highlights one of the basic flaws in its effort to use implied primary assumption to bar Coomer's claims, and it shows the importance of correctly identifying the risks and activity in each case. As explained above, what makes a risk "inherent" for purposes of this doctrine — and what distinguishes such risks from those at issue in an implied secondary assumption of the risk case — is that the risks are so intertwined (i.e., so "structural" or involved in the "constitution or essential character") with the underlying activity that the team cannot control or limit the risk without abandoning the activity. In *Cohen,* because the Mets could not control how fans reacted to the T-shirt launch, that reaction was an inherent risk — not of watching a baseball game but — of taking part in the T-shirt launch (which the plaintiff's work required him to do). Here, on the other hand, not only is being injured by Sluggerrr's hotdog toss not an inherent risk of watching a Royals game, it is not an inherent risk of the Hotdog Launch. As discussed below, the Royals concede that there are negligent *and* non-negligent ways of tossing a hotdog and that Sluggerr (for whom the Royals are responsible) can control which he uses.

Accordingly, the Court holds as a matter of law that the risk of injury from Sluggerrr's hotdog toss is not one of the risks inherent in watching the Royals play baseball that Coomer assumed merely by attending a game at Kauffman Stadium. This risk can be increased, decreased or eliminated altogether with no impact on the game or the spectators' enjoyment of it. As a result, Sluggerrr (and, therefore, the Royals) owe the fans a duty to use reasonable care in conducting the Hotdog Launch and can be held liable for damages caused by a breach of that duty.[20] Sluggerrr's tosses may — or may not —be negligent; that is a question of fact for the jury to decide. But the Royals owe the same duty of reasonable care when distributing hotdogs or other promotional materials that it owes to their 1.7 million fans in all other circumstances, excepting only those risks of injury that are an inherent part of watching a baseball game in person.

. . .

Conclusion

For the reasons set forth above, this Court vacates the judgment and remands the case. All concur.

---

[20] This observation highlights another — perhaps even more basic — flaw in the Royals' argument. From the very beginning, Baseball Rule cases holding that the home team has "no duty" to protect spectators recognized that balls and bats can go flying into the seats even though the batter, pitcher, or fielder is using reasonable care. The risk that is "inherent" in watching this game is that even careful players cannot always control the flight of the ball or keep control of the bat. To eliminate all risk of that occurring, the team's only choice is to change the game or the fans' access to it. Here, on the other hand, nothing (except the Royals) compels Sluggerrr to throw hotdogs at the spectators. Perhaps the Royals are correct and there is a non-negligent way to throw a hotdog at a patron, but safety *always* can be ensured simply by handing the food to the customer . . . as waiters, waitresses, and concessionaires prove millions of times every day. So, if Sluggerrr and the Royals decide to engage in the riskier conduct of throwing the food, they cannot complain that they have to persuade a jury that such conduct was reasonable anytime a fan is injured.

Notes and Questions

1. Be sure that you can explain the difference between express assumption of the risk, primary implied assumption of the risk, and secondary implied assumption of the risk.

2. Why would lawmakers choose to exclude a plaintiff's primary implied assumption of the risk from comparative negligence analysis? Why would they choose to subsume secondary implied assumption of the risk into comparative negligence analysis?

3. What are the procedural effects of the decision to characterize plaintiff's conduct as primary versus secondary implied assumption of the risk?

4. The Missouri Supreme Court in *Coomer* describes secondary implied assumption of the risk as including (a) circumstances in which the plaintiff himself or herself is reasonable in engaging the risk at issue, and (b) circumstances in which the plaintiff is unreasonable in engaging that risk. The classic hypothetical used to distinguish these two circumstances involves a plaintiff who runs into a burning building. The defendant's negligence caused the fire. Whether or not the plaintiff was reasonable depends on why he ran into the building. If it was to save a child, it is likely that a jury would conclude that he was reasonable—even a hero. On the other hand, if the man ran into the building to save a "favorite fedora," a jury would likely conclude he was unreasonable. See, e.g., Blackburn v. Dorta, 348 So.2d 287, 291 (Fla. 1977). What are or should be the legal implications of this distinction? Finally, based on this distinction you may sometimes see assumption of the risk divided into three categories instead of two: "secondary" implied assumption of the risk being used to describe a reasonable plaintiff and "tertiary" implied assumption of the risk being used to describe an unreasonable plaintiff. See if the following case helps you to understand the merits of this further division.

HEROD v. GRANT
262 So.2d 781 (Miss. 1972)

PATTERSON, Justice:

This is an appeal from a judgment of the Circuit Court of Montgomery County wherein the appellee was awarded $15,000 in damages for injuries received by him in falling from the appellant's truck. We reverse.

On the evening of October 24, 1969, Joseph Grant, plaintiff below, and Eddie Earl Herod, defendant below, engaged in a common enterprise to rid the appellee's bean field of predatory wild animals. Each equipped himself with a headlight and a rifle and at approximately 10:00 p.m. ventured into the appellee's bean field in the appellant's pickup truck. In scanning the field they observed a deer and the appellee seated himself in a cross-legged position upon a tool box situated in the bed of the truck immediately to the rear of the cab. The appellant then drove the truck not more than fifteen to twenty miles per hour along the rows of the field which had been combined that afternoon by the appellee. The deer, when it became illuminated by the lights of the truck and the headlights of the occupants, was twice fired upon by the appellee to no avail when the weapon jammed. He then obtained the rifle of the appellant in furtherance of his defense of the field when the deer, which had been running parallel to the truck, veered toward the vehicle, motivating the appellant, according to the appellee, to suddenly increase the speed of the truck in an attempt to run over the deer. This action, as well as a slight turn of the vehicle by the appellant, caused the appellee to fall from the tool box to the ground, seriously injuring him.

The testimony of the appellant is substantially the same with the exception that he denies the truck was rapidly accelerated or sharply turned from its path.

The sole issue before the Court is whether the appellee, by engaging in this activity, assumed the attendant risk attached to the endeavor.

In Elias v. New Laurel Radio Station, Inc., 245 Miss. 170, 146 So.2d 558 (1962), and Dendy v. City of Pascagoula, 193 So.2d 559 (Miss.1967), we quoted with approval the rule relative to the necessary elements of assumption of risk as set forth in 19 Mississippi Law Journal, Negligence-Automobile Accidents-Assumption of Risk as a Defense-Contributory Negligence Distinguished, at 370 (1948), wherein it is stated:

> . . . The elements which must be found in order to constitute a defense of assumption of risk are generally stated in some such terms as the following: (1) Knowledge on the part of the injured party of a condition inconsistent with his safety; (2) appreciation by the injured party of the danger in the condition; and (3) a deliberate and voluntary choice on the part of the injured party to expose his person to that danger in such a manner as to register assent on the continuance of the dangerous condition. . . .

The critical question for this Court to answer is whether the plaintiff comprehended a knowledge of the risk involved in riding in the rear of the truck. We have stated that the assumption of risk is governed by the subjective standard of the plaintiff himself whereas contributory negligence is measured by the objective standard of a reasonable man, and that the assumption of risk is a jury question in all but the clearest cases.

In considering subjective knowledge, 1 Blashfield Automobile Law and Practice, section 64.3 (3d Ed.1965), stated that:

> Subjective knowledge is more difficult to prove. Plaintiff may always claim he did not know of the facts creating the risk, or that he did not comprehend the risk involved. Evidence contradicting this is difficult to secure. The jury, having no external standard by which to judge his knowledge, must determine whether he is telling the truth. However, the courts have indicated a willingness to override such contentions of plaintiff where they find that any person of ordinary intelligence must, as a matter of law, have known and appreciated the risk. . . .

In discussing knowledge and appreciation of the risk, the textwriter in 57 Am.Jur.2d, Negligence, section 282 (1971) indicates that:

> Where the facts are such that the plaintiff must have had knowledge of the hazard, the situation is equivalent to actual knowledge and there may be assumption of the risk. In some cases the circumstances may show as a matter of law that the risk was understood and appreciated, and often they may present in that particular a question of fact for the jury. Also, the plaintiff may not close his eyes to obvious dangers, and

> cannot recover where he was in possession of facts from which he would be legally charged with appreciation of the danger.
>
> In cases involving the issue of assumption of risk, an understanding of the danger involved and consent to assume the risk may be shown by circumstances. However, in the absence of evidence that the injured person knew of the danger, or that the danger was so obvious that he must be taken to have known of it, it cannot be held that he assumed the risk of injury therefrom.

. . .

The case of De Winne v. Waldrep, 101 Ga.App. 570, 114 S.E.2d 455 (1960), presents a fact situation remarkably similar to that of the case at bar. In De Winne a party fell or was thrown from the back of a pickup while driving through open fields and hunting deer. The Georgia Court of Appeals held that one who knowingly and voluntarily takes a risk of injury to his person, the danger of which is so obvious that the act of taking such risk is and of itself amounts to a failure to exercise ordinary care and diligence for his own safety, cannot hold another liable for damages for injuries thus occasioned. The case at bar clearly presents a stronger fact situation for application of the assumption of risk doctrine than De Winne for the reason the parties here were defending, or hunting, at night and travelling through a cultivated field traversed by plowed rows.

We are of the opinion that Joseph Grant, by hunting deer from a seated position upon a tool box in the bed of the truck in the late evening hours in a cultivated field, assumed the risk that the vehicle might either pass over rough ground or that it might be accelerated or swerved in the excitement of the chase, or a combination thereof, none lending itself to safety, but rather all pointing directly to a precarious position from which injury could very easily flow. There being no relationship of master and servant, the appellee, a mature and reasonable man, assumed the risk of the endeavor for which no liability extends to the defendant.

We are of the opinion the trial court should have sustained the defendant's motion for a directed verdict at the conclusion of the plaintiff's testimony.

Reversed and rendered.

GILLESPIE, C.J., and INZER, SMITH and ROBERTSON, JJ., concur.

Notes and Questions

1. What was the defendant's assumption of the risk argument? What was the plaintiff's rebuttal?

2. At trial, the plaintiff was awarded $15,000.00 in damages. On the same facts and (uncomplicated) law, the Mississippi Supreme Court found in the defendant's favor; indeed, the Court held that the trial court should have found for the defendant as a matter of law at the close of the plaintiff's case. What accounts for these different views of the case?

3. Mississippi has long been a pure comparative negligence jurisdiction, but it only subsumed secondary implied assumption of the risk into its comparative negligence analysis in 1995. See Horton v. American Tobacco Company, 667 So.2d 1289 (Miss. 1995). This means that at the time *Herod* was decided, assumption of the risk remained a complete defense in negligence cases. If the same facts and arguments were made today, could the defendant's lawyer still achieve the same result, i.e., no liability and no damages due to the plaintiff?

III. COMPARATIVE FAULT AND COMPARATIVE RESPONSIBILITY

There have been two attempts to move beyond comparative negligence to doctrines that more fully encompass the various factors a jury might consider before reaching the damages phase of the plaintiff's case:

The first of these is comparative fault, which broadens the comparison beyond the parties' relative negligences to all fault-based actions—including negligence, gross negligence, willful and wanton misconduct, recklessness, and intentional conduct. Because comparative fault compares fault-based actions, actions that only qualify for strict liability (or no-fault) treatment are not be included in the comparison. As an example, consider a situation where a landlord failed to repair a gas leak he was substantially certain would cause an explosion and his tenant, despite smelling something odd, lit a match to light a decorative candle. Under a contributory negligence system, since the defendant's conduct was an intentional tort and the plaintiff's was ordinary negligence, these would not be compared. However, under a comparative fault system, both the intentional tort and the ordinary negligence would be considered by the jury in determining how responsibility for the damages would be allocated, presumably under an instruction that made clear that the severity of the fault should be considered by the jury in making their percentage allocation. According to the Reporter's Note following Restatement (Third) of Torts: Apportionment of Liability §1, though a significant number of states now include intentional torts in their comparison, it is not yet the majority rule.

The second move away from comparative negligence is comparative responsibility. At the risk of being tautological, this is a causation-based, rather than a fault-based approach to the comparison which focuses *both* on the parties' relative levels of fault (carelessness through intentionality) *and* on their relative causal contributions to the damages. For example, imagine that Defendant #1 shoots the Plaintiff but the bullet barely grazes his leg. Plaintiff is further injured when Defendant #2's truck, transporting gasoline on the highway, explodes in the next lane as Plaintiff is being transported to the emergency room. Finally, Plaintiff—who was in remarkably good shape when he finally arrived at the ER—dies in the operating room as a result of the gross medical negligence of Defendant #3, his surgeon. Defendant #1 committed an intentional tort—the worst form of fault along the fault continuum; however, his causal contribution to the Plaintiff's ultimate damages (including for death) might be said to be relatively small given that his bullet merely grazed the Plaintiff's leg. Defendant #2 committed a strict liability offense—assuming no accompanying negligence, a no fault tort; however, his causal contribution to the Plaintiff's ultimate damages were likely not negligible. Defendant #3 was grossly negligent—less "at fault" in terms of his mental state than Defendant #1, and more "at fault" than Defendant #2; however, his causal contribution to the Plaintiff's damages might be much more significant than either Defendant #1 or Defendant #2. As the Third Restatement suggests, comparative responsibility would permit the judge to instruct the jury to consider both relative fault and relative causal contributions:

Restatement (Third) of Torts: Apportionment of Liability §8: Factors for Assigning Responsibility

Factors for assigning percentages of responsibility to each person whose legal responsibility has been established include:

(a) the nature of the person's risk creating conduct, including any awareness of indifference with respect to the risks created by the conduct and any intent with respect to the harm created by the conduct; and

(b) the strength of the causal connection between the person's risk creating conduct and the harm.

Comment:

a. Assigning Shares of Responsibility. The fact finder assigns comparative percentages of "responsibility" to parties and other relevant persons whose negligence or other legally culpable conduct was a legal cause of the plaintiff's injury.

"Responsibility" is a general and neutral term. Assigning shares of "fault" or "negligence" can be misleading because some causes of action are not based on negligence or fault. Assigning shares of "causation" wrongly suggests that indivisible injuries jointly caused by two or more actors can be divided on the basis of causation. Assigning shares of "culpability" would be misleading if it were not made clear that "culpability" refers to "legal culpability," which may include strict liability.

Of course, it is not possible to precisely compare conduct that falls into different categories, such as intentional conduct, negligent conduct, and conduct governed by strict liability, because the various theories of recovery are incommensurate. However, courts routinely compare seemingly incommensurate values, such as when they balance safety and productivity in negligence or products liability law. "Assigning shares of responsibility" may be a less confusing phrase because it suggests that the factfinder, after considering the relevant factors, *assigns* shares of responsibility rather than *compares* incommensurate quantities. Nevertheless, the term "comparative responsibility" is used pervasively by courts and legislatures to describe percentage-allocation systems.

b. Causation and scope of liability. Conduct is relevant for determining percentage shares of responsibility only when it caused the harm and when the harm is within the scope of the person's liability.

. . .

c. Factors in assigning shares of responsibility. The relevant factors for assigning percentages of responsibility include the nature of each person's risk-creating conduct and the comparative strength of the causal connection between each person's risk-creating conduct and the harm. The nature of each person's risk-creating conduct includes such things as how unreasonable the conduct was under the circumstances, the extent to which the conduct failed to meet the applicable legal standard, the circumstances surrounding the conduct, each person's abilities and disabilities, and each person's awareness, intent, or indifference with respect to the risks.

The comparative strength of the causal connection between the conduct and the harm depends on how attenuated the causal connection is, the timing of each person's conduct in causing the harm, and a comparison of the risks created by the conduct and the actual harm suffered by the plaintiff.

. . .

Illustrations:

2. A is injured when A's and B's automobiles collide at an intersection with a four-way stop. In A's lawsuit against B, A is found negligent for taking his eyes off the road to attend to a child in the back seat, and B is found negligent for purposefully trying to beat A's automobile across the intersection after seeing it approaching. A's conduct and B's conduct are each found to have caused A's indivisible injury. The factfinder would be justified in assigning a higher percentage of responsibility to B because, between A and B, (a) B's conduct deviated more significantly from the legally required norm, (b) B had a more culpable state of mind, and (c) the other circumstances surrounding A's conduct were more forgivable.

. . .

Notes and Questions

1. To date, no jurisdiction has fully embraced the concept embodied in section 8.

2. By now you have a general understanding of jury instructions and verdict forms. Consider how substantive jury instructions and the verdict form might change when a jurisdiction moves from contributory to comparative negligence. Consider how both might change if a jurisdiction moves from comparative negligence to comparative responsibility. In both contexts, how might the jury deliberate differently?

CHAPTER EIGHT
STRICT LIABILITY

Strict liability, also known as no fault or absolute liability, is premised on the notion that in some kinds of cases the defendant ought to be liable simply for causing the plaintiff's harm regardless of the defendant's motivation or state of mind. In contrast with intentional torts and negligence, this means that strict liability claims are made out using a three-part prima facie case: proof of the existence of a qualifying fact pattern, causation, and injury. Because modern American tort law strongly prefers fault-based liability, this category has been reduced significantly in the last two hundred years. That is, liability for torts at common law was strict — they were all trespass-based — offenses; whereas today the claim exists only for certain cases involving animals, abnormally dangerous activities, and defective products.

I. ANIMALS

NASH v. HEROLD
Not Reported In A.2d, 2010 WL 2573764 50, Conn. L. Rptr. 45 (Conn. Super. 2010)

BLAWIE, J.

Introduction

This is a case in which Charla Nash (Nash or the plaintiff), allegedly sustained catastrophic and life-threatening personal injuries as a result of an attack by "Travis," a chimpanzee owned by Sandra Herold (Herold or the defendant). The incident occurred on February 16, 2009, while the plaintiff was an invitee on the grounds of the residence Herold shared with the chimpanzee at 241 Rock Rimmon Road, Stamford, Connecticut. The suit was commenced on the plaintiff's behalf by her twin brother, Michael J. Nash, who has been appointed the conservator of Nash's estate by the Stamford Probate Court. The complaint sounds in three counts. The first count, which is the subject of this memorandum of decision, asserts a theory of strict liability against the defendant for the keeping of a wild animal with dangerous propensities. The second count and third counts allege that Herold acted in a negligent and reckless manner, respectively, in her possession and housing of Travis, and by allowing the animal to roam outside Herold's home with knowledge of its violent and dangerous propensities and without regard for the safety of third parties such as the plaintiff.

If the strict liability count were to be sent to the jury, the plaintiff would have to prove by a fair preponderance of the evidence that the defendant knew of the chimpanzee's dangerous propensities, that she was injured by the defendant's chimpanzee, and that the actions of the chimpanzee were the proximate cause of those injuries. Under a theory of strict liability, if these elements are established, the plaintiff may be compensated for her injuries without regard to a finding of fault on the part of the defendant. Herold has moved pursuant to Practice Book § 10–39 to strike the strict liability count in the complaint. The defendant's argument is twofold: (1) that Connecticut does not recognize such a claim, and that the keeping of a chimpanzee does not rise to the level of an inherently dangerous activity; and (2) that the plaintiff has failed to allege facts sufficient to set forth a claim for strict liability. The plaintiff maintains that strict liability is a viable cause of action under Connecticut common law, and that sufficient facts are alleged in the complaint to set forth a cognizable claim.

Legal Standard

"The purpose of a motion to strike is to contest . . . the legal sufficiency of the allegations of any complaint . . . to state a claim upon which relief can be granted." (Internal quotation marks omitted.) *Fort Trumbull Conservancy, LLC v. Alves,* 262 Conn. 480, 498, 815 A.2d 1188 (2003). "It is fundamental that in determining the sufficiency of a [pleading] challenged by a [party's] motion to strike, all well-pleaded facts and those facts necessarily implied from the allegations are taken as admitted." (Internal quotation marks omitted.) *Gazo v. Stamford,* 255 Conn. 245, 260, 765 A.2d 505 (2001). "A motion to strike is the proper procedural vehicle . . . to test whether Connecticut is ready to recognize some newly emerging ground of liability." (Internal quotation marks omitted.) *Ortiz v. Waterbury Hospital,* judicial district of Waterbury, Docket No. CV 99 154112 (March 9, 2000, Pelligrino, J.) (26 Conn. L. Rptr. 547).

. . .

Discussion

The defendant was the owner of an adult chimpanzee named Travis, which the defendant acquired in its infancy. Herold had owned the animal for approximately fourteen years before the incident. The chimpanzee lived with Herold in her home and was treated in a quasi-familial manner. The defendant allowed Travis to ride in cars, drink wine from a stemmed glass, dress and bathe itself, and even use a computer. However, the chimpanzee had also displayed bouts of violent and erratic behavior on several prior occasions. Most notably, it bit a woman on her hand in 1996 and tried to drag her into a car. In 1998, it bit a man on his thumb. In 2003, Travis escaped from the defendant's vehicle and was at large roaming the area of downtown Stamford for several hours until it could be captured.

On February 16, 2009, Travis escaped from the house and/or was roaming the grounds of the defendant's Rock Rimmon Road property. Because Herold was unable to coax the chimpanzee inside, she telephoned Nash and asked for Nash's assistance in getting Travis back into the house. Nash complied, and shortly after she arrived at the defendant's property, the chimpanzee violently and without provocation attacked her. The attack caused Nash life-threatening and catastrophic injuries, including a traumatic brain injury, traumatic eye injury and the loss of both hands. Travis also damaged or destroyed significant portions of Nash's facial structure. Herold had called 911 for emergency assistance, and when the police and other emergency personnel arrived at the defendant's property, the chimpanzee fled. Travis returned shortly thereafter and attacked the police and emergency personnel, causing damage to a police car, and forcing an officer to shoot and kill the chimpanzee in self-defense.

The plaintiff alleges that the defendant is strictly liable for her injuries, in that they resulted from a dangerous propensity characteristic of wild animals such as a chimpanzee, and that the defendant knew of or had reason to know of such a propensity. The defendant advances several claims in support of her motion to strike the strict liability count. The defendant argues that while the legislature has provided for strict liability for personal injuries caused by dog bites, neither the legislature nor Connecticut courts have ever recognized a claim of strict liability for injuries caused by a wild animal. And further, that under Connecticut common law, it has been held that liability for injuries committed by a vicious animal is grounded in negligence only. The defendant also maintains that her chimpanzee was not a wild animal, nor was it an animal recognized as potentially dangerous pursuant to a statute in effect at the time the attack occurred on February 16, 2009.[5] The defendant asserts that she broke no laws, rules or regulations in having Travis live with her at her home. The defendant's brief also offers the unsubstantiated argument that, "Travis was exempted from the requirements of Connecticut General Statutes [§]26–55 [requiring permits for possessing wild mammals] because the state did not believe that he presented a public health risk."

The plaintiff contends that Connecticut common law supports holding an owner of an animal such as Travis to a strict liability standard. "Strict liability is available only when the legislature has provided for it or in those situations where the common law of the state has imposed such liability and the legislature has not seen fit to change it." *Torres v. Dept. of Corrections,* 50 Conn.Supp. 72, 78, 912 A.2d 1132 (2006); *Gore v. People's Savings Bank,* 235 Conn. 360, 363, 665 A.2d 1341 (1995). The defendant's brief in support of her motion to strike discusses inherently dangerous activities such as blasting and explosives, where it is clear that Connecticut courts have applied the theory of strict liability. The rationale underlying the application of the doctrine of strict liability in activities characterized as either "abnormally dangerous" or "intrinsically dangerous" is that "[a] person who uses intrinsically dangerous means to accomplish a lawful end, in such a way as will necessarily or obviously expose the person of another to the danger of probable injury [should be] liable if such injury results even though he uses all proper care." *Caporale v. C.W. Blakeslee Sons, Inc.,* 149 Conn. 79, 86, 175 A.2d 561 (1961).

However, a resort to holdings in cases involving ultrahazardous activities is of limited utility in resolving the specific issue before this court. The parties agree that no prior Connecticut case or statute directly addresses the issue of whether the private owner of a chimpanzee may be strictly liable for any injuries caused by the animal, and there appear to be no Connecticut cases construing the extent of liability for injuries caused by a wild animal. However, the traditional rule is that owners of wild animals are strictly liable. 4 Am.Jur.2d, Animals § 80, p. 327; 3A C.J.S., Animals § 171; Annot., 21 A.L.R.3d 603. Section 507 of the Restatement (Second) of Torts provides: "(1) A possessor of wild animals is subject to liability to another for harm done by the animal to the other, his person, land or chattels, although the possessor has exercised the utmost care to confine the animal, or otherwise prevent the animal from doing harm. (2) This liability is limited to harm that results from a dangerous propensity that is characteristic of wild animals of the particular class, or which the possessor knows or has reason to know."

---

[5] It is true that in the wake of this attack, the Connecticut legislature took action to change the law as to the possession of chimpanzees such as Travis. Public Act No. 09–198, among other things, amended General Statutes § 26–40a. That law prohibits the private possession of "potentially dangerous animals." A new provision, § 1(a)(4), expands the statutory definition of such prohibited animals to specifically include, "[t]he hominidae, including, but not limited to, the gorilla, chimpanzee and orangutan." However, because this new statute did not take effect until October 1, 2009, some seven months *after* the attack giving rise to these claims, the statute itself may not be used by the plaintiff as a basis for the imposition of strict liability in this case. The plaintiff's brief expressly disavows reliance upon any statutory authority for her claim.

Section 506 of the Restatement (Second) of Torts defines a wild animal as "an animal that is not by custom devoted to the service of mankind at the time and in the place in which it is kept." The commentary to § 506 states that, "[t]he fact that a particular animal is kept for a socially valuable purpose does not prevent it from being a wild animal; *the test is whether the animals are as a class recognized by custom as devoted to the service of mankind.*" (Emphasis added.) The court finds that chimpanzees are not a class of animals customarily "devoted to the service of mankind." This is a finding grounded not in a legal precedent, but in knowledge of custom and experience. The common law is the wellspring from which the plaintiff draws her strict liability count, and in his classic treatise on the common law, Justice Holmes noted, "The life of the law has not been logic; it has been experience." The Common Law, p. 1 (1881).

The rationale for the imposition of strict liability against owners for injuries caused by dangerous animals is discussed in W. Prosser & W. Keeton, Torts (5th Ed.1984). "Strict liability is appropriately placed: upon those who, even with proper care, expose the community to the risk of a very dangerous thing . . . The kind of 'dangerous animal' that will subject the keeper to strict liability . . . must pose some kind of an abnormal risk to the particular community where the animal is kept; hence, the keeper is engaged in an activity that subjects those in the vicinity, including those who come onto his property, to an abnormal risk . . . The possessor of a wild animal is strictly liable for physical harm done to the person of another. . . if that harm results from a dangerous propensity that is characteristic of wild animals of that class. Thus, strict liability has been imposed on keepers of lions and tigers, bears, elephants, wolves, monkeys, and other similar animals. *No member of such a species, however domesticated, can ever be regarded as safe, and liability does not rest upon any experience with the particular animal.*" (Emphasis added.) *Irvine v. Rare Feline Breading Center, Inc.*, 685 N.E.2d 120, 125 (Ind.App.1997), citing W. Prosser & W. Keeton, Torts, § 76, at 541–42 (5th ed.1984). In discussing strict liability principles relating to animals, Professor Prosser explains that the rule is an outgrowth of primitive law, in which the owner of an animal was so far identified with it that he was liable without any fault of his own for the damage the animal might inflict on his neighbors. Those who keep such animals for their own purposes are required to protect the community, at their peril, against the risk involved. The strict liability is, in general, co-extensive with the obvious risk. W. Prosser & W. Keeton, Torts, § 76, at 541–42 (5th ed.1984).

In a discussion of strict liability for ultrahazardous activity in *G.J. Leasing Co., Inc. v. Union Electric Co.*, 54 F.3d 379 (7th Cir.1995), Judge Posner drew an analogy to a wild animal that the court finds illuminating. "Keeping a tiger in one's backyard would be an example of an abnormally hazardous activity. The hazard is such, relative to the value of the activity, that we desire not just that the owner take all due care that the tiger not escape, but that he consider seriously the possibility of getting rid of the tiger altogether; and we give him an incentive to consider this course of action by declining to make the exercise of due care a defense to a suit based on an injury caused by the tiger — in other words, by making him strictly liable for any such injury." *Id.*, at 386.

While it is clear that a chimpanzee is not a tiger, the injuries here could not be more horrific if they were inflicted by a tiger, and it is equally clear that a principal objective of tort law is to determine whether or not to compensate for loss, and if so, how. Notwithstanding the sensational publicity attendant upon this incident, the fact that liability for personal injuries stemming from an attack by a chimpanzee has not heretofore been the subject of a civil suit for damages in Connecticut is a reflection of the relative rarity of the private possession of this species of animal in this country, rather than any novelty as to the legal theory underpinning a strict liability cause of action. In other words, this is not a "new" cause of action in the legal sense. This conclusion is reinforced by an examination of older editions of a treatise which was for many years in this state the seminal legal treatise in this area.

The 1956 edition of Connecticut Law of Torts by Douglass B. Wright includes the following language in its discussion of wild animals and strict liability:

> Most authorities hold that a harborer of a wild animal is liable without fault for injuries to person or property, although a small minority of jurisdictions is evidencing a tendency to base liability on negligence in the handling of the animal. In tort law a wild animal is sometimes defined as an animal with naturally vicious propensities; but the Restatement of the Law of Torts bases its definition of a wild animal on the utility of the animal and its adaptation to the service of mankind. Thus the custom of the locality may make an elephant or a camel a wild animal in one portion of the world and a domestic animal in another portion. The tort concept of a wild animal is different from the property concept, where the '*animus revertendi*' or the propensity to return on the part of the animal usually determines whether the animal is wild or domesticated.

D. Wright, Connecticut Law of Torts (1st ed.1956).

The court disagrees with the defendant's argument that the chimpanzee was not a "wild animal" within the legal definition of that term, or in the custom of the locality in this portion of the world (the State of Connecticut). As previously stated, Travis the chimpanzee is not of a class of animals recognized by custom as devoted to the service of mankind. The domesticated behavior the animal may have exhibited as alleged in the complaint, e.g., Travis' use of stemware, a computer, the wearing of clothing, or other human-like characteristics, while reflective of a more complex brain, does not change its essential animal nature. Over 130 years ago, the U.S. Supreme Court had occasion to rule in an action in which the plaintiff was injured by a powerful buck which roamed a park in Saratoga Springs, New York. The deer was part of a herd which had been domesticated to some degree by the defendant proprietor of that park. The plaintiff was visiting the park when she was attacked and seriously injured after being gored by the buck's antlers. The plaintiff alleged that the defendant knew the buck to be dangerous, but did not allege negligence on the part of the defendant. In finding no error, the court wrote, "Certain animals *ferae naturae* may doubtless be domesticated to such an extent as to be classed, in respect to the liability of the owner for injuries they commit, with the class known as tame or domestic animals; but inasmuch as they are liable to relapse into their wild habits and to become mischievous, the rule is that if they do so, and the owner becomes notified of their vicious habit, they are included in the same rule as if they had never been domesticated, the gist of the action in such a case, as in the case of untamed wild animals, being not merely the negligent keeping of the animal, but the keeping of the same with knowledge of the vicious and mischievous propensity of the animal." *Spring Co. v. Edgar,* 99 U.S. 645, 653, 25 L.Ed. 487 (1878).

This theme of a wild animal's reversion to form and the strict liability attendant thereto is echoed in Comment (c) to the Restatement (Second) of Torts Section 507, which notes that an owner of a wild animal, "may reasonably believe that it has been so tamed as to have lost all of these propensities; nonetheless he takes the risk that at any moment the animal may revert to and exhibit them. Thus a keeper of an elephant that for years has shown none of the dangerous traits common to elephants as a class is liable under the rule stated in this Section if the animal suddenly and unexpectedly exhibits these traits."

The court can discern no reason not to allow the plaintiff the chance to make out a case of strict liability. Where, as here, the defendant is alleged to have engaged in the activity of keeping and housing an adult male chimpanzee, a wild animal with a history of roaming and being known to have caused injury to third parties on prior occasions, the court can see no justification for relieving the defendant of strict liability. The owner of such an animal should properly bear the loss, rather than a third person such as the plaintiff Charla Nash, who has no connection to the chimpanzee, other than that of catastrophic personal injury. Venerable common law principles fully support strict liability against the owners of wild animals who cause harm to third parties, as an unreasonable risk of harm may be created merely by such possession.

Persons such as the defendant who choose to own such animals have the affirmative duty to keep and maintain them safely, and in a manner that avoids liability. This is a duty that existed at common law. Its existence is not dependent upon a statute, nor is that duty extinguished by the absence of an applicable statute. In addition to the claims of negligence and recklessness, a mutilation injury by a chimpanzee under these circumstances is the kind of harm that should be protected by a strict liability standard. The court's rationale is that strict liability should be imposed on the party best able to protect persons from the hazardous condition brought about by their ownership of such an animal in the first instance. Writing fully one hundred years[7] after its decision in the case of *Spring Co. v. Edgar, supra,* the U.S. Supreme Court observed, "The possibility that those subjected to strict liability will take extraordinary care in their dealings is frequently regarded as one advantage of a rule of strict liability." *United States v. United States Gypsum Co.,* 438 U.S. 422, 441, fn. 17, 98 S.Ct. 2864, 57 L.Ed.2d 854 (1978).

Conclusion

The plaintiff has stated a proper cause of action, and has alleged sufficient facts in support of her claim. For the reasons stated herein, the defendant's motion to strike the strict liability count from the complaint is denied. In doing so, the court is merely recognizing a cause of action that has long existed at common law. Moreover, the court is confident it is not running the risk of deterring any socially useful conduct.

SO ORDERED.

---

[7] It has been a century which has seen the expansion of the doctrine of strict liability, rather than its contraction. As Prosser notes, "[T]he last hundred years have witnessed the overthrow of the doctrine of 'never any liability without fault,' even in the legal sense of a departure from reasonable standards of conduct. It has seen a general acceptance of the principle that in some cases the defendant may be held liable, although he is not only charged with no moral wrongdoing, but has not even departed in any way from a reasonable standard of intent or care. In some instances, as where liability is imposed upon the keepers of animals, new reasons of social policy have been found for the continuance of an older rule of strict liability. . . . There is a strong and growing tendency, where there is blame on neither side, to ask, in view of the exigencies of social justice, who can best bear the loss and hence to shift the loss where there has been no fault." W. Prosser & W. Keeton, Torts, § 75, at 536 (5th ed.1984).

Notes and Questions

1. The Restatement (Third) of Torts, Strict Liability, § 22 Wild Animals, provides as follows:

> (a) An owner or possessor of a wild animal is subject to strict liability for physical harm caused by the wild animal.
>
> (b) A wild animal is an animal that belongs to a category of animals that have not been generally domesticated and that are likely, unless restrained, to cause personal injury.

How, if at all, is this updated provision different from that in the Restatement Second? If you were a plaintiff's lawyer, would you prefer the Restatement Second or the Restatement Third? What if you were a defense lawyer?

2. A tiger escapes from his enclosure dragging the chain attached to his collar behind him. The plaintiff, hurrying to get out of the tiger's way, trips on the passing chain and falls to the ground, breaking several bones. Her lawyer files suit against the owner of the tiger in strict liability. Since it is so clear that the tiger will be classified as wild, he does not bother also to file suit in negligence. Is this a smart move?

3. Charla Nash's litigation against Sandra Herold continued after this ruling. In May 2010, Ms. Herold died from a ruptured aortic aneurysm. Her lawyer was quoted as saying, "Ms. Herold had suffered a series of heartbreaking losses over the last several years, beginning with the death of her daughter who was killed in a car accident, then her husband, then her beloved chimp Travis, as well as the tragic maiming of friend and employee Charla Nash. In the end, her heart, which had been broken so many times before, could take no more." http://www.stamfordadvocate.com/default/article/Week-in-review-Chimp-owner-dies-505378.php

In November 2012, Ms. Nash settled with Herold's estate receiving cash, real estate, and other property worth about $4 million. http://www.stamfordadvocate.com/default/article/4-million-settlement-in-chimp-attack-lawsuit-4080943.php. No doubt Ms. Nash's case was strengthened by the facts that Ms. Herold had apparently dosed an agitated Travis with Xanax earlier in the day of the mauling and that Xanax was found in his system at the time of his necropsy. Xanax, which is used to treat anxiety and panic attacks in humans, had not been prescribed for Travis. Xanax "can . . . lead to aggression in people who were unstable to begin with." http://www.stamfordadvocate.com/default/article/Animal-experts-are-baffled-by-chimp-attack-109469.php

4. Ms. Nash also attempted to sue the State of Connecticut for knowing the chimp was dangerous but doing nothing about it. Several months before the attack, a biologist warned state officials in writing that the chimpanzee could seriously hurt someone if it felt threatened, saying, "It is an accident waiting to happen." Ms. Nash's petition to sue was denied in June 2013, because at the time of her attack it was not against the law to own a chimpanzee. She appealed the denial to the state's legislature, but her right to sue was finally denied in April 2014. See Sasha Goldstein, Charla Nash, mauled by Travis the chimp, denied the right to sue

Connecticut for $150M, April 2, 2014, available at http://www.nydailynews.com/news/national/charla-nash-mauled-bychimp-denied-sue-conn-150m-article-1.1743457

5. On May 28, 2011, Charla Nash had the third full face transplant in the United States as well as bi-lateral forearm and hand transplants. Five days later, the forearm and hand transplants were removed due to infections and other medical complications. According to her lawyer's website, the face transplant improved Ms. Nash's ability to eat, taste, and smell. Since the face transplant, Ms. Nash has also received cosmetic prosthetic eyes. She now lives in a nursing and rehabilitation facility. She hopes to again have bi-lateral hand and forearm transplants. Pre-mauling, post-mauling, and post-reconstruction photos of Ms. Nash can be found on the web. The post-injury photos are not for the squeamish.

SINCLAIR v. OKATA
874 F.Supp. 1051 (D. Alaska 1994)

ORDER

(Motion for Partial Summary Judgment)

HOLLAND, Chief Judge.

Plaintiffs have moved for partial summary judgment on certain aspects of their complaint. The motion is opposed. Oral argument has been requested and heard.

. . .

On June 4, 1993, Daniel Reinhard was bitten by Anchor, a two and a half year old German Shepherd dog. Daniel was two years old when he was bitten. Daniel's five year old sister, Michelle Levshakoff, witnessed the attack. It is a matter of dispute whether Daniel's mother, Katherine Sinclair, was present at the time of the attack or whether she arrived shortly afterward. Katherine Sinclair, individually and on behalf of minors, Daniel and Michelle, filed suit in the Superior Court for the Third Judicial District for the State of Alaska. The named defendants included Yoshitaka Okata, Kazuyo Okata and Yoshihide Okata. Defendants removed the case to federal district court. Jurisdiction was based on diversity. Plaintiffs are Alaska citizens. The Okatas are citizens of Japan. Plaintiffs, joined by Daniel's father, filed an amended complaint with this court. In their complaint, plaintiffs asserted causes of action based on negligence, strict liability, negligent infliction of emotional distress, and for loss of society and companionship. Plaintiffs seek compensatory and punitive damages.

. . .

Although some factual issues remain in dispute, there are many areas where there is no genuine dispute. It is not genuinely disputed that the Okatas owned the dog, Anchor, at the time that Daniel Reinhard sustained his injuries. It is also undisputed that Daniel sustained his injuries when Anchor bit Daniel's face. Both sides to the dispute agree that on June 4, 1993, Yoshihide Okata, the 17 year old son of Yoshitaka and Kazuyo Okata, arrived home without keys to enter the home he shared with his parents. With nothing else to do, Yoshihide decided to look through the owner's manuals to the new van his parents had recently purchased. While examining the manuals, Yoshihide heard the family's dog, Anchor, in the fenced backyard crying. Anchor was a two and a half year old German Shepherd. Yoshihide brought Anchor into the unfenced driveway where the van was parked and ordered the dog to "stay." The dog was not leashed, but Yoshihide stated that he believed Anchor would obey his command to stay. Yoshihide fell asleep in the van, with the dog still unleashed in the driveway. Yoshihide did not awaken until he heard Daniel Reinhard crying. He then spoke with Katherine Sinclair, Daniel's mother, who told Yoshihide that the dog bit Daniel.

. . .

There is also no dispute as to the fact that Anchor was involved in at least four previous biting incidents. On the first occasion, a young boy, Shane Perrins, was bitten after he approached Anchor in the Okata's yard. Perrins did not require medical attention, as he received only minor scratches and a small cut on his head. On another occasion, Mina Iinuma was bitten on the arm. Ms. Iinuma's injuries consisted of one or two small holes in her elbow, which did not require medical attention. The third biting incident involved Mizutaka Azuma. According to Azuma's declaration, he was bitten as he entered the Okatas' car after eating dinner with the Okatas. Azuma went to a doctor and received three stitches to his ear. A fourth incident involved Yumiko Seifert, who was bitten on her buttocks while she was a guest at the Okatas' residence. Kazuyo Okata drove Seifert to receive medical treatment. The physician's examination revealed "multiple bite marks", but there was no bleeding. Finally, there is evidence of a fifth incident involving another child, Miwa Inoue, who sustained an injury to her face requiring one stitch.

. . .

Beyond the bare facts of the four or perhaps five biting incidents, there is a marked dispute over the manner in which the incidents are characterized. Plaintiffs point to what they claim are five biting incidents to establish that Anchor had "dangerous propensities" and to establish that the Okatas had actual knowledge of Anchor's dangerousness. Defendants counter with evidence that each of the four admitted biting incidents were the result of natural instincts, not of any dangerous tendencies. They refer to the testimony of an expert who declared that each of the four biting incidents admitted to by defendants were the result of overstimulation, protective instincts and chase instincts. In Shane Perrins' case, defendants point to the fact that many children were playing near Anchor and were possibly shooting toy arrows at him when Perrins approached the dog. Defendants claim that the dog was merely excited by all the activity, and that he jumped on the boy because of the excitement, not because of any dangerous propensity. The declaration of Perrins' mother includes an opinion corroborating this characterization. Defendants next claim that the incidents involving Mina Iinuma and Mizutaka Azuma were caused by the people suddenly touching the dog. Both Iinuma and Azuma declared that they believed they were bitten because they surprised or frightened the dog. Finally, defendants claim that the incident involving Yumiko Seifert was caused by Seifert getting too close to the dog's food, then running from the dog when he barked at her. Seifert herself disputes this description of the event. She claims that she was bitten as she stood up from a table and crossed the room to examine some skis.

. . .

There is also a dispute as to the events leading up to Anchor biting Daniel. As discussed above, Katherine Sinclair has stated that the dog Anchor began running at Daniel and Michelle, but turned away. Then, as the children disappeared behind the van, Anchor is believed to have followed the children as they disappeared behind the van. This time, Michelle supposedly kicked at the dog in a defensive maneuver, and Anchor then attacked Daniel. In contrast, defendants believe that Anchor was provoked either by Michelle kicking at him or by Daniel playing with him. They believe that the children approached Anchor, not that Anchor chased after the children. They cite Weatherton's deposition testimony that she saw Daniel approach Anchor and pet him twenty minutes before Daniel was bitten. From this testimony, they infer that the children were attempting to pet the dog when Daniel was bitten.

Plaintiffs have moved for partial summary judgment on the issue of "liability."

. . .

Summary Judgment may be ordered on the issue of liability alone even though there is a genuine issue as to the amount of damages. Fed.R.Civ.Proc. 56(c). In support of the motion, plaintiffs have made three arguments: (1) that defendants are liable on a theory of strict liability; (2) that defendants are liable under a negligence theory; and (3) that defendants are liable under a theory of negligence *per se.*

A. WAS ANCHOR A DOG OF DANGEROUS PROPENSITIES?

In *Hale v. O'Neill*, the Alaska Supreme Court referred to "the doctrine of strict liability for injuries caused by a domestic animal with known dangerous tendencies." The court in *Hale* made passing reference to the elements of an action for strict liability based on an animal's known dangerous tendencies. The court first noted that "an owner of a domestic animal becomes liable, regardless of fault, for injuries caused by the animal which stem from a vicious propensity, known to the owner." In the same paragraph, the court described the elements of such an action as being: (1) the animal's owner knew or should have known of the animal's "dangerous tendency", and (2) that the dangerous tendency resulted in an injury to the claimant. *Hale* is the only Alaskan case discussing the requirements for strict liability for injuries caused by dangerous animals. More elaboration of Alaska law is required on certain points to decide plaintiffs' motion for partial summary judgment. This court, whose subject matter jurisdiction in this case depends on diversity only, must apply the law that it believes would be applied by the Alaskan courts.

. . .

The first issue presented under this theory of strict liability is whether Anchor had a dangerous propensity. Plaintiffs point to what they believe are five prior biting incidents to establish Anchor's dangerous tendencies. Defendants' response to this point is ambiguous. On one hand, defendants seem to argue that Anchor was not dangerous because he never intended to injure any of the biting victims. They write that, "viewed in the context of the reliable, competent evidence . . . it is apparent that a reasonable jury would conclude that Anchor was not a dog with dangerous and vicious propensities." They cite declaration testimony of some of the biting victims, who believed that Anchor was not "vicious" or "aggressive." Defendants cite authority for the proposition that "the biting of a person by a dog upon provocation is not sufficient to establish a vicious disposition of the dog." Defendants also state or imply, incorrectly, that the jury decides dangerousness in a strict liability situation.[44]

. . .

Defendants' argument fails on this point because it overstates the requirements for a finding that a dog is dangerous. A dog does not have to show a tendency to inflict grievous injury for it to be dangerous. Plaintiffs note that "[a]ny knowledge of the animal's propensity to bite or attack, whether in anger or play, is sufficient [knowledge]." In *Keane v. Schroeder*, cited by defendants, the court defined the term "vicious propensity" as:

> [A] propensity or tendency of an animal to do any act which might endanger the safety of person or property in a given situation. It is the act of the animal and not the state of mind of the animal from which the effects of a dangerous propensity must be determined. A dangerous propensity may, for example, be deduced from very playful conduct.

Plaintiffs cite further cases in support of the proposition that a dangerous or vicious propensity is a propensity to injure persons, whether by anger, viciousness or playfulness. This is the position taken in the Restatement of Torts as well.[49] It is likely that Alaska's courts would adopt this approach to assessing dangerousness of a domestic animal for purposes of strict liability. If Anchor did have a dangerous propensity, then it is immaterial whether this propensity was driven by anger, playfulness, affection or curiosity.

Defendants make a second type of argument which successfully raises a genuine issue of material fact on the issue of dangerousness. Throughout most of their briefing, plaintiffs engage in a qualitative analysis of the dog's behavior to determine whether the behavior was dangerous. They look to the four, perhaps five, previous biting incidents as evidence of dangerousness. This type of analysis is misplaced in a claim for strict liability. In a strict liability case, the first inquiry is always whether the activity engaged in was *abnormally* dangerous. Under the Restatement approach, "[a] possessor of a domestic animal that he knows or has reason to know has dangerous propensities *abnormal to its class*, is subject to liability for harm done by the animal to another, although he has exercised the utmost care to prevent it from doing the harm." Prosser and Keeton concur:

> A possessor of a domestic animal is not subjected to liability for harm simply and solely because it resulted from a dangerous propensity of the domestic animal. To be

---

[44] Defendants cite authority holding that the question of whether or not an animal has a dangerous or vicious propensity is a question for the trier of fact. *Keane v. Schroeder*, 264 N.E.2d at 99; *see also Giles v. Russell*, 255 S.C. 513, 180 S.E.2d 201, 203 (1971). As defendants point out, however, these two cases were negligence cases, not strict liability cases. In strict liability cases, the determination of whether an activity is abnormally dangerous is one for the court, not the jury. 7 Stuart M. Speiser, Charles F. Krause and Alfred W. Gans, *The American Law of Torts* § 19:2 at 8 (1990). Accordingly, if the issue is relevant at a trial, the court will make the determination of whether or not Anchor had dangerous propensities abnormal to its class.

[49] *See Restatement (Second) of Torts* § 509 cmt. c (1965) (indicating that the doctrine of strict liability applies even when "the animal is not vicious but has a dangerous tendency that is unusual and not necessary for the purposes for which such animals are usually kept.").

> strictly liable, the possessor must have known or had reason to know of a dangerous propensity or trait that was not characteristic of a domestic animal of like kind.

Again, it is likely that the Alaska courts would adopt this approach to assessing dangerousness in cases dealing with strict liability for injuries caused by domesticated animals. The question, then, becomes: is the dangerous propensity abnormal? Here, defendants are able to present a genuine question of fact. In their introduction, defendants characterize the prior biting incidents as "behavioral responses common to all dogs." Defendants' expert reviewed each of the four admitted biting incidents, and as to each one she concluded that Anchor's responses were "natural" or instinctive. Plaintiffs offer no evidence, through expert testimony or otherwise, to refute the opinion of defendants' expert. It may indeed be true that Anchor's reactions in the four or five incidents were abnormal in the sense that they were not reactions typical of domesticated dogs, but plaintiffs have not established that point beyond any reasonable dispute.

. . . Plaintiffs' motion for summary judgment on their strict liability claim is denied.

Notes and Questions

1. As *Sinclair* provides, at common law the owner of a domestic animal is only strictly liable when the animal exhibits vicious propensities abnormal to its class. Again at common law, this rule was often characterized as allowing dog owners "one bite free" — because it was not until the second bite that an owner would be on notice of his animal's abnormal propensity. *See, e.g.*, Bernstein v. Penny Whistle Toys, Inc., 40 A.D.3d 224 (N.Y. App. 2007). How did the defense propose to get around the fact that Anchor's owners knew he had previously bitten people?

2. In many jurisdictions, this common law rule has been abrogated by legislative action, generally a local ordinance. Such ordinances typically provide that dog owners are strictly liable for dog bites, without regard to whether the dog had previously shown vicious propensities. They are often directed at particular breeds. *See generally*, Dog Bite Law: Solutions for victims, lawyers, canine professionals and dog owners, available at dogbitelaw.com (developed by "the only attorney in the USA who does nothing other than represent people who have been seriously injured by dogs.")

II. ABNORMALLY DANGEROUS ACTIVITIES

The origins of modern strict liability for abnormally dangerous activities lie in trespassing farm animals. As described in the seminal British case Fletcher v. Rylands,

> [What] has most commonly occurred, and which is most frequently to be found in the books, is as to the obligation of the owner of cattle which he has brought on his land, to prevent their escaping and doing mischief. The law as to them seems to be perfectly settled from early times; the owner must keep them in at his peril, or he will be answerable for the natural consequences of their escape. . . .

(1865-66) L.R. 1 Ex. 265 (Court of Exchequer Chamber) (Blackburn, J.).* This principle, along with its exceptions or defenses, was extended to include "trespassing" water (and by extension other substances) in *Rylands*:

> We think that the true rule of law is, that the person who for his own purposes brings on his lands and collects and keeps there anything likely to do mischief if it escapes, must keep it in at his peril, and, if he does not do so, is primâ facie answerable for all the damage which is the natural consequence of its escape. He can excuse himself [only] by shewing that the escape was owing to the plaintiff's default; or perhaps that the escape was the consequence of vis major, or the act of God. . . . The general rule, as above stated, seems on principle just. The person whose grass or corn is eaten down by the escaping cattle of his neighbour, or whose mine is flooded by the water from his neighbour's reservoir, or whose cellar is invaded by the filth of his neighbour's privy, or whose habitation is made unhealthy by the fumes and noisome vapours of his neighbour's alkali works, is damnified without any fault of his own; and it seems but reasonable and just that the neighbour, who has brought something on his own property which was not naturally there, harmless to others so long as it is confined to his own property, but which he knows to be mischievous if it gets on his neighbour's, should be obliged to make good the damage which ensues if he does not succeed in confining it to his own property. But for his act in bringing it there no mischief could have accrued, and it seems but just that he should at his peril keep it there so that no mischief may accrue, or answer for the natural and anticipated consequences. And upon authority, this we think is established to be the law whether the things so brought be beasts, or water, or filth, or stenches.

Id. (finding a property owner strictly liable for flooding when water from his mill pond seeped through forgotten mine shafts and onto his neighbor's land).

Both at the time and going forward, it was significant that the defendant pond owner was found liable even though he had not been negligent — he had hired a reputable engineering firm to build his pond, and no one had reason to know of the old mine shafts; the point of the *Rylands* holding was that individuals' right to the undisturbed use of their own land was so highly valued that the law would protect it even as against non-negligent interventions. *Id.* (distinguishing activities such as driving along the highway which involve voluntary engagements with society and thus only negligence liability). Also significant going forward was that *Rylands* ultimately hinged on the fact that the defendant's use of his land was "non-natural" because the pond was engineered and not original to the land; the court distinguished water leakage through mine shafts due to rain which would not result in strict liability, and water leakage due to intentional flushing which would.

After some initial rejection by American judges, *see, e.g.*, Losee v. Buchanan, 51 N.Y. 476 (1873) (rejecting strict liability as the basis to claim against the defendant whose boiler exploded off of its land and onto the plaintiffs' on the grounds that Americans do not have the same fealty to the undisturbed use of land, especially in densely populated areas), the *Rylands*

* Editors' note: despite the advent of fault-based liability, consistent with *Rylands*, claims about trespassing animals remain in strict liability today: "[a]n owner or possessor of livestock or other animals, except for dogs and cats, that intrude upon the land of another is subject to strict liability for physical harm caused by the intrusion." Restatement (Third) of Torts: Strict Liability, § 21 Intrusion by Livestock or Other Animals.

rule was ultimately adopted in some form by jurisdictions across the country. Reflecting its extension beyond the agrarian setting of its origins, and then beyond land itself, the First, Second, and Third Restatements tracked the doctrine's evolution from trespassing "beasts . . . water . . . filth . . . [and] stenches" to "ultrahazardous" activities and then to "abnormally dangerous" activities. Paradigmatic abnormally dangerous activities in the modern period include blasting and the containment and transportation of fuels.

BRANCH v. WESTERN PETROLEUM, INC.
657 P.2d 267 (Utah 1982)

STEWART, Justice:

The Branches, the plaintiff property owners, sued for damages for the pollution of their culinary water wells caused by percolation of defendant Western Petroleum Inc.'s formation waters (waste waters from oil wells containing various chemical contaminants) into the subterranean water system that feeds the wells. A jury answered questions to special interrogatories, finding, inter alia, that the formation waters had contaminated plaintiffs' two wells and awarded damages of $8,050 for pollution of the well water, $700 for trespass, $10,000 for "mental suffering, discomfort and annoyance," and $13,000 punitive damages. The jury, over objection, was instructed on the theory of negligence; however, the trial court entered judgment on the basis of strict liability for the above amounts, except that damages for mental suffering, discomfort, and annoyance were disallowed.

Western appeals, arguing that the trial court erred in awarding damages for pollution of the wells on the basis of strict liability. It contends that negligence is the only valid legal theory upon which the judgment can be sustained and that the trial court erred (1) in not instructing on proximate cause; and (2) in not directing the jury to find the percentage of negligence attributable to each party as required by the Utah Comparative Negligence Act, U.C.A., 1953, § 78-27-38. Western also complains of the trial court's failure to reduce damages by the percentage of pollution "caused by other parties or conditions"; an improper selection of the jury venire; and the award of punitive damages without a showing that defendant's actions were willful and malicious. No attack is made on the judgment of $700 for trespass. On a cross-appeal, the Branches contend that the court erred in striking the jury award for mental suffering, discomfort, and annoyance.

I.

In December 1975, Western purchased forty acres of land in a rural area north of Roosevelt, Utah, which had previously been used as a gravel pit. Western used the property solely for the disposal of formation water, a waste water produced by oil wells while drilling for oil. Formation water contains oil, gas and high concentrations of salt and chemicals, making it unfit for culinary or agricultural uses. The formation water was transported by truck from various oil-producing sites and emptied into the disposal pit with the intent that the toxic water would dissipate through evaporation into the air and percolation into the ground. Alternative sites for disposing of the water were available to Western, but at a greater expense.

In 1976, the Branches purchased a parcel of property immediately adjacent to, and at an elevation of approximately 200 to 300 feet lower than, Western's property. The twenty-one-acre parcel had on it a "diligence" well, which had been in existence since 1929, some outbuildings, and a home. After acquiring the property, the Branches made some $60,000 worth of improvements to the home and premises. Prior owners of the property used the water from the well for a grade A dairy and later a grade B dairy. Both dairy operations required that the water be approved for fitness and purity by appropriate state agencies. The Branches, as had all prior owners since 1929, used water from the diligence well for culinary purposes. The water from the diligence well was described as being sweet to the taste and of a high quality until December of 1976.

Two months after purchasing the property, the Branches noticed that the well water began to take on a peculiar taste and had the distinctive smell of petroleum products. Soap added to the water would no longer form suds. They observed that polluted water from Western's disposal pit was running onto the surface of the Branches' property and, on one occasion, reached their basement, causing damage to food stored there. After testing the diligence well water and finding it unfit for human consumption, and after their rabbits and one hundred chickens had died, apparently from the polluted water, the Branches began trucking water to their property from outside sources. In November 1977, the Branches dug an additional well south of their home. Water from the new well was tested and found safe for culinary purposes. But after a few months, the new well also ceased producing potable water, and on advice of the State Health Department, the Branches ceased using the new well for culinary purposes and hauled water to their property almost until the time of trial.

The Branches requested Western to cease dumping formation water in the disposal pit, but Western refused unless the Branches would post a bond to cover the costs. Western did, however, agree to build a pond on its property to contain the escaping surface water and prevent it from flowing onto the Branches' land. In doing so, Western failed to establish the proper boundary line and built part of the pond on the Branches' land. After the Branches hired a surveyor to establish that Western had built the pond on their land, Western built another containing pond on its own property. The pond, however, was only partially successful in preventing the run-off onto the Branches' land from the disposal pit. Western caused additional damage by permitting its trucks to enter the Branches' property for the purpose of pumping out the containment ponds. When the discharge nozzles on the trucks were left open, polluted water was sprayed directly onto the Branches' land.

As a consequence of the unavailability of culinary water in her home, plaintiff Jeanne Branch returned to her original home in Colorado for a three or four month period so that she could "pull herself together." During this time, Lloyd Branch made weekly trips to and from Colorado to be with his family and otherwise tried to keep in contact with his wife on the telephone while he maintained his contracting business in Roosevelt.

Western's agents admitted that they did not know, and made no attempt to ascertain, what state law was with respect to permitting formation waters to seep or percolate into subsurface waters. Even after Western became aware of the laws relative to dumping, it still took no affirmative action to obtain approval of its ponds.

At trial the major issue was whether and how Western's formation waters caused the pollution of the Branches' wells. Western's expert, Mr. Ferris, a private geologist with approximately two years professional experience in the Rocky Mountain area, and the Branches' expert, Mr. Montgomery, a state geologist who had spent nine years working for the Utah Division of

Water Resources, agreed that the subsurface waters consist of shallow groundwater and a deeper aquifer known as the Duchesne Formation. The Duchesne Formation produces the culinary water which is tapped by the Branches' wells. The two experts also agreed that formation water in the disposal pit was percolating into the subsurface waters, but they disagreed on whether the polluted waters had merely entered the shallow groundwaters or had percolated down into the Duchesne Formation.

Ferris maintained that the formation water only entered the shallow groundwater and did not penetrate to the Duchesne Formation. He concluded that the formation water could have entered the Branches' original well only through cracks in the well casing at the level of the shallow groundwaters. He further testified that none of Western's polluted water entered the Branches' new well because there were no cracks in its casing. In addition, Ferris testified that since the shallow groundwaters were naturally contaminated and unfit for human use, Western's additional pollutants were of no consequence to the Branches. The new well, according to Ferris, contained naturally poor, although useable, water from the Duchesne Formation.

Montgomery, testifying for the Branches, admitted that the Duchesne Formation water was of relatively poor quality and contained many natural contaminants. However, he stressed that the natural contaminants were not sufficient to cause the well water to fall below the standards set by the Public Health Service for acceptable human use. He stated that the waters from Western's disposal water percolated below the shallow groundwater and through natural joints and cracks into the deeper Duchesne Formation, where it entered both of the Branches' wells and made them unfit for human use.

The jury obviously considered Montgomery the more convincing of the two experts. It found, in response to special interrogatories, that "defendant's use of the evaporation pit for the dumping of formation water [was] a cause of the pollution of the water in plaintiffs' [wells]," and that Western caused 66 percent of the pollution in Branches' original well and 52 percent of the pollution in the new well. The rest of the pollution was found to be caused by other unspecified "parties or conditions." The jury also found that Western was "negligent . . . in dumping formation waters in its evaporation pit," and had also committed a "trespass upon plaintiffs' land . . . other than the claimed pollution of [the] wells."

II.

The major substantive dispute is whether the trial court erred in entering judgment against Western on the basis of strict liability for pollution of the Branches' wells. Western argues that other states have based liability for pollution of subterranean waters on either negligence, nuisance, or trespass, and that since the Branches failed to allege nuisance or trespass, "the only accepted theory upon which this case could be based is negligence." Therefore, according to Western, the trial court erred in entering judgment on the basis of strict liability. Western further submits that since the court did not instruct the jury on proximate cause and comparative negligence, the judgment cannot stand. The Branches, on the other hand, take the position that Western created an abnormally dangerous condition by collecting contaminated water on its land for the purpose of having it seep or percolate into the groundwater and that, therefore, the law of strict liability controls.

This Court has not heretofore had occasion to consider the legal principles which govern liability for the pollution of subterranean waters by industrial wastes. Our survey of cases from other states and of legal scholars indicates that a variety of legal theories have been relied on. The theories that have been employed include negligence, private nuisance, public nuisance, negligent nuisance, nuisance without negligence, intentional nuisance, absolute nuisance, trespass, and strict liability. . . . The variety of approaches reflects numerous considerations, such as the general hydrological conditions in the state; the relative significance of promoting industrialization compared with the importance of promoting conservation of water; the nature of the particular state's water law; and, in particular, whether the doctrine of correlative rights applies to the use of water resources. *See* Davis, *Groundwater Pollution, supra*, at 119–37.

In England under the common law, percolating water was considered part of the freehold and subject to private ownership. In American law it is generally recognized that a landowner has no absolute right to pollute percolating waters. Annot., 38 A.L.R.2d at 1267. In this state, a landowner has no such absolute right because percolating waters belong to the people of the state. *J.J.N.P. v. State of Utah*, 655 P.2d 1133, No. 17183, Utah, (filed September 22, 1982). For that reason, and because percolating waters are migratory and the rights of the landowners to those waters are correlative, § 73-5-1, such waters are subject to the maxim that one may not use his land so as to pollute percolating waters to the injury of another. Annot., 38 A.L.R.2d at 1267.

As Utah is one of the most arid states in the union, the protection of the purity of the water is of critical importance, and the Legislature has enacted laws for the protection of both surface and subterranean waters. U.C.A., 1953, § 26-11-8 (Supp.1981); § 40-6-5; § 76-10-801; § 76-10-802; § 76-10-803(1)(d). Absent a permit, U.C.A., 1953, § 73-14-5 made it unlawful for any person to discharge a pollutant into waters of the state or to cause pollution as defined in section 73-14-2(a) which constitutes a menace to public health and welfare, or is harmful to wildlife, fish or acquatic life, or impairs domestic, agricultural, industrial, recreational or other beneficial uses of water, or to place or cause to be placed any wastes in a location where there is probable cause to believe they will cause pollution.

Two doctrines have developed in the common law to provide a remedy to a private landowner for nontrespassory injuries caused by another. The landmark case of *Rylands v. Fletcher*, 3 H. & C. 774, 159 Eng.Rep. 737 (1865), rev'd in *Fletcher v. Rylands*, L.R. 1 Ex. 265 (1866), aff'd in *Rylands v. Fletcher*, L.R. 3 H.L. 330 (1868), held that one who uses his land in an unnatural way and thereby creates a dangerous condition or engages in an abnormal activity may be strictly liable for injuries resulting from that condition or activity. Whether a condition or activity is considered abnormal is defined in terms of whether the condition or activity is unduly dangerous or inappropriate to the place where it is maintained. W. Prosser, Law of Torts § 78, at 506 (4th ed. 1971). That doctrine was the genesis of § 519 of the Restatement of Torts (1939), which, however, limited strict liability to "ultrahazardous activities." Prosser, *supra*, at 512.

Although *Rylands v. Fletcher* was initially rejected by a number of states, its influence has been substantial in the United States. According to the latest edition of Dean Prosser's treatise on torts, only seven American jurisdictions have rejected the rule of that case, while some thirty jurisdictions have essentially approved the rule. *Id.* at 509. Indeed, the strict liability rule of the Restatement of Torts was broadened in § 519 of the Restatement (Second) of Torts by making it applicable to "abnormally dangerous activities."

Nuisance law also protects property interests from nontrespassory invasions. Unlike most other torts, it is not centrally concerned with the nature of the conduct causing the damage, but with the nature and relative importance of the interests interfered with or invaded. The doctrine of nuisance "has reference to the interests invaded, to the damage or harm inflicted, and not to any particular kind of action or omission which has lead to the invasion." W. Prosser, *supra*, § 87 at 73–75. Since it is not the nature of one's conduct that generally is essential to an action for nuisance, a person whose interests have been invaded may have a claim for relief based both on nuisance and on the nature of the conduct producing the damage. *See Cities Service Oil Co. v. Merritt*, Okl., 332 P.2d 677, 684 (1958); *Wood v. Picillo*, R.I., 443 A.2d 1244 (1982). As the court in *Wood* stated:

> The essential element of an actionable nuisance is that persons have suffered harm or are threatened with injuries that they ought not have to bear. Distinguished from negligence liability, liability in nuisance is predicated upon unreasonable injury rather than upon unreasonable conduct. Thus, plaintiffs may recover in nuisance despite the otherwise nontortious nature of the conduct which creates the injury.

It is of no consequence that a business which causes a nuisance is a lawful business. The production of formation water is a natural and necessary incident to the business of producing oil and gas. A business such as Western, which collects and disposes of formation water, conducts a wholly legitimate business. But that does not give it a license to dispose of waste in a manner that for practical purposes appropriates the property of others by making it impossible for them to use water which they are entitled to use.

There are two separate, although somewhat related, grounds for holding Western strictly liable for the pollution of the Branches' wells. First, the facts of the case support application of the rule of strict liability because the ponding of the toxic formation water in an area adjacent to the Branches' wells constituted an abnormally dangerous and inappropriate use of the land in light of its proximity to the Branches' property and was unduly dangerous to the Branches' use of their well water. Several cases on comparable facts have applied strict liability due to the abnormal danger of polluting activity. For example, *Mowrer v. Ashland Oil & Refining Co., Inc.*, 518 F.2d 659 (7th Cir.1975), applied strict liability to the leakage of crude oil and salt water into a fresh water well; *Yommer v. McKenzie*, 255 Md. 220, 257 A.2d 138 (1969), applied the same rule to the seepage of gasoline from an underground tank into an adjoining landowner's well; *Cities Service Co. v. Florida*, Fla.App., 312 So.2d 799 (1975), applied strict liability to the escape of phosphate slime into a creek and river. *See also Bumbarger v. Walker*, 193 Pa.Super. 301, 164 A.2d 144 (1960) (strict liability for well pollution caused by defendant's mine blasting). *See generally Clark-Aiken Co. v. Cromwell-Wright Co.*, 367 Mass. 70, 323 N.E.2d 876 (1975) (strict liability applied to escape of impounded water); *Indiana Harbor Belt Railroad Co. v. American Cynamid Co.*, 517 F.Supp. 314 (N.D.Ill.1981) (strict liability applied to spillage of toxic chemical that resulted in property damage and pollution of water supply); W. Prosser, *supra*, § 78 at 512-13 and cases there cited. *See also Atlas Chemical Industries, Inc. v. Anderson*, Tex.Civ.App., 514 S.W.2d 309 (1974), *aff'd* 524 S.W.2d 681 (1975), where the Texas court, distinguishing a case relied upon by Western, *Turner v. Big Lake Oil Co.*, 128 Tex. 155, 96 S.W.2d 221 (1936), held the defendant strictly liable for polluting surface streams with industrial wastes. The strict liability rule of *Rylands v. Fletcher* was held to apply to pollution cases "in which the defendant has set the substance in motion for escape, such as the discharge of the harmful effluent or the emission of a harmful gas or substance." *Atlas Chemical, supra*, at 314.

. . .

We know of no acceptable rule of jurisprudence which permits those engaged in important and desirable enterprises to injure with impunity those who are engaged in enterprises of lesser economic significance. The costs of injuries resulting from pollution must be internalized by industry as a cost of production and borne by consumers or shareholders, or both, and not by the injured individual.

We think these reasons adequately support application of the rule of strict liability in this case.

The judgment of the trial court may also be sustained on the alternative doctrine of nuisance per se. The pollution of underground water has been held a nuisance by a number of courts. . . . When the conditions giving rise to a nuisance are also a violation of a statutory prohibition, those conditions constitute a nuisance per se, and the issue of the reasonableness of the defendant's conduct and the weighing of the relative interests of the plaintiff and defendant is precluded because the Legislature has, in effect, already struck the balance in favor of the innocent party. Defendant's violation of § 73-14-5 (See § 26-11-8 for corresponding current provision) and § 76-10-801 removed the issue of the reasonableness of its conduct compared with the nature of the injury inflicted from consideration in this case. The declaration of the Legislature is conclusive, and its determination will not be second guessed. The result for practical purposes is the same as strict liability.

We are aware that a nuisance theory was not presented to the trial court. Usually we will not consider on appeal a theory not presented to the trial court. However, nuisance per se is in reality just another term for strict liability. Furthermore, we may affirm a trial court's decision on proper grounds even though different than those relied upon by the trial court. . . .

In sum, the trial court properly ruled that Western was strictly liable for the damage which it caused the Branches. Since liability was properly based on strict liability, the failure of the trial court to give instructions on comparative negligence and proximate cause was not error. Contributory negligence is neither a defense to a nuisance action, *Mowrer v. Ashland Oil & Refining Co. Inc.*, 518 F.2d 659 (1975), nor to an action based on strict liability. The issue of actual causation was decided in favor of the Branches, and there was no issue of proximate causation to be decided.

We have already noted that the jury in this case was instructed, over the Branches objection, on a theory of negligence and that the jury's findings did not cover all the issues under a negligence theory. Nevertheless, the findings were sufficient as to all the factual issues under the law of nuisance per se and strict liability.

III.

Western also contends that the trial court should have reduced the damages awarded for the pollution of the wells by the percentage of pollution found by the jury to have been caused by other parties or conditions.

It is conceded by the Branches that the water in the area contains a high level of natural contaminants, although not so high as to make the water unsafe or unpotable. Federal health standards established 500 parts of solids per million as the highest safe level for the water.

Based on the latest chemical tests that were conducted, the Branches' diligence well contained 980 parts of solids per million and the new well 920 parts of solids per million. The jury found that Western was responsible for 66 per cent of the solids in the diligence well and 52 per cent of the solids in the second well.

The amount of contaminants in the diligence well attributable to Western, therefore, was 646.8 parts per million, leaving approximately 333 parts per million attributable to either natural or other causes. As for the new well, Western was responsible for 478.4 parts per million of the contaminants, and the remaining 441 parts were attributable to either natural or other causes. Thus, without the pollution caused by Western, the level of contaminants in both wells would have been within the limits of the federal safety standards. In other words, but for Western's pollution, the wells would have been useable.

Contrary to the implication of Western's argument, the injury to the Branches was not the total amount of contaminants in each well; it was rather the amount of contaminants above the safe level of 500 parts per million. The contamination above that level caused the whole injury, and as to that, Western was legally responsible.

IV.

Western also contends that the trial was defective on the ground that the jury venire was improperly chosen because those who wanted to go elk hunting were excused. Section 78-46-16(1) requires that a challenge to jury selection be made "[w]ithin seven days after the moving party discovered, or by the exercise of diligence could have discovered the grounds therefore, and in any event before the trial jury is sworn to try the case . . . ."

Western contends that it was not aware of the improper action prior to the time the jury was sworn and therefore was unable to file a motion challenging the selection of the jury within the statutory time period. Upon learning of the removal of those prospective jurors who desired to go elk hunting, Western filed with the trial court a motion requesting a new trial or a hearing to determine whether the jury selection was proper. The motion was denied, and no hearing was held.

Western's objection is not well taken. There are no affidavits indicating how many prospective jurors were excused or why Western did not find out about the facts sooner. We think the defect should have been discovered in the exercise of due diligence before the commencement of the trial as required by the statute.

Even assuming that the challenge was timely raised, § 78-46-16(2) requires a "substantial failure to comply with this act" and a showing that an "actual and substantial injustice and prejudice has resulted or will result to a party in consequence of the failure" to comply. Applying this latter requirement, Western's contention of prejudicial error fails. The jury panel was comprised of four males and four females. It consisted of a superintendent of schools, a highway patrolman, a former deputy sheriff (currently a Department of Transportation employee), a farmer-rancher, a county recorder, a high school secretary, and two housewives. There is nothing in the record to suggest that the prospective jurors who were excused were drawn from any particular religious, cultural, racial, sexual, or socio-economic class. Nor is there anything to suggest that the excluded group represented a belief or conviction, not otherwise represented on the panel, which was more sympathetic to the interests of Western.

Since there is no reason to suppose the elimination of a few elk hunters from the panel skewed the composition of the jury panel in any manner, and since the jury was passed for cause, there is no basis for finding prejudicial error.

V.

Western's final contention on its appeal challenges the award of punitive damages. It argues that punitive damages are appropriate only when willful and malicious conduct is shown and that the court erred in including the phrase "reckless indifference and disregard" in its instruction on punitive damages. However, in *Terry v. Zions Cooperative Mercantile Institution*, Utah, 605 P.2d 314 (1979), this Court held that punitive damages may be awarded when one acts with reckless indifference and disregard of the law and his fellow citizens:

> This presumed malice or malice in law does not consist of personal hate or ill will of one person towards another but rather refers to that state of mind which is reckless of law and of the legal rights of the citizens in a person's conduct toward that citizen. . . . In such cases malice in law will be implied from unjustifiable conduct which causes the injury complained of or from a wrongful act intentionally done without cause or excuse.

Id. at 327.

The evidence in this case meets that standard. Western discharged the waste water into the disposal pit intending that it seep into and percolate through the soil. Thus, the pollution of the percolating waters was willful and carried out in disregard of the rights of the Branches. Moreover, Western compounded the Branches' problems by its trespass on their land, the spraying of waste water over their land and the failure to comply with state law. In addition, Western continued its dumping activities even after the pollution of the diligence well. The punitive damage award was adequately supported by evidence of reckless indifference toward, and disregard of, the Branches' rights.

Furthermore, there is no merit to Western's contention that the award of punitive damages was excessive and influenced by passion or prejudice rather than reason. The jury was properly instructed that the purpose of exemplary damages is to deter defendant and others from engaging in similar conduct. In *Terry v. Zion's Cooperative Mercantile Institution, supra*, this Court stated:

> The purpose of a punitive or exemplary damage award is not to compensate the party harmed but rather to punish the wrongdoer, to deter him from similar acts in the future, and to provide fair warning to others similarly situated that such conduct is not tolerated.

Due to the purposes underlying the award of punitive damages many factors contribute in determining their appropriate measure. . . . The jury in its original decision or the court in its review of that decision must also consider the particular nature of the defendant's acts, the probability of those acts being repeated in the future, and the relative wealth of the particular defendant. The award of punitive damages is a matter in the first instance for the discretion of the jury, and the award was not excessive in relation to actual damages in either our view or the view of the trial judge whose judgment we accord considerable weight because of his firsthand knowledge of the evidence in the case.

VI.

The jury returned a verdict in favor of the Branches for mental suffering, discomfort and annoyance in the amount of $10,000. During the trial, the court dismissed the claim for such damages on the ground that "emotional distress and anxiety and upset concerning the matter is not compensable, per se. It may be in connection with exemplary, punitive damages. I don't know. But per se, there isn't a separate cause of action for that. And I grant your motion." Notwithstanding that ruling, the trial judge reconsidered, and at the conclusion of the trial, submitted a special interrogatory on the amount of damage suffered by the Branches as a result of "emotional distress, discomfort and annoyance." In response to that interrogatory, the jury found damages in the amount of $10,000. The trial judge initially entered judgment for that amount, but then struck that part of the judgment apparently on the ground that such damages could be recoverable, if at all, only under the doctrine of *Samms v. Eccles*, 11 Utah 2d 289, 358 P.2d 344 (1961). *Samms* dealt with the independent tort of intentional infliction of emotional distress, not with a nuisance case, and is therefore clearly inapplicable to this case.

It has, however, long been recognized that "a plaintiff may recover damages for personal inconvenience, annoyance and discomfort caused by the existence of a nuisance." *Wade v. Fuller*, 12 Utah 2d 299, 302, 365 P.2d 802, 805 (1961).

Admittedly, damages for inconvenience, annoyance, discomfort and mental distress are not capable of precise calculation, although those elements may reflect direct, immediate, and real injury. In this case the jury had evidence before it to justify the award of substantial damages of the type under consideration. The Branches testified to the emotional distress caused Jeanne Branch which culminated in her leaving her husband for a period of three or four months. In addition to that, the Branches were forced to truck water onto their property and to take numerous other steps to counter the nuisance created by Western.

For the foregoing reasons, we affirm the judgment of the trial court in all respects except with respect to the striking of the award of damages for mental distress, annoyance, and discomfort and remand for the re-entry of that award in the amount specified by the jury.

HALL, C.J., and OAKS and HOWE, JJ., concur.

DURHAM, J., does not participate herein.

Notes and Questions

1. Describe the strict liability rule adopted and applied by the Utah Supreme Court. Why did the court decide to adopt strict liability for percolating pollutants?

2. The court rejected the defendant's appeal from the trial court's decision not to instruct the jury on proximate cause. If you were the defendant's lawyer, why would you press this issue? What would be your proximate cause argument?

3. Based on the legal description provided in the opinion, state the prima facie case in nuisance. Why does the court say that the effect of nuisance per se is the same as strict liability? Notice that the court upheld the jury's award of mental distress, annoyance, and discomfort damages associated with the nuisance claim. What were the underlying or principal nuisance damages?

4. Why would the defendant challenge the jury venire on the grounds that elk hunters were improperly excused?

5. It is unusual for punitive damages to be awarded in strict liability cases, the facts of which are more typically like *Rylands* than like *Branch*. The *Branch* case shows that, depending on the jurisdiction, it is not impossible. *See also* Langan v. Valicopters, Inc., 567 P.2d 218 (Wa. 1977) (punitive damages upheld for wanton disregard of statute prohibiting aerial spraying of pesticides over neighboring property owner's home).

6. Polluted water and other waste impoundments may be classified as abnormally dangerous activities, even when they are common to an area. This is a typical application of *Rylands* in its original formulation. *See, e.g.*, Bunyak v. Clyde J. Yancey and Sons Dairy, Inc., 438 So.2d 891 (Fla. App. 1983) (liquified cow manure).

7. You may encounter the matter of water rights in your property class, including the differences among jurisdictions with respect to water ownership. This has long been an important (and fascinating) legal issue in Western states where water is relatively scarce. Due to changes in population density and climate change, water law is increasingly important in relatively wet states including along the Eastern seaboard.

ELMORE v. DIXIE PIPELINE COMPANY
245 So.3d 500 (Miss. App. 2017)

FACTS AND PROCEDURAL HISTORY

¶ 2. Dixie Pipeline Company ("Dixie") operates a buried pipeline through which liquid propane is transported. The pipeline, which was constructed in 1961, extends approximately 1,100 miles from Texas to North Carolina, and includes various sizes of pipe. The particular segment at issue consists of a 395–mile stretch of 12–inch-diameter pipe, which runs from the west side of the Mississippi River near Erwinville, Louisiana, eastward to Opelika, Alabama, and passes through Clarke County, Mississippi. Lone Star Steel Company manufactured the pipe using a low-frequency electric resistance welding (ERW) process.

¶ 3. In 1988 and 1989, the Pipeline and Hazardous Materials Safety Administration (PHMSA) issued an alert notice to all hazardous-liquid-propane operators who had in place ERW pipe manufactured before 1970. The notices advised of operational failures of pipeline constructed with ERW pipe manufactured prior to 1970. The notices included certain recommendations by the PHMSA. Neither notice required pipeline operators to cease operating pre–1970 manufactured ERW pipe, or remove and replace the pipe.

¶ 4. On November 1, 2007, the pipeline ruptured near Carmichael, Mississippi. As a result of the rupture, liquid propane was released, some of which vaporized and exploded. At the time of the explosion, Elmore owned a house located approximately 1.1 miles from the accident site. Elmore claims her house suffered structural damage as a result of the shockwaves from the explosion.

¶ 5. The National Transportation Safety Board (NTSB) investigated the pipeline rupture. The NTSB noted that the pipeline segment at issue was hydrostatically pressure tested in 1961, and again in 1984. Additionally, in-line inspections were subsequently performed in 1998, 2005, and 2006. Based on the inspections, the NTSB determined that no defects or anomalies in the subject pipe joint could be correlated with the 2007 rupture. The NTSB ultimately concluded that "the probable cause" of the subject pipeline rupture "was the failure of a weld that caused the pipe to fracture along the longitudinal seam weld, a portion of the upstream girth weld, and portions of the adjacent pipe joints." Importantly, the NTSB concluded that the following were not factors in the rupture: corrosion, excavation damage, the controller's actions, or the operating conditions of the pipeline.

¶ 6. In her amended complaint, Elmore asserted claims of negligence, strict-liability, and punitive damages against Dixie, as the operator of the pipeline. Following the agreed-upon discovery deadline, Elmore filed a motion to direct Dixie to produce the transcript of the corporate deposition taken in a case that involved the same pipeline rupture, but was litigated in Texas. The circuit court denied the untimely motion.

¶ 7. Dixie subsequently filed motions for summary judgment on all claims asserted by Elmore. The circuit court granted summary judgment in favor of Dixie on the strict-liability and punitive-damages claims, but denied the motion as to Elmore's negligence claim.

¶ 8. Dixie further filed a motion to exclude the opinions and testimony of Elmore's expert witness, Dr. Kendall Clarke. Following a hearing, the circuit court granted the motion, in part, and excluded Dr. Clarke from offering opinion testimony regarding the standard of care for pipeline operators, or any violation of that standard of care by Dixie.

¶ 9. Prior to trial, Dixie filed a renewed motion for summary judgment on Elmore's negligence claim. On reconsideration, and in light of the partial exclusion of Dr. Clarke's testimony, the circuit court granted summary judgment as to Elmore's negligence claim. Elmore now appeals and argues the circuit court erroneously: (1) denied her motion to produce the transcript of the corporate deposition taken in the Texas litigation, (2) excluded Dr. Clarke, (3) granted summary judgment on her strict-liability claim, (4) granted summary judgment as to her negligence claim, and (5) granted summary judgment on her punitive-damages claim.

ANALYSIS

I. The Denial of the Production of the Corporate–Deposition Transcript

¶ 10. Elmore first argues the circuit court erroneously denied her "motion to direct [Dixie] to produce the corporate deposition taken in the Texas litigation." "[Circuit] courts are afforded broad discretion in discovery matters, and this Court will not overturn a [circuit] court's decision unless there is an abuse of discretion." *Ashmore v. Miss. Authority on Educ. Television*, 148 So.3d 977, 981 (¶ 9) (Miss. 2014).

¶ 11. On February 27, 2014, an agreed order extending case-scheduling deadlines was entered by the circuit court, which extended the discovery-completion date to March 28, 2014. This was the second extension entered by the circuit court to allow the parties to complete discovery. On April 15, 2014, almost three weeks after the expiration of the agreed-upon discovery deadline, Elmore filed the subject motion and sought the production of "a true and correct copy of the deposition [transcript], with all exhibits, given by representatives of Dixie in the referenced Texas litigation."

¶ 12. Prior to the agreed-upon discovery deadline, Elmore propounded written discovery to Dixie and deposed two corporate representatives of Dixie. At no time before the close of discovery did Elmore request Dixie to produce prior corporate depositions taken in Texas. In fact, Elmore acknowledged that a formal request was not made until the filing of the motion at issue, which was after the expiration of the discovery deadline.

¶ 13. The circuit court "has the authority and indeed the duty to maintain control of the docket and ensure the efficient disposal of court business." *Douglas v. Burley*, 134 So.3d 692, 699 (¶ 20) (Miss. 2012) (emphasis omitted) (citing *Venton v. Beckham*, 845 So.2d 676, 684 (¶ 25) (Miss. 2003)). We find no abuse of discretion in the circuit court's denial of Elmore's untimely discovery motion.

II. The Exclusion of Dr. Clarke's Testimony

¶ 14. Elmore next argues the circuit court erroneously excluded the opinions and testimony of her expert, Dr. Kendall Clarke. "The standard of review for the admission or exclusion of expert testimony is abuse of discretion." *Patterson v. Tibbs*, 60 So.3d 742, 748 (¶ 19) (Miss. 2011). "This Court should find error in the [circuit] court's decision to exclude expert testimony only if the decision was arbitrary or clearly erroneous." *Id.*

¶ 15. The circuit court excluded Dr. Clarke's opinion testimony regarding the standard of care of pipeline operators, and the alleged breach of that standard by Dixie. Rule 702 of the Mississippi Rules of Evidence stated:

> If scientific, technical or other specialized knowledge will assist the trier of fact in understanding the evidence or determining a fact in issue, a witness qualified as an expert by knowledge, skill, experience, training or education, may testify in the form of an opinion or otherwise if (1) the testimony is based upon sufficient facts or data, (2) the testimony is a product of reliable principles and methods, and (3) the witness has applied the principles and methods reliably to the facts of the case.

In *Daubert v. Merrell Dow Pharmaceuticals, Inc.*, 509 U.S. 579, 589, 113 S.Ct. 2786, 125 L.Ed.2d 469 (1993), the United States Supreme Court held that expert testimony must be relevant and reliable. Thus, "[w]hen determining whether expert testimony is admissible, our [circuit] judges should act as gatekeepers and must determine whether the proposed testimony meets the requirements of Rule 702 and *Daubert*'s relevance and reliability prongs." *Patterson*, 60 So.3d at 749 (¶ 22).

¶ 16. Elmore retained Dr. Clarke, a metallurgical engineer, to offer expert opinions and testimony regarding Dixie's alleged negligence in its operation of the pipeline. In formulating his opinions, Dr. Clarke relied upon the NTSB report, the American Petroleum Institute (API)

Standards, and the American Society of Mechanical Engineers Standards. Dr. Clarke did not rely upon the federal safety regulations, including 49 C.F.R. § 195 (2015), "Transportation of Hazardous Liquids by Pipeline."

¶ 17. Elmore acknowledges that Dr. Clarke's opinions did not include a violation of the federal regulations. However, Elmore asserts that Dr. Clarke was not required to base his opinions upon the federal regulations and to opine whether or not the federal regulations had been violated since her case was "based on common-law tort claims" and not on the federal statute. We disagree.

¶ 18. The Dixie pipeline became subject to the federal safety regulations for hazardous liquid pipelines, codified in 49 C.F.R. § 195, upon enactment in 1969 by the U.S. Department of Transportation. Under these regulations, propane is classified as a highly volatile liquid. In his deposition, Dr. Clarke admitted that he had no familiarity with the federal regulations that govern integrity management for the pipeline. Additionally, Dr. Clarke admitted that he did not apply or consider those applicable federal regulations and standards in rendering his opinions in this matter. Instead, Dr. Clarke used "the API code because that applies in [his] business."

¶ 19. While the record indicates the pipeline was made of API-grade steel pipe and manufactured according to API standards, the pipe was not manufactured by Dixie. Instead, Dixie was the operator of the pipeline. The record shows the operation and maintenance of transmission pipelines is governed by federal safety regulations and standards. Indeed, the NTSB relied upon and cited 49 C.F.R. § 195 in its accident report.

¶ 20. Dr. Clarke, unlike the NTSB, never inspected the ruptured pipe joint, nor did he perform any testing or analysis on the ruptured pipeline segment. During his deposition, Dr. Clarke acknowledged that he had never been retained in any other case that involved a rupture in an interstate piping system that carried a highly volatile liquid. Dr. Clarke admitted that he had not "looked at a pipeline involving this type of stuff before" and further admitted that he had not "looked at a transportation pipeline governed by [the] DOT before this case." Moreover, Dr. Clarke testified that he had never before opined that a company failed to follow applicable standards or regulations for the integrity of its product.

¶ 21. Dr. Clarke opined the pipeline was running at too high a pressure, particularly given its age. However, the NTSB specifically determined that the operating conditions of the pipeline was not a factor in the rupture. Moreover, Dr. Clarke acknowledged that the pipeline can run up to maximum operating pressure 24 hours a day, 7 days a week, 365 days a year. Although Dr. Clarke stated it was not a "good practice," he admitted that such a practice was allowed.

¶ 22. Additionally, Dr. Clarke opined that Dixie should have either removed from service every anomaly identified in the in-line inspections and replaced it with new pipe, or de-rated the pressure in the pipeline to a lower maximum operating pressure. When asked the basis of his opinions, Dr. Clarke did not cite to any federal regulation or standard. Instead, Dr. Clarke stated, "I believe it's fair to say this is my opinion at this point based on all of my training from my doctorate on up." However, the NTSB, which spent nearly two years investigating this accident, did not reach the same conclusions. In fact, the NTSB determined that no defects or anomalies in the subject pipe joint could be correlated with the 2007 rupture. Moreover, the corrective measures suggested by Dr. Clarke were not required under the federal regulations, nor would such measures have been warranted, as there was no evidence a rupture was imminent on November 1, 2007.

¶ 23. The circuit court found:

> The people [who are] using the pipe, they have got to use it according to the government reg[ulation]s because they are transporting interstate liquefied propane. . . . And there are government regulations that are in place to say this is what you have got to do to do it safely in accordance with the regulatory guidelines. And I'm not hearing . . . Dr. Clarke or anybody else to say that Dixie violated any of those standards. What you are saying is, well, he said that — API standards say that whoever manufactured the pipe should do something different. Well, the people that are telling Dixie how to safely manage their facility that transports interstate — items interstate, I'm not hearing them say that they violated any standard.
>
> Dr. Clarke, however, it doesn't seem to me that he can — I mean, unless he — unless he states an opinion that relates to a violation of the applicable government regulatory standards, then I don't see how that applies to what you are dealing with.
>
> I think [Dr. Clarke] is a qualified metallurgist, and he can be qualified to make an opinion or render an opinion as to what happened there that resulted in an explosion. . . . I would allow him to testify about what happened in the pipeline that allowed the gas to escape. . . . He can testify to that. . . . As to violations of API standards[,] . . . I don't think that has any relevance. I think the relevant issue is whether Dixie was operating their pipeline in accordance with regulatory guidelines, and he has not expressed any opinion about that.

¶ 24. Since Dr. Clarke lacked familiarity with or understanding of the federal regulations and standards, the circuit court properly excluded his ability to opine as to the standard of care for pipeline operators or any violation of that standard of care by Dixie. As the circuit court noted, testimony regarding the violations of API standards would be irrelevant and would not assist the trier of fact. We find no error.

III. The Dismissal of Elmore's Strict-Liability Claim

¶ 25. In her amended complaint, Elmore alleged that "[b]ecause of the inherently dangerous product being transported through its pipeline by [Dixie] with the potential for a devastating loss of property and/or life in the event of an explosion[,] [Dixie] is strictly liable for [Elmore's] damages." Elmore's strict-liability claim is based on her assertion that the transportation of liquid propane is an ultrahazardous activity. The circuit court noted that Mississippi has not declared such an activity ultrahazardous, and therefore found strict liability inapplicable. Elmore now argues the circuit court erroneously granted summary judgment on her strict-liability claim.

¶ 26. "We employ a de novo standard of review of a [circuit] court's grant or denial of summary judgment and examine all the evidentiary matters before it." *Davis v. Hoss*, 869 So.2d 397, 401 (¶ 10) (Miss. 2004). Summary judgment is proper when "the pleadings, depositions, answers to interrogatories and admissions on file, together with the affidavits, if any, show there is no genuine issue as to any material fact and that the moving party is entitled to a judgment as a matter of law." M.R.C.P. 56(c). "The evidence is viewed in the light most favorable to the party opposing the motion." *Davis*, 869 So.2d at 401 (¶ 10). However, "an adverse party may not rest upon the mere allegations or denials of his pleadings, but his response . . . must set forth specific facts showing that there is a genuine issue for trial." M.R.C.P. 56(e).

¶ 27. In support of her claim, Elmore relies on *Donald v. Amoco Prod. Co.*, 735 So.2d 161 (Miss. 1999). In *Donald*, the plaintiff purchased a twenty-acre parcel of property from the bank, which had seized the property at foreclosure. *Id.* at 164 (¶ 1). The former owners of the property were in the oil business and had allegedly transported oil-field waste to the property and disposed of it. *Id.* The plaintiff sued the bank and claimed it had negligently misrepresented the condition of the property. *Id.* at 164 (¶ 2). The plaintiff further sued various oil companies for negligence, nuisance, trespass, breach of contract, waste, strict liability, and outrageous conduct. *Id.* The circuit court dismissed the strict-liability claim since oil-waste disposal was not considered an ultrahazardous condition. *Id.* at 171 (¶ 30).

¶ 28. On appeal, the Mississippi Supreme Court found that the plaintiff's strict-liability claim could be addressed without having to determine whether oil-waste disposal was an ultrahazardous activity since the plaintiff's nuisance, trespass, and strict-liability claims "[were] not separate theories of liability." *Id.* at 172 (¶ 33). The Court explained that "a plaintiff may recover damage by a physical invasion of his property on a simple showing that the defendant was responsible for the physical invasion . . . regardless of whether [the plaintiff] categorizes his claim of physical invasion as nuisance or strict liability or trespass[.]" *Id.* at 172 (¶¶ 33–34). Since the plaintiff "ha[d] alleged such a physical invasion for which the [o]il [d]efendants were responsible," the Court reversed the circuit court's dismissal of the plaintiff's strict-liability claim. *Id.* at 172 (¶ 34).

¶ 29. We find Elmore's reliance on *Donald* is misplaced. Here, Elmore does not allege a physical invasion of her property, nor does she allege nuisance or trespass. Instead, Elmore's strict-liability claim is based solely on the fact that the transportation of liquid propane is an ultrahazardous activity. However, as noted in *Donald*, "strict liability for ultrahazardous activity has only been found . . . in cases involving explosives." *Id.* at 171 (¶ 30). The fact that liquid propane can ignite and become explosive does not mean activities that involve it are ultrahazardous for purposes of strict liability. *See Lewis v. Kinder Morgan Se. Terminals LLC*, Nos. 2:07cv47KS–MTP, 2:07cv48KS–MTP, 2008 WL 3540174, at *10 (S.D. Miss. Aug. 6, 2008) ("There is no evidence to suggest that the storage of gasoline . . . and the use of a loading rack to load and unload gasoline into tank trucks is an ultrahazardous [condition].").

¶ 30. In *Searle v. Suburban Propane*, 263 A.D.2d 335, 700 N.Y.S.2d 588, 589–90 (2000), the plaintiff filed a products-liability action against the designer and installer of a custom propane-transmission system and sought damages for the death of the decedent killed in a propane explosion following a pipe rupture. The trial court entered partial summary judgment in favor of the designer and installer on certain causes of action, including strict liability and res ipsa loquitur. *Id.* at 590. On appeal, the supreme court, appellate division, affirmed. *Id.* at 592.

¶ 31. Specifically, the appellate court found that "the installation and maintenance of a propane gas storage tank, transmission system and fixtures d[id] not constitute an ultrahazardous activity so as to impose absolute liability." *Id.* at 591. In determining whether an activity was ultrahazardous, the court considered the six factors set forth in the Restatement (Second) of Torts section 520, which are:

(a) existence of a high degree of risk of some harm to the person, land[,] or chattels of others,

(b) likelihood that the harm that results from it will be great,

(c) inability to eliminate the risk by the exercise of reasonable care,

(d) extent to which the activity is not a matter of common usage,

(e) inappropriateness of the activity to the place it was carried on, and

(f) extent to which its value to the community is outweighed by its dangerous attributes.

Id. The court ultimately concluded, "[i]n view of the widespread use of propane gas as a commercial, consumer and household product, and the reasonable precautions that can be taken to prevent explosion, we are not persuaded to label it as an ultrahazardous activity." *Id.*

¶ 32. Additionally, in *Melso v. Sun Pipe Line Co.*, 394 Pa.Super. 578, 576 A.2d 999, 1003 (1990), a trial court found that the operation of a petroleum pipeline under a residential community was an abnormally dangerous activity so that Sun Pipe was subject to liability for harm, even if it took all reasonable care and the rupture was caused by the intervening act of a third party. The trial court determined that there was the potential that pipeline gasoline could cause an "environmental catastrophe of considerable magnitude" and "the pipeline transportation of large quantities of gasoline underneath a residential community is neither a matter of common usage, nor an activity appropriate to the place where it is carried on." *Id.*

¶ 33. On appeal, the Pennsylvania Superior Court reversed and found the transmission of natural gas and petroleum products by pipeline is "a common activity in a highly industrialized society such as our own." *Id.* The appellate court noted a jury instruction previously given, which stated:

> The measure of care is not that of an insurer to everyone who sustains loss by reason of gas escaping and exploding, but it is liable for an explosion where it knew or by the exercise of ordinary care should have known of the defect in its pipes or mains.

Id.

¶ 34. In *New Meadows Holding Co. v. Washington Water Power Co.*, 102 Wash.2d 495, 687 P.2d 212, 217 (1984), the appellate court found that a gas company was not strictly liable for damages involving the transmission of natural gas through underground lines. The court examined the factors set forth in section 520 of the Restatement (Second) of Torts and conceded factors (a) and (b). *Id.* at 216.

¶ 35. With regard to factor (c), the court stated:

> Some degree of risk of natural gas pipeline leaks will always be present. This does not mean, however, that the "high degree of risk" with which section 520 is concerned cannot be eliminated by the use of reasonable care. . . . Gas companies are subject to strict federal and state safety regulations.

Id. Accordingly, the court found that "the transmission of natural gas through underground lines can be eliminated by the use of reasonable care and legislative safeguards." *Id.*

¶ 36. The court found factors (d), (e), and (f) weighed against the imposition of strict liability. *Id.* Specifically, the court found "the transmission of gas is a matter of common usage, which is appropriate to the place where it is carried on." *Id.* The court further noted the widespread use of natural gas for residential needs. *Id.*

¶ 37. Additionally, the court compared the underground transmission of natural gas to the hauling of gasoline in commercial quantities upon public highways. *Id.* at 216–17. The court stated:

> Natural gas flows through a small (2–inch) pipe which is buried underground, away from the dangers of the surface world. There are no careless drivers, faulty brakes, or slippery roads with which to contend. The heightened danger resulting from the storage of a highly volatile substance in large commercial quantities, rolling at high speed on a well traveled highway, is also absent.

Id. at 217.

¶ 38. In *Kentucky Utilities Co. v. Auto Crane Co.*, 674 S.W.2d 15, 17 (Ky. Ct. App. 1983), the appellate court found the transmission of electricity was not an ultrahazardous activity for purposes of strict liability. The court noted that the transmission of electricity is a public necessity and stated, "the rules for strict liability for abnormally dangerous activities rarely apply to activities carried on in pursuance of a public duty." *Id.* at 18.

¶ 39. Here, our analysis of the Restatement factors leads us to conclude that the transportation of liquid propane is not an ultrahazardous activity for purposes of strict liability. As in *New Meadows Holding Co.*, 687 P.2d at 216, we too concede factors (a) and (b).

¶ 40. Regarding factor (c), Dr. Clarke opined Dixie's utilization of repeated pressure cycles and operating pressures caused the cracks to grow to critical length and depth. However, Dr. Clarke did not opine that the reduction of pressure cycles and operating pressures would reduce or eliminate the risk of a rupture. Importantly, the NTSB found that controller actions and operating conditions of the Dixie pipeline were not factors in the rupture. Moreover, the transportation of liquid propane is a regulated commercial activity, subject to state and federal regulations.

¶ 41. Additionally, factors (d), (e), and (f) weigh against the imposition of strict liability. The Dixie pipeline is a major pipeline through which liquid propane is transported from refineries in Texas, Louisiana, and Mississippi to customers all throughout the southeastern United States. The pipeline was built in 1961 and extends about 1,100 miles through multiple states from Texas to North Carolina. There is no evidence to suggest the placement of the pipeline was inappropriate. Moreover, the transportation of liquid propane is of great value to commerce and local, regional, and nationwide communities.

¶ 42. Overall, we find the transportation of liquid propane does not constitute an ultrahazardous activity. Accordingly, the circuit court did not err in dismissing Elmore's strict-liability claim on summary judgment.

IV. The Dismissal of Elmore's Negligence Claim

¶ 43. To succeed on a claim for negligence, the plaintiff must show "(1) the existence of a duty 'to conform to a specific standard of conduct for the protection of others against the unreasonable risk of injury,' (2) a breach of that duty, (3) [a] causal relationship between the breach and [the] alleged injury, and (4) injury or damages." *Donald*, 735 So.2d at 174 (¶ 42) (quoting *Meena v. Wilburn*, 603 So.2d 866, 870 n.5 (Miss. 1992)). "Duty and breach of duty are essential to finding negligence and must be demonstrated first." *Id.*

¶ 44. As previously noted, Elmore designated Dr. Clarke to offer expert testimony regarding the alleged negligence of Dixie. Dr. Clarke admitted that he has no familiarity with the federal regulations that govern integrity management for the Dixie pipeline. Thus, Dr. Clarke was not qualified to opine as to the applicable duty owed by pipeline operators or any breach of that duty by Dixie. Absent such evidence, there was no genuine issue of material fact to preclude summary judgment. Thus, Elmore's negligence claim fails.

¶ 45. Elmore asserts "this is a proper case for [the] application of the negligence doctrine of res ipsa loquitur." "Res ipsa loquitur, literally translated 'the thing speaks for itself,' is simply one form of circumstantial evidence." *Gray v. BellSouth Telecomm., Inc.*, 11 So.3d 1269, 1272 (¶ 11) (Miss. Ct. App. 2009). "Under the doctrine of res ipsa loquitur, negligence can be inferred in certain factual situations." *Id.* However, the doctrine should be applied cautiously." *Id.*

¶ 46. To apply res ipsa loquitur, the plaintiff must prove three elements:

> First, the defendant must have control and management of the instrumentality causing the plaintiff's injury. Second, the injury must be such that in the ordinary course of things it would not occur if those in control of the instrumentality used proper care. Third and finally, res ipsa loquitur only applies where the injury is not a result of the plaintiff's voluntary act.

Id. at 1272 (¶ 12). We find Elmore failed to demonstrate the second element.

¶ 47. The second element requires Elmore to show "that in the ordinary course of things, the injury would not have happened if [Dixie] had used proper care." *Id.* at 1272 (¶ 13). Here, there is simply no evidence that in the ordinary course of things, the pipeline would not have ruptured had Dixie used proper care. The record shows Dixie complied with the governing federal regulations for the operation and management of interstate pipeline. The NTSB found no substantive violations by Dixie and specifically found that controller actions and operating conditions were not factors in the rupture. Thus, Elmore's claim that the pipeline ordinarily would not have ruptured had Dixie "used reasonable care and caution in the operation of the pipeline" is without merit.

¶ 48. As there were no genuine issues of material fact regarding both negligence and res ipsa loquitur, the circuit court properly dismissed Elmore's claim.

V. The Dismissal of Elmore's Punitive–Damages Claim

¶ 49. Elmore last argues the circuit court "ha[d] no authority to grant summary judgment on the issue of punitive damages and committed reversible error in doing so." Since summary judgment was properly granted on Elmore's claims of strict liability and negligence, we decline to address the final issue of punitive damages, as the claim is moot.

CONCLUSION

¶ 50. Upon review, we find the circuit court did not abuse its discretion in denying Elmore's discovery motion or excluding Dr. Clarke. Additionally, as no genuine issues of material fact exist, we find the circuit court's entry of summary judgment was proper on Elmore's claims of strict liability and negligence. Accordingly, we affirm.

¶ 51. AFFIRMED.

Notes and Questions

1. What distinguishes the result in *Branch* from the result in *Elmore*? Are you comfortable that the two cases can be reconciled?

2. Be prepared to describe the relationship between strict liability and negligence, first at common law and then in the two jurisdictions at issue in the principal cases, i.e., in Utah and in Mississippi.

3. In the modern period, it is often suggested that a strict liability claim will not stand if a negligence claim would satisfy the plaintiff's need for compensation; and, that negligence law's res ipsa doctrine should ensure that the latter claim is available to plaintiffs even in explosion cases. (Explosions used to be considered classic strict liability fact patterns.) Why did this not work for the plaintiff in *Elmore*? Would it have made a difference had her expert actually been expert in the relevant questions? If not, how can plaintiffs expect to be compensated in cases like *Elmore*?

GEORGE CHRISTIE
AN ESSAY ON DISCRETION
1986 Duke L.J. 747, 767-69 (1986)

. . . In 1938, section 520 of the [First] Restatement of Torts subjected the operator of an 'ultrahazardous activity' to strict liability if the activity miscarried, and defined such an activity as one that (a) 'necessarily involves a risk of serious harm' to others and (b) 'is not a matter of common usage.' The common-usage exception was intended to accommodate Lord Cairn's declaration in *Rylands v. Fletcher* that the liability established in that case was limited to the 'non-natural use' of land. One practical implication of the common-usage exception posed some difficulties. What about fumigation of commercial buildings? It certainly was a common enough activity; indeed, in many cities it was required by law. Nevertheless, the Supreme Court of California held that although fumigation might be a common activity, only a very small number of professionals performed fumigation and thus it was not a matter of common usage. Accordingly, the court could appropriately classify it as an ultrahazardous activity subject to strict liability. The court cited the commentary to section 520 as support for its conclusion. The Oregon Supreme Court took a different approach, classifying cropdusting as an ultrahazardous activity despite the fact that the court considered it a matter of common usage. The court found the dangerousness of the activity alone sufficient to justify this classification.

When Volume III of the Second Restatement was published in 1977, several changes had been made in section 520. Instead of 'ultrahazardous activity,' the Second Restatement used the term 'abnormally dangerous activity.' More to the point, the Second Restatement replaced the two-pronged test of the Restatement with a factor analysis that included interest balancing. The full text of section 520 of the Second Restatement merits quotation:

> In determining whether an activity is abnormally dangerous, the following factors are to be considered:
>
> (a) existence of a high degree of risk of some harm to the person, land or chattels of others;
>
> (b) likelihood that the harm that results from it will be great;
>
> (c) inability to eliminate the risk by the exercise of reasonable care;
>
> (d) extent to which the activity is not a matter of common usage;
>
> (e) inappropriateness of the activity to the place where it is carried on; and
>
> (f) extent to which its value to the community is outweighed by its dangerous attributes.

This statement of the test leaves two overriding questions: who is to make the determination of what is an abnormally dangerous activity, and how is the required factor analysis and interest balancing to be done? As to the first question, the commentary to the Second Restatement declares that the judge, not the jury, is to decide whether an activity is abnormally dangerous. Although the commentary concedes that in a negligence case a jury might have to make a host of subjective determinations in deciding the reasonableness of an activity, it concludes that the decision whether an activity is abnormally dangerous is of a different type. The principal difference asserted is that, unlike a jury's decision in a negligence case, the classification of an activity as abnormally dangerous could destroy an entire industry. But of course a ruling that a product, say an airliner, is negligently designed could also destroy an industrial enterprise. Moreover, it seems to be generally accepted that, in actions brought on a theory of strict liability for defective products, the issue of product defect is submitted to the jury. Why should strict liability under an abnormally dangerous activity theory be treated differently than strict liability for a defective product?

The second question raised by section 520 of the Second Restatement, and the one that most immediately concerns this discussion, is how the court should weight the six factors that are to guide the determination whether an activity is abnormally dangerous. The commentary declares that the determination is to be made by the court, 'upon consideration of all the factors listed in this Section, and weight given to each that it merits upon the facts in evidence.' I submit that this is no weighting method at all. If taken literally, the commentary seems to suggest that each case is sui generis and that one need have no fear that an individual decision, whether made by a judge or by a jury, might ruin an entire industry. Thus, in any case involving an activity not covered foursquare by a precedent, one would have to litigate up to the highest court of the jurisdiction before knowing how the activity would be classified. The value of precedents covering other activities would be minimal. Whether or not one liked the old test, it was certainly easier to administer, since it asked only whether the activity involved 'a risk of serious harm' to others that 'could not be eliminated by the exercise of the utmost care,' and whether the activity was 'a matter of common usage.'

Some may object that the Second Restatement merely made explicit the factors courts already considered. This is not so. Of course, in any close case, a court is likely to consider individual equities like the comparative wealth of the parties and the social importance of the activity, and these factors will likely influence the decision. A court should never be expected to ignore individual equities. But to recognize that a court will be *influenced* by individual equities in deciding some legal issue is not the same as saying that these individual features themselves *are* the legal issue.

An enormous range of legal decisions could all be plausibly justified under section 520 of the Second Restatement. For example, it was held in Maryland that operating a neighborhood gas station, whose leaking storage tanks fouled the well of an adjoining landowner, was an abnormally dangerous activity. An Oregon court disagreed. In a Florida court, a mine operator seriously urged, again on the basis of the new version of section 520, that a mine producing phosphatic wastes was not an abnormally dangerous activity because of the location of the mine and its social importance. But the court ruled against the mine operator because of the size of the activity and the possibility of enormous damage if the activity miscarried.

Notes and Questions

1. How did strict liability test change from the First to the Second Restatement? Which version is truer to its origins in the *Rylands* case?

2. Professor Christie's main argument about Section 520 is that its factors approach permits courts unguided (and thus too much) discretion. Does the *Elmore* court's application of Section 520 support this argument?

3. Are the authors of the Restatement correct that a judge is more likely to make a good decision than a jury in cases that potentially involve the destruction of an industry?

Restatement (Third) of Torts
Strict Liability § 20 – Abnormally Dangerous Activities

(a) An actor who carries on an abnormally dangerous activity is subject to strict liability for physical harm resulting from the activity.

(b) An activity is abnormally dangerous if:

> (1) the activity creates a foreseeable and highly significant risk of physical harm even when reasonable care is exercised by all actors; and
>
> (2) the activity is not one of common usage.

Comment:

. . .

b. Relationship to negligence. The strict-liability rule set forth in this Section is concerned with activities that give rise to a highly significant risk of physical harm. The significance or magnitude of any risk relates to both the likelihood of harm and the severity of any harm that may ensue. However, even under negligence law, as the magnitude of the risk occasioned by the defendant's activity increases, so does the burden of precautions that the defendant is required to adopt while engaging in that activity in order to avoid being found negligent. If a highly significant risk of physical harm contributes to the case on behalf of strict liability under this Section, such a risk also facilitates the plaintiff's proof of the defendant's negligence . . . for failure to adopt appropriate precautions. Of course, in some instances the evidence will suggest that the defendant, though engaging in a highly risky activity, has adopted all reasonable precautions. In such cases, the issue of strict liability remains relevant. Indeed, a prerequisite for the strict-liability rule identified in this Section is not merely a highly significant risk associated with the activity itself, but a highly significant risk that remains with the activity even when all actors exercise reasonable care. Accordingly, at least at a general level, the issue of strict liability emerges at about the point at which the assignment of liability and losses in accordance with all actors' apparent negligence leaves off.

For many activities that initially entail a highly significant risk, the risks in question can be dramatically reduced by the exercise of reasonable care by all actors; moreover, the party immediately carrying out the activity is frequently the party whose exercise of reasonable care is most relevant. Consider an activity that is initially quite dangerous, but whose danger levels can be effectively minimized if the party carrying out the activity fully exercises reasonable care. When a harm-causing incident does occur in the course of that activity, the doctrine of res ipsa loquitur may well be available as a way of suggesting the defendant's liability under a negligence theory. Aviation, for example, is potentially quite dangerous; but a jury might believe that these dangers can usually be averted if the pilot and airline exercise reasonable care; accordingly, res ipsa loquitur can frequently be invoked against the airline. Of course, even in a case in which res ipsa loquitur is applicable, the defendant can avoid negligence by showing that the particular incident was brought about by factors unrelated to the actor's negligence. In such a case the issue of strict liability can become salient. Arguments on behalf of strict liability, then, tend to begin with the premise that the accident has happened even though the defendant has fully exercised reasonable care while engaging in the activity.

Yet even if the defendant who engages in an activity has taken all reasonable precautions, one possible negligence argument remains. If all the risks entailed by an activity even when reasonable care is exercised outweigh all the advantages that the defendant and all others derive from the activity, it may be unreasonable and hence negligent for the defendant to carry on the activity at all, or at least to carry it on at the particular location. However, if the defendant's decision to engage in the activity is in fact negligent, the issue of the defendant's strict liability recedes in importance. Accordingly, this Section's discussion of strict liability tends to assume that the defendant is not negligent in engaging in the activity — that the advantages of the activity are sufficient to justify its risks.

. . .

l. Function of court. Whether the activity is abnormally dangerous is determined by the court, applying the factors in Subsection (b). When appropriate, the court can rely on judicial notice in order to acquire information about a particular activity. Alternatively, that information can be provided by evidence, especially expert testimony. While factfinding may be involved, the process of factfinding is properly assigned to the court rather than to the jury. The facts in question commonly concern an entire class of activities within society, rather than the conduct of the particular defendant. Moreover, the factual findings determine the very standard of liability that applies to the conduct of the defendant, rather than merely the application of a previously specified standard of liability to the circumstances of a particular defendant. In addition, the decision as to the standard of liability applicable to an activity is likely to have a broad societal impact. . . . Indeed, it is desirable for courts clearly to identify those activities that are abnormally dangerous, so as to give parties fair notice, avoid unequal results, and reduce subsequent litigation costs. For all these reasons, the responsibility is properly entrusted to the court for conducting the inquiry under Subsection (b) that leads to the judgment as to whether an activity is abnormally dangerous.

Notes and Questions

1. Compare the Restatement Third to the Restatements Second and First. How has the doctrine evolved still further from *Rylands*? What remains of that rule?

2. The authors of the Restatement Third apparently agreed with Professor Christie's preference for the First Restatement's simpler strict liability test; that is, the Restatement Third's new formulation appears to return to that simpler approach. Does it also solve Christie's concern with the unguided judicial discretion inherent in the Restatement Second's factors test?

Problem Twelve: From Virus to Vaccine

P is a small private company whose business is pharmaceutical research and development. In particular in this period, P is working on two projects, both Ebola-related. The first is a vaccine designed to protect inoculated individuals from catching or experiencing the serious effects of the virus. The second is a drug designed to alleviate its symptoms once it is contracted. To do this work, P has been allocated a small number of live samples of the Ebola virus from the Centers for Disease Control and Prevention (CDC). Because the CDC only provided samples to four companies, which are in competition to produce the safest and most effective products the most quickly, and because regulators' and investors' interest seemed to be focusing on P's prospects in particular, P's stock value doubled as soon as the allocation was announced publicly.

Because the virus is deadly, because it can spread quickly, and because there is as yet no cure, the transportation, handling, and storage of the samples all must be executed with extreme caution. D is a company that specializes in (among other things) the transportation and transfer of sensitive substances. Earlier this year, P and D entered into a contract which provided that P would retain D's specialized services to transport and transfer Ebola virus samples from a CDC secure storage facility to P's laboratories, and in turn P would pay D for its services. Among other things, the contract also contained a performance and payment schedule and a liability waiver providing that each party agreed to hold the other harmless for injuries and damages to third persons occasioned by any unintended release of the virus while the samples were in its custody.

Custody documents provide that when the samples designated for P were transferred by the CDC to D for transport, they were in intact, sealed vials, and the vials themselves were properly lodged in additionally sealed containers. There is no evidence to the contrary. The documents further provide that P received the samples from D in undamaged containers with intact CDC seals, and that P immediately stored these securely and according to protocol. There is also no contrary evidence in this respect. The evidence is murkier with respect to the conditions of the transportation and transfer of the containers themselves. On the one hand, the manager who supervised the employees who actually transported the samples has provided an affidavit indicating that each step of the transportation and transfer protocol was followed and that they did not report anything unusual along the way. On the other hand, the two employees in question no longer work for the company and apparently cannot be located. In any event, when P's laboratory technicians opened the containers to begin to process the included samples, it quickly became clear that most of the vials were cracked or broken. And unfortunately, although the area was evacuated with all due care, in that process somehow some of the virus leaked out not only of the laboratory but of the facility itself so that neighboring businesses also had to evacuate their premises and remain away until CDC inspectors finally declared the area safe. (Although the Ebola virus is not believed to be airborne, concerns that it might become so are significant enough that evacuations and inspections are relatively routine.)

These events have left P in bad shape: Existing research and development work stopped during the period of the evacuation; no new research and development work can begin until the CDC provides it with new samples; and in the meantime, based on news of the work stoppages associated with the event and evacuation, its market share has plummeted seventy-five percent. And it has been sued by its neighbors for the financial losses associated with their time away from their premises. Their accountants have established these losses to the point where P is convinced they are significant.

We have agreed to represent P. P would like to sue D for indemnification of any damages it has to pay out to its neighbors, and for its own losses, which include the lost profits and market share P claims it likely would have garnered had it been able to continue to conduct the expected Ebola-related research and development. Its accountants are able to document the drop in market share they claim is associated with the lost research and development opportunity, and they have developed models which purport accurately to reflect lost profits.

Let me know if there is a claim or claims we might develop for P that could potentially result in recovery of these different losses, and if so, how the D might respond.

III. PRODUCTS LIABILITY

The third strict liability category concerns defective products. Because this is a specialized area of law that is difficult properly to capture in a few first-year class sessions, and because it is generally taught as a stand-alone upper level course, we do not attempt to do more here than introduce you to the subject. The reading we have selected for this purpose, written by Professor Joanna Shepherd and published in the Vanderbilt Law Review, provides an excellent overview of the relevant history, evolution, and current state of products liability law. If you are interested in the subject, we encourage you to consider taking the specialized course as part of your upper level curriculum.

JOANNA M. SHEPHERD
PRODUCTS LIABILITY AND ECONOMIC ACTIVITY: AN EMPIRICAL ANALYSIS OF TORT REFORM'S IMPACT ON BUSINESSES, EMPLOYMENT, AND PRODUCTION
66 Vand. L. Rev. 257, 262-78 (2013)

. . .

I. The Evolution of Products Liability Law

Products liability law as we know it began in the 1960s. Prior to that period, products liability cases were rarely brought and plaintiffs rarely won the cases that were brought. However, the widespread adoption of strict liability in the 1960s and the development of new proplaintiff theories in the 1970s expanded products liability law and increased plaintiffs' recoveries. The tide turned again in the early 1980s with the enactment of state-level legislation that limited the scope of products liability law. This prodefendant trend continued into the twenty-first century with several industry-specific reforms adopted at the federal level. In this Part, I briefly describe the ebb and flow of U.S. products liability law from its roots in English common law to the present.

A. Early American Law

The early development of products liability law was greatly impeded by two powerful doctrines borrowed from England: caveat emptor and privity of contract. Caveat emptor translates to "let the buyer beware." Under this doctrine, sellers were not responsible for product defects and buyers bore the risk for product-related injuries. Hence, plaintiffs had no recourse under the law for injuries they sustained from either obvious or hidden defects. Reflecting the nation's commitment toward free enterprise and protecting infant industries during the Industrial Revolution, all states but South Carolina strictly adhered to the caveat emptor doctrine until the turn of the nineteenth century. Caveat emptor persisted in the majority of jurisdictions until the Uniform Sales Act of 1906 obligated an implied warranty of quality that made sellers responsible for many product defects.

Despite legislatures imposing implied warranties of quality after 1906, manufacturers often were still able to avoid liability with privity defenses. The doctrine of privity required manufacturers and consumers to be in a contractual relationship for a valid products liability claim to lie. Thus, it comported with the realities of the preindustrialization economy when products were typically sold directly by the manufacturer to the consumer. However, as industrialization and mass production expanded, goods were increasingly sold through intermediate retailers. As a result, manufacturers no longer entered into contractual relationships with consumers, and they could use the ready-made defense of no privity of contract to avoid liability in products liability cases.

As manufacturers became increasingly remote from consumers in the expanding economy, the harshness of the privity doctrine became obvious. The privity requirement began disappearing from products liability claims in 1916, when the New York Court of Appeals decided MacPherson v. Buick Motors. Explaining the liberation of tort law from contracts, Judge Cardozo proclaimed:

> We have put aside the notion that the duty to safeguard life and limb, when the consequences of negligence may be foreseen, grows out of contract and nothing else. We have put the source of the obligation where it ought to be. We have put its source in the law.

Although most states quickly followed New York's lead in eliminating the privity requirement, it remained in a few states well into the second half of the twentieth century.

As the majority of states eliminated the doctrines of caveat emptor and privity of contract in the early 1900s, products liability claims began to increase across the nation. However, plaintiffs still had to overcome significant hurdles to prevail in these cases. Because negligence was the basis for products liability claims, the injured party had to prove that the manufacturer was negligent in producing the product and that the negligence caused the subsequent injuries. Plaintiffs rarely prevailed in these cases because they were usually unable to produce evidence of manufacturers' negligence, which often occurred years before the product caused an injury.

B. Modern American Law

The tide began to turn in favor of plaintiffs in the early 1940s. In the first, 1941 edition of the most influential treatise ever published on tort law, Dean William Prosser argued for strict liability for manufacturers of defective products. Three years later, in Escola v. Coca Cola Bottling Co. of Fresno, the Supreme Court of California upheld a res ipsa loquitur verdict against Coca Cola for an exploding bottle, eliminating the need for plaintiffs to provide evidence of manufacturers' negligence in situations where accidents would not normally occur without negligence. Moreover, in his concurrence, Justice Roger Traynor argued for strict products liability using many of Prosser's arguments: "[I]t should now be recognized that a manufacturer incurs an absolute liability when an article that he has placed on the market, knowing that it is to be used without inspection, proves to have a defect that causes injury to human beings."

However, it was not until 1963 that strict products liability was adopted by the Supreme Court of California. In Greenman v. Yuba Power Products, Inc., the court upheld a judgment for a plaintiff that had been injured by a defective power tool. Although Justice Traynor had alone argued for strict liability in his concurrence in Escola nineteen years earlier, he authored the majority opinion for a unanimous court in Greenman: "A manufacturer is strictly liable in tort when an article he places on the market, knowing that it is to be used without inspection for defects, proves to have a defect that causes injury to a human being."

Just two years later, in 1965, the Restatement (Second) of Torts helped propagate strict products liability to virtually every jurisdiction. The American Law Institute ("ALI") had started revisions on the Restatement of Torts chapter that applied negligence to the liability of sellers in the 1950s. Fortuitously, Dean Prosser was chosen as the Reporter for the Second Restatement. Consequently, a year after Greenman was decided in his home state of California, Prosser presented the ALI with a revised draft that incorporated the principles of strict products liability found in both Greenman and his own torts treatise. The American Law Institute adopted the revision in 1965 as section 402A of the Restatement. Section 402A made products liability "strict" because sellers could be liable even if they had exercised "all possible care" and thus were not negligent.

From 1965 to the early 1980s, court after court, along with several state legislatures, adopted strict liability for manufacturers and sellers of defective products. The development of new theories, such as enterprise and market-share liability, further facilitated suits by consumer-plaintiffs. The end result was a body of products liability law in 1980 that was significantly more plaintiff friendly than it had been in the days when negligence was the basis for liability and caveat emptor and privity of contract were valid defenses.

C. The Liability "Crisis"

Largely as a result of the proliferation of strict products liability, products liability trials and awards increased significantly beginning in the 1970s. Although only data on federal cases are available during this period, the data reveal that products liability cases increased by an average of forty percent per year during this period. Whereas only 2,393 products liability cases commenced in federal court in 1975, the number of these cases had increased to 14,145 by 1987. Moreover, this number drastically underestimates the true number of products liability claims because many tort claims are brought in state courts and the vast majority are settled before trial.

Furthermore, although litigation in general increased during this time, products liability litigation increased at a significantly higher rate. In 1975, products liability cases represented 2.04 percent of all civil cases. However, by 1987, that share had almost tripled, rising to 5.92 percent.

Awards in products liability cases increased as well. The average verdict of $563,438 in 1980 more than doubled by 1987, to $1,325,443. Similarly, the median verdict, which may be more informative because it is not influenced by a few unusually large awards, increased from $225,000 in 1980 to $430,000 in 1987.

Increases in both the number of products liability cases and the awards in those cases increased the expected liability for manufacturers, distributors, and product sellers. As a result, insurance companies increased the premiums for liability coverage for these industries. When section 402A was published in 1965, total liability premiums in the United States were $881 million. By 1987, this figure had increased by over two thousand percent, to $20.9 billion. The average annual growth rate during this period was over sixteen percent, and in some years, premiums grew by over seventy percent.

D. A Period of Reform

Although the causes of the explosion in premiums are debatable, there is little doubt that the more consumer-friendly products liability law was at least partly to blame. As a result, manufacturers, insurers, and other businesses declared the situation a "crisis" and pushed for legislation, either at the state or federal level, to protect the interests of manufacturers and businesses. Their activism was extensive, ranging from industry papers to nationwide advertising campaigns to testimony before both Congress and state legislatures.

The proponents of immediate reform argued that proconsumer products liability doctrines resulted in unfair harassment of businesses by opportunistic consumers and plaintiffs' lawyers. They claimed that burdensome liability costs and insurance rates had dramatically increased the cost of doing business and were forcing many manufacturers and sellers out of business. Moreover, they argued that state-by-state variation in products liability laws resulted in a competitive disadvantage for businesses operating in high-liability states. Thus, the arguments were generally cast in terms of restoring balance to an area of law that had become lopsided in favor of plaintiffs.

The outcry in the business community won over some courts. Although courts did not commonly overturn prior decisions, they regularly rejected arguments to further expand products liability boundaries. Moreover, many courts began to question whether strict liability was the appropriate standard for evaluating a product's warnings and design. The Restatement (Third) of Torts, published in 1998, eventually validated this doubt and grounded liability for design and warning defects in the principles of negligence.

However, a more significant attack on products liability law came during the 1980s from state legislative bodies enacting tort reform. The state legislatures were persuaded that products liability reforms would solve the liability and insurance crisis and fix an imbalanced system. Moreover, they believed that reforming the system would improve their local state economies: a more business-friendly legal environment would bring business to their states, creating jobs and strengthening the state economy. State after state enacted legislation designed to curb the crisis by limiting the scope of liability and damages. Next, I discuss the most significant reforms that the states adopted to limit the scope of products liability.

1. Statutes of Repose

One of the most frequent reform measures passed by the states limits the period during which suits can be brought. All civil suits are subject to a statute of limitations. However, the statute of limitations for most torts is only one or two years. Because the act for which defendant manufacturers are traditionally liable is manufacturing defective products, a two-year statute of limitations poses a problem for plaintiffs injured by products purchased several years earlier. Thus, rather than leave plaintiffs without a remedy when they were injured by products purchased years earlier, many courts adopted a "discovery" rule. Under a discovery rule, the statute of limitations begins to run when the plaintiff actually discovers the injury, instead of when the defective product was purchased.

However, under the discovery rule, manufacturers' exposure to liability can last for the life of the product. Consequently, some manufacturers are subject to liability for injuries caused by products that are twenty and thirty years old. To counteract this open-ended liability, many states have adopted so-called statutes of repose that specify the number of years after a product is first sold within which suit must be filed. Instead of beginning to run when the injury is discovered, the repose period begins to run when the product is first marketed. Thus, a statute of repose may expire, precluding a lawsuit, even before an injury occurs and a statute of limitations begins to run. Most repose periods are set at ten years; thus, suits for injuries caused

by products purchased over ten years earlier are barred under statutes of repose. Twenty-seven states have adopted these reforms that significantly reduce manufacturers' exposure to liability.

2. Reforms to Product-Seller Liability

Another popular reform adopted by the states involves the liability of nonmanufacturer product sellers such as wholesalers, distributors, and retailers. Under traditional products liability laws, nonmanufacturer product sellers can be held strictly liable like product manufacturers for injuries caused by product defects. Although innocent sellers can subsequently recover from manufacturers under traditional law, this creates significant transaction and litigation costs. Thus, several states have enacted reforms that eliminate strict liability for wholesalers, distributors, and retailers that do not manufacture products. Under these reforms, nonmanufacturer sellers may be held liable only for their own negligence or breach of warranty. Thus, these reforms relieve nonmanufacturer sellers from the significant costs associated with defending products liability claims. Twenty-two states have enacted reforms that eliminate strict liability for product sellers.

3. Reforms to Joint and Several Liability

Several states have also reformed joint and several liability rules in products liability cases. Under traditional joint and several liability, a plaintiff can recover the full cost of her injury from any party who is partially responsible for the injury, no matter how small the party's responsibility. The rule ensures that plaintiffs are fully compensated, but ignores whether each codefendant pays his or her portion of the damages. As recently as 1973, joint and several liability was universally applied in every state.

Unfortunately, traditional joint and several liability rules encourage plaintiffs to seek out a "deep-pocket" defendant, even if that defendant contributed only modestly to causing the damages. Although the deep-pocket defendant can seek contribution from the other tortfeasors for their share of the damages, such cross claims are often fruitless when the other tortfeasors lack resources. Reformers argue that the traditional rule unfairly requires a single defendant to pay the entire damage award, even when that defendant is only remotely responsible for the harm. As a result, thirty-one states have eliminated joint and several liability in products liability cases so that each responsible defendant is liable only in proportion to its relative share of responsibility.

4. Reforms to the Collateral Source Rule

Other states have modified the traditional collateral source rule. The traditional rule prevents the admission of evidence at trial that shows that a plaintiff's losses have been compensated by other sources, such as insurance or workers' compensation. The rationale for the traditional rule is that a defendant should not benefit from something paid for in advance by the plaintiff.

Although the rule promotes efficient deterrence by requiring a tortfeasor to pay damages even when a victim has received payments from a source other than the tortfeasor, it allows plaintiffs to potentially recover twice for the same injury. Moreover, even if providers of the collateral benefit have a contractual or statutory right to subrogation — allowing them to recover the value of the benefit from successful tort claimants — subrogation involves significant transaction costs to determine the providers' rights.

Thus, several states have adopted reforms that include allowing evidence of collateral source payments or completely offsetting awards by the amount of collateral source payments. Thirty-six states have adopted such reforms that modify the traditional collateral source rule in products liability cases.

5. Noneconomic Damage Caps

Limitations on damages have been passed by many states as an additional way to treat the products liability crisis. Most reforms are aimed at either noneconomic damages or punitive damages. Noneconomic damages are damages for nonpecuniary losses such as pain and suffering, loss of consortium, emotional distress, and other intangible losses. Thus, unlike punitive damages, noneconomic damages are compensatory, even though they are frequently difficult to compute. Moreover, noneconomic damages serve an important deterrent function because they make potential tortfeasors internalize the nonpecuniary harms they impose on others.

However, critics claim that these damages are often excessive and unpredictable, increasing both the level and variation of expected liability costs. For example, one study suggests that the severity of harm explains only about forty percent of the variation in noneconomic damage awards in personal injury cases. This leaves enormous award variation that is random and unexplained. For example, awards for the most serious permanent injuries range in value from approximately $147,000 to $18.1 million. This unpredictability produces several harms. It makes settlement more difficult because accurate prediction of jury awards is impossible. It increases insurance premiums as insurers charge potential tortfeasors "ambiguity premiums" to cover the increased risk. Moreover, the risk of significant noneconomic damage payments may result in manufacturers curbing innovation or production to reduce their exposure to catastrophic judgments.

In addition, critics claim that, because prices reflect expected liability costs, a tort system that provides noneconomic damages effectively requires everyone in society to pay for insurance to cover such losses. Critics argue that most people do not want this mandatory insurance for nonpecuniary losses because they do not purchase insurance coverage for other nonpecuniary harms.

State legislatures have listened to the critics, and twenty-four states have adopted caps on noneconomic damages in products liability cases. However, the reforms vary tremendously. Not only do the amounts of the cap differ by state, but some reforms impose a fixed dollar cap while others are indexed to inflation. Some reforms impose different caps for different types of defendants or different severities of injury. The reforms also vary in what kinds of cases are covered or excluded from the cap.

6. Punitive Damage Caps

Punitive damages are meant to deter willful, wanton, and malicious conduct. Although they are not awarded to compensate victims, punitive damages may be necessary to achieve adequate deterrence of either especially egregious behaviors or behaviors where the probability of detecting negligence is low. When victims only discover their harms and/or file claims in a fraction of suits, damages in the few suits that are filed must exceed the compensatory level to achieve adequate deterrence.

However, critics argue that increasing punitive damage awards have led to excessive litigation and windfall gains for plaintiffs. They insist that the grounds for punitive damage awards are inappropriately expanding in many areas. Moreover, probusiness groups argue that excessive and arbitrary punitive damage awards have increased the cost and reduced the availability of insurance. Many blame punitive damages for producing unjustifiably large awards and forcing otherwise viable industries out of business. Many state legislatures have been persuaded that business competitiveness depends on reasonable and predictable liability costs. As a result, twenty-three states have adopted caps on punitive damages in products liability cases.

7. Comparative Negligence

Other states have reformed laws regarding comparative fault. Historically, in an action claiming negligence on the part of the defendant, contributory negligence disallowed any recovery by a plaintiff whose own negligence contributed, even minimally, to causing the damages. In contrast, contributory negligence was not recognized as a defense to strict liability.

Critics argue that contributory negligence is overly harsh to negligent plaintiffs in negligence actions. As a result, forty-six states have adopted comparative negligence that reduces the plaintiff's recovery in proportion to his percentage of responsibility.

Although these comparative negligence reforms were intended to increase recovery for negligent plaintiffs, they have accomplished the exact opposite in strict liability actions. Whereas contributory negligence was not a defense to strict liability, comparative negligence is recognized as a defense in these actions. Hence, in products liability cases under contributory negligence, defendants' damages are never reduced to reflect plaintiffs' negligence, but under comparative negligence, defendants' damages are routinely reduced to account for plaintiffs' negligence.

8. Other State-Level Reforms

States have experimented with other reforms to varying degrees. Although the specific reforms vary by state, they all serve to limit manufacturers' liability. For example, "The patent danger rule relieves a manufacturer from liability for failure to warn or to redesign if the dangerous aspect of the product is obvious to the reasonable person." Although adopted by a few states, many have rejected the rule as a complete defense and, instead, consider an obvious danger as one factor to consider when determining liability.

Another reform adopted by some states relates to the "state of the art," or the feasibility of safety measures when a product was developed. These reforms have taken various forms, though most allow the introduction of evidence about the state of the art at the time the product was developed.

9. Federal Reforms

In response to the perceived liability crisis of the 1970s and 1980s, numerous federal tort reform bills were also introduced in Congress. The vast majority of these bills stalled in committee, faced filibusters, or passed in one chamber but not the other. As a result, for years states were the primary source of legislative efforts to reduce the scope of products liability.

However, in the 1990s, Congress successfully enacted a series of products liability reforms that shielded manufacturers and product sellers in specific industries. For example, the General Aviation Revitalization Act of 1994 created an eighteen-year statute of repose for manufacturers of general aviation aircraft and their component parts. Similarly, the Biomaterials Access Assurance Act of 1998 limits the products liability of biomaterials suppliers of raw materials and medical-implant component parts. Likewise, the Y2K Act provides liability relief and limits on punitive damages for defendants in legal actions arising from year-2000 computer failures. The Homeland Security Act of 2002 limits the liability of both manufacturers and administrators of the smallpox vaccine and sellers of antiterrorism technology. Similarly, the Protection of Lawful Commerce in Arms Act shields manufacturers, distributors, dealers, and importers of firearms or ammunition from liability resulting from the misuse of their products by others.

Despite reformers' success at enacting various industry-specific reforms, efforts to adopt comprehensive federal tort reform have failed. Although numerous bills that reduce the scope of products liability across all industries have been proposed in Congress, they have yet to be enacted. The bills are often successful in one chamber but fail in the other. One bill was even passed by both chambers, but Congress subsequently failed to override President Clinton's veto of the bill. Proponents of federal tort reform argue that, despite state tort reforms, many judgments are still excessive. In addition, they argue that national uniformity in products liability law is necessary to prevent distortions in the cost of doing business across states. Comprehensive federal tort reforms continue to be proposed every few years, and several powerful business interest groups continue to campaign for them.

CONCLUSION

This book and course have focused on the fundamentals of tort law including both the concept of the fault continuum, which underlies all of legal responsibility, and the substantive claims along the continuum: the intentional torts through negligence to strict liability. Most torts litigation involves these claims in their basic forms. And all "advanced torts" including constitutional, business, and dignitary torts are based in their structures and elements. For example, civil rights claims under 24 U.S.C. §1983 are generally intentional torts committed by a state actor where the injury is a violation of the individual plaintiff's federal constitutional rights; products liability, interference with business relationships claims, and privacy torts are based in negligence or strict liability or a combination of the two; and breach of fiduciary duty claims including constructive fraud claims are generally negligence-based. The knowledge you have developed has thus prepared you for further study of and work with both the basic and advanced torts.

The book and course have also focused on the fundamentals of the litigation process including claims development, rebuttal, and defense; the relationship between substance and procedure; the difference between normative and case-specific decision-making; the significance of facts as evidence; and using evidence to meet or defeat the burden of proof. As applied to tort law, the scales of justice that cover this volume are a metaphor both for this process and for the formal role of this area of the law in providing compensation, deterrence, and some measure of retribution according to prevailing social norms about reasonable behavior. Ultimately, though, these essential lessons are all portable beyond torts: law and the practice of law generally are grounded in the same process and understandings.

Finally, like most if not all of your other 1L classes, the book and course have inevitably provided lessons in lawyering skills; that is, in "thinking like a lawyer" or what used to be called "the legal method." Because Torts is a particularly obvious vehicle for this purpose, however, we have been intentional in our focus on skills-building. Thus, we have worked with you on reading carefully and instrumentally within and across cases to extract rules; on developing analytical rubrics and outlining to organize and understand large amounts of complicated information; and on tackling problems, issues, or questions using some variation on the FIRAC paradigm, where the "rule" is common law or statute-based or else simply a governing principle, and the "analysis" is well-structured, creative, evidence-based, and persuasive. Our expectation is that you will have also have been intentional about developing your lawyering skills, recognizing similar and complimentary lessons from your other 1L courses, so that your foundations in substance, process, and method are as strong as possible going forward.

APPENDIX: PRACTICE PROBLEMS

The problems that follow were either in previous versions of this book or on one or another of our final exams, mostly the latter. Although you don't have to do practice problems as part of your exam preparations, many students find this to be a helpful study tool. If you do, we strongly recommend that you not work on them until you've outlined the entire course so that you take them on at the point when you are fully prepared to tackle the expected issue triage, rule choices, and analysis. In other words, in our view, doing practice problems should be the final or next-to-final stage of your exam preparation process.

CORRECT/INCORRECT

(DLC)

1. The causation rule in Summers v. Tice works equally well no matter how many defendants there are; regardless of their number, they will be jointly and severally liable for the plaintiff's damages.

2. When the Plaintiff gets a res ipsa loquitur instruction, breach is established as a matter of law.

3. There is a difference between factual foreseeability and reasonable foreseeability.

4. Modern parents have two lines of argument against battery claims brought by their children: they have a threshold parental immunity argument and the discipline defense; either or both will ensure that they are not liable in tort.

5. A plaintiff in a medical malpractice case against a specialist based in a clear medical error must retain an expert who will testify to the national standard of care.

6. The reasonable person standard is based on the "average" person in the community, not the person "born hasty and awkward" or the person with special expertise.

7. The government is generally immune from liability in ultrahazardous activity cases and, barring a statute or constitutional provision to the contrary, also has a complete defense against trespass actions justified by public necessity.

8. Words alone can be the basis for an IIED claim.

9. The best defense against a lost chance medical malpractice case is proof that the plaintiff never actually had a chance; this will ensure the defendant has no liability whether the jurisdiction uses causation theory under the Restatement or the majority rule damages theory.

10. Employers are vicariously liable for the torts of their employees committed during working hours.

11. The United States Supreme Court has established that punitive damages, generally a matter of state law, will violate the due process clause of the federal Constitution anytime they exceed single digit ratios.

12. Good Samaritan statutes typically abrogate the common law negligence duty of a volunteer rescuer.

13. Risk-utility analysis (or the BPL formula) is sometimes an aspect of the rule for duty, the rule for breach, and the rule for proximate cause.

14. The exclusive remedy provision of worker's compensation statutes generally precludes suits in negligence for on-the-job injuries.

15. Children who are charged with negligence or contributory negligence are held to the standard of a reasonably prudent child of their age, intelligence, temperament, and experience.

16. Business custom, like medical custom, is dispositive of the standard of care in negligence.

17. Assuming no last clear chance facts, a plaintiff who is more at fault than the defendant or the defendants combined can hope to recover something for their injuries only if they are in a pure comparative negligence jurisdiction.

18. Private necessity is not a complete defense to a trespass claim.

19. The government has generally waived sovereign immunity in negligence cases; this means that plaintiffs can sue the government under the public duty doctrine.

20. Baseball will always be protected by primary implied assumption of the risk where a patron is hit by a flying bat or a flying baseball.

YES/NO
(DLC)

1. Thirteen-year-old D rides his dirt bike through P's recently planted flower garden, damaging the landscaping. Afterwards, he is asked why he did this and he explains that the P "is a jerk who deserved it." P sues D and D's parents for trespass. P explains that D's parents are at least partly responsible because he's their kid and separately, they didn't raise him right. D's parents disagree with P's take on their parenting but they write P a check. Is this the right result?

2. D's dog Ruby is trained first to bark and then, if the intruder proceeds in the face of the barking, to bite anyone who tries to climb the fence D has installed between the edge of his property and his house. D trained Ruby to do this because he lives in a high-crime neighborhood and a few of his neighbors have recently been robbed at gunpoint by thieves trying to enter their homes. Ruby bites a thief who is climbing the fence as he's leaving D's property. Ruby didn't bark first because she was distracted by something else. Should D write P a check?

3. David owns and manages a grocery store. He sees Patricia put her hand near a box of breakfast bars and then into her pocket. Because of this, he believes she has stolen a breakfast bar. As Patricia is moving toward the exit, David places himself in the doorway, tells Patricia that he suspects her of stealing the bar, and tells her to stop and wait while he calls the police. Patricia stops, tells David he is wrong, and they argue for about 5 minutes until the police arrive. When they do, Patricia empties her purse and pockets to show that she has not stolen the bar. David apologizes for his mistake and Patricia leaves. Patricia sues David for false imprisonment and asks for nominal damages. Does David need to write the check?

4. D owns and operates an excavation business in full compliance with federal and state workplace safety laws. Nevertheless, it knows from one of its in-house engineers that there is an 85% chance that a particular section of one of its excavations projects is vulnerable to collapse. In order to stay on schedule, D decides to proceed with the project. The side does collapse and several workers die as a result. Does the exclusive remedy provision of the state's workmen's compensation statute bar an eventual suit by their representatives in battery?

5. A deer named Bambi runs across the road in front of D. D loves wild animals and her new car. She makes an instantaneous decision based on these preferences — and self-preservation, of course — to avoid hitting the deer by swerving off of the road onto P's lawn. Is she likely to have to pay for the damage to the lawn?

6. P1 knows nothing about investing and so hires D, an investment adviser and broker, to advise and invest his money for him. As part of the initial interview, D asks P1 a set of questions designed to establish P1's tolerance for risk — is P1 willing to lose money in exchange for the possibility of greater gains? P1 tells D that he wants half of his funds put into very low-risk investments but that he'd like to take more of a chance with the other half. D agrees to invest P1's funds with these parameters in mind. A month later, thinking she has just received very good insider information that a particular high-risk investment is actually a safe one, D puts all of P1's funds in that high-risk situation. This was a mistake. She loses all of P1's money. Does P have a claim for fraud?

7. Same facts as above. Does P1 have a claim for breach of fiduciary duty?

8. Same facts as above, except that we are working with P2. When P2 heard that P1 had hired an investment advisor and broker, he gave P1 his savings and asked P1 to put it with the funds P1 was giving to D. P2 didn't have very much and wasn't in a position to hire his own advisor. P1 and P2 were good friends and so P1 agreed. Does D owe P2 a duty in negligence?

9. Ps are victims and representatives of victims of a high school shooting. They learn that the shooter, a student at the school, was an avid player of a particular first-person shooter game; and that what he did on the day of the school shooting exactly replicated the game's storyline. Their lawyers are thinking of developing a negligence claim against the game's developers and distributors. In fact, they think this is such a great idea they will be able to ride it to riches and retirement, like the plaintiffs' lawyers who developed the claims against Big Tobacco. Are they right?

10. Despite a fixed schedule that has roller coaster cars taking off from their starting point one minute apart to avoid possible collisions, two cars collide on the same stretch of track; specifically, one hit the other from behind. P was a passenger in one of the cars and her back was injured in the collision. D is the owner and operator of the ride. P sues D in negligence and wants to introduce an expert in amusement park safety standards who would testify that D violated those standards. P asks the judge to admit her expert and to instruct the jury that this testimony is conclusive on the issue of breach. The judge admits the expert but refuses the requested instruction. Is this the right call?

11. Same facts as above except the judge refuses to admit the expert. P has no other evidence of breach and there are no obvious prospects on the horizon, i.e., asking for more time to develop such evidence is not an option. D moves for summary judgment. Should the judge grant it?

12. P has an invasive brain tumor. D is his neurosurgeon. During the operation, D mistakenly leaves a small instrument in the surgical cavity. This "retained instrument" is visible in a routine post-operative brain scan. P sues D for malpractice. D moves for summary judgment on the ground that P has not retained an expert in neurosurgery who will testify that D violated the applicable standard of care. Should the judge grant the D's motion?

13. Same facts as above except that D's alleged malpractice was in failing to remove all of the tumor despite their pre-operative agreement that this was necessary to P's long-term chances of survival. D explained to P that during the surgery, she made the decision not to touch that tissue because doing so

would have posed too great a risk of stroke and death. P is upset because she really wanted the tumor entirely removed. She files a malpractice claim and hires a different neurosurgeon to provide expert testimony in support of that claim. At trial, on direct examination, P's expert testifies that despite the risk of stroke and death, she would have removed all of the tumor. In her words, "the tumor itself risks death so on balance, it would have been best to remove it all." On cross-examination she testifies that it would also have been reasonable to skirt the area. In her words, "Yes, reputable surgeons could disagree about this, both options were viable in the circumstances." D moves for a directed verdict. Should the judge grant D's motion?

14. Same facts as above. When P retained D as her neurosurgeon, she had a 25% chance of survival. Had the tumor been completely removed, she would have had a 60% chance of survival. Because it was not completely removed, her post-op chances of survival are 45%. She's (still) upset about this less-than-expected result. Assuming it was malpractice not to remove all of the tumor, would a suit seeking damages for a 15% lost chance of survival be successful?

15. A developer buys a piece of land with an old office building on it. The plan is to remove that old building and put up a new one. The developer hires a building company to do the job. The building company hires a subcontractor to demolish and then to remove the resulting debris from the old office building. As is the standard, that subcontractor uses explosives to do the demolition work. That work is done negligently and people unrelated to the project are injured. They sue the developer on the theory that it is vicariously liable for their injuries. Are they right?

16. P sues D, the local employee of the Internal Revenue Service who mishandled the audit of his 2015 federal tax return which led to the forced but unnecessary tax sale of his home and consequent severe emotional distress. The suit is in negligence. D moves to dismiss the suit on the grounds that as a federal employee, he is not subject to suit in negligence. Is he right?

17. Federal agents damage part of P's home in the course of apprehending a terrorism suspect. The damage was authorized, but it turns out they had the wrong house: the tip received by the government properly indicated the suspect was hiding out at 110 John Street, but by mistake the agents went to 110 Jane Street. P sues the government for negligence resulting in property damage. The government defends on the ground of public necessity. Is this a good argument?

18. Same facts as above. When the federal agents entered P's home, they were initially confronted by P's German Shepherd. Not taking any chances, they shoot it and it dies. P sues the government in battery for the death of his dog. D files a motion to dismiss for failure to state a claim. Is this a good argument?

19. Same facts as above. Assume P can make out a claim for the death of his dog. The issue is damages. The dog was three years old, scheduled to live for at least seven more assuming no unexpected injuries or diseases. He was a terrific pet especially because he was dangerous looking but actually totally harmless. P is devastated by his loss. The government says it's sympathetic but denies it's responsible for more than nominal damages for the dog's death since the dog had no market value and because he's dead, there are obviously no repair costs. Is this a good argument?

20. Same facts as above except that it turns out the address error was intentional. The agent who received the tip hates P and so used this as an opportunity to harm him. He sent the team to P's address on purpose. P sues the government in trespass for this separate act. The government claims sovereign immunity. Is this a good argument?

21. D is found guilty of rape in a criminal proceeding. His victim, P, subsequently sues him for assault and battery. A jury finds D liable and awards $160 to compensate her for the insurance co-pays she advanced for her associated medical expenses, $1M in pain and suffering damages, and $25M in punitive damages. (The D is wealthy and according to state law, the jury properly heard evidence to this effect.) A state statute has capped non-economic damages at $300,000. Based on this, D asks the trial judge to issue a remittitur in the amount of $700,000. Should the trial judge grant it?

22. Same facts as above. The D appeals the punitive damages award on the ground that it violates the due process clause. Is this a good argument?

23. P and D enter into a contract which includes an exculpatory clause. The clause has P waiving liability for any and all claims he may otherwise have had in torts, and limits any damages arising under the contract to those specified in its separate damages clause. In the course of their relationship, D engages in fraud that costs P significantly, beyond the amounts provided in the damages clause. P files a torts claim against the D seeking to recover the full amount of his losses. D files a motion to dismiss the claim on the ground that it is precluded by their contract. Should the trial judge grant D's motion?

24. A tourist from abroad comes to the United States and goes to a professional baseball game for the first time in her life. She knows nothing about baseball. She is hit by a bat mistakenly released by a player during batting practice. She files suit against the player, his team, and the owners and operators of the stadium seeking damages for her resulting injuries. None of the Ds appears in court to defend the suit. The court *sua sponte* dismisses her claim. Is this the right result?

25. P is injured. The jury determines that P is negligent and D is strictly liable. And it allocates responsibility 45% to P and 55% to D. D writes a check for 55% of the total. Does P accept it?

IN "REASONABLE" FEAR OF DEADLY FORCE?
(DLC)

Read the following hypothetical, developed by Professor Jody Armour:

> It is a stormy night in a combined residential and commercial neighborhood in a predominantly white upper-middle-class section of a major city. The time is 10:30 p.m. Although most of the fashionable shops and boutiques in the neighborhood have closed, the neighborhood bank contains an automatic teller. The machine is located in a lobby between two sets of glass doors; the first set opens directly into the bank and is locked at closing each day, while the second leads to the public sidewalk and remains open twenty-four hours.
>
> A middle-aged resident of the neighborhood enters the bank's lobby, inserts her bank card into the machine, and requests $200. As she waits for her transaction to be processed, the woman suddenly notices a figure moving directly toward the lobby from across the street. Focusing her full attention on the approaching figure, she notes that the person is a young man (at most twenty-something); that he is wearing a trench coat with an upturned collar and a tarpaulin hat pulled down even with his eyes (perhaps in deference to the pouring rain); and that he is black.

> The trench coat-clad young man glances down the deserted street as he reaches the lobby and then enters, pushing his right shoulder against one of the swinging glass doors. As he pushes the door open, he unbuttons the collar of his trench coat with his right hand and reaches into the coat in the direction of his left armpit. With his eyes focused on the space beneath his coat into which he is reaching, he takes hold of something and begins to withdraw it.
>
> Panic-stricken at the image before her and conscious of the rhythmic clicking of the automatic teller counting out ten fresh clean twenty-dollar bills, the woman pulls a pistol from her purse and levels it at the entering figure. As the young man looks up from his coat, he sees the pistol trained on him and reflexively thrusts his right hand — which now contains a billfold retrieved from his inside breast pocket — out in front of him while shouting at the woman not to shoot. Perceiving what she takes for a handgun thrust in her direction, together with the man's unintelligible loud shouts, the woman shoots and kills the black man.

Jody D. Armour, Race Ipsa Loquitur: Of Reasonable Racists, Intelligent Bayesians, and Involuntary Negrophobes, 46 Stan. L. Rev. 781 (1994).

How would the plaintiff's estate make out its assault and battery prima facie cases on these facts? How would the defendant rebut those prima facie cases? What is the best argument you can make for the defendant that her use of deadly force against the plaintiff was appropriate in the circumstances? What is the best argument you can make for the plaintiff that the defendant used excessive force? As you are developing your arguments, consider the perspectives offered in the following two essays:

(1) Brent Staples, Black Men and Public Space, available at http://mshobday.weebly.com/uploads/1/6/9/9/16992572/blackmeninpublicspaces.pdf

(2) Phylisa Wisdom, I'm Sick of Being Afraid to Walk Alone at Night, Role Reboot (August 18, 2014), available at http://www.rolereboot.org/life/details/2014-08-im-sick-afraid-walk-alone-night/

MOSQUITO WARNINGS REQUIRED
(dlc)

Duke Academy is a private, non-profit college preparatory school in Durham, North Carolina. The school was founded in the 1920s and has long been considered the best elite private school in the area. Mostly because of the regional demographic — which is chock full of professional parents with advanced degrees including those who are on the faculties of the many nearby universities — the school's admissions standards are tough, its curriculum is extensive and rigorous, and its placement rates at the most elite colleges and universities are excellent. Parents of children who might attend DA are willing to pay a lot of money in tuition to afford their children this educational opportunity. Indeed, like most parents, DA parents are typically willing to do almost anything to give their children a leg up in life.

One of the things DA does especially well is balance its curricular and co-curricular offerings. And so, among other things, the children enrolled there can take advantage of terrific in- and out-of-session academic enrichment programs. The latter in particular are a highlight of the school's marketing efforts. For example, the current admissions "viewbook" features students on various day and overnight field trips to places within and outside of the United States. Consistent with the school's forward-looking pedagogical philosophy, these field trips are designed to be interdisciplinary and team-oriented; in other words, they are designed to mirror the academic and career skills that will be the basis for the students' success in college and beyond.

Peter and his parents were attracted to DA because it is the best school in the area, but they were especially happy that it offered an optional summer program at the Yachana Ecolodge in Ecuador. The on-site program includes Spanish lessons as well classes in rainforest biology, ecology, and conservation. Although it was still early in his high school career, Peter planned to apply to colleges with strong Latin American Studies programs, and he and his parents believed that going on the school's Ecuador trip would demonstrate to college admissions officers that he was sincerely interested in the field. The fact that DA's Advanced Placement (AP) Spanish and Biology teachers were chaperoning the trip and co-teaching the lessons at Yachana was also significant for Peter and his parents because it would give Peter an additional opportunity outside of school to cultivate their interest in him, which would hopefully result in favorable recommendation letters to include in his college applications.

And so in the spring of Peter's sophomore year, when he was fifteen, he and his parents signed him up and paid in advance for that coming summer's trip to Ecuador. Among the documents in the trip packet were the following:

DA's standard "waiver and release of liability" which all three of them signed before Peter left for Ecuador. This contract did not contain information and warnings specific to the trip to Ecuador; other than a filled-in line specifying the destination and dates of the trip, the form was the same the school used for all other trips and off-campus activities.

A brochure published by the Yachana Ecolodge and provided to the school which included the following F.A.Q.s:

> Do I need a yellow fever shot? Ecuador recommends that travelers get a yellow fever shot before coming to the country but it is not a requirement. This is more as a measure to try to rid the entire continent of yellow fever than as a prevention of catching the fever. There have not been any yellow fever cases in the region for many years. The decision on whether to take the shot or not is entirely up to you. But you need to be aware that the yellow fever vaccine is a live vaccine and can cause a reaction.
> Am I going to see snakes? We hope you will. Snakes are beautiful and are an important part of the ecosystem. There are poisonous snakes so one needs to be careful, but we have never had a visitor bitten by a poisonous snake.
>
> Am I going to get bitten by insects? There is that possibility. You ARE in the jungle. Taking basic precautions will help to minimize bites. These consist of always using your rubber boots, that we provide, when you leave the lodge walkways. The more square meters of flesh exposed the higher probability of getting bites. So it helps to use shirts that cover your back and shoulders, long sleeves and long pants. Bring insect repellent and an antihistamine if you really have problems with bites.

Because the school assumed the students and their parents were intelligent and educated and thus would carefully consider its contents, none of the information in the trip packet was discussed by the school with the families in advance of the trip.

The DA contingent arrived at Yachana late in the afternoon. While they were waiting for their scheduled lodge orientation, Peter and his biology teacher spotted a gorgeous green tree snake hanging lazily from the limb of a tree which stood several meters off of one of the Lodge's raised wooden walkways. Excited to see the beast up close, the two made their way from the walkway into the tall grasses just beneath the tree limb. They took photographs of the snake and also a few selfies of themselves and the snake, which they later proudly posted on the school's Facebook site. The photographs show two happy people in their shorts and t-shirts on either side of a gigantic green snake. A few days later, Peter reported that he had a lot of what he assumed were mosquito bites and that he didn't feel well, but he and his teachers all thought it was best to wait to get back to Durham to be checked out by a doctor. A few months later, Peter's doctors at Duke Children's Hospital — where he had been a deteriorating in-patient since his return from Ecuador — explained to his parents that he had liver disease which was likely caused by the yellow fever virus which was, in turn, likely contracted in Ecuador from a mosquito bite. They were provided with this further information about the yellow fever virus from the Centers for Disease Control:

> Yellow fever virus is found in tropical and subtropical areas in South America and Africa. The virus is transmitted to humans by the bite of an infected mosquito. Yellow fever is a very rare cause of illness in U.S. travelers. Illness ranges in severity from a self-limited febrile illness to severe liver disease with bleeding. Yellow fever disease is diagnosed based on symptoms, physical findings, laboratory testing, and travel history, including the possibility of exposure to infected mosquitoes. There is no specific treatment for yellow fever; care is based on symptoms. Steps to prevent yellow fever virus infection include using insect repellent, wearing protective clothing, and getting vaccinated.

In the spring of the following year Peter's parents filed a lawsuit against DA. For themselves they sought damages for the costs of the trip to Ecuador, his medical care, and the loss of his consortium. For Peter, they sought damages for his physical injuries, his pain and suffering, and for future lost opportunities since it was expected based on his condition that Peter's life prospects would be reduced as a result of his illness. Specifically, the claim alleged that DA was negligent in failing to warn all three of them of the possibility that Peter would be exposed to mosquitos that could carry the yellow fever virus, and of the steps they could all take to reduce his chances of contracting yellow fever; it alleged that had they been specifically warned in this respect, they would have taken the most conservative precautions in all respects because this is the sort of people they are; and they alleged that had they taken these precautions, it is unlikely that Peter would have been bitten by a mosquito that carried the yellow fever virus and thus unlikely that he would have suffered severe liver disease as he does today.

Over DA's lawyers' objections and motions to dismiss, for summary judgment, and for directed verdicts, the trial court judge allowed the case to go to trial and then to a jury. In response to special interrogatories, the jury found that:

> 1. DA was negligent in failing to warn Peter and his parents about the risk of contracting mosquito-borne yellow fever virus on the Ecuador trip, and about the protective measures they could have taken to reduce this risk.
>
> 2. DA's negligence was the actual and proximate cause of their injuries.
>
> 3. Peter was not an actual or proximate cause of his illness.

4. Peter did not assume the risk of his illness.

5. The general "waiver and release of liability" was unenforceable.

6. The plaintiffs were due compensatory damages in the amount of $44 million dollars—four million dollars for Peter's parents, and forty million dollars for Peter.

DA's motions for judgment notwithstanding the verdict and for a new trial were denied and the court of appeals affirmed the trial court in all respects.

DA wants to appeal these decisions to the State Supreme Court: From the school's and its insurer's points of view, this appeal is necessary because of the precedent it would set if it stands. Separately, because the school's insurance policy has a maximum "per occurrence" payout of one million dollars, its remaining liability — $43 million dollars — would be crippling.

Our firm has been retained to handle the appeal. The jury's findings provide the basis for us to work on several issues, but for various reasons we are only interested in trying to convince the Court of two things: (1) that the school had no duty to warn Peter and/or his parents of the risk of contracting the yellow fever virus on the Ecuador trip, or of the precautions that one could take to avoid this risk; and (2) that the school was not the proximate cause of Peter's injuries. Develop these arguments and advise as to their weaknesses and our likelihood of success.

THE MARKSMAN
(DLC)

D, an expert marksman, raised his gun, aimed it at P's head, and pulled the trigger. Because P and D had been friends for a long time, P knew of D's expertise. Witnesses say that P saw D raise and aim his gun, and that P seemed to smirk and maybe even laugh, but that he also ducked. In the process of ducking, P tripped and fell, hitting his head on a sharp rock that had fallen out of a landscaper's truck and onto the otherwise clear parking lot earlier in the day. P died instantly. When interviewed by the police after the fact, D acknowledged that he and P had recently had a very public argument over very personal matters, but he insisted there were no bullets in his gun when he pulled the trigger. There is no evidence contradicting D's assertion.

Develop P's estate's strongest claim in battery against D. What is D's best rebuttal?

D moves for summary judgment and the trial court grants his motion. P appeals. What should the court of appeals do and why?

THE GOOD SAMARITAN
(DLC)

Like a majority of people in the community, P is a ___ist / ite / phobe. Fill in the blank with whatever group you prefer to work with, e.g., racist, anti-Semite, Islamophobe, transphobe, whatever. For exam purposes, I assure you and so believe me that your choice will have no effect on the arguments you can develop.

P has filed a battery claim against D who saved him from drowning and, once back on land, gave him mouth-to-mouth resuscitation. P is deeply disturbed because even though D — a member of the group P rejects — rescued him from the water, she didn't step aside when P's Friend volunteered to take over the rescue effort. Like most people, even those who are not ists / ites / phobes, P cares a lot about his bodily integrity and autonomy, especially in regard to its intimate parts — the mouth, of course, included.

Friend can't swim but knows cardiopulmonary resuscitation (CPR). D, who was at one time a certified lifeguard, was following standard protocol.

D didn't know P or his Friend before the rescue. She was just acting on instinct and training, basically being a Good Samaritan. Although she was relatively new to the area, having recently moved there for a new job, she was aware of the general sense of discomfort with and sometimes outward hostility toward people like her. Indeed, when she was considering the move, the overall sociopolitical environment was a clear negative factor which was ultimately overcome by the incredible job opportunity with which she had been presented and the professional respect and personal kindness exhibited by her employers and co-workers.

What is the P's best case for battery, what are the D's best arguments in response, and how might a court justify both sending it to and pulling it from the jury on a dispositive motion?

BALINT ENTERPRISES
(DLC)

Balint Enterprises is a gun manufacturer. Since 1977, it has made a version of the AR-15 rifle. AR-15s have been used in a number of recent mass shootings, including the shooting at Sandy Hook Elementary School in 2012, and at Stoneman Douglas High School in 2018. Balint estimates that its market share is about 10% of legal sales.

According to Wikipedia:

> An AR-15 style rifle is a lightweight semi-automatic rifle based on the Colt AR-15 design. After Colt's patents expired in 1977, an expanded marketplace emerged with many manufacturers producing their own version of the AR-15 design for commercial sale. They are referred to as modern sporting rifles by the National Shooting Sports Foundation, a firearms industry trade association, and by some manufacturers. Coverage of high-profile incidents where various versions of the rifle were involved often uses the shorthand AR-15.

Rolling Stone Magazine explains further that:

> The AR-15 assault rifle was engineered to create what one of its designers called "maximum wound effect." Its tiny bullets — needle-nosed and weighing less than four grams — travel nearly three times the speed of sound. As the bullet strikes the body, the payload of kinetic energy rips open a cavity inside the flesh — essentially inert space — which collapses back on itself, destroying inelastic tissue, including nerves, blood vessels and vital organs. "It's a perfect killing machine," says Dr. Peter Rhee, a leading trauma surgeon and retired captain with 24 years of active-duty service in the Navy.
>
> Versions of the AR-15 have been the U.S. military's standard-issue assault rifle in every war since Vietnam. But only in the past dozen years have semi-automatic models become a fixture of American life. Gun-makers — emboldened by Congress and cloaked in the Second Amendment — have elevated the AR-15 into an avatar of civilian manhood, independence and patriotism. In the process, this off-patent combat rifle has become an infinitely customizable weapon platform that now accounts for nearly one in five guns sold in America. The federal government has deemed them "semi-automatic assault rifles" with magazine capacities that serve "no sporting purpose." But the National Rifle Association now simply calls the AR-15 "America's Rifle."

You work for a plaintiffs' firm. One of the partners thinks it's possible, especially in the current climate, to develop a successful strict liability claim against manufacturers of the AR-15. To test the idea, she assigns you to prepare a memo sketching out the claim, its weaknesses, and how they might be overcome. For illustrative purposes, she has told you to imagine that we will represent the students at Stoneman Douglas High School who died and were injured by the shooter, Nikolas Cruz, and that we will sue Balint Enterprises. You do some state law research and understand that the relevant law is in flux in your jurisdiction. Write up to two pages responding to the assignment.

IT'S IN THE BAG
(DHB)

Jim Packer [JP] was having a hard day on the Friday after Thanksgiving, Black Friday in 2014. JP was 35 and had Down's Syndrome [DS]. [1] He lived in the Duke DS Group Home and they had gotten him his job as a grocery packer at the Wal-Mart Supercenter. On Black Friday, JP thought the shoppers were being mean to him and his Wal-Mart co-workers. JP was at his crankiest by 4:45 p.m., with 15 minutes left in his shift.

William Shopper [WS] and Lynn [LS] Shopper, a husband and wife, retired and in their mid-60's, were holiday shopping together at the Wal-Mart. After loading their purchases into the car, their conversation turned to that night's dinner. Agreeing on their exhaustion from shopping, and that neither wanted to "cook," they decided to have an easy meal of heated canned LaChoy brand Chow Mein over Kraft Minute® rice. They often ate this meal when they wanted a quick dinner with few pots and pans. Also, their only child, Mark, an adult son was visiting. Chow Mein was a meal he, too, enjoyed. So, back into Wal-Mart they went.

In the grocery department, WS selected four two-pound cans of Chow Mein from the shelf and put them in their cart. LS brought a five-pound box of Kraft Minute® rice from further down the aisle. As the couple passed through the beer and wine section they added bottle of white wine. And then, after getting into a lengthy line, WS remembered they were low on eggs, so he went and got a dozen while LS waited on line.

As WS and LS were checking out at 4:45 p.m. and talking to each other, WS said something about President Trump that JP overheard and apparently found offensive because he later complained about the remark to the checker in his lane. JP was a fan of the President's TV show, "The Apprentice," and often would joke with people who made a mistake at work and say, "You're fired." Despite WS's remark, JP continued to pack their purchases in a single plastic grocery bag, putting the heaviest items at the bottom and the eggs at the top. As he loaded in the eggs, he thought to himself it would be justice for WS's remark about the Mr. Trump if the eggs fell out and broke on WS. To ensure that the bag did not tear when JP lifted it from the checkout counter, JP slipped his hand and arm under bag to support the box of rice and cans in the bag and slid his hand and arm out as he gently placed the bag in the Shoppers' cart.

Wal-Mart teaches packers about packing. The company's instructions are:

- Never waste plastic bags.
- Heaviest items go at the bottom; fragile items go on top.
- Plastic bags can hold up to 14 pounds if there's nothing in the bag likely to rip it
- Try not to put more than ten pounds without double bagging[2] or dividing the customer's purchases between two bags.

---

[1] Down syndrome [DS] is a genetic disorder caused by the presence of all or part of a third copy of chromosome 21. JP, like most DS people had physical growth delays, characteristic facial features, and mild to moderate intellectual disability. In JP's case, he had an IQ of about 50, speech delays and functioned, intellectually, at about a 4th grade level.

[2] "Double bagging" is putting one bag inside another before filling them.

When the Shoppers got to their car, WS picked up the bag by its handles at the top, and lifted it out of the cart. As he was lifting it out, he saw the corner of the box of rice tear through the bottom of the bag and watched one of the LaChoy cans fall on LS's right foot causing a deep cut. The couple went immediately to the local hospital's emergency room where LS received stiches and was diagnosed with a broken toe. Within days, LS's cut and her broken toe bone became infected with an aggressive type of infection that responds, if at all, to only one antibiotic. Two surgeries amputating the toe first and then the foot, and months of the correct antibiotic were ineffective. The infection spread throughout LS's body. She died 11 months after the injury. An autopsy was conclusive that the infection was the cause. Since she died, the family has learned that the antibiotics she received for the first two weeks were from a bad batch that were wholly ineffective for the treatment of the infection. Later batches she received were full strength but unfortunately ineffective against the infection.

WS has come to you seeking legal advice about all potential claims from LS's injury other than those against the drug manufacturer. You are aware of all the information above either from WS directly or from an interview with the checker done by a government agency at WS's request. In addition, WS kept the torn bag and you had it tested. The expert's report you received said that the bag exceeded industry standards for design and had no manufacturing defects. Based on the evidence you have, analyze the strengths and weakness of the claims that could be brought for any plaintiff arising out of these events. You need not consider any questions relating to damages.

Assume that the state uses the majority rule (or if no majority rule, the plurality rule) for all things tort-related and that no statutes apply.

EVERYBODY LOVES SUSAN

(DHB)

There's an old joke in real estate that begins with "What are the three things that matter in real estate?" The answer is "Location, location, location." In Dukeville, the primo location was Garden Hill and the realtor with the most listings of houses for sale there was Susan Valley. She was also the realtor who was most often contacted by people who wanted to buy in that neighborhood. Needless to say, she, too, was a valuable property in the Dukeville real estate market.

Susan had started to tell her fellow high-end realtors that she was tired of the hassle of owning her own real estate agency and wanted to join another agency who would be responsible for all of her administration. In return, she was willing to commit to work five more years and give up one third of her annual profits for each of those years. Those profits had averaged more than $1,000,000 a year for the past five years and had risen about five percent each year during that period.

Hearing word of Susan's availability, Jack B. Nimble at Nimble Real Estate immediately reached out to Susan and they made the deal described above first orally and then reduced to it to writing. John C. Lately, who had the biggest agency in Dukeville, got wind of the deal between Nimble and Susan before it was publically announced. He had one of his agents who was close with Susan run into her at the Garden Hill Country Club bar where both were often found. The agent, following Lately's instructions, let Susan know that Nimble was facing charges before the Real Estate Board for fraudulent practices. This was true, but Lately only knew about the confidential charges because he served on the Board. In disclosing them, he violated the Board's rules. The agent told Susan that she should "talk to Lately." Susan did. Lately confirmed the charges and asked Susan what her deal was with Nimble. Susan told him. In response, he offered to match Nimble's deal and add a $100,000 signing bonus. When Susan worried aloud about what Nimble would do, Lately promised to indemnify Susan if she was sued by Nimble. Within a day Susan signed a contract with Lately and notified Nimble that she was not going to come to work with him. She told him that she had heard "things" about him that made her uncomfortable in going ahead with the deal. Nimble, who was later cleared of the Real Estate Board charges, sued Susan for breach of contract. That case settled. He also sued Lately. The trial court dismissed Nimble's claim for failure to state a legally recognized cause of action. The Court of Appeals affirmed. The case is now before the state's Supreme Court on a writ of certiorari.

Your jurisdiction has not previously considered a case like this. You are clerking for a judge on the State Supreme Court. She is of the view that the conduct identified above should be actionable as some kind of a tort. She would like you to, in effect, create the tort, identify its elements and address the issues you see with the tort should it actually be recognized by the Court. She has told you that she does not want you to consider claims for defamation, libel, slander.

BAD SPORT
(DHB)

Able takes Baker, his 9-year-old soccer-playing daughter, to her recreational league game at a busy local multi-purpose park with soccer and baseball fields, running paths, walkways, and gardens. Charlie, a former collegiate soccer player who is 5'10" and 160 pounds and still competitive in adult leagues, coaches the opposing team. This game will decide which team goes on to the league championship game.

The score is tied at the end of the game. Ties are broken by a "shoot out" in which the teams alternate free kicks.[3] The winner is the first team whose successful kick is followed by the other team's unsuccessful kick. Charlie's team kicks first and is successful. Baker is the best player on her team and will be making their first free kick. If she misses, Charlie's team wins; if she is successful, the alternating kicks continue.

Baker places the ball on the ground, steps a few yards back from it, and starts her run to kick the ball. After her first step, Charlie screams out, "Hey Baker, your shoe is untied." Baker stops running, looks at her shoes, and realizes the laces are still tied. Her face turns bright red to gales of laughter from the opposing team. She backs away from the ball to compose herself. After a couple of deep breaths, she starts her second run to kick the ball. And again, just as she starts to the ball, Charlie shouts "Hey Baker, your lace really is untied." Baker never stops and continues to the ball, but her kick goes far wide of the goal to more laughter from the opposing team. Baker is in tears and inconsolable.

Able, who is 6' tall, 240 pounds and paunchy, is outraged. He walks purposefully towards the sideline where Charlie stands amidst his celebrating players. He yells towards Charlie from about 30 feet away, "I'm going to use your head for kicking practice." Charlie responds, "If you think you can catch me, couch potato, go for it." Able, who at this point is only 10 feet from Charlie, clenches his fists and

[3] In a free kick, the ball is placed 12 yards from the opposing team's goal, which is defended by that team's players--all of whom have to be more than ten yards from where the ball is placed. The kicker then kicks the ball from its spot, trying to get it past the opposing players and into the goal.

starts running at him. Charlie immediately takes off running away from Able through a large group of players and parents who are leaving the field after the game. In complete frustration that he will never be able to catch him, Able takes a pair of cleated soccer shoes off the shoulder of one of Charlie's players and throws them towards the escaping Charlie knowing they will never reach him. The shoes land well short of Charlie, but hit the face of a woman out for her daily run. She did not see them coming because she was texting while she was running. The woman's cornea is injured.

For a couple of weeks after these events, Baker had trouble getting to sleep, wasn't eating well, and had frequent stomach aches for which she received medical attention and medications. She is doing well now. After Able and other parents complained to recreation league officials, Charlie was banned for life from coaching in the league.

For those people discussed above who have any tort claims, analyze those tort claims. For those who would be sued for those torts, analyze their defenses. Consider only claims and defenses covered this semester using majority or plurality rules if they exist.

TARGETED DRONE STRIKE
(DHB)

The Basker family home in Durham has a swimming pool secluded behind an eight-foot-tall hedge. On sunny summer afternoons, Kay Basker, 16, and her best girlfriend, Ashley, sunbathe by the pool. Robert Flier lives next door to the Baskers. Robert is technologically gifted and can figure out anything electronic, is a superstar at video games requiring eye-hand coordination, but overall is only a fair student because he tends to "hyper-focus" according to his teachers. What he does is focus on some things while ignoring others. In the past, for example, he has forgotten to eat while immersed in reading, and walked into a wall while playing videos on his phone.

For his 12th birthday, Robert's aunt gives him a Z-10 Camera Drone (photo above) bought from Drones Unlimited on the advice of salesperson Sam Seller as being appropriate for Robert. When a camera drone flies over something it transmits color video back to its remote controller's screen along with GPS information about its location, route, height, and speed. Drones of the Z-10's weight are regulated by the Federal Aviation Administration [FAA]. Its regulations require the drone be registered with the FAA, but impose no minimum age for pilots. The FAA also requires that the drone fly neither closer than one mile to an airport nor over 400 feet. Robert's house is more than ten miles from any airport. The Z-10's box repeats the FAA limitations and also includes language saying, "For ages 14 and older." Robert's father, dubious about drones generally, lets Robert keep the Z-10 when Robert promises not to use it to annoy anyone. Robert's drone was never registered.
Very quickly Robert masters piloting the drone. Occasionally, he ignores the yellow light on the controller indicating the battery is low, and the battery runs out while the drone is in the air. When that happens, the Z-10's rotors stop, it crashes, and its plastic rotor blades break on impact with the ground. After Robert breaks several rotors, his father starts keeping spares in the house.

Robert only flies the Z-10 from his backyard. One day as it flies over the Baskers' house, its video shows Kay and Ashley by the pool. Thereafter, while careful not to fly low or hover over Kay's pool, Robert routinely flies the drone over the pool on its way to and from his backyard. When she notices it, Kay smiles and waves.

On this sunny day Robert is piloting his drone back to his house at about 10 miles an hour and 450 feet. As it passes above Kay's pool, Robert becomes particularly curious about what Kay and her friend are wearing while sunning. While hovering the drone and closely examining the video on his screen, Robert fails to notice the the yellow light. The drone's battery runs out and the Z-10 crashes, striking Ashley and giving her a nasty gash on her face. While in the hospital being treated, Ashley is exposed to Necrotizing Fasciitis [NF], the flesh eating bacteria. NF infects a scratch she got when Kay, who was helping Ashley into the house after Ashley was hit by the drone, tripped over Kay's own purse that she had left on the ground by the door to the pool. While Ashley's medical treatment was perfect and contracting NF is a known risk of hospitalization, Ashley ended up losing her leg. Her facial gash, however, healed perfectly with plastic surgery.

You are a 1L summer associate. Your firm is considering representing Ashley. The partner you work for picks you to write the memo, knowing you just took Torts. Her request is that, based on the facts above, you analyze Ashley's potential tort claims and relevant defenses. She asks you to accept as true [despite what you know] that North Carolina uses the majority or plurality rule for all matters tort-related. She also asks that you ignore how any damages would be allocated among any parties found responsible.

THE DOG SILENCER

(DLC)

The Practical Sound Waves Corporation (PSW) manufactures various products that use sound waves to solve everyday problems. One of its most popular products is the Dog Silencer.[4] PSW's website pitches the Dog Silencer as follows:

> Stop barking with our newest, most powerful ultrasonic bark control device to date. Whether it's your dog or the neighbor's dog, the Dog Silencer will help you regain the peace and quiet that's been disrupted by nuisance barking. This revolutionary device automatically detects and stops barking with special sound frequencies and works up to 6X Farther than the competition!
>
> When the Dog Silencer detects barking it immediately sends a high-pitched sound heard only by the dog. Using this proven method, dogs are safely and humanely discouraged from barking. Relax while the Dog Silencer quietly trains your dog, your neighbor's dog or even multiple dogs!
>
> Our humane training technique uses an age-old principle that teaches dogs to associate their barking with the irritating frequencies. Unlike shock collars that are painful and can be used only on one dog, the Dog Silencer can be used virtually anywhere without you having to ask permission from your neighbors. The Dog Silencer trains dogs to stop nuisance barking

[4] There is a real product called the Dog Silencer. The block quote above comes from a real website which advertises the real Dog Silencer. The rest of the fact pattern, including the details about my Dog Silencer, is entirely a product of my imagination, made up for this exam. Call it fair use, literary license, or satire, so long as we all understand that I'm sure the real Dog Silencer — which I otherwise know nothing about — is a perfectly fine product. DLC

(boredom and attention-getting barking) but is designed to have no effect on instinctual or protective barking.[5]

Nadia learned about the Silencer from a close friend who had used it successfully in the past. "It's fantastic," her friend said. "The neighbors don't know you're using it, so you maintain friendly relations, and their dogs stop barking. Correction: When the dogs hear something or need to bark, they bark once but then they stop. Before, they would have gone on and on all day and night."

This was exactly what Nadia needed. Nadia is a writer who works from home. She earns a good living at it. But after Master P moved in to the house next door with his standard poodle Beau, Nadia hadn't been able to concentrate on her work. Beau barked a lot, and the particular sharp sound he made really got to Nadia. Nadia discussed the situation with some of the other neighbors who agreed that Beau was disruptive, but because they don't work from home and Beau seemed to settle down at night, the situation was not really problem for them during the weekdays. Weekends were different. Everyone seemed to max out on Beau's barking then, to the point that people started thinking twice about cookouts and other common backyard activities. An emissary from the neighborhood tried to see Master P about it, but no one answered the door at his house and after that everyone tried to deal with the situation the best they could. One day, Nadia decided that she was done dealing with it and so purchased and set up the Silencer. As she aimed it toward Master P's house, she re-read PSW's promotional material, smiled, and said aloud to herself, "Love the gun metaphor. Bang! No more 'attention-getting barking'!" Nadia's Amazon Echo replied, "I'm sorry, I don't understand. You want me to bark?"[6]

A month later, the administrator of Master P's estate went to see a lawyer. The administrator had learned from neighbors that Nadia may have been using a Silencer to stop Beau's barking. It turns out that Beau is a service animal and he barks a lot both because standard poodles tend to do that — it's a breed-typical behavior — and because this was what he had been trained to do when his disabled owner, Master P, was in distress. The administrator had also learned that on the day Nadia set up the Silencer, smoke from the private ceremony commemorating the launch of the also-adjacent Church of Cannabis wafted throughout the neighborhood causing the uninitiated — not including Nadia — to experience "lethargic stupor and overwhelming couchlock."[7] In any event, Beau barely barked and the systems that were in place to rescue Master P failed. He died as a result.

What claim or claims might you develop if you worked for P's estate? Explain any weaknesses in the current state of your evidence and the additional evidence you would hope to get through discovery so that you could survive any defense motions for summary judgment.

---

[5] Id.

[6] Nadia likes gadgets. She also recently purchased and installed an Amazon Echo. Amazon's website explains that "Echo is a hands-free speaker you control with your voice. Echo connects to the Alexa Voice Service to play music, provide information, news, sports scores, weather, and more — instantly. All you have to do is ask. Echo has seven microphones and beam forming technology so it can hear you from across the room — even while music is playing." Like Apple's Siri, and Google Home, Echo responds to voice commands and will tell you when it does not understand a command. According to Wired Magazine, "Whenever you make a voice request, Google Home and Alexa-enabled devices record or stream audio clips of what you say. Those files are sent to a server — the real brains of the operation — to process the audio and formulate a response. The recorded clips are associated to your user account, and that process is enabled by default."

[7] Master P Cannabis Strain, www.cannasos.com, last accessed on April 25, 2017.

JUSTICE CARDOZO REINCARNATED

(DLC)

You are the reincarnation of Justice Cardozo. You have been asked to contribute a short essay to a prominent law review explaining why, from your (Justice Cardozo's) perspective, Judge Lord was correct to deny the defendant's motion for a JNOV in Barker v. City of Philadelphia. Write that essay.